CW00348071

Territorial Soldiering in the North-east of Scotland During 1759-1814

Aberdeen University
Studies : No. 68

Territorial Soldiering

University of Aberdeen.

COMMITTEE ON PUBLICATIONS

Convener: Professor JAMES W H TRAIL, F R S, Curator of the Library

UNIVERSITY STUDIES

General Editor: P J ANDERSON, LL B, Librarian to the University

Alexander 4th Duke of Gordon.

PAINTED BY SIR HENRY RAEBURN

Territorial Soldiering

in the North-East of Scotland

during 1759-1814

By

John Malcolm Bulloch, M.A.

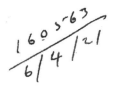

Aberdeen

Printed for the University

1914

EPISTLE DEDICATORY

To His Grace the Duke of Richmond and Gordon, K.G.

My Lord Duke,

If the Epistle Dedicatory has fallen into desuetude, the grim business of battle is so far from being in abeyance that we have been compelled to turn the pæan of Peace with which the centenary of the Treaties of Paris and of Ghent was to have been celebrated into the pursuit of the greatest War the world has ever seen. And in the event, this book has been unconsciously transformed from a mere historical excursus into a practical demonstration of what our ancestors did to meet the national crisis of a hundred years and more ago.

That crisis has found Your Grace in the active ranks of recruiters, precisely as the menaces of 1759-1814 found your forefathers. You have spent your energy in summoning the youth of your Northern home to the colours. You have sent all your three sons to the front, losing the youngest of them almost within hail of Quatre Bras, to the field of which Wellington and his officers hurried from your great-grandmother's famous ball in Brussels. The gallant Regiment of Highlanders which your great-great-grandfather, the 4th Duke of Gordon, with the help of his incomparable consort, raised, has fought and bled on the fields of France and Flanders, as its predecessor fought at Quatre Bras and Waterloo; and your domains are sending more men and still more to fill up the gaps in its decimated ranks.

But Your Grace needed no such impetus as actual War to help you to carry on the traditions inherited from the Gay Gordons as well as from the line of Lennox. You yourself became an officer in the Guards

vii.

just fifty years ago: you saw service in South Africa in command of the 3rd Royal Sussex: for years, as President of the Territorial Associations of Banff and of Elgin, you have been closely identified with our measures for defence: and by rearranging and inventorying the unique collection of weapons, battle trophies, and colours at Gordon Castle which have been handed down to you from your ancestors, you have put students of military history under a debt of gratitude to you.

As for myself, I shall not readily forget the sympathetic courtesy which prompted Your Grace to allow me to examine in my limited leisure the great array of documents from your archives bearing on the history of the four regiments which your ancestor, the 4th Duke of Gordon, raised between the years 1759 and 1794. That invaluable material, which was not at the disposal of any other historian of those regiments, is the foundation of the present volume; and it has proved the main inspiration to carry my investigations, chiefly at the Public Record Office, to all the military forces raised in the counties of Aberdeen and Banff.

And so, by reason of the military achievements of your House—Gordon and Lennox alike—and in virtue of your own and your sons' work in the War of 1914, this account of what the North did in the War which ended in 1814, falls most naturally to be inscribed to Your Grace by your obedient servant,

JOHN MALCOLM BULLOCH.

123 Pall Mall, S.W.,
December the First,
MDCCCCXIV.

CLASSIFIED CONTENTS OF THIS BOOK.

ILLUSTRATIONS.

ALEXANDER, 4TH DUKE OF GORDON - - - - - - *Frontispiece*

The 4th Duke of Gordon (1743-1827) raised four of the regiments dealt with in this book, besides supplying one company each to two others This picture was painted by Sir Henry Raeburn (1756-1823) and hangs in the Manchester City Art Gallery, which acquired it from Agnews on June 9, 1902, being reproduced here in Annan photogravure by kind permission of the Corporation.

GORDON HIGHLANDER OFFICER - - - - - Facing page 192

This picture, by L Mansion and St Eschauzier, was drawn for Spooner's Upright Series (1833-40) The original size is 10⅝ in. by 9 in It was reproduced 7¾ in by 6½ in for Mr. Ralph Nevill's " British Military Prints," issued in 1909 by the "Connoisseur," to the publishers of which I am much indebted for the loan of the (three) colour blocks These blocks have been slightly pared to suit the size of the present page They have been printed by George W Jones, at the Sign of the Dolphin in Gough Square, Fleet Street, London (See p 431)

BANFFSHIRE LOCAL MILITIA - - - - - - - Page 442

This represents the actual size of a (brass) part of the uniform It was picked up by Mr James Grant, County Clerk of Banffshire, and presented by him to J M Bulloch

A GENERAL SURVEY OF TERRITORIAL SOLDIERING.

The year Nineteen Hundred and Fourteen will never be forgotten. Not only did it witness the outbreak of the greatest war in history, but it marked a series of anniversaries bearing on war. This wonderful year was the six hundredth anniversary of the Battle of Bannockburn, which not only set Scotland free, but forms a landmark in the art of war by showing that Infantry is the backbone of an army. This year was the two hundredth anniversary of the accession of the House of Hanover, which, by rousing a large part of Scotland to arms on behalf of the Stuarts, made the subsequent commandeering of the Scot for the purposes of national defence at once timely—and timorous. And this year was the hundredth anniversary of the Peace with France and with America, thereby closing down a prolonged period of real national defence, which made Scotland feel acutely for the first time the full price of the Union with England.

But although all these historic events have an inter-dependent connection beyond the facile similarity of date; although we are once more discussing for the thousandth time the subject of defence and citizen service as a problem of current politics; and although men are writing naval and military history and compiling regimental records at a rate unknown to us before—almost as if to checkmate the Angells who are piping for Peace—this book has not been planned as a *livre de circonstance*, however "topical" its appearance at this particular moment may be, except in as much as none of us can escape from streams of tendency.

Nor has it been primarily conditioned by my keen interest in the House of Gordon, which has contributed so largely to the whole art of war. On the contrary, my absorption in the family of Gordon has arisen from a previous and boyish interest in soldiering, for I was writing, in 1887 and 1888, on the history of the Wapinschaw, the Covenanting skirmishes in Aberdeenshire, the Jacobites and the Volunteers before I ever tackled the enormous subject of Gordon genealogy;

and my immediate re-introduction to the latter was the professional necessity of having to describe the part played by the Gordon High-landers in the capture of the heights of Dargai in October, 1897

But the subject of soldiering had attracted me long before any of these things. One of the earliest recollections of my childhood is a slender, blue-boarded quarto, in the centre of which stood a gilded isosceles triangle bearing the words—spelt phonetically as if for nursery use—YE NOBELL CHEESE-MONGER At that time, of course, I did not know what an isosceles triangle meant, or that the appella-tion " Cheese-monger " had any touch of the ludicrous, but the first page of the volume, printed in colours, was irresistibly comic to my childish eye It showed a crowd of coatless Lilliputians tugging grotesquely at ropes to pull down backwards the martial-cloaked, clean-shaven figure of the Duke of Gordon from his granite pedestal in the Castlegate, while another group in front was engaged with equal enthusiasm in elevating towards the about-to-be vacated site the figure of a dumpy man in a green uniform and bushy whiskers, looking a little alarmed at the honour that was being thrust upon him I say this picture struck my childish fancy, not from the retrospective stand-point of one of those psychological prodigies of Mr Henry James's imagining, but because the anonymous artist, Sir George Reid, had sketched unerringly an irresistibly comic situation, of which the bearded Joey and Harlequin is the *locus classicus.* Besides this, the rare occasions on which the book was shown to us—for it was one of six copies produced (in 1861)—was enough to make the occasional perusal of it something like a red-letter day, and, furthermore, I used to "play at soldiers" in a tunic and belt, with the word "Bon-Accord" on it, which my father had worn as a fellow member with the aforesaid artist of the Cheese-monger's Volunteer corps

In picturing the Duke as a Prometheus, bound helpless before the advance of the Cheese-monger, the satirist—it is strange that he rarely, if ever, again lent his pen to humour—was instituting no comparison between the social status of his Grace and the grocer. While he was primarily aiming at pitting the amateur, the Volunteer, against the professional, he was also viewing both from the standpoint of the civilian of that period, just as *Punch* itself was doing, thereby, with a keen, though perhaps unconscious, sense of history, seizing on our traditional and deep-seated attitude as a nation to the business of soldiering. To take but one example, everybody knows the difficulty which was experienced in establishing a Standing Army, for it figures to this day in the preamble of the Army Annual Bill, by which the Army is rhetorically renewable year by year:— "Whereas the raising or keeping of a Standing Army within the United Kingdom of Great Britain and Ireland in time of peace, unless it be by the consent of Parliament, is *against the law*."

As a people we do not understand the Army *qua* Army; we recognise it as but one of the instruments of State, the purpose of which is to uphold the honour of the Nation. When that honour is not at stake, the instrument always tends to become rusty. When danger arises, we begin sharpening the old instrument and improvising new ones for the emergency; the South African War was an absolutely typical example, and precisely the same thing has been done in the war of 1914.

It is of such improvisation that this volume treats. It is not a history of Highland regiments like Stewart of Garth's classic work. It is not an account of Scotland's military system from early times after the manner of Lady Tullibardine in the case of Perthshire. It is not an application of Mr. Fortescue's 1803-1814 treatment of the County Lieutenancies; and it is not a history of the Volunteers, the force to which we have come to apply the term Territorial. It is an account of how two counties, Aberdeen and Banff, contributed to the herculean efforts put forth by the United Kingdom from 1757 to 1814 to extend her frontiers and to hold what she already possessed. I have confined myself to these two counties (except in including the two Strathspey regiments) because Kincardine was always associated with Forfarshire and Elgin and Nairn with Inverness, as Banffshire itself became in the matter of Militia. Indeed, Aberdeenshire alone of the north-east counties has always been a distinct unit.

I have used the word Territorial,* not in the modern restricted use which connotes the old Volunteering, but because the whole effort of recruiting—and not the subsequent tactical disposition of the forces so

---

* The Nottinghamshire Regiment (now the 1st Battalion of the Derbyshire Regiment), raised in 1779, initiated the Territorial system (Fortescue's *History of the British Army*, iii., 291).

raised—in the north during the period under review was conducted with. a frank recognition by the State of local conditions First, in the case of Regular regiments it was carried out under the aegis of the great territorial.lords , later on, in the case of some of the Fencible regiments, under the influence of professional soldiers who had some local connection , then, in the case of the Militia, Volunteers and Local Militia under the management of the Lord Lieutenants, with or without the compulsive aid of the ballot My last, main aim has been not to describe the actual service of these forces when raised, but to show the mechanism used to raise them, for, difficult as it is to find the data, this is really the most useful fact for the modern reader to understand In this introduction I shall sketch the general principles under which the various regiments in the north-east of Scotland from 1759 to 1814 were raised

The spirit of territorialism, not to say parochialism, was the pivot of this mechanism , indeed, it was so dominating that the ultimate reason why the mechanism was set in motion tended to become obscured The opening statement of Mr Fortescue in his *County Lieutenancies and the Army* is to a large extent true of Scotland— " The military system of England from the close of the Middle Ages to the Nineteenth Century was practically, though with superficial differences, the same To every place which required a garrison a small permanent force was indissolubly attached, and for the purposes of war an army was improvised" Thus a place like Aberdeen had its "blockhouse," under the control of the Town Council , and the Army, such as it was, was as visible, as local, a fact as any other aspect of municipal control.

In the country districts the laird became the pivot, and the raising of troops was as much a. personal matter as the levy of the old feudal lords.in return for tenure of land The Highland regiments recall the fact to this day better than any other type of troops, for they wear in their. uniforms the mottoes and the badges of the individual families concerned in their creation, such as " Bydand " and the stag's head of the Gordon Highlanders, and the appearance of the arms of the company commanders, for the time being, on the pipe banners Many other instances might be cited , suffice it for the moment to say that the spirit of territorialism with all its idiosyncracies conditioned, in varying degree, all the troops raised in the north-east of Scotland during the period, 1759-1814, under review, and it has been strongly reasserted on four subsequent occasions—the raising of the Volunteers in 1859, Cardwell's allotment of infantry regiments to territorial recruiting districts in 1872 (when the Gordons got " Bydand " and the stag's head in lieu of the Sphinx and the word " Egypt " for cap badge), Childers' linked, or rather "welded," battalion system of 1881, and Lord Haldane's Territorial and Reserve Forces Act of 1907, which aims at making national defence an integral part of local government

Now in view of these facts it is very curious that soldiering has not been considered a matter of real territorial interest among us Nothing proves this point more clearly than its meagre treatment in local newspapers and the indifference shown by nearly all local historians —past masters of the minute as they are—to anything dealing with defence, or what is called " the military," a phrase which sums up the separateness of the army from citizenship   Thus a book like the late Mr A M Munro's history of Old Aberdeen has nothing to tell us of the Aulton Volunteers, and Dr. Cramond confined his reference to the subject in Banff to a nonpareil note hidden away among the Town Council minutes   The irony of Sir George Reid in " Ye Nobell Cheese-monger " was thoroughly characteristic of the attitude of his period Not only has the subject been treated with indifference, but in actual practice soldiering for long encountered active opposition   So far as Regular soldiering is concerned, every man of middle age can recall that in his youth it was almost anathema, and will recognise the verisimilitude of Mr R J MacLennan's wit in his volume of Aberdeen sketches, *In Yon Toon*.—

Miss Macpherson—" It's a terrible thing aboot Mrs Thomson's loon, isn't it ? "

Mrs. Simpson—" O, fit was that   I'didna hear o't "

Miss Macpherson—" He's jined the sojers "

Mrs Simpson (raising her hands heavenwards)—" Jined the sojers, has he ?   Eh, my good !   An' his mither will be richt pitten aboot Aye, an' this her washin' day, too   Eh, my ! "

This point of view has largely changed in recent years, and it would no longer be possible to re-create a Nobell Cheese-monger, yet the spirit underlying such incidents, and exhibiting antagonism to the centralised military ideal has not been wholly exorcised, as the policy

c

of the Aberdeen Town Council on the use of the Links as a rifle range has served to show us   That attitude is due to no unpatriotic contrariness; it is created by local conditions, which were much more antagonistic in the period dealt with by this inquiry

It has therefore been far from easy to get at data for the present volume, especially in reference to the mechanism employed in raising troops   Luckily there is a large number of documents at Gordon Castle dealing with the regiments raised by the 4th Duke of Gordon, and I have to thank the Duke of Richmond and Gordon for the privilege of examining them at my leisure   The charter chests of other families engaged in raising men might furnish similar papers, but I have not been able to get access to them   Such documents, of course, tell us little or nothing about regiments once they had been handed over to the State   Here we must consult the War Office papers now housed at the Public Record Office, London , and extensive as the data are, the wholesale destruction of documents in the past shows us that the military authorities could be as indifferent as the civilian local historian   The old system by which regiments kept their own records, carting them about with other impedimenta, was thoroughly bad and involved serious —and from some points of view, not unnatural—destruction from time to time *   Many of the documents that have been preserved have not been seen by students   This was especially the case with the series of Volunteer pay rolls, all of which had to be specially stamped for me to examine, showing that they had never been given out to the

---

* A classic case which has recently occupied the attention of the Royal Commission on Public Records has been kindly cited for me by the Secretary, Mr Hubert Hall, of the Record Office , and it is interesting as showing that the Horse Guards seem to have had a different point of view from the War Office   On April 10, 1824, the Adjutant-General wrote from the Horse Guards to the officer commanding the 24th Regiment that he had heard that "almost the whole" of the Regimental Records of that corps had been destroyed —"I am commanded by H R H to call upon you to state distinctly by whose authority so unmilitary and unwarrantable a proceeding has taken place, in order that the Commander-in-Chief may visit the author of it with some mark of his serious displeasure "   A few days later he communicated with the Deputy-Secretary at War to whom he wrote again on October 22, 1824 —"I have the honor to transmit herewith the Draft of a General Order which it is proposed to issue to the Army, requiring Commanding Officers of Regiments on embarking for Foreign Service, to leave at their Depôts in this country the Books and Records for the antecedent five years which may not be required for frequent reference at the Headquarters, but which are necessary to be preserved "   I deal (p 228) with the almost miraculous preservation of the first Description Registers of the 92nd

public before.   I have also examined minutely the Home Office series
of documents known as " Internal Defence," the trackless desert of
which was first traversed, and to such good purpose, by Mr. Fortescue
in *The County Lieutenancies and the Army* (1909), his journey throughout the whole 326 volumes and bundles being, of course, much more
exhaustive and exhausting—he says it was " maddening " to write his
book—than one confined to two counties.   These documents alone form
my excuse for dealing with the Militia and Volunteers, for both forces
had already been tackled by Colonel Innes and Mr. Donald Sinclair.
That, however, has only added to my difficulty, for I have had to incorporate the new material without rewriting their work and thus
cumbering space needlessly.

The personal side of the subject remains most imperfect in the
absence of Description Registers and the biographies of officers.   To
follow that up completely would require a knowledge as extensive as
Mrs. Skelton's in *Gordons under Arms*, plus a genealogical equipment
such as probably no individual scholar possesses.   The greatest difficulty
is presented by the Volunteers, as if these officers had been shy of
publicity, foreseeing the ridicule cast by Mr. Meredith on the great Mel,*
the tailor in *Evan Harrington*, which was published in the very year
that Sir George Reid immortalised the Cheese-monger.

I am very well aware that some of my conclusions on the influence
of territorialism may be regarded by some readers, especially professional soldiers, as highly controversial.   But there can be no doubt whatever that national aspirations and local idiosyncracies largely conditioned
the efforts to raise troops in the middle of the eighteenth century.   We
are all familiar with the facile theory that when Great Britain set out on
her sixty years of world-conquest in 1757, she had only to beckon to
her northern people and that soldiers sprang to attention like gourds,
if only because the spirit of military adventure satisfied the martial
hunger of a race that had been reared on fighting, but had been

---

* " At that period, when threats of invasion had formerly stirred up the military
fire of us Islanders, the great Mel, as if to show Napoleon what character of being a
British shopkeeper really was, had, by remarkable favour, obtained a lieutenancy of
militia dragoons : in the uniform of which he had revelled, and perhaps for the only
time in his life felt that circumstances had suited him with a perfect fit.   His solemn
final commands to his wife . . . had been that, as soon as the breath had left his
body, he should be taken from his bed . . . and in that uniform dressed and laid
out."—(Chap. ii.).

deliberately starved for forty years by reason of its exploits on behalf of Jacobitism There could be no more misleading interpretation of history, no greater blindness to the essential territorial fact, for the simple reason that the half century of Union had not obliterated Scotland's individual consciousness, her point of view still differed greatly from that of the dominant partner

In the first place, Scotland had been friendly on political, temperamental and dynastic grounds with England's traditional enemy, France When the fruits of the Union seemed likely to be spoilt by some of the Scots' preference for the essentially French line of Stuart, France had become unusually friendly to these aspirations, so that we find a Scots officer, Thomas Gordon, who had been transferred to the English Navy, deliberately using his professional opportunities to make French aid to the Jacobites the more available But even if she had been inspired with the English bias, Scotland was far removed from that strip of Channel which kept England constantly on the alert Indeed, so far from rousing Scotland, the sea had a terrifying effect at any rate on the Highland levies, and more than one mutiny arose out of the soldiers' intense dislike, even horror, of ships When at last Scotland was threatened by France as part and parcel of the United Kingdom, the danger, as the minister of Aberarder plainly told the Duke of Gordon in a remarkable letter of 1778, was "too remote" to make some of the inland districts worry Indeed, from every point of view, the reasons why Scotland should buckle on her armour against France were far less obvious than in the case of England

The Effect of Jacobitism

The reasons why Scotland was not so predisposed as England was to take to soldiering went further than the greater absence of motive For ten years before the opening of the great campaign for the possession of India in 1757, the best part of warlike Scotland had been deliberately dispossessed of whatever arms she possessed, the dominant partner being thoroughly frightened at the possibility of another pro-Jacobite attempt, despite the fact that the disarming Acts of 1716 and 1725 had actually contributed to encourage the hopes of the exiled house of Stuart The Act of 1746 (19 Geo II cap 39) "for the more effectual disarming the Highlands in Scotland"—an extraordinarily "absent-minded" move seeing that the interrupted campaign in the Low Countries against the brilliant Marshal Saxe was being renewed at this very moment—was even more drastic, involving part of Dumbarton and Stirling, and the whole of Argyll, Perth, Forfar, Kincardine, Aberdeen, Banff, Nairn, Elgin, Inverness, Ross, Cromarty, Sutherland and Caithness. The prohibition of the Highland dress—not removed till 1782—was another blow in the same direction; while the Heritable Jurisdictions Act of 1747 broke up the feudal power of the great landowners in such a way as to frustrate their later desire to raise troops. The fear of the Highlanders rising again is brought out in a letter which Lord Findlater wrote to the Duke of Newcastle on July 8, 1748 (*Add. MSS.*, 32,715 f. 323):—

It is said that ther is an intention to turn the two Highland Regiments [the names are not given] into Independent Companies to be sent to the Highlands. . . . I am sure it wou'd prove a most pernicious scheme, for it wou'd effectively spread and keep up the warlike spirit there and frustrate all measures for rooting it out. . . . It would be dangerous to scatter such a number of military Highlanders in their own country. . . . No Highlanders ought to be employed in the Highlands, but a small number of pick'd ones to serve for guides for the regular troops.

The disarming edict affected whole communities as well as individuals. Thus, Aberdeen was deprived of its ordnance in 1745, lest it should fall into the hands of the rebels, and this led to a strong protest from the Provost, July 11, 1759, when the coast towns were becoming frightened of France, all the more as Regular troops had been withdrawn to fill up the gaps in our scattered army. On July 12, 1759, the Lord Provost of Edinburgh, as præses of the Convention of Burghs, memorialised the Secretary of State, Lord Holdernesse, as follows (*P.R.O.*; *S.P. Scotland*: series 2: bundle 45: No. 59):—

The Burroughs of Scotland which are situated on the East Coast from the river Tay northwards, having represented to the annual Convention of the Royal Burroughs now mett here, that in consequence of the orders given to the troops gathered among them to march thither, they will be in a very dangerous situation; for, being disarmed by law, they are altogether unable to defend themselves from the enemy, who may attack them successfully even with ships of very small force.

The Convention having heard their representative, and being desireous that something may be done for their safety and security

while the troops are removed at a distance, have directed me as their
præses humbly to lay their case before your lordship

We are far from complaining of the measure of the removal of
the troops, being sensible that these orders have been given for weighty
and good reasons   We only beg your lordship will have the goodness
to represent to our most gracious Sovereign the present defenceless,
and, therefore, dangerous state of these burroughs, that he may be
pleased to give out orders for their safety as he shall see proper, and
which the public security will best admitt of   If a 40- or a 20-gun
ship could be spared from the service, and ordered to cruize from
Fifeness to Buchanness, we are hopefull that the evils we dread would
hereby be effectually prevented   But this we humbly suggest with the
greatest submission

Even when the luck turned in our favour, as in the capitulation of
Quebec, and after arms had been sent—400 stand were given to the town
in August, 1759 (*W O* 1, 614)—Aberdeen felt as nervous as ever,
because the people did not know how to use these arms   Thus, the
Magistrates wrote to Holdernesse on October 21, 1759 (*Ibid.* No 84) —

It is with great reluctancy we presume to trouble your Lo'p at this
critical juncture, when you are overburdened with publick affairs   But
necessity obliges us to have recourse to your Lo'p for relieff and
assistance, when we are threatned with such immediate danger

Your Lordship knows there are no troops on the East Coast of
Scotland betwixt the Murray ffrith and the Frith of Forth, so that this
town, being a place of the greatest consequence for the number of its
inhabitants and manufactures betwixt the two ffriths, and situate centri-
cally betwixt them in an open sandy bay, where a number of troops
could be landed in a very short space of time, and so we are much
exposed to the invasion of a forreign enemy, and there is great reason
to believe, may be the first place that will be attacked   And tho' His
Majesty and the Ministry have been graciously pleased to furnish us
with some arms and ammunition, yet, our citizens having been long
out of use of arms, it cannot be expected that they are in case to
oppose a forreign enemy without the assistance of regular troops

We are making the best use we can of the arms sent us, and are
learning our citizens to the proper exercise of them, and, were there
regular troops to mix with them, and animate them to action, we are
hopeful they would do great service

As we are presently so much exposed and in a defenceless state,
we must implore His Majesty and the Ministry to order a regiment of
Regular troops to be cantoned along our coast, and make this the head
quarters, so as they may quickly repair to any place that may be

attacked. It will likewise be most necessary to order as many as can be spared of the King's Ships to cruize along our Coast, and protect us against the invasion of a forreign enemy with which we are daily threatened.

Not only was Aberdeen robbed of arms, but it was deprived of the men who could have borne them, for the memorial goes on to state :—

We have of late furnished a vast number of men, as well for the land as the sea service, and gave large bountys for their encouragement ; and, as we pay our taxes regularly, we humbly apprehend we are entitled to the Government's protection. And therefore we beg leave once more to implore His Majesty and the Ministry to comply with this our most humble and earnest request.

A case in point is quoted in the *Aberdeen Journal*, March 16, 1756, which shows how compulsion was forced on the local authorities :—

On Tuesday last [March 9, 1756] there was a very hot Press for mariners and seafaring men, which was conducted with the greatest secrecy, vigilance and activity. The Provost, having received Orders from above, concerted the plan of operation with Colonel Lambert, commanding Holms's regiment here ; and in the forenoon of that day parties were privately sent out to guard all the avenues leading to and from the town, as also the harbour mouth ; and, immediately before the Press began, guards were placed on all the ports of the town. A little after two o'clock, the Provost, Magistrates, Constables and Town Sergeants, with the assistance of the military, and directed by Colonel Lambert, laid hold on every sailor and seafaring man that could be found within the harbour and town, and in less than an hour, there were about 100 taken into custody, and, after examination, 35 were committed to gaol as fit for service. Since that time several more sailors have been apprehended, as also land men of base and dissolute lives ; and on Sunday last [March 14] were brought in from Peterhead and committed to gaol six sailors who were sent to town under a guard of General Holms's regiment. There are now from 40 to 50 in prison on the above account, and the Press still continues.

Nothing could show more poignantly—if you have any imagination —the intense hunger for fighting men ; but this kind of raid appeased only one form of the hunger, namely the clamant necessities of the State, which ran to earth any kind of men, anywhere and anyhow. But it left two other maws, mainly local, not only unsatisfied but more hungry than ever. If it appeased the great, and mostly unseen, campaign of aggression carried on by the nation at large, it neglected

the less showy necessities of internal defence, leaving the coastwise
communities robbed of their manhood, and consequently panic-stricken
at the thought of invasion   Then it starved the great landlords, who
for very definite reasons of their own were beginning to raise regiments
from among their vassals, very much as the feudal squires had been
doing centuries before, and who found men increasingly difficult to get,
until at last their personal and financial resources became thoroughly
exhausted in the process and their task had to be taken up by the
local authorities

Faced by the local fact, the Government at last began attacking
the problem, so far as the north was concerned, on much more sympathetic lines by recognising that territorial needs must be met by
territorial means and that it was highly advisable to raise infantrymen
by consent instead of by the hole-and-corner and antagonising tyranny
of the Press Gang for a service which was really alien to the genius
of the people

The new policy was opened in 1757, the year after the Press Gang
raid which I have described, which witnessed the inauguration of Clive's
decisive campaign in India   The old fear of Jacobitism was going (as
we see by the interesting fact that even old Glenbucket's grandson,
William Gordon, was granted permission by the Sheriff Depute of
Banffshire to wear arms again), and the new hope of arming the Highlanders for the service of the State was begun   On January 4, 1757,
the Hon Archibald Montgomerie, 11th Earl of Eglinton (1726-96) got
a commission to raise a regiment (the 77th), while the 78th was raised
by the Hon Simon Fraser, *de jure* 12th Lord Fraser of Lovat
(1726-82), under commission dated January 5, 1757   Of course, neither
Montgomerie nor Fraser invented the idea of utilising the Highlander
for soldiering. That must be credited to the Black Watch which, I
believe, Mr Andrew Ross is right in tracing back, not to 1725 as
Stewart and all his imitators state, but to 1667, when the 2nd Earl of
Atholl got a commission to raise men to be a constant guard for
securing the peace in the Highlands, and "to watch upon the braes"
The idea had also been taken up again in 1745 when the 4th Earl of
Loudon raised a Highland regiment which fought at Prestonpans and
was afterwards taken to Flanders   But the Rebellion put a complete
end to this kind of military experiment, and nothing more was done

until 1757, when Montgomerie and Fraser got their commissions to raise two Highland regiments of the line, the 77th and 78th, to help the nation in the ambitious adventures afoot on the Indian and Canadian continents.

The necessity of the nation was just the opportunity that the Highland chiefs wanted. Montgomerie, of course, was a Lowlander, though he was connected by marriage with the Highlands, and had always been loyal. But Fraser had been reared in the atmosphere of rebellion, and had served under the Prince in the 'Forty-Five, being attainted like his father, the notorious Lord Lovat. The rebel chiefs had come to see that something more was necessary than a sulky acceptance of the new House of Hanover; they felt that they must do something positive; and their territorial position, even if the feeling of clanship was on the wane, gave them the chance of helping the State in its great hour of need.

Montgomerie tapped Aberdeenshire for two companies—one of them being commanded by a son of the 3rd Earl of Aboyne—as we learn from the "state" of his regiment, dated Nairn, March 9, 1757 (*W.O.* 1 : 974). The amazing point about this return, which shows 10 companies, is the number of men rejected, 472 recruits being "not approved" out of a total of 1,029.

Company Commander.	Men raised.	Approved.	Not approved.	Where raised.
Lieut.-Colonel Montgomery	109	102	7	Athole and Strathdearn.
Major Grant	230	230	—	Strathspey and Urquhart.
Major Campbell	80	—	80	West Highlands.
Capt. Sinclair	110	—	110	Sutherland and Caithness.
Capt. Hugh Mackenzie	83	60	23	Glasgow and Ross-shire.
Capt. [Hon. John] Gordon [of Glentanner.]	76	30	46	Edinburgh and Aberdeenshire.
Capt. Alexander Mackenzie	117	—	117	Perthshire and Aberdeenshire.
Capt. M'Donald	43	23	20	Edinburgh and Skye.
Capt. Munro	112	112	—	Fairn Donald.
Capt. Roderick M'Kenzie	69	—	69	Kintail.
	1,029	557	472	

"The draughts intended for sergeants and corporals are not included in the above return."

Fraser kept more to his native county of Inverness, but he, too, had a Gordon officer—Cosmo Gordon, of unknown origin, who was killed at Quebec in 1760.

d

Nothing more was done for two years; but in 1759 the growing necessities of the situation—the compaigns against the French in India and Canada, and the threat of invasion—called for further efforts. The Secretary at War, Lord Barrington, issued a memorandum which strikingly illustrates the clamorous need for soldiers (*Add. MSS.* 32,893, f. 62):—

Whereas the King's Dominions are publickly threaten'd to be invaded by the French, who are making great and expensive preparations for that purpose: And, whereas some of His Majesty's Corps of Troops in Great Britain are not so full as at such a juncture might be wish'd, especially at a season of the year when it can not be expected that they should be immediately compleated by the usual methods of recruiting;

Declaration is hereby made that any man *may* inlist in the Army on the following conditions:

He shall not upon any account or pretence whatever be obliged to go out of Great Britain, even tho' the Regiment wherein he serves should be sent abroad:

He shall be intitled to his discharge on demand at the end of the War, or sooner in case it shall appear to His Majesty that the French have lay'd aside their design of invading Great Britain.

The North tackled the problem much more energetically by raising three totally new regiments—the 87th (Keith's); the 88th (Campbell of Dunoon's); and the 89th (the Duke of Gordon's). It is with the last that I start this book, for though Aberdeenshire contributed both to Montgomerie's in 1757 and to Keith's, the 89th was the first complete corps produced by the north-east of Scotland. I may add that I have gone into the foreign service of the 89th at greater length than that of any of the other regiments dealt with for the simple reason that it has hitherto been much neglected by military historians, although it did excellent work in India under Hector Munro.

From the moment in 1759 when these big efforts were put forward, down to 1814, when the Peace with France and with America called a long halt, the north-east of Scotland was perpetually thinking of soldiers. The necessities of the national situation synchronise exactly with local efforts as the following parallel statement of outstanding events prove:—

THE NATIONAL PROBLEM.	THE TERRITORIAL SOLUTION.
1759—French lose Quebec.	1759-63—87th : Keith's Highlanders
„ defeated, Quiberon Bay.	Fought in Flanders.
1760— „ invade Ireland.	1759-65 —89th : (Gordon's Highlanders)
„ defeat at Wandiwash.	Fought in India.
1761— „ lose Pondicherry.	1760-63—101st : Johnstone's Highlanders
„ lose Belle Isle.	Partly recruited and officered
1762—War declared with Spain.	in Aberdeenshire.
1763—Peace of Paris.	
—Patna : Mir Cassim defeated.	
1764—Buxar : Nabob of Oude defeated.	
1775-82—American War.	1775-83—71st : Fraser's Highlanders
1778-83—War with France.	4th Duke of Gordon raised Coy.
1779-82—Gibraltar besieged.	1777-83—77th : Atholl Highlanders
1779-83—Spain wars on Britain.	Commanded by Col. Gordon.
1779-81—1st Mahratta war.	1777-83—81st : Aberdeenshire High-
1781-83—War with Holland.	landers.
1780-84—1st Mysore war.	1778-83—Northern Fencibles
1783—Peace (of Versailles) with France.	Raised by 4th Duke of Gordon.
1789-92—2nd Mysore war.	1790-91—Black Watch Company
1792-97—1st Coalition against France	Raised by 4th Duke of Gordon.
(Austria, Prussia, and Great	1793-99—Northern Fencibles.
Britain).	1793-99—Strathspey Fencibles.
1797—Spain defeated : Cape St. Vincent.	1793-95—97th : Strathspey Regiment.
Naval mutiny at the Nore.	1794—100th (afterwards 92nd) : Gordon
Dutch defeated : Camperdown.	Highlanders.
1798-9—Irish rebellion.	1794-95—109th : Aberdeenshire Foot
1798—French defeated : Nile.	Raised by Alexander Leith-
1798-9—3rd Mysore war.	Hay.
1801—French defeated : Alexandria.	1794-1803—Aberdeenshire Fencibles
Danes defeated : Copenhagen.	Raised by James Leith.
1802—Peace (of Amiens) with France.	1794-1802—Volunteers
	Aberdeenshire had 33 Companies.
	Banffshire had 20 Companies.
	1798-1802—Banffshire Fencibles
	Raised by Hay of Montblairy.
	1798—Aberdeenshire Militia
	Now 3rd Battalion Gordon
	Highlanders.
1803—France declares War.	1803-8—Volunteers
Emmet rising in Ireland.	Aberdeenshire had 53 Companies.
1803-6—2nd Mahratta war.	Banffshire had 2 Battalions.
1805—Battle of Trafalgar.	1808-14—Local Militia
1806—Sepoy mutiny at Vellore.	Aberdeenshire had 5 Regiments.
1807—Danes defeated : Copenhagen.	Banffshire had 1 Regiment.
1808-14—Peninsular war.	
1809—Walcheren expedition.	

1814, April 11—Peace with France (Treaty of Paris).
1814, July 6—Volunteers and Local Militia disbanded and thanked by Parliament.
1814, December 24—Peace with America (Treaty of Ghent).
1859, May 12—Volunteer Force revived (to counter France).
1908, April 1—Territorial Army inaugurated.

Such were the vast enterprises undertaken by the State, and such the aid afforded by our district   On the one hand you find a grandiose Foreign Policy (the one local newspaper contained little else than foreign " intelligence," its information about the soldiering that was going on being of the most meagre kind), on the other, you are confronted, and some readers may be bewildered, by an extraordinary particularism, based on a complete, and perhaps necessary, submission to local conditions.   This, of course, was not the monopoly of the district, it was national, for, if Seeley's doctrine of the absentmindedness of our " expansion " seems too obvious to some critics, there can be little doubt that the policy of defence was one long series of experiments in the art of opportunism to suit the ideals of an island race, reaching a climax in 1803 in Addington and his Secretary for War, Lord Hobart, whose " blindness," " weakness " and " folly," evoke the wrath of Mr Fortescue   The War Office was conditioned by this particularism, by the mental outlook of the Scot in general and the Highlander in particular, first in the matter of getting men, and secondly in the art of keeping them once they had been got, and the authorities had to pay a heavy price for any attempts, conscious or not, to over-rule local sentiment

First, with regard to getting men, the State was confronted by everything making for clannishness   It must be remembered that the Highlanders were essentially home birds, devoted to their own district, to their own friends and leaders ; the world-famous wandering Scot was almost exclusively of the Lowland type   The Celt's love of his native soil, which has informed so much of our politics, and which is so finely expressed in the " Canadian Boat Song," was so intense that it strongly militated against the success of such a small adventure as the Jacobite march to Derby, even though the clans were intensely interested in the main object of the exploit   Therefore when they were asked to support a scheme in which they did not feel themselves personally involved and which meant not merely a departure from their native glens but a journey across the seas, it became very difficult to induce the Highlanders to support it   If they agreed to go, it was only on condition that they did so with the people they knew and under the command of the leaders they respected, so that casual recruiting among them would have been next to useless, you had to recruit the whole clan, as it were, and establish a Highland Regiment, which considered itself as much a unity in the heart of the whole army as a foreign embassy remains inviolable territory in the capital in which it is placed. This feeling remained potent for a long time after the original impulse of the Highland regiments had become obscured. A picturesque example of it is cited by Sergeant Robertson in his interesting *Diary*. Speaking of the Battle of Orthes (February 27, 1814) he says (p. 129):—

Here the three Highland regiments met for the first time—namely the 42nd, 79th and 92nd; and such a joyful meeting I have seldom witnessed. As we were almost all from Scotland, and having had a great many friends in all regiments, such a shaking of hands took place. The one hand held the firelock and bayonet, while the other was extended to give the friendly Highland grasp, and the three cheers to go forward. Lord Wellington was so much pleased with the scene that he ordered the three regiments to be encamped beside one another for the night as we had been separated for some years, that we might have the pleasure of spending a few hours together and make inquiry about our friends and to ascertain who survived and who had fallen.

But even within a Highland regiment there were differences between different septs to be reckoned with, so that we find groups of men of one surname declining to march to a rendezvous with groups of men of a different name, with whom there may have been long outstanding controversies. And when they reached such a rendezvous there were cases—even so late as 1793, as the Northern Fencibles had to reckon with—when a Highland officer demanded that the men he had raised should be confined to his company, the military exigencies of distributing men over the whole regiment being quite incredible to him. Another great difficulty in getting men arose out of the jealousies of the leaders who set out about raising regiments. The War Office did not raise them, in the beginning at least, directly. It assigned the task to individual magnates, under licence, and simply took over the regiment when completed. How the regiment was actually gathered together was a matter of small concern to the War Office. The consequence was that rival recruiters vied with each other in offering inducements, so that bounties increased with the necessity for troops until the price rose in some cases to as high as £50 and £60 a head. One recruiter would invade the territorial domain of another and annex men by hook or by crook, local jealousies being fanned to a sort of civil war—waged, ironically enough, because of the common enemy of the State. Aberdeenshire affords two striking cases in point —the conflict in 1778 between the Northern Fencibles, raised by the Duke of Gordon, and the 81st Regiment, raised by his kinsman, the Hon. William Gordon. Again in 1794 the Duke was seriously hampered in raising the Gordon Highlanders by the efforts put forth by Leith-Hay to raise the 109th, the houses of Gordon and of Leith rallying round their respective leaders, while the Corporation of Aberdeen inclined to favour Leith-Hay. Both the 81st and the 109th soon disappeared, but that was because the influence of their organisers was not sufficiently strong with the authorities, as the Duke's was, to keep them going. The story of these conflicts, represented of course entirely by private documents and not in the War Office archives, makes extraordinary reading. It need hardly be said that human nature took full advantage of such a situation, until recruiters were faced by all sorts of compulsions from their quarry. For instance, small farmers would agree to give a son in return for an enlargement of their holding, or a greater security of tenure or some similar *quid pro quo*; while the laird also would exercise pressure by threatening tenants guilty of small offences, such as annexing wood or game, or doing something that was more or less punishable. It is necessary to underline these facts because Stewart of Garth, who has been copied by nearly every writer on the subject, gives a point blank denial. Ever on the defensive so far as the Highlanders were concerned, he lays it down (*Sketches of the Highlanders*, ii., 308) :—

It has been alleged that these services [of tenants in the field at the call of the lairds] were not unbought, as the sons of tacksmen and tenants were sent by their parents to fill up the ranks of Highland regiments on a direct or implied stipulation of abatement of rent, or on some pecuniary or other advantage to be received, for the service of the youths who came forward to take up arms at the call of their chiefs and lords. Circumstances do not confirm this view of the subject.

In reply to which you have only to read the letters sent to the Duke of Gordon by tenants in purely Highland districts; letters which I have little doubt could be matched by others in the charter chests of the great landlords, for there is no reason to believe that the Duke's tenants were more worldly wise than those of other landlords.

If it was difficult to raise men, it was nearly as difficult to retain them, even when they passed into the keeping of the State For a long time, indeed, the Highlanders were unable to differentiate the two factors—the individual subject who induced them to join and the nation as a whole for which their services were required The State spoke through the voice of the individual, and the individual was expected to keep to the terms which he proposed, and which tended to vary with national exigencies   Here we see an inevitable clash between national temperaments, between the Scot's logicalness and the inherent opportunism of the dominant partner, just as strong to-day as it was then, when the force of events made it almost necessary   Thus, if a 'regiment was raised on the Fencible plan to serve in Scotland and an attempt was made to march it across the Border or transport it to Ireland, the rank and file simply declined, greatly to the amazement of a man like Colonel Woodford, commanding the Northern Fencibles of 1793, who had been trained in the obedient school of the Grenadier Guards In the case of regiments of the line, attempts made to draft men from one corps to another were equally repudiated, while the efforts to get the Highland corps to sail abroad led to open mutiny The classic case is that of the Black Watch in 1743, which has been set forth so sympathetically by Mr Duff MacWilliam   The War Office, applying the legal standard, shot three of the resisters and drafted a great many of them—" victims of deception and tyranny," to whom Mr MacWilliam proudly dedicates his book   " The indelible impression " which this made on the minds of " the whole population of the Highlands, laid," as Stewart of Garth is bound to admit, " the foundation of that distrust in their superiors which was afterwards so much increased by various circumstances " A full corroboration of Stewart's statement occurs in the remarkable letter written by the minister of Aberarder in 1778, to which too much attention cannot be paid —

The people have been successfully deceived since the middle of the last war by all the recruiting officers and their friends It has constantly been, since that period, the common cant that the recruits were only enlisted for three years or a continuance of the war, yet, they saw or heard of those poor men being draughted into other regiments after their own had been reduced, and thus bound for life, instead of the time that they were made to believe   The people will

not be convinced, not even by giving them written obligations. . . .
They have been so often cheated that they scarce know when to
trust.

So disastrous indeed was the effect of penalising the Black Watch,
that when the Atholl Highlanders, commanded by the Laird of
Farskane, took up the same attitude exactly forty years later, Parliament and the authorities declined to punish a single man. Intensely
pro-Highland and patriotic, and imbued with the theirs-not-to-reason-
why of the old soldier, Stewart is compelled to devote a whole chapter
to eight of these mutinies—"very distressing events" he calls them
—extending from 1743 to 1804; and his whole tone is that of
sympathetic apology for the "peculiar disposition and habits of the
Highlanders."

One of these "peculiarities" was a fierce resentment against the
infliction of the brutal punishments then meted out to soldiers. Stewart
insists again and again that Highlanders had to receive preferential
treatment, not so much because their "crimes" were less serious, but
because their temperament made such expiation highly prejudicial to
the State's chance of gaining the services of their countrymen. He
maintains for instance (ii., 313):—

The corporal punishments which are indispensable in restraining the
unprincipled and shamelessly depraved, who sometimes stand in the
ranks of the British Army, would have struck a Highland soldier of
the old school with a horror that would have rendered him despicable
in his own eyes and a disgrace to his family and name. The want of a
due regard to, and discrimination of, men's dispositions has often led
to very serious consequences.

The more minute investigations of modern historians completely cor-
roborate Stewart's attitude.

It is extremely important to note that even after the territorial
organiser of a regiment had placed his corps on the "Establishment," his
influence with the men remained and was made use of. Thus, when
Colonel Woodford failed to make anything of the Northern Fencibles,
he had to send post-haste to Gordon Castle for his brother-in-law, the
Duke of Gordon, to go south and pacify the men; and similarly when
the Strathspey Fencibles became restive at Dumfries in 1795, Sir James
Grant, who had raised the regiment, was sent for, "but unfortunately
he arrived too late."

A City of Aberdeen Regiment Declined.

So far, I have been dealing with regiments raised under the personal influence of the great landed magnates ; for little was done to encourage corporate bodies. A striking case of this refusal was experienced by the City of Aberdeen, which got thoroughly alarmed like the rest of the country after the disastrous surrender of Burgoyne at Saratoga in October, 1777. Early in December the town of Manchester volunteered to raise a battalion of eleven hundred men at its own expense. Liverpool shortly afterwards followed this example, and was immediately imitated by Glasgow, Edinburgh and Aberdeen, and the offers of all except Aberdeen were accepted. The Aberdeen offer* was forwarded to Lord Suffolk, the Secretary of State for the North, by Provost Jopp on January 10, 1778, as follows (Aberdeen Town Council Archives) :—

My Lord,—The City of Aberdeen, having on many occasions given the strongest assurances of their zeal and attachment towards His Majesty's person and government ; and having beheld with indignation the rise and progress of a rebellion and revolt in the British Colonies in America, which seems to be grown to an alarming height :

Have resolved at this critical juncture most humbly to offer to His Majesty every assistance in their power for the better enabling Government to prosecute with vigour the American War and for reducing the rebellious Colonies to their former state of allegiance and subordination. And I have the honour to inform your Lordship that they have opened and are now carrying on successfully and with all possible dispatch a subscription for the purpose of raising a body of men for His Majesty's Service.

I have taken the liberty to inclose for your Lordship's perusal a Memorial on this subject, and have to request that your Lordship will be pleased to lay the same before His Majesty for his gracious acceptance. If this Memorial should contain anything improper, it must be imputed to my having had no opportunity of knowing what conditions Government has been pleased to allow other Corporations in like cases.

I must beg leave to remark to your Lordship that the circumstances

---

* Fortescue's *British Army*, iii., 245. Mr. Sinclair (*Aberdeen Volunteers*, p. 23), seems to consider that the offer referred to a Volunteer Force, apparently because it was proposed to call it the "Aberdeen Volunteers" ; but as Captain Sebag-Montefiore points out (*History of the Volunteers*, p. 101), the term Volunteer was applied only to the method of its formation. The Aberdeen regiment was to have been "from the date of incorporation on a footing of equality with the regular forces of the Crown," like the regiments of Manchester, Liverpool, Edinburgh, and Glasgow, which were numbered respectively the 72nd, 79th, 80th, and 83rd. The proposals of Aberdeen made on April 30, and August 26, 1778 (*infra*, p. lv.), were for local defence only.

of a new corps [the 81st Regiment] of one thousand men to be raised by Colonel [the Hon. William] Gordon, whose officers are mostly named from this corner and county, may render the immediate procuring of recruits more difficult, and may require that the period for completing any corps we may be able to raise be not limited, or at least not to a very short space. At the same time, assuring your Lordship that every effort will be made for carrying this design into execution with all possible dispatch; we hope that your Lordship will be pleased to signify to us His Majesty's pleasure as soon as may be.

The City's proposals were embodied in the following memorial:—

1. That a body of men shall be enlisted at the expense of this City to be put upon the Establishment as a separate Corps, provided they shall amount to 500 or upwards, and, if under that number, to be embodied in Independent Companies.

2. That the community be allowed to recommend officers who are to be approved by His Majesty, vizt.; If 500, a Lieutenant-Colonel Commandant, Major, Captains and Subalterns for the different Companys; it being understood that no Officers above the rank of Lieutenants shall be recommended but such as are of approved merit and have served with reputation in the Army, several of whom have already offered their services on this occasion.

3. If 700 or upwards, a Colonel, Lieutenant-Colonel, Major, etc.

4. Pay to commence from the time allowed to other Corps now raising.

5. Cloathing, arms, etc., to be furnished by Government.

6. The Order from War Office for inlisting to be addressed to the Provost of Aberdeen with the ordinary power of delegation.

N.B.—In order to be able to procure men with more facility, might engagement be made that such as desire it may have a discharge at the end of the American War?

To this enthusiastic offer, Lord Suffolk returned a polite refusal on January 23, 1778:—

Having had the honor of laying before the King your letter of the 9th [sic] inst. with the Memorial enclosed in it, I am now to inform you that the fullest sense is entertained of the zeal and attachment of the City of Aberdeen towards His Majesty's person and government as well as of the constitutional principles which induce the Corporation to the proposal of enlisting a body of men at their own expense to be put upon the Establishment as a separate Corps.

As, however, it is not at present intended to accept any new levies beyond what are already under the consideration of Parliament, I am on this account to decline the offer: at the same time that I once more assure you on the justice done to the loyal and constitutional motives from which it originates.

The Fencible Movement of 1778 and 1793.

To anyone who considers the magnitude of our operations at this time and the complications arising out of France's alliance with America (February), with the declaration of war on us (July 10, 1778), the refusal of the Government to accept the help of Aberdeen may seem extraordinary. As a matter of fact, it was thoroughly typical of the hugger-mugger, hand-to-mouth management of our military pre-parations throughout the whole period. It is true that the new levies to which Suffolk referred included twelve regiments of the line—the 72nd to the 83rd inclusive—of which nine were Scots, but it is also true that for some time before this date the difficulty of getting men had been growing so acute that a compulsive measure, known as the Comprehending Act (18 Geo. III. cap. 53), had to be passed; and a less exigent type of troops, the Fencibles, was raised, in the absence of Militia, which Government declined to allot to Scotland till 1797, though England had had its Militia Act in 1757. One of these Fencible regiments was raised in 1778 by the 4th Duke of Gordon, who found out that nineteen years of Regular soldiering had more or less satisfied his vast tenantry. The conditions of service in the Fencibles were voluntary enlistment (for a Government bounty of three guineas per man). The service was confined to Scotland, except in the case of the invasion of England. The men were not to be drafted; and the officers were to be chosen by the raiser of the regiment. Perhaps it was the belief in the discrimination of the individual magnate to choose good officers, as compared with the conflicting views of a corporation, that made Government favour the recruiting proposals of the former; in any case, the State's refusal was not a happy way to treat municipal enthusiasm, and may account for much of the antagonism that has not infrequently existed between the War Office and Town Councils.

In 1782 a bill was introduced into Parliament " for the better order-ing the Fencible Men in that part of Great Britain called Scotland." It provided for 12,500 privates being "annually formed into corps, companies, and battalions to learn the use of arms, and to qualify themselves in case of actual invasion, or rebellion existing within Great

Britain, to march out, and act within Scotland, against any rebels and invading enemies." The quotas of the northern counties were :—

Aberdeen	1,148
Banff	380
Elgin	303
Nairn	56
Inverness	587
Caithness	219
Ross	423
Cromarty	50
Sutherland	208
Kincardine	227
Total	**3,601**

This spurt in regiments lasted only five years, for with the Peace of Versailles, 1783, many regiments were disbanded, including the 77th, the 81st, and the Northern Fencibles, and then the old laxness set in until the next crisis ten years later. The situation has been admirably summed up by Mr. Fortescue (*County Lieutenancies*, p. 3):—

From 1784 until 1792 Pitt allowed the military forces of the country to sink to the lowest degree of weakness and inefficiency, and in 1793 he found himself obliged to improvise not merely an army, but, owing to the multiplicity of his enterprises [with Austria and Prussia against France], a very large army. He fell back on the old resources of raising men for rank [which signified the grant of a step of promotion to all officers and of a commission to all civilians who would collect a given number of men], and calling into existence new levies, allowing the system to be carried to such excess that the Army did not recover from the evil for many years. Never did the crimps reap such a harvest as in 1794 and 1795 ; and never was a more cruel wrong done to the Army than when boys fresh from school, in virtue of so many hundred weaklings produced by a crimp, took command of battalions and even of brigades, over the heads of good officers of twenty and thirty years' standing. In 1793, the bounty offered to men enlisting into the line was ten guineas; within eighteen months the Government was contracting with certain scoundrels for the delivery of men at twenty guineas a head, and long before that the market price of recruits had risen to thirty guineas.

The new crisis in national affairs was met by the raising of twenty-two corps of Fencibles,* including the Duke of Gordon's Northern Fencibles and James Leith's Aberdeenshire Fencibles ; and a great many

---

* The cost of the Fencibles and Militia of the United Kingdom was as follows :— June-December, 1793 (43 Companies), £773,378 : 1794, £787,693 : 1795 (54 Companies), £1,109,837 (*W.O.* 24 : 586 and 592).

regiments of Regulars—thirty thousand were enlisted between November, 1793, and March, 1794—to which the North-East contributed
the 100th (Gordon Highlanders) and the 109th   Besides that, a totally
new force was created in 1794, namely the Volunteers, which I shall
describe more particularly later on.   In addition to these, Sir James
Grant raised the 97th and the Strathspey Fencibles, which, though
rather out of our district, have been included because the Grants were
rivals of the Gordons and because both these corps exhibit strong traces
of the vicious system to which Mr. Fortescue refers   The method of
raising men for rank had hitherto been confined to Independent Companies, and had therefore led to no higher rank than that of Captain.
But it was now extended to the raising of " a multitude of battalions,
which, for the most part were no sooner formed than they were disbanded and drafted into other corps," thereby showing that the
personal' principle animating the earlier territorial corps had broken
down   Mr Fortescue describes the vicious situation (*British Army*,
vol. iv, part 1, p 213) —

   The Army-brokers   carried on openly a most scandalous
traffic   " In a few weeks," to use the indignant language of an officer of
the Guards, "they would dance any beardless youth, who would come
up to their price, from one newly raised corps to another, and for a
greater douceur, by an exchange into an old regiment would procure him
a permanent situation in the standing Army"
   The evils that flowed from this system were incredible.   Officers
who had been driven to sell out of the Army by their debts or their
misconduct were able after a lucky turn at play to purchase reinstate-
ment for themselves with the rank of Lieutenant-Colonel   Undesirable
characters, such as keepers of gambling houses, contrived to buy for
their sons the command of regiments, and mere children [you may
remember the story of the baby-Major " greetin' for his parritch "] were
exalted in the course of a few weeks to the dignity of field officers
One proud parent, indeed, requested leave of absence for one of these
infant Lieutenant-Colonels on the ground that he was not yet fit to be
taken from school.

The Gordon Highlanders

   In this sordid and inept welter, the Gordon Highlanders, first
numbered the 100th and then the 92nd Regiment, stand forth with
flying colours, and remain with these colours flying to the present day ;
whereas their immediately local rivals, Grant's 97th and Leith-Hay's

109th, vanished a few months after they were raised, as victims of the vicious system by which they were partly officered. Indeed, of all the many regiments raised in our district in the period under discussion the 92nd with the Aberdeen Militia alone have survived, and few British regiments have captured the public imagination like the Gordons.

I should like to add one word of explanation about this distinction. It has been said that the fame of the Gordons is due to the indiscriminating praise of " Cockney " war-correspondents, especially at the time of Dargai. It has also been hinted that my own work on the house of Gordon has had an influence in " booming " the regiment. Both suggestions only prove the inadequate historical equipment of critics who make them. The Gordon Highlanders from the very first have been popular, and have always been " boomed."* The best proof of this statement is to be found in the bibliography appended to the present volume. The 75th Regiment, now forming the 1st Battalion of the Gordons, came into existence in 1787, seven years before the 92nd. It has had a splendid fighting career; and yet not one single monograph, not even of pamphlet size, has been written about it. Almost the only attempt to tell its story is that made by Lieutenant-Colonel Greenhill Gardyne in his *Life of a Regiment*, where he devotes some chapters to the old 75th as the 1st Battalion of his main subject. The same holds true of the iconographia of the two corps, for beyond Eschauzier's print of 1833 there is scarcely a picture of the 75th.

Why should this be the case? The Gordons are not the oldest Scots regiment; they do not possess the longest " honours "; they have not been unduly praised by Aberdeen writers—rather, indeed the contrary, for we pride ourselves on our sense of proportion, and it is only of comparatively recent years that the Gordons have been intimately associated with their present depot. The main reason of their popular fame is that they have always had the touch of personality about them, and have not merely been a unit in an indiscriminating

---

* The Great War of 1914 has afforded a characteristic example of the popularity of the Gordons. Thus, one of the posters utilised by the recruiting authorities, and previously used to advertise the film of "Our Army," showed a (nondescript) Gordon Highlander in the foreground with a Lancer and R.H.A. gunners behind. Furthermore, the " National Christmas Card " (price 6d.), entitled "Defenders of the Empire," issued by Raphael Tuck on behalf of the Prince of Wales's National Relief Fund, in November, 1914, showed one Highlander, a Gordon sergeant (drawn in colour by Harry Payne), in the foreground of a group illustrating seventeen types of our Army.

military organisation   This personal touch was imparted to them with the raising of the regiment, which was enthusiastically forwarded by the Duke of Gordon and all the members of his family, notably by his brilliant consort, Jane Maxwell, who is said to have kissed the recruits.   Whether that is true or not, it has become an integral part of a sort of saga, and is now boldly illustrated in the official recruiting literature of the regiment   The personal touch was continued by the service of the Duke's popular and handsome heir, the Marquis of Huntly; immortalised in Mrs Grant of Laggan's "Highland Laddie." Again, this personal feeling was greatly aided by the fact that the first recruits were to a large extent Highland, and the officers have been mostly Scots.   The Gordons, indeed, are to my mind a splendid example of what the best type of territorialism can do for a regiment—to preserve traditions and *esprit de corps*, and to ensure a continuity and preservation of individuality, which are of first rate value in forming the character of a regiment in the British Army

The Grampian Brigade

Before passing on to the next type of military force which was raised, namely the Militia, reference must be made to an abortive scheme to raise a new combination of Highlanders, which was to be called the Grampian Brigade   Nominally promulgated by the Duke of York, it was forwarded on February 22, 1797, as a circular letter to the Duke of Gordon by his great friend, Dundas, then Home Secretary (*Gordon Castle Archives*) —

I submit to your Grace's view a plan which the Duke of York has put into my hands   I own I was very much struck on the perusal of it

Perhaps at the time the laws were made for restraining the spirit of clanship in the Highlands of Scotland the system might be justifiable by the recent circumstances which gave rise to that policy   It has for many years been my opinion that those reasons, whatever they were, have ceased, and that much good, instead of mischief, may on various occasions arise from such a connexion among persons of the same Family and Name   If this sentiment should be illustrated by the adoption of any such measure as the accompanying paper suggests, I shall have reason to be still more fortified in that opinion   I have not, however, thought it right to give His Royal Highness any advice on the subject without having some ground to judge how far there was a likelihood of its being carried into existence   The most obvious method of doing so is by addressing myself to your Grace and to other persons suggested as the proper cements [sic] of the different classes of Families referred to.

If the plan takes place it does not occur to me there can be any reason of distinguishing such a levy as this from other Fencible corps in respect of establishment and pay.

The Plan was to raise 16,000 men for internal defence by embodying the Highland Clans to be employed in Great Britain or Ireland in case of actual invasion or civil commotion or the imminent danger of both or either. Each clan was to be formed into distinct corps not exceeding 600, nor less than 200 private men in each.

There were to be nine separate brigades, utilising the clans in the following proportions :—

Brigade.	Privates.
1st or the Isles Brigade—Lord Macdonald, brigadier - - -	1,600
2nd or Caithness and Sutherland Brigade—Earl Gower, brigadier -	1,500
3rd or Ross Brigade—Mackenzie of Seaforth, brigadier - -	1,300
4th or Inverness and Moray Brigade—Sir James Grant, brigadier -	1,400
5th or the Grampian Brigade—Duke of Gordon, brigadier -	1,900
6th or Argyll Brigade—Duke of Argyll, brigadier - - - -	2,100
7th or Perth Brigade—Duke of Atholl, brigadier - - -	1,800
8th or Aberdeen and Angus Brigade—Ogilvie of Airlie, brigadier -	1,200
9th or Stirling and Dumbarton Brigade—Duke of Montrose, brigadier	1,200
	14,000

The 5th or Grampian Brigade, 1,900 strong, with the Duke of Gordon as brigadier, was to be constituted thus :—

Macdonnells on the mainland, including the families of Glengarry, Morar, Keppoch, and Glencoe - - - - - -	500
Camerons - - - - - - - - - - -	400
Gordons - - - - - - - - - - -	400
MacPhersons - - - - - - - - - -	300
MacIntoshes - - - - - - - - - -	300
Total - - - - - - - - -	1,900

The Aberdeen Angus Brigade was made up in this way :—

Ogilvies, etc.—Commanded by Ogilvie of Airlie and Lord Findlater -	600
Farquharsons— „ „ Farquharson of Invercauld - -	300
Forbeses— „ „ Lord Forbes - - - -	300
	1,200

The total of officers and men in the nine brigades and 40 battalions was to be —

Captains	· · · · · · · ·	244
Subalterns	· · · · · · · · ·	508
Sergeants	· · · · · · · ·	762
Corporals	· · · · · · · ·	762
Drummers or pipers	· · · · · ·	247
Privates	· · · · · · · ·	14,000
Total	· · · · · ·	16,523

The Plan was accompanied by some explanatory "remarks" disclosing the theory underlying it —

The Plan now proposed for embodying the Highland Clans is formed upon the principles which seem calculated to obtain the unanimous approbation of all ranks of people in the Highlands and to make it a popular measure

The Highlanders have been, and still are, warmly attached to their Chiefs and ancient customs, particularly in regard to the ranking and marshalling of the Clans   The present arrangement completely embraces these views, as each Clan forms a distinct Battalion, commanded by their natural Chief or Leader, more or less in a number according to the strength of the Clan, whilst the dignity of the great Chiefs and proprietors is equally supported by placing each at the head of a Brigade

Considerable attention is also paid in forming each Brigade of Clans which are naturally attached from local situation or otherwise to one another, as well as to their Brigadier

From the ordinary avocations of the Highlanders in general it is obvious that no equal number of men in any one district in the Kingdom can be employed with so little injury to agriculture and manufactures   At this moment they may be justly considered the only considerable body of men in the whole kingdom who are as yet absolutely strangers to the levelling principles of the present age, and therefore they may be safely trusted indiscriminately with the knowledge and use of arms

They admire the warlike exploits of their ancestors to a degree of enthusiasm , and, proud to see the ancient order of things restored, they will turn out with promptitude and alacrity

As all the Clans have a number of men in the present Fencible Regiments, each Chief will be allowed to complete his serjeants and corporals from among his kinsmen in those corps for the purpose of drilling his battalion expeditiously ; and, moreover, that each regiment may be furnished with some officers of knowledge and experience, the

f

Chiefs will be permitted to take a certain proportion of their Officers from the Line, or the half pay list. This will be attended with no difficulty, as there is no Clan which has not a number of gentlemen in the Army; and in order to induce officers of the Line to enter into the Clan levy, it will be a subject for consideration whether one step of promotion may not be given to them. It will, likewise, be subject for future consideration what the rank of the field officers commanding corps shall be, and what the proportion of staff officers shall be to each corps.

When the Duke received the scheme, he immediately transmitted it to the chiefs of whom he was, as it were, the superman, and he did so in a thoroughly tentative spirit, for the time had long gone past when he could ride roughshod over them as his ancestor, the first duke, had done. The replies of the heads of the great Highland families on his estates—namely, the Macphersons, the Mackintoshes, the Macdonnells, and the Camerons—must have soon convinced him that the scheme would not work. These documents are remarkably interesting. Macdonnell, dating from Glengarry House, March 7, was cautious:—

Having seen only parts of the Plan, [I] must defer remarks for the present, as I purpose doing myself the honour of waiting on your Grace in about twelve or fourteen days hence at furthest.

Macpherson, dating from Cluny, March 6, was sceptical:—

Your Grace must be very sensible that this country has already been much drained by different levies—so much so that, if the number now proposed were taken out of it, there would be a great danger of a totall stop being made to the operations of husbandry; and, tho' I have not the smallest doubt of the loyalty of the inhabitants, I have my fears that they would not readily agree to leave their homes in the manner proposed. But if the Plan of enrolling into volunteer companys be thought a good measure, I have no doubt (should there be no interference) that six companys of 50 men each would readily turn out in this country; by which is meant the Lordship of Badenoch, from Lochaber to Strathspey, these companys to be supplied with light arms, accoutrements, and clothing by Government, to be drilled, separately, two days in the week as near their own homes as possible, being paid for these days, and not to be called from hence on any account except in case of invasion, and that we confine our service to the coast 'twixt Inverness and Aberdeen; and that such services are not to be expected or demanded but during an invasion or civil commotion within that district.

These, my lord, are my ideas on the subject, and I take them from my knowledge of the state of the country and the sentiments of the people But should your Grace think of a better plan, or one more conciliating to the minds of the people, I shall readily and chearfully concur with you, as far as I can, in any way your Grace may think most effectual for thwarting the views of our inveterate enemy against our Gracious Sovereign, our Country and happy constitution

The [Volunteer] Company, tho' drilled separately for the conveniency of the inhabitants, will march and act in a body, should there be occasion for it

Æneas Mackintosh, writing on March 16 from London, whither he had taken his wife for the benefit of her health, was also dubious

I feel myself at this distance—without any communication with the other Gentlemen, heads of families—incapable of giving a decided opinion Although I have every inclination to give effect to any Plan that may be suggested   yet, upon the first idea being suggested, it appears to me that from the great drain the country has already sustained, it will be almost impossible to raise the body of men proposed, if they are liable to be sent to England, but especially to Ireland And, I conceive, I need not remind your Grace how little influence the chieftains retain at this day in comparison of what it was half a century ago Whatever arrangement it may ultimately be decided to carry into effect for the real internal defence of Scotland, your Grace may rely its having my best wishes, and any personal aid in my power shall not be wanting

A very different tone was adopted by Cameron of Lochiel, who wrote a significantly rude letter from Glasgow, by return of post, March 6 · —

[I] am clearly of opinion that every exertion in the present time must be used by those who have power and interest in the Highlands , and, as far as relates to myself, I am ready to come forward not only on account of the situation of my country, but the great satisfaction I shall feel at leaving your Grace's regiment [the Northern Fencibles],· which I am perfectly dissatisfied [with], and am not the only one , I am convinced if all the circumstances were known to you, you would not be surprised

In reply to your Grace's question whether the men would go to Ireland, I don't know what they would do, They have already been asked by Lieutenant-Colonel Woodford [the Duke's brother-in-law who commanded the Fencibles] and refused him Nothing, my Lord Duke, would have induced me to be in this corps but the idea of affording my neighbour, the Duke of Gordon, every assistance in my power, which, I hope, will always be the case Therefore, should it so happen that

I am called on by your Grace to come forward according to the Plan proposed, I shall expect that same friendly assistance from you by which each of us ought at all times to be governed.

Whatever the Duke may have thought, his uncle, Lord Adam Gordon, then Commander of the Forces in Scotland, had summed up the Celt in his own mind, for he wrote, August 5, 1795, giving as one of his reasons for opposing the proposal to commute in part the loaf of wheaten flour to oatmeal " the suspicious nature of the Highlanders " and their jealousy.

Perhaps it was to this Grampian Brigade proposal that, according to a letter from Lord Fife to his Deputies, November 9, 1803, the Lord Lieutenancy of Banffshire had proposed in March, 1797 (H.O. 50 : 59), to fix alarm signals along the coast to announce the approach of an enemy by erecting flagstaffs at Trouphead, Melrose Head, the Hill of Redhyth, Logiehead and Portknockie Head. The alarm signal for calling out the people in the more inland parts of the county was to be by the ringing of the church bells, "which were directed to be rung at funerals and on other occasions in knells only ; but when used as a signal to be rung in loud peals." But this idea, like the Brigade itself, melted away, for, the alarm "having subsided, the only signal post that was ever erected in consequence of the resolutions was one on Trouphead, put up by Mr. Garden of Troup," who about the same time built a fort at his own expense (H.O. 50 : 94).

Although the raising of the Gordons showed that the personal equation was still a factor in territorial soldiering, the reception of the Grampian Brigade scheme proved that the wholesale raising of Highland regiments was played out. Indeed, for that matter, the system of entrusting the organisation of troops to private individuals was coming to an end—only two Highland regiments were raised after this date— and the task was transferred to the local authorities, equipped with the compulsive machinery of the ballot. It was not merely that the financial resources of individuals were becoming unequal to the strain, but the need for men was increasing at an enormous rate and no one could see the end of it. So the State, which had been so chary of entrusting the task of raising troops to Corporations in Scotland, was at last driven to that expedient.

The Militia

So great had the strain become that in February, 1797, the Bank of England was compelled to suspend cash payments   In the same month, a French fleet bore down on Wales, and in May a mutiny broke out in the Navy at the Nore.   True, Jervis had defeated the Spaniards at Cape St Vincent, February 14, and in October, Duncan was to defeat the Dutch at Camperdown , but the year opened in panic, and part of that panic resulted in the extension on July 19, 1797, of the Militia Act (37 Geo III cap 103) to Scotland

The measure involved the most serious aspect that soldiering had yet presented, with the exception of the Comprehending Act of 1778 It approximated the conditions of Territorial soldiering as we know it to-day in point of the administrative body, the Lords Lieutenant, entrusted with raising it, though by introducing the ballot—which differentiated the Militia from the Fencibles—it relied on a new machinery

Mr Fortescue says that in Scotland the Militia had been unknown until 1797 , but this is not quite correct   There had been a sort of a Militia since September 23, 1663—Mr Andrew Ross traces its tangled history minutely in the *Military History of Perthshire* (1, 104-124)—when a force of 20,000 Foot and 2,000 Horse was raised. In October, 1678, it was reduced to one fourth , but even at that, a "Method of turning the Militia of Scotland into a Standing Army," was advocated in a pamphlet of 1680 (in the British Museum)   The measure of 1797 differed considerably from this early Militia, though, curiously enough, it authorised the raising of a force only a little larger than the 1678 Militia

England had been equipped with a Militia in 1757 by an Act, which provided for passing the entire manhood of the nation through the force by ballot in terms of three years, though it was not strictly enforced and lost much of its value   Attempts to extend the measure to Scotland were made in 1760, 1776, 1782 (when the Marquis of Graham's bill was thrown out), and 1793 , but they all failed—at first because the spectre of Jacobitism had not been exorcised from the English mind, and later on for other reasons.   So forty years were allowed to elapse before the system was actually extended to Scotland, under the intense pressure of the country's difficulties in the field

The Act (consisting of 56 sections) fixed the quota of Militia to be supplied by Scotland at 6,000 men, and its administration was entrusted to the Lords Lieutenant.   Mr. Ross summarises its conditions neatly : —

In every parish a return was made of all men between the ages of 19 and 23 inclusive, and after omitting therefrom all who could plead exemption, *viz.*, those serving in the Volunteers and Yeomanry, all professors, clergymen, schoolmasters, constables, indentured clerks, apprentices, seamen and men with more than two legitimate children, a ballot for the required quota was taken.   When a sufficient number of men volunteered no ballot was necessary.   Substitutes were allowed. [Mr. Fortescue points out that "these substitutes were precisely the men who, but for the heavy bounty which they could gain from serving comfortably at home, would gladly have enlisted in the Army."]   The men were enlisted to serve within Scotland during the war and for one calendar month after the proclamation of peace.   The field officers were nominated by the Crown, the other officers by the Lords Lieutenant, and all were to have a certain property qualification [so that the force was practically in the hands of the landed gentry].

These land qualifications, which proved a stumbling block, provided that a Colonel or Lieutenant-Colonel should be possessed or be heir apparent to a person possessed of a landed estate of £400 Scots value rent in Scotland.   A Major or Captain had to have a similar qualification to the extent of £300 a year, and a Lieutenant or Ensign one of £100 a year.   It was provided that, if a sufficient muster of persons could not be found to accept commissions as Lieutenants and Ensigns, officers in the Army or those who had held commissions in the Regular, Fencible, or Volunteer forces could be appointed.   Peers or their heirs apparent having places of residence in the county might act without being qualified, and the acceptance did not involve vacating a seat in Parliament.

From the very first the Act proved unpopular.   Mr. Ross thinks this was due to the "blundering fashion in which the measure was placed before the people "; but, as we shall see, it went deeper down than that.   The first consequence was that it became necessary by a second Act to postpone the initiation of the force from August 1, 1797, to March 1, 1798, and to reduce the quota from 6000 to 5468.   But that number was further reduced, for a return of 1797 (no month or day is stated) speaks of His Majesty " having determined to call out at present only 3,000 men."   The apportionment from the various counties was as follows, Dumfries, Clackmannan, and Orkney being omitted as no returns had been received (*H.O.* 50: 29):—

Edinburgh County	115	Fife	176
„ City	41	Dumbarton	42
Linlithgow	37	Bute	16
Haddington	72	Argyll	136
Berwick	76	Inverness	95
Peebles	26	Perth	263
Selkirk	13	Forfar	185
Roxburgh	78	Kincardine	52
Kirkcudbright	66	Aberdeen	244
Wigton	47	Banff	65
Ayr	180	Elgin	47
Renfrew	98	Nairn	12
Lanark	283	Cromarty	11
Stirling	102	Ross	81
Kinross	13	Sutherland	27
	Cromarty	35	
Total			2,734.

In the south of Scotland the raising of the force actually led to riot. Dundas, who was then Secretary at War, was greatly disgusted with his countrymen, writing on August 27, 1797 (*H.O.* 50: 29):—

When I left Dalkeith, I had no idea the execution of the Militia Law could cause any disturbances in the county [Midlothian]. If I could have foreseen it, I should have remained upon my post. On Sunday the 20th [of August], I was informed that some persons had pulled down the list [of ballotable men] from the church door in the parish of Canonby, and that the parish registers were to be burned next day [because they contained the material necessary for the collection of men]. Immediately on Monday, I got together about thirty of the heads of families in the schoolhouse to endeavour, if possible, to prevent any further violence. I was soon informed that about 200 young men had, on the night of Sunday, or early in the morning of Monday, taken by force the books from the schoolmaster's house. The mob have been most outrageous, insulted the Deputy Lieutenants, driven them from the meeting, exacting oaths and promises that they will not proceed further in the business.

The attack on dominies is also referred to by the Duke of Roxburghe who, writing on September 1, 1797, says that many individuals were "frightened at the idea of being militiamen," and he adds—"The schoolmasters are intimidated, and I am afraid that we shall not procure new lists without making examples of some of them" (*H.O.* 50: 29).

David Hay, a Deputy Lieutenant for Dumfries, wrote on September 1 to the Duke of Queensberry—"old Q," the "degenerate Douglas" of Wordsworth's sonnet—that the opposition to the Act was "general in Scotland, and nowhere more so than in this part of the country" (*H.O.* 50 : 29) :—

There is not one of your Grace's Deputies who has not been threatened with Distruction, as Sir William Maxwell [of Springkell?], Colonel Dirom, and Mr Grahame of Moss Knowe, Deputies, had a meeting the other day in their district, and were most grossly insulted by a enraged mob, and before they were allowed to depart were forced to sign an obligation on Stamped Paper, that they would never interfere in the business again.

On the same day, Dundas wrote that the counties of Fife and Lanark had followed the example of those in the south.

Lord Adam Gordon, Commanding the Forces in Scotland, took the Regular soldier's point of view, for he wrote from Edinburgh to Dundas on September 1, 1797 (*H.O.* 50 : 29) :—

There surely must be, as you say, incendiaries, and of the worst description, behind the curtain and at the bottom of this bad business. Otherways, so much system and sameness could never appear in so many different and distant places at once, or nearly at once. But there can be but one opinion—*viz.*, that, at all hazards, and cost what it may, this opposition to the law of the land must be subdued, and full obedience to the civil magistrate enforced ; else there is an end of government.

On the previous day he had written to Lieutenant-General Musgrave, Commanding the North-Eastern District (*H.O.* 50 : 29) :—

Since I wrote you last by Saturday's post, the situation of things here [Edinburgh] has become so much more critical as to make it absolutely my duty to request that *without delay*, you would send into Scotland by Berwick, Coldstream, Kelso, and Carlisle a reinforcement of 3,000 men of which the more cavalry the better.

P.S.—English Fencibles would suit us better than Scotch ones at this time.

A very different attitude was adopted by George Haldane of Gleneagles. His letter is peculiarly interesting because, though his name was really Cockburn (of the Ormiston family), his mother, Margaret Haldane, was the great grand-aunt of Lord Haldane, who has grasped the Territorial principle more completely than any of our War Ministers. Writing to Dundas on September 8, 1797, he said (*H.O.* 50 : 29) :—

The state of the country is at present such that I feel a strong inclination to trouble you with some intelligence with regard to it, which I think you should be acquainted with.

The new Militia Act has been among them [the people] for a fortnight past, and endeavours used to get it executed, but without effect, as it has occasioned much commotion and even outrage, from the oposition it has met with from the People—1st, Because not understood: (there is a defect in promulgating our lawes which you would do well to bring in a bill to remove); 2nd, The People, being grown more opulent and at their ease, *now* expect to be treated with more attention; to be in some measure advised with, and not totally neglected, as if only born to pay Taxes; so far has the Democratical spirit prevailed generally! 3rd, Evil designing people spread amongst them, laid hold of and inflamed their prejudices, perswading them that they were all to be made Soldiers (the very name of which they hate), and sent abroad with other troops ; and that Government would not keep faith with them, tho' they should promise it; and point out to them instances of the Fencibles and other corps who have been sent out of the country contrary to their engagement at enlisting. If there is any truth in this it should be carefully guarded against, as it does *much ill*.

Another thing which has been laid hold of to irritate them much and has done a deal of mischief was that they had on the first mention of an invasion, they had [repeated thus] in many parts of the country zealously and voluntarily made repeated offers to come forth as Volunteers whenever called upon; but that their offers to enter such had been slighted or rejected. Besides, they were told that they behoved to serve without any pay on the days of training, and all other occasions, excepting on actual service or on invasion, which they complained of as a great hardship, as they also thought it was not to be allowed to serve under such officers of their own country as they chose, a thing they prize much. They also complained much that they could be ordered away from their own homes, perhaps in harvest time, or to the total neglect of their own affairs, to any the most distant part of the country without pay or reward; and even their sons taken away from them, who are necessary to them for carrying on their farms, and no bounty to be given to them, which the Army always has. They had many other objections ariseing from Ignorance, Stupidity, and Obstinacy, which I will not trouble you with, but which I, as well as others, took much pains to rebuke; and, at last, by explaining things to them made some impression on them. As I knew their dispositions to be at bottom good and that the bulk of them were loyal and ready

g

to serve their country, and especially against a foreign enemy, I wrote and dispersed among them two printed papers explaining the Act and answering their objections, and also caus'd print another paper sent me by the Duke of Montrose which he had published in Stirlingshire for the same purpose. And I am confident I could, if necessary, carry out with me 200 good men from this parish, and at least as many from the adjoining parishes where my property lies.

At the same time, I am not sure that all their objections are removed, for in sum of the neighbouring parishes where the strong hand has been too hastily, as too far, tryed it has had bad effects, as has happened to our friend Sir William Murray, who has been very ill-used in his parish of Foulis by carrying there with him a troop of Dragoons to get the lists made up and posted on the church door. This being done on a Sunday and by the military so exasperated the mob that they fell upon him when he had seized one of them, and trampled him down till he was relieved by the soldiers who cut some of them down with their swords, and thus made the thing worse, as there is nothing now heard of thro' the country but breach of the Sabbath day and being cut to pieces by the soldiers; whereas I am certain that nothing will do with them but gentle and soft measures and soothing, rather than offending, them; at least it must be first tryed. And I do conjure you to attend to this, least a spirit which might be led should be drove into madness and fury and occasion much mischief, for these wild people have an unconquerable spirit, and will never be quelled by dragoons. I think it right to presume to give the caution to you, whose opinion is likely to be followed. Remember Pentland and Bothwell Bridge, and keep your Dragoons to yourself. You may have need for them. As one of the Deputy Lieutenants, I thought it proper for me to write to the Lord Lieutenant to the above purpose, and proposed to his grace to bring another method, *viz.*, to try rather the Clause in the Act, p. 27 [section] 29, which allows volunteers to be accepted of, instead of the quota of militia men to be imposed under the Act. The first with a moderate bounty will be more easily raised than the Act inforced by Dragoons, and will answer the purpose as well or better, and keep all quiet. This will not be giving up the Act, which I was always keen for, but only taking an easier method, and a little more time, during which the Volunteers might be learning the use of arms to make them really useful: for which purpose half pay officers and drill sergeants may be sent down, and this would help soon to reconcile the people and introduce the Act among them *by degrees*; the only way in which it ever will be done—by gentle usage and the just confidence they have in the Government.

The Duke of Hamilton, adopting the persuasive method, took up another point of view, namely that Scotland had been insulted by not being allowed to have a Militia force of its own. He issued a printed broadside dated September 4, 1797 (preserved at the Record Office— H.O. 50: 29), in which he pointed out that the pay, 1s a day, was better than that of most day labourers and of "many kinds of tradesmen." He proceeds :—

It is notorious that many persons, who are strongly against every measure of Government whatever, have gone from County to County with the avowed intention of inflaming the minds of the people upon this occasion ; and there is every reason to think that it is owing to the instigation and misrepresentation of such persons that so much clamour has been raised against a measure so natural and so necessary, and which only puts Scotland upon a footing with England, which has long enjoyed the Constitutional Defence arising from a Militia, and thus taken away a distinction which has long been reckoned odious and dishonourable to Scotland. Had Government refused to grant Scotland a Militia and to trust us with arms for our own defence, then, indeed, there might have been cause of discontent.

It would surely, therefore, be a stain upon Scotchmen should they refuse to step forward to defend Scotland within Scotland after matters have been cleared up and explained. Let all men consider how happily they live under the protection of the Laws of their Country . . . but let them also consider that if, by tumultuous meetings and acts of violence they break those laws, they thus forfeit their protection and become liable to punishment to the great loss of themselves and their families.

Whether there were any similar difficulties in Aberdeenshire, I am unable to say, for no documents at the Record Office bear on the point, but I think it quite likely, all the more as the county had been such a prey to unscrupulous recruiters in the preceding years.

The total cost of the Scots Militia for the year 1798 ran up to £175,492, as follows (W.O. 24: 604):—

1st or Argyllshire - - - - - -	£17,980
2nd or Ross-shire - - - - - -	13,714
3rd or Lanarkshire - - - - - -	17,018
4th or Dumfries-shire - - - - -	20,542
5th or Fifeshire - - - - - -	18,210
6th or Aberdeenshire - - - - - -	18,635
7th or Ayr and Renfrewshire - - - -	16,751
8th or Forfarshire - - - - - -	15,603
9th or Perthshire - - - - - -	16,376
10th or Edinburghshire - - - - -	19,658
Difference of pay to paymasters - - -	1,000

In spite of the Peace of Amiens the difficulties of the country did not diminish: still more troops were required: so on June 26, 1802, a new Act (42 Geo. III. cap. 91) was passed increasing the Scots Militia to 7,950 men and the ten original battalions to fifteen, the counties being redistributed as follows, the figures in the right-hand column indicating the number of the new battalion:—

1797.	1802.
1st or Argyll, *i.e.*, Argyll, Dumbarton Bute, Inverness	7 Argyll and Bute. 15 Dumbarton, etc. 13 Inverness, etc.
2nd or Ross, *i.e.*, Ross, Elgin, Nairn, Cromarty, Sutherland Caithness	9 Ross, Caithness, Sutherland, Cromarty. 13 Elgin, Nairn, etc.
3rd or Lanark, *i.e.*, Lanark	4 Lanark.
4th or Dumfries, *i.e.*, Dumfries, Selkirk, Peebles, Roxburgh Kirkcudbright Wigtown	10 Dumfries, Selkirk, Roxburgh. 8 Peebles, etc. 14 Kirkcudbright, Wigtown.
5th or Fife, *i.e.*, Fife, Stirling Kinross, Clackmannan	3 Fife. 15 Stirling, Kinross, Clackmannan, etc.
6th or Aberdeen, *i.e.*, Aberdeen, Banff	1 Aberdeen. 13 Banff, etc.
7th or Ayr, *i.e.*, Ayr, Renfrew	2 Ayr. 6 Renfrew.
8th or Forfar, *i.e.*, Forfar, Kincardine	12 Forfar, Kincardine.
9th or Perth, *i.e.*, Perth	5 Perth.
10th or Edinburgh, *i.e.*, Edinburgh Linlithgow, Haddington, Berwick	11 Edinburgh. 8 Berwick, Linlithgow, Haddington, etc.

The new measure proved quite as unpopular as its predecessor, and far more so than in England. Summarising the Scots counties in the bulky volumes of correspondence on the subject at the Record Office ("Home Office Papers: Internal Defence"), Mr Fortescue gives a succinct account of the dislike created by the measure (*County Lieutenancies*, 48):—

From almost every county in Scotland, even before the war broke out, came the same tale of difficulty in obtaining not only men but officers, and of perfunctory conduct, or worse, on the part of the Deputy-Lieutenants. In Aberdeen ballotted men invariably paid the fine for exemption, and no gentleman would accept even a captain's commission when offered to him. In Banff, again, only one duly qualified gentleman could be persuaded to become a captain. In Haddington there was the like dearth of officers, and in Peebles the like unwillingness of the men. In Bute there were only five men in the

Militia who had not been drawn from other counties, and not one single ballotted man had been enrolled.   From Ross came the report that the Highlanders would have nothing to do with the Militia; that the most mountainous district had not produced a man; that the Militia laws were ill understood by magistrates and Deputy Lieutenants and that, being an innovation, they were detested by the Highlanders as an intolerable grievance.   In Stirling the Lieutenancy had done its work so ill that in several cases the same man had been enrolled and had received bounty from several sub-divisions.   In Selkirk the Lord Lieutenant despaired of providing his quota of twelve men for the Supplementary Militia, though he could count upon payment of the fines.   Forfar could show but one principal to every six substitutes, and to every five men that paid the fine for exemption.   From Kirkcudbright the Lord Lieutenant reported that almost the whole of the Militia would be substitutes and that the insurance societies [which insured men for the price of the exemption fine] had been largely patronised in the towns. In Perth it was a case of few enrolments and many fines.   In fact, the service was not only unpopular but suspected; for it was bound up with an oath and a red coat, and it was hard to make the cautious Scot believe that this combination did not signify compulsory military service for life.

The difficulty experienced in handling the Militia at its start was experienced throughout the whole course of its earlier career.   Its administration, indeed, was one long muddle.   A few points may be noted. In 1807, when an Act was passed to permit enlistment into the Line, Scotland sent only 3,890 out of the 4,160 men qualified to enlist, the deficiency from Aberdeen being 12.   In 1810 "the general hatred of the Militia in Scotland," to use Mr. Fortescue's phrase, came out when the Government permitted the deficiency caused by enlistment into the Line to be filled for a period by Volunteering.   In 1811 the price of substitutes had risen in Forfar to from £50 to £80.   In 1813 many substitutes put forward a claim—Mr. Fortescue says it was engineered by "some pettifogging lawyers in various parts of Scotland"—to be discharged on the completion of ten years' service, five for themselves and five for their principals, although the wording of the Act was adverse to any such claim.   On January 1, 1813, a petition on these lines, signed (most illiterately) by 607 men of the Aberdeenshire Militia stationed at Glasgow, was sent to "Prince George of Wales," an appeal to the Lord Lieutenant having failed (*H.O.* 50: 292); while 182 men of the Inverness-shire Militia, stationed at Hillsea, sent a similar petition. But the "men were easily persuaded of their folly," and the agitation was stamped out.   In view, then, of all those difficulties in its early history, and of the neglect into which the force was allowed to fall between Waterloo and the Crimea, it is remarkable that the Militia should be the only corps, besides the Gordon Highlanders, that has survived out of all the numerous regiments raised in the north-east of Scotland during the period under review.

The Volunteers.

Great as was the help arising from the organisation of a Militia force in Scotland, the supply of men did not equal the demand, and so the Government, in April, 1798, had recourse by Act of Parliament (38 Geo. III. cap. 27) to another type of troops of a less military character—the Volunteers.   This force, as its name implies, was not raised under compulsory measures, which made the Militia as much disliked as the Regular Army, and therefore it was popular.   But this very popularity was constantly militating against the existing forces, and in consequence Government had to go on tinkering with other types of troops to keep the Volunteers in check, until you get a mosaic of muddle in which it is very difficult to trace the pattern.   I cannot do more here than indicate some of the main currents in the history of the Volunteers.

In the first place, it was not really a new force in 1798.   What the Act of that year did was to put the Volunteers and the Armed Association so closely connected with them more in touch with the existing military machine, creaking as it was ; to make them more available for the State, the Act describing itself " as applying in the most expeditious manner and with the greatest effect the voluntary services of the King's loyal subjects for the defence of the Kingdom."

It is necessary to go back a little and see what were the voluntary services available.   This is not easy to do, for the beginnings of the Volunteers are exceedingly obscure, so that Mr. Fortescue washes his hands of any attempt to describe the force between 1794 and 1801 : the documents "are so scanty and imperfect that it is impossible to speak of them except in general terms."   Suffice to say that the Volunteers started in a characteristically makeshift manner, coming into existence from the common man's desire to defend himself rather than from the resolution of the State to defend him.   There had been " Armed Associations " in England as early as 1745 ; but the Volunteers proper had been born out of our disaster at Saratoga twenty years before the Act of 1798, and got their greatest fillip in Ireland—which, as we have seen with our own eyes, has a genius for raising Volunteers   Aberdeen, as we know, had also been moved by the Saratoga tragedy, and had been baulked by the Government in an offer of a regiment of the Line   A few weeks later (April 30, 1778), the Town Council resolved to arm suitable citizens with the weapons that had been forwarded by the Government for the defence of the town in 1759   The organisation so created was called the " Aberdeen Associates," but the Government vetoed the movement and demanded that the arms should be given up, and so the Associates declined (August 26) to " embark again on an undertaking on which so harsh a negative was formerly put "   The Government took up exactly the same attitude in regard to Ireland's desire to arm, and when the Mayor of Belfast applied for troops to defend the town he was told that only half of a troop of dismounted horsemen and half a company of Invalids could be spared   But the Town Council of Belfast lacked that sense of obedience to authority which had made the Town Council of Bon-Accord acquiesce in the return of the Associates' arms   " The people at once flew to arms, sudden enthusiasm, such as occurs two or three times in the history of a nation, seems to have passed through all classes "—how history repeats itself in Ireland—and " all along the coast Associations for self-defence were formed under the direction of the leading gentry "   It is not part of my business to trace the history of the Irish Volunteers of this period   I mention the movement simply to show that volunteering was no new idea and that it disproves the claim made by the Hon Archibald Fraser,* the youngest son of the notorious Lord Lovat, that the " Cale-

* Fraser, elected M P for Inverness-shire, March 28, 1782, seconded on June 17, following, the Marquis of Graham's motion for leave to bring in a bill to repeal the Disarming Act of 1746 (so far as its veto of the kilt was concerned), and his bill received the royal assent on July 1   On June 10, the House of Commons rejected Lord Graham's bill to establish a Militia in Scotland   On September 5 a meeting was held in Edinburgh to consider a plan for raising a Volunteer Corps, the Caledonian Band, of ten companies, to serve without pay until called out on actual service, and to be clothed in the Highland dress, with Graham as Colonel, Lord Buchan as Lieutenant-Colonel, and Fraser as one of the Captains , and it was hoped that this example would be followed by the principal counties and towns in Scotland, so as to supersede the necessity of raising a Militia   But the proposal does not seem to have met the views of Lord Shelburne, and appears to have been dropped (*Scots Magazine*, September, 1782   *Edinburgh Evening Courant*, September 7, 1782, and notes from Mr Andrew Ross, Ross Herald)

donian Band at Edinburgh," of 1782, were the "first Volunteers in the
Empire" (*H.O.* 50: 209).

The next attempt to organise a Volunteer force took place in 1794,
when, in addition to war abroad, there was trouble at home in the
spread of republican doctrines from France. The dilemma induced
several bodies of citizens to come forward with offers of service to the
Government, the first to be enrolled being the Five Associated Companies of St. George's, Hanover Square, London, in the Spring of 1794.
Government, ever slow to move, took time, and in April an Act (34 Geo.
III. cap. 31) was passed, limited to the duration of the war, authorising
the raising of Volunteer corps.

The new force had two drawbacks from the tactical point of view.
It was not only a unit, independent of and, owing to its recruiting conditions, antagonistic to the existing military forces of Regulars, Militia,
and Fencibles, but it was a series of units, inside and independent of
its own main unit, for the individual corps were run by local
"Associations" and financed by private subscription.

The antagonism to the existing military forces arose, as I have
said, from the fact of the exemption from service in the Militia of men
producing a certificate that they had attended exercise punctually during
six weeks previous to the hearing of appeals against the Militia list.
Each parish had now the choice of raising its quota of defence by means
of the Militia ballot, or by the formation of distinct companies of
Volunteers, and the latter system very naturally won the day, as being
much less exigent.   This disassociation of the Volunteers from the
Militia is for Mr. Fortescue "a great and disastrous blunder which has
never (he was writing in 1906) been thoroughly repaired."

The Volunteers were also units within this unit, for while the Act
reserved to the King the manner in which Volunteers should in any case
be employed in the event of being called out on active service, it made
no attempt to limit or define the conditions of service under which a
particular corps should be formed. No corps was subject to military
discipline, nor was it entitled to pay unless and until called into actual
service.   Mr. Fortescue points out that "the corps made their own conditions of service, were supported by private subscriptions, and were
directed by committees of subscribers, who were not necessarily holders
of commissions. These committees addressed the Secretary of State

directly, and it was an open question whether they or the officers were the true commanders of the corps" Small wonder that he is chary of attempting a history of the 1794 movement

An attempt to codify the regulations relating to the movement and to co-ordinate its efforts was made in June, 1794, by Archibald Fraser of Lovat, who circularised the magistrates of Scotland about "A Permanent Loyal and Constitutional Defence" He propounded the following propositions —

(1) Such Force should consist of two kinds one *Moveable* at his Majesty's orders to any spot within Great Britain and to consist of a Volunteer Enrolment with levy money as a votive offering, according to the size, situation and state of each Shire, with great attention on the part of the Shire to the character of the individuals enrolled

(2) The other Defensive Force to be *Local*, and confined to each Shire or its near neighbourhood, at the call of the Lord Lieutenant and his Deputies, for the purposes of procuring and maintaining good order and obedience to the Laws, the individuals to be enrolled from a selection of Freeholders and Feuars of Land and their relations and relatives resident upon the lands of others, who, having acquired fortunes by their industry and abilities, although they have not land, have property to lose, and lastly, thriving Tenants, specially recommended, in writing, to the Shire, by Freeholders and Feuars of Land, or acting for such, as representing them in their absence

(3) This Local Defence to be enrolled without levy money, and, when required, to act on horseback, to find their own horse, having all cattle to carry them to kirk and market

(4) To be subject to a scrutiny of character and test oaths, and, when called together, to be subject to Military Laws, and, of course, intitled to these liberal encouragements already secured by Act of Parliament, 17th April, 1794, Chap 24

(5) Local enrolment within Boroughs for the like laudable purposes to consist of substantial Burghers and inhabitants known to the Magistrates and by them recommended in writing

(6) That if an Uniform, for the sake of good appearance and œconomy, is adopted, it should be of the plainest kind, such as plain blue with a red cape and cuff, and each Shire or Stewartry to be distinguished only by the name of the Shire on their buttons

(7) That the Discipline and weapons of Defence be adapted to the natural and local situation of each Shire, with due attention to the maritime interests, where there is sea coast, islands, creeks or harbours

h

(8) The mode of Assembly may be, in hilly counties, by Smoke by day and Fire by night from eminent places, and in thick weather by the Bugle Horn or by written orders only of the Lord Lieutenant and his Deputies

(9) This mode of Internal Local Defence interferes not with recruiting or military service, but may greatly aid it, as it embraces all persons of property, having fixed residences and good characters, and includes Land Proprietors, Commissioners of Supply, Justices of the Peace, and Half-pay Officers

Fraser's proposal came to nothing, and Scotland simply followed the helter skelter arrangements of England, "Volunteer Associations" organising corps by private subscription   Aberdeen came forward in 1794 with one Battery Company and one Infantry Battalion, Peterhead followed with a corps in 1795, and Fraserburgh in 1797   But in the absence of War Office data it is impossible to present anything like a complete account of the force in Aberdeen   A statement in the *Aberdeen Journal* of April 11, 1797, gives a glimpse of the activity of the district:

The farmers on the Earl of Aberdeen's estates in the County of Aberdeen have come forward with great alacrity and made a voluntary offer of their services in the event of invasion, expressive of their regard and attachment to the King and Constitution, and their resolution to exert their utmost efforts for the defence of the country   Fifteen hundred and seventy-two of them have already enrolled and agreed to serve without pay under his Lordship or the Deputy Lieutenants of the district where they reside, and in the meantime to be trained in the use of arms   They have also engaged to furnish their horses, carts, and servants for conveying, without expense to Government, troops and military stores through the county   In his Lordship's estates 1,200 carts and 2,400 horses can be procured for this purpose, and the white fishers and seafaring people in the sea towns of Auchmedden, Cairnbulg, and Boddam belonging to the Earl, amounting to 93, have also enrolled and offered their services either by sea or land as may be judged most effectual for the defence of the Country

But more than enthusiasm was necessary   The increasing stringency of the situation abroad and the unrest in Ireland compelled a greater co-ordination of effort, or, as Dundas put it, "a general direction to the zeal of the country"   This was attempted, as I have noted, by the passing (in April, 1798) of an Act (38 Geo III cap 27) "for applying in the most expeditious manner and with the greatest effect the voluntary services of the King's loyal subjects for the defence of the Kingdom" It is very difficult to summarise the history of the conversion*, for we not only have very few documents to go upon, but those that exist show that the Government had not made up its mind what it wanted, and consequently chopped and changed It may, however, be broadly claimed that the Act of 1798 made an effort to unify the various Volunteer companies and Armed Associations and to arrange them on a more tactical basis, the parish and county giving place to the idea of a "military district" In certain respects the Volunteers and the Armed Associations were antagonistic in conception, and the Government instituted a difference between them in consequence, by granting pay and exemption from the Militia ballot only to the Volunteers On the other hand, it cut down the pay and the clothing allowance of the Volunteers who were formed after the passing of the Act Ultimately the majority of the local corps conformed to the conditions prescribed by the War Office, and a force of from 1,400 to 1,450 companies of Volunteers was formed in Great Britain, with about 75 in Ireland, with 78 district corps formed by Voluntary Associations for Defence, but Mr Fortescue, who finds it difficult to speak with certainty (*History of the Army*, iv, 894), thinks it "extremely doubtful whether all the Volunteers could have put above 60,000 into the field"

The 1798 force was dissolved with the thanks of Parliament (April 6) on the conclusion of the Peace of Amiens (March 25, 1802), yet so undecided was Government and so distrustful of the continuance of the Peace, that we find Lord Hobart writing (April 26) to Lord Pembroke about the advisability of encouraging the continuance of the Volunteers On May 4, the Secretary at War, sought leave to bring in a bill "to enable his Majesty to accept of the offers of service" of the Volunteers—thereby creating a precedent for maintaining a Volunteer force in time of peace, while on June 22, 1802, an Act (42 Geo III cap 66) was passed to this end The measure, which granted exemption from the hated Militia ballot, proved an immediate success, the Aberdeenshire companies rising from 33 to 53 On March 31,

---

* The most succinct account of the Volunteers under the Act of 1798 is given in Captain Sebag-Montefiore's *History of the Volunteer Forces*, pp 187-225 See also Lady Tullibardine's *Military History of Perthshire*, i 194-200

1803, the Government invited offers from additional Volunteers* and outlined the plan on which it intended to act, adding that "it must be considered with reference to a permanent system rather than to a situation of emergency", previously the force had been raised to last the length of the war These additional men brought up the force by December, 1803, to 450,000—"unregulated, undisciplined, unorganised, but irrepressible" with the result that the price of substitutes for the Militia rose to as high as £100 Two Aberdeenshire cases illustrating the point may be cited On July 22, 1803, the Duke of Gordon wrote to the Secretary of State (*H O* 50. 57) —

The whole Militia Force, including the Supplementary Militia number appointed to this county have been duly ballotted for, although the effective strength of the regiment is yet by no means complete, from the circumstance of a very great proportion of the persons drawn having paid the penalties incurred by the Act The most strenuous exertions will, however, be used to procure men from the amount of these penalties.

Again on February 8, 1808, Andrew Affleck, of the Loyal Aberdeen Volunteers, wrote to Colonel Finlason that two drummers, Alexander Morice and George Pine, had asked for their discharge so that they might enter as Substitutes into the Militia, for which they were to receive £40 They were willing to pay £20 each for their discharge

In the face of all this sort of thing, many expedients were invented, one of these being the creation of an "Army of Reserve" It proposed (43 Geo III cap 83) to raise men under the Militia Ballot, applying that measure to catch those who had not joined the Volunteers before the passing of the Act (July 6, 1803) The force so raised differed from the Militia in that the men were drafted into second battalions of the Regulars † In 1804, the measure was drastically transformed into the Permanent Additional Force Act, which apportioned 10,666 men to

---

* The compelling power of the period was fear of Napoleon The following memorial of sixty-one youths who joined the Inverness Volunteers, August 10, 1803, is typical (*H O* 50 59) —"We the subscribers hereto aroused, with the consideration of our country's danger in the present perilous crisis, when our dear native land is threatened with the chains of a Corsican tyrant, aided by a blinded and enslaved people, a people over-awed by a mercenary, unprincipled, and predatory army . ."

† The best attempt to disentangle the constantly changing measures dealing with the Volunteers of 1803 is made by Mr Fortescue in his *County Lieutenancies and the Army*, pp 59-125 See also Captain Sebag-Montefiore's *Volunteers*, pp 228-300

be raised in Scotland. It dispensed with the ballot: gave a bounty of £12 12s. to each Reservist and £10 10s. more on his joining the Regulars, which made it much more advantageous for him to do so through the Reserve than directly, as the Regular recruit got only £16 16s. It shifted the expense of bounty from the parochial funds to the Imperial Treasury, and turned parish officers into recruiters, the parishes having to pay £20 for every man deficient after a certain date. Both measures failed. The parish officers, making up their minds that the Government wanted only the fines, christened the second measure " The Twenty Pound Act." The Lords Lieutenant hated the Army of Reserve, because it created friction with the military authorities.

The attitude of the North was exactly the same as it was all over the country. Thus, the Lord Lieutenant of Aberdeenshire wrote to the Secretary of State, September 16, 1805 (*H.O.* 50: 125):—

Notwithstanding the exertions made by the heritors and their agents in compliance with the Order in Council, no men have been procured in any of the parishes for making up the numbers they were required to furnish.

Banffshire was even bolder, for Lord Fife, circularising his Deputies, October 17, 1805, showed clearly why no men could be got (*H.O.* 50: 125):—

1st—The smallness of the Bounty; it being hardly to be expected that men who recently before the passing of the Additional Force Act had been offered £40 and £45 and even more as substitutes in the [Army of] Reserve, would (at any rate for some time) accept of a Bounty of twelve guineas.

2nd—Because even this Bounty of twelve guineas is not payable at once at the time of enlistment, but at different periods and partly in necessaries—which recruits are not fond of.

3rd, and principally—The impossibility of getting parish officers and other fit persons to embark in this business, or to undertake recruiting on any terms.

4th—The want of recruiting officers and parties in the county to assist in procuring men, and the want of a receiving officer to pass and take charge of the men when procured.

5th—The restriction contained in the 22nd section of the Act, which only allows men to be raised within certain confined limits.

I am in hopes, from the representations which have partly been made by other Counties as well as by this, that measures will be adopted by Government for removing, or at any rate in part obviating, the obstacles which have hitherto retarded the levy   But, whether this shall be the case or not, it becomes an object of the very utmost importance—as well on account of the public service, as to avoid the penalties which must continue to be periodically assessed [£20 for every man deficient]—that every possible exertion should be used to procure men   In the letter written to the Subdivision Clerks to be laid before you, the necessity of this has been strongly pointed out, and I take the liberty of again earnestly and particularly pressing it on your attention

Independent of the anxiety, which I am satisfied we all feel, to give effect to every measure of Government in the present arduous struggle, it is the obvious interest of every individual to use his best endeavours to promote the object in view to the utmost of his power, because one half of the assessment of penalties affects all tenants of lands and occupiers of houses, and will continue to do so, while any deficiency exists either in the Militia Quota, or in that of the Additional Force for the County of Banff   I therefore persuade myself that you will meet with the zealous co-operation of all ranks of the community in a matter in which *all* are so fraternally concerned

Fife's earnest desires were of no avail, for he wrote to Lord Hawkesbury, the Home Secretary, November 22, 1805 (*H O* 50, 125) — "Great exertions have been made [for the Permanent Additional Force] by the Lieutenancy and other Gentlemen of the County, but I am sorry to say that they have been able to procure no men   . The penalties are a very heavy burden on the County" So the Reserve Army vanished into thin air six months later

While the scramble for men was going on, the Navy appeared on the scene as a rival recruiter, and gave the local authorities much trouble   Thus on August 23, 1803, the naval lieutenant in charge of raising sailors wrote from Fraserburgh to the Provost of Banff (*Banff Town Council Archives*) —

It is with regret I learn that some of the fishermen have expressed themselves as determined not to appear before me for the purpose of being enrolled and furnishing one man out of six for the Navy, especially at a place call'd Buckey   If you will have the kindness, send to the Chief Magistrate or principal person in that town and inform him that he may acquaint the fishermen that, unless they come before me in a peaceable, orderly manner and be registered as all the other fishermen have been, I will order a cutter to cruise off Buckey and send three Press Gangs into that Town, and to remain there until every fisherman in it is impressed   I will also offer a reward of twenty shillings to any of His Majesty's troops who may apprehend any of them in the country. I would fain hope they will not bring upon themselves and their families so severe a chastisement.

The Local Militia.

The last important change in our efforts at soldier-raising was the introduction of the system of Local Militia (48 Geo. III. cap. 150, June 30, 1808), designed to replace the Volunteers. The men were selected by ballot ; and no substitution or bounty to ballotted men was to be allowed, a move which is described by Mr. Fortescue as " perhaps the most notable point of the whole of our administrative military history." Corps of Volunteer Infantry might transfer themselves bodily to the Local Militia.   Mr. Fortescue says that, " speaking generally," the Volunteer corps seem to have been backward in transferring, but Aberdeenshire and Banffshire showed no such dislike, almost the entire Volunteer force going over to the Local Militia without difficulty, though trouble broke out in the Garioch. Within a year Scotland produced 66 regiments with 45,721 men.

In 1809 the germ of the Territorial system, as we know it, was suggested by the Adjutant-General, Sir Harry Calvert, who proposed to make the Local Militia part of the Line regiment belonging to its county ; but Castlereagh did not adopt the idea.

The administration of the Local Militia was as tortuous as that of its immediate predecessors, and the competition between the various types of troops was extremely demoralising. One of the most vivid pictures of the state of affairs is afforded by an Aberdeen writer, John Milne (1791-1865), the Aberdeen letter carrier who wrote *The Widow and Her Son, or the Runaway* (Aberdeen, 1851). In the autobiographical introduction, speaking of the clamour for men in the period immediately following the end of the Peace of Amiens (1803-9), Milne, who enlisted in the Artillery in 1813, says (pp. 38-41) :—

Scarcely a male from 18 to 55 could escape from being enrolled as belonging to some corps, and liable to be called out on an hour's warning, in defence of his king and country. To remain entirely a civilian, tradesmen could not, without a pecuniary sacrifice, frequently to a great extent. To obviate the risk of the Militia ballot, members of insurance clubs were often obliged to lodge money to the amount of £10 yearly. If, however, anyone was enrolled as a Volunteer in a corps belonging to the county town, it proved his "ground of exemption " from the ballot. . .

The strength of the Regular Militia regiments was kept up, in general, by being supplied out of the Locals with substitutes for those ballotted for the Regulars. The bounties—or rather the value of a substitute—rose from £30 to £60, £70 and in some cases to the extent of £100. Men, young or old, at that period were of value. The Government contracts made trade brisk; the demand for clothes and shoes for the Military, with canvas and other stores for the Navy, could scarcely meet a supply. I have known weavers then earn from thirty to forty shillings a week; no other tradesmen could make above two-thirds, unless calico printers, but they, too, soon experienced an overwhelming reverse. Farm-servants' wages rose to £10 for six months. But neither farmers, master tradesmen, nor employers of any description could depend upon the services of the men employed a week upon end. Whenever a young man differed from his master, or had any dispute with his mother, his wife or sweetheart, off he went to the depot for substitutes, passed the doctor, and went through the formula of swearing in, and then laid his hands on £60 or £70, or, in proportion, more or less, with the urgency of the conscriptions.

The large amount of capital thus circulated may be said, negatively, to have done good and evil. It was a heavy burden on the country, which many felt; while it had a tendency to demoralise the recipients, by coming into the possession of so much money, so easily acquired at the time. They no doubt gave it circulation again. Many articles were purchased which continued necessary for the family use for several years; for, by the original Militia Act, men with large families were not excluded from serving as substitutes. Indeed, at that time, the wives and so many children of those serving, whether sub-stitutes or principals, were entitled to what was called county money, when residing at a distance from their husbands, and it was generally the case that, when an unmarried man took the bounty, he was not long in procuring a female partner to assist him in its disposal. There were some young men who, from prudent motives, deposited their money at interest, and derived benefit from it to themselves and their relations many years afterwards. But the worst feature in the disposal of this suddenly acquired wealth, was the reckless conduct of many others, who, upon the principle of "light come light gone," embraced the period allowed them previous to joining their regiments as a fitting time for revelling in all the grossest scenes of debauchery and dissipation.

The taprooms and low public houses derived for a number of years no small emolument from the free-and-easy manner in which the foolish young men parted with their money. Some landlords were agents for the Militia Clubs, both in town and country; and their commission on procuring a substitute would have amounted, in a case of emergency, to twenty or twenty-five per cent Besides, it was a practice with some of the silly fools to keep an open table for all comers, by giving the landlord a one pound note to stick up on the wall, and, whenever Boniface was pleased to pronounce the amount spent, it was replaced by another And it was an established fact at the time, that one individual was so reckless in endeavouring to get clear of the money given him in lieu of his freedom as to munch a leopard cat (Aberdeen bank note) along with the buttered toast and a Welsh rabbit

This Militia mania continued from 1803 until 1813. In 1809, I was compelled, on account of being liable to the ballot, to enter the Local Militia, of which there were two regiments for the city, commanded by Colonels Finlayson and Tower These were embodied annually for twenty-eight days training, but, in case of invasion, were liable to be put in actual service, at fourteen days' notice There was generally at this period some other Regiment stationed in the Barracks I have seen, on some occasions, upwards of three thousand Military occupying the city * Such a congregated mass of men, all under the oath of allegiance to the British Crown, seemed as if the war had been the only art or science worth studying, in order to secure the stability of the Empire Such an extensive war establishment conveyed to many thousands of its conscripts the idea that they had likewise become privileged libertines Swearing, drinking, and all kinds of debauchery, they considered the probationary course they had to study, before becoming brave soldiers Even the annual enrollment of the Local Militia was considered as the commencement of a carnival in honour of Mars, Venus, and Bacchus, and the disembodiment of the Corps generally terminated in fighting and drinking, with a transfer of, perhaps, twenty or thirty to the Regulars

Although I had in a great measure become acquainted with the low ribaldry, the loose slang, and hectoring bravadoes frequently made use of by young recruits, or soldiers-at-will, as Local Militiamen might have been called, I had kept aloof for four or five years from becoming a soldier in reality The idea never struck me of entering the Regular Militia, although offered repeatedly from £60 to £70 as a substitute

This picture, fully corroborated as it is from many other sources,

---

* Aberdeen got a sharp taste of what "the military" could do by the running amok of the Ross and Cromarty Rangers on the King's Birthday, June 4, 1802, when an old soldier, John Ross, was shot dead in the street The colonel, a captain, and two sergeants were tried for murder, but were acquitted, January 10, 1803 The report of their trial was published in Aberdeen, 1803 (pp 198). A short account of the regiment, with a list of all its officers, was given by the present writer, in the *Aberdeen Weekly Journal*, August 28, 1914

was not a pretty state of affairs, and shows that the war, so far from
chastening the people, had come to demoralise them thoroughly.
Happily it all came to an end in 1814, first by the Peace with France
(April 11) and then with the United States (December 24). On July
6, 1814, the thanks of Parliament were voted to the Local Militia and
the Volunteers.* The Volunteers were at once disbanded, but it was
not till 1816 that the Local Militia was formally dismissed.

The destruction of Napoleonism at Waterloo in 1815 made the Peace
of Paris doubly secure, and Great Britain returned to her normal self
in allowing her Auxiliary forces to fall into abeyance. The work which
the machine had been constructed to perform was done, and as has
always happened among us, the machine was permitted to become rusty
and practically useless. Had we lived on anything but an island this
would probably not have happened. As it was, for nearly forty
years the subject of home defence was, as Captain Sebag-Montefiore
says, relegated "to the category of abstract questions of military
policy."

The Duke of Wellington sounded a note of alarm in 1847, but
it was not until 1859 that fear of France roused the nation to arms and
re-established the Volunteers—amid a great deal of chaff from
large and well-to-do sections of the community, as the pages of *Punch*
and *Ye Nobell Cheese-Monger* serve to remind us.

Since that time we have seen much neglect and many experiments ;
but through it all there has been a steady drift towards the principle
of Territorialism, both in regard to the Regular Army and the Auxiliary
forces. We have seen in Aberdeen, for instance, the Regular battalion
of the Gordon Highlanders much more identified with the town in every
way, notably in the establishment of the Institute in Belmont Street ;

---

*Had space permitted, I would have printed the names of all the Volunteers in
the counties of Aberdeen and Banff from 1797 to 1803 as preserved at the Public
Record Office. As it is, only the names of the commissioned officers have been given
in this volume. The names of the rank and file, to the number of very nearly 6,000,
have been printed (April-Dec., 1914) by Mr. William Will and myself in 49 issues of
eight weekly newspapers in Aberdeen, Peterhead, Fraserburgh, Huntly, Banff, Portsoy,
Keith, and Buckie, so that in some cases they have appeared side by side with the
"Rolls of Honour" of 1914. This represents all the Volunteer organisations in the
two counties except in the towns of Aberdeen and Banff which supply some 3,000
more. The printing of the former commenced in the *Aberdeen Weekly Journal* of
December 18, 1914 ; and the latter will be issued in the transactions of the *Banff Field
Club*. An inventory of the rolls already published will be found *infra*, (pp. 420-421).

while round the Regular regiment the old Militia and Volunteer battalions have been grouped: the whole being designed to fit in with tactical necessity.

The necessity created by the Great War of 1914 has resulted in the seven battalions of the Gordon Highlanders being increased to fifteen, the four Territorial battalions being duplicated for reserves, while four new battalions, Nos. 8, 9, 10, and 11, have been raised as part of "Kitchener's Army." This expansion, which Lord Haldane's scheme fully provided for, has been wise, for civilian recruiters in Banffshire have discovered that the best way of getting men for the new armies has been by assuring them that they would join "the Gordons," where they would meet their kith and kin; whereas it has been very difficult to induce recruits to join other regiments or different branches of the Service.* This is an exact repetition of the experience of the first recruiters for the Highland regiments, which were essentially battalions of "pals." Much the same thing has been experienced elsewhere, for it was announced on December 1, 1914, that the War Office "have now decided to ear-mark all men recruited hereafter for the New Army to the local units where they enlist, thus making the Territorial principle a reality, and not letting it degenerate into mere matter of nomenclature." A more primitive form of Territorialism was sketched by Lord Kitchener on August 14, 1914, in the matter of the "Home Defence Territorial Forces," to be trained on a system "by which leave can be given for those serving to look after their urgent private affairs somewhat on the Commando principle which prevailed in South Africa."

Professional soldiers have been rather doubtful about the value of the Territorials, but the Messines charge of the London Scottish—who were attached to the Gordons in South Africa—dispelled that doubt;

---

* The Highland regiments quite obsess the imagination of the German caricaturists, for, although we have only five kilted corps in the Regular Army, a kilted soldier appears in almost every German cartoon. A powerful drawing, in four colours, which appeared in the well-known Munich weekly *Jugend*, on August 18, 1914, showed two Highland soldiers, in white tunics, with Gordon glengarries and sporrans, but a rather indiscriminate tartan. The picture was called "Albions Söhne," and the legend beneath it, in verse, ran:—"Outside—picturesque tunics and a costume full of beauty. Inside—the allies of Cossacks and barbarians. Like other queer folk, you cannot tolerate with Germany's development. With all your beautiful Highland uniform, what sadness there is in your hearts!" It may be noted that Mr. Neil Munro, writing from France as correspondent to the *Daily Chronicle* (Dec. 2), says that the kilt is the "ideal dress for warfare," especially in the trenches.

while the verdict of Sir John French in his Despatch of November 20 is conclusive :—

The conduct and bearing of these [nine Territorial] units under fire, and the efficient manner in which they carried out the various duties assigned to them have imbued me with the highest hopes as to the value and help of Territorial Troops generally.

In developing the Army on the lines of the genius of our own people (and not merely on Continental models), taking full advantage of our unceasing experiences in India, Egypt, and Africa, we have been proved supremely right. In saying this we have the authority of the leader of the Expeditionary Force of 1914, who, in a memorable Army Order issued on Sunday, November 23, says to his soldiers :—

I have made many calls upon you, and the answers you have made to them have covered you, your regiments, and the Army to which you belong with honour and glory.

Your fighting qualities, courage, and endurance have been subjected to the most trying and severe tests, and you have proved yourselves worthy descendants of the British soldiers of the past who have built up the magnificent traditions of the regiments to which you belong. You have not only maintained those traditions, but you have materially added to their lustre.

It is impossible for me to find words in which to express my appreciation of the splendid services you have performed.

The present volume, if it shows anything, proves that there is no "degeneracy" in the national temper. "In Scotland," says Mr. Fortescue, writing of the year 1806, "the people were more military," than in England, "and the Volunteers more efficient": and the crisis of 1914 has found North Britain heading the percentage in recruiting. If this book only helps us to understand that the Soldier must take into consideration the psychology of the Civilian when requesting his services, it will have achieved a purpose which rarely falls within the province of the New Spalding Club.

TERRITORIAL SOLDIERING IN THE NORTH.

THE EIGHTY-NINTH REGIMENT OF FOOT.

1759: RAISED BY THE 4TH DUKE OF GORDON: DISBANDED 1765.

The Eighty-Ninth Foot, raised in 1759, and one of the four complete regiments organised by Alexander, 4th Duke of Gordon, in the course of half a century, was not a body of Territorial troops as we understand the system to-day. It was a regiment of the line—the first attempt of the north-eastern counties of Scotland to contribute directly to the armed forces of the Crown; and it affords a striking example of the two great factors which formed the guiding principle of these achievements. On the one hand, it was the result of individual family pride; on the larger issue, it was a local contribution to the necessities of national defence.

To understand the situation one must tell a little family history. Alexander, 4th Duke of Gordon, was born in 1743 and succeeded his father, Cosmo, the 3rd Duke, at the age of nine. Luckily for his boyish Grace, he had a strong-minded mother to guide his footsteps, for, a Gordon herself, she had dowered him with a double dose of the blood of that reckless race. She had not only married into a family suspect of Jacobitism, but on the maternal side she had come out of a Jacobite hotbed, as this table will show :—

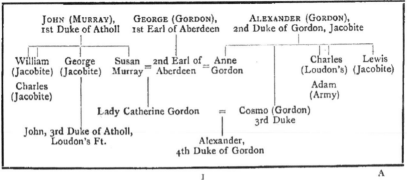

Lady Catherine (the step-niece of her own husband !), found herself at the age of thirty-four with six young children on her hands, three boys and three girls. The temper of the boys may be gauged from the fact that the second, Lord William, was yet to bolt with Lady Sarah Bunbury, and the youngest, Lord George, was to make the town ring with his riots against "Popery," and to die in Newgate as a Jew. She clearly felt that the origins of herself and of her boys were not such as to speak in her favour. Three of her Murray uncles had come to grief over both the Jacobite Risings—one of them died in the Tower, and the other an exile in Holland. Her father-in-law, the 2nd Duke of Gordon, had fought at Sheriffmuir, suffered imprisonment, and died in an atmosphere of suspicion; while her brother-in-law, the gallant Lord Lewis Gordon, had died a Jacobite exile in France. These ugly blots had been partly wiped off the slate by another brother-in-law, Lord Charles, joining Lord Loudon's Foot, the first of the Highland regiments raised after the '45, and his brother, Lord Adam (who married Lady Catherine's aunt, the widow of the 2nd Duke of Atholl), was an officer in the 3rd Foot Guards, and shaping to become Commander-in-Chief in Scotland. So, with a clever woman's wit—strangely enough, all the five Duchesses of Gordon had more force of character than their consorts—she seized on her widowhood as an occasion for sympathetic treatment by the Crown, and got into touch with the Duke of Newcastle, then Secretary of State for the South. She wrote him the following ingeniously conceived epistle (*Add. MSS.* 32,729 f. 256,) from London, September 1, 1752, that is to say, within a month of her husband's death :—

My Lord,—The melancholy event of the death of my Lord the Duke of Gordon is the occasion of my giving your Grace the trouble of this letter: to beg you would do me the honour to take a proper opportunity of acquainting the King of my intention of educating my children in whatever way shall be thought most agreeable to his Majesty, being induced theirto as well by my own principals as by a know-ledge of the great attachment and zeal my deceas'd Lord had to his Majesty and Government, as also a most sincere gratitude for the honour his Majesty did in bestowing so many marks of distinction on him; which I can assure your Grace he always had the highest value for, and expressed himself in the strongest terms, even in his last moments of his earnest desire to have his children brought up under his Majesty's protection, and the same good principals inculcated in them which he had   And allow me to say that his Majesty had not a more faithfull subject   My Lord was very sensible of his obligations to your Grace, and on all occasions expressed his gratitude and the confidence he had in your opinion.

May I therefore beg your Grace's assistance in representing to his Majesty the earnest desire I have of my children and I being taken under his Majesty's protection and to beg for the continuance of the pention which my Lord had to me and for the benefite of my younger children who are left unprovided for?   I hope your Grace will forgive this trouble and excuse me if I have erred in making this application in a wrong stile.   If so, it's from ignorance and the unhappy situation of my mind at present, and not from any intention—so flatters my self with the thoughts your Grace will have the goodness to advise me what is right, and forgive me if I have done wrong.

[I] shall stay in town hoping for the honour of a letter from your Grace, and then shall either go to Scotland to settle my affairs their and return against the winter, or shall waite here the King's arrival as your Grace shall judge most proper, for, as my Lord (through a know-ledge of my principals being the same with his own) did me the honour to put an entire confidence in me, boath as to the education of his children and the management of his eldest son's estate, so [I] would be sorry to think I could be capable of doing anything to betray so great a trust as to take any step with regard to my conduct that was not approved by your Grace: and would fain flatter myself that, if my eldest son lives to be a man and have the same good principals that his father and I joined in wishing him, that he won't be thought unworthy of the protection of his Majesty

Forgive my detaining your Grace so long on this melancholy subject, and I beg leave to conclude with throwing myself under the protection of his Majesty and your Grace, which obligation shall be most gratefully acknowledged on all occasions by her who has the honour to be with the greatest respect and esteem, My Lord, your Grace's most obedient and most faithfull humble servant,

K GORDON

It does not transpire whether Newcastle did anything in particular at the moment, but her Grace did something for herself—she began to look out for a husband, who could help her to manage the boys Horace Walpole suggests that she made a bid for Stanislas Poniatowski, the last King of Poland—his great-grandmother had also been a Lady Catherine Gordon—who visited England in 1754.   He was fourteen years her junior, but the " Highland goddess "—whom Walpole compared to a " raw-boned Scotch metaphysician that has got a red face by drinking water"—introduced her boys, the Duke and Lord William, to him as Cupids with bows and arrows, while she herself reposed on a couch, a "sea-born Venus." Luckily for her, the young Pole passed her by—ultimately for another strong-minded Catherine, the Empress of Russia. But the Duchess still stuck to her purpose, and married on March 25, 1756, a young American officer, Staats Long Morris, who was twelve years her junior. This alliance set her thinking on the army. In order to give her youthful consort some position, the Duchess wrote on September 18, 1758, from Upper Grosvenor Street to his Grace of Newcastle (*Add. MSS.*, 32,884 f. 49):—

Dutchess of Gordon presents her respectfull compliments to the Duke of Newcastle, and as she intends to set out soon for Scotland, hopes his Grace will be so good as to do her the honour to let her have an opportunity to say a few words to his Grace befor she goes, at any time that he pleases to apoint.

The motive of her desire to interview his Grace, who possibly did not reply—Sir Robert Walpole once declared that "his name was Perfidy"—is frankly stated in another letter, which she wrote to him on October 24, 1758, from Upper Grosvenor Street (*Add. MSS.*, 32,885 f. 66):—

I had the honour of sending a message to your Grace some time ago, to let you know that I intended to set out for Scotland, and wanted to have say'd a few words to your Grace at any time that was most convenient; but, as it may have sliped from your memory and I not have an opportunity of seeing your Grace before I go, I now take the liberty to ask your commands with regard to the ensueing elections of the several countys and boroughs in Scotland that I have an interest in, as I am strongly solicited by different candidates, and as I have always acted in the way I thought was most agreeable to your Grace, I shall think myself honoured to have your instructions at this time, which I will obey with pleasure.

I am now soliciting my Lord Barrington and Lord Legonier to get Mr. Morris removed into the Guards, and I beg leave to remind your Grace of the application of my brother, the Earl of Aberdeen, made to you for him before he left London, and at the same time to interest your Grace's assistance.

Her Grace's interest in soldiering was soon stirred to a much more personal issue, for the country, immersed in war, was clamouring for soldiers, and she saw a great opportunity, not only for finding a billet for her young husband, but also for rescuing the Gordon name from a long spell of reproach. She would raise a regiment for her son. True, the capture of Quebec, September 13, 1759, had brought a lull: we were winning. "We are forced to ask every morning what victory there is, for fear of missing one," wrote Horace Walpole. But in the early part of the year the country had been shaken to its foundations, and Aberdeen had suffered from something very like a panic owing to the withdrawal of troops from the coast. On July 11, 1759, John Duncan, Provost of Aberdeen, had forwarded to Lord Holdernesse, Secretary of State, the following memorial on behalf of the city (*P.R.O., S.P. Scotland:* series 2, bundle 45; No. 58):—

THAT it has been the practice of having at least three regiments of foot always cantoned along the coast from Inverness to the Firth of Forth.

THAT the whole foresaid coast is now left entirely destitute of troops, they being all moved to the incampment as aforesaid.

THAT the City of Aberdeen, justly reckoned the third tradeing town in Scotland, cannot help thinking themselves exposed to the most imminent danger from the enemy, as one hundred men from any of the enemy's privateers may enter their port and ravage and destroy every thing before them without the least opposition.

THAT untill the year 1745 the said city had a Block-house at the mouth of their harbour mounted with thirteen guns, mostly twelve pounders, and at the same time had at least two hundred stand of small arms for the use of the citizens on all emergencies. These cannon and armes were in the month of September, 1745, at the earnest desire of Sir John Cope, then commanding the forces at Aberdeen, delivered up to him (least they should fall into the hands of the rebells), and accordingly were shipt off with his army at Aberdeen and landed at Dunbar; so that at present there is neither cannon nor small arms in or about the City of Aberdeen to make the least defence.

THAT it is notour that the harbours of Aberdeen, Montrose, and Peterhead are the three most exposed of any on the East Coast of Scotland to the invasion of enemies, all the other seaports on the east coast of Scotland being within firths where an enemy would not venture so boldly to approach; and for a proof of this it is well known that in the late unnatural Rebellion these were the only three ports where troops or implements of war were landed to support the rebells.

The above facts being duly considered call loudly for the assistance and protection of the Government, and if at this critical juncture troops cannot be spared to be cantoned along the foresaid part of the Eastern Coast, it is at least hoped that some forty- and-twenty- gun ships of war should be stationed along the same in order to deterr enemies from approaching, for, should that part of the coast be left entirely destitute of protection either by sea or land and an enemy once got a footing on shoar, it's hard to know what progress they may make or how the Event may turn out.

It is therefore prayed that the Right Honourable the Lord Holdernesse will lay the foresaid memorial before the most Honourable his Majesty's Privy Council and also before the Lords of the Admiralty, that they may grant such Relief in the premises as to them shall seem best.

Meantime, the Duchess knew that some of the great families had raised troops—the (Loudon) Campbells, the Frasers, the Keiths, the (Dunoon) Campbells, the (Argyll) Campbells, and the noble Sutherlands —the last four organising regiments in this very year, 1759. The Gordons must not be left out; so she set to work, immensely aided, of course, by the youth of her first-born. The task had its difficulties, for even the presence of national enemies did not silence family enmities; so the Duke of Argyll opposed the proposal. Stewart of Garth states that the Duchess "dreaded the authority" of Argyll, representing "the youth of her son and the danger that would result should his political influence in his minority be directed to another family, and especially to that family between which and her own so many ancient feuds had subsisted, the seeds of which still remained, if not in the minds, at least in the traditions, of many. Greater exertions were, in consequence, made to support what the Duchess called the cause of her son and the honour of his family" (*Highlanders*, 2nd ed., ii., 36). Argyll's opposition, as we shall see, did not end here.

The official mandate for the creation of the regiment (*Add. MSS.* 33,056 f. 36) is undated and unaddressed, but it clearly had been sent to the Duke of Newcastle, who was Prime Minister at the time. It was as follows:—

Captain Morris, of Lord Robert Manners' Regiment, husband to the Duchess of Gordon, proposes to raise a regiment of Highlanders for foreign service, with the assistance of the Duke of Athol, Lord Finlater, Lord Desford, Sir Ludovic Grant, and other Highland chief[s]. He asks no levy money and desires no rank for himself or officers till the battalion is completed and approved on a review by the end of April next or sooner.

The undertakers for other Highland corps had three pounds per man levy money, and had their commissions immediately. They did not undertake to raise the men within a limited time. If Captain Morris succeeds in this attempt he expects to command the corps with the rank of Lieutenant-Colonel, like Montgomery and Fraser. The Duke of Gordon will have a company.

The first commissions of the officers are all dated between October 13 and October 23, 1759 (*W.O.*, 25; 138, pp. 105, 114, 118, 124, 127, 170: *W.O.*, 25; 209, p. 178: Stewart's *Highlanders*, 2nd ed., ii., 37; *Aberdeen Journal*, Dec. 5, 1759):—

COLONEL.

Staats Long Morris, October 13, 1759. He was M.P. for the Elgin Burghs, 1774-89; became a general; and died as Governor of Quebec (a post to which he was gazetted *vice* Johnstone, deceased, on December 15, 1797), April 2, 1800, being buried in Westminster Abbey.

MAJORS.

George Scott, October 13, 1759; he became a general in 1798, and died in 1811.

Hector Munro, October 13, 1759. Born in 1726, he suppressed the mutiny at Patna, 1764, won the battle of Buxar, 1764, captured Pondicherry, 1778; was knighted 1779; and died in 1805.

CAPTAINS.

Alexander, 4th Duke of Gordon, October 13, 1759; the real begetter of the 89th.

Alexander Duff of Davidston, October 14, 1759. Born in 1725, he was the son of John Duff of Culbin (one of the few unlucky Duffs) by Mary, daughter of James Gordon, the first of the first set of Gordons of Ellon; her nephews James and Andrew Gordon were both officers in the army. Alexander Duff married in 1771 his first cousin Magdalen, daughter of William Duff of Muirtown, and his son John (1772-1836) succeeded to Drummuir. Alexander died in 1778 (Taylers' *Book of the Duffs*, 391). In 1759 he was the only Duff holding a commission in the Army. His grandmother, Katherine Duff of Drummuir, declared that " soldiers is but slaves " (*Ibid.*, 475).

Ludovick Grant, of Knockando, October 17, 1759.

Normand Lamont, October 18, 1759; son of the Laird of Lamont.

William McGillivray, October 16, 1759; brother of Alexander McGillivray of Drumnaglass, who was killed leading the Mackintoshes at Culloden, and whom he succeeded.

Duncan Macpherson, October 19, 1759; afterwards of the 42nd and 71st Regiments; died 1807.

George Morison, October 15, 1759; son of Theodore Morison of Bognie. He held the estate of Haddo, married in 1767, Jean, daughter of General Abercromby of Glassaugh, and died at Banff, April 1, 1777

(Temple's *Fermartyn*, 156). His widow married in 1781, Admiral Robert Duff of Logie (*Book of the Duffs*, 102, 317, 475). His brother, Alexander Morison of Bognie, married Catherine, the step-sister of George's fellow captain, Alexander Duff (Temple's *Fermartyn*, 157).

CAPTAIN-LIEUTENANT.

Archibald Dunbar, October 13, 1759 (from ensign, 56th). A member of the Northfield family: died before March 30, 1762.

LIEUTENANTS.

William Baillie, October 18, 1759; killed in India, 1779, while commanding a detachment of Sir Hector Munro's force.

George Campbell, October 22, 1759. Came from Rothes.

Alexander Duff, October 12, 1760. Duff, who was a natural son of Alexander Duff, II. of Hatton, entered the 58th Regiment in 1772, was honorary Colonel of the Banffshire Volunteers, laird of Mayen, and died in 1816 (*Book of the Duffs*, 273).

William Finlason, October 20, 1759. Son of John Finlason (born at Dysart, 1708) by his wife, Anne, daughter of Alexander Gordon of Aberdour, he spent nearly 60 years in the Army, and died in Aberdeen, 1817. A long account of his career was given by J. M. Bulloch in the *Aberdeen Weekly Journal*, August 7, 1914.

John Forbes, January 24, 1765.

James Fordyce, April 21, 1760.

Alexander Godsman, October 19, 1759.

Charles Gordon, October 13, 1759; fought at Buxar, where Sir Hector Munro praised him—" my A.D.C., for his brave and spirited behaviour; this officer had his horse shot under him in action." Captain-Lieutenant, March 30, 1762. He was the son of William, I. of Sheela-green, and commanded the Atholl Highlanders, 1782-3. Died unmarried, 1789 (*Gordons under Arms*, No. 303).

John Gordon, October 23, 1759. Son of Alexander, Collector of Customs, and brother of Sir Alexander, of Lesmoir. Died 1761 (*Gordons under Arms*, No. 887).

Lord William Gordon, October 13, 1759. Brother of the 4th Duke of Gordon. Born 1744; d.s.p.m., 1823 (*Gordons under Arms*, No. 1401).

Ludovick Grant, October 16, 1759; preferred.

Ralph Hanson, October 21, 1759; probably a relative of Catherine, daughter of Oswald Hanson, of Wakefield, Yorkshire, wife of the 3rd Earl of Aberdeen.

Lawrence Leith, October 14, 1759. Son of Alexander Leith, of Bucharn, a cadet of the Leith-hall family. He was afterwards in the Aberdeenshire Fencibles, and died at Bucharn unmarried, December 17, 1795.

John Macdonald, October 25, 1759. He was Lieutenant-Colonel of the 81st Regiment in 1783.

—— Macleod, October 27, 1759. He was superseded by Alexander Duff.

Angus McNeil, October 29, 1759; cancelled February 12, 1760.

Alexander Macpherson, October 26, 1759.

William Macpherson, October 28, 1759.

Rotrus Thomas Richard Maitland, March 20, 1760.

Robert Munro, April 25, 1760.

Alexander Stewart, October 15, 1759. He was a Captain in the Garioch Volunteers of 1798. Laird of Lesmurdie; died before July 4, 1785, when his widow, Jean Gordon, died at Burghead.

Alexander Stuart, October 17, 1759. Laird of Tinninver.

ENSIGNS.

James Bennet, October 13, 1759. He was Quartermaster.

Matthias Calvert, October 14, 1759. Lieutenant, November 18, 1761.

Alexander Donald, October 13, 1759. He was Adjutant: Lieutenant, April 28, 1764.

Alexander Donald, November 16, 1761.

John Edwards, October 18, 1759.

Harry Gilchrist, October 20, 1759.

Alexander Gordon, October 16, 1759. Only son of George, of Cults; he was occupant of Tilliethrowie.

Lord George Gordon, October 13, 1759; Lieutenant, March 30, 1762. Brother of the 4th Duke of Gordon. Born in 1751, he entered the Navy, became notorious as the anti-Catholic rioter; and died unmarried in Newgate, 1793.

James Gordon, October 15, 1759. He entered the 48th Foot as Lieutenant, October 26, 1763 (*Gordons under Arms*, No. 710).

John Innes, April 29, 1764.

John Macpherson, October 19, 1759.

Cæsar Morison, April 28, 1764.

Alexander Munro, January 26, 1765.

John Nairne, April 26, 1764.

William Nairne, April 27, 1764.

Patrick Ogilvy, October 17, 1759. Brother of Ogilvy of East Milne.

James Willox, March 30, 1762.

CHAPLAINS.

Rev. Alexander Chalmers, October 13, 1759. He was minister of Cairnie (1747-98), and married Lady Anne Gordon, daughter of the 3rd Duke of Gordon. He died s.p. October 2, 1798, aged 78.

John Pritchard, March 30, 1762.

B

SURGEONS.

James Arthur, October 13, 1759. He was the son of a farmer near Bathgate. On April 4, 1756, he married, privately, the daughter of John Gourlay, maltman, Stirling. She afterwards raised an action to be acknowledged as his legal wife (*Add. MSS.* 36,174).

Alexander Findlay, M.D., King's College, Aberdeen, 1760, succeeded Arthur.

Agent—Drummond, Spring Gardens, London.

Patrick ("Tiger") Duff (1742-1803), of the Torriesoul family, was a "gentleman volunteer" in the 89th, but he transferred to the H.E.I.C. in 1762 (*Book of the Duffs*, 474). His mother was a Letterfourie Gordon.

Though we know the motives for raising the regiment, we have very few data about the measures adopted to achieve the task, for not only are there no documents on the subject in the Gordon Castle archives, but there is not a single muster roll at the Public Record Office. The accounts of the recruiters' success differ considerably. Stewart of Garth says that "in a few weeks, 960 men assembled at Gordon Castle." The *Aberdeen Journal* of November 24 says that several of the officers were "so popular in places where they reside that they have already raised a considerable number of recruits," and on December 5 it tells us that the regiment was filling up "apace," and that, if the war continued, Morris was to raise three more companies, "which, when compleated, 'tis reckoned will make as good an appearance as any in the British Establishment." On the other hand, Lord Adam Gordon, the uncle of the youthful Duke, writing to the Lord Register from Prestonhall, January 8, 1760, says (*Add. MSS.*, 32,901, f. 160):—"I hear Morris's Corps goes on slow, the numbers not exceeding 300." Yet the pay list from October 13, to December 24, 1759, was for nine companies, or 1,035 men, and amounted to £3640 (*W.O.* 24: 356).

The Duchess went north to help in the project, though by doing so she endangered her chances of getting the reversion of the Countess of Stair's pension of £400 a year, for, writing to Newcastle on November 26, she says (*Add. MSS.* 32,899 f. 126):—"I would have done myself the honour to have solicited your Grace [to get Lady Stair's pension] in person, but forwarding the raising of Mr. Morris's battalion requires my attention here [Gordon Castle]."

It is certain that her Grace did not resort to the compulsive and crimping methods of the period, of which she had had an unpleasant personal experience, as this letter which she wrote on May 11, 1757, shows (*W.O.* 1: 973):—

A few days ago, Thomas Williams, my postilion, was impressed into His Majesty's Service, and I have made application for his discharge [granted May 12] to the Commissioners, who inform me I cannot have him released without further orders from your Lordship. Therefore, I take the liberty to request of you, if it is consistent with His Majesty's service to give the proper orders for his discharge, which will much oblige [me].

We get one or two glimpses of the mechanism employed in raising men.* Thus, Alexander Duff of Davidston, wrote from Inverness, December 5, 1759, to William, Lord Fife (*Book of the Duffs*, 392):—

I beg ten thousand pardons for not waiting of your Lordship and my Lady Fife, when I was last in the East Country. I was then solliciting for a Company in Coll. Morris Highland Regiment, and was in such a hurry and confusion, that I scarce knew what I was doeing. . . . I have at last, with some difficulty, procured a Company, but I have the burden of 60 men upon my shoulders. Mr. George Morrison [his brother-in-law] haveing got a Company in the same Regiment makes my recruiting more difficult, as his brother [the laird of Bognie] will give him all the assistance which I might have expected if Mr. George had not been in the field.
We are told by the Collnl. that, if we do not raise our quota of men, we shall be superceded. I am the only one of the Clan that is a capn. in the Army. I hope they will stand by a Clansman, and not see him affronted. Our rank in the Regiment depends upon our raseing our quota of men. If your lordship would be so kind as give me your countenance, it would be doeing me a verry signall service, and laying me under ane obligation never to be forgott by myself or ffriends. I have a few men already and will with all my heart give 5 guineas for every good man. I depend on your Lordship's goodness in my present situation.

The Dunbar family also invoked the Quality to help them, as appears from a letter which Lord Moray wrote to Mackintosh, his

---

* When the 89th was being recruited, the *Aberdeen Journal* of December 25, 1759, recorded this curious case : " Last week a young girl, who lives near the town of Keith, drest herself in man's apparel and enlisted in the Royal Volunteers, having received four guineas bounty money. At bed-time, she took the opportunity to slip out and shifted to her proper dress : but, being discovered, she was obliged to return the money."

chamberlain at Inverness, December 27 (Dunbar's *Social Life in Former Days*, 2nd series, pp. 161-2) :—

As Mr. Dunbar of Duffus his son has gott a commission in Collonel Morris's Batalion, he will immedeatly sett about recruiting. I am informed that [William McGillivray of] Drumnaglas [whose elder brother Alexander had been killed at Culloden, where he commanded the Mackintoshes] has got a company in said batallion. I do call upon you and all those under your care who pretend freindship and regard for me and my family to be aiding and assisting to Captain Dunbar ; and if any other recruiting party, or officer should interfere with him, I desire that my weight may be throwen into Captain Dunbar's scale, where the terms are equall ; and if I hear (and hear I will) that after you receive this letter any recruits are gone out of the Lordship of Petty and not unto Captain Dunbar's Company, I will not easily forgett nor forgive it to those who have had the smallest hand in contributing towards it. You may let my vassals know that they cannot come to me with a stronger claim to my freindship than by giving me proof that they deserve it by giving substantial assistance to Captain Dunbar, notwithstanding the pretext of Drumaglash his company. Be active in this affair as you wish to oblige your assured freind,

Moray.

The truth seems to be that even at this early date, before recruiting rivalry became acute, men were not easy to get. Certain it is they were not easy to hold, as the desertions advertised in the *Journal* show :—

1759, December 4.—Captain Morison's Company—John Beverley, born in the parish of Old Aberdeen, and lately servant to James Christie, horse-hirer in Aberdeen. Beverley is about twenty-five years of age, full six feet high, brown bushy hair, broad shoulders, stoops a little ; had on when he deserted a drab colour coat with metal buttons. Whoever shall apprehend the said deserter, and deliver him to Alexander Morison, younger of Bognie, Esq., at Frendraught, or to Daniel Freeman, Captain Morison's sergeant in Aberdeen, shall have 20s. sterling reward, over and above the 20s. allowed by Act of Parliament for apprehending deserters. If the said deserter deliver himself up voluntarily to the said Sergeant Freeman before Saturday next, he shall be pardoned, for this his first desertion. If any person receive the said Beverley to their service, or conceal him, they will be prosecute with the utmost rigour of law.

1760, January 1.—From Captain Morison's Company—John Gordon, born in the Parish of Belhelvie, a tailor, about 22 years of age, about 5 ft. 8 in. high, black hair, a genteel thin lad ; had on when he deserted a dark blue coat with a velvet neck, scarlet belt, black plush breeches, large silver buckles on his shoes.

1760, January 15.—From Captain Morison's Company—Alexander M'Intosh, born in Ross-shire, but an inhabitant of Marnoch since he was 4 years of age; a labouring servant, late of George Hay of Montblairy; about 24; 5 ft. 5½ in., black, bushy hair, thick and able-bodied; had on when he deserted a short grey coat and waistcoat, and brownish breeches. To be delivered to Alexander Morison of Pitfaucie at Frendraught, or Robert Shand in Conland, Captain Morison's sergeant in Forgue, or to Sergeant Freeman in Aberdeen.

1760, February 12.—From Captain McGillivray's Company— William Young, 33, a tinker, 5 ft. 3; black complexion, black hair, black eyes, thin black beard, wearing a red freize coat, an old tartan vest and philibeg, and worsted stockings.

George Smith, 19, labourer, in the Parish of Cairney; 5 ft. 2½ in.; brown complexion, black hair, gray eyes; had a sinew broke on his left hand; stooped forward in his walking; had on when he deserted a gray coat and tartan waistcoat, gray breeches and stockings. Collector Finlason, Aberdeen [father of the future Colonel William Finlason], was to be applied to for the reward for apprehending the deserters.

1760, March 25.—Lieutenant Charles Gordon's Company—John Archibald, 40, shoemaker; native of Parish of Insch; enlisted at Sheela-green on February 1, 1760, and went off from Duncanstone, in Leslie, the place of his abode, on Monday, March 17, in a short brown coat, and old green waistcoat, blue breeches with black buttons, and black striped stockings, with a broad saddle girth round his middle. A squat, well-made man, brown complexion, and ash brown hair, a little bald.

To begin with, at any rate, the regiment was called "Lieutenant-Colonel Commandant Staats Long Morris's Highland Battalion of Foot," and it was thus that the officers were gazetted (*W.O.*, 25; 138; p. 114). But it got the number Eighty-Ninth, in point of precedence, being the first regiment in the British Army so designated. By a happy coincidence, the modern 89th, which was raised in 1793, now forms the second battalion of the Royal Irish Fusiliers, of which the first battalion is the old 87th, a number first assigned to Keith's Highlanders, raised in the same year as the Duke of Gordon's 89th.

Stewart asserts that the regiment marched from Gordon Castle to Aberdeen in December, 1759. As a matter of fact, the uniforms and swords did not arrive in Aberdeen till January 8, and it was only during that month that some of the men began to arrive there. The Duke himself was "expected by February 1," and when he arrived, he appeared "every day in the Highland dress"—it is not, however, clear whether the regiment wore the kilt—"which becomes him extremely well."

The Regiment was divided into two sections, of five and four companies respectively. On February 5, 1760, Lord George Beauclerk, commanding the Forces in Scotland, wrote a most significant letter to Lord Barrington, the War Minister, from Edinburgh (*W.O.* 1 : 614):—

I have this day received a letter from Lieut. Col. Morris acquainting me that five companies of his Battalion will be the first week of this month at Aberdeen. It likewise contains an unprecedented request, which I could by no means think of complying with, tho', by way of giving it the greater weight, he pleads that it was agreeable to what your lordship had desired of consulting him upon these and other occasions. His proposal, most warmly insisted upon, is that the Companies shall be reviewed at Aberdeen before they begin their march from thence to embark at Leith.

I have given him the following reasons for my not concurring with this measure, *viz.*, that I must look upon the several officers to be respectively responsible for the men they shall have raised till reviewed, and, consequently, the most effectual tye on these officers to give all possible attention to prevent desertion. For this single reason, I have, as a measure universally approved of, had all the Highland Corps reviewed as near the place of embarkation as possible.

The reason is obvious; it is well known that men who are raised in the Highlands enlist from the principles of personal regard and attachment to their officers, and, of course, look upon themselves as particularly bound to adhere to those officers as long as they are thus answerable for them. The officers, too are, on their part, equally bound to exert every influence to prevent any bad consequences, as none of their men are sustain'd till reviewed; and, therefore, the later both officers and men are released from their reciprocal engagements, the more it must tend to the good of the service. I thought it proper to acquaint your Lordship with those facts, that, in case you should have any different representation of this matter, you may see it in all its lights.

The five companies did not remain long at Aberdeen, but set out for Edinburgh, via Kirkcaldy, some men deserting on the road to the Lang Toun, so that Morris had to advertise for them in the *Journal* of March 3. The section was reviewed at Kirkcaldy, on February 18, by Lieutenant-Colonel Tayler, who reported as follows (*W.O.* 1 : 614):—

OFFICERS—Of a very good appearance, young, and extremely fit for service.

NON-COMMISSIONED OFFICERS—In general, tall and young men, and very fit for service.

DRUMMERS—Young boys, and learning to beat.

MEN—Front ranks of a good age and size. The rear ranks mostly young, and unexceptionable, as are most of the center ranks, according to the instructions for raising, which allow of low size, if well limbed. About twenty boys, rather too young, but straight, well limbed, and show signs of spirit and marched well from the North.

ARMS—About three hundred swords and pistols only given out; the rest in store or at the makers. Those I saw are good and new.

CLOATHING—Very good and laced. Only three hundred suits issued; the rest reported in London.

ACCOUNTS—None.

COMPLAINTS—Not any.

In countersigning this, February 28, Beauclerk wrote—" Upon the whole, a great number of the men in the Prime of Life for service, and no indulgence shown but to a few boys, on account of their spirit and appearance of being very soon quite unexceptionable."

Four transports were employed to take them from Burntisland to the Nore, namely the " Betsy," " Hopetoun " (with 330 men), and the " Carolina " and " Helen " (with 180)—seventeen of the passengers belonging to Colonel Parslow's regiment. Lord George announced to the War Minister that the five companies " sailed from Leith Road, on Sunday morning," March 2. As a matter of fact, one of the transports broke down and did not sail till March 16, when the contractor, David Loch, put in a bill for £40 for the demurrage of 378 tons, in addition to the £919 which he charged, of which £369 went in fares (at 15s. a man), and £382 for food. Loch's statement of his charge from March 6 to March 16 makes curious reading (*W.O.* 1: 614):—

To extraordinary charge taking up and fitting with the greatest despatch a larger ship, one of the transports being damaged by a storm; and, though she was immediately and effectually repaired, yet the Highlanders, from their being intirely unacquainted with sea affairs, would not embark on board the transport from an unreasonable conception of her still being leaky and insufficient, tho' the contrary was attested by the Naval officers and ship's carpenters sent by Commodore Boys at Lord George Beauclerk's desire to examine said ship.

As we shall see, part of the regiment was to return to England in a storm, so that the 89th got a good taste of the sea. On March 22, the commander-in-chief ordered two of the companies to march to

Petersfield and three to Chichester, which has since become so closely identified with the ducal family of Richmond and Gordon (*W.O.* 5: 47, p. 344).

Morris himself did not sail on March 2, for Beauclerk wrote to Barrington on March 6 (*W.O.* 1: 614):—

I have this day received a letter from Lieut. Col. Morris, acquainting me that your Lordship desires the four remaining companies of his battalion shall be at Spithead by the 20th, and leaving it to him to have them forwarded from hence by sea or land. As he thinks it best for the service to have them embarked at Aberdeen, the sooner I receive your Lordship's instructions on this head it will be much the better, that noe delay may be occasioned on the part of the transports which, he says, can now be got at Aberdeen, time enough for that purpose.

He told me when here that your Lordship did not intend they should be reviewed previous to their embarkation, of which your Lordship will likewise be pleased to inform me and whether any muster of them is necessary in Scotland.

Lord Barrington wrote the following instructions on the back of this letter:—

Acquaint Lord George that I had the honour of writing to his Lordship upon the subject of this letter by last post. I told Lieut. Col. Morris that, if I received a good report of the five companies, I would issue the commissions to the officers of the remaining four as soon as they were returned compleatt, without waiting till they were reviewed. However, I always intended that they should be reviewed before they embarked, as your Lordship may have observed from my last letter. I do not think it necessary that they should be mustered, as the other companies were not. Acquaint Lieut. Col. Morris that, from a letter I have received from Lord Geo. B., I apprehend he has misunderstood a passage in my letter to him of —— relative to the four last companies of his Battalion.

With regard to the other four companies, two entered Aberdeen on March 31, 1760, and Beauclerk ordered them to be embarked there by April 6, so that they might be reviewed and sail from Aberdeen by the 10th. It was not till June 15 that they sailed under convoy of H.M.S. "Tartar" (*W.O.* 1: 614). Here again there was a bungle, for James Burnett, the contractor, put in an extra claim, as he had bought provisions at a dear rate and "in a hurray" for thirty days for 400 men, but, "by a deficiency of men," the greater part of the provisions was thrown on his hands. The fares to Portsmouth cost £150 and the victualling £117, while there was a charge of £5 for the use of ten boats from the beach to the transports.

Meantime, Loch put in another claim for taking the five companies, which had been despatched from Burntisland, from the Nore to Portsmouth. These sailings did not absorb the whole regiment. Part of it went by road, for the War Office informed Lieutenant Fordyce, November 24, 1760—"It is His Majesty's pleasure that you cause the party belonging to Col. Morris's Highland Battalion under your command to march from Berwick by the shortest and most convenient route to London" (*W.O.* 5: 48, p. 93).

Of course, the 89th was a regiment of the line, and, unlike the Fencibles, liable to be sent abroad, but raw as it was, it received a shock on being ordered to sail for India. This is said to have been the doing of Argyll. According to Walpole—

Duke Archibald [of Argyll] was undoubtedly a dark, shrewd man. I recollect an instance, for which I should not choose to be quoted just at this moment, though it reflects on nobody living. I forget the precise period, and even some of the persons concerned; but it was in the minority of the present Duke of Gordon. A regiment had been raised of Gordons. Duke Archibald desired the command of it to a favourite of his own. The Duchess-Dowager insisted on it for her second husband. Duke A. said, "Oh, to be sure, her Grace must be obeyed"; but instantly got the regiment ordered to the East Indies—which had not been the reckoning of a widow re-married to a young fellow.

A corroboration of Walpole's story comes from the Duchess of Gordon herself. On March 3, 1760, she wrote from London to the Duke of Newcastle as follows (*Add. MSS.* 32,903 f. 57).

My Lord,—I am sorry to be under the necessity of troubling your Grace with a letter on a subject that I would have wished to have spoke on to you, could I have flattered myself to have had an opportunity. But, as it is too interesting for the wellfair of my family to admit of silence or delay, I am obliged to take this method to express to your Grace the surprise it gives me to hear that the regiment, which Mr. Morris has been raising on my son the Duke of Gordon's estate, is intended to be sent to the East Indias.

I must acquaint your Grace that how soon his Majesty approv'd of this regiment being raised, from that unwearied zeal I have always show'd to his Majesty's person and government I imedetly exerted myself to assist Mr. Morris to have this regiment properly officer'd and as quickly recruited as possible; and I flatter myself the success has

C

attended (in spite of many difficultys) will show the confidence his
Majesty was gratiously pleased to bestow on us was neither misplaced
nor abused. And the chearfullness exprest by my son's vassells and
tenants in assisting this measure of government will testify my son's
influence over them and readyness to exert himself in his Majesty's
service, for I brought him to Scotland on purpose to forward the recruiting service, well knowing his presence would be of the greatest
consequence.

    Your Grace must be sensible after this exertion of my family and
the readyness of my son's tenants in chearfully inlisting that nothing can
equal the shock that it gives me to hear they are intended for the East
Indias—a measure that must deeply affect the interest of my young
family upon this first essay of their early zeal for his Majesty's person
and government (in which I hope they will always distinguish themselves); and your Grace must permit me to mention how greatly it
must hurt them and affect the confidence of their tenants to find themselves order'd to the East Indias, so contrary to my hopes and expectations, as I always flatter'd myself they wer to have served his Majesty
in Germany, or at home. My anxious concern on this occasion obliges
me to apply to your Grace (whose protection and countinance my family
has experienced) to intreat that you'll be so good as give such directions
as you shall judge proper to change the intended destination of this
regiment, which I hope you will the more readily comply with, as I
can assure your Grace no measure could be more hurtfull to Government
in our part of the world as well as to my son's interest, of which, I
would soon convince you had I an opportunity of a few minutes conversation with your Grace.

Whether Newcastle put in a plea for the Duchess is not clear.
Probably he did not, for she frequently troubled him with her demands ;
but, if he did, he failed, for the regiment was packed off to India.

    Stewart makes the statement that the youthful Duke of Gordon
(then only sixteen) "left College [which one ?] with the intention of
embarking with his friends for the East Indies " :—

    This spirited resolution, however, was checked by George II., who
recommended the Duchess to send her son back to finish his education.
There being only nine Dukes in the kingdom of Scotland, he could not,
he said, suffer him to leave his native country ; and, commending his
spirit and patriotism, he added that he had more important services in
view for him than any he could perform as captain of a company in the
East Indies. This advice, so like a mandate, was, of course, followed,
and the Duke remained at home.

    Stewart has given wide vogue to the statement that the 89th

embarked at Portsmouth for the East Indies " in December, 1760, and reached Bombay in November, 1761." Mr. Fortescue gets nearer the truth when he says that " half a regiment [sic] of Morris's Highlanders under Major Hector Munro," arrived at Pondicherry on September, 2 (*History of the Army*, ii., 481). As a matter of fact, the 89th, or part of it, reached the scene of the great siege in August, for Major William Gordon, of the 84th Foot, who died as Governor of Pondicherry in 1761, writing (to an unknown correspondent) from L'Oulanget Camp, near that town, on October 27, 1760, says (*Add. MSS.* 35,917 f. 44):—" The reinforcement of four additional companies, 600 marines, and six companies of Morris's Highland Regiment, who joined in August last, was very seasonable, as the two preceding months were sickly ; our hospitals full ; numbers died." The 89th was subsequently stationed in different parts of India.

Part of the regiment sailed from Bombay in an old tub, H.M.S. "Elizabeth," and had a dreadful voyage home, the passage occupying from December 16, 1763, to July 11, 1764. Indeed, the voyage was one of the most trying on record, and Mr. Edward Fraser, the naval historian, tells me that the saving of the ship " is one of the most wonderful stories of the sea." It was an ironic fate for a race like the Highlanders who disliked the sea, and, not improbably, the tradition of it may have had something to do with the subsequent refusal of Highland regiments to embark on foreign service.

The " Elizabeth " had been launched on November 29, 1737, being partly built out of the timbers of an earlier " Elizabeth," which had been taken to pieces in 1734. She was of 70 guns (afterwards reduced to 64), and 1,124 tons. She had fought with Vernon in the West Indies and elsewhere, finally in the East Indies in the Pocock-D'Ache series of battles 1759-60, and her last commission—part of it under the captaincy of Kempenfelt of " Royal George " fame—was at Bombay, with the voyage homewards. She was taken to pieces at Chatham in 1765. The whole story of her terrible voyage home is told with technical minuteness by the captain (*P.R.O.: Captains' Logs*, 307).

On December 15, 1763, the vessel embarked " 100 Highland soldiers," eight sergeants and eight corporals, besides officers, and the fort " saluted Colonel Morris with 15 guns as he was leaving the shore. We," says the log, " saluted with 13 at his coming aboard." An unsigned letter in the *Aberdeen Journal* (June 25, 1764), says that Morris was accompanied by the following officers :—

Captains Morison, Lamont and Leith ; Lieutenants Stuart, sen. and jun., Finlason, Hanson and Fordyce ; Ensign Donald, and about 100 soldiers. " Major [Hector] Munro and the other officers at Bombay could not be accommodated in the ' Elizabeth,' and remain till another opportunity, which probably would happen in the month of February last."

The " Elizabeth " weighed anchor on December 16, and found Admiral Cornish's fleet on the coast of Malabar. Bad weather began to be experienced on January 31, in latitude of 20 degrees south, between Madagascar and the African coast. The gale was so furious that on February 1 the Captain hove four guns overboard to save the ship. " She strained so much," he says, " that all the brickworks of the copper and grates fell down," and there was 6 ft. $8\frac{1}{2}$ ins. of water in the hold. On February 2, he struck the top mast. The *Journal* correspondent continues the story :—

It was with the greatest difficulty we could keep the crazy old ship from sinking, although four chain pumps were constantly employed during the gale. The seams opened by the violent motion of a high sea, and, to compleat her misfortune, the rudder hinges gave way, and were obliged to be cut away ; and she was preserved from sinking only by a number of people at the pumps, and wrapping her round with cables and hawsers, to prevent her from parting asunder. After the gale, a machine was contrived to supply the defect of a rudder, but answered so badly that it was six weeks before we reached the Cape, although the common passage was not 14 days from the place we lost our rudder in. [Cape Town was reached on March 9.]

After our arrival at the Cape, Colonel Morris and Ensign Fordyce took their passage on board the " Osterley," Indiaman, from Bengal, and the admiral had resolved to bring the " Elizabeth " home, contrary to the opinion of every officer belonging to the ship, except the captain. To stop her leaks was impossible, as they were occasioned by an universal defect in her timbers and planks ; and they had begun to cover her outside with tarred canvas, when the " Osterley " left the Cape on March 21. The admiral gave leave to four of our officers to take their passage on board the " Chatham," a good ship ; and Leith and the two Stuarts had the good fortune to draw lots for the " Chatham." Captain Morison, as commanding officer, was indulged with his choice, which he made for the " Chatham."

I hope the " Elizabeth " will meet with fair weather. If she has such fine weather as we have met in the " Osterley " and which she has reason to expect, there will be no great damage. But if she encounters a gale of wind, I should be much afraid of her. The admiral intended to sail from the Cape the end of April.

As a matter of fact the "Elizabeth" was in such a bad condition that she had to lie up at the Cape for repairs from March 9 to April 17, and stopped at St. Helena, May 3, 4, 5. It was not until July 11 that England was reached, the troops being disembarked on July 12.

Meantime, greater things were in store for Munro and the remnant of the regiment, for just as he was on the point of embarking for England, he was summoned back to succeed Carnac. He brought with him the remains of his own regiment, the 89th, and of Morgan's, the 90th, and in August, 1764, reached Patna, which was in a highly mutinous state. Early in the following month he broke the mutiny, and blew twenty-four of the mutineers from guns under thrilling circumstances. Munro achieved a far greater success at Buxar, a few weeks later, October 23, when he completely defeated the huge army of Oude.

It is not known when the remainder of the regiment came home, but Stewart says it was disbanded in 1765. He is also responsible for the statement that "an uncommon circumstance attended their service," in the fact that, although five years embodied, four of which were spent in India, or on the passage going and returning, "there was neither death, promotion, nor any change whatever among the officers except that of Lieutenant Lord William Gordon," promoted, and that of his successor to his lieutenancy. As there are no muster rolls or other data, it is difficult to check this statement. But we know that one of the officers, John Gordon, of the Lesmoir family, died on September 1, 1761, being buried the same day in St. Mary's Cemetery, Madras. Death certainly occurred among the rank and file. An advertisement in the *Aberdeen Journal* of November 2, 1764, names the following soldiers of Colonel Morris's regiment and Captain Morison's company—James Annan, James Bonnyman, Thomas Fraser, John Jopp, and William M'Donald, who died during the absence of the regiment from Britain. "Captain Morison gives notice to the nearest relatives of these men that upon proving their propinquity he will pay them the money due to the deceased."

The second "uncommon circumstance", which struck Stewart as "more remarkable and in itself highly honourable to this respectable corps," was that not one man in the regiment was "brought to the halberts or deserted during the five years." The first statement may be true ; but the second, as we have seen, was certainly not : but it affords Stewart the opportunity of ending his pioneer account of the 89th with a peroration on the peril of "infamous punishments," a favourite subject with him, which proves him to have been far in advance of his time.

It only remains to add that there was no 89th in our army again till 1779, when a regiment was raised, to be disbanded in 1783. Another arose in 1793 and exists to this day as the second battalion of the Princess Victoria's (Royal Irish Fusiliers), who share with the Seaforths the distinction of wearing two collar badges.

THE EIGHTY-SEVENTH: OR KEITH'S HIGHLANDERS.

1759: RAISED BY ROBERT MURRAY KEITH: DISBANDED 1763.

As this regiment was partly raised in Aberdeenshire by a Kincardine man who was descended from a noble Aberdeenshire family, and who was afterwards of great service on the continent of Europe to Aberdeenshire soldiers, one is justified in referring to it briefly.

The 87th owed its origin to Robert Murray Keith (1730-95), son of Robert Keith (died 1774), the British Ambassador at Vienna, by his wife Agnes, daughter of Archibald Murray, of Blackbarony. He was descended from William (Keith), 2nd Earl Marischal (died 1526), whose third son, John, got the estate of Craig, and whose male line died out (at Hammersmith) in the person of the raiser of the 87th. Keith began his career in the Scots Brigade in Holland, where he must have heard much of his distant kinsman, Field Marshal James Keith, the inventor of Kriegsschachspiel, who fell at Hochkirch in 1758. As his native land was in danger, he came back to it to raise a corps in Scotland.

Stewart gives little or nothing about the origin of the corps, which he treats in conjunction with the 88th, or Campbell's Highlanders; and there are no muster rolls at the Public Record Office. It is true that the Notification Books there give the officers, but they give these officers and those finally allotted to Campbell's Highlanders as all having been gazetted to Keith's, and it is only when we come to the Succession Books, constructed at a later period, that we are able to see the particular regiment to which each officer was assigned.

Keith's own appointment to be "major commandant of a corps of Highlanders to be forthwith formed," is dated August 20, 1759 (*W.O.* 25: 138, p. 44). On the following day, August 21, he wrote to Pitt as follows (Mrs. Gillespie Smith's *Memoirs of Sir Robert Murray Keith* i., 99):—

I got access to Mr. Pitt, who inquired into my situation with a generous and friendly concern. He sd. he wished yr. family well, and wd. serve me whenever it was in his power. Soon after it was determined, though not without some opposition, to form a little corps of Highlanders and send them to Germany. Three hundred supernumeraries of Lord J[ohn] Murray's corps [the 42nd] were ready at Newcastle. Mr. Pitt *removed all obstacles*, and gave me the sole command of them. This Corps is to be augmented to five companies and to belong entirely to me, with the rank of Major-Commandant. I kissed hands to-day; am to embark the three first companies, as soon as possible, for Embden. They are to be in Highland dress, and be called the Highland Volunteers.

While the supernumeraries of the Black Watch formed the nucleus of the corps, two additional companies were formed by Keith, who recruited some of them in Aberdeenshire. A return of the regiment shows that out of five companies, two were at Aberdeen in April, 1760, commanded by Captain Murray (77 men), and Captain the Hon. William Boyd (54 men); other companies were in Glasgow, Ross-shire and Caithness (*W.O.* 1: 614). The recruiting in Aberdeenshire was done by Captain Boyd, who like Keith had also an Aberdeenshire origin, which had resulted in his brother, Lord Boyd, succeeding (August 19, 1758) their great-aunt as 15th Earl of Erroll, though, of course, he did not succeed to the forfeited titles of his own father, the Earl of Kilmarnock, who had been beheaded in the Tower twelve years before. Boyd fell out with a citizen, Alexander Clerk, though he was exonerated by the following memorial from the magistrates to Lord George Beauclerk, May 1, 1760 (*W.O.* 1: 614):—

Understanding that complaint has been made to Lord Barrington, Secretary at War, upon the Hon. Captain William Boyd, of Major Murray Keith's Regiment, of his turbulent behaviour while recruiting in this city and neighbourhood; and that Lord Barrington had advised your lordship thereof,

We reckon ourselves in duty bound to certify your lordship that Captain Boyd during his residence here for some months past in the recruiting way has on every case behaved with the greatest civility and discretion as a gentleman. There were indeed mutual processes betwixt him and Alexander Clerk, one of our burghers, for a breach of the peace, as to which a precognition of the facts will probably be laid before your lordship. We shall therefore say nothing further about it; only that it is now amicably settled.

In justice to Captain Boyd's character, we could not omitt troubling your lordship with this letter, so that when you have occasion to correspond with Lord Barrington relative to Captain Boyd, you will be so good as acquaint his lordship what is our real sentiments of [sic] Captain Boyd's character; and we have the honour to be, with real regard, your lordshipp's most obedient and most humble servants—John Duncan, Provost; George Shand, James Jopp, Alexander Raitt, Baillies.

As I have said, the Notification Books (*W.O.* 25: 138: pp. 44, 52, 66, 82, 87, 103, 135, 147, 164, 188) gazette all the officers to Keith's corps, which was first in the field (August, 1759), Major John Campbell of Dunoon, who commanded the 88th, not being gazetted till January 1, 1760.

It looks as if Keith's corps was so successful that it had to be split up into two commands. The Succession Books (*W.O.* 25: 209: pp. 176-178) disintegrate the original commissions into the two regiments as finally embodied. It is these I follow, retaining those officers in the 88th who were killed and wounded (detailed by Stewart, ii. 35), and the Aberdeenshire officers.

COMMANDANT.

Robert Murray Keith (from the 73rd), major-commandant, August 20, 1759; lieutenant-colonel com. May 10, 1760.

MAJORS.

Alexander Maclean (from captain, 88th), July 14, 1761; went back to the 88th.

88th—Archibald MacNab (of Leighton's), December 11, 1759; wounded at Fellinghausen, July, 1761; succeeded April 26, 1762, by MacLean. Laird of Macnab?

John Pollock (from captain, 72nd), February 19, 1760; killed at Camphen, October 15, 1760 (Stewart's *Highlanders*, ii. 28, 35).

CAPTAINS.

Hon. William Boyd (from the 52nd), January 3, 1760; joined the 114th, October 17, 1761. Born, 1728, he was the fourth son of the 4th Earl of Kilmarnock (beheaded 1746), and died unmarried, 1780 (*Scots Peerage*, v. 181).

Archibald Campbell (from the 42nd), August 18, 1759, *vice* Roy; Major, December 20, 1760, *vice* Pollock; wounded at Camphen, October 15, 1760, and at Fellinghausen, July, 1761. Stewart (*Highlanders*, ii. 26, 27, 32) says he was "brother to Auchallader, whose classical learning and accomplishments attracted the notice of Lord Lyttleton."

88th—Patrick Campbell, September 29, 1759; wounded at Brucher Mühl, September 21, 1762.

Finlay Farquharson, October 11, 1759.

D

John Gorry (from lieutenant, 72nd), October 27, 1759.

John Gunn (from the 65th), January 6, 1760; died before June 26, 1760, when he was succeeded by Clunes.

Alexander MacLean (from the 42nd), August 20, 1759; major, April 26, 1762, *vice* MacNab; killed at Brucher Mühl, September 21, 1762.

John Murray (lieutenant, 42nd), August 26, 1759; major, April 26, 1762.

William Roy (from the 51st), August 18, 1759; succeeded on the same day by Archibald Campbell.

CAPTAIN-LIEUTENANTS.

Patrick Davidson (from lieutenant, 103rd), May 3, 1762.

James Fraser, (from the 42nd), October 8, 1759; succeeded December 20, 1760, by Gordon Clunes.

1ST LIEUTENANTS.

Gordon Clunes (of the 42nd), August 26, 1759; captain-lieutenant, December 20, 1760; captain *vice* Gunn, June 26, 1762; wounded at Camphen, October 15, 1760.

Patrick Drummond, September 27, 1759; resigned before August 4, 1762.

Alexander Duff (from ensign, 69th), August 29, 1759; captain, *vice* Boyd, May 3, 1762.

88th—James Farquharson, October 11, 1759. Probably son of Gustavus Farquharson of the Allargue family, whose son, Lieutenant James, died at Nether Coulie, Monymusk, May 12, 1787, aged 58 (A. M. Mackintosh's *Farquharson Genealogies*, No. 1, p. 38).

Patrick Gall, September 26, 1759.

James Grant, September 11, 1760. Stewart says John [sic] Grant was killed at Fellinghausen, July, 1761.

James Grant, April 29, 1762, *vice* Ross, deceased; became adjutant.

Archibald MacArthur (from the Dutch Service), August 27, 1759; adjutant, August 29; wounded at Fellinghausen, July, 1761. Captain, 105th, October 18, 1761.

George MacGill, April 21, 1760.

George Mackay (lieutenant, Sutherland Fencibles), November 11, 1763, *vice* Robertson.

Donald Mackenzie, January 27, 1760.

George Mackenzie, October 26, 1759.

Angus Mackintosh, February 19, 1760; wounded at Camphen, October 15, 1760; killed at Fellinghausen, July, 1761.

William Mackintosh (from ensign, 42nd), August 28, 1759; captain, April 26, 1762.

88th—James Mercer (of Home's), January 4, 1760. Son of an Aberdeenshire laird; afterwards in the Northern Fencibles of 1778.

Duncan Robertson, September 29, 1759; quartermaster, April 26, 1762, *vice* John Robertson.

John Robertson, January 28, 1760; adjutant and quartermaster.

George Ross, January 28, 1760; resigned by April 28, 1762.

William Ross, October 27, 1759; killed at Fellinghausen, July, 1761.

Robert Sutherland, sen., January 6, 1760.

Robert Sutherland, jun., January 7, 1760. One of these Roberts transferred to the Sutherland Fencibles.

George Vaughan, November 27, 1763, *vice* MacArthur.

2ND LIEUTENANTS.

Volunteer Walter Barland, August 27, 1759; 1st lieutenant, December 20, 1760, *vice* Clunes; wounded at Camphen, October 15, 1760; and at Brucher Mühl, September 21, 1762.

Oliver Campbell, April 27, 1762.

Ronald Campbell, July 15, 1761, *vice* Ogilvie, deceased.

William Davidson, April 28, 1762.

Volunteer Donald Fraser, December 20, 1760, *vice* Barland.

Volunteer James Garioch, August 4, 1762.

Patrick Handasyde, January 28, 1760; 1st lieutenant, April 28, 1762, *vice* Ross, resigned.

John Johnston, May 24, 1762, *vice* Cameron.

Angus Mackintosh, February 19, 1760; 1st lieutenant, April 28, 1762, *vice* Ross, deceased.

Alexander MacLeod, October 27, 1759; 1st Lieutenant, April 22, 1762.

Donald Macleod, July 16, 1761, *vice* Fraser, deceased.

William Ogilvie, August 29, 1759; wounded at Warburg, July 31, 1760; dead by April 21, 1762. Ogilvie was appointed surgeon, August 29, 1759; probably volunteer the same.

John Reid, April 26, 1762, *vice* Duncan Robertson.

Duncan Robertson, September 29, 1759; 1st lieutenant, April 26, 1762, *vice* William Mackintosh; quartermaster, April 26, 1762, *vice* John Robertson.

William Rose, January 3, 1760; 1st lieutenant, August 6, 1762, *vice* Drummond.

William Ross, June 30, 1760.

CHAPLAIN.

James Milne, January 27, 1761.

It is stated that Alexander MacGregor Murray, brother of Sir John Murray of Lanrick, joined the corps at the age of 14 as a volunteer. He commanded the Royal Clan Alpine Fencible Infantry, 1798-1802 (*Military History of Perthshire*, i., 181-4).

On August 27, 1759, Keith's corps was ordered to be called the "Highland Volunteers" (*W.O.* 4: 58: p. 474), but it was usually called Keith's Highlanders, and officially the 87th.

On April 10, 1760, Beauclerk sent a return of the strength of the corps, " which from their dispersed situation I have given an order for assembling such of them as are now employed in recruiting in Aberdeen" (*W.O.* 1: 614). The report stated:—

Non Commissioned Officers—In appearance fit for service, young and tall.

Men—Front ranks mostly young and good men. The center and rear ranks in general very good—some few old men and boys not fit to be objected at this time when men are very difficult to get.

The regimental pay for 802 men from January 24 to December 24, 1760, was £12,782 (*W.O.* 24: 356).

On May 9, Keith's men sailed from Burntisland for Germany—154 and 18 horses on the "Desire," and 183 on the "Charming Polly" —to join the army of Prince Ferdinand. Here they fought side by side with Campbell's Highlanders, the 88th, losing very heavily in the seven fierce battles waged between January 1760 and September 1762. The two regiments, which had seven officers and 109 rank and file killed, and 13 officers and 171 rank and file wounded, are treated together by Stewart (*Highlanders*, ii. 23-35). They returned home in 1763, and Keith's was reduced at Perth.

THE 101ST: OR JOHNSTONE'S HIGHLANDERS.

The recruiting for the Duke of Gordon's regiment and Keith's Highlanders was quickly followed in Aberdeenshire by the recruiting for the Independent Company which Peter Gordon of Knockespock was commissioned to raise. He was one of five gentlemen so commissioned, the others being Colin Graham of Drainie, James Cuthbert of Milncraigs, Ludovick Grant of the Rothiemurcus family, and Robert Campbell of Ballivolin.

Peter Gordon was the son of George Gordon of Knockspock, by Jean Leith of the Harthill family, and younger brother of a distinguished officer of the Engineers, Colonel Harry Gordon (d. 1787), who succeeded to Knockespock. Peter—who probably got his name from the Leiths—entered the Army in 1755 as Ensign in the 54th Foot, and became a Lieutenant in the 51st three years later. He served with his regiment in Germany, and was wounded at the battle of Minden, August 1, 1759.

On October 28, 1760, he was appointed Captain Commandant of an Independent Company, and set about recruiting in Aberdeenshire, having his headquarters in the town of Aberdeen. He was associated with two other officers—Lieutenant James Campbell and Lieutenant Richardson McVeagh. The latter was related in a round about way with Gordon, for he was the nephew of Hugh McVeagh, the Huntly bleacher (who was the son of Dr. Ferdinand McVeagh, founder of the McVeaghs of Drewston, Co. Meath, described in Burke's *Landed Gentry*), who had married Gordon's cousin, Margaret Lumsden of the Cushnie family. Richardson McVeagh afterwards died in Bengal.

The companies were to consist of five sergeants and 105 privates each. Gordon was so successful that, according to a return of December 3, 1760 (*W.O.* 17: 792), 70 men had been enlisted " of which 40 [were] sent to ye Company," and 28 remained in recruiting quarters, while two had deserted. On January 26, 1761, Gordon advertised in the *Aberdeen*

Journal "for four or five men to compleat" his Company. He offered "seven or eight guineas for very clever young men. He wants two sergeants and a corporal and will give two guineas to any person that brings him a recruit." One of the recruits, Alexander Duncan, born in Strathbogie, deserted, and was advertised for in the *Journal* of July 12, 1762.

Gordon got command of the Company on March 1, 1761. The various companies were marched to Perth, numbered the 101st (McVeagh becoming Adjutant), and given to James Johnstone to command. Johnstone (1721-1797) succeeded to the baronetcy of Westerhall, Dumfries, in 1772, and was succeeded by his brother, William (1729-1805) the greatest American stock-holder of his day.

The regiment, which twice prepared to go abroad and was countermanded on each occasion, was reduced in August, 1763. Gordon subsequently served in the 63rd and 70th and went to Grenada, where he was killed in a duel by Mr. Proudfoot, Member of the House of Assembly, June 1768 (*Gordons under Arms*, No. 1,149). The regiment is eulogistically sketched by Stewart (*Highlanders*, ii., 40-43). There are, unhappily, no muster rolls at the Record Office.

THE SEVENTY-FIRST: OR FRASER HIGHLANDERS.

1775: RAISED BY THE HON. SIMON FRASER: DISBANDED 1783.

The 4th Duke of Gordon's second experiment in recruiting was carried out in 1775, when he raised a company for the Fraser Highlanders. This was the second body of Fraser troops. The first (78th Regiment) was raised in 1757 by the "Hon." Simon Fraser, *de jure* 12th Lord Fraser of Lovat (1726-82), elder son of the notorious Lord Lovat. It greatly distinguished itself at Quebec, where it lost 59 killed (including an unidentified lieutenant, Cosmo Gordon) and 156 wounded, and was reduced in 1763. Its history has been told by Stewart (*Highlanders*, 2nd ed., ii. 18-23), in *Notes and Queries* 11 S. viii., 354-5, and by Edward Kelly in *The Fighting Frasers of the 'Forty-Five and Quebec*, 1908 (pp. v., 57).

The second regiment of Fraser Highlanders (the 71st) was raised (two battalions) in 1775 by the same Simon, and disbanded 1783. Its history was elaborately done by Stewart (2nd ed., ii. 43-80). The mandate for the raising of the regiment was addressed "to our trusty and well-beloved Simon Fraser, Esq., Major-Generall of our Forces and Colonell of a highland regiment of foot to be forthwith raised":—

George III.—Whereas we have thought it fit to order a Highland Regiment of Foot of two battalions to be forthwith raised under your command; each battalion to consist of ten companys of four sergeants, four corporalls, two drummers, and one hundred private men in each company, with two pipers to each of the grenadier companies, besides commissioned officers;

These are to authorise you by beat of drum or otherways to raise so many men in any county or part of our Kingdom of Great Britain, as shall be wanting to compleat the new Regiment to the above mentioned numbers. And all Magistrates, Justices of the Peace, Constables and other, our civill officers, whom it may concern, are hereby required to be assisting unto you in providing quarters, impressing carriages, and otherways as there shall be occasion.

Given at our Court of St. James's, the 25th day of October, 1775, in the 16th year of our reign.

By His Majestie's command.

Barrington.

The 4th Duke of Gordon became interested in it through his wife, Jane Maxwell, whom he had married in 1767, because her brother, Hamilton Maxwell, second son of Sir William Maxwell, 3rd bart. of Monreith, desired a commission and had therefore to raise a company. The task which the Duchess set herself was by no means easy, and she encountered many disappointments. Despite her husband's power as a great landlord, she met with small success among the Macphersons, to take but one class of tenant. The Rev. Robert Macpherson, Aberarder, writing on April 6, 1778, says that "no person appeared in the country for Captain Maxwell, to take upon him the horrid drudgery of drinking whysky and to act the recruiting sergeant among the people. Besides, the few remaining sparks of clanship had by that time been kindled into a flame, which with their sympathy for Clunie's misfortunes made them enlist with their chieftain in preference to all mankind. But the fit did not last long." Her Grace had also the mortification of encountering rivals. Thus a certain David Mackay, who had been enlisted at Grantown market, was not attested, "being carried off by a son of Galloway's." A party spent three days looking for him (at a cost of £18). He finally listed with Ensign Grant.

The formula of the recruit is illustrated in the following case :—

I, John Sharp, do make Oath that I am a Protestant and by trade a Taylor, and to the best of my knowledge and belief, was born in the parish of Mortlich in the County of Banff; that I have no rupture, nor ever was troubled with fits; that I am no ways disabled by lameness or otherwise, but have perfect use of my limbs; and that I have voluntarily enlisted myself to serve His Majesty King George the Third as a private soldier in General Fraser's new highland regiment and in Captain Maxwell's Company; and I have received all the enlisting money which I agreed for. As witness my hand, this 29th day of Dec., 1775.

John Sharp.

The men were largely raised at markets, pipers and drummers being used to attract them. The most active recruiters were Sergeant Peter

Thomson; David Tulloch, who got a shilling a day and a guinea a recruit; J. Stewart; and Peter Wilkie. The accounts, which with the muster roll are at Gordon Castle, contain such items as the following:—

By cash to a piper to Glass Mercatt	£0	7	0
To William Hamilton, piper, employed from Dec. 7, 1775,			
to Feb. 17, 1776, at a shilling a day	3	12	0
For dirk to him	0	10	6
For a kilt for him	0	5	9
To extraordinary drink at Elgin market	1	5	0
To the recruits to drink upon the Duchess's setting out for			
London, Feb. 12, 1776	1	10	0

A sum of 5s. 6d. was paid for "three boys coming from Keith to list with Her Grace, [but] not fit for service." Another curious item is £1 1s. to "Miss Annie Gordon, doctress, for medicine to different recruits in Captain Maxwell's Co'y."

The company was uniformed by Alexander Umphray, Fochabers, and by A. Forsyth and Son, the clothing including tartan, scarlet cloth, silver lace, gilt buttons. Some of the items included in Umphray's bill for the recruiting sergeants under date December 13, 1775, were as follows:—

To 11 yards tartan	£1	0	2
„ 1 blue bonnet	0	1	10
„ 13 yards yellow ribbon	0	7	10
„ 4 yards tartan for a philabeg	0	7	4
„ 4 yards tartan for hose	0	8	0
„ 4 pairs garters	0	2	0
„ ½ dozen yellow buttons	0	0	6
„ 12 yards tartan for a plaid	0	13	0
„ 1 pair shoe and knee buckles	0	2	0

In another account we find a sum of £11 2s. 8d. paid for tartan for the recruits.

The raising of the company cost the Duchess from first to last the sum of £587 5s. 3d., of which £366 19s. 8d. went in bounties (varying from 7s. 6d. to £6 per man); and £129 3s. 6d. in "subsistence" from November 12, 1775, to March 24, 1776.

At last the quota was complete, 89 men in all, of whom 73 were

E

for her brother, Captain Maxwell, and t6 for Lieutenant Francis Skelly (formerly of the 25th Foot), the Duke's first cousin Only two of the 89 men had red hair Maxwell's men (67 strong) marched from Fochabers on February 26, 1776, under the command of Sergeant Peter Thomson, and two days later the Duchess received the Muster Roll.

The Muster Roll of the Duchess's company preserved at Gordon Castle shows that the average height of the eighty men was 5 ft 5 17416 inches

Name	Age	Height.	Birthplace	Trade.	Date	And Place of Enlistment
Anderson, David	19	5 ft 5 in	Kennethmont, Aberdeen	Heckler	Jan 1, 1776	Fochabers
Anderson, John	22	5 ft 4 in	Elgin, Moray	Labourer	Jan 30, 1776	,,
Andrew, Alexander	16	5 ft 3 in	Watten, Caithness	,,	Dec 25, 1775	,,
Brymer, John	23	5 ft 4½ in	Fochabers, Moray	,,	Jan 10, 1776	,,
Burnet, Robert	20	5 ft 4 in	Inverkeithny, Banff	,,	Feb 10, 1776	Huntly
Cameron, Evan	25	5 ft 5 in	Kilmalie, Inverness	,,	Dec 20, 1775	Lochaber
Davidson, George	20	5 ft 5 in	Fordyce, Banff	Mason	Jan 8, 1776	Fochabers
Duncan, James	18	5 ft 10½ in	Rothiemay, Banff	Labourer	Dec 23, 1775	,,
Duncan, William	27	5 ft 5½ in	Drumblade, Aberdeen	Tailor	Jan 9, 1776	Huntly
Forbes, Robert	32	5 ft 6 in	Aberdeen City	Tobacconist	Feb 14, 1776	Banff
Forsyth, William	19	5 ft 6¼ in	Keith, Banff	Labourer	Jan 10, 1776	Huntly
Fraser, Alexander	32	5 ft 5 in	Inverness City	Butcher	Nov 12, 1775	Fort William
Fraser, James	16	5 ft 3½ in	Rulcarlatie, Inverness	Labourer	Dec 25, 1775	Fochabers
Fraser, John	18	5 ft 4½ in	Rafford, Moray	Shoemaker	Feb 10, 1776	Huntly
Garrow, George	24	5 ft 4½ in	Keith, Moray	,,	Feb 8, 1776	Fochabers
Geddes, Alexander	19	5 ft 6 in	Drainie, Moray	Labourer	Dec 20, 1775	,,
Geddes, James	22	5 ft 6½ in	Drainie, Moray	,,	Dec 20, 1775	,,
Gilberton, John	27	5 ft 5½ in	Olrig, Caithness	,,	Dec 12, 1776	,,
Gillan, Alexander	16	5 ft 3½ in	Urquhart, Moray	,,	Dec 18, 1775	,,
Gilzean, James	16	5 ft 3½ in	Fochabers, Moray	,,	Dec 8, 1775	,,
*Gordon, Alexander	18	5 ft 6 in.	Duffus, Moray	,,	Dec 13, 1775	Elgin
Gordon, John	17	5 ft. 4 in	Fochabers, Moray	Gardener	Dec 20, 1775	Fochabers
Gow, James	17	5 ft 2½ in	Kilmalie, Inverness	,,	Dec 18, 1775	'
Grant, Absalom	17	5 ft 4 in	Kirkmichael, Banff	Labourer	Dec 30, 1775	,,
Grant, Alexander	16	5 ft 4½ in	Duthell, Inverness	,,	Dec 25, 1775	,,
Gunn, John	20	5 ft 4½ in	Creach, Sutherland	,,	Jan 2, 1776	,,
Gunn, John	32	5 ft 9½ in	Durness, Sutherland	,,	Feb 14, 1776	Banff
Hay, George	20	5 ft 5 in	Gartly, Aberdeen	,,	Dec 16, 1775	Fochabers
Hay, John	18	5 ft 8½ in	Keith, Banff	Gardener	Dec 26, 1775	,,
Herrygerry, James	17	5 ft. 4½ in	Culsalmond, Aberdeen	Labourer	Dec 20, 1775	,,
Holm, Donald	19	5 ft 5 in	Rosskeen, Ross	,,	Dec 26, 1775	,,
Howie, James	20	5 ft 4 in	Birnie, Moray	,,	Dec 27, 1775	,,
Ingram, William	27	5 ft 4½ in	Gartly, Aberdeen	,,	Dec 11, 1775	,,
Ingram, William	20	5 ft 7½ in	Bellie, Banff	,,	Feb 1, 1776	,,
Innes, Robert	18	5 ft 5 in	Keith, Banff	,,	Jan 8, 1776	,,
Kennedy, John	20	5 ft 6 in	Kilmanivaig, Inverness	Lint dresser	Jan 8, 1776	,,
Kingsley, Robert	28	5 ft 11½ in	Boston, Lincoln	Wool comb'r	Dec 21, 1775	Fort William
Logie, John	16	5 ft 5½ in	Elgin, Elgin	Labourer	Dec 13, 1775	Fochabers
M Coase, William	18	5 ft 4 in	Marnoch, Banff	,,	Jan 8, 1776	Elgin
M'Commachie, Patrick	23	5 ft 9 in	Mortlach, Banff	,,	Jan 8, 1776	Fochabers
M Donald, Donald	26	5 ft 5 in	Apin, Argyle	Tailor	Jan 18, 1776	,,
M'Donald, William	19	5 ft 6 in	Marnoch, Banff	Labourer	Feb 21, 1776	Fort William
M'Gregor, Patrick	19	5 ft 8 in	Cromdale, Inverness	,,	Dec 9, 1775	Banff
M'Kay, Donald	17	5 ft 3½ in	Roggart, Sutherland	,,	Dec 13, 1775	Fochabers
M'Kay, Hugh	19	5 ft 4 in	Kincairn, Ross	Squarewri't	Dec 8, 1775	,,
M'Kay, Hugh	19	5 ft 2½ in	Rosekeen, Ross	Labourer	Jan 13, 1776	Gordon Castle
M'Kay, Murdoch	39	5 ft 6 in	Lewis, Ross	,,	Feb 5, 1776	Fochabers
M'Kay, Neill	19	5 ft 3½ in	Wick, Caithness	,,	Dec 13, 1775	,,
†M'Kenzie, Kenneth	15	5 ft 7½ in	Old Aberdeen, Aberdeen	Fiddler	Jan 1, 1776	,,
Mackie, William	26	5 ft 10½ in	Marnoch, Banff	Tailor	Dec 12, 1775	,,
‡M'Lean, John	22	5 ft 5½ in	Lochbroom, Inverness	Labourer	Jan 16, 1776	,,

* Sent to 42nd as a deserter
† Deserted
‡ The Duchess sent his wife a boll of meal

Name.	Age.	Height.	Birthplace.	Trade.	Date.	And Place of Enlistment.
M'Pherson, Dougald ..	18	5 ft. 4 in.	Ardnamurchan, Argyle	Miner	Jan. 13, 1776	Fort William
{M'Pherson, Dun[can]..	24	5 ft. 5½ in.	Ardclach, Nairn	Labourer	Jan. 16, 1776	Fochabers
M'Pherson, Evan ..	17	5 ft. 4 in.	Alvey, Inverness	Tailor	Dec. 22, 1775	,,
M'Queen, Alexander ..	15	5 ft. 4 in.	Moye, Inverness	Shoemaker	Jan. 23, 1776	,,
Man, William ..	23	5 ft. 6½ in.	Auch, Inverness	Labourer	Jan. 26, 1776	,,
Melville, Alexander ..	16	5 ft. 4 in.	Boharm, Banff	Labourer	Dec. 18, 1775	Huntly
Morrison, James .:	17	5 ft. 4 in.	Deskford, Banff	Heckler	Dec. 13, 1775	Fochabers
Nicholson, Robert ..	17	5 ft. 6 in.	Ardersier, Inverness	Chapman	Dec. 19, 1775	,,
Phimister, William ..	18	5 ft. 4½ in.	St. Andrews, Moray	Merchant	Dec. 21, 1775	Elgin
§Raeburn, Thomas ..	19	5 ft. 6½ in.	Boyndie, Banff	Labourer	Jan. 8, 1776	Fochabers
Rainie, Charles ..	17	5 ft. 8 in.	Knockando, Moray	Weaver	Dec. 9, 1775	Huntly
Reid, Alexander ..	23	5 ft. 6½ in.	Bellie, Banff	Labourer	Feb. 12, 1776	Banff
Robertson, John ..	25	5 ft. 6 in.	Deskford, Banff	,,	Jan. 30, 1776	Fochabers
Rose, Hugh ..	20	5 ft. 2½ in.	Kincairn, Ross	,,	Jan. 24, 1776	,,
Rose, John ..	18	5 ft. 6 in.	Tarbart, Ross	,,	Jan. 8, 1776	,,
Sage, James ..	18	5 ft. 5 in.	Auldearn, Nairn	Merchant	Feb. 21, 1776	Elgin
Sampson, Edward ..	38	5 ft. 7 in.	Long Setton, Lincoln	Brickmaker	Jan. 10, 1776	Fochabers
Sinclair, Charles ..	17	5 ft. 4½ in.	Latheron, Caithness	Labourer	Jan. 8, 1776	,,
Sinclair, Francis ..	18	5 ft. 5 in.	Latheron, Caithness	,,	Feb. 14, 1776	Banff
Smith, Peter ..	18	5 ft. 5½ in.	Inveralian Inverness	,,	Jan. 8, 1776	Fochabers
Smith, Robert ..	18	5 ft. 4 in.	Cairnie, Aberdeen	,,	Jan. 8, 1776	,,
Stalker, James ..	18	5 ft. 3 in.	Raffart, Moray	,,	Dec. 18, 1775	,,
Stephen, William ..	16	5 ft. 5 in.	Elgin, Elgin	,,	Dec. 25, 1775	Elgin
Stewart, Allan ..	19	5 ft. 4½ in.	Cromdale, Moray	,,	Jan. 1, 1776	Fochabers
Stewart, James ..	16	5 ft. 3½ in.	Kirkmichael, Banff	,,	Jan. 6, 1776	,,
Sutherland, James ..	19	5 ft. 4½ in.	Elgin, Moray	,,	Dec. 13, 1775	Elgin
Sutherland, Neill ..	16	5 ft. 4 in.	Latheron, Caithness	,,	Dec. 15, 1775	Fochabers
Syme, Alexander ..	29	5 ft. 4 in.	Grange, Banff	,,	Dec. 29, 1775	,,
Taylor, James ..	18	5 ft. 3½ in.	Elgin, Moray	,,	Dec. 25, 1775	Elgin
Thomas, Alexander ..	18	5 ft. 4 in.	Fochabers, Moray	,,	Dec. 20, 1775	Fochabers
Thomas, James ..	16	5 ft. 3 in.	Fochabers, Moray	,,	Dec. 20, 1775	,,
Thomson, Peter, Sergt.	35	5 ft. 6½ in.	Dyke, Moray		Dec. 7, 1775	,,
Torrie, James ..	17	5 ft. 4 in.	Dundurcas, Moray	Labourer	Dec. 29, 1775	Huntly
Tulloch, David ..	25	5 ft. 8 in.	Ardclach, Nairn	Squarewri't.	Dec. 14, 1775	Gordon Castle
†Tulloch, John ..	20	5 ft. 6½ in.	Ardclach, Nairn	Labourer	Jan. 18, 1776	Fochabers
Tulloch, Robert ..	29	5 ft. 4 in.	Nairn, Nairn	—	Dec. 8, 1775	,,
Watson, Donald ..	18	5 ft. 4½ in.	Rosemarky, Ross	Daylabourer	Dec. 8, 1775	,,
Watt, John ..	40	5 ft. 5 in.	Kennethmont, Aberdeen	Labourer	Feb. 6, 1776	Huntly

The 71st was reduced in 1783, and Captain Maxwell afterwards entered the 74th Regiment, It is a curious fact that the 71st now forms the first battalion of the Highland Light Infantry, while the 74th is the second battalion. It may have been Maxwell's connection with the 74th that led his brother-in-law, the 4th Duke of Gordon, to enlist six men for Captain Twysden's company of the 74th in 1787, as follows:—

			Age.	Height.			Bounty.		
Nov.	4.—John Duncan, hosier, Speymouth . .		16	5 ft.	4 in.	£5	5	0
,,	19.—William Mitchell . .		24	5 ft.	9 in.	5	5	0
,,	20.—Hugh Gordon . .		29	5 ft.	6 in.	3	8	0
,,	20.—John Bonniman . .		30	5 ft.	5½ in.	3	8	0
,,	27.—Hugh Ellis . .		17	5 ft.	4½ in.	5	5	0
Dec.	3.—Sergeant Alexander Sutherland; not attested, but supposed absent . .		30	5 ft.	11 in.			

---

† Deserted.
‡ The Duches s sent his wife a boll of meal.
§ Discharged—having an ulcer on his thigh.

It only remains to add that Captain Maxwell died in India in 1794. He was buried in the compound of the Church of England, Oldtown, Cuddalore, where a stone commemorates him :—

Beneath this stone are deposited the remains of Hamilton Maxwell, son of Sir William Maxwell of Monreith, Bart., aide-de-camp to the King, and Lieut.-Col. of H.M.'s 74th Highland Regiment of Foot, who died, universally regretted by all who knew him, at the house of his friend, John Kenworthy, Esq., at Newtown, on June 8, 1794, in the 40th year of his age. In testimony of the affection they bore their gallant commander, and as a tribute to his talents and many virtues, this monument is erected by the officers of the 74th.

THE 81ST: OR ABERDEENSHIRE HIGHLANDERS.

1778: RAISED BY THE HON. WILLIAM GORDON: DISBANDED 1783.

The raising of the 81st Regiment forms a highly illuminating study of some of the guiding principles which underlay the efforts of the Quality to aid the Nation. Behind the impulse of patriotism, there was nearly always the personal equation, which constantly made its appearance under the strain of terror created by the crisis in America.

The year 1777 was particularly critical, witnessing Burgoyne's capitulation at Saratoga, and the recognition of the States by our old enemy, France. Our answer was the raising of several regiments. In Scotland, the 73rd, 74th, 76th, 77th, 78th, 81st, and Northern Fencibles came into being. Lord Macleod, who raised the 73rd, was the exiled son (1727-89) of an attainted peer, George, 3rd Earl of Cromartie (1702-66). Lord Macdonald put Macdonell of Lochgarry, the scion of a strong Jacobite group, in command of the 76th. Lord Macleod and Macdonell both had Gordons for mothers—representing respectively the families of Invergordon and Glenbucket. The 78th was raised by the (restored) Earl of Seaforth, whose grandfather, the 5th Earl, had been attainted in 1716. The house of Murray, which raised the Atholl Highlanders, had given several sons to the Jacobite cause.

A personal equation of a different kind influenced the Hon. William Gordon in raising the 81st. It was a family quarrel, the cause of which is obscure, but which was shared not only by Gordon and the Duke, but by a group of antagonistic supporters. For instance, Pryse Lockhart Gordon, a faithful follower of the Duke, wrote a "powerful satire" on the laird of Fyvie for his well-known *Personal Memoirs* published in 1830. These pages, however, were suppressed, as we learn from the will (December 26, 1868) of Pryse's son, George Huntly Gordon, who bequeathed them to his son, Huntly Pryse Gordon. "Never was a more perfect prototype of Polonius than our Groom of the Bedchamber," wrote Pryse Gordon of William Gordon, "and, though the King sometimes hit him rather hard, yet he was a great favourite."

The Hon. William Gordon, who was eight years the Duke's senior, and son of the 2nd Earl of Aberdeen, was at once the cousin and the step-uncle of the Duke of Gordon, being the son of the Duke's aunt, and half-brother of his Grace's mother. Such a mixture of relationship was sure to give trouble. Nor did it end with the rivalry in recruiting in 1777-8; it began with the Duke's second brother, Lord William, in 1777, and extended to the Duke's youngest brother, Lord George, the Rioter, whom the Hon. William threatened in the House of Commons (June 2, 1780) to transfix with his sword—an incident repeated almost word for word in *Barnaby Rudge.*

The Hon. William, unlike some of the regiment-raisers, had no Jacobite kink to straighten out, for the Gordons of Haddo had discountenanced the Jacobite movement. It is said that, as a little boy of ten, he had been taken by his mother to see the Duke of Cumberland on the march to Culloden. His Royal Highness assured the lady (who was the sister of the Jacobite Lord Lewie Gordon) that he would live to see the boy " a good Hanoverian"; and he did, for William entered the 11th Dragoons as a cornet in 1756. He then became a captain in the 16th Light Dragoons in 1759; major in the 84th Foot in 1760; and in 1762 he became lieutenant-colonel of the 105th Foot, which was disbanded in the following year, leaving him idle and on half pay. He occupied his leisure by entering politics, representing Woodstock in 1767, and Heytesbury in 1774, and in 1775 he became one of the Grooms of the Bedchamber of George III., a pro-Hanoverian attachment which even Cumberland, his Majesty's uncle, may not have foreseen. Gordon therefore approached the national crisis of 1777 from the standpoint of the soldier, the politician, and the courtier; and he saw an opportunity of assisting to solve it as a territorial magnate, for he was laird of Fyvie, and could raise a regiment of his own.

The Duke of Gordon says that William got the regiment through his interest. It is not quite clear what this means, for one would have thought that William was as near the ear of the King as the Duke. However that may be, the Duke thought that Gordon should do something for his brother, Lord William Gordon, who had given the family a great deal of trouble. Having bolted in 1769 with Lady Sarah Bunbury and repented in a sensational way by a pilgrimage to Rome, Lord William had decided to settle down, and his family thought a bit of soldiering would be a good way of completing his expiation. In the first instance, the Duke applied to Lord North for a billet for Lord

William worth a thousand a year, a transaction which is mysteriously dealt with in a pamphlet by Junius entitled *A Serious Letter to the Public on the late transactions between Lord North and the Duke of Gordon*, in which it is noted that His Grace was keen on getting a commission in the army for Lord William   The *Political Magazine* suggests (June, 1780) that the Minister offered the post, " if Lord George [Gordon] would vacate his seat for Luggershall in Wilts "—a proposal which Lord George afterwards characterised in the Commons (April 13, 1778) as ." villainous," demanding at the same time that North should call his " butchers and ravagers from the colonies "   As Colonel Gordon was in a position at Court, the Duke then seems to have approached him in reference to the raising of Fencibles and to getting a commission for Lord William, but it miscarried, for North, writing on December 12, 1777, to his devoted supporter, Lord George Germain, afterwards Lord Sackville, who has been credited with the authorship of " Junius," says (*Stopford Sackville Papers*, Hist. MSS Com , 9th report, part iii p 88) —" The Duke of Gordon's and Lord William's letters are intended to be sent to your Lordship, and will show you that Colonel [the Hon William] Gordon's plan is likely to fail, and I much question whether the King will consent to the Duke of Gordon's proposal in the extent he desires but, perhaps, if Lord William is put at the head of the corps, his Grace will willingly consent to the necessary restrictions "

The King did not consent   Not only so, but the Hon William stepped into the breach   The Duke was furious, and on New Year's day, 1778, he wrote from London, to James Ross, his factotum at Gordon Castle, a letter which breathed anything but the good-will-to-men spirit of the season   The letter, which is preserved at Gordon Castle, runs —

I have been hurried most amazingly since I came here about this affair of the Regiment   The King having absolutely refused to give Lord William Gordon the rank, Fyvie was appointed after having assured Lord George Germaine that he was to have my interest and support—and indeed he was sure of it, had he behaved properly—but he had named most of his officers and had wrote to them before he was sure whether he or Lord William was to command the battalion, and by that means made it impossible, if Lord William had got the command, to have changed one of Fyvie's nomination without making them enemies to him and friends to Fyvie , and you will see that he had an eye to Aberdeenshire in the list he has named   To this hour he has never had the civility to offer me the appointment of one officer, tho' Lord Adam

[Gordon] has named three and George Ross has named your namesake and his for a Major, who was tried lately at Inverness.

Fyvie passed me on the road, but we did not meet. When I came here, I went to the Ministry, all of whom told me there was no intention of putting a slight upon the Duke of Gordon and that it was certainly more desirable for them to treat with the head of the family than any branch of it; that, as Colonel Gordon had assured them of my support, they thought he would certainly consult me as to the proper officers; that they gave him the Regiment upon the faith of it through my interest; and that he would not have been named otherwise. This is the language both Lord George Germaine and Lord North held to me. The former told me if he had met me in the streets he would have asked me how my Regiment was going on; and the latter said he thought Colonel Gordon was gone to Scotland to consult me as to the nomination of the officers.

I was advised by Lord North to tell my story to His Majesty, which I did yesterday. I also shewed him Col. Gordon's letter and the list he sent me of officers he had wrote, even before he had got the Regiment. His Majesty and Ministers are much displeased. Lord George Germaine told me he had wrote to Colonel Gordon last night, in which he said that he was commanded by His Majesty to mark his disapprobation of Colonel Gordon's conduct.

These are the words you are at liberty to tell all my friends. The affair ends here for the present. What is to be done after Colonel Gordon's answer comes I don't know. I entreat you will tell the whole story and write it to all my friends as soon as possible. Let me know what every body says and your opinion as to raising men.

I forgot to tell you that when Sandy Gordon [the future Lord Rockville] delivered me Fyvie's letter at Edinburgh with the list of officers, I was very angry and said I was surprised at his brother's conduct in having got a regiment through my interest and not giving me the nomination of one officer. He answered in a huff :—" Well, by God, we can raise it without you!" This was a fine speech from a man who I have been plagueing all the Ministers these two or three years to get a gown for.

From this letter you may judge of my feelings and act as to recruiting as your own sense will direct you. Pray write me fully what Colonel Gordon's friends give out with regard to his having got the Battalion and why he did not give me the offer of a single commission.

Lord George Germain, to whom the Duke also wrote, replied next day, January 2, from Pall Mall (*Gordon Castle Papers*):—

My Lord,—Your Grace asked me yesterday whether His Majesty had said anything relating to the conduct of Colonel Gordon in consequence of your audience on Wednesday.

I told your Grace that I had been directed by the King to write Col. Gordon and to acquaint him that His Majesty was dissatisfied with the little attention which he had shewn to your Grace in not applying to you for your assistance previous to his appointment, and in not leaving the nomination of any Officers of your Grace's in a Battalion which His Majesty understood was to be raised with your approbation and under your Grace's influence, and it was upon that supposition he was appointed Colonel.

This is what I wrote by the King's order. I gave him my opinion upon the matter very fairly and very clearly, and if he follows my advice nothing will be omitted on his part to give your Grace every satisfaction you could desire.

I shewed the King the whole of my letter, which he was pleased to approve, and permitted me to inform your Grace that I had written by His Majesty's order in the manner I have had the honour of stating to you.

Whatever the explanation of Colonel Gordon's tactics, the Duke was put on his mettle, and set about raising a regiment of his own, for on January 14 he attended a levee at St. James's Palace, and had a long conference with the King on the subject of the Northern Fencibles. The difficulty of raising one regiment in a district was severe enough, but to raise two was almost an impossibility. Nothing could give a clearer idea of the accumulated difficulties of the position than a memorial of 1778, which stated that :—

A proprietor of a considerable land estate in Scotland, altho' desirous to promote the King's Levys when directed to the proper objects and conducted fairly without violence or oppression, finds it necessary to protect his people from the rapacity of adventurers now recruiting ; many of whose commissions depending upon the number of men they can entangle, the greatest abuses are frequently committed, and which may grow to an intolerable excess if not properly checked.

It was bad enough when an " adventurer " swooped down with his head full of heroics and his pocket full of money in the shape of extravagant bounties ; it was worse when one's own neighbour and relative set up rival schemes and poached on one's own preserves. That was precisely what Colonel Gordon did. He carried war into the enemy's country by sending out recruiting parties into the Duke's special territories. To checkmate this bold move, the Duke sent a warning to all his tenants, and on January 30 it was reiterated with emphasis by his factor, Alexander Milne, Braehead. The sound advice of Charles

F

Gordon of Braid, the lawyer in Edinburgh, was also asked, for on February 28 he wrote to the Duke's factotum, James Ross —

I am aware of the difficulty of protecting the Duke's highland territory, but the proper means must, no doubt, be used; and the residents should exert themselves to discourage adventurers   I early foresaw and suggested that the Duke's country, being so extensive, would be in greater danger of distress from his having no battalion to raise than if he had patronised a corps, because in that case he would have had the arrangement and distribution of the officers to his mind, who would have directed their operations under his authority to the proper objects for His Majesty's service, and in that case adventurers would have fled elsewhere   Indeed, I never doubted but this would have happened to our wish, but there was a misunderstanding in the outset of Col Gordon's corps, which certainly interfered.

The county took sides in the quarrel, the non-Gordon lairds rallying to the laird of Fyvie, not because they cared so much for him, but they had the chance of wiping off some old scores with the head of the house   They could not have done anything more irritating to his Grace than to invade the town of Huntly, which as the cradle of the Gordons in the north, was regarded by his Grace as sanctuary   William Bell, Coclarachie, reporting progress to Ross on January 25, gives a vivid picture of the position (*Gordon Castle Papers*) —

Lady and Captain Leith, Leithhall, and the two Captains Leith of Bucharn were in Huntly [on January 22]   Leithhall and Alexander Leith and all the recruits they could muster made a grand procession thro' the town, and had punch on the streets   They beat up, but I did not come so near them as to know what they offered, but a little before that his sergeant offered 20 guineas   I was told [Gordon of] Wardhouse came to them that day.   At night there was another procession thro' the town with flambearers, and music, etc   Leithhall arrived at Huntly before the post on Thursday and brought the news that was in the papers about the Duke's conference   They were in Huntly all Friday and got some youngsters there   I have not learned who it was, but some or other made an excursion into the streets and pulled down all the signs in the town except one   Leithhall was angry at it   There has been a bonfire in the Square, I was told it was the boys that made it   Yesterday [January 24] the three Captain Leiths and Wardhouse set out for Turriff   Leithhall has now enlisted four men in Huntly From the parade that has been made and the temptation of gold, I am surprised they are not more

Lady Leithhall told us that the difference between the Duke and

Colonel Gordon was amicably made up.   It must be from that supposition that they have made such a parade at Huntly.   They all knew how averse the Duke was to any recruiting party being at Huntly, etc., and it was never yet said that the Duke would take no concern in recruiting men.   Therefore they must know of some channel or other thro' which they can satisfie his Grace, or they do not mind whether he may be pleased or not.   It is true Leithhall recruits fairly and honourably.   He says he will have none but volunteers.

I forgot to tell you they recruited a female in men's clothes at Drumblade.   She was kept a day or two and dismist.

Bell reports further progress to Ross a few weeks later.   Writing on February 13, he expresses the fervent wish that the Leith recruiting party would leave Huntly.   "The parades they make and the great bounty given draw many to them.   I do not know where it is to end.   I wish the Duke's mind were known, and how far his Grace disapproves of the conduct of some of his tenants that have received so many favours from him."   Two days later (February 15), he writes once again (*Gordon Castle Papers*):—

There was never men so earnest as the Leiths at Huntly.   On Friday night [Feb. 13] they made an appearance on the street.   Merchant Deason and his son Cosmo, with others, were then both much intoxicated, as I am told.   The merchant offered 25 guineas to any man that would enlist, and asked his son if he had any money.   He said he had, and would give the same terms, but, alas!   Mr. Deason's flow of spirits soon got a checke.   That very night one of his sons, a very fine young man, was drowned in Isla, crossing that river from Nether Mills to go home.   There was a flood in the river.   Some say he was intoxicated with liquor; others that he was not.

The Huntly people are in great spirits on the notice the Duke has taken of their offer to raise a company.   They hardly expected it.   They might as well have proposed to raise a battalion.   They could never have performed either.

The conduct of Captain Leith, Bucharn, and Charles Leith is very unaccountable.   Even supposing they act conform to law, they know it must be disagreeable to the Duke.   What many bystanders think the best construction that can be put upon it is that the Duke is not serious.

Precisely the same state of matters was found in other parts of the Duke's dominions, to the heads of which his factor, Alexander Milne, Braehead, had sent a letter (on January 30), "repeating the Duke's order anent preserving and protecting his men from being imposed upon by any recruiting party." A typical case in Ruthven is cited by Charles Stewart, Drumin, whose own servant, Davidson, was caught :—

On the 22nd ult. (January), I sent Davidson to a burial from Inverurie, when [Rev.] Mr. Farqrson made up to him and recommended a military life in the strongest terms, and he says promised to procure him a halbert, which he agreed to accept of ; then carried Davidson with him from the churchyard to the Manse, and from that to Ruthven.

Glenlivet was more fortunate, as William Gordon, Minmore, showed in a letter dated February 2 (*Gordon Castle Papers*) :—

There has none as yet appeared in Glenlivet in that character [of recruiter], and the country is at present quite peaceable, and the people following their ordinary and respective occupations unmolested : which is a particular happiness, considering how some of our neighbours are used at present. I understand the Strathaven people are not so very quiet. Doctor Farquharson, now Lieutenant, and his namesake the parson has enlisted some people in that country. . . . In order to prevent giving recruiting parties any handle for giving trouble, I have caused my servants and advised my neighbours to lay aside everything peculiar to the highland garb.

Tho' I have a Beating Order, I am determined not to accept of a single man belonging to his Grace the Duke of Gordon, nor any in his land, but will do all in my power to protect them from oyrs. . . . I am still of opinion that this country will be as safe as any in Scotland ; nor can I believe that any will attempt to contradict his Grace's order, but will do to the outermost of their power to suppress recruiting ; and indeed I hope there will be but little to do, as I know not a country has more aversion to a military life.

Milne, the factor, himself thought " there's little to be feared from any, except it bees for Mr. Farquarson, minister of Strathaven, or Doctor Farquarson ; which, I hope, the country will discourage as much as possible." As a matter of fact, much more forceful tactics were adopted by the Leiths, as the difficulties of recruiting increased. An extraordinary story is told by James Ross in a letter to his brother dated March 4, in which John Wright, whom he had dismissed from the position of Baron Baillie Depute at Huntly, figures unpleasingly (*Gordon Castle Papers*) :—

A constable and party from Old Meldrum came to Huntly with a warrant from Mr. Urquhart of Meldrum, as a Justice of Peace of the County, to apprehend and carry before him a lad accused of forgery. They accordingly did apprehend him, and were setting off for Old

Meldrum, but were attacked in broad daylight in the publick street of Huntly by Leithhall's serjeant and a posse of recruits, who after a pretty smart struggle, overpowered and deforced the constable and party, and carried off the prisoner. He soon agreed to enlist with Leithhall, and Baillie Wright, tho' the only man in the burgh who pretended to any civil authority, instead of taking measures to support the laws of the country and some degree of order and police in the place, went to a publick house, in obedience to a call from the serjeant, sat down and drank with him and his posse ; and, in a short time after the riot had happened, attested the prisoner as a recruit for Leithhall. . . . I supposed that this serjeant and recruits who were guilty of so publick and gross a violation of the law of the country or some such others might have laid hands upon any inoffensive countrymen who came to Huntly about their private affairs, forced them into an ale-house and sent for Baillie Wright; and I consider in how pitiable a situation an ignorant simple country fellow, averse to a military life, would be when impannelled before such a judge, surrounded by such a posse.

Disputes between the recruiting parties of the rival regiments were of frequent occurrence. One case which gave a good deal of trouble was that of John Couper, a Knockespock man, whose story is set forth in a memorial signed by Ensign John Gordon (Coynachie) of the Northern Fencibles (*Gordon Castle Papers*):—

Upon Tuesday [June] at a market in Clett, John Couper was enlisted as a soldier by Ensign John Gordon, of the Duke of Gordon's ffencibles. About an hour after Couper's enlisting, one Innes, a Serjeant of a recruiting party belonging to Captain Leith of the 81st, interfered with him, said he was a ffool for engaging with the ffencibles ; it would be much better for him to enlist with his Captain, who would pay the smart money to Mr. Gordon, give him 15 guineas and his obligation for a halbert. However, at this time Couper resisted the temptation and went home perfectly satisfied with his bargain with Ensign Gordon. When the market was over, Serjeant Innes ffollowed Couper to Knockespick, persuaded him to go to a publick house in the neighbourhood, and there prevailed on him to go immediately to Mr. Gordon's quarters and offer the smart money. And accordingly that instant Couper set out and came to Mr. Gordon's bedside [in the house of George Gordon, Rhynie] with two witnesses, said he had repented, left a twenty shillings note upon a table and went off. Next forenoon (Wednesday) Innes went and informed his Captain of the transaction with Couper. He approved of his Serjeant's conduct, upon ffriday had Couper brought before him, and bargained with him very much on the same terms which his Serjeant offered when he prevailed on Couper to offer the smart money to Mr. Gordon.

A court of inquiry was held in Edinburgh, when it was reported (October 13) that Gordon had asked Leith's pardon for any improper expressions he may have made in his memorial, on the ground that they were solely owing to his inexperience in the service. Leith declared himself satisfied, but the court could not proceed further, as Gordon's witnesses were in the north and could not be brought up until after the harvest. Meantime the unfortunate Couper was left at Edinburgh till the claim to him could be decided.

Another market case which gave much trouble was that of John Ryver, who had been enlisted by the Leiths at Drumblade, Ryver writing several letters of protest to the laird of Freefield and Morison of Bognie.

Nothing could show the fierceness of the competition for recruits better than the case of William Stephens, a weaver in Huntly, who had a great grievance against the Leiths. Born in Aberdeenshire, he had served his apprenticeship as a bleacher with Hugh M'Veagh in Huntly. In 1761 he listed in the 66th Foot, and served till 1774, when he got a three months' furlough to look out for two recruits in lieu of his discharge. During this furlough, Alexander Leith of Freefield, who was an ensign in the 66th, promised to get his discharge, if Stephens would become his servant in the regiment, an arrangement which lasted till 1777. Having by this time married, Stephens again sought his discharge on the two-recruit basis. He got his men, but found that one of them was claimed as a deserter by the 11th Foot. He was requested to find another man or pay five guineas, and he was allowed to go, his actual discharge being deferred until he had found another man. So he settled down at Huntly in August, 1777, with his wife and child. Soon after, Leith looked him up, and promised to get the final discharge if Stephens would help the recruiting for Colonel Gordon's regiment. He actually found ten men, and ultimately went to Aberdeen, "to assist for a little in cloathing and instructing them," staying till March 2, 1778. When he wanted to return to his wife, Leith put him under arrest, reporting him as a "serjeant in the 73rd regiment." Stephens complained to the Aberdeen magistrates that he had never been enlisted in the 73rd. Leith thereupon charged him as a deserter from the 66th. Of course he had no discharge, and so he was cast into prison. As a matter of fact, Leith had got a blank discharge, which he had filled in with the condition that Stephens should enter Colonel Gordon's regiment. Stephens was sent off on April 16 as a prisoner with Colonel Gordon's regiment, and his wife applied in a piteous letter to James Ross at Fochabers, promising that if her husband were set free he would assist in recruiting for the Duke's own regiment.

What is to be thought of the tactics of sitting outside a jail door waiting for a prisoner to be handed over? Yet this was done apparently, for Lieutenant Finlason, writing to Ross on August 6, 1778, says :—

I beg you will inform the Duke that one of the people concerned in the late meal riot in the Mearns and now sentenced to some [four] months' imprisonment and afterwards to be banished has been enlisted for me. I am inform'd he would make a good soldier, could he be liberated and the punishment remitted. An officer of Fyvie's corps sollicited strongly that I would give up my claim to him, as in that case he had reason to say from a conversation he had with the Sheriff-Substitute of the county that the punishment would be remitted upon his being forced into a marching regiment. They deemed it none, his going into the Fencibles. This request I absolutely refused.

Of course there may have been quite another side to this view of the 81st Regiment, for I have had access only to the Duke's own papers. Even these contain a memorial from Lieutenant Charles Grant of the 81st, who, writing to General Skene (October 12), maintained that he had enlisted a tailor named Robert Grant on February 10. The man deserted in March, and was enlisted by the Duke. Lieutenant Grant requested his Grace to surrender him, but the Duke replied that he fell under the proclamation pardoning deserters who returned to their duty, and declined to deliver him up.

In spite of these exciting and exasperating attempts at recruiting in Aberdeenshire, the regiment had anything but a local look so far as the surnames of the privates are concerned. In the absence of any such muster rolls as are preserved at Gordon Castle, it is impossible to indicate the origins of the men, for the muster rolls at the Record Office (*W.O.* 12; 8,250, 8,251) simply add " B " for British and " I " for Irish. It is notable that out of the 1,120 non-commissioned officers and men, only six bore the name of Gordon—Charles Gordon, corporal in the Hon. John Gordon's company; Thomas Gordon, sergeant in Lord Strathaven's, and Hugh, a private in John Ferguson's, while Peter Gordon, the future laird of Abergeldie, brought three with him—

William, senior and junior, and James, all privates. · The only company in which the captain had (to judge from nomenclature) a sort of clan following was that of the major, Alexander Ross, who brought 33 men named Ross (besides two officers), and 27 " Macs." Twenty-six of the Ross privates remained to the very last of the regiment. Stewart of Garth proudly cites the case of Ross, and apparently bases on it the statement that about 650 of the regiment were " from the mountains." He even says that as an inducement to the young men to enter more readily, the Highland garb, " to which they were then extremely partial, although prohibited by severe penalties," was to be the regimental uniform. I have found no official documents bearing on the uniform.

Colonel Gordon himself might have been expected to have been able to enlist a large local following, but this was not so, as a glance at the names of the privates in his company in June, 1778, serves to show (the I stands for Irish):—

Alerton, William (I).
Alexander, Andrew.
    „   John.
Anderson, Alexander.
    „   George.
Arnot, Alexander.
Bane, Archibald.
Bell, Archibald.
Bengo, Ralph.
Bennet, Nicholas.
Bruce, John.
Campbell, James (I).
Clinton, Michael (I).
Corrigen, Patrick (I).
Crane, Edward (I).
Donald, Nathaniel.
Dowall, Richard.
    „   Stephen.
Eason, John.
Edward, Alexander.
Fawns, James.
Ferly, Dennis (I).
Finlayson, Alexander.
Fitzsimmons, William (I).
Fordyce, George.
Glen, John.
Gordon, Alexander.
    „   John.
Grahame, Alexander.
Gray, Andrew.

Grieve, Andrew.
Hardy, James.
Hutcheon, Andrew.
Irvine, Alexander.
Johnston, James.
    „   John.
Livingstone, Daniel.
Lyon, Charles.
Macdonald, Hugh.
    „   John.
    „   Ronald.
Macgill, John.
    „   Samuel.
Mackenzie, Luke.
McKimmie, James.
McLean, Donald.
McPetrie, James.
McPherson, Alexander.
Millar, John.
Milne, David.
Minton, Patrick (I).
Mitchell, John.
More, Alexander.
Morrison, John.
Murray, John.
Neish, James.
Norvall, Alexander.
O'Hara, Dennis (I).
Paterson, John.
Rea, James (I).

Reed, James.
Renny, Robert.
Robertson, Donald.
    „   Duncan.
Ross, Donald.
    „   James.
    „   John.
Rugan, Barnabas (I).
Scott, John.
Skene, John.
Shovelbright, Robert.
Stapleton, Isaac.
Stedman, William.
Stewart, Daniel.
    „   James.
    „   John, senr.
    „   John, junr.
Strachan, James.
Strange, George.
    „   John.
Thomson, James.
Tindal, Evan.
Trevor, Michael (I).
Tyrie, James.
Ward, James.
Webster, Alexander.
Wilson, Robert.
Wishart, John.
Wright, Alexander.

Another feature of the corps was the large number of professional soldiers who got commissions (*W.O.* 25; 148, p. 150; *W.O.* 25; 116, p. 125; *W.O.* 211; *W.O.* 212). On August 2, 1778, Colonel Gordon wrote from Kinsale to the Secretary of War that there was discontent among the officers because they did not get rank from the date of their beating orders (*W.O.* 1 : 997). The officers throughout the career of the regiment were :—

COLONEL.

The Hon. William Gordon, December 19, 1777. As noted, he had between the years 1756 and 1763 held commissions in the 11th and 16th Dragoons, and in the 84th and 105th Foot. After the reduction of the 81st, he held commissions in the 60th, 7th, 71st and 21st Foot in turn. He died unmarried at Maryculter, May 25, 1816, aged 81 (*Gordons under Arms*, No. 1,397).

LIEUTENANT-COLONELS.

Robert Farquhar, November 9, 1778, *vice* Gordon; previously in the 32nd Foot; retired before December 16, 1782.

The Hon. John Gordon, December 19, 1777. Between 1746 and 1757 he held commissions in the 1st, 62nd (recruiting for the latter in 1757, 76 men), and 52nd Foot. A son of the 3rd Earl of Aboyne, he was born in 1728 and died in 1778 (*Gordons under Arms*, No. 880).

John Hamilton (from Major, 21st), April 4, 1783, *vice* Macdonald.

MAJORS.

John Dickson, March 4, 1782, *vice* Ross; previously major, 68th.

John Macdonald, December 28, 1777; previously captain, 26th Foot; joined 103rd before March 4, 1782.

Stephens Howe, April 22, 1783, *vice* Leith; previously captain, 96th.

Alexander Ross, December 19, 1777; previously captain, 71st.

CAPTAINS.

John Ferguson, December 19, 1777; previously in the 3rd Foot; retired by November 23, 1782.

Adam Gordon, December 21, 1777; previously in the 66th Foot. Son of the 8th Viscount of Kenmure, he formed an interesting link between the Gordons of the south and the Gordons of the north. He became Collector of Customs at Port Patrick, where he died, 1806. (*Gordons under Arms*, No. 97.)

George (Gordon), Lord Strathaven, December 26, 1777; formerly of the 1st Foot Guards; joined the 9th Dragoons by April 13, 1782. Born 1761, he was the son of the 4th Earl of Aboyne, and succeeded to the Marquisate of Huntly. He commanded the Aberdeenshire Militia from 1798 till his death in 1853 (*Gordons under Arms*, No. 518).

G

Peter Gordon, December 20, 1777 ; previously in the 114th and 13th Foot ; retired before April 30, 1781. Born 1751, he was laird of Abergeldie, and died 1819 (*Gordons under Arms*, No. 1,150).

James Horn, December 25, 1777 ; formerly of the 14th Foot ; apparently of the Westhall family.

Alexander Leith, December 22, 1777 ; late of the 66th Foot. Laird of Leithhall and Rannes ; assumed the additional name of Hay, 1789 ; raised 109th Foot, 1794 ; general, 1813 ; died 1838. Father of Sir Andrew Leith Hay (1785-1862).

John Macdonald, December 28, 1777 ; formerly of 26th Foot ; Lieutenant-Colonel, December 16, 1782, *vice* Farquhar.

George Moncrieff, December 23, 1777. Lady Tullibardine says he was a son of Major-General Moncrieff of Myres and Reedie. He entered the 10th Foot, November 23, 1773 ; became captain, 11th Foot, December 20, 1786 ; and Lieutenant-Colonel, 90th Foot, November 10, 1794. He was the father of General George Moncrieff of the Scots Fusilier Guards, who, in turn, was the father of Lieutenant-General George Moncrieff of the same regiment (Notes from the Duke of Atholl).

CAPTAIN-LIEUTENANT.

William Duncan, December 24, 1777 ; late 66th Foot ; captain, April 13, 1782, *vice* Lord Strathaven.

LIEUTENANTS.

Charles Baillie, December 23, 1777 ; joined Independent Company before December 18, 1782.

Thomas Bell (from Cornet, 12th Dragoons), June 29, 1782, *vice* Campbell.

F. G. Bowins (from Lieutenant, 103rd), *vice* Ross, jun., December 18, 1782.

William Burnett (from Ensign, 26th), December 10, 1781, *vice* Garden, captain.

Archibald Campbell, December 27, 1777 ; joined Independent Company before June 29, 1782.

Dunbar Douglas, January 8, 1778.

Henry Dunn, December 22, 1777 ; joined Independent Company before August 4, 1781.

Nicoll Ewing, December 29, 1777.

Gregor Farquharson, January 3, 1778 ; joined Independent Company before December 18, 1782.

Robert Garden, December 20, 1777 ; joined Independent Company before December 10, 1781.

Charles Grant, January 5, 1778.

John Hay, January 1, 1778 ; died before July 25, 1778.

William Johnston, December 31, 1777; joined the 90th before June 29, 1780.

Alexander Keith, December 21, 1777; Captain-Lieutenant, April 13, 1782.

William Kelso, December 28, 1777; joined the 98th before June 29, 1780.

Arthur McLachlan, December 25, 1777.

Lachlan McLean, January 7, 1778.

William McLeod, January 6, 1778.

William Newall, December 23, 1777; retired by January 14, 1783.

Walter Ridley (from Ensign, 51st), December 18, 1782, *vice* Farquharson.

Sir Alexander Sinclair, January 4, 1778; resigned before March 8, 1780. Third baronet of Dunbeath; d.s.p. on the passage from Jamaica to Malaga, 1786; succeeded by his great-uncle, Benjamin Sinclair.

George Skene, December 19, 1777; promoted captain *vice* P. Gordon, April 30, 1781. Laird of Skene; died unmarried, April 28, 1825 (*Family of Skene*, 45-7).

Alexander Taylor, December 26, 1777.

Andrew Wellwood, December 10, 1781, *vice* Ryan.

ENSIGNS.

James Abernethy, December 25, 1777; became lieutenant, 92nd.

David Andrew, February 11, 1783, *vice* Stewart, lieutenant.

John Braid, April 2, 1783.

Donald Cameron, December 22, 1777; joined 95th before June 29, 1780.

Archibald Campbell, March 26, 1783, *vice* John Campbell.

John Campbell, March 25, 1783, *vice* Johnstone; retired same or next day.

James Church, September 8, 1780, *vice* Abernethy.

William Duncan, August 12, 1779, *vice* Stewart; lieutenant, August 2, 1781, *vice* Dunn.

Cecil Edgworth, June 29, 1780.

James Farquharson, March 25, 1783, *vice* Johnston.

James Fortescue, September 8, 1780, *vice* Gordon; lieutenant, December 18, 1782, *vice* McLean.

Thomas Francis, April 23, 1783, *vice* Montresor.

John Gordon, December 23, 1777; lieutenant, June 29, 1780, *vice* Kelso; lieutenant, June 29, h.p. 1783; entered Perthshire Volunteer Brigade, 1803; residing at Corstoun, 1841 (*Gordons under Arms*, No. 903).

Donald Grant, June 29, 1780, *vice* Cameron.

Andrew Irvine, March 8, 1780 (surgeon's mate); lieut., April 13, 1782.

James Irvine, January 31, 1780; joined the 67th before November 19, 1781.

David Johnston, February 19, 1783, *vice* Moore; joined a company of Fencibles before March 25, 1783.

William Johnston, February 19, 1783.

James Leith, lieutenant, August 1, 1781, *vice* Skene, captain: captain, November 23, 1782, *vice* Ferguson. Leith (1763-1816) was the brother of Alexander Leith Hay. He distinguished himself in the Peninsular War, particularly at Corunna, and died of fever as Governor of the Leeward Islands at Barbados.

John Lister, April 13, 1782; joined Waller's Corps before March 12, 1783.

Robert MacLachlan, December 18, 1782.

Norman Maclean, December 24, 1777; retired before December 18, 1782.

Roderick Maclean, December 30, 1777.

Thomas Gage Montresor, March 12, 1783, *vice* Lister; joined 104th Foot before April 22, 1783.

Pierce Moore, March 31, 1782, *vice* Pemberton; lieutenant, December 18, 1782, *vice* Burnet, captain.

William Moore, February 19, 1783, *vice* Trevor, lieutenant.

Robert Styles O'Brien, September 1, 1781, *vice* Duncan.

Henry Pemberton, June 2, 1781, *vice* Grant; joined Independent Company before March 31, 1782.

William Rattray, October 6, 1778; joined Independent Company before May 26, 1780.

George Harrison Reade (from Ensign of Invalids), November 19, 1781, *vice* Irvine; lieutenant, December 18, 1782, *vice* Leith, captain.

Thomas Richardson, May 26 1780, *vice* Rattray.

James Ronaldson, December 20, 1777; lieutenant, March 8, 1780, *vice* Sinclair resigns.

John Ross, December 21, 1777; lieutenant, January 2, 1778, *vice* Johnston; joined 103rd before December 18, 1782.

John Ryan, December 19, 1777; lieutenant, July 25, 1778 *vice* Hay.

George Skene, March 25, 1783, *vice* Reade, lieutenant.

Alexander Gordon Stewart, October 9, 1778, *vice* Ryan.

Charles Stewart (from ensign, Northern Fencibles), April 13, 1782, *vice* Wellwood, lieutenant.

Hugh Trevor, April 13, 1782, *vice* Edgworth, deceased; lieutenant, January 14, 1783.

Andrew Wellwood, June 2, 1781, *vice* Church; lieutenant, December 10, 1781, *vice* Ryan.

CHAPLAIN.

Rev. John Stark, December 19, 1777.

ADJUTANT

William Duncan, December 19, 1777, succeeded by Q M Evermy on January 8, 1783

SURGEON

William Braid, December 19, 1777, previously mate in the 25th Foot His mates were Robert Coupar and Andrew Irvine George Gordon was appointed October 1, 1782

QUARTERMASTERS

James Evermy, September 1, 1781, *vice* Ryan, was previously a sergeant, adjutant, January 8, 1783, *vice* Duncan

—— Gunn, January 8, 1783, previously sergeant-major in the 66th Foot

John Ryan, December 19, 1777

The officers were assigned to companies in the following combination as noted in the first pay list, June 5, 1777 (*W O* 12, 8,250) —

COMMANDANT	LIEUTENANT	ENSIGN
Lieut -Col The Hon John Gordon.	Arthur McLachlan. / Lachlan McLean	John Gordon
Major Alexander Ross (had 33 Rosses as privates)	Charles Baillie / John Ross.	John Ross.
Captain John Ferguson	Alexander Keith / Roderick McLean	Norman McLean
Captain Adam Gordon (Son of "8th Lord Kenmure ")	William Newall / Dunbar Douglas	
George (Gordon), Lord Strathaven 9th Marquis of Huntly	Alexander Taylor / Archibald Campbell	Donald Cameron
Captain Peter Gordon (Of Abergeldie)	William Johnston / William McLeod / Gregor Farquharson	
Captain James Horn.	Robert Garden / John Ryan	
Captain Alexander Leith. (Only Company with papers)	William Kelso / Nicol Ewing	Charles Grant
Captain George Moncrieff. (In America)	Henry Dunn / Sir Alexander Sinclair	James Ronaldson

The 81st had no territorial connection with the north of Scotland in point of service. Stewart gives it the alternative title of " Aberdeenshire

Highlanders," but the pay rolls at the Record Office call it "H.M. 81st Regiment of Foot, commanded by the Hon. William Gordon."

The corps was certainly not complete when it went south, for on May 18, 1778, Duncan, the adjutant, wrote a letter from Greenock to such captains as it concerned as follows (*W.O.* 1 : 997) :—

Sir,—I am commanded by Col. Gordon to acquaint you that it has been signified to him by the Secretary at War that His Majesty will not sign the commissions for the officers of this Regiment until it is compleat in numbers, according to the Establishment mentioned in your Beating Order. The Colonel, therefore, desires that you will exert yourself in compleating your quota and expects that you will have it done in two months from the date thereof at farthest. Otherwise, he will be obliged to name another gentleman for the commission you was [sic] to have had in his regiment. And the Colonel further directs that you do acknowledge the receipt of this letter by the next post after it comes to your hands, addressed to him at Kinsale.

It was marched to Stirling and then shipped to Kinsale, seven companies landing in January, and the rest on June 6, 1778; but it left a recruiting party behind, for Ensign James Gordon of the Northern Fencibles wrote to the Duke of Gordon from Benholm, July 24—" There is a party of Colonel Gordon's in this country, but they have not got a single man." When the regiment landed in Ireland the companies, instead of having 100 privates each, had only the following complement of men :—

COMPANY.	PRIVATES.	COMPANY.	PRIVATES.
John Ferguson	73	Hon. William Gordon	95
Adam Gordon	80	James Horn	85
Lord Strathaven	80	Alexander Leith	98
Hon. John Gordon	77	George Moncrieff	88
Peter Gordon	95	Alexander Ross	96

Some recruiting was done in Ireland itself, for in July, 1778, there were seven Irishmen in Colonel Gordon's own company, but three of them, enlisted in July, had deserted by September of the same year. On August 2, 1778, Colonel Gordon wrote to the Secretary of War from Kinsale :—" I could have enlisted a great many men in this country, but as I knew they would not remain long with us, I have only taken on seven or eight, who were well recommended " (*W.O.* 1 : 997).

The regiment was quartered in Dublin till June 30, 1780, then went to Cashel till September 30, and from there to Kilkenny. The companies broke up in the following year, two being quartered at Youghal, two in Cloyne, two in Clonmell, two in Middleton, one in Kilkenny and one in Cashel. In July, 1782, eight of the companies were in Limerick, and by September the whole regiment was at Monkstown.

Stewart of Garth is responsible for the statement that in "the end of 1782," the 81st crossed over to England, and in March, 1783, were embarked at Portsmouth,

with the intention of sending them to the East Indies, immediately after the preliminaries of peace were signed, although the terms on which the regiment had enlisted were that they should be discharged in three years or at the conclusion of hostilities. The men, however, made no objections or complaint, and embarking very cheerfully remained quietly on board, waiting the orders for sailing and apparently overlooking, or indifferent about, the conditions of their engagement. At length, however, a very opposite feeling evinced itself, when it was known that the Atholl Highlanders had insisted [January 27] on the performance of the terms of their agreement and [had] refused to embark. The example, as might have been expected, spread rapidly, and the Aberdeenshire regiment, following that of the Atholl Highlanders, called for the fulfilment of their agreement and requested to be disembodied and marched back to their own country to be there discharged. This request being conceded, the regiment marched to Scotland and was disbanded at Edinburgh in April, 1783.

As a matter of fact the 81st left Ireland in 1782, and had begun their march back to Scotland by March, 1783. Their movements are set forth with great minuteness in the War Office records (*W.O.* 5 ; 64 ; pp. 320, 322, 358, 394, 416-8, 424-5, 451, 485-8, 506 ; 65 ; pp. 4 and 10). On December 23, 1782, the order was given to Lord George Lennox at Portsmouth :—"As soon as the 68th and 81st Regiments are embarked, you cause the 36th to march into Hillsea Barracks" (where Andrew Wood, of Captain Duncan's company of the 81st, was left "sick"). On December 24, they were to embark on board the vessels which had been "prepared for their reception." The next order, January 25, 1783, bids the 81st on arrival at Spithead be disembarked and marched to Hillsea Barracks. Here the regiment remained till near the end of February, when it was sent on the march in pairs of companies ; one pair on February 19 to Petersfield ; another on February 20 to Waltham ; a third on February 20 to Petersfield ; and the last pair on February 21 to

Waltham. Four companies then met at Bagshot from which they set out on March 17 for Newark (reached April 1), marching two days at a time and halting the third. The second division, of two companies, set out from Alton in March 18 for Grantham. The third division set out on March 19 for Stamford. On April 11, the regiment set out in two divisions from Newark, reaching Newcastle April 26, via Doncaster, Ripon, Northallerton, Darlington and Durham. Berwick was reached in May, via Morpeth and Alnwick; so that during the five months' sojourn in England, the 81st saw more of the world than during all its four years in Ireland.

The War Office records stop at Berwick. The regiment, or rather the dregs of it, went to Edinburgh, where the final disembodiment took place on May 10 and May 13. Stewart says that it was reduced in April. As a matter of fact the men had begun to be discharged as early as December, 1782, and dropped off in batches on the march northwards. The state of Captain Dickson's muster in Edinburgh on May 10 is typical, there being only 24 privates present, and 61 "casuals since September 10," 1782. Forty-seven discharges took place as follows (the company being finally reduced on May 10):—

1 in December 1782.	1 on April 22, 1783.
21 on February 28, 1783.	2 on April 28, ,,
1 on March 15, ,,	4 on April 29, ,,
1 on March 20, ,,	1 on April 30, ,,
1 on March 22, ,,	14 on May 3, ,,

The discharges in the companies in the last muster were as follows (*W.O.* 12; 8,251):—

Company Commanders.	Present, May 10, 1783.	Casuals since Sept. 10, 1782.	Final Discharge.
Hon. William Gordon	19	72	May 13
Lt.-Col. Hamilton	53	34	
Major John Dickson	24	61	May 10
Capt. William Burnett	27	55	May 10
,, William Duncan	24	63	May 13
,, Adam Gordon	22	65	May 13
,, James Horn	33	53	May 13
,, Alexander Leith	19	42	
,, James Leith	32	66	May 10
,, George Moncrieff	19	71	May 13
,, George Skene	26	62	May 10

Of the original company commanders only five remained, namely the Hon. William Gordon, Adam Gordon, James Horn, Alexander Leith and George Moncrieff.

The Number 81 was revived in 1793 for the Loyal Lincoln Volunteers, which regiment continues to this day as the second battalion of the Loyal North Lancashire Regiment.

THE SEVENTY-SEVENTH: OR ATHOLL HIGHLANDERS.

1777: RAISED BY THE 4TH DUKE OF ATHOLL: DISBANDED 1783.

Whether the 81st Regiment of Foot did or did not follow the example of the Atholl Highlanders in declining to sail for "foreign parts," it is well to understand the action of the latter themselves, for it throws a flood of light on the attitude of the Scots territorial regiments to national exploits.

This is not the place to describe the raising of the 77th, or Atholl Highlanders, which was a Perthshire regiment. Its history has been told in detail by the Duke of Atholl in his exhaustive *Atholl Chronicles*, and also in his daughter-in-law's book, *A Military History of Perthshire, 1660-1902* (pp. 70-78). Stewart of Garth discusses it in the section of his book devoted to "Mutinies of the Highland Regiments" (*Sketches of the Highlanders*, 2nd ed. ii. 405-8). Garth got his first commission in the Atholl Highlanders on April 21, 1783, after the mutiny, but never joined, and remained on half pay till 1787, when he was appointed to the 42nd. Curiously enough he makes no reference to the fact.

But if the regiment was Perthshire, several of the officers were Aberdeenshire, including John Farquharson (Lieutenant, January 10, 1778), who was a son of Lieutenant Alexander Farquharson, Micras, late of the 42nd; John Farquharson, paymaster (Lieutenant, December 30, 1777), who was a son of Invercauld's factor; and probably Charles Farquharson, who was gazetted a Lieutenant, December 31, 1777. Strangely enough they brought few Farquharsons with them, but the regiment tried to recruit in the north, as the following letter, written by Charles Stewart, sergeant in the Atholl Highlanders, to Charles Stewart, Drumin, serves to show. It was dated Inverlochy, January 31, 1778, but Drumin felt convinced that from its "glassed ink," it had been written elsewhere. It runs (*Gordon Castle Papers*):—

Honoured Sir,—Upon my returning from Strathspey from attesting as a Serjeant with Lieutenant Farqrson of the Athole Highlanders, it seems an information has been given you that I was trepaned and carried away by force, which out of great friendship made you take the trouble to come up here in order to relieve me, for which I return you most thankful acknowledgments; and in justice to Lieutenant Farqrson and others who might perhaps be blamed in decoying me, take this opportunity of informing you that no bad usage was offered me and that I was, as I still am, most desirous and happy of the opportunity I have got of being a Serjeant with an acquaintance; and the reason of my leaving the country by night was to be kept from being pestered by women, who, I dare say, wished me well and might have thought I was drunk, which was not the case.

All I regret is that I took the step without consulting you, and hope you will not be offended or blame anyone but myself, as I wrote my attestation with my own hand. I would have seen you at Drimmin in a few days, but have orders to go over to Strathdon, as my master has gone to Strathspey, who is good enough to say will dispense with me most freely if any of my friends could procure me to a higher rank in the army, which I have an ambition for. I will give myself the pleasure of seeing you upon my return from Strathdon, if I thought you are not offended.

A much nearer local association, however, arose from the fact that an Aberdeenshire laird, Charles Gordon of Sheelagreen, in the parish of Culsalmond, became major of the 77th on October 24, 1778, and assumed command in November, 1782. Gordon, who was born in 1741, had begun his career in the 89th, raised by the Duke of Gordon, getting his lieutenancy, October 13, 1759. He became captain in March 1762, and was A.D.C. to Hector Munro at the battle of Buxar. He got a captaincy in the 11th Foot in April, 1767, and became major of the 31st in May, 1776; so that he came to the Atholl Highlanders with much experience. He also had a nephew in the regiment, for he wrote from Dublin to Colonel Murray, May 3, 1781 (Atholl archives):—

I shall also request the favour [i.e. from the Lord Lieutenant] of an ensigncy for Donald MacGregor, but, should not my application have effect, you will be pleased to mention him and my nephew, Charles Gordon [whose parentage I have not discovered] for the first two vacancies. I do not know that my nephew should be any burden on the regiment, as I shall immediately appoint him lieutenant to [Robert] Duff's [Independent] Company as soon as the notification is made out.

Young Gordon got his ensigncy May 26, 1781, became lieutenant January 28, 1782, and was placed on half pay 1783, his name appearing in the army lists till 1798. Robert Duff's father, James (1700-79), was Land

Surveyor of Customs at Dundee (but had come from the north, being a son of Robert Duff of Hillockhead, fourth son of George of Edindiach), who married Christian Innes, daughter of James Innes of Knockorth, Provost of Banff (*Book of the Duffs*, 431, 433, 435). There was thus a fair admixture of northern officers in the regiment.

Like the 81st, the Atholl Highlanders spent most of their service in Ireland; but in August, 1782, the regiment embarked for Bideford, and found its way to various places in Hants. In November, Murray was promoted major-general, and the command devolved on Gordon, who, however, was not gazetted until February 28, 1783.

Early in January, 1783, the 77th received orders to proceed to India, and was marched to Portsmouth for that purpose on January 25. On that very day, the news reached the town that the preliminaries of peace between France and Spain had been signed, but notwithstanding this the order for embarkation was not countermanded. The regiment declined to budge, and its attitude has become historic.

Stewart of Garth, anxious to say everything possible in favour of the Highlanders generally, glozes the facts when he tells us the men of the 77th " showed no reluctance to embark, nor any desire to claim their discharge," though he admits that the Letters of Service entitled them to do so. " On the contrary, when they came in sight of the fleet at Spithead, as they marched across Portsdown Hill, they pulled off their bonnets and gave three cheers for a brush with Hyder Ali. But no sooner were they quartered in Portsmouth to wait till the transport should be ready than distrust and discord appeared."

Stewart even goes the length of criticising Gordon's leadership. The Atholl Highlanders, he says,

had every advantage of discipline while commanded by Colonel Gordon, an officer of great experience and firmness of character, though too much of the German school for a Highland regiment. But although he was of a temper to trust little to the native character of his men, and too apt to enforce his orders with a strictness which did not always yield to circumstances, he seldom had occasion to resort to corporal punishment. It is creditable to the character of the regiment that under so close an observer of their discipline, too much accustomed to look on soldiers without thought or reflection beyond the immediate orders they received, very few punishments were inflicted, and that these were only of the kind usually inflicted on Highland regiments of that period.

Having criticised the Colonel, Stewart goes on to suggest that the mutiny was really caused by " emissaries from London," who " expatiated on the faithlessness of sending them such a distance when their time of service had expired." But Garth himself devoted a whole chapter to " Mutinies of the Highland Regiments "—" a series of very distressing events," of which the classic case is that of the Black Watch in 1743, when two corporals, natives of Laggan, and a private from Strathspey were shot, and 104 men drafted to other regiments, for declining to go upon foreign service. The whole story has recently been set forth at great length by Mr. Duff MacWilliam in his *Official Records of the Mutiny in the Black Watch* (pp. cxxviii., 237), with the conviction that it " contributed largely " to the Forty-Five. Certain it is, that it had become a tradition in the Highlands, and must have been well known to the Atholl Highlanders. I set forth their action chronologically from various contemporary accounts :—

January 23.—On this day [a Thursday] one of the greatest scenes of confusion happened at Portsmouth that ever was remembered in that town. The Highland, or 77th Regiment, now quartered here were ordered on Sunday [January 26] to be ready to embark for the East Indies the next morning [January 27] (*Gent.'s Mag.*, vol. 53, p. 89; not quoted in Lady Tullibardine's book.)

January 26.—On this day some of the men sent a letter to Lord George Gordon informing him that they were to be sent to the East. " It is known that Lord George sent back an answer assuring them of his support in all legal proceedings, and he doubtless encouraged them in their mutinous conduct " (*Military History of Perthshire*, p. 74) Maidment apparently did not know of Lord George's intervention, for in annotating the ballad about the emeute he suggests his Lordship's uncle " Adam."

January 27.—In obedience to order they assembled on the parade, but with determined resolution not to embark, alleging as a reason that their arrears were not paid, and that they were enlisted on the express condition to serve only three years or during the American war : and, as they conceived these conditions were fulfilled, and that they were not intended for the East India Company's service, where none of their officers were going, they declared that they would stand by each other to the last, and would not be compelled to embark for the East Indies, as they believed their officers had bartered them away to that Company. The Colonel was not present, but the Lieutenant-Colonel and the other officers insisted that they should embark ; in consequence of which the soldiers surrounded them, violently beating the Lieutenant-Colonel and

several others, who narrowly escaped with wounds and bruises: after
which they repaired to the magazine or storehouse for the regiment,
which they broke open and furnished themselves with several rounds of
powder and ball. A party of Invalids were ordered out to prevent the
Highlanders possessing themselves of the parade guard-house, but,
being discovered before they gained that place, the Highlanders fired on
them, killed one, and wounded one or two others, which compelled the
Invalids to retreat. In short, the whole was a scene of the utmost
drunkenness, riot, and confusion. Sir J. Pye and Sir J. Carter, the
Mayor, took every step in their power to appease them, and on their
promising they should not be embarked until further orders were received,
they separated and returned to their quarters in the evening tolerably
well satisfied, and this morning [January 27] they have been informed
their embarkation will not be insisted on (*Gent.'s Mag.*, vol. 53, p. 89).

January 28.—Writing on this date from Haslar Hospital to General
Murray, Colonel Gordon practically corroborates this account (*Military
History of Perthshire*, p. 73):—" On Sunday [January 26] at 12 o'clock
the whole Regiment was paraded with arms and accoutrements, which,
after inspecting very narrowly, I told them by Companies to be upon the
publick parade by 10 o'clock on Monday following in order to embark
on board the 'Indiaman,' that I hoped for the credit of the regiment that
there would be no absentees nor a single man the worse for liquor.
Upon which I dismissed the regiment and found some of the men
grumbling; but particularly the Grenadier Company. . . .

" I went to the parade by 12 o'clock yesterday, it being put off on
acc[oun]tt of rain, when a great many of the Reg[imen]t was assembling
with their arms. I observed a good many of the Grenadiers the worse
of liquor and noisy: I went up to the Comp[an]y and commanded silence,
when they told me unanimously they wou'd sooner loose their lives than
go on board of ship, and that they were sold like so many bullocks to
the India Company. That they had made good their agreement by
serving during the American War.

" Whilst I was endeavouring to convince them of their being misled
by some people who did not wish well to the service, they suddenly
attacked me with their firelocks, knocked me down several times, and
with the utmost difficulty, by the assistance of L[ieu]t. Farquharson, senr.
(who I am sorry to find is much cut in the head) and a few of the men,
I was carried into a house near to the Parade, where they endeavoured
to force the door. I was determined, with the few men with me (who
were much attached) to sell my life as dear as I could, but finding they
were firing in the town, and the very small probability of our being able
to prevent them from breaking in to the house, I thought of an expedient
which had the desired effect, by desiring one of the men to inform them
that the L[ieu]t. Col. was in that house, but from the blows he received

he was breathing out his last   Soon after they dispersed, by which means I made my escape

"They broke open the stores, took out ammunition and their swords In that distracted state the Reg[imen]t is now in   Had Lord Grantham's letter [announcing that the preliminaries of Peace had been signed] been published a few days later, they would, I'm certain, have embarked with the greatest cheerfullness   I can only say that every step was taken to prevent these irregularities; the uneasiness it gives me and the corps you may easier conceive than I can possibly describe"

January 31—The *Gentleman's Magazine* correspondent continues the story as follows —"The 77th or Scotch Regiment continued to parade the streets attended by their sergeants and corporals, but without their officers   They appeared to be entirely free from intoxication and behaved with so much decency as to remove from the inhabitants every apprehension of danger   Since which, the 68th Regiment, embarked on board transports for the West Indies, hearing that the Highlanders were not to be sent to the East Indies, made a determination that they would disembark, and in consequence, very early in the morning of the 30th past, they were discovered getting the transports under way to run them into the harbour, but were all prevented by a man-of-war firing on them, except one transport, the mate of which was compelled by the soldiers, amounting to about 300, to bring his vessel so near the southern beach that they all got ashore, marched to the town with the intention to demand quarters of Lord George Lennox, who met them and ordered them to return, which they refused   His Lordship would not permit them to have quarters, but sent them to Hillsea barracks, where they were to remain till orders were received from London   To quiet these disorders, Lord Maitland interposed, and produced an order from the War Office of the 16th Dec, 1775, signed Barrington, and published in the *London Gazette*, by virtue of which all those who should enlist in any of His Majesty's marching regiments after that date should be bound to serve only for the term of three years, or during the rebellion   This produced an explanation of His Majesty's said order, which explanation, dated War Office, Feb 4, and published in the *London Gazette* of the 4th inst, declares that all men now serving in any marching regiment, or corps of infantry, who have been enlisted since the date of the said order, should, on the ratification of the definite treaty of Peace, be discharged, provided that they shall have served three years from the dates of attestations   and all men enlisted, and serving as above, who have not so completed their full time of service, shall be discharged at the expiration of three years from the dates of their respective attestation, and that, in the meantime, no person enlisted under the condition above mentioned shall be sent on any foreign service, unless he shall have been re-enlisted into His Majesty's service"

The present Duke of Atholl in his account of the affair says that as soon as General Murray heard of the "mutiny" he started for Portsmouth in the hope of restoring order, but was advised by the officers not to show himself to the regiment. "A few days later he was present on parade, and did all he could to convince the mutineers that he had never done them any injury: but to this 'they gave very little faith.' He then made an effort—through the medium of Captain William Robertson—to persuade them to disavow the mutiny, but only two companies could be prevailed upon to do this."

There is an interesting extract from a letter from Portsmouth in the *Morning Chronicle* of February 6, 1783, dated February 2, bearing on this:—

The Duke of Athol and Col. Murray, and Lord Geo. Lennox, Commander in Chief in Scotland, have been down here; but the Athol Highlanders are still determined not to go to the East Indies. They have put up their arms and ammunition into one of the magazines and placed a very strong guard over them, whilst the rest of the regiment sleep and refresh themselves. They come regularly and quietly to the Grand Parade, very cleanly dressed, twice a day. Their Adjutant and other Officers parade with them. One day it was proposed to turn the great guns on the ramparts against the Highlanders; but that scheme was soon overruled. Another time it was suggested to send for some marching regiments quartered near this place; upon which, the Highlanders drew up the drawbridges, and placed centinels at them.

The 81st, another Highland regiment aboard the Indiamen, have also insisted upon being disembarked, and we hear that they are to be disembarked on Tuesday.

An English regiment embarked for the West Indies, insisted likewise on being re-landed, and cut the cables of their transports, and are now in the barracks here. The Athol Highlanders are quartered among the town's people; they do not all appear to be Highlanders. There are indeed some of Struan Robertson's men amongst them, and a few of the Glin Ammon people, and Stuarts of Appin, and Camerons of Lochiel; but they chiefly consist of young lads from Perth, Glasgow, Dundee, and Montrose, amounting in the whole to near 1000 men. The most of them attend the worship of God to-day, it being Sabbath, and placed centinels all round for fear of being surprised.

The inns are full of company from London, and the country people from Sussex and twenty miles round flock in to see the Highlanders.

The affair was debated on January 29 in the House of Commons, the following report being constructed from various sources, including the

Morning Chronicle of January 30 and February 1, 1783, and the *Gentleman's Magazine*, vol. 53, pp. 89-90 :—

Mr. [Robert] Vyner, M.P. for Lincoln, spoke of the riot as " of a most dangerous nature "; the particulars he had not heard, but he understood some blood was shed, and the riot was not quelled when the express came away. If he was rightly informed, he said the men were, in some measure, justified in what they had done (if it was possible for men to be justified for mutiny). The men had been enlisted for three years, or during the war; therefore, when they found they were going to be sent to the East Indies, they mutinied, and, he understood, had killed one of the officers, and wounded several others. If the men had been enlisted on these terms, the hon. gentleman insisted that faith ought to have been observed with them, and they were not, in his opinion, liable to be punished as persons who were guilty of mutiny without a provocation. He called upon His Majesty's ministers to declare what they had heard or knew of the matter.

Mr. Thomas Townshend, Secretary for War, afterwards Viscount Sydney, said he had heard of the unfortunate affair, and was fearful that the officers who enlisted the men were to blame. He knew, he said, that it was frequently practised by officers, who wished to gain rank, to offer to men terms which they were not authorised to do, in order to get them to enlist. In those cases, the officers undoubtedly deserve the severest reprehension; but that, having made those terms with the men, the conditions ought to be duly observed, and the men set at liberty when the term was expired.

If he was rightly informed, he said, the 77th Regiment was raised not to stay at home, but to be sent wherever His Majesty's service should require. Certainly they were as proper a regiment to be sent to the East Indies as any other; but he desired the House to remember that he was always against raising those levies or regiments in the manner the 77th was raised, and he still thought it was a dangerous and impolitic mode. The attestations of many of the men at Portsmouth, he said, had been examined, and found to be for three years, or during the war; and certainly those men should not be considered in the light they would have been, had no such attestation been given.

Mr. Burke reprobated the mode used by many officers of enlisting some men for three years, others for five, and in fact on any terms; and insisted that peace having taken place, the men who had enlisted for " during the war," were to all intents and purposes perfectly right in not going to the East Indies.

General Smith desired it might not be set forth to the world that it was an aversion to go to the East Indies, for he knew of the 23rd

Regiment, that was quartered either at Guernsey or Jersey, being on the parade, turned out for church, when the orders came to them to go to the East Indies; they went to church, and returned thanks for their appointment.

Mr. Burke said he did not mean to convey the idea that the East Indies was a bad place for a soldier; on the contrary, he believed it to be the best.

Lord Maitland (8th Earl of Lauderdale), M.P. for Newport, Cornwall, ("Citizen Maitland") said he perfectly well remembered the regiment being raised, and he knew many of the men did not understand English; but he was certain that it was the general idea held out to them at the time of their enlisting that it was for three years, or during the war. He read the copy of an advertisement signed "Barrington," from the *London Gazette* of December 26, 1775, the purport of which was "to order that all men to be enlisted in any of his Majesty's marching regiments of foot after that day, should be enlisted on the express condition of being discharged at the end of three years, or at the end of the rebellion, at the option of His Majesty." Therefore, he was not surprised to find men averse to be sent abroad, from whence, in all probability, they would never return, especially at a time when war was said to be at an end; but he should like to be at a certainty on what conditions the men were raised. He therefore moved, "That the Letters of Service for raising the 77th Regiment be laid on the table." Mr. Vyner seconded.

Mr. Secretary Townshend wished it to be postponed, as a person was gone down to inquire into the business.

Mr. [George] Dempster of Dunnichen, M.P. for the Forfar Burghs, was likewise of opinion it would be better to postpone the business until the return from Portsmouth of General Murray.

Lord North said that with regard to the point of their [the 77th] being raised for home service only, he well remembered that was not the condition. They were not fencibles, and the House must know that those regiments raised for home service in Scotd., were all fencibles. The 77th was raised at the same time as the Edinburgh regt., the Glasgow regt., Lord Macleod's, and several others; all of them to be employed wherever the King's service should require. As to the stipulatn. that they were to serve only three years, he did not recollect any such conditn., and if the fact was that the officers concerned in raising them, had taken upon themselves to go the length of holdg. out conditions to them, wh. Government neither meant to have held out, nor authorised such officers to promise, he should think the officers highly culpable.

Sir R[ichard] Hotham, M.P. for Southwark, said that though the riot was over, something speedy should be done in the business, as keeping the Indiamen there was a great expense to the proprietors.

Sir P[hilip] J[ennings] Clerke, formerly Lieutenant-Colonel of the Horse Guards and M.P. for Totnes, spoke in favour of the men; and hoped, if any delay was caused, that they would not suffer or be shipped off until the matter was inquired into.

General Sir G[eorge] Howard, M.P. for Stamford, who had commanded the Buffs at Falkirk and Culloden, said he understood that the men were raised, as described, for three years, or during the war; and that it was testified on the back of their attestations.

General Henry Seymour Conway, who had been dismissed the services for opposing George III.'s arbitrary measures in 1764, and was Commander-in-Chief, 1782-3, said that he was responsible for appointing the 77th to foreign service. He chose it because it was complete, and most of the other regiments were weak and incomplete. Peace came suddenly, and the regiment was ordered upon the service abroad before the Peace was known. He did not know that any condition of serving for three years, or till the end of the war, was in the terms of their enlisting.

Mr. William Eden, M.P. for Woodstock (formerly represented by the Hon. William Gordon of the 81st), afterwards created Baron Auckland, spoke up both for men and officers. He had had the 77th immediately under his observance during sixteen months of their garrison duty in Dublin; and although they were the largest regiment in the King's service, and employed during so long a period in a city not remarkable for its police, he must say that their conduct had been regular and exemplary. Their officers, too, were not only men of gentlemanly characters, but peculiarly attentive to regimental discipline. Mr. Eden added, that having once, upon the sudden alarm of an invasion, sent an order for the immediate march of this regiment to Cork, they shewed their alacrity by marching at an hour's notice, and completed their march with a dispatch beyond any instance in modern times, and this without the desertion of a single soldier.

The Letter of Service was produced, and ordered to lie on the table until the arrival of General Murray, on receiving a promise from Mr. Secretary Townshend that the men should not be sent abroad until an inquiry was made into the business.

Lady Tullibardine defends the attitude of Murray to the regiment. She says (*Military History of Perthshire*, p. 413) that he resisted the nomination of officers to the 77th by successive Lords-Lieutenant of Ireland, pointing out that his corps was " not only national but provincial in character, and that if his men were to be commanded by officers whom they did not know, he would not be able to get another recruit." The refusal of the regiment is said to have " added half a score to his looks."

It was a "blow" to him to think that the men should believe him capable of selling them to the East India Company.

A ballad of the period called "The Athole Highlanders," quoted in Maidment's *Scottish Ballads and Songs*, 1859 (pp. 236-244), takes a very different view of Murray from that held (naturally) by the family historians, and it is not referred to by them. Maidment tells us in a prefatory note that the song, which was printed at Edinburgh under the title of "The Athole Highlanders' (or LXXVII. Regiment's) Triumph, or General Murray and Colonel Gordon's Lamentation," was written by one of the privates of the 77th. It was printed by subscription, and each of the soldiers who subscribed got a copy. "From its fugitive nature it is now almost entirely unknown. As a national record of the very remarkable circumstances that gave rise to it, and as a song of triumph on the part of the Highlanders, who were on this occasion on the right side of the question, it has been placed in this volume." The ballad runs as follows :—

> The twenty-seventh of January,
> The year seventeen hundred and eighty-three,
> The Highland boys would not agree
>   To ship for Colonel Gordon.
>
> CHORUS :
>
> Charley [Gordon] are you waking yet?
> Or are you sleeping, I would wait ;
> The Highland drums to arms do beat,
>   Will you go on board this morning?
>
> To the East Indies we were sold
> By Murray for a bag of gold :
> But listen awhile and I'll unfold
>   How he did blast his glory.
>
> At Portsmouth we were shipped to be,
> To serve the East India Company ;
> But the Highland lads would not agree
>   To go on board that morning.
>
> Were it to fight 'gainst France and Spain,
> We would with pleasure cross the main,
> But like bullocks to be sold for gain
>   Our Highland blood abhors it.

Charley appeared upon the plain,
And thus he did address his men;
"The first that refuses shall be slain,
    To go on board this morning."

The Highland boys did him deny,
Said, "We will fight until we die,
But you and Murray we defy;
    We'll comb your hair this morning.

"To the East Indies we won't go
To join Eyre Coote or Hector Munro;
Our time is out, and home we'll go
    In spite of all your saying no."

The name of Murray I do suppose
Should stink in every Scotsman's nose;
To king and country they were rogues,
    As witness traitor Geordy.

Your father commanded in Forty-five,
The young Pretender could not thrive,
As witness many men alive,
    How treacherously he sold them.

Our fathers you sold at Culloden field,
The Isle of Man you up did yield,
But the 77th have hearts of steel,
    Go ask it of Colonel Gordon.

As witness bears his bloody head,
I would not wish the poor wretch dead;
But when my grinders can chew bread,
    The Murrays I abhor them.

If writing keeps his memory,
His deed shall not forgotten be,
It makes my blood run chill in me
    To think on Murray's roguery.

Upon the earth short shall he dwell,
But like all traitors go to hell,
Who thought the 77th to sell,
    But God detects his roguery.

Then General Smith came to the plain
And ask'd him where was his men?
"The pox on me if I do ken,
    They comb'd my hair this morning."

Our Major, like a soldier bold,
He said, "My lads, you shan't be sold,
For of your hands I'll take a hold
    And bring you off this morning."

Sir Robert Stewart of birth and fame,
And long may he maintain the same,
To be an honour to the name,
    May all that's good come o'er him.

Messrs. Vinner and Maitland too,
To them our hearty thanks is due ;
Our cause they stood to, firm and true,
    In spite of Murray's roguery.

When the news to London went,
Lord George Gordon down was sent
To look upon the men's complaint,
    How they were us'd that morning.

Lord George Lennox, a soldier brave,
How generously he did behave,
His word of honour to us gave
    That we should not be sent away.

Lord George Gordon should not be forgot,
Who is a true and a trusty Scot,
But may damnation be their lot
    Who approves of Murray's roguery.

Now to conclude and make an end
Of these few lines that I have penn'd.
May peace and plenty be the end,
    God bless our own King Geordy.

The India captains they did cry :—
"Where are our men that we did buy?"
Then Murray said : "If they should die,
    They'll go on board this morning."

They cried to Murray : "Where's your men?"
He swore and said : "I do not ken,
But they have alter'd all my plan,
    As they would not ship this morning."

The price was struck at a high rate,
The bargain struck without debate
That Athole men to India be sent
    To stop your Hyder Ali.

May Sir Eyre Coote and brave Munro
Make that savage villain know
That Britons are his mortal foe,
    And let them twist him fairly.

We Athole men go home to rest,
For sure we are we've done our best,
But her nainsell has been opprest
    By Murray who fairly sold us.

There have been traitors you may see
In Forty-Five and Eighty-Three,
But let Murray still branded be,
    And all good men abhor him.

Thy father, Murray, died in disgrace,
And now his son fill'd up his place :
Judas and Murray got yon place
    Where gold cannot restore them.

Now, dad and son, I am to end
This new song that I have penn'd.
May all the traitors high be hanged,
·   For Athole men abhor them.

Whoever was responsible for the conditions creating the dispute, the " mutineers " were very leniently dealt with, almost indeed in the spirit exhibited by Mr. Duff MacWilliam, who dedicates his book to the " brave [42nd] Highlanders, victims of Deception and Tyranny." The authorities had clearly learned the Black Watch lesson, for not a single man of the Atholl Highlanders was brought to trial or punished. The present Duke of Atholl suggests that the order for embarkation was countermanded the more readily because Lord George Gordon had interested himself in the affair and a popular outcry might have had to be faced if they insisted on sending the regiment to the East. " The Government first offered them a chance of re-enlisting for a bounty : but, as they would not advance the money until 500 men had offered their services and refused to give it before the men were safely on board, the offer was rejected by the mutineers " (*Military History of Perthshire*, p. 75). Meantime, the Highlanders sent a letter of thanks to Lord George Gordon and " it may therefore be concluded that they believed they owed something to his intervention."

The 77th got orders, in February, to march down to Scotland in four divisions, and on its arrival at Berwick in April and May, 1783, it was disbanded by companies. On March 11, Colonel Gordon severed his connection with it by becoming Lieutenant-Colonel of the 61st Regiment. He died unmarried in 1789.

THE NORTHERN FENCIBLES, 1778-83.

1778: RAISED BY THE 4TH DUKE OF GORDON: DISBANDED 1783.

The Duke of Gordon's effort in recruiting, seriously handicapped as it had been by the rivalry of his kinsman, was not so ambitious as the Hon. William Gordon's; for while the latter raised a regiment of the line, the Duke organised a Fencible force. That, as it happened, was a much more direct thing to do. The way had been led by His Grace of Atholl, who was followed by Henry Scott, the young Duke of Buccleuch, in the following spring (of 1778). Buccleuch and Gordon were almost of one age, and their careers had run almost in parallel lines :—

	3rd DUKE OF BUCCLEUCH.		4th DUKE OF GORDON.
Born	1746	-	1743
Succeeded	1751	-	1752
Married	1767	-	1767
Raised Fencibles	1778	-	1778
Died	1812	-	1827

Buccleuch's influence on His Grace of Gordon is clearly set forth in a circular letter which the latter wrote from Upper Grosvenor Street, on April 8, 1778 :—

Sir,—The Duke of Buccleugh gave in a proposal a few days ago to the King's Ministers for raising in the Southern Counties of Scotland 2,000 Fencible men for the defence of the country, never to be sent [out] of this Island upon any account whatever, and not to march out of Scotland, except in case of an actual invasion in England; and when that service is over is to be march'd back, so as when disembodied they shall be disembodied in Scotland; to be cloath'd and accouter'd and paid by the public, but the officers to have rank and pay only whilst embodied.

Upon information of this proposal, I thought it my duty to make a similar proposal in every respect for the Northern Counties, whose zeal in the King's service ought not to appear, what I am sure it is not in reality, inferior to that of their southern brethren. I have reason to believe the proposals will be accepted either in whole or in part, and I flatter myself I shall be honor'd with your aid and support in carrying into execution this measure calculated for the honor as well as the safety of our Country.

The Duke of Buccleugh and I are to be colonels of our respective corps. I propose setting out for Scotland as soon as the particulars are settled.

The Duke of Gordon got his mandate for raising the Northern Fencibles, under Letter of Service dated April 14, 1778:—

My Lord,—I am commanded by the King to acquaint your Grace that His Majesty approves of the plan of raising a Battalion of Fencible Men for the internal protection of North Britain, on the terms proposed by your Grace, as follows:—The Regiment shall consist of eight Battalion Companies, one Company of Grenadiers, and one of Light Infantry. The Battalion Companies are to consist of one Captain, two Lieutenants, one Ensign, five Sergeants, five Corporals, two Drummers, and 100 Private Men each. The Grenadier Company of one Captain, three Lieutenants, five Sergeants, five Corporals, two Drummers, two Pipers, and 100 Private Men. The Light Infantry Company of one Captain, three Lieutenants, five Sergeants, five Corporals, two Drummers, and 100 Private Men, with the usual Staff Officers.

The Regiment is to have the Field Officers undermentioned, *viz.*, one Colonel, one Lieutenant-Colonel, and one Major, each having also a Company, and one Major without a Company, receiving an allowance of ten shillings per diem in lieu thereof and five shillings per diem as Major; but it will be a matter of future consideration whether, in case of the death or promotion of such additional Major the pay of such additional Major shall not cease upon the establishment. The Regiment to be made under your Grace's command as Colonel. [The Duke's commission, signed Suffolk, is dated April 14.]

The Recruits are to receive subsistence from the respective days of their attestation, and one guinea is to be paid to each man enrolled on his arrival at the rendezvous of his Company.

The King leaves to your Grace the recommendation of all the Officers, being such as are well affected to His Majesty, and most likely by their interest and connections to forward the complement of the corps; a list of whom your Grace will be pleased to transmit to me as soon as convenient, for His Majesty's information.

None of the Officers appointed to this Regiment are to have rank longer than while it remains on the Establishment; nor, when reduced, are they to be entitled to half-pay. Both these circumstances are, I know, perfectly understood by your Grace; yet I must take the liberty of adding that your Grace cannot too fully explain the matter respecting rank to the gentlemen you mean to propose for commissions, that they may not in future conceive they have derived any claim whatever to permanent rank in the Army from their services in your Grace's Regiment   It may be proper to mention that, if your Grace takes any Officers from half-pay, they will be replaced thereon on the reduction of your Regiment

In all respects of pay, clothing, arms, and accoutrements, the corps is to be on the same footing as His Majesty's other marching regiments

The Beating Order to authorise this levy, being made out in the usual form, allows the recruiting to be carried on in any part of Great Britain, it is meant, notwithstanding, to be confined to the counties of Scotland proposed by your Grace, and specified in the margin hereof

The Regiment is to serve in any part of Scotland, but not to march out of it except in the case of invasion on the more southern parts of the Kingdom   The men are not to be drafted; and in the event of their being ordered into England, His Majesty consents that they shall not be reduced there, but be marched back in a corps and disembodied in Scotland

The King hopes that the corps will be completed within three months, the period mentioned by your Grace, and, though it has been customary in new levies to stipulate that the recruits shall not be under 5 feet 4 inches, nor under 18 or above 30 years of age, yet His Majesty thinks it unnecessary to prescribe these limits on the present occasion, in full confidence that from your Grace's zeal for his service and regard for your country, every exertion will be used to recruit the corps with men fit for active and immediate duty

In the execution of this service, I take leave to assure your Grace of every assistance that this office can afford —I have the honour to be, my Lord, your Grace's most obedient and most humble servant, Barrington.

The Beating Order gives authority to the Duke in the following terms —

George R —Whereas we have thought fit to order a Regiment of Fencible men to be forthwith raised under your command, which is to consist of ten companies, of five sergeants, five corporals, two drummers, and one hundred private men in each, with two pipers to the grenadier company, besides commissioned officers, which men are not to be sent out of Great Britain'   These are to authorise you by beat of drum or otherwise to raise so many men in any county or part of our Kingdom of Great Britain as shall be wanting to compleat the said regiment to the above mentioned numbers   And all Magistrates, Justices of the Peace, and Constables, and other Civil Officers whom it may concern are hereby required to be assisting unto you in providing quarters, impressing carriages, and otherwise as there shall be occasion   Given at our Court at St. James's, this 14th day of April, 1778, in the 18th year of our reign. By His Majesty's command, Barrington.

[Endorsed]—To our Right Trusty and Right Entirely Beloved Cousin, Alexander, Duke of Gordon, Colonel of a Regiment of Fencible Men to be forthwith raised, or to the Officer appointed by him to raise men for our said Regiment.

The Duke of Buccleuch approached the task by issuing a manifesto "to the Brave Lowlanders," a copy of which is at Gordon Castle. It ran as follows :—

In the present alarming condition of this country, whilst France, united with America, threatens invasion and descent upon the coast of Britain, some of the Peers of Scotland, zealous for the safety and honour of their native land, have offered to raise regiments of FENCIBLE MEN, and to serve with them in person during the present war: the King, with signal marks of approbation hath accepted the offer, and issued warrants for that purpose. These regiments are called the South, the West, and the North Fencibles. His Majesty, and the noble commanders of these regiments, considering the circumstances of the levy and trusting to the zeal and valour of the Scots, do not purpose to bribe men to enter into this service by such sums of money as have been given to those who enlisted to leave the kingdom, and to serve abroad ; nor is it reasonable they should, for these regiments have many advantages : they are not to march out of Scotland, except in case of an actual invasion, and then to England only, to assist their brethren against their common enemy. Private men, by enlisting in these regiments acquire all the privileges and immunities of soldiers ; such as freedom of burghs and corporations etc. They are to be commanded by gentlemen of their own country, born and bred amongst those whom they command ; and when the regiments are once formed and taught their exercise, every possible indulgence, consistent with their duty will be given to the private men ; they will be allowed to work for themselves during hay time and harvest, (and at all other times, when they are quartered in places where work is to be had, to as great a degree as the circumstances will permit) so that the men who enlist in these regiments do not become soldiers in the common sense of the word, but are furnished with arms, accoutrements, clothing and pay and taught military exercise to be ready at a call to defend their country and their own families from the invasion, rapine and plunder of the most cruel and treacherous of enemies.

One of these regiments, (the South Fencible) is commanded by COLONEL HENRY DUKE OF BUCCLEUGH, and it is hoped and expected that the men of the Low countries will not be backward in offering themselves to serve in this regiment. The Low-landers, it is well known were once famous for their valour; they were reckoned in ancient times the bravest and most warlike of all the Scots; led by their own chiefs, they defended their country with success against much braver enemies than the French or Americans can pretend to be; but these enemies are now become their firmest friends: the happy Union has made the Scots and the English one people. If they unite in sentiment and action upon this great occasion, and manfully resist the confederacy formed for the downfall of Britain by the perfidious French and ungrateful Americans, Britain will rise greater from her dangers. The English are already arrayed, it is high time for the Scots to arm at this important period. Regulars, militia and fencible men, are equally the defenders of their country.

N.B. A ship of war, manned with Frenchmen and Americans, has landed men in sundry places in England and Scotland to plunder, burn and destroy.

His Grace of Gordon did not venture on any such rhetorical appeal, but at once set about the serious task of recruiting, getting James Ross, his cashier at Gordon Castle, to send out this circular letter, dated April 25, 1778:—

Sir,—I have the pleasure to acquaint you that the King has given the Duke of Gordon a warrant for raising a Regiment of Fencible men in the Northern Counties of Scotland, to consist of ten companies of 100 private men each. . . .

The raising of this Regiment must be attended with great trouble and very considerable expence to His Grace; but, as he undertook it for the good of the country, which would otherways have been quite defenceless, 'tis hoped he will meet with the approbation and hearty assistance of every man of property and consequence in it.

The Duke writes me of the 17th that he intended to set out for Scotland in about eight days after, in order to take measures for raising this regiment, and that he hoped and expected, not only his particular friends, but also every person of influence in the country would exert their best endeavour to get the corps compleated as expeditiously as possible, that it may be the sooner fit for the purpose intended, especially as all the regular troops are so withdrawn from the north upon the present emergency.

The first thing to be done will be the appointment of the officers, of whom His Grace writes there are none fixed but Lord Haddo and Mr. Campbell of Calder: for, tho' he had many applications, his answer was that he must first see his friends in the north to consult with them.

I, therefore, in compliance with His Grace's desire, and while he is upon the road, take the liberty to bring this circumstance into your view, that you may lose no time in applying to His Grace in case you or any of your friends wish to have a commission in his regiment. The first nobility in England are just now taking the lowest commissions in the Militia, prompted by an emulation to appear in the defence of their country at this critical time: and it is to be expected that our country-men will not fall short in point of spirit upon the present occasion.

One of the first tasks of the Duke was to find officers. There was certainly a keen desire among some gentlemen to get commissions, but they were not the type of officer his Grace wanted, for many of them had no influence. All the first commissions, forty-three in number, bear the same date, April 14, 1778, as the mandate for raising the regiment, but that does not imply that the appointments were actually made on that date, for the list was not complete on July 3, and the first official announcement was not made till September 17, when the War Office issued the list (*W.O.* 25; 148: p. 236). The fact is the commissions were antedated. On July 3, 1778, His Grace wrote to Lord Barrington, Secretary of War (*W.O.* 1; 997):—

I have met with some very unexpected disappointments by the defection of several officers I had appointed. My officers are not all named owing to the disappointment I have mentioned, which is the reason of my not having sent you a Return of them. But if your Lordship desires it, I shall send a list of such as I have named and have reason to think will be entitled to commissions in my regiment.

Some of the applications for commissions were very curious. Thus Cameron, of Fassifern, suggests Lochiel's son, a "fine stout boy of 10," and he offered to do duty for three or four years until the boy was ready to take post.

John Macleod, of Rasay, writes on May 12, that he had "two boys at Aberdeen Colledge," the eldest being about 17, and "would be happy in having him under His Grace's protection so early in life."

Alexander Gordon, of Whiteley, proposed Sir William Gordon of Park, "who is indeed a very sensible worthy man." Sir William had been attainted for his share in the Jacobite Rebellion, but 20 years had apparently sobered him, and he was ready to support the House of Hanover.

Patrick Grant, Inverness, writes:—"Old as I am to begin in the military line, if his Grace would honour me, I think I should renew my age."

William Todd writing from Ruthven on April 27, gives the Duke a useful hint :—" If his Grace has any passion for a parcel of real genuine Highlanders, he should offer a commission to Glengarry, whose men are yet entire and the best in the whole country." As to his own district he says, "there is not a piper in all this country but Cluny's, and he is too old, and I am afraid too great for service." Todd offered his own son as a subaltern, and mentioned the sons of his neighbours, Butter and Macgregor.

Malcolm Macpherson, Ardylach, George Macpherson, Aberdeen, and the brother of Hugh Rose, Nigg, all sent applications.

Sir Robert Abercromby offered from £1,200 to £1,400, and added " if the Duke wants a Chaplain for his Regiment I should put in for it " —apparently on behalf of a friend. Abercromby of Birkenbog was also anxious for a commission.

One of the most curious of all the applications, however, came from a minister and schoolmaster named Robert Gordon. His memorial dated Rhynie, July 1, runs as follows (*Gordon Castle Papers*):—

That your memorialist has been for some years a Preacher of the Gospel, and for many years Schoolmaster at Rhynie, a laborious and painful occupation of which he feels himself very weary.

That he wou'd be extreamly happy to accept of the honour of any employment under your Grace in the regiment now raising, and of which your Grace has the command, as he has but a very remote prospect of any provision in the line of life in which he was educated.

That if your Grace cou'd honour him with a lieutenancy in that regiment, he wou'd be anxious by every honest method in his power to promote the interest of the service with the utmost zeal, and tho' he cou'd not promise on raising the number of men usually given for that office, he nevertheless thinks that in consequence of his acquaintance and connection in this corner he cou'd be of some service, the rather as a Brother of his has had some success in that way here, and has still a prospect of doing something more effectual.

Your Memoralist begs leave to add that his father and friends have been time immemorial tenants to Your Grace's family in this corner.

May it therefore please Your Grace to take the Memoralist and his Memorial under your consideration.

The poor, bored dominie did not get a commission, but he escaped from the drudgery of his "squeel" by ultimately becoming minister of Drumblade, presented to him by the Earl of Kintore in 1794. He had his military ambition realised in his issue, for one of his daughters

married an officer (Captain Henry), another daughter had a son in the
Black Watch, a daughter married a general (John Gordon, Culdrain),
and a second an admiral (Charles Gordon).

One can easily understand the desire of a young man, cooped up
at home and engaged in a dull round of duty, to get a commission.
A very interesting letter bearing on such a case was written to Ross
by John Macpherson, Inverhall, dated June 6.   He says:—

My son hinted to me the beginning of the winter that he wou'd
go into the new levies upon some footing or oyr, and entreated I wou'd
co-operate wt. him in raising a lieutenant's comp[lemen]t of men.   I
told him I did not chuse that line of life for him, as none of his broyrs.
were in Britain to assist me in my old age.   This had not the desired
effect, tho' his uncles Banchar and Mr. Robt. McP. [minister of Aberarder?] endeavoured to influence him to stay.   At last, I promised to
indulge him providing his Grace, who, as was then expected had got a
regiment and that he wou'd be pleas'd to appoint him an off[ice]r.   This
proposall prevailed upon [him] to renunce every oyr. prospect.   But
the misfortune now is that, tho' the boy is still possitive, I cannot engage
for any number of men, the country being so drained by repeated recruiting.   If his Grace will be pleased to give him a comm[issio]n, I
hope he never will have cause to charge him with ingratitude or
cowardice.   Mr. Tod well knows the strugle I had to keep Andrew from
the army, and that I wou'd upon no oyr. terms agree to part wt. him
unless his Grace got a regiment.   Ffrom this plain narrative of the
affair I expect you will be so kind if the D[uke] does not provoid for
him that you will reconcile [him] to stay in good humour wt. me.

The biggest disappointment the Duke met came from Sutherland,
which took this opportunity of finally jettisoning his influence.   He may
have thought that his patriotic endeavour would once more make him a
Cock of the North.   But that was not to be, for not only had his over-
lordship been broken long before he was born, but the county of
Sutherland was expecting to be called on to raise a regiment of Fencibles
of its own, which it did in 1779, under the colonelcy of William Wemyss
of Wemyss (1760-1822), the first cousin of the Countess of Sutherland.

The Gordon influence in Sutherland had come with one Elizabeth,
Countess of Sutherland, and it went with another.   The house of
Sutherland had borne the surname of Gordon from 1501, the probable
date of the birth of Alexander, Master of Sutherland, son of Elizabeth
(Sutherland), Countess of Sutherland, who married, about 1500, Adam
Gordon, second son of the 2nd Earl of Huntly.   Gradually, however,

the family began to repudiate allegiance to the Gordon family, and in 1713 they roused the latter's fury by dropping the name of Gordon and reverting to that of Sutherland. The Jacobite struggle put another gulf between the two houses, for, while the ducal Gordons were tentatively Jacobite, the Sutherland line was staunchly Hanoverian, and in the 'Fifteen the Earl of Sutherland actually invaded the Duke's domains. The final break came in 1771, when the claim of Sir Robert Gordon of Gordonstown to the peerage of Sutherland as heir male of the Gordon Earls was dismissed in favour of the sixteen-year-old Elizabeth, who was under the tutelage of her aunt Lady Elizabeth's husband, the Hon. James Wemyss of that Ilk, whose granddaughter, Elizabeth Brodie, was yet to marry the last Duke of Gordon. The fact that the young Countess's father had raised a Fencible regiment in 1759, the same year as the Duke, and that her mother, like the Duke's wife, was a Galloway Maxwell, may have encouraged His Grace to look to her for help; but while not directly antagonistic, the Sutherland family was not enthusiastic. The Duke put himself into communication with the Countess's guardian, James Wemyss of that Ilk, to whom he wrote as follows, on May 18, 1778 (*Gordon Castle Papers*):—

I received your obliging letter. Believe me I never entertained an idea of interfering with Lady Sutherland in the event of a corps being destined for her country. But by this time, I presume you will know that mine is the only one fixed for the North; and, as it would give me particular pleasure to embrace this opportunity of distinguishing with commissions such of my Lady Sutherland's friends as her managers approve, I therefore deem it a favour to have this permission to take into my regiment Captain James Sutherland at Dunrobin, or any other person more agreeable to Lady Sutherland's friends. I have a company at their service and perhaps a majority if the attention necessary to be paid to my friends in this country can admit of it.

As this undertaking of mine requires despatch, may I beg the favour of an answer directed to me at Gordon Castle as soon as convenient.

On the same day the Duke wrote to Captain James Sutherland at Dunrobin (*Ibid.*):—

I have received your obliging letter of 25th April. Mr. [Charles] Gordon [of Wardhouse] wrote to me from Edinburgh, 19th, that he had delivered my letter to Mr. Wemyss, who, after expressing much friendship for me, told him that he expected you at the Wemyss early last

L

week, and would, upon your arrival, write on a particular answer to my letter.

I have since been in daily expectation of hearing from Mr. Wemyss, and upon that account have delayed arranging some of the commissions in my regiment, being very desirous to reserve such as might be agreeable to you or any other gentleman by Lady Sutherland's managers. But, as the business I am embarked in does not admitt of much longer delay in filling up all my commissions ; and as I have just now heard a report that you have not yet left Dunrobin, I send this by express, and must beg to know by the return of the bearer what part you and Lady Sutherland's other friends chuse to take in my Regiment. I have kept one of the majoritys open for your acceptance. It will be very obliging to have your final resolution by the return of the bearer, and, if you don't find it convenient to accept, I beg you will not mention the offer.

I had almost forgot to mention that I have already appointed a paymaster, but I hope Mr. Gordon will still accept of a company. My paymaster [William Finlason] was appointed before I left London ; otherways I should have been happy to have bestowed it on my namesake.

I daresay your friends, when once they embark, will have the honour of the corps so much at heart as not to make it necessary for me to commend it to them to raise their men as soon as possible that we may not be behind the other Fencible Regiments in Scotland.

On May 21, 1778, Sutherland wrote from Edinburgh to James Ross, the Duke's cashier (*Ibid.*) :—

I am favoured with your letter and the reason of my delay in not acknowledging it before now was the expectation I had of a Sutherland regiment being raised. But, as this is now over, I can with truth assure you that I wish success to the Duke of Gordon's regiment ; and if his Grace will procure me an order from the Countess of Sutherland and her guardians, I can in ten days' time send his Grace two or three hundred fine young fellows ; and on this present emergency I hope every gentleman in the northern counties will exert their endeavours to have the Duke's corps completed with the soonest.

I only arrived here [Edinburgh] last night, and, when I go next week to wait on Mr. Wemyss, I shall mention to him the propriety of his and Lady Sutherland's other tutors assisting the Duke of Gordon on this occasion.

The Duke wrote again to Wemyss on May 26, 1778, dating from Gordon Castle (*Ibid.*) :—

After writing to you the other day, I was exceedingly happy to receive your letter this morning. I am much obliged to you for the friendly part you have used upon this occasion. I shall be ready to do anything on my side to keep up the connection that has so long subsisted between the ffamily of Sutherland and mine.

I am very glad to have it in my power to name Captain Sutherland one of my majors, and Mr. Charles Gordon, or any other you think proper, for a company, with four lieutenants and two ensigns to be named by you—making in all the whole officers for two companies; taking it for granted that they are to bring their quota of men, agreeable to my recruiting instructions, copies of which with Beating Orders, etc., I shall leave with Captain Sutherland's agent at Inverness, for which I set out this evening on my way to Lochaber.

As a matter of fact, Captain Sutherland held his commission only for a fortnight. "It was a disappointment to me, you may easily believe," wrote the Duke, " particularly in losing him." And on June 17, 1778, he wrote to Sir Adolphus Oughton:—

I have met with some great disappointments in gentlemen resigning their commissions after having accepted them a fortnight. The greatest is the family of Sutherland, who had undertaken for 200 men, and, if they had stood to their first engagements, I should now have been 600 strong.

The Duke, however, managed to get one Sutherland, namely John Sutherland of Dunbeath, to whom he gave a lieutenancy. On June 8, 1778, Sutherland wrote from Dunbeath to the Duke that he had got eight men and hoped soon to have more. He asks whether he might make one or two sergeants, as he had got in view one or two young men of education. He also asks for some more attestation papers with a few of the printed obligations, "as the young men in this country are so affraid without them that they think they're not safe." On September 16, 1778, Sutherland, who had now got a company, wrote again from Dunbeath to the Duke (*Gordon Castle Papers*):—

I've the honour to inform your Grace that I have got 20 men attested for your Grace's regiment, and would have got all my complement had I not been continually thwarted by some of the county gentlemen, who never lose an opportunity to disappoint me, Freswick only excepted, to whom I appeal for my conduct. Shall use every fair means to compleat my complement with all possible speed.

With less excuse, the Duke also tapped Caithness, possibly arguing that, if his own domains were invaded, he might as well invade other people's. Luckily for him, the Reay country was not called on to produce a Fencible regiment till 1794, so that he found greater friendliness among the Mackays. On May 18, 1778, the Duke wrote to the Hon. George Mackay, of Skibo, who had been captain in Loudon's Independent companies in the 'Forty-Five, and who was the father of the 7th and 8th Lords Reay (*Gordon Castle Papers*):—

I had the honour to receive your letter of the 29th April, and beg to return my best thanks for your obliging expression of attachment to me and my family.

I presume you are by this time acquainted that mine is the only corps of Fencible men to be raised in the North, and consequently that you find yourself at liberty to assist in raising it. I therefore beg to know by the return of the bearer what concern it will be agreeable to you to take in that matter, and whether you have any relatives you would wish to appoint officers. As the business does not admitt of delay, I have been obliged to promise away the greatest part of the commissions, but shall endeavour to keep some open till I have the pleasure of hearing from you.

Skibo got his namesake, George Mackay of Bighouse, who had been in the army and was now on half pay, to take the matter up, and wrote from Tongue to the Duke, on May 30, 1778 (*Ibid.*):—

The express with your Grace's letter of the 26th came here last night, and, as your Grace desires, I send this by express to Fort William to acquaint [you] that I chearfully agree to raise a company for your Grace's regiment, as does Mr. Mackay of Bighouse to have command of a company, which we have no doubt will be completed in a few weeks. I have not yet fixed on the proper persons for subaltern officers. [I] will do so soon, and acquaint your Grace in course after they are fixed on.

I intended to have set out for Edinburgh next week. I now delay till the company is compleated. Bighouse and I will soon after do ourselves the honour to waite of your Grace at Gordon Castle. He desires me to make offer of his most respectful compliments to your Grace; says he cannot easily find money for bills in Aberdeen, but that he can for bills in Edinburgh, and therefore wished to have credit in Edinburgh for the money necessary to raise the company. He wished to know the head musters of the regiment in order to his sending the weekly returns to the commanding officer there, also to have the form of a return sent him.

Then Ross, the cashier at Gordon Castle, took up the tale, writing to Bighouse on July 22, 1778 (*Ibid.*):—

I was happy when I understood that you were to have a company in the Duke's regiment, as it must afford us opportunitys of renewing our acquaintance, which I shall always be glad to cultivate.

Your drummers and piper are expected daily at the general muster in Elgin.

I don't know if your old acquaintance Major Mercer wrote you of his appointment to the regiment, and beg your assistance to get him some men after your own complement was filled up. He has been very successful in recruiting at Aberdeen, and as he is very anxious to make up a decent number, it will be doing him a great favour to help him to some. Perhaps the execution of the Comprehending Act may put this more in your power.

But a great deal was quite out of Mackay's power, for Bighouse wrote July 25, 1778, to the Duke about the Comprehending Act Commissioners' meeting at Wick on July 22 :—"I find your Grace has little to expect from the County of Caithness. The gentlemen of this county think the country very much drained of men already, and that they have no men who can come under the description of the Comprehending Act." He adds, however, that he has got a "pipper" for the ducal corps.

As a matter of fact, the Duke had to rely largely on his own estates, especially on his vast acres in Inverness; and I shall now show the mechanism of the various endeavours he put forward, and the answers that were made to his call—truly an illuminating glimpse into human nature, even under the stress of possible invasion. In the first place, there were his officers, who brought men in consideration of getting posts in the regiment. Hardly less important were his estate agents and officers, notably James Ross, his cashier at Gordon Castle; William Todd (1745-1821) his factor in the Enzie, who married a sister of Professor William Ogilvy, the pioneer land reformer, and gave several sons to the army (*Scottish Review*, xvii., 117-8); and James Bell, another factor, who farmed Coclarachie, where he died on August 13, 1790.

The instructions to the officers were scheduled in a definitive form (*Gordon Castle Papers*):—

The Officers are referred to the annexed copy of the Letter of Service for their guidance in general; but, as the Country has been much drained of men by the new regiments lately raised, and a latitude is on that account given for recruiting the Fencible Regiment somewhat below the usual standard of the Army, his Grace therefore proposes the following particulars in addition to the Letter of Service.

1. That men be enlisted of any age from 15 to the period that obvious infirmity and age render them unfit for active service, and on receiving a certificate (previous to their being attested) from a surgeon, that, after inspection, they appear free from diseases or weakness, that can prevent their marching and actively wielding their arms.

2. Tho' the recruiting of this Regiment is meant to be carried on in the particular counties specified in the Letter of Service, yet if any man, from any other county of North Britain, then resident in the specified counties, should offer to serve in this regiment, such man may be accepted.

3. The guinea proposed to be paid to each man enrolled (on his arrival at the rendezvous of their respective companies, after the above specified inspection and attestation) may be paid, in order to provide the recruit with necessaries, which ought to consist of three good shirts, and two pairs of shoes and hose (including ammunition ones) if the recruiting officer thinks it will forward the service, and chooses to risque the advance; but this immediate advance (considered actually as inlisting money) is on no account and at no time to exceed a guinea.

4. In consideration of such risque, and other contingencies, which the recruiting officer may be liable to, he is to be allowed for every recruit, who shall be brought to Head-Quarters, and approved of by a Field Officer of the regiment as fit for service, a sum not exceeding twenty shillings; but no allowance whatsoever is to be made for any recruits who may die, desert, or be discharged before or rejected on their being brought to Head-Quarters. The officers are individually assured, his Grace will generously apply the utmost extent (and withhold no part) of whatever is allowed by Government for the proposed useful Purpose.

5. In order to carry on the recruiting service with greater facility, money will be lodged with Captain Finlason, who is appointed paymaster, and now residing at Aberdeen, on whom the recruiting officers may draw bills at the rate of £40 at a time for each Field Officer, or Captain, and £20 at a time for each subaltern. When the first sums so drawn are expended, or nearly so, an account of the expenditure must be sent to the said Captain Finlason, who will from time to time honour such farther bills as may be drawn during the continuance of the recruiting, on receiving the accounts of the expenditure of the former sums, and finding they are regularly conducted, and intitled to approbation.

6. Returns agreeable to the annexed form to be sent to the Commanding Officer at Head-Quarters every Monday, signed by the Officers commanding at the respective recruiting quarters.

7. It is strongly recommended to the officers to pay all possible attention to the health and morals of their recruits, by keeping them clean, sober and orderly, and enjoining their being attentive to a regular and wholesome diet, either in messes, or boarded, and discountenancing riots and disputes with inhabitants or parties of other Corps.

8. To initiate the recruits in discipline and regularity, they should, from the earliest period, be directed to parade twice (if not thrice) every day, punctually, at certain specified hours of roll-calling; where the officers as well as non-commissioned officers in the respective quarters of course will attend and inspect the appearance and good behaviour of their men.

Lastly, all possible exertion on the part of the recruiting officer is requested; and those who are most successful shall be considered accordingly in classing them by seniority, in their several ranks, when the regiment is compleat and their commissions are made out. The proportion of numbers to be levied by the officers in their several ranks is expected to be as follows, *viz.*, 75 by each Field Officer, 50 by each Captain, 25 by each Lieutenant, and 15 by each Ensign.

The officers are directed to publish the very favourable terms on which this regiment is formed, and the full and unquestionable security the men will individually receive, that they are never to quit their native country, the event of an invasion on England excepted, which obligation authentically vouched by his Grace, will be delivered to each recruit on his being attested and passed.

P.S. It is recommended to such Officers as have acquaintance with officers in the army, to endeavour to procure from the marching regiments two or more Corporals fit to be made Serjeants, and two or more Privates fit to be made Corporals.

In putting forward these instructions, the Duke reduced Buccleuch's rhetoric to the simple statement that the Regiment was raised for "the loyal and spirited purpose of protection to the North of Scotland." That was a very plain issue, but the difficulties encountered in getting men clearly show that this significance was largely lost on his tenantry. The imminent danger which faced the country drained of its troops for America, and the threat of invasion from France which followed the coalition, gave intense anxiety to statesmen and induced something like panic in all the dwellers in the coast towns, who scanned the horizon daily for signs of a hostile sail. It can easily be understood, however, that the same terror did not affect the people living in the remote glens of which the Duke was over-lord. There were other deterrents of a more practical nature which impeded his progress. In the first place, the country had been drained dry by previous recruiting projects. Indeed, it had been squeezed to such an extent that agriculture seemed destined to come to a standstill for lack of hands. Thus, John Macpherson writing to Ross on June 6, declared that he had not a single man servant :—"They are so scarce in the country," he wrote, "that I have no more prospect of being accommodated at this time."

A remarkable picture of the situation is drawn by the Rev. Robert Macpherson, parish minister of Aberarder, Inverness-shire, to whom the Duke applied for help as "the oracle and adviser of the whole clan." The Macphersons had long been difficult to deal with, for if the noble house of Gordon was their over-lord in the legal sense, they had never regarded it as their chief in any clan sense. First, the kindred clan Mackintosh had given difficulty, because the promise of the lordship of Badenoch by Morton in 1572 had not been implemented. The situation became complicated by the dispute in 1672 between Andrew Macpherson of Cluny and Lachlan Mackintosh for the chieftainship of the Clan Chattan. The ennobled Gordons had wobbled and pleased neither party, the vendetta being viciously pourtrayed in Æneas Macpherson's polemic, "The Loyall Dissuasive." When the Duke of Gordon, feeling unequal to the difficulties of the case, put Gordon of Glenbucket into the baillieship of Badenoch, and gave him a wadset there, the Macphersons almost assassinated the old man in 1724, and practically drove him back to Donside, so that Alexander Pennecuik lashed them with a doggerel whip :—

> May that accursèd clan up by the roots be pluckéd,
> Whose impious hands have killed the great Glenbucket !

The immense power of the Macphersons is shown by the intervention of the old Chevalier in this particular case, for he felt that if the Duke of Gordon went on pursuing Glenbucket's assailants, the Clan Macpherson would not rally to the ducal banner in the coming Jacobite attempt. As an example of the delicate way in which the Macphersons had to be handled, one has only to note a statement by Charles Gordon of Braid and Cluny, who, writing to the Duke of Gordon's people from Edinburgh, May 13, 1778, said :—" I find there are about 150 Highlanders of the Duke of Hamilton's Regiment chiefly mustered by the Macphersons. They have declared they would never put on breeches, and are left behind, in order to be, it is supposed, the ffoundation of additional companies."

The Gordons had not learned their lesson in handling the Macphersons, for when William Todd, the Duke's factor, wrote on behalf of his Grace's corps to the minister of Aberarder, he hinted at what would be expected of the Macphersons "upon this occasion," and what would be the "consequences of their not exerting themselves." Whereupon, the minister replied (April 6, 1778) in a remarkable letter, which may be regarded as the *locus classicus* of the great recruiting campaign of the period in the north (*Gordon Castle Papers*):—

I am perfectly of your opinion that neither the honour of the country nor attachment to the Duke of Gordon can easily procure a decent number of Volunteers in this country for his Grace's Fensible Regiment. The Duke will therefore have, seemingly, great reason to complain of his tenants in this country, and it will confirm the prejudices he already appears to have, unhappily, conceived against them.

Clunie's and Captain Duncan Breckachie son's success in recruiting two years ago, and the number lately levied by officers from this country for the Hamilton Regiment and other new corps, will rivet the belief that our fault will proceed more from the want of inclination and attachment than the want of ability or power to raise men at this time for his Grace's Regiment. However, I beg leave to observe that when the two first-mentioned companies were raised, the country was full of people, and the times were so bad that many of them were starving, or obliged to go to the Low Country to serve as labourers. The two gentlemen, Ralea and Captain Duncan Breckachie, who conducted that recruiting, were indefatigably active. The principal tacksmen and gentlemen, tho' they could give them no assistance, lay by, and allowed every art to be used to inveigle and entrap every man that could be most easily spared. Emissaries were sent to the Low Country, who soon picked up all the natives of this that had straggled thither. A dozen clever fellows, being thus once engaged in a cause, which at that time appeared the less allarming from the frequent emigration to America which immediately preceded it, soon infused a proper spirit into others. The recruiting their complement became no arduous task. Indeed, the emulation at that time between the several clans engaged (who should first make out their complement of men) had its weight with the common people. I can positively affirm that there was not a gentleman in this country except Captain John Bellachroan, for a week or two in the beginning, who took an active concern for Cluny and still less for Breckachie's son upon that occasion: nor, if they had, would it have answered any good purpose.

The spirit of clanship has absolutely ceased, as to its more important consequences, all over the Highlands, and more especially in this country. The principal heads of families have very much fallen off for their circumstances, and proportionable to that is the decrease of their influence among the common people. These, again, are now happily aiming at independence, and trust to their own industry and protection of the law more than to the precarious support formerly afforded them

M

by their demagogues or heads of tribes. The only instance where gentlemen interfered in Clunie's recruiting soon convinced them of their folly and of the change of spirit among the people : and Ralea soon discovered that the only way for this gentleman was to take no seeming concern, but to leave him to follow his own measures.

Captain Maxwell's success here [in raising 67 men for the Fraser Highlanders in 1775], tho' so powerfully recommended [by his sister, Jane Maxwell, Duchess of Gordon], can be easily accounted for from what I have already observed. The gentlemen and principal tacksmen had, really, little or nothing in their power. There was no person appeard at the time in the country for him, to take upon him the horrid drudgery of drinking whisky and to act the recruiting serjeant among the people. Besides, the few remaining sparks of clanship had, by that time, been kindled into a flame, which, with their sympathy for Clunie's misfortunes, made them enlist with their Chieftan in preference to all mankind. But the fit did not last long. It was truly fortunate for him that his preferment did not depend upon his success in the recruiting, as was once expected at this time. As to the last recruiting we had in this country I need say nothing. You know perfectly well how little credit was due on that occasion to the active concern and influence of our Gentlemen. The all-powerful influence of whisky, uncommon address, to give it no worse name, and the lucky circumstance of your being detained for some time in the Low Country, after the recruiting began, rendered Captain John Bellachroan's and other officers' indefaticable and persevering industry very nearly effectual in raising their complement of men. Yet the half of them were not of this country. Poor passengers and men picked up in other parts of the Highlands and Low Lands composed the bulk of the *kind* of recruits they brought to the Hamilton Corps.

Though the condition to which we are already reduced for want of servants and labourers is deplorable, yet I wish you clearly [to] see that private interest as well as our credit and honour should, upon this occasion, powerfully stimulate us to promote the recruiting in support of his Grace's Patriotic Plan. And it is my opinion that the most effectual method will be that which was practised two years ago in recruiting for Cluny—that two Gentlemen of address and character should be pitched upon, one in each end of the country. The whole executive power should be devolved on these : that all the tacksmen should be called to a meeting and separately required to give up upon oath, if found necessary, the name of every man of bad fame or even ambiguous character in the several parishes, and such other hands as could be most easily spared. The feuars should be applyed to for the same purpose. When the list is made out, the recruiting gentlemen should cause all these to be apprehended, *brevi manu*, and if any interfere to protect them these and only these should become obnoxious to his Grace, and be made to feel the weight of his resentment. It would be unfair to execute a general and undistinguishing vengeance upon a number of people whose greatest failure will, I maintain, be occasioned by their poverty, and, consequently, their want of influence over their former dependents and followers.

Distressed as we really are for want of servants, I am possitive, if the country was well sifted, it might still supply his Grace with a decent number of recruits without much injury to the honest industrious farmers.

Volunteers need hardly be expected. The danger is too remote to raise any apprehensions in the common people of the country's being attacked by a foreign enemy. It is of little consequence what the Gentlemen may think in regard to it; unless they take up arms and engage in the cause, they will not be believed. The people have been successfully deceived since the middle of the last war by all the recruiting officers and their friends. It has constantly been, since that period, the common cant that the recruits were only enlisted for three years, or during a continuance of the war. Yet, they saw or heard of these poor men being draughted into other regiments after their own was reduced, and thus bound for life, instead of the time that they were made to believe. This was a deceit practised more than ever in raising the late levies; but it has now little effect. Nor will it have much where it ought to have it. The people will not be convinced, not even by giving them written obligations that the Fensible Regiments will not be draughted or kept up longer than till the war is over. They have been so often cheated that they scarce know whom to trust. I have already been using my best endeavours with some of them. Their answer was that for any difference they saw between one regiment and another, they never would take a guinea of levy money from any man, and refuse twenty and even thirty which the Duke of Athole and others are presently offering to good recruits: and that, for any thing they know, the promises of the one may be equally depended upon with that of the other in respect to the time of their service.

Some such plan as I have proposed must, I suspect, be followed both in this country and Lochaber. Indeed, the tenants in that country have much the advantage of us here. I am well informed there were only sixteen men carryed away from his Grace's Lochaber estate to the new levies, and not nearly that number about two years ago [for the Fraser Highlanders]. We have been drained in this country at those two periods, and in the interval of them, of some more than two hundred to his Majesty's service.

Mr. Macpherson's views were actually put into force in the shape of an "Act for the more Easy and Better Recruiting of His Majesty's

Land Forces and Marine" (18 Geo. III. cap. 53, passed in 1777-8; repealed by 19 Geo. III., cap. 10), known for short as the Comprehending Act. It might well have been called the Apprehending Act, for it was absolutely compulsive in its methods. It divided suitable recruits into three classes:—

1. VOLUNTEERS.—Men who entered the service of their own accord before May Day, 1779, came under this category. Each Volunteer received £3 by way of bounty, and could claim discharge at the end of three years' service.

2. LOAFERS.—"All able-bodied, idle, and indifferent persons who cannot, upon examination, prove themselves to exercise and industriously follow some lawful trade or employment, or to have some substance sufficient for their support and maintenance," could be impressed.

3. SMUGGLERS.—"Any fit and able person who shall be convicted of running goods to the value of not exceeding 40s." could be enlisted in lieu of punishment.

No person with a Parliamentary vote could be taken, and harvest hands were exempted from May to October on obtaining a certificate. No person under 17 and over 45 years of age was eligible, and none under 5 ft. 4 ins. "without shoes."

The officials charged with carrying out the Act were various local authorities. They were summoned by the High Sheriffs in England and by the Sheriffs in Scotland on a mandate from the War Secretary. Churchwardens and specially-appointed constables were then chosen, who had power to search for and apprehend the type of persons enumerated by the Act, and then to bring them before a Justice of the Peace, who could lodge them in jail if necessary. The persons thus apprehended were then forwarded to the Commissioners for approval; the last stage of all being the handing over the persons so approved to the military authorities on certain payments. The inhabitants of any parish were bound to assist, a bounty of 10s. accruing to any parishioner who apprehended a man.

The Act came just in time for the Duke of Gordon as he recruited for his Northern Fencibles, but, as he found difficulty in grasping its details, he sought the advice of the Lord Advocate, who took a different view of its provisions from that adopted by the Commander-in-Chief in Scotland, Sir James Adolphus Oughton, once described by Boswell as "a man of boundless curiosity and unusual diligence." As Sir James's interpretation was the one probably followed, his letter to the Duke, dated Edinburgh, July 1, 1778, may be quoted (*Gordon Castle Papers*):—

My Lord,—In order to put in execution the Act passed in last session of Parliament for the more Easy and Better Recruiting His Majesty's Land Forces and Marines, Your Grace is immediately to order 13 Officers of the Regiment under your Command to repair to the Towns [sic]:—1. Kincardine; 3. Aberdeen; 3. Inverness; 1. Banff; 1. Caithness and Sutherland; 2. Ross and Cromarty; 1. Elgin and Nairn; 1. Forfar—where they are to apply to the Sheriff-Depute or Substitute, to know the days and districts named by the Commissioners, for putting the Act in force, which they are regularly to attend, and to make weekly returns to the Adjutant-General of North Britain, of the raised, as per the Form in the Act of Parliament.

For every Volunteer you are to pay £3 that comes of his own accord and inlists; and for every man declared a Volunteer by the Commissioners, after being apprehended by the constables, £3 and 20s. to the constables for their trouble, and 2s. to the clerk.

To every impressed man 20s. as expenses to the constables and 2s. to the clerk, and a sum not less than 10s. and not exceeding 40s. to the parish.

Every man fit for service, as expressed in the Act, you are to receive, but upon no account to take men incapable of His Majesty's service.

No officer at his peril to offer a man cited to appear before the Commissioners more than £3, on any pretence whatever, and no Fencible to offer above a guinea and a crown. If any does, he shall be brought to a general court martial and tried for disobedience of orders.

The officers of the Fencible Regiments now raising in North Britain are only to give a guinea and a crown to each Volunteer, and cannot be entitled to any of the impressed men.

Every Volunteer to have it in his option to go to the Fencible Corps at a guinea and a crown or to the Marching Regiments at £3, as he chooses, before the Commissioners begin their examination, but after the examination he cannot be received as a Volunteer, if adjudged within the law.

As there are few officers in North Britain at present to attend the different districts that may be appointed to meet, Sir Adolphus Oughton recommends to the officers of the Marching Regiments and Fencibles to be aspiring to one another in the execution of this service, and the officers are to beg of the Commissioners to regulate their meetings in such a way as one or two of them can attend every meeting, especially where the Regular Regiments and Fencible Regiments interfere.

N.B. for Volunteers.—The Fencibles must pay the 20s. to the constables likewise if apprehended by them.

A meeting of the Justices of the Peace and Commissioners of Supply was held at Aberdeen on July 29, 1778, convened by the Sheriff for putting the Act into execution, when the county was divided into eight districts, which, with the dates of the sittings of the Commissioners, were as follows :—

Kirkwood of Crimond	- - - - -	August 10, 17.
Ellon - - - -	- - - - -	„ 11, 18.
Kincardine - -	- - - - -	„ 10, 17.
Boat of Forbes - -	- - - - -	„ 11, 18.
Aberdeen - - -	- - - - -	„ 10, 17.
Craigsley - -	- - - - -	„ 12, 19.
Turriff - - -	- - - - -	„ 13, 20.
Huntly - - -	- - - - -	„ 15, 21.

As a type of the mandate issued to a constable, one may quote the precept sent to Arthur Sivewright (great grandfather of Sir James Sivewright), who was the constable for the parish of Bellie (*Ibid.*) :—

We, the Commissioners subscribing, do hereby command and require you Arthur Siveright, Constable named and appointed for the Parish of Belly, that you furthwith pass and make dilligent search within the said parish, for all able bodied, idle, and disorderly persons, who do not exercise and industriously follow some lawful trade or employment, and who have no subsistence sufficient for their support and maintenance, who are free from ruptures and every other bodily disability, who are not under the age of seventeen, nor above forty five years old, and who are not under the size of five feet four inches without shoes : all which persons you are desired to bring before us or any three or more of the Commissioners of the Elgin district upon the 20th day of August current, at a meeting then to be held within the Town house of Elgin in Elgin. On the execution of which service you are hereby empowered to call for the assistance of all the inhabitants within the said parish ; but with certification that if you willingly neglect your duty herein, you will be fined, imprisoned, and punished as the law directs. Given under our hand at Elgin the sixth day of August, 1778 years.

ARTHUR DUFF.
WILLIAM GORDON.
WILLIAM BRODIE.

It would seem as if some of the officers engaged in raising Fencible regiments declined to avail themselves of the Act. Among these was Lord Frederick Campbell, who thought it " beneath the idea of Fencibles to incorporate Comprehensibles with them." Recording this decision to the Duke of Gordon, Charles Gordon of Braid wrote to his Grace on July 11, 1778, as follows (*Ibid.*):—

I understand he is mighty anxious to get ahead of your Grace. I hope in this he will be disappointed ; but, as I understand your Grace is now scrupulously nice on the quality of your Fencibles, might it not be proper, in the view of being just compleated, to reserve your weeding until you have supernumeraries?

The Duke, himself, had some of Campbell's scruples, for he wrote on July 5 :—

It will be no disappointment to me if I don't get such men as may be adjudged under the authority of the Comprehending Act. Hitherto I have none but real volunteers, and my wish is not to admit any other into my corps.

There is ample evidence that the Act was not popular with the authorities, and many little difficulties cropped up. Major Mercer, for example, had a strong objection to a recruiting sergeant named Gunn, who had been appointed by the Duke's uncle, Lord Adam Gordon, to attend the meeting of officers engaged in carrying out the provisions of the Act. Mercer describes Gunn (July 19, 1778) as "the most consummate recruiting hero of the age," adding, as if to keep up his reputation as a scholar:—"I do not believe that Julius Cæsar would be a match for Serjeant Gun at the drum head." At Aberdeen on August 17, no men were brought before the Commissioners.

Captain A. P. Cumming of Gordonstoun thought (July 26) that the gentlemen of Elgin should "engage in their business with more spirit than at present they seem inclined to do," and he was, "hurt at their being so lukewarm." Elgin was divided into three districts. "'Twill be necessary," wrote Cumming on the same occasion, "a great number of Constables shou'd be made by way of showing we are in earnest."

Then there was the rivalry of different gentlemen recruiting different corps. At the meeting in Huntly, August 15, Gordon of Craig "expressed some words that Leith-hall," who was interested in the raising of the 81st regiment, "took exception at, which caused the company to break up very abruptly." Leith-hall, wrote William Bell of Coclarachie, "seemed to carry the matter, I thought, very high. I wish there may not be a challenge in the case." In some cases the "comprehended" were divided. Thus at Craigsley on August 20, one of three men was handed over to Captain Leith for the 81st; two others went to Lieutenant Mowat on behalf of the Duke's Fencibles. Mowat tells us that

At Huntly [on August 22] there were three men brought before the Commissioners; but upon examination were not found to come within the description of the Act of Parliament, and therfore were released. The Provost of Aberdeen ordered one, Donaldson, to be taken up, who afterwards inlisted with him for us [the Northern Fencibles].

Notwithstanding the help suggested by the Comprehending Act, the Duke had to fall back on the bounty, though several of his correspondents felt that it was too small. Indeed, it seems to have increased, for the Forsyths of Huntly, writing on May 22, speak of £2 1s. allowed by the Duke for recruits. Alexander Baillie writing from Cradlehall on April 30, declared that the very high bounty, which had drained his part of the country, would have an effect, "which will be severely felt by all recruiting officers for some time to come." A practical experience of this prophecy is given by Alexander Milne, Drumin, who writing on May 3 relates the result of a meeting he called in Deskrie public house (*Gordon Castle Papers*):—

When a little warmed, the greater part of them declared their strongest attachment to His Grace, and would do all in their power to promote his honour that way; and severalls of them proposes to go with me to wait on His Grace, and also goes with me to Tomantoul upon Tuesday first in order to shew their zeal, attachment and readyness to follow His Grace in any station he was pleased to appoint them; but at the same time complained of the smallness of the enlisting money as our country had greater aversion to recruiting or recruiting parties.

Very much the same feeling was experienced by Lieutenant Godsman, who, writing from Dunain, May 3, said (*Ibid.*):—

I have made proposalls to those nearest at hand, who I thought might be induced to enter into the service; but when they are informed of the bounty money they broke off further treaty. . . . This part of the country has been the seat of recruiting for this long while past, and the officers have been very often obliged to give such extravagant bounty money that the idea of receiving great sums cannot be defaced from the minds of the people.

Nor did this inducement end with mere money payment. Recruits constantly insisted on a *quid pro quo* in the shape of an advantage in their leases, or some other benefit, and the wheedling by whisky was practically universal. A case in which both factors operated was that of John Gordon in Auchmair in the Cabrach, who told his story in a petition to the Duke (*Ibid.*):—

That about three weeks ago when your Grace was at Hardhaugh, your petitioner attended there as the rest in the country did. He must acknowledge that your Grace used him very kindly. But after he had got himself a little in liquor, Mr. Bell plyed him verry hard to inlist, being informed that he had served for some years in the last French war. At last, he offered to serve your Grace as his chief, upon condition that he would get his ffather's tack at the expiry therof without any hight [sic] or grassome: and that he should be entred as a sergeant. But this Mr. Bell sayed that your Grace could not do, as there were too many sergeants already promised, but that your petitioner should get a letter of tack upon his ffather's possession, be entered as a corporall, and the first sergeant that hapned to be broke in the regiment he should be sure of his place. Your petitioner must plainly tell your Grace that he was so much overtaken with liquor that he does not particularly remember what after hapned—which he now greatly repents. That your petitioner presently possesses a reasonable possession, and, thank God, is in verry good circumstances, and had no occassion to enter into the Army. Besides, he has a verry well behaved discreet woman to his wife, a gentleman's daughter, who by his late bad conduct and behaviour has done her more hurt than possibly she will ever recover: and, therefore, if your Grace will not appoint him a sergeant, he is determined not to go into your regiment as a privat man, be the consequence what it will. Therefor, he beggs your Grace will take his case to your consideration, and either appoint him a sergeant, or allow him the same pay, or dispense with him alltogether.

This may be the John Gordon, concerning whom Major Mercer writes from Elgin on August 9 (*Ibid.*):—

Gordon, who refuses to do the duty of a private man, was confined about half an hour ago. He has just sent word to me that he will fall into the ranks if his Grace will give him an obligation in writing that he shall have the farm which his father once had upon the demise of the present possessor. I only mention this circumstance to show you what a dog the fellow is. I think he should certainly be tried and punished.

John Stuart offered his services (July 24) on condition that the Duke gave his father, Charles, and his brother full possession of Bachonish and Badgaish against Whitsunday, his father farming only half of Bachonish.

Sometimes the conditions were made by tenants who promised to get recruits. James Cameron writes from Kinrara, July 11, that

N

There is an honest namesake of mine possess'd of one of the Knocks of Kincardine. He is doing his best to get a man for the Duke, but has hitherto been unsuccessfull. I frequently hear that he is to be dispossess'd of his farm. I well know that I am not entitled to ask favours (for myself or another): yet, my anxiety for my poor namesake has made me muster up resolution to begg a singular favour, if convenient, to let me know what is to be the fate of this same Cameron.

The Camerons were not "blate," for James Cameron, younger of Kinlochleven, wrote in May (*Ibid.*):—

If your Grace will give me the farm of Kilmanivaig and Brackletter for five years, I can furnish your Grace two handsome men to-morrow. I would be glad to give my assistance to your Grace without those terms, but, as it is not in my power to accomodate the freinds of those who go, I am oblidged to ask these, as I [have] no lands of my own.

There were cases when a man bargained for his rank. Thus Donald McBain from Bon-naughton "spoke" to going into the ranks on condition of being appointed a sergeant and getting a new lease of his farm. Another case was that of Donald McDonald. On June 15 he had been sent by Lieutenant Godsman with a letter to Ross asking the latter to give him all encouragement "as he was teaching a school before, and is capable of writting, compting, and teaching of both languages." Ross was in Aberdeen when McDonald arrived at Fochabers; so he was taken by Ross's clerk to the Duchess. She advised him to enlist, which he did; but he petitioned the Duke to give him a better position than that of a "single soldier only."

The conciliation of the women had also to be taken into account. For instance, the Rev. Alexander Cameron, Findron, wrote to Ross, on September 28, that a woman from Corgarff, who had three handsome sons in the Fencibles and who was totally destitute in consequence of their absence, wanted a croft in the Findron neighbourhood. He adds that he "gloried" that of his "small congregation," 16 and 17 had 'listed, "which in my narrow sphere I did all in my power to promote." A peculiar case was that of Duncan Campbell, who entered as a volunteer upon account of Mrs. Todd. He had occupied a pendicle with his brother at the east end of Garvabegg. A Mrs. Clark, who had the principal tack and possessed the other end, was so angry at his 'listing instead of entering her service that she threatened his brother-in-law "with the utmost severity of oppression." Campbell petitioned Ross to get his pendicle in his own name and that of his brother-in-law. This was not a solitary case of danger threatening a recruit in his absence: Duncan McGregor had 'listed on the understanding that he was to have the fourth part of the farm of Blairacuran in Lochaber. But in his absence he found that it had been "set upon by two young lowse lads," and he petitioned Ross, July 18, to restore his rights.

The Duke on his part frequently gave his recruits written obligations. For instance he wrote to a man, June 2 (*Ibid.*):—

As you have just now furnished me with five men for my regiment of Fencible men, I hereby promise and engage that, at the end of James McBarnet's lease upon the farm of Kyllichownet and Inachan at Whitsunday, 1784, you shall be put in possession of the same with the usual sheallings. . . . In the meantime . . . . I have ordered you to be put in possession of the farm of Auchacharr and the grazing of Craigguanach for six years.

Here is another more formal obligation, signed by the Duke at Drumin, July 11 (*Ibid.*):—

In respect William Stewart, son of the deceased Donald Stewart in Mains of Achriachan, has frankly entered as a volunteer in my regiment, and that he is connected with several respectable people in my estate of Strathaven, I hereby promise that when the current leases expire, I shall give him a preference upon equal terms to some farm in that estate of equal extent, as may be suitable to the circumstances, providing he behaves himself properly so long as he continues in my regiment.

A natural feature of the recruiting of farming folk was the demand they made to get off at harvest time. Cosmo Gordon, a recruit from Glenlivet, who had left no one on his croft but his fifteen-year-old daughter, sent a petition from Fort George on September 7 (*Ibid.*):—

I hope yo'll consider my circumstance, as I have my crop without any mankind to take care of it. I have my cattle at the same time as ever I had, for I did not dispose of anything I had for this year; but, plase God, it shall not be so another year the same way. In the mine time, I'm affraid that his Grace has forgot me. It sinks my heart much in the time, and I hop in God his Grace shall never allow me to wear this common regementels no more at present.

On the very same date, September 7, William Macpherson in sending some men from Invereshie begged Major Mercer to look after them (*Ibid.*):—

As all of them have some cattle to look after in the country and some of their parents are poor farmers who would require the assistance of their sons at some seasons in the year, I flatter myself that they will be indulged with as frequent and long furloughs as the service will permit.

Charles Stewart, Drumin, writes to Ross, September 22, that Thomas Cruikshank's wife is his " daily stranger [sic], wanting him to return for a few weeks to help her to shear their puckle corn."

The familiarity of the tenants towards the Duke was a relic of the old feeling of loyalty towards the chief which still lingered in spite of the Rev. Robert Macpherson's pessimistic outlook. Thus we find Lieutenant Godsman writing (May 3) that the Duke's own presence on the different parts of his estate would " make the business go on most successfully." Alexander Macpherson, writing on May 9 from Fort William, says that the people " in general " expressed the desire " of offering their services to the Duke personally rather than any other way " : and Baillie Macpherson wrote that a hundred men might be got in Lochaber, " provided the Duke was to appear in person to demand them." A similar expression of opinion appears in a letter which Captain George Mackay of Bighouse wrote to the Duke on August 13 (*Ibid.*) :—

The people in this country are so much attached to their masters that with them they do not scruple going to any distant country. But I was afraid, should I send a part of the men away and I do not go with them . . . . they would take it in there heads they were to be sent to other regiments, and not to your Grace's ; which would occasion a great stagnation in my recruiting.

On August 14 (so great was the urgency of the case), he wrote to Ross (*Ibid.*) :—

I am certain, was I to send any men from this country and I not go with them, as they are unexperienced as yet with any kind of discipline, it would put a totale stope to my geting any more men in the North to his Grace's Regiment.

Captain Lachlan McIntosh writes on similar lines from Craighouse, June 27 (*Ibid*) :—

I must particularly beg that your Grace will not call for any of my recruits till such time as I am compleat, in any event nearly so : otherwise, my success in the recruiting would totally be at an end, as still the country people entertain strong doubts of my at all intending going alongst with them myself : so that ordering my men out of the country untill I am called for wou'd confirm them in such opinion, and consequently prevent my getting a single man: and the more so, as your Grace is sensible how much this country is already drained of men.

The same spirit of recognition of chieftainship comes out in a letter which Angus McDonell wrote from Inch to Ross on July 8, thanking him and the Duke for looking after his son when the latter was ill (*Ibid.*):—

May heaven reward his Grace for his humanity and condescension in taking such notice of him. It was really very great and noble. Believe, his Grace's goodness on that occation has laid me under the greatest obligation: so much [so], that if I can get the mother to agree to my sending another son under the Duke's banner, I will send him with the greatest pleasure. But this is what I cannot immediately propose to her considering her present grief.

If these Highlanders were grateful, there is clear proof that their services were appreciated, their presence giving certain distinction and character to a corps. Thus we find Charles Gordon (of Braid?) writing to the Duke from Edinburgh, on July 6 (*Ibid.*):—

I wish your Grace had found room for the Camerons and Macphersons. They were generally great feathers in the wings of your family, and Lochiel in all probability will soon have what formerly belonged to his predecessors. Your Grace will have full credit for any exertion made by such auxiliarys as parts of your natural following: whereas, such a potentate as McEssic, who knew how to make the most of every part of his consequence, may be apt to make his own account with the publick.

So much from the vassals' point of view: but just as they bargained with his Grace, so the Duke, or his representatives, used his power as landlord to bring pressure to bear on the tenants. Of this there is ample evidence in several very interesting letters. Thus Alexander Cameron, Letterfinlay, writes, July 29, about the case of one Alexander Breck:—

I hope he had not the assurance to tell that he did it [enlist] willingly. To the contrary, it was with the outmost compulsion I offered him twice in your presence to engage and I wou'd continue him upon the same ffooting with the rest of the subtenants of the Lo[rds]h[i]p. I repeated[ly], times thereafter, endeavoured to prevail with him. His return always was a fflat denyall; upon which, I have sett his lands to other people and threatned to eject him instantly:. which was the only cause that induced him to go to serve.

In the same spirit Todd, of Ruthven, had indicated to the Rev. Robert Macpherson " what would be expected of the Macphersons," and "what would be the consequences of their not exerting themselves ": while Ross wrote to Captain Mackintosh, July 22 (*Ibid.*):—

Tho' I do not doubt but next post may bring a compleat return of your complement of 50, yet I flatter myself you think it incumbent upon you to make a proper compensation of several men you have got, who would have come the Duke's way, if you had not been in the play. And besides, I imagine your father and you would not chuse to be behind with your neighbours, Invereshie and Benchar, who, tho' not concerned in the regiment, are bestirring themselves to raise recruits for the Duke upon this occasion. Don't suspect me of joking on this subject.

It was, indeed, nearly impossible that a laird in recruiting should resist bullying methods, for the State had placed in his hand various schemes, notably the Comprehending Act, for putting on the thumb-screw, so that as Bell of Coclarachie wrote (May 18) that the people in his part of the country were in " a kind of panic, imagining they were to be laid hands upon." Although the Duke declared his dislike of the Act as a method of recruiting for the Northern Fencibles, men were brought to him under its provisions. Even in Aberdeen itself, which was out of the Duke's direct jurisdiction, and where the " Devil " had "got into the fellows," Lieutenant Finlason told Ross (July 26) that " a number of them begin to shake now that they see the Press Act over their heads." Lieutenant John Spens of the Black Watch wrote on September 24, that he had been in Orkney and received the "impressed men." He got William Taylor to go to the Duke's regiment, handing him over to Lieutenant Sutherland, Dunbeath. On July 21, Macpherson of Invereshie offered the Duke a deserter from the Black Watch itself. Here is an example where the Comprehending Act was recommended. Robert Willox wrote from Gaulrig, August 26 (*Ibid.*):—

There is one Robert Cruickshank from this countree that listed with Braehead. What made him list was in order to proteck his son from being a shogeer. The son is a very handsome recruit. Three years ago I mett him hunting and took his gun, which I delivered to the Duke of Gordon. The fellow thought to shut [shoot] me, and brunt priming at my breast. I think this brings him within the Comprehending Act. If you think proper, I shall cause apprehend him and send him to his Grace's regiment.

On August 22, Bell of Coclarachie wrote to Ross about another case (*Ibid.*):—

There is one James Gray in Collithie will be brought before the [Comprehending Act] Commissioners for taking the Duke's birk wood in Tulliminate, taken in the act by John Pirie, the forester. He is an ill tongued fellow, and I hope you will insist against him. He will pretend lameness, but Dr. Shand said he might be a sudier [soldier]. Also John Wright for taking wood this summer; proved by William Malcom in Greenhaugh. There is one Walker also for cutting wood some years ago, accused by Captain Leith, whom he attempted to strike with the ax when he took him cutting the wood. There is one Stewart taken up in Mill-hill. He has a bad character and the country, almost in one voice, want to be clear of him. The particular matter against him is stealing peats. William Martin was in the hands of the constable, one you know. These are the men that ought to be made examples of in the first place.

Several cases of acts of this kind appear. The Duke himself caught five men—James Morison, James Hay, Alexander Forbes, and Thomas Morison all in Nether Dallachy, and Peter Scott in Achinhalrig—in the act of pilfering his potatoes (November 20). Instead of prosecuting them, he gave them the option of choosing one of their number for the Fencibles. They agreed to draw lots: each of the other four agreeing to pay to the one chosen the sum of 25s. over and above the Duke's bounty. Lieutenant Shaw wrote, July 27, that there were " severals in Badenoch and on Deeside that has been in constant use of killing your Grace's deer that the country could well spare; a list of whom I shall send to your Grace, if agreeable."

The Act sometimes defeated itself through the over-zealousness of those who put it into practice. A case is brought out by Ross, who complained (August 14) to William Milne, factor, Braehead, that the constables had brought in men who would not have been adjudged had they been brought to trial (*Ibid.*):—

I am afraid this will have a bad effect on the recruiting in Strathaven and Glenlivet, and am therefore laid under the disagreeable necessity of desiring you to take another jaunt into these countrys in order to do something that may tend to rouse such of the people as are thought fittest for entering the military life.

What I wish is that you go there the beginning of next week, and, after informing yourself from the Gentlemen who know the characters and circumstances of the people best, that you cause the constables to apprehend one or two persons who really fall within the description of the Act; whom I would have kept in custody and brought before the Commissioners. Nor would I be sorry that one was actually adjudged and delivered over to a marching regiment, as I'm persuaded it would have a great effect upon others, who presently keep off, in hopes that they will not be disturbed or at most only forced to enter with the Fencibles at last. At the same time I have no objection to your endeavouring to frighten others, who, tho' not falling literally within the description of the Act, may be well spared from the country; of whom I imagine there are many; and I shall be glad that Ensign [William] Gordon of Minmore get the benefit of these operations.

While you are in that country, I beg you will get me exact and certain intelligence of the characters and circumstances of the people who granted bills for the wood penalties, because such of them as are not able to pay and are fit for being Fencibles ought to inlist accordingly; and others of them in better circumstances who do not furnish men must lay their account with paying directly.

The recruiting officers found difficulty in administering the Act through the opposition of the women relatives of its victims. An exciting experience is recounted from Inverness on October 9, by Lieutenant Shaw (*Ibid.*):—

The Constables, assisted by me and two of my men, apprehended one McBean, a residenter on McIntosh's estate. He is a remarkable stoute fellow and his conduct plainly brings him within the description of the Press Act. But, as no other supporter of irregularities could then be had, and notwithstanding McBean's being of the laird of McIntosh's people, Captain John Dow McPherson's lady appear'd on [sic] the head of upwards of sixty men and women with staves and stones sufficient to attact Tingal himself. Their Godess declar'd McBean should not move a step further, and all said in the words of the Ephesians that blessed was the words of their Diana. I behaved with all possible politeness to her, being a woman, and though she had a bad cause; but the sacrament had been that day administered to her; her violence led her so far as to call me an eternal scounderal etc.! I should have made her bow, but, being so unexpectedly attacted, an ungarded spark kindled in my breast that led me to tell her that none but an ill bred hissie durst tell me so; you know she is Uire's [?] own daughter. However the Justices was under a necessity to interfeer. McBean's tryall commenced and, as the proof will come out cleare against him, he will be worth some three to the Duke.

All this pressure told not merely on the people and through them on the Duke, but the opposition of rival recruiting projects impinged even more severely upon him.   Besides the competition of his kinsman, the laird of Fyvie, the Duke had to face the fascinations of the Atholl and Hamilton Regiments, for the latter of which Lieutenant John Macpherson (formerly Ensign in the 6th Regiment) had raised 45 men, two of them from the Duke's estates.   Lieutenant John Grant in Rippachie, writing Ross on July 12, gives a typical instance (*Ibid.*):—

Two light-head fellows, fine recruits, servants of my own, on Friday last at the fair of Tarland, has [sic] it seems, been tampering with some recruiting party, who pretends to have given them money, but which they deny receiving.   They offered the smart in due time, but it was refused.

On July 13, James Grant writes from Tomintoul (*Ibid.*):—

As I was passing by Tomintoull, I enterfeired with a young lad, who declared to me before Glenbucket and severall oyrs that he was willing to goe volanteir to serve his Grace without taking money for to goe for any oyr man whatever.   James Cameron in Billanlish had been offerring him money for to goe for him.   Glenbucket and I enterfeired for the young lad's goeing volentier to his Grace, which the lad agreed to before all that was present.

Lieutenant John Rose, of Calder's Company, wrote to the Duke from Nairn, July 5, that the express he had sent to McDonnell younger of Barrisdale with the beating order had been "trepanned" and made a soldier for the McDonnell Regiment.

Perhaps the Duke, himself, was not free from blame.   At anyrate, James Macgregor wrote to Ross from Pittyvaich on July 31 that a part of his Grace's recruits had carried off one of Lord Fife's tenants "in a forcible manner," and he complained specially of Sergeant Charles Gordon.

Coming to the normal conditions of recruiting we find whisky in universal use.   The minister of Aberarder had groaned over the "horrid drudgery" of whisky drinking, and Charles Gordon of Braid advised the Duke (May 13) on going to the Highlands to "enliven the different musters of the different districts with one or two good pipers.   The musick and the whisky," he adds, "are powerful in rousing the martial spirit and even creating it, I find."   The Duke in fact tried all devices, including a request to the learned and non-martial Dr. Beattie to help him in recruiting.   It is significant that only one man advocated the use of the newspaper.   Advertisement had been used from the

O

outside, for on December 7, 1778, a professional recruiter informed the citizens of Aberdeen through the *Journal* that he would help:—

Whereas a speedy supply of able recruits are often wanted in the established regiments, new raised regiments, and corps of Fencible men, a gentleman, resident in London, who has served in the army a number of years with reputation, and who is at this period employed under the Secretary at War in recruiting, undertakes in the most expeditious manner, directly or indirectly, to raise any number of able men for His Majesty's service on the most reasonable terms. Address for A. B., to be left at Ashley's Punch House, Ludgate Hill, London.

Captain Lachlan McIntosh, writing from Inverness, July 3, says that some of the townsfolk suggested advertising for recruits and offering the freedom of the town to anyone who enlisted in the writer's company. Others suggested that the town should pay two guineas to anyone who brought a recruit. The sum total of all the devices was, however, a pretty uphill fight.

Let us look at the results in certain districts. One would have thought that the Enzie as essentially Gordon land would be enthusiastic, but when Alexander Gordon at Landends called a meeting of his fellow tenants, the attendance was "thin." A second meeting was called, but, according to Alexander Chalmers, Tynet, in a letter to the Duke, July 30, "not many attended" (*Ibid.*):—

As each tenant had little chance of procuring a man, it was agreed to associat ourselves into parties, and that each party should endeavour to procure by all fair means one or more men for your Grace's service. Agreeable to this concert, I associat myself with Mrs. Reid and her son in Resting-hillock, Alexander and William Gordons in Landends [and four others], and we present to your Grace a man, who, we hope, will fitt the service, and you will find very willing for the service. This we propose as a beginning, and every one in our society have agreed to go on in using all fair endeavours to procure as many men as we can, and such as we know the country can best spare.

Lieutenant Shaw gives a rather gloomy account of his experience in Badenoch (*Ibid.*):—

I enlisted men, but their original superiors, always watchful behind the curtain to thwart my measures, lodged smart money for them without their own knowledge or consent, tho' they afterwards prevail'd upon them to acknowledge it as a lawful deed: some of whom have been sent to His Grace the Duke of Gordon as if enlisted at St. Comb's market. They only enlisted a few days before they were sent down. One of them, according to my information, inlisted the very day they set of from Badenoch.

On July 1 William Macpherson of Invereshie wrote to William Todd in a pessimistic mood :—

I do not believe that there is a single man in Badenoch who will now accept of a commission in the Fencibles on the condition of raising the ordinary complement of men over and above the men that have and that will be sent to the Duke, because I am of opinion that none of them would now accomplish it without taking a very wide range and expending more money than would be either expedient or prudent.

If it was difficult to get recruits in the territory where the Duke was a power from his position as a landlord, it was still more difficult for him to succeed in Aberdeen, where he was of little or no importance. The invitation to the people of Aberdeen to join his banner was done by dispersing handbills, the town sergeants, who accomplished the distribution, being accompanied "with the sound of drums, fifes, bag-pipes, sackbuts, psalteries and all kinds of musical instruments." Even the town, however, expected a *quid pro quo*, for the Provost intimated (May 11) that the Town Council would raise a company, provided the town could have the call on 50 or 100 men in case of emergency. Not-withstanding this arrangement, progress was slow. On June 2, Major Mercer wrote (*Ibid.*) :—

My prospect of success in the recruiting way is at present extremely poor, for I must say that the people in office here seem to testify much indifference upon the subject. As the interest of His Grace and my honour are at stake, I thought it necessary to write him freely on the occasion. I am extremely sensible of the honour which the Duke has done me, and I am sincerely attached to his person and interest, for which reason I will never join with my townsmen, the Magistrates, in carrying on a farce when real exertions are requisite. I am, therefore, resolved to speak forth early, in order that His Grace may have time to adopt, if necessary, a new plan, and to form connexions, which may be of more advantage to the recruiting of the Regiment, than those in which he is at present engaged with me and my lukewarm constituents.

You will soon hear of a public procession, that is to be made here on Friday next in favour of the Regiment. My friends will certainly attend upon that occasion, but, altho' they are numerous and respectable in this place, I much doubt whether they are the sort of people who will be able to do my business, and I am still afraid that I shall be in the unhappy predicament of the hare with many friends. Sir Adolphus

Oughton, after praising the good intentions of the people of the good town of Aberdeen, has in a late letter to our Provost ordered our town's militia to be disbanded, the mode of their proceedings being found contrary to Act of Parliament. In the close of his letter he signifies that the zeal of Aberdeen will be most acceptable to Government, if directed towards promoting the levies of the Fencible Regiments; but I do not imagine that this hint will be attended with any immediate good effect, as the people who had enrolled themselves in the trainbands will for some time continue outrageous at being deprived of the use of their firelocks. Mr. Findlayson has been very successfull in his recruiting, for as he started long before Mowat and me; he had an opportunity to engage in his interest all those myrmidons who are commonly in the pay of recruiting officers, and, whilst the Town Council continues inactive, I can boast no advantage over any recruiting party.

On June 19 the Magistrates, accompanied by the principal citizens, made a parade through the streets, along with Major Mercer and Lieutenant Mowat and their recruiting party, for the purpose of encouraging recruits to enter the city company. Accordingly, several " stout fellows " entered with the Major, and when the procession was over the Magistrates ordered a hogshead of Rigg's fine home brewed porter to be distributed among the "populace." On July 5, Mercer is in quite a hopeful mood, for he writes (*Ibid.*) :—

When I got to Aberdeen, I found the whole town ringing with the fame of the Duke's recruits. A number of people came about me to learn the truth of the matter, and some of Seaforth's officers in particular asked me if the Fencible recruits were as handsome as their company of Grenadiers: to which I answered with much appearance of modesty that all I could say of the Duke's recruits was that they had the persons of men and the faces of angels. Everybody admired the extreme caution and reserve with which I expressed my sentiments: but [the] Lord Provost seems to me to be a good deal crestfallen.

On the other hand, Lieutenant Finlason was quite pessimistic when he wrote, July 26, that " the Devil has got into the fellows here, for no pains or means I can devise will make them enlist." Even Mercer returned next day to his earlier mood (*Ibid.*) :—

Mr. Bruce told me what I well knew from experience to be true : that men are at present very difficult to be had, and added that, if his ill success continued, he would upon the expiration of a fortnight or thereabouts relinquish his military views. The poor man seemed much embarassed, and, I am persuaded, looked upon me at the beginning of our conversation to be one of his bitterest enemies on account of some squabble which had happened in the course of our recruiting. I must do Provost Jopp the justice to say that he got me a recruit last week.

Bruce, writing on July 29, says he is not astonished that the Duke's patience is "nearly run out":—

I am in greate degree myself astonished and find much more difficulty than I could ever have apprehended. My want of success was not owing to remiss trifling. The real scarcity of men is the ingenious cause.

As late as November 11, he was penning the same sort of jeremiad (*Ibid.*):—

I have done the outmost in my power and to no purpose. After proclaming publickly with the drum and ofring six pounds ster. for a man, Aberdeen seems to be entirely drain'd, both toun and country, that I am diffident of suckseding.

Deeside proved an equally uphill task. Lieutenant Shaw, who recruited in the Invercauld and Abergeldie country, told the Duke, July 13, that in the absence of the lairds of these places he had found it hard to convince "the vulgar" of the constitution of the Duke's regiment. "They are not pretty much satisfied that they are not to go out of the kingdom. . . . The prettiest young lad in the country I have inlisted this day. He is but 18 years of age, and measures 5 feet 10½ inches. He writes and figures and comes of respectable parents: from all which I have ventured to promise him a halbert." Shaw soon gave up Deeside, leaving it to friends, who, however, did "not act agreeable to their promise." He then turned his attention to Sutherland, only to find that Captain Sutherland, Dunrobin, had persuaded "all his country" that they were soon to have a regiment of their own. Shaw ultimately worked his way down to Badenoch, where he was hardly more successful. On July 7, Lord Haddo set out from Aberdeen with Gordon of Hallhead, for Cromar, "to enlist, attest and depopulate the whole of it." But his success was not alarming. One of the men he got (June 18) was Charles Gordon (age 26: height 6 feet) described as a "writer," and born at Glenmuick. He was made a sergeant. The Duke, however, set his face against incompetents, for despite all his difficulties he announced himself (August 28) as being "positively determined against appointing any one who is not fit for actual service, even altho' there should be precedents in other Fencible corps."

So slowly did the recruiting go that the Duke wrote to Lord Barrington on July 3, 1778, for an extension of time (*W.O.* 1 : 997):—

I received your Lordship's letter of the 4th June, enclosing a copy of your letter to Sir Adolphus Oughton [the commander-in-chief in North Britain] relative to the enforcing of the recruiting Act in North Britain, and I have received several letters upon the subject from Sir Adolphus, all of which I shall attend to. Several circumstances prevented me from setting the recruiting business agoing immediately after I had the honour to receive His Majesty's Letter of Service, and since my arrival in this country I have met with some very unexpected disappointments [in the officers]. Notwithstanding which, I made a return the 1st of this month to the Adjutant General at Edinburgh, of 543 men including sergeants and drummers and I flatter myself the recruiting will now go on very successfully. I am sensible, however, that it will not be in my power to compleat my Regiment within the time expressed by my Letter of Service ; and therefore I now entreat your Lordship to prolong the period and to continue the pay of the establishment as an aid to recruiting for some months longer. At the same time your Lordship may be assured that I shall exert myself to the utmost to compleat the corps as soon as possible.

The first men had been enlisted in April, which produced but 21. The figures gradually rose as follows (*Gordon Castle Papers*):—

			Sergeants.	Drummers.	Rank and File.
July 1 -	-	-	22	7	514
July 18 -	-	-	24	8	613
August 1	-	-	29	15	704
August 16	-	-	36	17	786
August 30	-	-	38	17	869
September 13 -	-	-	40	17	933
September 27 -	-	-	41	18	962

Even as late as December 30, 1778, the regiment was not complete, for on that date the Duke wrote from Gordon Castle to Barrington's successor at the War Office, Charles Jenkinson, the future Lord Liverpool (*W.O.* 1 : 997):—

I am sorry to give you this trouble so soon after your coming into office ; but, as Lord Barrington by his letter of the 14th of this month has ordered that my Agent should commence the non-effective account of my Regiment from the 25th of October, I must request of you to give me a little further indulgence, and that the non-effective fund may be continued in aid of recruiting to the 25th of this month [Dec.]. I hope you will not think this an unreasonable demand, considering the small bounty money we are allowed to give and the unavoidable expense I have been at in raising my Regiment.

I only want 45 men to make me quite compleat, and I flatter myself I shall soon be able to raise them, tho' the very great bounties that the officers in other regiments are giving is certainly a great prejudice to us, who are only allowed to give a guinea.

Probably as a fillip to the recruiting, we find Alexander Duthie, Aberdeen, paying the following amounts to Alexander Gunn, late sergeant in the 26th Foot; £20 on December 29, 1778; £10 on December 30; and £40 on January 4, 1779. Another undated item shows that he got £10 "towards recruiting expenses for the Dutchess of Gordon," proving that she lent her aid towards getting men.

The regiment is variously titled. The first muster roll (*W.O.* 13: 3,900) calls it "H.M. Regiment of North Fencible Highlanders." The Notifications Book (*W.O.* 25: 148) in announcing the first commissions calls it the "Northern Regiment of Fencible Men." The Army List of 1782 calls it the "Northern Regiment of Fencible Men in North Britain." As a rule, it is called the "Northern Fencibles." Stewart of Garth simply uses the word "Gordon."

The regiment was dressed in Highland costume. Apart from any desire the Duke of Gordon may have had to play the chief, this was a highly politic move considering the character of his recruits, for nothing had wounded the pride of the clans so much as the suppression of the philabeg in 1746. As a matter of fact, this harsh measure was not repealed until 1782, by an Act in which occurs the first official record of the kilt. There was something, therefore, very ironic in the Government's uniforming some of its regiments in the garb of old Gaul. Unfortunately we do not know what tartan was adopted. On May 29, the firm of W. and A. Forsyth, Huntly, wrote regretting that "so much time is lost in resolving on the patterns of plaids." The hose were of scarlet.

The men wore blue bonnets with plumed feathers, the sergeants wearing "ostridge" ones. This decision was not reached without careful consideration. On August 28, the Duke wrote to Arthur Mair, of Cox and Mair, the Army Agents, that, "while he did not wish to bring unnecessary expense on himself, or the men, he thought they would look better with feathers." He requested Mair to determine whether the cock's feather, or worsted, would be "the most proper." Mair replied that a cock's feather would look better, and its cost was only sevenpence.

The Grenadiers had caps with silver-plated fronts, scarlet tassels, cockades with buttons, and loops with a touch of yellow round the cockades. The Light Infantry had caps with swordproof crowns, and " fur round."

The equipment of the regiment was a fine thing for the local manufacturers, who were not slow to remember the value of this aspect of territorial soldiering. Thus, the Forsyths of Huntly supplied plaids for 1,010 privates and 22 drummers. Forsyth of Elgin, Umphray of Fochabers, McVeagh of Huntly, and Ross, tailor in Fochabers, supplied various goods, the last named charging only sixpence for the making of a kilt. James Philp, junior, and James Shepherd, Fochabers, offered to make goat skin knapsacks at five shillings and calf skin ones at four-and-six. Besides these, the more elaborate parts of the uniform came from Bray and Fraser of Brewer Street, London, and from William Dickey, London, who despatched his goods from London by the " Charlotte " on August 14, the remainder coming on by a smack " Duke of Gordon," which arrived on September 20. The initial bill for clothing and equipping the regiment ran into £4,712 odd, allotted as follows :—

Alexander Forsyth & Son, Elgin	.	.	.	£15	3	1
W. & A. Forsyth, Huntly (tartan)	.	.	.	1,779	2	0
Harry McVeagh & Co., Huntly (shirts)	.	.	192	11	10
William Dickey, London (facings, etc.)	.	.	1,284	8	11
Alexander Umphray & Sons, Fochabers	.	.	10	16	11
Bray and Fraser, London	.	.	.	.	1,330	15	1½
Total of equipment in 1778	.	.	.	.	£4,712	4	3½
Recruiting expenses in 1778	.	.	.	.	1,304	4	11
Expense of Raising the Regiment	.	.	.	£6,016	9	2½

Between April, 1779, and January, 1780, a further sum of £3,468 18s. 11d. was paid for clothing ; and between 1778 and March 11, 1780, the paymaster disbursed £8,725 19s. 8½d.

The Highland character of the regiment was further emphasised by the employment of pipers—Roderick Mackenzie, attested March 15, 1778, and John Macpherson, attested April 16. One reads with surprise in a letter by Alexander Milne, Drumin, March 3, that " there is only one man in these countrys that plays on the pipe." On August 1, Major Chisholm wrote to the Duke from Moniack :—" My brother has as good a Highland piper as is now in the north. He has consented to let your Grace have him for a few years if you are not already provided with one. The piper himself is very willing to serve your Grace, provided he could get his son along with him (as he is now teaching him the pipes) as a drummer or fifer." Fifes were also used, for Alexander Godsman, Dunain, wrote that Blair, music master, Inverness, was willing to teach the boys to play the fife at 10s. 6d. a month each, giving them two lessons a day. Major Donaldson suggested on June 12 that the drummers should be taught by Corporal Donald Munro of the 42nd.

The first muster of the regiment took place at Elgin on August 3, 300 men assembling, but the Duke found that Elgin was a "very improper place for forming a new regiment," and he requested it to be sent on to Fort George, which was immediately done, Lieutenant Charles Gordon, Wardhouse, declaring on September 6 that they were the best-looking men in the Fort.

The organisation of the regiment, however, left much to be desired, as a letter written by Captain John Gordon, Laggan, on September 1 shows (*Gordon Castle Papers*):—

When we came from Elgin there was no roll of those enlisted by the Duke. No person knew their numbers. [Charles Gordon of] Wardes had got an old roll from Mr. Munro, but it was neither exact nor distinct. Severalls had never been entered in it, and a number absent without any mark, whether on furlough or otherwayes. We had no rule to go by but to make a roll of those we had within the garrison, which, including seven sergeants, eleven corporals and two drummers, ammount to 224. . . . There may even have been desertions on the road without our knowledge. . . . The right of the Duke's, by name the Colonel's company, [is] commanded by me, and the left, the Lieutenant Colonel's, by Wardes. In every other thing, we go hand in hand, except that Wardes drew cash at Ffores for paying the Duke's men, and consequently has the name of paymaster. . . . What I scrouple most is being obliged to act as quartermaster for the A companys, doing a man's duty I know nothing about and by far the most troublesome in the garrison.

The lads still continue to behave well and are very tractable and obedient. I must let you know Mr. Fraser, the barrackmaster's, report to the Governor respecting their barracks:—"There have been thirteen regiments in this garrison since I had concern with it; I never saw barracks so clean and in so good order as those presently possessed by the Duke of Gordon's men, tho' they received them but two days since from the Macdonalds in a way I am ashamed to mention."

On Friday I had the honour to mount Guard with the Fencibles for their first appearance on duty, and, making some allowance for our

P

awkwardness, which must be expected from raw recruits, the officers and whole garrison said old soldiers could not behave with more decency and attention, which has been the case with any one of our guards mounted since. If we are keept together but a short time, I hope you will hear of our being a pattern regiment.

Wardhouse wrote, September 23, "I wish to God we were formed into Companys for the trouble of paying them in their present troubled state is prodigious." There was friction even among the officers, for Captain A. P. Cumming, afterwards Gordon-Cumming of Altyre, wrote to the Duke from Altyre asking His Grace to summon Lieutenant Cumming of his company to headquarters: "Whilst I am fagged about like a post horse, he seems to enjoy his ease and venison at Calder."

The first officers' commissions are dated April 14, 1778, but they were not officially published till September 17, 1778, when they appear in the Notifications Book in the War Office (*W.O.* 25; 116: p. 132: *W.O.* 25; 148: pp. 236-7):—

COLONEL.

The 4th Duke of Gordon, April 14, 1778.

LIEUTENANT-COLONEL.

Lord William Gordon, April 14, 1778. Brother of the Duke.

MAJORS.

James Chisholm (from major in the 21st Foot), April 14, 1778.

James Mercer, April 14, 1778. Son of Thomas Mercer, Aberdeen (d. 1770): and brother of David Mercer of Auchnacant (d. 1787), whom he succeeded. He was born February 27, 1734; entered the 88th, leaving the army as major in 1772. He was a cultivated man, publishing a volume of *Lyric Poems* in 1794, and a friend of Beattie. He married in 1763 Katherine Douglas, daughter of the laird of Fechil and sister of Lord Glenbervie, and died at Sunnybank, Aberdeen, November 27, 1804. He left two daughters, one of whom, Katherine, married, 1781, Charles Gordon, of Wardhouse (a fellow officer of her father in the Northern Fencibles), who divorced her, 1797. (See Appendix " Q," Forbes's *Life of Beattie; Thanage of Fermartyn*, 603-4; Walker's *Bards of Bon-Accord*, 333-337; J. F. George's article on the " auld hoose " of Sunnybank, built by Mercer, in the *Book of Powis*, 1906; *Aberdeen Journal Notes and Queries*, ii., 351, iii., 16; *Life of General Hugh Mercer*, by John T. Goolrick, New York, 1906).

CAPTAINS.

John Campbell, April 14, 1778; joined the Cardigan Militia and was replaced by John Grant, April 8, 1779.

Alexander Penrose Cumming, April 14, 1778 (from 13th Foot), afterwards in the Strathspey Fencibles　Created a baronet, 1804, died, 1806, founder of Gordon-Cumming family (*Gordons under Arms*, Nos 1,521-1,535)

Sir William Forbes, April 14, 1778, resigned by September 13, 1780. Born in 1755, he was 5th bart of Craigievar, married 1780, Sarah, daughter of the 13th Lord Sempill; and died 1816

Alexander Fraser, April 14, 1778 (from captain, 78th Regiment) Laird of Culduthil, dead by December 26, 1778

James Fraser (from the 87th), January 8, 1779, *vice* Fraser, joined the 71st by April 8, 1779

George (Gordon), Lord Haddo, April 14, 1778　Born 1764, he was son of the 3rd Earl of Aberdeen, had six sons in the services (*Gordons under Arms* Nos 196, 323, 541, 961, 1,797), and Robert (not mentioned there), who had a commission in the 3rd Aberdeen Local Militia in 1813

George Mackay, of Bighouse, April 14, 1778; from half pay

Lachlan Mackintosh, April 14, 1778　Younger of Belnespick

Captain-Lieutenant

William Finlason, April 14, 1778, captain, April 8, 1779, *vice* James Fraser　He had previously been in the 89th Foot, 1759-1763

Lieutenants

George Abercromby, April 14, 1778; resigned by October 18, 1780 Laird of Birkenbog (?)

Robert Cumming, April 14, 1778, resigned by May 5, 1782

Donald Forbes, April 14, 1778, resigned by May 5, 1782

—— Fraser, April 14, 1778 (*W O* 25 211)

Charles Gordon, April 14, 1778, captain, May 29, 1782, *vice* Lord Haddo, resigned.　Laird of Wardhouse (*Gordons under Arms*, No 307)

James Gordon, April 14, 1778, resigned by March 15, 1782 (*Gordons under Arms*, No 721)

John Gordon, April 14, 1778, captain, September 12, 1782　Son of James, in Laggan (*Gordons under Arms*, No 906)

William Gordon, April 14, 1778　Son of Robert Gordon, Achness (*Gordons under Arms*, No 1,408)

William Graham, April 14, 1778, resigned by March 23, 1779

Alexander Grant, April 14, 1778

John Grant, April 14, 1778 (from half pay); captain-lieutenant, April 8, 1779, *vice* Campbell　Of Rippachie

Donald Mackay, April 14, 1778; resigned by May 19, 1780

William Mackintosh, April 14, 1778, resigned by January 1, 1781.

Andrew Mowatt, April 14, 1778

George Munro, April 14, 1778.

George Reynolds, April 14, 1778, *vice* Fraser, declines.

John Rose, April 14, 1778; joined the 42nd by March 18, 1782. Of Holm.

John Rose, jun., April 14, 1778.

Thomas Russel, April 14, 1778 (from half pay); captain-lieutenant, January 19, 1780; captain, September 13, 1780. He was subsequently in the Banff and Rosehearty Volunteers, 1794-8. Laird of Rathen; died at Banff, 1827, aged 85. His career is given minutely in the *Aberdeen Weekly Journal*, October 16, 1914.

James Shaw, April 14, 1778; captain-lieutenant, September 13, 1780. He had a nephew, James Shaw, a sergeant in the regiment, and asked a cadetship for his own son, Æneas, who was with him at Inverness.

John Sutherland, April 14, 1778. Of Dunbeath.

ENSIGNS.

Charles Adamson, May 5, 1782, *vice* Huoy.

Angus Cameron, April 14, 1778; Lieut., May 5, 1780, *vice* Gordon.

Colin Chisholm, January 8, 1779, *vice* Fraser, who declined; lieutenant, September 13, 1780.

Alexander Clerk, April 14, 1778; lieutenant, April 8, 1779; joined the Marines by November 21, 1781.

Alexander Dunbar, September 15, 1782, *vice* Smith, lieutenant.

Alexander Forbes, July 20, 1781; lieutenant, March 15, 1782, *vice* James Gordon.

——— Fraser, April 14, 1778.

Thomas Fraser, May 5, 1782; lieutenant, September 29, 1782, *vice* Todd, resigned.

Adam Gordon, January 1, 1781; lieutenant, May 29, 1782.

Adam Gordon, September 29, 1782. Son of John Gordon of Florida and South Carolina, who died at Bordeaux, March 4, 1778 (*Gordons under Arms*, No. 101).

George Gordon, April 8, 1779. Entered 1st Dragoons, May 1780. Natural son of the 4th Duke of Gordon; lived at Glentromie (*Gordons under Arms*, No. 512).

John Gordon, April 14, 1778; lieutenant, March 23, 1779, *vice* Graham, resigned; captain, September 15, 1782. Son of James Gordon in Laggan, which John subsequently farmed; died 1799 (*Gordons under Arms*, No. 906).

John Gordon, April 14, 1778; lieutenant, April 10, 1779; joined Independent Company, February 13, 1782; captain-lieutenant, Gordon Highlanders, February 12, 1794. Farmed Coynachie; died 1827 (*Gordons under Arms*, No. 909).

John Gordon, March 18, 1782, *vice* Rose, lieutenant, May 12, 1782, *vice* J Gordon, jun , captain, September 15, 1782, *vice* Mackay, resigned Son of James Gordon in Croughly, died 1788, at Croughly, aged 25 (*Gordons under Arms*, No 917) Five of his brothers entered the Army, and thus laid the foundations of the Service achievements of this farmer-family which has from first to last produced 28 officers (*Ibid* p xxxiv)

Lewis Gordon, June 15, 1782, *vice* Stewart Son of John Gordon, IV. in Minmore, secretary to the Highland Society, died unmarried 1839 (*Gordons under Arms*, No 1,093)

William Gordon, April 14, 1778, lieutenant, January 19, 1780 Son of John Gordon, IV in Minmore, brother of Lewis, *supra*, died 1829 (*Gordons under Arms*, No 1,407)

Charles Grant, May 19, 1780, lieut, November 21, 1781, *vice* Clarke

James Grant (1), April 14, 1778, lieutenant, January 19, 1780, *vice* Mowatt, February 7, 1780

James Grant (2), April 14, 1778

George Hoy, March 15, 1782, resigned by May 5, 1782 Son of the Duke's "Meteorologist"

Alexander Innes, November 21, 1781, lieutenant, May 5, 1782, *vice* Forbes

William Knox, September 13, 1780

Thomas Livingstone, March 23, 1779, joined the 98th before July 12, 1780 Probably son of Dr Thomas Livingstone, Aberdeen (1728-85), who was accoucheur to the Duchess of Gordon

Hugh Mackay, February 7, 1780, lieutenant, January 1, 1781, *vice* Mackintosh

Robert Mackay, April 14, 1778 (by purchase), lieutenant, May 19, 1780, *vice* Donald Mackay, 2nd lieutenant, 21st Foot, June 13, 1781 Married at Limerick, February 10, 1786, and had a son and two daughters, living at Jersey, 1828 (*W O* 25 766 p 9)

Andrew Macpherson, May 29, 1782

Robert Campbell Macpherson, January 17, 1782, lieutenant, May 5, 1782, *vice* Cumming

Colin Mathieson, May 5, 1780, lieutenant, July 20, 1781, *vice* Mackay, who joined the 21st

John Mathieson, May 12, 1782

James Meik, June 16, 1780, *vice* Gordon

Alexander Rose, October 18, 1780

Simon Simpson, September 6, 1780, *vice* Francis Stewart, lieutenant, January 17, 1782, *vice* Grant

Charles Smith, May 5, 1782, lieutenant, September 15, 1782

Charles Stewart, July 12, 1780, *vice* Livingstone; joined the 81st by June 15, 1782.

Francis Stewart, January 19, 1780; joined the 48th by September 6, 1780. Laird of Lesmurdie; died 1824.

Alexander Todd, January 19, 1780; lieutenant, October 18, 1780, *vice* Abercromby, resigned; resigned by September 29, 1782. Son of William Todd, the Duke's factor.

CHAPLAIN.

Rev. James Gordon (1728-1809), April 14, 1778. Son of George, of Fifthpart of Dundurcus (*Gordons under Arms*, No. 709).

SURGEON.

John Gordon, April 14, 1778. Son of John in Minmore, as above. He was succeeded, January 8, 1779, by George French ("*vice* Gordon, declines"), who was Professor of Chemistry at Marischal College from 1793 till his death in 1833. It was he who urged Sir James McGrigor to enter the army (McGrigor's *Autobiography*, p. 7).

MATES.

James Meik, January 8, 1779; ensign, June 16, 1780.

William Knox, January 8, 1779; ensign, September 13, 1780. Probably the William Knox who took the M.D. of Marischal College in 1785, and entered the H.E.I.C.S.

ADJUTANT.

George Reynolds, April 14, 1778.

QUARTERMASTER.

Thomas Russel, April 14, 1778.

AGENTS.

Cox, Mair and Cox, Cray's Court, London.

The officers were apportioned to companies as follows:—

COMPANY.	LIEUTENANT.	ENSIGN.
Col. Duke of Gordon.	George Munro.	William Gordon.
Capt. John Campbell.	Robert Cumming. John Rose, sen. John Rose, jun.	
Major James Chisholm.	William Graham.	Angus Cameron.
Capt. A. P. Cumming.	Andrew Mowatt. Alexander Grant. John Grant.	James Grant.
„ Sir William Forbes.	George Abercromby. Thomas Russel.	Robert Mackay.
„ James Fraser.	Simon Fraser. William Mackintosh.	Colin Chisholm.

COMPANY.	LIEUTENANT.	ENSIGN.
Capt. George, Lord Haddo.	{ James Gordon. { John Gordon. { William Gordon.	
„ Lord William Gordon.	{ Charles Gordon. { George Reynolds.	John Grant.
„ George Mackay.	{ Donald Forbes. { Donald Mackay.	Alexander Clerk.
„ Lachlan Mackintosh.	{ James Shaw. { John Sutherland.	James Grant.

The ten companies averaged 93 men. Their names are given in the first muster roll of the regiment, preserved at the Record Office, for the period September 26—December 24, 1778 (*W.O.* 13: 3,900). It contains the bare names only. But fortunately there is a list full of facts concerning 13 sergeants, 13 corporals, 13 drummers and 278 privates, at Gordon Castle. Of the privates, I discover by comparison with the War Office roll that 88 belonged to the Duke's company (four being missing), and 84 to Lord William's (ten being missing in the Gordon Castle roll). The Gordon Castle roll is a carefully written MS. folio, and is entitled " Roll of men inlisted for the Duke of Gordon," and gives (1) name of soldier; (2) date of enlistment; (3) by whom or where enlisted; (4) age; (5) height; (6) description of complexion; (7) colour of hair; (8) colour of eyes; (9) trade; (10) where born. Although I am well aware that items 6, 7, and 8 are extremely interesting from the eugenics point of view, I have not (on the ground of space) included them. I have transposed items 9 and 10. Several details from other lists, more or less fragmentary, in the possession of the Duke of Richmond, have been added in brackets.

The average height of the 295 men for whom statistics are given is 5 feet 6.02544 inches.

Name.	Age.	Height.	Born.	Trade.	By whom or where Enlisted.	Date of Enlistment.
SERGEANTS.						
Cormack, Donald ..	27	5 ft. 3 in.	Wattin, Caithness	Labourer	Mr. Bell	May 28
Duffus, James	31	5 ft. 10 in.	Fordyce, Banff	Sh'maker	Mr. Ross	May 16
Gordon, Charles ..	29	5 ft. 10½ in.	Bellie, Banff	Mason	The Duchess	June 10
Gordon, John	49	5 ft. 9½ in.	Loth, Sutherland	Labourer	Mr. Munro	April 21
Grant, Francis	19	5 ft. 10½ in.	Mortlich, Banff	Student	The Duke	July 13
Horn, Peter ..	37	5 ft. 6½ in.	Fordyce, Banff	Hairdr'ser	Mr. Ross	April 28
M'Honachy, Wm. ..	23	5 ft. 7 in.	Mortlich, Banff	Farmer	Gordon of Laggan	May 23
M'Kinlay, Alex. ..	20	5 ft. 8½ in.	Inverness	Labourer	Mr. Munro	May 2
Maclay, Wm. ..	31	5 ft. 7 in.	Forres, Murray	Merchant	Mr. Bell	April 28
M'Phail, John ..	30	6 ft. 2 in.	Dunlichty, Inverness	Farmer	The Duke	June 6
Moffat, James ..	25	5 ft. 6 in.	Urquhart, Murray	Taylor	Gordon of Laggan	May 26
Steuart, Peter ..	38	5 ft. 11½ in.	Leathret, Caithness	....	....	June 1
Young, William ..	40	5 ft. 7 in.	Paisley, Renfrew	Soldier	Lord Adam Gordon	Sept. 28

Name.	Age.	Height.	Born.	Trade.	By whom or where Enlisted.	Date of Enlistment.
CORPORALS.						
Cameron, Donald ..	25	5 ft. 9 in.	Kilmanivaig, Inverness	Labourer	The Duke	May 30
Elder, William ..	23	5 ft. 7½ in.	Marnoch, Banff	Labourer	Mr. Munro	May 4
Gordon, George ..	23	6 ft. 2 in.	Inveraven, Banff	Labourer	The Duke	July 10
Grant, William ..	22	5 ft. 9 in.	Kincardine, Inverness	Labourer	His Father	June 8
Greenwood, Paul ..	36	5 ft. 9 in.	Wadsworth, York	Taylor	Mr. Bell	May 2
Innes, Robert ..	30	5 ft. 7½ in.	Dipple, Murray	Labourer	Mr. Bell	May 6
M'Donell, Donald ..	30	5 ft. 5½ in.	Kilmanivaig, Inverness	Farmer	Colonel Campbell	June 8
M'Intyre, Patrick ..	23	5 ft. 11 in.	Fortingale, Perth	Labourer	Colonel Campbell	June 3
M'Kenzie, Alex. ..	39	5 ft. 5½ in.	Kirkhill, Inverness	Labourer	The Duke	July 1
M'Pherson, Andrew	19	5 ft. 11 in.	Alvie, Inverness	Farmer	Colonel Campbell	June 8
Pitullo, Patrick ..	20	5 ft. 7½ in.	St. Martin, Perth	Mason	Mr. Bell	June 9
Romans, William ..	19	5 ft. 9½ in.	Keith, Banff	Labourer	Fochabers	May 23
Sutherland, Alex. ..	21	5 ft. 10⅝ in.	Bellie, Murray	Gardener	Fochabers	June 15
DRUMMERS.						
Duff, William ..	..	....	....	....	Lieut. James Gordon	....
Duncan, Peter ..	12	....	Huntly, Aberdeen	....	....	July 1
Forbes, William ..	16	....	Inverness, Inverness	Labourer	....	June 3
Fraser, William ..	13	....	Fordyce, Banff	Labourer	....	May 13
Garrow, John ..	14	5 ft. 2 in.	Mortlich, Banff	Sh'maker	....	June 20
Gordon, Adam ..	13	....	Farr, Sutherland	....	....	June 26
Horn, James ..	15	....	Bellie, Murray	Flaxdr'ser	....	May 22
Horn, John ..	14	....	Bellie, Murray	Flaxdr'ser	....	April 28
Kerr, John ..	..	....	....	....	Lieut. James Gordon	....
M'Kenzie, John ..	11	....	Kirkhill, Inverness	....	....	July 1
M'Leod, Donald ..	..	....	....	....	Captain Mackay	....
M'Millan, Peter ..	14	....	Kenmuir, Perth	Sailor	....	Oct. 3
Weir, William ..	15	....	Monquiter, Aberdeen	....	....	Sept. 28
PRIVATES.						
Alexander, Wm. ..	28	5 ft. 10 in.	Forgue, Aberdeen	Labourer	Laggan	June 9
Allardyce, John ..	17	5 ft. 3 in.	Gartly, Aberdeen	Labourer	Huntly	June 19
Anderson, Alex. ..	18	5 ft. 7 in.	Forgue, Aberdeen	Labourer	(Lieut. Gordon), Wardhouse	July 30
Anderson, Charles ..	16	5 ft. 6 in.	Forgue, Aberdeen	Labourer	Brideswell	June 10
Anderson, James ..	18	5 ft. 6 in.	Bellie, Banff	Labourer	Fochabers	June 10
Anderson, William	30	5 ft. 5½ in.	Rathven, Banff	Labourer	Fochabers	June 8
Bain, William ..	40	5 ft. 6 in.	Thurso, Caithness	Labourer	Minister of Belly	June 30
Barron, William ..	22	5 ft. 4 in.	Meldrum, Aberdeen	Sh'maker	Dr. Gordon	July 28
Beg, James ..	16	5 ft. 3 in.	Grange, Banff	Labourer	Sergeant M'Lay	May 27
Black, John ..	46	5 ft. 6 in.	Kilmanivaig, Inverness	Labourer	The Duke	June 8
Black, William ..	17	5 ft. 7 in.	Elgin, Murray	Labourer	(G. Munro), at Elgin	Aug. 12
Blair, John ..	23	5 ft. 11 in.	Cromdale, Murray	Labourer	Laggan	May 1
Bowman, William ..	16	5 ft. 3 in.	Inveraven, Banff	Labourer	Mr. Grant, Minmore	June 22
Bremer, Edward ..	17	5 ft. 6 in.	Bellie, Murray	Labourer	Fochabers	May 7
Bremer, John ..	16	5 ft. 7 in.	Bellie, Murray	Labourer	Fochabers	May 5
Bremer, Joseph ..	20	5 ft. 9 in.	Bellie, Murray	Labourer	Fochabers	May 16
Brodie, Peter, sen.	35	5 ft. 6½ in.	King-Edward, Ab'd'n	Miller	Sergeant M'Lay	Aug. 28
Brodie, Peter, jun.	16	5 ft. 3 in.	Tillynessle, Aberdeen	Taylor	Sergeant M'Lay	Aug. 29
Brown, Thomas ..	17	5 ft. 4 in.	Kirkmichael, Banff	Weaver	Gordon, Clashmoir	July 23
Burges, James ..	22	5 ft. 8½ in.	Boharm, Banff	Mason	The Duchess	June 10
Cameron, Alex. ..	17	5 ft. 3 in.	Kilmalie, Inverness	Labourer	Blairachurn	May 30
Cameron, Alex ..	17	5 ft. 3 in.	Kilmanivaig, Inverness	Labourer	Neil Cameron, Rattichmore	May 30
Cameron, Alex ..	19	5 ft. 5½ in.	Kilmalie, Inverness	Labourer	Terindriesh	June 3
Cameron, Alex. ..	20	5 ft. 7 in.	Kineardin, Inverness	Labourer	W. Cameron	July 1
Cameron, Alex.Breck	30	5 ft. 3 in.	Kilmanivaig, Inverness	Labourer	Glenturat	July 17
Cameron, Allan ..	17	5 ft. 3 in.	Kilmanivaig, Inverness	Labourer	Cameron, Lindilly	June 1
Cameron, Donald ..	23	5 ft. 7½ in.	Inveraven, Banff	Labourer	Rob. Stuart, Desky	July 6
Cameron, Donald ..	36	5 ft. 4½ in.	Kilmanivaig	Labourer	Tacksman of Annat	June 2
Cameron, Donald ..	18	5 ft. 4 in.	Kilmalie, Inverness	Labourer	Blairehurn	June 3
Cameron, Donald ..	18	5 ft. 4 in.	Kilmanivaig, Inverness	Labourer	Glenturat	May 30
Cameron, Donald ..	17	5 ft. 3½ in.	Kilmanivaig, Inverness	Labourer	Glenevas	June 3
Cameron, Donald ..	18	5 ft. 4½ in.	Kilmanivaig, Inverness	Labourer	Annat	June 11
Cameron, Donald ..	20	5 ft. 2 in.	Kilmanivaig, Inverness	Labourer	Letterfindlay	June 15
Cameron, Donald ..	19	5 ft. 5 in.	Contine, Ross	Labourer	Mr. Bell	May 28
Cameron, Duncan ..	30	5 ft. 6¾ in.	Kilmalie, Inverness	Labourer	Letterfindlay	June 2
Cameron, Duncan ..	25	5 ft. 8 in.	Kilmanivaig, Inverness	Labourer	Blairachurn	May 30
Cameron, Ewen ..	35	5 ft. 4½ in.	Kilmanivaig, Inverness	Labourer	Gordonsburgh	May 30
Cameron, Ewen ..	21	5 ft. 6 in.	Kilmanivaig, Inverness	Labourer	Stronobad	June 1
Cameron, Ewen ..	18	5 ft. 8 in.	Kilmanivaig, Inverness	Labourer	Tomcharie	June 13
Cameron, Ewen ..	16	5 ft. 7½ in.	Kilmanivaig, Inverness	Labourer	(Corpl. Donald Cameron, etc)	Aug. 8
Cameron, John ..	16	5 ft. 4 in.	Kilmalie, Inverness	Labourer	Kennedy, Leinachanmore	June 5
Cameron, John ..	19	5 ft. 3½ in.	Kilmanivaig, Inverness	Labourer	Glenevas	June 3

Name.	Age.	Height.	Born.	Trade.	By whom or where Enlisted.	Date of Enlistment.
Cameron, John (added as 277th man)					Mr. Grant, Tombreackachy	....
Cameron, Martin ..	30	5 ft. 9½ in.	Kilmanivaig, Inverness	Labourer	Rattichbeg	May 30
Cameron, Martin ..	30	5 ft. 6 in.	Kilmanivaig, Inverness	Labourer	Likroy	May 30
Campbell, Duncan ..	30	5 ft. 7¼ in.	Kingussie, Inverness	Labourer	Mrs. Tod	June 6
Cantley, James ..	28	5 ft. 6 in.	Fordyce, Banff	Wheelwright	A. Gordon, in Landends	Aug. 1
Cattach, Alexander	15	5 ft. 2 in.	Mortlich, Banff	Labourer	Lieut. Gordon, Laggan	June 29
Cattanach, Alex. ..	50	5 ft. 3½ in.	Kingussie, Inverness	Labourer	John Grant, in Achnarrow	Aug. 17
Cattanach, Findley	20	....	Inch, Inverness	Labourer	Inveresby	June 26
Christie, Peter ..	41	5 ft. 6 in.	Fordyce, Banff	Gentm'n's servant	Mr. Bell	July 3
Clark, Alexander ..	24	5 ft. 6½ in.	Keith, Banff	Labourer	Fochabers	May 15
Copland, John ..	40	5 ft. 7 in.	Rathven, Banff	Farmer	....	Dec. 1
Corbet, Robert ..	44	5 ft. 3½ in.	Mickle Govan, Lanark	Gunsmith	Hugh Murray, Strichen	July 1
Craig, James ..	32	5 ft. 7 in.	Kinnethmont, Aberdeen	Flaxdr'ser	Forsyth, Huntly	May 1
Craigie, Nathaniel ..	22	5 ft. 6 in.	Towie, Aberdeen	Soldier	Lord Adam Gordon	Sept. 28
Cruickshank, Robert	40	5 ft. 8 in.	Kirkmichael, Banff	Square wright	Mr. Miln, Braehead	May 22
Cruickshank, Thomas	32	5 ft. 8 in.	Inveraven, Banff	Labourer	Drummin	July 23
Cumming, James ..	17	5 ft. 7 in.	Inveraven, Banff	Labourer	Achorachin	July 10
Davidson, Alexander	16	5 ft. 2⅜ in.	Mortlich, Banff	Taylor	Laggan	June 17
Davidson, Farquhar	36	5 ft. 6 in.	Inch, Inverness	....	Inveresby	June 20
Davidson, James ..	22	5 ft. 5 in.	Kingussie, Inverness	Labourer	Raits	June 8
Davidson, John ..	30	5 ft. 6 in.	Ellon, Aberdeen	Labourer	Fochabers	Aug. 13
Davidson, John ..	25	5 ft. 5½ in.	Forgue, Banff	Weaver	Ensign J. Gordon (Coynachie)	July 23
Dawn, Alexander ..	35	6 ft. 1 in.	Glass, Banff	Labourer	Lieut. Gordon, Wardhouse	July 3
Desson, James ..	28	5 ft. 6½ in.	Huntly, Aberdeen	Weaver	Ensign J. Gordon (Coynachie)	June 29
Donald, George ..	34	5 ft. 7¼ in.	Deskford, Banff	Labourer	Mr. Ross	July 13
Downie, Robert ..	37	5 ft. 4 in.	Urquhart, Murray	Labourer	(Lieut. Gordon), Laggan	June 1
Duncan, Robert ..	38	5 ft. 7 in.	Rhynie, Aberdeen	Labourer	Huntly	July 1
Duncan, William ..	18	5 ft. 3 in.	Dumbennan, Aberdeen	Labourer	Thomas Miln	April 28
Fife, George ..	40	5 ft. 5 in.	Boyndie, Banff	Labourer	Ensign J. Gordon (Coynachie)	July 2
Fife, Patrick ..	17	5 ft. 2 in.	Elgin, Murray	Flaxdr'ser	Fochabers	July 14
Findley, Alexander .	30	5 ft. 4 in.	Forres, Murray	Labourer	Mr. Bell	May 28
Forbes, Alexander ..	20	5 ft. 6 in.	Belly, Banff	Labourer	Fochabers	Nov. 21
Forbes, John ..	26	5 ft. 6½ in.	Bellie, Murray	Labourer	Fochabers	May 23
Forsyth, William ..	30	5 ft. 4 in.	Inveraven, Banff	Carpenter	(Wm. Grant, Tombrackachy)	Aug. 10
1Forrester, John Stewart	..	....	....	Discharged	....	July 14
Fraser, James ..	16	5 ft. 4½ in.	Cromarty, Inverness	Labourer	Fochabers	June 4
Fraser, James ..	24	5 ft. 5½ in.	Fordyce, Banff	Labourer	Ensign J. Gordon (Coynachie)	July 14
Fraser, John ..	45	5 ft. 7½ in.	Strathdon, Aberdeen	Labourer	Wm. Gordon, Lettoch	July 24
Gartly, John ..	27	5 ft. 6½ in.	Gartly, Banff	Labourer	Ensign J. Gordon	June 25
Gordon, Alexander .	18	5 ft. 5½ in.	Kingussie, Inverness	Labourer	Benchar	June 12
Gordon, Andrew ..	25	5 ft. 6 in.	Guthrie, Angus	Labourer	Mr. Bruce	June 5
Gordon, Cosmo ..	36	5 ft. 7 in.	Inveraven, Banff	Farmer	W. Grant, Minmore	July 1
Gordon, Duncan ..	18	5 ft. 3½ in.	Kingussie, Inverness	Labourer	Fort-William	June 1
Gordon, James ..	18	5 ft. 4½ in.	Kincardin, Inverness	Miller	Kincardine	June 18
Gordon, John ..	36	5 ft. 5 in.	Cabrach, Banff	Farmer	Hardhaugh	July 13
2Gordon, Theodore .	34	5 ft. 9½ in.	Forgue, Aberdeen	Merchant	Fochabers	June 5
Grant, Alexander ..	26	5 ft. 8 in.	Marnoch, Banff	Wright	Fochabers	May 29
Grant, Duncan ..	40	5 ft. 4 in.	Abernethy, Murray	Labourer	John Grant, Achnahyle	Aug. 12
Grant, James ..	17	5 ft. 4 in.	Cromdall, Banff	Labourer	Ensign W. Gordon (Minmore)	June 27
Grant, James ..	18	5 ft. 3 in.	Kirkmichael, Banff	Labourer	Robert Grant, Cults	June 30
Grant, John ..	19	5 ft. 6 in.	Inveraven, Banff	Labourer	(Lieut. Gordon), Laggan	May 10
Grant, John ..	20	5 ft. 5 in.	Kirkmichael, Banff	Labourer	Mr. Miln, factor	May 28
Grant, Robert ..	34	5 ft. 6 in.	Inveraven, Banff	Taylor	R. Grant, Ruthven	May 8
Grant, Robert ..	30	5 ft. 6 in.	Kirkmichael, Banff	Farmer	Claimed by 81st	May 5
Grant, Robert ..	16	5 ft. 1 in.	Elgin, Murray	Sh'maker	(G. Munro), Elgin	Aug. 21
Grant, William ..	35	5 ft. 4½ in.	Inveraven, Banff	Labourer	R. Willox	June 17
Grant, William ..	22	5 ft. 6½ in.	Cromdall, Inverness	Labourer	R. Willox	June 12
Grant, William ..	28	5 ft. 6 in.	Cromdall, Murray	Labourer	Fochabers	June 28
Gray, William ..	21	5 ft. 6 in.	Fetteresso, Mearns	Brazier	Fochabers	June 30
Graysick, James ..	33	5 ft. 6 in.	Strathdon, Aberdeen	Labourer	(Lieut. Gordon, Wardhouse)	July 7
Gregor, James ..	34	5 ft. 5 in.	Daviot, Inverness	Labourer	Huntly Market	June 16
Gregory, James ..	36	5 ft. 10 in.	Keith, Banff	Sh'maker	Lieut. Godsman	April 26
Hay, John ..	27	5 ft. 5½ in.	Cabrach, Banff	Farmer	Hardhaugh	July 13
Hay, William ..	45	5 ft. 10 in.	Inch, Aberdeen	Labourer	Mr. Bell	June 11
Hay, William ..	18	5 ft. 9½ in.	Keith, Banff	Fowler	Fochabers	June 27
Hay, William ..	46	5 ft. 5 in.	Elgin, Murray	Labourer	(The Duke), Elgin	Aug. 27

1 The size list enters John Stewart, age 40, 5 ft. 7 in., fowler, " not yet [July 18] attested."
2 In Captain Fraser's company.

Q

Name.	*Age.*	*Height.*	*Born.*	*Trade.*	*By whom or where Enlisted.*	*Date of Enlistment.*
Hepburn, Alexander	25	5 ft. 7½ in.	Meldrum, Aberdeen	Baker	(The Duke), Fochabers	Aug. 13
Hosack, Alexander .	20	5 ft. 6½ in.	Bellie, Murray	Labourer	Fochabers	May 23
Inch, Alex. McDonell	23	6 ft. 0 in.	Kilmanivaig, Inverness	Farmer	His Father	June 1
Inch, John	23	5 ft. 3 in.	Dipple, Murray	Labourer	Fochabers	June 8
Innes, John	34	5 ft. 6½ in.	Leslie, Aberdeen	Sh'maker	(Lieut. Gordon, Wardhouse)	July 6
Innes, John	29	5 ft. 5 in.	Bellie, Murray	Sh'maker	Fochabers	May 22
Jopp, John	24	5 ft. 7½ in.	Rathven, Banff	Labourer	(The Duke), Fochabers	July 30
Kennedy, Alexander	24	5 ft. 6¾ in.	Inch, Inverness	Labourer	Invereshy	June 18
Kennedy, Angus ..	17	5 ft. 4 in.	Kilmalie, Inverness	Labourer	Mr. Butter	June 3
Kennedy, John ..	19	5 ft. 3 in.	Kingussie, Inverness	....	Benchar	June 11
Kennedy, William ..	21	5 ft. 5¼ in.	Kingussie, Inverness	Labourer	Invereshy	July 20
Kennedy, William ..	17	5 ft. 6 in.	Inch, Inverness	Labourer	Benchar	June 13
Lawson, John ..	20	5 ft. 8 in.	Alford, Aberdeen	Labourer	Mr. Gordon, son of Jas. Gordon, Brae of Scurdargue	July 27
Leslie, William ..	24	5 ft. 6¼ in.	Rhynie, Aberdeen	Millwri'ht	G. Gordon, Rhynie	June 15
Logie, James ..	23	5 ft. 6½ in.	Longbride, Murray	....	....	May 16
Lumsden, John ..	26	5 ft. 8¾ in.	Ruthven, Banff	Labourer	A. Gordon, Landends	July 30
McArthur, Charles .	34	5 ft. 7¾ in.	Laggan, Inverness	Labourer	M'Donald, Garoymore	June 6
McBain, William ..	19	5 ft. 11 in.	Inverness, Inverness	Taylor	Fochabers	July 14
[3]McBain, Peter ..	22	5 ft. 6 in.	Rothymurcus, Inverness	Labourer	The Duke	July 8
McConachie, William	22	5 ft. 5 in.	Mortlich, Banff	Taylor	(Lieut. Gordon), Laggan	May 23
McDonald, Alex. ..	20	5 ft. 0 in.	Tarves, Aberdeen	Labourer	....	Oct. 17
McDonald, Alex. ..	49	5 ft. 4 in.	Inveraven, Banff	Labourer	(Lieut. Gordon, Wardhouse)	Aug. 8
McDonald, Alex. ..	24	5 ft. 8 in.	Kirkmichael, Banff	Labourer	Ensign Wm. Gordon, (Minmore)	June 13
McDonnell, Alex. ..	20	5 ft. 5 in.	Kilmanivaig, Inverness	Labourer	Chyleonach	June 2
McDonald, Allan ..	20	5 ft. 10½ in.	Moidart, Inverness	Labourer	Thos. Gordon in Achlochrach	Aug. 22
McDonald, Angus ..	15	5 ft. 2 in.	Kilmanivaig, Inverness	Labourer	Blairachurn	Sept. 3
McDonald, Archibald	36	5 ft. 4½ in.	Slate, Inverness	Labourer	....	July 8
McDonald, Archibald	22	5 ft. 7 in.	Laggan, Inverness	Labourer	McDonald, Galway	June 8
McDonald, Archibald	17	5 ft. 3½ in.	Kilmanivaig, Inverness	Labourer	Keppoch	June 10
McDonald, Charles .	21	5 ft. 8 in.	Kilmanivaig, Inverness	Labourer	Keppoch	June 10
McDonnell, Donald	19	5 ft. 4 in.	Daviot, Inverness	Schoolm'r	....	June 19
McDonald, Donald. .	22	6 ft. 1 in.	Nigg, Ross	Labourer	Chas. Grant, Tombreahachy	June 11
[4]McDonnell, Donald	20	5 ft. 7½ in.	Kilmanivaig, Inverness	Labourer	Inveroymour	June 2
McDonnell, Donald .	20	5 ft. 8½ in.	Kilmanivaig, Inverness	Labourer	Chyleonach	June 2
McDonnell, Donald .	32	5 ft. 7 in.	Kilmanivaig, Inverness	Labourer	Chyleonach	June 2
McDonald, Ewen ..	30	5 ft. 5 in.	Kincardin, Inverness	Labourer	Captain Grant	Aug. 12
McDonald, John ..	20	5 ft. 3½ in.	Slate, Inverness	Labourer	McDonald, Galway	July 4
McDonald, John ..	18	5 ft. 3½ in.	Laggan, Inverness	Labourer	McPherson, Blargymore	June 6
McDonald, William	20	5 ft. 6 in.	Kincardine, Inverness	Labourer	John Stuart	June 1
McDougald, Duncan	30	5 ft. 7 in.	Appin, Argyle	Carpenter	McDonell, Glenco	June 1
McGillowray, Arch.	18	5 ft. 6 in.	Botriphney, Banff	Labourer	(G. Munro), Elgin	Aug. 22
McGregor, Donald ..	20	5 ft. 3 in.	Kilmalie, Inverness	Labourer	Colonel Campbell	June 2
McGregor, Duncan .	21	5 ft. 2 in.	Kilmalie, Inverness	Taylor	Blairachurn	May 30
McGregor, James ..	30	5 ft. 3 in.	Edinkeelly, Murray	Labourer	Mr. Godsman	July 15
McGregor, John ..	15	5 ft. 2 in.	Perth, Perth	Labourer	Ensign J. Gordon, (Coynachie)	June 29
McGregor, Peter ..	27	5 ft. 5½ in.	Kirkmichael, Banff	Labourer	Strathavon, Mr. Ross	June 11
McGregory, William	18	5 ft. 2 in.	Perth, Perth	Labourer	Watt, Mill of Gartly	July 6
McInnes, Angus ..	35	5 ft. 6 in.	Kilmalie, Inverness	Labourer	Mr. Gray, Barrackmaster	June 3
McIntosh, James ..	19	5 ft. 6 in.	Duthell, Murray	Labourer	Grant, Delmore	July 10
McIntyre, Alexander	20	5 ft. 7½ in.	Alvie, Inverness	Labourer	Invereshy	July 21
[5]McIntyre Alexander	20	5 ft. 5 in.	Laggan, Inverness	Labourer	Glentrim, his father	May 30
McIntyre, Angus ..	24	....	Inch, Inverness	Labourer	Invereshy	July 6
McIntyre, Donald ..	16	5 ft. 3½ in.	Kincardine, Inverness	Labourer	J. Stuart	May 28
McIntyre, Duncan .	17	5 ft. 3 in.	Kilmalie, Inverness	Labourer	Drumfour	June 8
McIntyre, Ewen ..	18	5 ft. 3 in.	Kilmalie, Inverness	Labourer	Drumfour	May 30
[6]McIntyre, Malcolm	30	5 ft. 9 in.	Kingussie, Inverness	Forrester	....	June 16
McKay, Alexander .	17	5 ft. 4 in.	Glass, Banff	Labourer	Sergeant McLay	June 4
Mackie, John ..	25	5 ft. 5 in.	Huntly, Aberdeen	Labourer	Malcolm, Westertown	May 20
McKay, John ..	30	5 ft. 6 in.	Kingussie, Inverness	Labourer	Benchar	June 16
Mackie, Neil ..	16	5 ft. 2 in.	Marnoch, Banff	Labourer	Malcolm, Westertown	May 26
McKay, Peter ..	21	5 ft. 11 in.	Inch, Inverness	Blacks'th	Inveresh[illegible]	June 16
McKenzie, David ..	28	5 ft. 2 in.	Dornoch, Sutherland	Labourer	(The Duchess's grieve)	Aug. 5
McKenzie, Donald ..	17	5 ft. 6 in.	Kilmalie, Inverness	Labourer	Jno. Kennedy, Lienachanmore	June 2
McKenzie, Duncan ..	21	5 ft. 4½ in.	Kilmalie, Inverness	Labourer	McDonald, Tillcorat	June 4
McKenzie, John ..	25	5 ft. 9 in.	Kilmalie, Inverness	Labourer	Fassfearn	July 6
McKenzie, John ..	30	5 ft. 4 in.	(Contine, Ross)	Labourer	Serjt. McLay	May 28

[3] Peter M'Bain was the son of the late John M'Bain and his wife, Isobel Grant.
[4] Did not join.
[5] The size list says he was replaced on July 6 by his brother, Malcolm.
[6] Malcolm McIntyre, deserted (*Aberdeen Journal*, March 8, 1779).

Name.	*Age.*	*Height.*	*Born.*	*Trade.*	*By whom or where Enlisted.*	*Date of Enlistment*
McKenzie, William .	30	5 ft. 4 in.	Contine, Ross	Labourer	Mr. Bell	May 28
McKinnon, Duncan	34	5 ft. 7½ in.	Glenelg, Inverness	Labourer	Terindriesh	June 4
McLachlan, Alex. ..	20	5 ft. 7 in.	Kilmalie, Inverness	Labourer	Fassifearn	June 2
McLean, Alexander	22	5 ft. 8 in.	Alvie, Inverness	Labourer	Invereshy	June 22
McLean, John ..	21	5 ft. 4 in.	Inveraven, Banff	Weaver	(Lieut. Gordon), Laggan	July 11
McLeod, William ..	28	5 ft. 3 in.	Inverness, Inverness	Taylor	Elgin Market	June 10
McMaster, Donald	18	5 ft. 6 in.	Kilmalie, Inverness	Labourer	Cameron, Lindilly	June 3
McMaster, Donald	18	5 ft. 3 in.	Kilmanivaig, Inverness	Labourer	Drumfour	May 30
McMaster, Donald	35	5 ft. 6 in.	Kilmanivaig, Inverness	Weaver	Lindilly	June 1
McMaster, Donald	16	5 ft. 4½ in.	Kilmanivaig, Inverness	Labourer	William Mitchel	June 2
McMaster, John ..	40	5 ft. 4¾ in.	Kilmalie, Inverness	Labourer	Inch	June 3
McMillan, Hugh ..	30	5 ft. 5 in.	Kilmalie, Inverness	Labourer	Mr. Butter	June 3
McNeil, John ..	25	5 ft. 10 in.	Kilmanivaig, Inverness	Labourer	McDonald, Achtriachan	May 30
McPherson, Alex. ..	20	5 ft. 6 in.	Kingussie, Inverness	Labourer	Benchar	June 13
McPherson, Alex.	17	5 ft. 3 in.	Laggan, Inverness	Labourer	(McPherson), Ralia	Aug. 21
[7]McPherson, Charles	18	5 ft. 6 in.	Kirkmichael, Banff	Labourer	Old R. McPherson	May 6
McPherson, Donald	25	5 ft. 6½ in.	Kingussie, Inverness	Labourer	Dalenich, Badenoch	May 30
McPherson, Donald	17	5 ft. 4 in.	Kingussie, Inverness	Taylor	Deserter from 71st	June 8
McPherson, Donald	22	5 ft. 2¾ in.	Laggan, Inverness	Taylor	McPherson, Ballochmore	June 8
McPherson, John ..	22	5 ft. 4¾ in.	Kirkmichael, Banff	Gardener	Lach's Son	June 29
McPherson, John ..	20	5 ft. 4 in.	Kilmalie, Inverness	Labourer	Baillie McPherson	May 30
McPherson, John ..	35	5 ft. 7 in.	Kingussie, Inverness	Farmer	(McPherson), Ralia	July 20
McPherson, John ..	17	5 ft. 7 in.	Laggan, Inverness	Labourer	Pressmuchrach, Bad.	May 30
McPherson, Lachlan	48	5 ft. 9½ in.	Kirkmichael, Banff	Labourer	Lach Dowl	June 29
McPherson, Malcom	17	....	Inch, Inverness	Labourer	Invereshy	June 23
McPherson, Murdoch	35	5 ft. 7 in.	Kingussie, Inverness	Labourer	....	June 6
McPherson, William	30	5 ft. 8 in.	Kingussie, Inverness	Labourer	Benchar	June 4
McQueen, Alexander	33	5 ft. 6 in.	Inverallan, Inverness	Labourer	R. Willox	June 12
McQueen, Alexander	22	5 ft. 11 in.	Kincardin, Inverness	Labourer	His Father	June 8
McWilliam, Robert	16	5 ft. 3 in.	Mortlich, Banff	Labourer	(Lieut. Gordon), Laggan	May 21
McWilliam, William	19	5 ft. 4¼ in.	Mortlich, Banff	Labourer	(Lieut. Gordon), Laggan	July 13
McWillie, John ..	19	5 ft. 9½ in.	Botriphney, Banff	Mason	The Duchess	June 10
McWillie, John ..	19	5 ft. 7 in.	Bellie, Banff	Labourer	Minister, Bellie	June 29
Maitland, William..	26	5 ft. 10 in.	Kinnoir, Aberdeen	Farmer	The Duke, Huntly	May 12
Marcus, George ..	28	5 ft. 5 in.	Deskford, Banff	Blacks'th	(G. Munro) at Elgin	Aug. 13
Mearns, Alexander	33	5 ft. 6 in.	Leslie, Aberdeen	Labourer	(Lieut. Gordon, Wardhouse)	Aug. 20
Mennie, George ..	40	5 ft. 10 in.	Culsamond, Aberdeen	Carpenter	(John) Bruce, Aberdeen	May 22
Miller, William ..	31	5 ft. 5½ in.	Dundurcas, Murray	Labourer	Fochabers	May 19
Milne, James ..	..	....	....	....	Forsyth, Huntly	May 16
Milne, John ..	42	5 ft. 5 in.	Forglen, Banff	Sh'maker	Fochabers	July 13
Milton, George ..	20	5 ft. 5 in.	Fordyce, Banff	Labourer	Ross, Fochabers	May 13
Milton, John ..	27	5 ft. 5¾ in.	Deskford, Banff	Labourer	Fochabers	Nov. 9
Mitchel, James ..	34	5 ft. 6 in.	Kennethmont, Abdn.	Farmer	Mr. Bell	July 2
Mitchell, Robert ..	19	5 ft. 6 in.	Kincardin, Inverness	Labourer	J. Stuart	May 6
Munro, John ..	50	5 ft. 2½ in.	Nigg, Ross	Labourer	(G. Munro) at Elgin	Aug. 12
Murray, Donald ..	22	....	Keith, Banff	Turner	Invereshy	June 23
Murray, George ..	19	5 ft. 5¼ in.	Deskford, Banff	Labourer	(John Forbes, recruit)	Aug. 10
[8]Murray, John ..	45	5 ft. 0 in.	Abernethy, Inverness	Labourer	En. W. Gordon	Aug. 22
Oxford, James ..	29	5 ft. 4 in.	Elgin, Murray	Labourer	(Lieut. Gordon), Laggan	June 3
Newton, David ..	24	5 ft. 5 in.	West Church, Lothian	Stocking maker	(John Steuart, forester of Strathdown)	Aug. 18
Proctor, George ..	34	5 ft. 4 in.	Kennethmont, Aberdeen	Labourer	(Lieut. Gordon, Wardhouse)	Aug. 19
Reid, John	20	5 ft. 7½ in.	Mortlich, Banff	Cartwrght.	Keith Market	June 16
Riach, Donald ..	30	5 ft. 6 in.	Kirkmichael, Banff	Labourer	Tomintoul	June 30
Riddle, Alexander ..	..	....	....	....	G. Gordon, Rhynie	May 29
Robertson, Alex. ..	18	5 ft. 11½ in.	Cabrach, Aberdeen	Labourer	Mr. Bell	July 2
Robertson, Alex. ..	24	5 ft. 6 in.	Laggan, Inverness	Labourer	Parson R. McPherson	June 6
Robertson, James ..	30	5 ft. 0 in.	Kirkmichael, Banff	Labourer	(Wm. Grant), Tombrackach)	Aug. 10
Robertson, William	35	5 ft. 4 in.	Cabrach, Aberdeen	Labourer	(Lieut. Gordon, Wardhouse)	July 3
Robson, William ..	17	5 ft. 3 in.	Manchester, Chester	Weaver	Deserter of Glasgow Vols.	July 29
Ronald, James ..	18	5 ft. 7½ in.	Gartley, Aberdeen	Labourer	Mr. Reynols	Aug. 2
Ross, Angus ..	24	5 ft. 2 in.	Dornoch, Sutherland	Labourer	Elgin Market	Aug. 5
Ross, Thomas ..	25	5 ft. 6 in.	Kilmalie, Inverness	Sh'maker	Mr. Ross, minister	June 10
Ryley, Bryan ..	32	5 ft. 9½ in.	St. Tringans, Glasgow	Labourer	(John) Bruce, (Aberdeen)	May 27
Scott, William ..	30	5 ft. 4 in.	Drainie, Murray	Labourer	(Lieut. Gordon), Laggan	June 1
Shaw, Lachlan ..	20	5 ft. 8¼ in.	Inch, Inverness	Labourer	Invereshy	June 22
Shaw, William ..	23	5 ft. 7 in.	Kirkmichael, Banff	Labourer	Priest of Strathaven	July 10
Shearer, George ..	28	5 ft. 8 in.	Glass, Banff	Labourer	(Lieut. Gordon, Wardhouse)	July 15
Siveright, James ..	28	5 ft. 5 in.	Rhynie, Aberdeen	Labourer	G. Gordon, Rhynie	June 17
Siveright, John ..	26	5 ft. 8 in.	Keith, Banff	Labourer	The Duchess	July 4

7 The size list says he replaced, October 20, his father, Robert, farmer, who enlisted May 6, aged 60.
8 John Murray did not join.

Name.	Age.	Height.	Born.	Trade.	By whom or where Enlisted.	Date of Enlistment.
Smith, Alexander ..	23	5 ft. 4 in.	Ruthven, Aberdeen	Flaxdr'scr	Fochabers	June 2
Smith, George ..	20	6 ft. 1 in.	Belhelvie, Aberdeen (discharged 16 Nov.)	Square wright	....	June 19
Smith, James ..	24	5 ft. 2½ in.	Rhynie, Aberdeen	Labourer	Smith, Aberdeen	July 6
Smith, Robert ..	18	5 ft. 4 in.	Kincardine, Inverness	Labourer	His Father	July 11
Smith, William ..	25	5 ft. 3 in.	Huntly, Aberdeen	Weaver	Fochabers	April 26
Smith, William ..	39	5 ft. 3½ in.	Elgin, Murray	Taylor	Stewart	May 23
Steenson, James ..	34	5 ft. 5 in.	Fordyce, Banff	Gardener	Fochabers	June 13
Stephen, Thomas ..	23	5 ft. 6 in.	Alves, Murray	Labourer	Fochabers	April 29
Stephen, William ..	21	5 ft. 5 in.	Alves, Murray	Blacks'th	Fochabers	May 5
Stewart, Alexander	21	5 ft. 6 in.	Mortlich, Banff	Labourer	Rob. Stuart, officer's son	July 13
Stewart, Charles ..	15	5 ft. 3 in.	Kirkmichael, Banff	Labourer	Tomintoul	July 10
Steuart, Alexander	29	5 ft. 3 in.	Inch, Inverness	Labourer	J. Stuart	June 8
Steuart, Donald ..	17	5 ft. 4 in.	Inveraven, Banff	Labourer	James Gordon, Achnastank	July 20
Steuart, Donald ..	17	5 ft. 3½ in.	Kirkmichael, Banff	Labourer	John McPherson, Tomach-laggan	Aug. 10
Steuart, John ..	19	5 ft. 5 in.	Inveraven, Banff	Labourer	Chas. Grant, Tombreackachy	Sept. 8
Steuart, John ..	30	5 ft. 7 in.	Mortlich, Banff	Labourer	Capt. Grant, Lurg	Aug. 22
Steuart, John ..	24	5 ft. 3½ in.	Abernethy, Inverness	Farmer	His Father	July 31
Steuart, John ..	21	5 ft. 6½ in.	Kilmanivaig, Inverness	Weaver	Gordonsburgh	June 3
Stewart, Lewis ..	24	5 ft. 5½ in.	Kirkmichael, Banff	Labourer	Rob. Smith, Dell	July 15
Steuart, William ..	?	5 ft. 10 in.	Kirkmichael, Banff	Labourer	C. Stewart, Drummin	June 24
Stewart, William ..	21	5 ft. 8 in.	Kirkmichael, Banff	Labourer	Tomentoul	July 11
Sutherland, Robert	15	5 ft. 3 in.	Rothlemay, Banff	Labourer	Ensign J.Gordon (Coynachie)	June 29
Sutherland, William	15	....	Kildonan, Sutherland	Labourer	Elgin Market	Aug. 7
Taylor, William ..	20	5 ft. 5½ in.	Ruthven, Aberdeen	Labourer	Fochabers	June 1
Taylor, William ..	40	5 ft. 7 in.	Ruthven, Aberdeen	Labourer	Laggan	June 6
Thomas, James ..	21	5 ft. 4 in.	Bellie, Murray	Labourer	Fochabers	May 4
Thomson, John ..	(22)	5 ft. 9 in.	Raine, Aberdeen	Wright	(Lieut. Gordon, Wardhouse)	July 3
Thomson, William ..	26	5 ft. 5 in.	Elgin, Murray	Labourer	Elgin	June 12
Webster, Arthur ..	30	5 ft. 7½ in.	Forglen, Banff	Gardener	(John) Bruce, (Aberdeen)	June 4
Whinton, John ..	29	5 ft. 5 in.	Inverkeithny, Banff	Labourer	Laggan	June 4
Wilkie, Peter ..	25	5 ft. 9¼ in.	Glass, Banff	....	....	May 16
Wood, Robert ..	45	5 ft. 6 in.	Stitchel, Tweedale	Taylor	Huntly	July 8
Wrachan, John ..	..	....	....	....	....	
Yeats, John ..	19	5 ft. 7 in.	Aberlour, Banff	Labourer	(Lieut. Gordon, Wardhouse)	July 29
Young, John ..	28	5 ft. 6 in.	Fordyce, Banff	Blacks'tn	Fochabers	June 30

The Highland character of the corps is shown by the fact that 348 of the 930 privates bore surnames beginning with "Mac." There were 26 Camerons (19 being in the Duke's company), 24 Grants (15 in Cumming's company), over 20 Frasers (17 in Fraser's company), and only 7 Gordons; Sergeant Charles Gordon, of Haddo's company, is entered as "in prison." In the Duke's and Lord William's companies there are 83 different surnames, out of 186 different privates. Of these, the only English ones are Oxford and Reynolds. It is rather strange that 18 of the 930 privates were returned dead in the September-December muster roll (five occurring in Campbell's company), and there were two desertions. The following summary of the first muster roll discloses some interesting facts at a glance:—

COMPANY.	STATION.	PRIVATES.	PRIVATES EFFICIENT.	"MACS."
Duke of Gordon ...	Fochabers	... 94	... 91	... 37
Lord William Gordon	Fort George	... 94	... 94	... 16
John Campbell ...	„	... 92	... 89	... 40
James Chisholm ...	„	... 92	... 91	... 27
A. P. Cumming ...	„	... 91	... 90	... 22
Sir William Forbes ...	„	... 93	... 90	... 12

COMPANY.	STATION.	PRIVATES.	PRIVATES EFFICIENT.	"MACS."
James Fraser... ...	Fort-George ...	92 ...	90 ...	45
Lord Haddo	,, ...	93 ...	93 ...	35
George Mackay ...	,, ...	93 ...	93 ...	65
Lachlan Mackintosh	,, ...	96 ...	90 ...	49

It is not very easy to follow the early movements of the regiment. One company seems to have been stationed in October, 1778, in Cromarty, and the entire regiment marched through Aberdeen in May, 1779, for Ayr, from which the companies radiated in several directions. Then the second set of musters at the Record Office for the period of 182 days, ending June 24, 1779, discloses these facts :—

COMPANY.	PLACE.	PRIVATES.	PRIVATES EFFICIENT.
Duke of Gordon - -	Ayr - -	96 -	94
Lord William Gordon -	Ayr - -	96 -	93
James Chisholm - -	Irvine - -	96 -	84
John Campbell - -	Ayr - -	96 -	84
Alexander Penrose Cumming	Greenock -	96 -	82
William Finlason -	Kirkcudbright -	96 -	86
Sir William Forbes -	Irvine - -	96 -	85
Lord Haddo - -	Ayr - -	96 -	91
George Mackay - -	Greenock -	96 -	91
Lachlan Mackintosh -	Kirkcudbright -	96 -	81

The Northern Fencibles never moved out of Scotland, but were simply shifted from town to town, mostly in the south. They were on duty in Glasgow when the news of the riots instigated by the Duke's crazy brother, Lord George, reached Gordon Castle in June, 1780. The Duchess was living alone in the Castle, and on hearing the news she hurried off to Edinburgh to be nearer the sources of information. There she found Beattie, the poet, who went on with her to Glasgow, where she remained till the review of the regiment was over, after which she and the Duke set off for London. The details of its five years of life, however, were not in any case exciting. Stewart (*Highlanders*, 2nd ed. ii. 305) says that the regiment was "so healthy and efficient," that "only 24" of the men died during its five years' existence.

In 1781 and 1782 the regiment, or part of it, seems to have been stationed in Aberdeen, for the *Aberdeen Journal* (August 6, 1781, p. 4, col. 3) records a mysterious mutiny, of which I can find no official records :—

On Friday last a general Court Martial was held here, for the trial of John Fraser and William Kennedy, soldiers in the North Fencible Regiment, for being actively concerned in a mutiny among the soldiers of that corps, on Sunday evening the 15th of July. His Grace the Duke of Gordon was President, and Sir James Dunbar, Judge Advocate of the Court, which was composed of officers from the North Fencibles and Sutherland Fencibles. The trial continued Friday and Saturday, and is to go on this morning.

The *Aberdeen Journal*, July 29, 1782, records another event at Aberdeen :—

Deserted yesterday morning from the Northern Fencible Regiment quartered here, John Cameron, aged 24, 5 feet 6 inches high, fair complexion, fair hair, grey eyes, born parish Kincardine and county of Inverness, and Euan McPhic, aged 33, 5 feet 9 inches high, brown complexion, brown hair, blue eyes, born in the parish of Kilmalie, Inverness-shire.

At last the order for the disbandment of the regiment was made on March 20, 1783, as follows :—

George R.

Whereas We have thought fit to order our North Regiment of Fencible Men under your [Duke of Gordon's] command to be disbanded, and have appointed Our Trusty and Well-beloved Lieutenant General Mackay to attend the doing thereof : Our will and pleasure is that upon the arrival of the said Lieutenant General Mackay or such person or persons as he shall appoint for this service at the quarters of Our said Regiment in North Britain, you take care that the several companies thereof be dismissed our service in such manner and according to such instructions as we have signified to the said Lieutenant General Mackay in that behalf.

Given at Our Court at St. James's this 20th day of March, 1783, in the twenty third year of our reign.

The final muster roll (of which there are 11 bundles at the Record Office, W.O. 13: 3,900) is for the 118 days ending April 21, 1783, although some of the companies had been disbanded before that. The dates of the disbandment were as follows :—

COMPANY.	PRIVATES.	DISBANDED.	PLACE.
Duke of Gordon -	92	April 12	Aberdeen
Lord William Gordon -	62	„ „	„
James Chisholm -	87	May 30	Fort George
Alexander Penrose Cumming	85	„ „	„
William Finlason -	62	April 12	Aberdeen
Charles Gordon -	49	„ „	„
John Gordon -	94	April 22	Fort George
John Grant -	60	„ „	„
Lachlan Mackintosh -	46	May 30	„
Thomas Russel -	27	April 12	Aberdeen

The Duke's patriotic services were appreciated by his neighbours, for the Aberdeen Town Council sent him a letter of thanks in April 7, 1783, and the Magistrate of Peterhead, the batteries of which town were in charge of one of his sergeants, also thanked him. The Aberdeen letter ran as follows:—

My Lord Duke,—Being informed that Your Grace's Regiment of North Fencibles is ordered soon to be disembodied, before that event takes place, We think it our indispensable duty in name of this City and Community to express the just since [sense] we entertain of not only of the laudable and spirited exertion made by Your Grace in first raising of the Regiment for the internal defence of the Country, at a period, when its situation so much called for a protection, but also of the good conduct and behaviour of the Corps since their establishment, by which they have upon all occasions done so much honour to themselves.

We are no less particularly sensible of the exact discipline and good order which has uniformly been maintained by all the Officers, as well as of the regular and peaceable deportment of the Soldiers, during the long time we have had the happiness of the Regiment's head quarters being at Aberdeen, in so much that we are convinced, they are all lookt upon and esteemed as good citizens, equally as well disciplined Military.

Impressed with these sentiments, We beg leave in this manner to communicate them to Your Grace, and to request that you will be so good as convey them to the Officers and Corps, in any manner that Your Grace shall think most suitable and proper.

We have only to add that We sincerely wish all happiness and prosperity to Your Grace's illustrious Family, and that we have the honour to be with the most profound respect and esteem My Lord Duke, Your Grace's most faithfull and most obedt. Servts.,

W. YOUNG, Provost.

The Duke replied to this epistle, dating from Aberdeen the same day (April 7):—

Gentlemen,—I have the honor of your very polite letter of this date, and I take the earliest opportunity to assure you that it is highly flattering to me and to the Officers under my Command to have our conduct approved of by a Body so respectable as the Lord Provost and Magistrates of Aberdeen.

We do, Gentlemen, most sincerely thank you for this publick testimony of your esteem. It does infinite honor to the Corps, and confers a lasting obligation upon us all.

I in particular, am proud to find that the measures I pursued for the internal defence of this Country have given satisfaction to those who constitute so distinguished a part of the Community   I am highly obliged to you, Gentlemen, for your good wishes in favour of my family and I beg leave to assure you that upon every occasion I shall have entirely at heart the Interest and Prosperity of the City of Aberdeen

LORD HUNTLY'S BLACK WATCH COMPANY.

1790: RAISED BY THE 4TH DUKE OF GORDON: DISCHARGED 1791.

The fourth of the Duke of Gordon's six experiments in recruiting was the Independent Company, raised nominally by his son, the handsome young Marquis of Huntly, but really under the powerful ægis of his Grace himself, and taken to the Black Watch in 1790. It is of peculiar interest, for the Black Watch suggested the tartan adopted by the Gordons, a Huntly manufacturer adding the famous yellow stripe.

The return of the Black Watch from America was one of the sensations of the autumn of 1789. Landing at Portsmouth in October after an absence of 14 years, it was visited by hundreds of people as it marched northwards over Finchley Common, where it had had a lamentable experience in 1743; and when it reached Edinburgh in the summer its reception was most enthusiastic. Owing, however, to difficulties in the Highlands, the attempt to increase its strength failed. It was probably this which made the Marquis raise his Independent Company, although, on the other hand, he may have enlisted it to serve with any regiment of his choice. As a matter of fact, he took it to the Black Watch, having exchanged with Captain Alexander Grant.

The Letter of Service for the raising of the company does not seem to have been preserved at Gordon Castle, but it would appear to have been sent to the young Marquis on October 13, 1790, for, writing from Gordon Castle on November 8, 1790, to Sir George Yonge, Secretary for War, he says (*Gordon Castle Papers*):—

I had the honour to receive your letter of the 13th October conveying His Majesty's commands for my raising an Independent Company of Foot upon the terms therein mentioned; of which I accept with pleasure and expect soon to be able to return my complement compleat.

I beg leave to offer my compliments and best thanks and also to present my compliments and thanks to Lady Yonge for the cockade which her ladyship was so attentive as to send me some posts ago.

The Marquis put out all oars, getting help from every side. The earliest correspondent on the subject was James Saunders, who wrote to Todd, the Duke's factor, from Edinburgh on October 30, 1790, as follows (*Ibid.*):—

As I most heartily wish the Marquis success in his recruiting business, a thought has struck me that I may be of use to him, and also to that vagabond, my ffriend, Jock of Lurg. He is certainly one of the best serjeant kites in the kingdom. I therefore sent for him this afternoon, and pointed out to him where he might find a more powerful advocate as to his possession of Campdel than any man in the island, and that was the Marquis of Huntly. Bringing his Lordship ten or a dozen recruits, he might wipe off a deal of that stigma that is presently out against him, and perhaps might obtain the deed warrant recalled that is presently issued against him. He seemed to relish the thought much, and proposes setting out from this Monday, and to be with you at Pitmain Wednesday morning; but, as I know from experience that he is not a very true tryster, I trouble you with this in case he does not take the Badenoch route, that you may, if the Marquis approves of it, please send for him and conferr on this subject. I know perfectly if he embarks in this business he will save the Marquis and you both a world of drudgery. I have told Lurg that liberal bounty money will be allowed.

They are most extravagant here in that article. Lord Dalhousie [who had entered the 3rd Dragoon Guards in 1788] is giving 20 guineas for some stout fellows. But I hope the Marquis will beat all of our south country down, and show himself to be the Cock of the North, and that his country produces men and not sheep.

Naturally enough, the town of Huntly was deeply interested in the Marquis's efforts, and William Forsyth, the designer of Gordon tartan, took special pride in the recruiting. On November 6, he informed Menzies that he had got a recruit named Mackie for 5½ guineas. "We are now twelve men strong." He hopes to keep pace with Fochabers. "Sergeant Gordon, who is very active, wants a sword and belt, and the lads understand you give a decent shirt, so that there will be a great demand for shirts; which attend to." Forsyth, who supplied shirts to the extent of 150 yards of linen, had, you see, an eye to business. On November 9, he again reports progress (*Ibid.*):—

There is some difference between Sergeant Gordon and George Donald. The latter says he was promised Sergeant's pay and wishes to walk with ye sergeant. We can't spare Gordon. He's a diligent, honest fellow. Say what's to be done. We have a lad of five feet 7½ inches in treaty. . . .

Since yesterday [November 16] at 4 o'clock we have danced in the street and publick house to one o'clock this morning. By dint of drink and bank notes [we] have got five good recruits, all sober this morning and duly attested.

In still another letter, which is undated, he writes (*Ibid.*):—

We had a very handsome, well-dressed party beating about yesterday. Depend that every exertion will be made to promote ye Marquis's plan of getting recruits. I'm as much disposed to œconomie as any, but find that it will be necessary to give high bounties—from five to ten guineas. You can't judge what effect money has among a lower class. . . . . The whiskie is not quite out of my head. The party requir'd a good deal.

Coming to Glenlivet, we get a very interesting letter from William Gordon, Minmore, who got a commission in the regiment. Writing to the Duke on November 16 (*Ibid.*):—

When I had the honour of waiting on your Grace some time ago at Glendiffich upon a report that your Grace was to be concerned in raising a regt., I requested the honour of being recommended for an ensigncy in that event. Tho' your Grace has not engaged on the plan then expected, as I understand the Marquis is raising an Independent Company, I hope your Grace will pardon my presuming to request my earnest desire and ambition to serve under any of the Noble Family, particularly one whose transcendent virtues attract the love and admiration of all who have the honour to approach his person.

If, therefore, the ensigncy is not promised, I will venture to request of your Grace, in addition to numberless other favors, to be recommended for it. If men were an object to his lordship, I think I could undertake for the ordinary compliment [sic]. At least, I am convinced my chance would be as good as any from this quarter, and, could I assure them that I were to be engaged, I believe I have half a dozen ready to follow me, whom I have tried in vain on any other footing. But I will urge nothing farther on the subject. An accumulation of favours have established in me such unbounded confidence in your Grace, that if the appointment is not promised, I will venture to hope for a favourable answer.

The (undated) petition of Duncan Gordon in Glenfeshie to the Marquis is also another pleasant document (*Ibid.*):—

Humbly sheweth: That his lot in the world has been various and uncertain—the first periode of his life in afluence. He has been twice married: has two sons by his first wife in the Artillery at Giberalter. Their appearance would please your lordship, and according to your petitioner's information their conduct would intitle them to your lordship's patronage and protection. That your petitioner through old age and infirmities is not only reduced to indigent circumstances, but is now unable to work for the support of his second wife and her issue, the bearer hereof being their second son and best support. Notwithstanding, they think him well bestowed when their Chief has use for him.

May it therefore please your lordship to take the bearer not only under your protection, but also to consider him as your lordship's own, to do with him as may seem best to your lordship. That your lordship may long live to support friends and suppress enemies shall ever be the prayers of Duncan Gordon.

As in all the recruiting experiences of the Gordons, Lochaber (where the Duke owned 110,494 acres) proved helpful, producing 15 men, including seven Camerons, one of whom is described as " a present from Lochiel." Besides these, the " Gentlemen " offered 16 more men. Whether these were forthcoming does not appear, but a note on the Lochaber list says :—" Many of the above Gentlemen offered 15 and even 20 guineas for a man to present to his lordship." Over and above the 16, Captain Macdonell of Keppoch " undertook to give four men for Keppoch and two for himself " ; but upon Keppoch's being appointed ensign, the Marquis dispensed with them. As it turned out, however, Alexander Macdonell of Keppoch was able to produce only one man. Writing on November 30, he says (*Ibid.*) :—

What hurts me most is that I fear the Marquis of Huntly may, from my want of success in recruiting, be dubious of my attachment to his interest. The truth is that I have not the method myself ; neither have I the young men. My nephew finds I could not even collect them together for the purpose of concerting some plan of getting men for him : and for the lower class the same aversion to the service runs through the whole. Some people are still out with recruiting orders. What their success may be I know not : but, if they bring in any recruits, they shall be sent to meet the Marquise's party at Edinburgh when my nephew will have the honour of paying his respects to him.

My nephew was on his way to Edinburgh when at Fort William he mett with some of his tutors, who advised him to remain in the country till he was honoured with further instructions from the Marquis, as letters were said to have been received to put a stop to the recruiting of the Independent Companies.

No person can have a more gratefull sense of the many essentiall favours conferred upon the family of Keppoch than I ; and doubt not but that I can point out to you where his Grace the Duke of Gordon might pocket near £1,000 yearly more than his present rent roll, if his

Grace did not prefer his present sett of tenants to strangers. But that and the ingratitude of the people upon the ffarms which my nephew holds by His Grace's goodness, I shall defer at present and shall mention only one man who ask'd no less a sum than £100 sterl. The offers I have made to many I would be ashamed to own.

A somewhat similar plaint was made by James Glashan, who wrote from Keith, December 7, about William Davidson, late servant to James Grant, merchant there. In the previous month Davidson had received from his master in the house of Robert Gordon, vintner, Keith, half a guinea by way of enlisting money (*Ibid.*):—

But before he left the room he repented and threw back the half guinea: and which has since been in the keeping of one Ffraser, another recruit . . . Under all these circumstances, Davidson, rather than to have the matter judicially cognosed before the Justice [Gordon of Cairnfield], chose to refer himself to the Marquis and to acquiesce in what his lordship should determine: for which purpose he goes just now to Gordon Castle.

This disinclination was, however, by no means universal. Thus, Captain John Grant, writing to Menzies from Tammore, November 19, cites a very different case (*Ibid.*):—

If ye Marquiss is not provided in drummers, I was induced to inlist one for him, a very fine hansome boy with an excellent eer, who would not part with his comrade, one of ye lads I attested. He tear'd [cried?] like a child to enlist.

Again John Stuart, Pityoulish, wrote (December 4) about another case (*Ibid.*):—

The bearer, Rhanald McDonald (who got a man for the Marquis at Grantoun) I have prevailed upon to offer himself to the Marquis; a stoute man who, I hope, will answer. If so, please hyre a horse for him at my expenses, untill he wins up with ye rest of the men. The man has been a soldier before. In the event he hands a man to his lordship, he expects the Marquis sometime or other may procure the pension for him.

The personal touch was very important in all these recruiting endeavours. Thus, James Glashan, writing from Keith, November 30, gives it as his and Gordon of Coynachie's opinion that the Marquis's " riding into Banff would have a very good effect."

The Marquis had spread his net as far south as Edinburgh, the family friend, Charles Gordon of Braid, keeping his eyes open. He wrote from Edinburgh to Braid on November 22 (*Ibid.*):—

Sir,—I last night fell in with two very stout old Fencibles, who were willing to inlist under Lord Huntly's banners. I took the liberty of calling at your house [in] Princes Street at rather a late hour, as I was afraid they might not be so keen when some borrowed spirit had left them. [The men were apparently Alexander McKinlay, formerly a sergeant in the Fencibles, and Donald McDonald, the latter of whom drew back.]

One of the greatest obstacles encountered by the Marquis was the attitude of the employer of labour, especially in the case of indentured apprentices. Thus, when Isaac Watson, Abraham Craib and Walter Milton, apprentices of Provost George Robinson, stockingmaker of Banff, enlisted, that worthy strongly objected. Watson had been a servant with James Milne of Boyndie. On December 2, 1789, he entered a seven years' apprenticeship with Robinson's firm. On November 20, (1790), he went to Gordon Castle and offered himself as a recruit to the Marquis's company, receiving a bounty of five guineas and 6s. to drink the King's health. He then returned to Banff on holiday, and was arrested. He wrote to Menzies from Portsoy on November 24, as follows (*Ibid.*):—

Sir,—I most inform you that last night ay was taken prisener about seven aclock at night. P[l]eas send word to reliv me, as shone [soon] as posoble. You wil ableadg your humb[l]e servant.

On December 1, 1790, the Robinsons presented a petition to the Banff Justices of the Peace, who decided that Watson must return to his work, under a penalty of £30, and forbade the Marquis of Huntly to molest him under a penalty of £50. The Marquis intervened in the case, "not upon the distinguished character as eldest son of one of the first peers of the realm . . . but simply as captain of the company." Robinson on his side declared that he raised the case not because he wanted to retain Watson personally, but because he thought it would have a bad effect on his other apprentices. He wrote to Huntly, November 25 (*Ibid.*):—

I am compelled to adopt these measures to deter the rest of my apprentices from leaving their service after they have been taught their business with much labour and expense. I should be sorry to do anything to interrupt your Lordship's success in recruiting. On the contrary, nothing would give me more pleasure than to forward it by any means in my power. At the same time, I trust the circumstance will shew the indispensable necessity of making examples of these apprentices.

Another apprentice case occurred with a certain Mr. Thurburn, who, writing from Drum, December 6, said (*Ibid.*):—

Mr. Thurburn returns his most respectfull compliments to the Marquis of Huntly, acknowledging the great honour done him by the card of yesterday.   It is Mr. Thurburn's sincere wish that Siveright may do the Marquis more honour as a soldier than he has given him satisfaction as an apprentice.   As to any money due to him by Mr. Thurburn, that method appears to have been totally misrepresented.   Instead of this, Mr. Thurburn has incurr'd more expence (now useless), and suffer'd more loss than his apprentice is ever likely to repay; of which Mr. Thurburn will chearfully give the Marquis the most satisfactory proof, if he should condescend to enquire into it.

Masters sometimes took much pains to keep an apprentice.   Thus, John Grant, Keith, writes (November 25) to Menzies about a "truely handsome boy" named Davidson:—"His master, John Stables, has kept him out of the way, but ye lads that are here will find him out and bring him down if he keeps Keith."

Sometimes the recruits were undesirable for other reasons.   On December 5, William Marshall wrote to Menzies from Keithmore (*Ibid.*):—

It seems that Peter Steuart, who has enlisted himself with My Lord Huntly, means to defraud him [Thomson in Mains of Balveny] of a just debt which he has his bill for, and the purport of this is to see if you can be of any service to him in trying to recover it before Steuart leaves the country: which, I hear, will be soon.

In spite of the letters quoted here of a later date, a halt seems to have been made in the recruiting, under a circular letter of November 22, which was sent from Gordon Castle to Captain Godsman; Captain Grant, Rippachy; James Gordon, Portsoy; Gordon, Coynachie; George Bell, Cocklarachie; and William Forsyth, Huntly.   It announced (*Ibid.*):—

All recruiting for the Marquis of Huntly's Company being now stopped, in consequence of orders from the War Office, I at his lordship's orders request the favour of you to forward here immediately on receipt all the lads you may have enlisted, and in course of post to transmitt me their attestations and a particular account of the levy money, etc., paid by you.

Forsyth advises Menzies, November 23, that a kind of rendezvous for the recruits had been fixed at Ruthven market, that day (*Ibid.*):—

They will all be collected and make their appearance tomorrow [at Gordon Castle] before the Marquis, except Brodie whose wife's in labour. She's so bound up in Johne that she wou'd realy lose her reason. He's a good recruit and very steady and willing, and will appear when a young soger is brought forth.

The total cost of the recruits to the Marquis between October 27, 1790, and March 12, 1791, was £1,054 6s. 8d., including the following expenses :—

Bounty Money	.	.	.	.	.	.	.	£492 7 6
Incidental Expenses	.	.	.	.	.	.	492 17 0
Subsistence	.	.	.	.	.	.	.	132 1 2

The company marched south in the beginning of December, the *Aberdeen Journal* (of December 13) recording :—

Last week passed through this place the Marquis of Huntly's Independent Company, under the command of Lieutenant Gordon. The Company is more than complete, was raised in about three weeks: and we do not exaggerate when we say that a company of finer young fellows never carried arms. Such was their zeal and attachment to their noble young lord that few, if any, would accept the King's bounty [though they did not hesitate to accept the Marquis's as we have seen].

The Marquis got his commission in the Black Watch, January 25, 1791, and brought his Independent Company with him, much to the joy of the Regiment (then at Edinburgh Castle), which had failed in its own endeavours to recruit at this time. The Marquis's contingent numbered 93 men, and they figure for the first time in the regimental muster, December, 1790-June, 1791 (*W.O.* 12 : 5,480). Strange to say, however, only 43 were retained, for 40 were discharged on February 21, 8 on March 5 ; 1 on May 27 ; and 1 on June 13, 1791. The names of 58 figure in the collection of papers at Gordon Castle dealing with the company, and give details of bounties and some interesting facts. Of these 58, however, eighteen never reached the regiment at all, and three at least, all bearing the name of Macraw, soon deserted. The following roll is made up from the Gordon Castle data and from the official muster roll (*W.O.* 12 ; 5,480) :—

MEN.			REMARKS.	BOUNTY.	DISCHARGE.
Alexander, Peter	-	-	......	......	Feb. 21, 1791
Aver (?), John	-	-	*Gordon Castle List*: not in *W.O.* 12: 5480	£5 5/-	......
Beaton, Angus	-	-	......	......	Feb. 21, 1791
Bisset, Thomas	-	-	*Gordon Castle List* - - -	£5 5/-	......

MEN.	REMARKS.	BOUNTY.	DISCHARGE.
Brodie, John	whose wife was " in labour "	......	Feb. 21, 1791
Buchanan, John	......	......	Mar. 5, 1791
Cameron, Alexander	son to Donald Moir, viz., Cameron, at Lochroy, Inverness	......	......
Cameron, Allan	Enlisted by Cameron of Fassifern	£5 6/-	......
Cameron, Allan	from Mr. Steuart, Lochaber. One of these Allans is not in *W.O.* 12 : 5480	......	......
Cameron, Donald	may perhaps be Duncan in *W.O.* 12 : 5480	......	Feb. 21, 1791
Cameron, Duncan	from the Ballichbeg tenants, Lochaber	......	......
Cameron, Duncan	from the Ballichmore tenants, Lochaber	......	.....
Cameron, James	from the Ballichmore tenants, Lochaber	......	......
Cameron, John	from Macdonell, Inch, Lochaber	......	Feb. 21, 1791
Cameron, Martin	son of Cameron of Letterfinlay, not in *W.O.* 12 : 5480	......	......
Chisholm, Roderick	from McLenachar Moir, Lochaber	......	Feb. 21, 1791
Clark, Andrew	......	......	Feb. 21, 1791
Clark, Duncan	......	......	Feb. 21, 1791
Craib, Alexander	......	£6 5/-	Feb. 21, 1791
Cruickshank, James	died Jan. 22, 1791	......	......
Cumming, George	......	£5 10/-	Feb. 21, 1791
Davidson, John	......	£3 3/-	Feb. 21, 1791
Davidson, Thomas	not in *W.O.* 12 : 5480	£5 5/-	......
Davidson, William	enlisted by Sergeant Gordon late servant to James Grant, merchant, Keith	£13 13/-	Feb. 21, 1791
Donald, George	Sergeant: not in *W.O.* 12 : 5480	£5 5/-	......
Donald, John	brother of George	£3 3/-	Feb. 21, 1791
Donaldson, James	......	......	Feb. 21, 1791
Dumbreck, John	......	......	......
Dunbar, John	......	......	......
Duncan, William	......	......	Feb. 21, 1791
Fraser, Alexander	......	......	Feb. 21, 1791
Fraser, John	......	......	Feb. 21, 1791
Fraser, Simon	......	......	Feb. 21, 1791
Fraser, William	......	......	Feb. 21, 1791
Gilbert, John	......	£5 5/-	Mar. 5, 1791
Glass, James	......	......	Mar. 5, 1791
Gordon, Alexander	......	......	Feb. 21, 1791
Gordon, James	......	......	......
Gordon, John	......	......	Feb. 21, 1791
Grant, Duncan	......	......	......
Grant, Lewis	......	£5 5/-	Feb. 21, 1791
Henry, James	......	......	May 27, 1791

S

MEN.	REMARKS.	BOUNTY.	DISCHARGE.
Horne, George - -	......	......	......
Kennedy, Neil - -	Lochaber - - - - -	£10	......
Lyon, John - - -	......	£5 5/-	......
McArthur, Alexander -	not in *W.O.* 12 : 5480 -	......	......
McBain, Duncan - -	"McBean" in *W.O.* 12 : 5480 -	......	......
McDonald, Alexander -	Glencoe - - - -	......	Feb. 21, 1791
McDonald, Archibald -	......	......	......
McDonald, George -	......	......	......
McDonald, James-	......	......	Feb. 21, 1791
McDonald, James (2) -	......	......	Feb. 21, 1791
McDonald, John - -	......	......	Feb. 21, 1791
Macdonell, Forbes -	recommended by Achtriachton, not in *W.O.* 12 : 5480	......	......
MacDowall, James -	......	......	Feb. 7, 1791
McEachan, Alexander -	......	......	......
McEdward, Donald -	......	......	Feb. 7, 1791
McGregor, Alexander -	......	......	......
McKay, William - -	......	......	......
Mackie, William - -	enlisted by William Forsyth -	£5 15 6	Feb. 21, 1791
Mackenzie, Donald -	*W.O.* 12 : 5480	......	Feb. 21, 1791
Mackenzie, Duncan -	may be the same as Donald -	£5 11/-	......
Mackenzie, Thomas -	sergeant, not in *W.O.* 12 : 5480	£5 5/-	......
Mackenzie, William -	......	......	Feb. 21, 1791
McKinlay, Alexander -	formerly in a regiment of Fencibles, not in *W.O.* 12 : 5480	£5 5/-	......
McLachlan, Robert -	......	£7 7/-	Feb. 21, 1791
McLeod, Alexander -	Age 20, height 5 ft. 5 ins. ; labourer, Killearnan ; enlisted Nov. 18; not in *W.O.* 12 : 5480	......	......
McLeod, Donald - -	Duncan, in *Gordon Castle List* -	......	......
McLeod, Neil - -	from Mr. Ross, Lochaber - -	......	Feb. 21, 1791
Macpherson, Allan -	age 23, height 5 ft. 8 ins., born at Alvie ; enlisted Nov. 8; not in *W.O.* 12 : 5480	......	......
Macpherson, Duncan -	......	£5 5/-	......
Macpherson, John (1) -	......	......	......
Macpherson, John (2) -	......	......	Feb. 21, 1791
Macpherson, Malcolm -	......	......	Feb. 21, 1791
Macpherson, William -	not in *W.O.* 12 : 5480 - -	......	......
Macraw, Donald - -	age 22, height 5 ft. 9½ ins. ; labourer, Kintail ; enlisted Nov. 2 : deserted.	......	......
Macraw, Farquhar -	age 23, height 5 ft. 8 ins. ; labourer, Glenelchaig, Ross ; enlisted Nov. 12 : deserted	£3 3/-	......
Macraw, Murdoch -	from Achriachton, Lochaber ; not in *W.O.* 5480.	......	......
Macraw, Murdoch -	age 25, height 5 ft. 6 ins. ; labourer, Glenelchaig ; enlisted Nov. 12, at Inverlochy; deserted	......	......
Mathieson, William -	......	......	Feb. 21, 1791

MEN.		REMARKS.	BOUNTY.	DISCHARGE.
Mathieson, William	-	may be the same as the other -	......	Mar. 5, 1791
Murray, William -	-	......	......	Feb. 21, 1791
Nicholson, James -	-	......	......	......
Patello, William -	-	......	......	Feb. 21, 1791
Porterfeld, James -	-	......	£5 5/-	......
Robb, James	-	......	£5 5/-	......
Robertson, Duncan	-	age 18, height 5 ft. 6½ ins. ; born in Dumbarton; calico printer; enlisted Nov. 20, not in *W.O.* 12 ; 5480.	......	......
Ross, Hugh -	-	......	£5 5/-	......
Ross, John -	-	drummer: not in *W.O.* 12 : 5480	£3 3/-	......
Roy, James -	-	his master got 21/-	£3 3/-	Feb. 21, 1791
Shaw, Angus	-	......	......	Feb. 21, 1791
Shaw, John -	-	......	......	Mar. 5, 1791
Sivewright, John -	-	......	......	June 13, 1791
Slorach, George -	-	......	£3 3/-	Mar. 5, 1791
Smith, Thomas -	-	......	......	Mar. 5, 1791
Stewart, Alexander	-	age 16, height 5 ft ; labourer, Kingussie ; enlisted Nov. 1 ; not in *W.O.* 12 : 5480	......	......
Stewart, John -	-	......	......	Feb. 21, 1791
Stewart, William -	-	......	£3 3/-	Feb. 21, 1791
Sutherland, William	-	......	......	Mar. 5, 1791
Thomson, Peter -	-	......	£5 5/-	Feb. 21, 1791
Wiseman, John -	-	......	£5 5/-	......

The regiment was reviewed in Edinburgh in June, 1791, by the Marquis's grand uncle, Lord Adam Gordon, who was then Commander of the Forces in Scotland, and marched north in October, companies being sent to Fort George, Dundee, Montrose, Banff and Aberdeen, to the last of which two were allotted.   The Marquis paraded these companies on the Links of Aberdeen, August 2, 1792, and gave them "a handsome gratuity for drink money."   A jingle which became a sort of catchword at the time ran :—

> Cock o' the North, my Huntly braw,
> Whaur are ye wi' the Forty Twa?

The Marquis was so proud of his uniform that he was presented at Court in it, and tartan soon became the rage of Society in London, his mother, the enterprising Duchess, introducing it in silk, and being caricatured in a famous print of 1792 as the "Tartan Belle."   To this period of his career we also owe a notable portrait of the Marquis, by Kay, the caricaturist, entitled "A Highland Chief."   Later on, when he became colonel of the Black Watch, he was painted (1806) in the uniform by Andrew Robertson, the miniaturist. It is a charming bit of work, and coloured prints of it engraved by Holl are now very scarce. It shows the Marquis's bust, with the red coat and the blue facings of the Black Watch.

THE NORTHERN FENCIBLES, 1793-99.

1793: RAISED BY THE 4TH DUKE OF GORDON: DISBANDED 1799.

The raising of the Northern Fencibles of 1793 found the Duke of Gordon quite an expert in equipping regiments, for it was his fifth experiment in the art. France declared war on Holland and ourselves on February 1; the country had been drained of men; and the Duke found himself competing against two regiments of the line, the 78th and 79th. His was one of six Fencible regiments being raised, one of which cut him off finally from Sutherland, and another, the Strathspey Fencibles, came very near his own doors.

The Letter of Service authorising the Duke to raise a Regiment of Fencibles was dated March 1, 1793, and ran as follows:—

George R.
George the Third, by the Grace of God, King of Great Britain, France, and Ireland, Defender of the Faith, &c. To Our Right Trusty and Right Entirely Beloved Cousin, Alexander, Duke of Gordon, K.T. Greeting: We, reposing especial trust and confidence in your loyalty, courage, and good conduct, do, by these presents, constitute and appoint you to be a Colonel of our Northern Regiment of Fencible Men and to the rank in the Army during the establishment of the said regiment only, and likewise to be Captain of a company in our said regiment. You are therefore to take our said regiment as Colonel and the said company as Captain unto your care and charge, and duly to exercise as well the officers as soldiers thereof in arms, and to use your best endeavours to keep them in good order and discipline; and We do hereby command them to obey you as their Colonel and Captain respectively; and you are to observe and follow such orders and directions from time to time as you shall receive from Us or any other your superior officer, according to the rules and discipline of war, in pursuance of the trust We hereby repose in you. Given in Our Court at St. James's, the first day of March, 1793, in the thirty-third year of Our Reign.

By His Majesty's Command,
Henry Dundas.

Entered with the Comsry.-General of Musters,
Tho. Butts.
Alexander, Duke of Gordon, Colonel of the
Northern Regiment of Fencible Men.

The necessary authority was given to his Grace in the following Beating Order:—

George R.

Whereas We have thought fit to order a regiment of Fencible Men to be forthwith raised under your command, which is to consist of 8 Companys, of 3 Sergeants, 3 Corporals, 2 Drummers, and 60 Private Men in each, with 2 Pipers to the Grenadier Company, besides a Sergeant-Major and Quarter-Master-Sergeant, together with the usual officers, which men are not to be sent out of Great Britain:

These are to authorize you to beat the drum or otherwise to raise so many men in any county or part of Our Kingdom of Great Britain as shall be wanted to complete the said regiment to the abovementioned numbers. And All Magistrates, Justices of the Peace, Constables, and other our Civil Officers, whom it may concern, are hereby required to be assisting unto you in providing quarters, impressing carriages, and otherwise as there shall be occasion. Given at Our Court at St. James's, this 1st day of March, 1793, in the 33rd year of our Reign.

By His Majesty's Command,

Geo. Yonge.

Fuller particulars of the regiment were given in a letter Sir George Yonge wrote to the Duke from the War Office on March 2, 1793.

I am commanded by the King to acquaint Your Grace that his Majesty approves of your Grace's offer to raise a corps of Fencible men for the internal protection of North Britain on the following terms:—

The Corps shall consist of six Battalion companies, one Company of Grenadiers and one of Light Infantry; the Battalion Companies to consist of one captain, one lieutenant, one ensign, three serjeants, three corporals, two drummers and 60 private men, in each: the Grenadier Company of one captain, two lieutenants, three serjeants, three corporals, two drummers, two pipers, and 60 private men: the Light Infantry Company of one captain, two lieutenants, three serjeants, three corporals, two drummers, and 60 private men, with the usual staff officers, and with a serjeant major and quarter master serjeant, exclusive of the serjeants above mentioned.

The regiment [is] to have the Field Officers undermentioned, vizt. one Colonel, one Lieutenant Colonel and one Major, each having also a company; and to be under Your Grace's Command as Colonel. The Captain-Lieutenant is, as usual, included in the number of Lieutenants above mentioned.

The pay of the officers is to commence from the dates of their commissions, and the pay of the non-commissioned officers and private men from the dates of their respective attestations.

Three guineas are to be paid to each man enrolled, on his arrival at the rendezvous of his company, which will be issued from time to time to the agent of the Regiment.

The King leaves to Your Grace the recommendation of the officers, being such as are well affected to His Majesty, and most likely by their interest and connexions to forward the completion of the corps ; a list of whom you will be pleased to transmit to Lord Amherst as soon as convenient for His Majesty's information.

None of the officers appointed to this corps are to have rank longer than while it remains on the establishment ; nor when reduced are they to be entitled to half pay (the adjutant and quarter master excepted, who will be allowed half pay agreeably to the pre-cedent at the end of last war).   Both these circumstances are, I know, perfectly understood by your Grace, yet I must take the liberty of adding that you cannot too fully explain the matter respecting the rank to the gentlemen you mean to propose for commissions, that they may not, either now, or in future, conceive they have derived any claim whatever to permanent rank in the Army, or to half pay from their services in this Regiment.   But it may be proper to mention that officers taken from half pay into the situation of Field Officers or Captains of com-panies in the Fencible Regiments will be replaced on their former half pay upon the reduction of the corps : and such half pay officers as may be appointed to the subaltern or staff commission will be allowed to receive their half pay together with the pay of these commissions.

In all respect of pay, clothing, arms, accoutrements and allowances for bread and necessaries, the corps is to be on the same footing as His Majesty's other marching regiments of infantry.

The beating order to authorize this levy, being made out in the usual form, allows the recruiting to be carried on in any part of Great Britain.   It is meant, notwithstanding, to be confined, according to your Grace's proposal, to the counties of Inverness and to such other counties wherein your Grace's estates and superiorities are, and to the neighbour-hood hereof.

The regiment is to serve in any part of Scotland, but not to march out of it, except in case of invasion of the more southern parts of the kingdom.   The men are not to be drafted : and in the event of their being ordered to march into England, His Majesty consents that they shall not be reduced there, but be marched back in a corps and disem-bodied in the country where they were principally raised, or as near thereto as possible.

The King hopes that the Corps will be compleated within three months, the period mentioned by you : and although it has been custom-ary in new levies to limit the age and size of the recruits, yet His Majesty thinks it unnecessary to prescribe such limits on the present occasion, in full confidence that from the zeal of your family for his service, and their regard for their country, every exertion will be made to recruit the corps with men fit for active and immediate duty

In the execution of this service, I take leave to assure you of every assistance that this office can afford

The Duke's difficulty on this occasion was not so much in getting men—he was asked only for 480 privates, and the regiment was returned as complete on April 14, that is to say six weeks after the mandate for its creation, it lay first in the handling of the men after he had got them, due, as we shall see, to a variety of causes, including the attempts of other landed magnates to denude his ranks, Sir James Grant trying to get men from him in 1794, and Cameron of Lochiel in 1798

There was little of the compulsion exercised between the Duke and the recruit and between the recruit and the Duke, such as marked the raising of his previous Fencible Regiment in 1778 One of the few cases in which compulsion operated was in the matter of the tenants of the Eight and Forty Dauch of Huntly, who took concerted action, clearly under pressure of the Duke's displeasure at their previous tepidness, for George Bell, Cocklarachy, wrote to Menzies on April 1 :—

We, inhabitants of the Aucht and Forty, are resolved to remove the umbrage His Grace has taken at them, and, if possible, procure some men who are, absolutely, inconceivably scarce   There is a fund established for doubling the bounty to all volunteers living in the Aucht and Forty, and different houses opened for inlisting them and at least it is hoped that the Duke and the world shall see it is not our faults if there is not a few handsome fellows to present from the Lordship of Huntly

The tenants managed to induce seventeen men to join the regiment

The Duke on his part felt the touch of compulsion from the recruits in at least one case, for he gave this undertaking to Charles Stewart (alias Derg) on April 18 —

You have voluntarily enlisted into my regiment, I promise to appoint you upon the reduction of the corps one of my foresters with a salary of twelve pounds sterling a year, or to some other appointment of equal emolument

The first recruiting was done by the Duke's son-in-law, Sir Robert Sinclair—the husband of Lady Madelina Sinclair, who had just sustained a fall from her horse at Elgin, "but is now [February 19] quite well"

On February 28, he wrote from Forres that he had just " 'listed on the road-side John Macknockiter from Edinkillie, and a lad, Angus Cameron from Dallas." " I gave them a card to you," he writes to Menzies, " written on the roadside." On April 21, Sir Robert wrote from Fort George :—

Considering the many fine boys that will be rejected under size, it would be a very fine nursery for the Duke's regiment to get leave to form a company from 5 feet 2 to 5 feet 4, to be armed as a light infantry carrying carabines instead of firelocks.

His Grace quickened the recruiting by a visit in April to Glenfiddich, where he received deputations of people from Auchindoun, Glenrinnes and the Cabrach, who had got recruits. He also went to Tomintoul, where a man named Robert Grant insulted him in some way. Grant afterwards apologised through John Grant, the minister of Kirkmichael, throwing the blame of his "improper conduct" upon "fasting in the morning, a little whisky in the afternoon, and the crowd round him at the time attacking him all at once." Grant begged the minister to forward his application to enlist, but the minister was shy, for he " never wished to give a recommendation to any person that could be guilty of giving the least offence to his Grace, who is the father of his people." The Duke himself 'listed 21 men in Badenoch, 58 in Lochaber, and 6 in Huntly. In the east of Aberdeenshire he had the support of the Earl of Erroll, who offered the reward of a guinea over and above His Majesty's bounty to every man on his estate who enlisted with Captain Gordon-Cuming of Pitlurg.

Although the regiment was returned complete on April 14, the men did not all assemble until May 13, as some of them had to come a long way. It was then found that 62 had to be discharged on account of size, age, consumption, lameness and other troubles, and one or two of them for being " unsightly," while 11 men either deserted or never joined. The figures are as follows :—

Officers.				Discharged.	Deserted.
Major John Baillie -	-	-	-	7	...
Captain Donald Cameron	-	-	-	14	4
Lieut. Francis Charteris -	-	-	-	1	...
Captain James Fraser -	-	-	-	11	...
„ John Gordon-Cuming	-	-	-	3	...
Lieut. John Gordon	-	-	-	1	1
„ Pryse Lockhart Gordon	-	-	-	2	...
				39	5

T

Officers.			Discharged.	Deserted.
			39	5
Lieut. William Gordon -	-	-	2	2
„ Alexander Harvey	-	-	7	2
Captain William Mackintosh -	-		9	...
„ Hugh Macpherson	-	-	5	2
			62	11

The allocation of the enlistments was as follows:—

By Captain Finlason	-	·	-	·	·	98
In Lochaber -	-	-	·	·	·	59
By Macpherson of Invereshie		-	·	·	30
At Gordon Castle -	-	·	-	·	·	26
At Fochabers	-	·	-	·	·	24
By the Duke in Badenoch	-	·	-	·	21
By Gordon, Coynachie -	-	·	-	·	19
By the Strathbogie farmers	-	·	·	·	17
At Tomintoul	-	·	-	·	·	15
In Strathaven, Glenlivet, Auchindoun		-	·	13
By John Stuart, Pityoulish	-	·	-	·	7
By the Duke at Huntly -	-	·	-	·	6
By Captain Godsman	-	·	-	·	·	3
By Gordon in Croughly -	-	·	-	·	2

The precedence of the corps was decided on June 9 at a meeting held at Holyrood Abbey, apparently in the quarters of Lord Adam Gordon, the Duke's uncle, who was then Commander-in-Chief in North Britain (*W.O.* 1 : 1,059); the Duke's regiment being called the "6th Northern Fencibles." The first list of officers was announced on June 25, though the commissions were antedated to March 1, 1793, the date of the Letter of Service (*W.O.* 25 : 156, pp. 193-194). In this document the regiment is called the "Northern Regiment of Fencible Men." The first officers were:—

COLONEL.

Alexander (Gordon), 4th Duke of Gordon, March 1, 1793.

LIEUTENANT-COLONEL.

John Woodford, March 1, 1793. Brother-in-law of the Duke, having married, December 28, 1778 (as his second wife) his Grace's eldest sister, Lady Susan Gordon (1746-1814), widow of the 9th Earl of Westmoreland. By this marriage he had two sons—Field Marshal Sir Alexander George Woodford (1782-1870), and Major-General Sir John George Woodford (1785-1879). Colonel Woodford died at Edinburgh, April 18, 1800, and was buried in Holyrood Abbey (See *D.N.B.* and *Brief Memoir of Major-General Sir John George Woodford*, by J. Fisher Crosthwaite, 1881, printed at Keswick, pp. 63, xi.).

MAJOR.

John Baillie, of Dunain, March 1, 1793. Raised the Loyal Inverness Fencible Highlanders, 1795, of which John Gordon-Cuming was Lieutenant-Colonel. Baillie died 1797.

CAPTAINS.

Donald Cameron, of Lochiel, March 1, 1793; Major, November 28, 1795; left the Northern Fencibles to become Colonel of the Lochaber Fencibles, 1799. He had been restored to his estates under the General Amnesty Act; married, 1795, Anne, daughter of Sir Ralph Abercromby; and died 1832.

James Fraser, March 1, 1793; Major, March 7, 1794, Rothesay and Caithness Fencibles. Laird of Culduthel.

Daniel Gordon (from Lieutenant, h.p. 60th), October 18, 1798, *vice* Charteris. Captain, May 1, 1799, Aberdeenshire Militia. Son of William Gordon, III. in Minmore; born 1768; died at Aberdeen, February 23, 1831 (*Gordons under Arms*, No. 396).

John Gordon-Cuming-Skene, March 1, 1793; Major, February 17, 1794; Brevet Lieutenant-Colonel, November 21, 1794; Lieutenant-Colonel, October 21, 1795, Loyal Inverness Highland Fencible Infantry; raised by his fellow officer, Major Baillie of Dunain (*supra*); Lieutenant-General, June 4, 1813. Son of John Gordon-Cuming of Pitlurg; died 1828 (*Gordons under Arms*, No. 1,536).

William Mackintosh, March 1, 1793. Of Aberarder.

Hugh Macpherson, March 1, 1793; joined 97th before November 28, 1795. Of Inverhall.

CAPTAIN-LIEUTENANT.

Charles Gordon, March 1, 1793; Captain, February 17, 1794. Paymaster, 1st Foot, 1798. Laird of Beldorney and Wardhouse; born 1750; began soldiering in the Northern Fencibles of 1778: died at Gordonhall, 1832 (*Gordons under Arms*, No. 307).

LIEUTENANTS.

Donald Cameron, March 1, 1793; Captain-Lieutenant, November 28, 1795, *vice* Gordon. Of Glennevis.

John Cameron, March 1, 1793. He gave a lot of trouble, which resulted in his being court-martialled.

Francis Charteris, March 1, 1793; resigned by October 18, 1798. Born 1772, he was the son of Francis, Lord Elcho (1749-1808), whose mother, Lady Catherine Gordon, was a daughter of the 2nd Duke of Gordon. He was A.D.C. to his grand-uncle, Lord Adam Gordon; was created Baron Wemyss in 1821, and died in 1853.

John Gordon, March 1, 1793; Captain-Lieutenant, June 6, 1794.

Son of John Gordon, IV. in Minmore; died 1819 (*Gordons under Arms*, No. 907).

Pryse Lockhart Gordon, March 1, 1793. The well-known diarist, 1762-1845 (*Gordons under Arms*, No. 1,164). He tells us in his *Memoirs* (i., 141) that, "not liking the pay of drilling a new levy," he "preferred being Quarter Master, which with my Lieutenancy would give me the emolument of a Captain." He got his Captaincy, June 21, 1794, and was succeeded in the Quartermastership by his seven-year-old son, William!

William Gordon, March 1, 1793; Ensign, resigned by February 17, 1794. Son of Alexander Gordon of Aberdour, of which he became laird; died 1839 (*Gordons under Arms*, No. 1,419).

William Alexander Gordon, March 1, 1793; Ensign, 112th Foot, October 11, 1795. Rejoined Northern Fencibles, August 26, 1798, as Captain, *vice* Cameron. Son of James, in Croughly (*Gordons under Arms*, No. 1,474).

Alexander Harvey, of Broadland, Rattray, died 1817 (Henderson's *Aberdeenshire Epitaphs*, 78-80; *Family Record of the Name of Dingwall Fordyce*, vol. ii., p. xcii.).

Humphrey Grant (from Ensign, Ross-shire Fencibles), October 31, 1798, *vice* White.

John Hay, May 7, 1796, *vice* James Stuart; joined the 11th Foot by May 27, 1797.

James Hoy, February 17, 1794. He wrote to the Commander-in-Chief from Hastings, September 25, 1795, asking for a commission in a regiment of the line at home or abroad, without purchase (*W.O.* 1 : 1,088). Probably a son of the Duke's "meteorologist."

Alexander Macdonald (from Captain, h.p.), February 17, 1794; Captain, November 28, 1798, *vice* Hugh Macpherson.

Forbes James Macdonell (from Ensign), February 17, 1794; was surgeon's mate; joined the 100th (then the number of the Gordon Highlanders) by November 28, 1795.

John Macdonell (from Ensign), February 17, 1794.

Ronald Macdonell, November 28, 1795, *vice* Smith.

James McKilligin (from 101st), February 17, 1794.

Adam Macpherson, March 1, 1793. Son of Colonel Macpherson.

Donald Macpherson (from Lieutenant, 71st), February 17, 1794.

Duncan Macpherson, February 17, 1794.

Robert Barclay Macpherson, February 17, 1794; joined 88th by November 28, 1795.

William Mitchell (from h.p., 5th West Indian Regiment), June 5, 1798, *vice* Robertson.

Alexander Munro, February 17, 1794.

Alexander Robertson (from late 89th), February 17, 1794, *vice* Gordon; Captain, June 23, 1798, *vice* H. Macpherson.

Peter Simpson, November 28, 1795, *vice* R. B. Macpherson; joined 11th by May 27, 1797.

Robert Smith, October 10, 1794, *vice* Dowle; Captain-Lieutenant, November 28, 1795, *vice* Cameron.

William Smith, November 28, 1795, *vice* Alexander Macdonald.

Patrick White, February 17, 1794; resigned by August 29, 1798.

ENSIGNS.

George Anderson, May 27, 1797, *vice* Macpherson; Lieutenant, August 29, 1798, *vice* Brown.

Thomas Bennet, May 19, 1798, *vice* Gordon.

James Bisset, May 19, 1798, *vice* Allan Cameron (deceased).

Allan Cameron, February 17, 1795; resigned by January 9, 1796.

Allan Cameron, December 24, 1796, *vice* Milne; died by May 19, 1798.

Douglas Campbell (from Sergeant-Major), May 27, 1797, *vice* White.

George Cumine (from Sergeant), October 31, 1798, *vice* Gordon.

William Dalrymple, March 1, 1793; joined 81st, February 14, 1794.

Charles Dowle, March 1, 1793; Ensign, July 19, 1794, Gordon Highlanders. Killed in Egypt, 1801.

James Fraser, January 17, 1795, *vice* W. W. Fraser.

W. W. Fraser. Left the corps by January 17, 1795.

Charles Gordon, January 7, 1796, *vice* George Todd.

John Gordon, March 1, 1793; Lieutenant, November 28, 1795, *vice* F. J. Macdonell; Ensign, February 26, 1799, 1st Foot. Eldest son of John Gordon, Milltown of Laggan, cadet of Beldorney; killed, February 27, 1818, by the Killedar of Talneir, who was shot in consequence (*Gordons under Arms*, No. 932).

Robert Gordon, May 27, 1797, *vice* Todd; Lieutenant, September 1, 1798, *vice* White; 1st Lieutenant, July 1, 1800, Strathdon Volunteers. Son of James Gordon in Croughly; born 1780; died 1828 (*Gordons under Arms*, No. 1,215).

Robert Gordon, August 29, 1798, *vice* A. G. Macdonald; Lieutenant, July 18, 1803, Aberdeenshire Militia. Son of Alexander Gordon of Invernettie and Glendaveny, cadet of Sheelagreen; *d.s.p.*, July 27, 1827 (*Gordons under Arms*, No. 1,217).

John Henderson, March 1, 1793; Lieutenant, December 11, 1793. Joined 100th (afterwards the 92nd) by November 7, 1795.

Alexander Macdonald, October 31, 1798, *vice* Cameron

Archibald Gordon Macdonald, Ensign; Lieutenant, June 23, 1798, *vice* Woodford

John Macdonell, February 14, 1794, *vice* Dalrymple

Alexander Macpherson, March 1, 1793, Lieutenant, February 17, 1794, *vice* Cameron, Captain, November 28, 1795, *vice* John Gordon, joined the Gordon Highlanders by November 28, 1798 Of Blairagrie

Alexander Macpherson, jun, March 1, 1793, Lieutenant, February 17, 1794, *vice* P L Gordon Of Strathdearn

Donald Macpherson, November 28, 1795, *vice* Stuart; joined 39th by June 10, 1796

Duncan Macpherson, March 1, 1793, Lieutenant, February 17, 1794

John Macpherson, November 28, 1795, *vice* Hutcheons, Lieutenant, May 27, 1797, *vice* Milne

William Marshall, January 7, 1796, *vice* Todd, Lieutenant, May 27, 1797, *vice* Hay

George Milne, June 14, 1796, *vice* Donald Macpherson, Lieutenant, December 24, 1796, *vice* Richard Stewart, joined 11th Foot by May 27, 1797

Alexander Stewart, August 29, 1798, *vice* Anderson

James Stuart, March 1, 1793, Lieutenant, February 17, 1794, joined 45th

George Sutherland, May 27, 1797, *vice* Marshall, resigned by August 29, 1798

Alexander Taylor, August 29, 1798, *vice* Sutherland

Alexander Todd, February 17, 1794, *vice* Alexander Macpherson, jun (*W O* 25 224), Lieutenant, May 27, 1797, *vice* Simpson

Alexander Todd, January 9, 1796, *vice* Allan Cameron (*London Gazette*)

George Todd, February 17, 1794, *vice* Alexander Macpherson, sen , joined 29th by January 9, 1796 These Todds were probably the sons of William Todd, the factor.

William Ramsay White, February 17, 1794; Lieutenant, May 27, 1797, *vice* Hutcheons

John George Woodford, February 17, 1795; Lieutenant, November 28, 1795, *vice* Alexander Macpherson, left by June 23, 1798 Second son of Lieutenant-Colonel John Woodford (*supra*)

CHAPLAINS

Samuel Copland, March 1, 1793 Minister of Fintray; died 1795

John Thompson, May 12, 1795, *vice* Copland

SURGEONS.

James Brown, November 8, 1798, *vice* Caldwell.

Ralston Caldwell, May 27, 1797, *vice* Hutcheons; resigned by November 8, 1798, having got into trouble with the Colonel.

Daniel Hutcheons, from (second mate) September 24, 1796, *vice* Stewart; Lieutenant, November 28, 1795, *vice* Munro; joined 68th by May 27, 1797.

Richard Stewart, March 1, 1793; Lieutenant, November 28, 1795, *vice* Charteris; joined Cinque Ports Fencible Cavalry by September 24, 1796. M.D. Marischal College.

ADJUTANTS.

James Brown (from Sergeant-Major), June 23, 1795; Lieutenant, November 7, 1795, *vice* Henderson; Lieutenant, October 15, 1803, Peterhead Volunteers.

John Henderson, March 1, 1793.

George Reynolds. 1st Lieutenant, Huntly Volunteers, October 15, 1803.

QUARTERMASTERS.

Pryse Lockhart Gordon, March 1, 1793.

William Abercrombie Gordon, June 6, 1794, *vice* his father, P. L. Gordon. Born 1787; died 1808 (*Gordons under Arms*, No. 1,473).

The first official muster roll of the regiment, preserved at the Public Record Office (*W.O.* 13: 3,900), is for the period from the dates of attestation to May 31, 1793, and was returned from Edinburgh Castle, November 27, 1793. Luckily, all the attestations are given, and the names of the rank and file are arranged alphabetically, though they are not told off in companies. Besides this there is a roll at Gordon Castle, and numerous notes which supplement it. The roll at Gordon Castle gives 240 names, together with the heights (of 216) and other particulars. This is the roll printed here, though I have supplemented it with the names of all the sergeants, corporals and drummers, from the Record Office. The height of the 216 rank and file averaged 5 feet 6.25572 inches. At the first muster 407 were present and 193 absent, and there was one "casual."

The Highland character of the corps is proved by the large number of purely Highland surnames. Thus, out of 669 rank and file in the first muster roll, 229 bore surnames beginning with

"Mac," and 80 were Camerons. The distribution of surnames was as follows :—

Cameron	80	McAlpine	1	Mackay	13	McTavish	2
Campbell	8	McArthur	2	Mackinnon	9	McVicar	1
Cattanach	2	McBain	9	Mackintosh	18	Manson	3
Chisholm	3	McCommie	2	Maclachan	4	Mitchell	6
Davidson	5	McCraw	3	Maclean	10	Munro	6
Farquharson	1	Macdonald	40	Maclennan	4	Murray	2
Forbes	1	Macdonell	6	Macleod	4	Robertson	11
Fraser	1	McGillivray	2	McMaster	3	Ross	13
Gordon	11	McGregor	5	Macmillan	12	Sinclair	2
Grant	11	McInnes	2	Macpherson	39	Smith	4
Innes	5	McIntyre	8	McPhie	6	Stuart	16
Kennedy	8	McIsaac	1	McQueen	5	Sutherland	7

There was one each of the following Mac- surnames :—

McAddie	McEdward	McGlashan	McHaffie
McCraig	McEwan	McGuinness	McHardie

Name.	Age.	Height.	Residence.	Enlisted by	Date of Enlistment.
SERGEANTS.					
Brown, James, Sergt.-Major	..	....	....	....	April 1
Cameron, Alexander	.. ..	....	....	....	March 20
Cameron, Allan	.. ..	....	....	....	March 13
1Cameron, Hugh	.. ..	....	....	Cameron, of Lochiel	March 10
Cameron, John	.. ..	....	....	....	March 5
Crammond, James	.. ..	....	....	....	April 13
2Gordon, James	.. ..	....	Tomintoul	Lieut. John Gordon, Tombae	March 8
Grant, John, Q.M.S.	.. ..	....	....	....	April 29
Hutchinson, John	.. ..	....	....	....	March 23
Innes, James	.. ..	....	....	....	March 12
Littlejohn, James	.. ..	....	....	....	March 19
MacIntyre, Peter	..	38	5 ft. 11 in.	Lochaber	....	April 9
Mackay, Hugh .. (d. Nov. 22)	.. ..	....	....	....	March 21
Mackay, Kenneth	.. ..	....	....	....	March 11
Mackenzie, William	.. ..	....	....	....	April 5
Mackintosh, William	.. ..	....	....	....	March 15
Macpherson, Alexander	..	....	....	....	March 20
Macpherson, Duncan	.. ..	....	....	....	March 20
Macpherson, Ewan	.. ..	....	....	....	March 20
Macpherson, John	.. ..	....	....	....	March 8
Macqueen, William	.. ..	....	....	....	March 7
Mathieson, William	.. ..	....	....	....	March 8
Miller, Alexander	.. ..	....	....	....	April 8
Miller, John	.. ..	33	5 ft. 6½ in.	....	The Duke, at Edinburgh	March 13
Ross, John	.. ..	....	....	....	April 20
Ross, John	.. ..	....	....	....	April 26
CORPORALS.					
Baillie, William	.. ..	....	....	....	March 15
Boyd, Alexander	.. ..	....	....	....	April 8
Brown, James	.. ..	....	....	[Discharged, July 7, 1793]	April 4
Cameron, Alexander	.. ..	....	....	....	March 12
Cameron, Angus	.. ..	....	....	....	March 20
Cameron, Donald	.. ..	....	....	....	March 19
Cameron, William	.. ..	....	....	....	March 9
Campbell, William	.. ..	....	....	....	March 27
Davidson, James	.. ..	....	....	....	March 20

1 Sergeant in the Lochaber Fencibles, 1799-1802; then became drill sergeant in the 42nd. Lochiel requested, 5 November 1804, that he should be appointed Adjutant of the Fort-William Volunteers (H.O. 50 : 94).

2 Nephew of Col. Gordon, Dart [Dort? Holland].

Name.	Age.	Height.	Residence.	Enlisted by	Date of Enlistment.
Donald, George	.. ..	....	....	....	March 10
Kennedy, William	.. ..	....	....	....	March 8
Macdonald, Ronald	.. ..	....	....	....	March 9
McGlashan, John	.. ..	....	....	....	March 30
Mackay, William	.. ..	....	....	....	March 22
Mackintosh, Alexander	..	....	....	....	March 20
MacLellan, Roderick	.. ..	....	....	....	March 29
Macmillan, John	.. ..	....	....	....	March 20
Macpherson, Alexander	..	....	....	....	April 12
Ross, Thomas ..	.. 30	5 ft. 8 in.	Lochaber	....	April 10
Ross, William ..	.. ..	....	....	....	April 4
3Stewart, Alexander	.. ..	....	....	....	March 8
Wilson, William	.. 39	5 ft. 8 in.	....	The Duke, at Stirling	March 30

PIPERS

Name.	Age.	Height.	Residence.	Enlisted by	Date
Mackenzie, Roderick	.. ..	....	....	....	March 15
Macpherson, John	.. ..	....	Badenoch	....	April 16

DRUMMERS.

Name.	Age.	Height.	Residence.	Enlisted by	Date
Andrew, William	.. ..	....	....	....	April 19
4Baxter, John ..	.. 15	5 ft. 0 in.	....	....	March 25
Cameron, Duncan	.. ..	....	....	....	April 29
Cowan, Thomas	.. 16	5 ft. 3 in.	....	....	April 3
Davidson, James	.. 18	5 ft. 0 in.	....	....	March 25
Elmslie, John ..	.. ..	....	....	....	April 1
Fraser, John ..	.. ..	....	....	....	March 26
5Gordon, Cosmo	.. ..	....	....	....	April 5
6Gordon, James	.. ..	....	....	....	April 1
McConnochie, Samuel	.. ..	....	....	....	March 14
Macdonald, John	.. ..	....	....	....	April 20
Macqueen, Alexander	.. ..	....	....	....	March 16
Mathieson, William	.. ..	....	....	....	April 9
Ross, John ..	.. ..	....	....	The Duke, at Huntly	March 29
Shaw, Donald, ..	.. ..	....	....	....	April 2
Thomson, John	.. ..	....	....	....	April 8

PRIVATES.

Name.	Age.	Height.	Residence.	Enlisted by	Date
Beaton, Malcolm	.. 26	5 ft. 6 in.	Lochaber	....	March 17
Bell, Alexander	.. 17	5 ft. 5 in.	....	Capt. John Macpherson, of Invereshie	March 18
7Bonniman, George	.. 15	5 ft. 4 in.	....	Lieut. John Gordon, Coynachie	March 8
Boyd, Alexander	.. 24	5 ft. 7 in.	Lochaber	....	....
Brodie, John ..	.. 25	5 ft. 4½ in.	....	Farmers of Strathbogie	April 6
Brotchie, Francis	.. 26	5 ft. 3 in.	Dunnet	....	March 26
Buchan, George	.. 17	5 ft. 4 in.	....	Farmers of Strathbogie	March 20
Burges, James ..	.. 26	5 ft. 6 in.	Lochaber	....	....
8Cameron, Alexander	.. 24	6 ft. 0 in.	....	Baillie Cameron and Col. Campbell	....
Cameron, Alexander	.. 26	5 ft. 5 in.	Lochaber	....	....
Cameron, Allan	.. 20	5 ft. 8 in.	....	Baillie Cameron and Col. Campbell	....
Cameron, Allan	.. 20	5 ft. 7 in.	Lochaber	....	....
Cameron, Angus	.. 17	5 ft. 3½ in.	....	Capt. John Macpherson, of Invereshie	....
Cameron, Angus	.. 30	5 ft. 9 in.	Lochaber	....	....
Cameron, Benjamin	.. 23	5 ft. 9½ in.	....	Capt. John Macpherson, of Invereshie	....
Cameron, Donald	.. 36	5 ft. 10 in.	Lochaber	....	....
Cameron, Duncan	.. 21	5 ft. 8 in.	Lochaber	....	....
Cameron, Duncan	.. 18	5 ft. 5 in.	Lochaber	....	....
Cameron, Ewen ..	.. 17	5 ft. 5 in.	Achorachan	....	April 1
Cameron, Ewen ..	.. 30	5 ft. 6½ in.	Lochaber	....	....
Cameron, Ewen ..	.. 27	5 ft. 8½ in.	Lochaber	....	....
Cameron, John ..	.. 17	5 ft. 5 in.	....	The Duke, in Badenoch	....
Cameron, John ..	.. 15	5 ft. 4 in.	Tombreck	Gordon Castle	April 6
Cameron, Murdoch	.. 20	5 ft. 7½ in.	....	Capt. John Macpherson, of Invereshie	March 18
Cameron, Murdoch	.. 23	5 ft. 6 in.	....	Capt. John Macpherson, of Invereshie	March 18
Cameron, William	.. 17	5 ft. 4 in.	....	Pityoulish and his brothers	....
Campbell, John	.. 24	5 ft. 8 in.	....	Capt. John Macpherson, of Invereshie	....
Cattanach, Duncan	.. 20	5 ft. 3½ in.	....	Capt. John Macpherson, of Invereshie	March 26
Cattanach, John	.. 19	5 ft. 4 in.	....	Capt. John Macpherson, of Invereshie	March 16
Chisholm, William	.. 26	5 ft. 5 in.	....	Capt. Godsman	March 21
Cormack, Joseph	.. 15	5 ft. 4 in.	....	Farmers of Strathbogie	April 12

3 Died, July 3, 1793.
4 Discharged, November 22, 1793.
5 and 6 Sons of Sergeant Gordon.

7 Drummed out.
8 Ground officer's son.

U

Name.	*Age.*	*Height.*	*Residence.*	*Enlisted by*	*Date of Enlistment.*
Coutts, John	18	5 ft. 5½ in.	....	Gordon of Croughly	April 2
[9]Cowan, John	22	5 ft. 0 in.	....	Gordon of Cairnfield	March 23
[10]Cowan, William ..	18	5 ft. 7 in.	....	Gordon of Cairnfield	March 13
[11]Cruickshank, James	..	....	....	Lieut. John Gordon, Tombae	April 1
[12]Cumming, Duncan ..	22	5 ft. 5 in.	....	Farmers of Strathbogie	March 21
Currie, Alexander ..	18	5 ft. 6 in.	....	Farmers of Strathbogie	April 17
Dallas, Alexander ..	25	5 ft. 7 in.	....	Capt. John Macpherson, of Invereshie	....
Davidson, George ..	24	5 ft. 5 in.	....	Farmers of Strathbogie	March 29
Dean, James	..	....	Aberlour	Lieut. John Gordon, Tombae	March 17
Dey, James	18	5 ft. 7 in.	Achriachan	....	April 13
Dobbie, George ..	20	5 ft. 8½ in.	....	The Duke, at Edinburgh	March 13
Donald, John	20	5 ft. 6¾ in.	....	Lieut. John Gordon, Coynachie	March 8
Donald, George	..	....	Huntly	Lieut. John Gordon, Tombae	....
Douglas, David	16	5 ft. 3 in.	Caithness	....	April 4
Dow, James	30	5 ft. 4 in.	....	The Duke, at Huntly	March 27
Duncan, William ..	16	5 ft. 7½ in.	Bower	....	March 29
Duncan, William ..	..	....	Aberlour	Lieut. John Gordon, Tombae	March 25
Elder, John	18	5 ft. 2½ in.	Reay	....	March 29
Fleming, James ..	24	6 ft. 2 in.	....	At Tomintoul	April 13
Fleming, Robert ..	18	5 ft. 7 in.	....	Gordon of Croughly	April 9
Fraser, Alexander ..	30	5 ft. 5½ in.	....	Capt. Godsman	....
Fraser (*alias* Bruce), Andrew	23	5 ft. 4 in.	....	Gordon Castle	April 3
Fraser, John	18	5 ft. 5 in.	....	Farmers of Strathbogie	April 9
Fraser, John	20	5 ft. 6 in.	....	Mr. Gordon, in Forres	April 8
Fraser, William ..	31	5 ft. 10 in.	Lochaber	....	....
Gairn, John	21	5 ft. 3 in.	Boat of Brig	Fochabers	March 8
Garrow, Peter	16	5 ft. 4 in.	....	Lieut. John Gordon, Coynachie	March 8
Glass, John	34	5 ft. 5 in.	....	Minister of Urquhart	March 16
[13]Gordon, Alexander ..	16	5 ft. 3 in.	Badenoch	Duncan Gordon	March 25
Gordon, John	24	5 ft. 4 in.	....	The Duke, at Huntly	March 27
Gordon, John	30	5 ft. 7 in.	....	Lymavoir	April 13
[14]Gordon, Wm., jun. ..	..	....	Tomachork	Lieut. John Gordon, Tombae	March 12
[15]Gordon, Wm., sen. ..	..	....	Achnarrow	Lieut. John Gordon, Tombae	March 10
Grant, Charles	19	5 ft. 4 in.	....	Farmers of Strathbogie	March 20
Grant, James	20	5 ft. 6 in.	Lochaber	....	March 10
Grant, James	18	5 ft. 7 in.	....	Lieut. John Gordon, Coynachie	March 8
[16]Grant, James ..	..	....	Abernethy	Lieut. John Gordon, Tombae	....
Grant, James	21	5 ft. 9 in.	....	Tombreakachy	March 16
Grant, John	20	5 ft. 5 in.	....	Findron	April 13
Grant, John	22	5 ft. 10 in.	Glenlivat	At Gordon Castle	March 20
Grant, Peter	19	5 ft. 6 in.	....	Lieut. John Gordon, Coynachie	March 13
Grant, William ..	22	5 ft. 8 in.	....	Capt. John Macpherson, of Invereshie	April 13
Grant, William ..	19	5 ft. 7 in.	Tombreachachy	....	April 13
Green, Robert	19	5 ft. 9 in.	....	Lieut. John Gordon, Coynachie	March 8
[17]Gregory, John ..	17	5 ft. 4 in.	....	....	April 2
Hay, James	..	....	Huntly	....	April 26
Hay, Peter	22	5 ft. 11 in.	....	Lieut. John Gordon, Coynachie	March 8
Henderson, Donald ..	18	5 ft. 3 in.	Halkirk	....	March 29
Imlach, William ..	30	5 ft. 6 in.	Spynie	Minister of Speymouth	March 30
Ingram, Alexander ..	22	5 ft. 7 in.	....	Farmers of Strathbogie	April 9
Ingram, John	20	5 ft. 6 in.	Inverurie	Gordon Castle	April 2
Innes, Alexander ..	25	5 ft. 10 in.	Glenlivat	Gordon Castle	March 20
Innes, James	17	5 ft. 8½ in.	Achlichny	Gordon Castle (enlisted voluntarily)	March 12
Innes, Robert	17	5 ft. 3¾ in.	Reay	....	April 1
Kennedy, Angus ..	34	5 ft. 6 in.	....	Capt. Ewen Macpherson	March 19
Kennedy, Ewen	20	5 ft. 6 in.	Lochaber	....	April 4
Kennedy, John ..	28	5 ft. 6½ in.	....	Capt. John Macpherson, of Invereshie	March 3
Kennedy, John	25	5 ft. 10 in.	....	Capt. Ewen Macpherson	March 20
Kennedy, Neil	23	5 ft. 6 in.	Lochaber	Lady Madelina Sinclair	....
Kennedy, William ..	24	5 ft. 0½ in.	....	Capt. John Macpherson, of Invereshie	April 4
Kerr, John	22	5 ft. 6 in.	Labourer at Gordon Castle	....	April 2
Laing, Alexander ..	15	5 ft. 4 in.	Boat of Bogue	James Logie	March 26
Lawson, John	16	5 ft. 4 in.	....	Farmers of Strathbogie	March 2
Leslie, Joseph	17	5 ft. 4 in.	....	Lieut. John Gordon, Coynachie	March 8
M'Bain, Gillies	17	5 ft. 9 in.	....	Capt. John Macpherson, of Invereshie	March 22
M'Bain, William ..	19	5 ft. 10 in.	Lochaber	....	....
M'Cadie, James ..	20	5 ft. 6 in.	....	Capt. John Macpherson, of Invereshie	March 8

9 and 10 Brothers.
11 Servant to Kininvie.
12 Discharged, October 14, 1793.
13 Had a brother in the 42nd.
14, 15, and 16, Servants to Lieut. Gordon.
17 Carpenter at Gordon Castle.

Name.	Age.	Height.	Residence.	Enlisted by	Date of Enlistment.
M'Combie, Alexander ..	18	5 ft. 7 in.	....	Lieut. John Gordon, Coynachie	March 8
M'Craw, Donald ..	17	5 ft. 5½ in.	....	The Duke, in Badenoch	....
Macdonald, Angus ..	23	5 ft. 9 in.	Lochaber	....	....
Macdonald, Angus ..	23	5 ft. 0 in.	Lochaber	....	....
M'Donald (alias M'Edward), Donald ..	..	....	....	....	March 28
M'Donald, Donald ..	..	....	....	Mr. Smith, Nairn	....
M'Donald, George ..	17	5 ft. 7 in.	Glack	....	....
M'Donald, Gregor ..	22	5 ft. 5 in.	Tomintoul	Mr. Smith, Campdell	April 14
Macdonald, John ..	24	5 ft. 9 in.	Serv't to Tombae	Gordon Castle	April 6
M'Donald (alias M'Alister), William	..	....	Aberlour	Lieut. John Gordon, Tombae	....
Macdonell, Alexander..	32	5 ft. 8 in.	Lochaber	....	....
Macdonell, Alexander..	30	5 ft. 7 in.	Lochaber	....	....
Macdonell, Angus ..	19	5 ft. 8 in.	Lochaber	....	....
M'Donell, Angus (alias Boyle) ..	30	5 ft. 10 in.	....	Baillie Cameron and Col. Campbell	....
M'Donell, Donald ..	22	5 ft. 6 in.	Lochaber	....	....
18 Macdonell, Donald ..	30	5 ft. 9 in.	Unachan	The Duke, at Gordon Castle	....
M'Donell, John ..	18	5 ft. 5 in.	Lochaber	....	....
Macdonell, John ..	24	....	Lochaber	....	....
Macdonell, Paul ..	25	5 ft. 7 in.	....	The Duke, in Badenoch	....
Macdonell, Ranald ..	22	5 ft. 8 in.	....	Capt. Cameron, in Kinrara	....
Macdougall, Alexander	25	5 ft. 8 in.	....	Capt. Cameron, in Kinrara	....
M'Guirman, William ..	18	5 ft. 6 in.	.... [aven	Capt. Godsman	March 29
MacGregor, James ..	19	5 ft. 5 in.	Gaubig, Strath-	The Duke, at Tomintoul	March 18
19 M'Gregor, John ..	..	....	Blairfindy	Lieut. John Gordon, Tombae	....
M'Gregor, John ..	36	5 ft. 6½ in.	Lochaber	....	....
M'Hardy, Alexander ..	..	....	Demickmore	Lieut. John Gordon, Tombae	March 13
M'Intosh, Duncan ..	25	5 ft. 7 in.	....	Capt. Ewen Macpherson	....
20 M'Intosh, William ..	..	....	Achnarrow	Lieut. John Gordon, Tombae	....
M'Intyre, Ewen ..	30	5 ft. 5 in.	Lochaber	....	....
M'Intyre, John ..	30	5 ft. 4½ in.	....	Capt. John Macpherson, of Invereshie	....
M'Intyre, Malcolm ..	18	5 ft. 7 in.	....	Baillie Cameron and Col. Campbell	....
Mackay, George ..	17	5 ft. 3½ in.	Reay	....	March 26
M'Kay, John ..	23	5 ft. 7 in.	....	Capt. John Macpherson, of Invereshie	....
Mackenzie, Alexander..	22	5 ft. 5 in.	Cairny	....	April 5
Mackenzie, Donald ..	24	5 ft. 8 in.	Lochaber	....	....
M'Kenzie, John ..	34	5 ft. 9 in.	Lochaber	....	....
M'Kenzie, Patrick ..	30	5 ft. 10 in.	....	Capt. Ewen Macpherson	....
M'Kinnon, Alexander..	24	5 ft. 6 in.	Lochaber	....	....
M'Kinnon, Donald ..	22	5 ft. 8 in.	Lochaber	....	....
M'Lachlan, Donald ..	17	5 ft. 6 in.	....	Duncan Gordon	....
M'Lachlan, Ewen ..	18	5 ft. 5 in.	Lochaber	....	....
M'Lean, Alexander ..	21	5 ft. 4 in.	....	The Duke, in Badenoch	....
21 M'Lean, James ..	21	5 ft. 5 in.	Fochabers	....	April 6
M'Lean, John ..	25	5 ft. 8 in.	Lochaber	....	....
M'Lean, John ..	21	5 ft. 8 in.	Lochaber	....	....
M'Lean, John ..	29	5 ft. 9½ in.	....	Capt. John Macpherson, of Invereshie	....
Macleod, Neil ..	20	5 ft. 7¾ in.	Assint	....	March 29
M'Mahon, Alexander ..	25	5 ft. 7 in.	....	Capt. Ewen Macpherson	....
M'Martin, Donald ..	18	5 ft. 7 in.	Lochaber	....	....
M'Master, John ..	27	5 ft. 10 in.	Lochaber	Lady Madelina Sinclair	April 4
M'Millan, Donald ..	19	5 ft. 4 in.	....	Baillie Cameron and Col. Campbell	....
M'Millan, Duncan ..	..	....	Glennevis	....	....
M'Millan, Ewen ..	29	5 ft. 4 in.	Lochaber	....	....
M'Millan, John ..	17	5 ft. 5 in.	Lochaber	....	....
M'Millan, John ..	30	5 ft. 6 in.	....	Baillie Cameron and Col. Campbell	....
M'Neil, Donald ..	20	5 ft. 6 in.	Lochaber	....	March 23
Macpherson, Alexander	20	5 ft. 4½ in.	....	Capt. John Macpherson, of Invereshie	....
Macpherson, Angus ..	19	5 ft. 4 in.	....	The Duke, in Badenoch	....
Macpherson, Angus ..	20	5 ft. 6 in.	....	Capt. John Macpherson, of Invereshie	....
Macpherson, David ..	..	....	Shirabeg	....	....
Macpherson, Donald ..	38	5 ft. 5 in.	Lochaber	....	....
Macpherson, Donald ..	18	5 ft. 4 in.	....	The Duke, in Badenoch	....
Macpherson, Ewan ..	20	5 ft. 8 in.	....	Capt. Ewen Macpherson	....
Macpherson, James ..	16	5 ft. 2 in.	....	The Duke, in Badenoch	....
Macpherson, James ..	26	5 ft. 7 in.	....	Capt. Ewen Macpherson	....
Macpherson, James ..	19	5 ft. 3½ in.	....	Capt. John Macpherson, of Invereshie	....

18 Had been in a Fencible Regiment before.   20 Servant to Lieut. Gordon.
19 Servant to Minmore.   21 Servant to John Smith, vintner, Fochabers.

Name.	Age.	Height.	Residence.	Enlisted by	Date of Enlistment.
Macpherson, John	23	5 ft. 5 in.	....	Capt. John Macpherson, of Invereshie	....
Macpherson, John	20	5 ft. 4 in.	....	Capt. John Macpherson, of Invereshie	....
Macpherson, John	19	5 ft. 3½ in.	....	Capt. John Macpherson, of Invereshie	....
Macpherson, John	22	5 ft. 8 in.	....	Capt. John Macpherson, of Invereshie	....
Macpherson, Lachlan	20	5 ft. 7 in.	....	The Duke, in Badenoch	....
Macpherson, Murdoch	17	5 ft. 5 in.	....	Capt. John Macpherson, of Invereshie	....
Macpherson, Thomas	20	5 ft. 5 in.	....	The Duke, in Badenoch	....
Macpherson, William	19	5 ft. 5 in.	....	....	April 13
Macpherson, William	18	5 ft. 4½ in.	....	Capt. John Macpherson, of Invereshie	....
Macpherson, William	25	5 ft. 5 in.	....	The Duke, in Badenoch	....
MacPhie, Angus	28	5 ft. 6 in.	Lochaber	....	....
M'Queen, Lachlan	..	....	....	Mr. Smith, Nairn	March 27
Manson, Charles	21	5 ft. 7½ in.	....	Lieut. John Gordon, Coynachie	March 8
Manson, Peter	18	5 ft. 4½ in.	Bower	....	March 29
Mathieson, William	22	5 ft. 8 in.	....	Lieut. John Gordon, Coynachie	March 8
Mitchell, Andrew	32	5 ft. 6 in.	....	Pityoulish and his brothers	March 12
Mitchell, James	22	5 ft. 6 in.	....	Pityoulish and his brothers	March 28
Mitchell, John	30	5 ft. 5 in.	....	Pityoulish and his brothers	March 28
Morrison, Donald	23	5 ft. 7½ in.	....	Farmers of Strathbogie	April 14
Munro, Alexander	18	5 ft. 5 in.	....	Farmers of Strathbogie	April 14
Munro, William	19	5 ft. 5 in.	....	Lieut. John Gordon, Coynachie	March 8
Murray, Marcus	27	5 ft. 6 in.	....	Farmers of Strathbogie	April 2
Mutch, John	..	..	....	Mr. McHardie	....
Paul, William	..	....	....	Mr. Black	March 30
Phyn, John	18	5 ft. 7½ in.	....	Lieut. Gordon, Minmore	March 21
Riach, John	22	5 ft. 10 in.	Argeith	....	April 18
Robertson, Donald	29	5 ft. 6 in.	....	The Duke, in Badenoch	March 18
Robertson, Donald	23	5 ft. 4 in.	....	Pityoulish and his brothers	March 27
Robertson, John	21	5 ft. 6½ in.	....	Capt. John Macpherson, of Invereshie	....
Robertson, Thomas	20	5 ft. 2½ in.	....	The Duke, in Badenoch	March 26
Ross, Charles	21	5 ft. 10 in.	Strathaven	Lady Madelina Sinclair	March 28
Ross, James	25	5 ft. 5 in.	....	Charles Grant, in Blairfindy	March 11
Roy, James	18	5 ft. 6 in.	....	Lieut. John Gordon, Coynachie	March 8
Sinclair, John	15	5 ft. 2¾ in.	Reay	Reay	March 29
Skinner, Alexander	25	5 ft. 7 in.	....	Lieut. John Gordon, Coynachie	March 14
Smith, Alexander	22	5 ft. 5½ in.	....	Farmers of Strathbogie	March 3
Smith, James	22	5 ft. 10 in.	....	The Duke, at Huntly	March 28
Smith (alias Gow), Thos.	23	5 ft. 5 in.	Strathaven	Gordon Castle	March 27
Smith (alias Gow), Thos.	22	5 ft. 5 in.	....	Wm. Smith	April 14
Stitchell, John	18	5 ft. 6 in.	....	The Duke, at Huntly	March 8
Stuart, Alexander	21	5 ft. 7½ in.	....	Lieut. Gordon, Coynachie	March 8
Stewart, Charles (alias Derg)	28	5 ft. 11 in.	....	Tomintoul	April 13
Stuart, Donald	19	5 ft. 4 in.	....	Capt. John Macpherson, of Invereshie	....
Stuart, Gaven	18	5 ft. 6 in.	....	Lieut. John Gordon, Coynachie	March 8
Stuart, John	18	5 ft. 6 in.	Caithness ?	....	April 1
Stuart, John	25	5 ft. 11 in.	....	Pityoulish and his brothers	....
Stuart, John	17	5 ft. 7 in.	Newmill	Rippachy (" in exchange for a chief ")	March 6
Stewart (alias M'Lea), Lewis	..	..	Desky	Lieut. John Gordon, Tombae	....
Stuart, Murdoch	20	5 ft. 7½ in.	....	Capt. John Macpherson, of Invereshie	March 18
22Stuart, Peter	24	5 ft. 9 in.	....	....	....
Stuart, Robert	28	5 ft. 6 in.	....	Lieut. John Gordon, Coynachie	March 8
Stuart, Robert	25	5 ft. 11 in.	Tomintoul	Mr. Smith, Campdell	April 14
Steuart, William	22	5 ft. 5 in.	....	A. Forbes, in Cuttlebrae	March 23
Sutherland, George	35	5 ft. 7 in.	Buckie	Skipper Geddes	March 22
Taylor, William	20	5 ft. 8 in.	Keith	Serjeant Reid	March 22
Thomson, Alexander	20	5 ft. 5½ in.	....	Farmers of Strathbogie	April 17
Thomson, George	34	5 ft. 4 in.	....	Farmers of Strathbogie	April 10
Thomson, James	21	5 ft. 8 in.	Labourer	Gordon Castle	March 19
Tulloch, John	20	5 ft. 6 in.	.... [more	Pityoulish and his brothers	March 16
Turner, John	..	....	Nether Clash-	Lieut. John Gordon, Tombae	....
White, James	17	5 ft. 6½ in.	....	Mr. Thomson, in Hardbaugh	April
Wilson, Patrick	22	5 ft. 9 in.	....	Lieut. John Gordon, Coynachie	March 9
Wilson, Thomas	19	5 ft. 5 in.	....	Lieut. John Gordon, Coynachie	March 8
Wiseman, John	40	5 ft. 10 in.	Garmouth	Minister of Bellie	March 25
Young, John, sen.	40	5 ft. 6 in.	Buckie	Gordon Castle	March 29
Young, John, jun.	16	5 ft. 4 in.	Buckie	Skipper Geddes	March 21

22 Brother of Charles Stuart, Derg.

G. III. R.

I *Niel Kennedy* do make oath,
That I am no apprentice, nor belong to any regiment of militia, or
to any other regiment or corps in his Majesty's service; that I am by
trade a *Labourer* and to the best of my information
and belief, was born in the parish of *Kilmannan* in the
county of *Invernes* and kingdom of *Scotland* and
that I have no rupture, nor ever troubled with fits; that I am no way
disabled by lameness, or otherwise, but have a perfect use of my limbs;
and that I have voluntarily inlisted myself to serve his Majesty King
GEORGE, as a private soldier, in the regiment of North Fencibles,
commanded by the DUKE of GORDON, and that I have received all
the inlisting money which I agreed for, as witness my hand, this
ninth day of *April* 1793

Niel Kennedy

Witness

THESE are to certify, That the forefaid *Niel Kennedy*
aged *twenty three* years, *Five* feet *Six* inches high,
Fair complexion, *Fair* hair, *blue* eyes,
came before me, *Justice of peace for the County of Invernes*
and acknowledged, that he had voluntarily inlisted himself to serve his
Majesty King GEORGE, in the above-mentioned regiment: He also
acknowledged he had heard the second and sixth sections of the Articles of War read unto him, against Mutiny and Desertion, and took
the Oath of Fidelity mentioned to him in the said Articles of War.
Sworn before me, at *Ft William* this *Tenth* day of
April 1793 years

J. P.

I have examined the above named man, and find him without
Rupture, Lameness, or any defect of Body or Limb.

Surgeon.

AN ATTESTATION PAPER FOR THE NORTHERN FENCIBLES, 1793.

The regiment had two colours, both of which are at Gordon Castle. The King's Colour, first Union (6 feet by 5 feet 6 inches), has in the centre the circle, cross, and figure of St. Andrew, surmounted by the crown. Above this is a scroll with the words, " North Fencible High-landers "; and beneath the figure is another scroll inscribed *Clue le Cruadal* (a phonetic spelling of *Cliù le Cruadail*—" Renown with Hardihood "), surmounted by the first Union wreath of roses and thistles. The Regimental Colour (6 feet by 5 feet 8 inches) is of yellow silk with the first Union canton, and is emblazoned like the royal. A reproduction of it appears in the *Catalogue of Weapons, Battle Trophies, and Regimental Colours* [at Gordon Castle]: re-arranged by Charles, 7th Duke of Richmond and Gordon, 1907 (facing p. 32).

One of the most interesting facts about this Regiment of Northern Fencibles is this, that it was for its benefit that Gordon tartan seems to have been designed. The tartan was suggested by the Black Watch plaid, just as the Highland regiments altogether had been more or less modelled on the 42nd. When the Marquis of Huntly took his company to the Black Watch in 1791, he had startled London by wearing its tartan at Court. There was, therefore, a close connection between the Black Watch and the territory from which the Duke of Gordon was now recruiting. Indeed one man, Thomas Smith, who had been enlisted for the Marquis of Huntly's Black Watch Company by John Grant of Tarmore, made an application to be appointed a sergeant in the Northern Fencibles. On April 15, William Forsyth, the manu-facturer of Huntly, wrote this very interesting letter :—

When I had the honour of communing with His Grace the Duke of Gordon, he was desirous to have paterns of the 42nd Regiment plaid with a small yellow stripe properly placed. Enclosed [are] three paterns of the 42nd plaid all having yellow stripes. From these I hope his Grace will fix on some of the three stripes. When the plaids are worn the yellow stripes will be square and regular. I imagine the yellow stripes will appear very lively.

On April 20, the Duke fixed on pattern 2—" that's to say the same with the 42nd Regiment, with the alteration of the yellow stripe properly placed ; the quality of the plaid [the] same in every other respect."

William Dickie of Caroline Street, Bedford Square, London, who had uniformed the previous Northern Fencibles, had offered to clothe and accoutre the present regiment for £2,982 16s. 4d.

The regimental band consisted (in 1798) of fifes, flutes, a clarinet, a triangle, a horn—and pipes.

On June 1, the regiment was reviewed in Aberdeen by General Leslie, and on June 4, it was drawn up on the Plainstones at the rejoicings over the King's birthday. Later in the month, on the occasion of the Duke's birthday (June 18, old style), the officers and their ladies had an "elegant" dinner at the New Inn (the Duke's headquarters in Aberdeen), a ball and supper being given in the evening, while the privates had hogsheads of porter given to them on the Castle Hill.

On July 2, 1793, the Duke wrote to Lord Amherst from Gordon Castle :—

Altho' I am persuaded that in the arrangement of the rank of Colonels in the Fencible regiments, your lordship will fully consider all our pretensions, yet I beg to submit to your consideration that, having been an old colonel of Fencibles, I hope to have rank given me over those colonels who have not been in that situation before. From my never having resigned my commission as Captain in the 89th Regiment, and having been accordingly put on the half pay list, I cannot but consider myself in the same situation, and must hope that I shall not have my claim to priority of rank on that ground lessened, because I did not chuse to receive the annual stipend of the half pay, more especially as from an order in this late war for the posting of the officers in my regiment those even who had served at all in the army were to take rank of those who had never been in the Fencibles. I shall hope your Lordship will take these pretensions into your consideration and regulate accordingly the rank I ought now to hold as Colonel of the Northern Fencible Regiment.

On July 9, Lord Amherst assured His Grace that his rank with respect to the other colonels would be laid before the King on any occasion that might require it, "which does not alter in any degree the rank of the Fencible Regiment which they have drawn lots for. Officers who served in the army certainly take the place of those who have not served."

On August 21-22, the Fencibles marched from Aberdeen to Edinburgh via Perth, and were stationed at Edinburgh Castle till March, 1794.

The expense of the Regiment from June 1 to December 24, 1793, was as follows (*W.O.* 24 : 578, p. 29) :—

Pay	£5,624 11 10½
Clothing	1,083 8 2
Agency	103 9 3½
Allowances	361 7 1
Accoutrements	64 15 4

On February 17, 1794, Sir George Yonge of the War Office wrote to the Duke authorising an increase in the men to 1,000 :—

My Lord [Duke]—I have the honour to acquaint you that His Majesty has been pleased to direct that the Northern Regiment of Fencible Men under your Grace's Command shall be augmented by the addition of 1 Major, 1 Captain, 12 Lieutenants, 2 Ensigns, and 1 Surgeon's Mate : that 2 Battalion Companies shall be added thereto each of the following numbers viz.: 4 Serjeants, 4 Corporals, 2 Drummers, and 100 private Men : and that the former Companies shall be augmented to the same Establishment : so as that the Regiment when completed, shall consist af the numbers specified in the margin. I am to add that the Surgeon's Mate to be appointed must be previously approved by the Physician and Surgeon-General, and the Inspector of Regimental Hospitals.

This order would have brought up the numbers of the regiment to this strength :—

1 Colonel	1 Capt.-Lieut.	1 Adjutant	42 Sergeants
1 Lieut.-Colonel	21 Lieutenants	1 Quartermaster	40 Corporals
2 Majors	8 Ensigns	1 Surgeon	20 Drummers
6 Captains	1 Chaplain	2 Surgeon Mates	2 Pipers
		1000 Privates	

As a matter of fact, the increase never took place, though Pryse Gordon was sent to Aberdeen with a recruiting party. On the contrary, the numbers dwindled, as the muster rolls show :—

June 1–24, 1793	601	June–December, 1794	547
June–December, 1793	619	December, 1794–June, 1795	550
December, 1793–June, 1794	588	December, 1795–June, 1796	467

This declension in figures was undoubtedly due to those difficulties in handling the men which I have referred to as the real crux of the Duke's 1793 experiment in soldiering. The price of men all over the country had steadily advanced; but there was a further reason why the Highlanders should have become more difficult to manipulate. As the suppressive measures which followed the 'Forty-Five receded into the page of history, the clans involved slowly regained self-consciousness ; all the more as the Government had come to regard them with special consideration, as the case of the Atholl Highlanders had clearly demonstrated. This consciousness had the effect of making some of the clansmen in the Duke's regiment revert to the attitude, never wholly suppressed, of resenting his "superiority," and insisting on their own clan customs and rights, quite apart from his legal hold over them. This was brought out in the attitude of one officer in particular, Captain John Cameron, who rebelled at Edinburgh in 1794, and was court-martialled there for a fresh offence four years later.

Nothing could illustrate more vividly the tetchy traditions of the Highlanders and the clash between the clan and the feudal ideals than the episode narrated almost truculently by Pryse Lockhart Gordon (*Personal Memoirs* i., 141-2). When the serious business of drilling the men at Edinburgh Castle began,

the forming of the flank companies excited no small jealousy among several of the Highland officers, especially to one young chief, who had no conception, when he brought four score of his clan as volunteers, that they were to be disunited : on the contrary, he took it into his head that his own levy was to be solely under his own control, and one day foolishly declared at the mess table "that if the commanding officer [Woodford] *dared* to draft any of his men, he would order his pipers to sound his gathering and march them back to Lochaber "; commenting at the same time on the great superiority of his mountaineers over the *Botich a Brechich* (fellows with breeches), and that this was the first time his clan's standard had been unfurled in unison with the Gordons'; finishing this sensible harangue by adding that "his men were *gentlemen*, with whom he was in the habit of associating "!

Pryse Gordon, who heard him, suggested that this doctrine had become old-fashioned, and added—" Should you continue to keep company with your *soi-disant* 'gentlemen,' the breeches men will not associate with *you*. . . . Such declarations have a tendency to excite mutiny in a young corps." The chief "changed countenance more than once, and before I concluded was pale with rage. . . . At length, he started on his legs, and, laying his hand on his sword, I followed his motions and got on mine, being also armed with a good Andrea di Ferrara." Captain M'Intosh thereupon intervened, in support of Pryse Gordon, but this had the effect of infuriating Cameron :—

He stammered out something by way of explanation (which in the hubbub was not intelligible, if meant to be so), and, turning to me, said in a subdued tone, which he probably thought was prudent, "that I was welcome to repeat on the parade ground what he had said." To this I only replied "that I was not in the habit of repeating in public private conversations, but I considered it my duty to inform the Lieutenant-Colonel of his sentiments, and without asking his permission." To this I was not honoured with a reply; but he immediately withdrew, followed by his *tail*, for he had introduced half a dozen yahoos in great jackets and tartan trews.

As it might be considered invidious in me to be the talebearer, M'Intosh undertook to communicate the affair to Woodford, who summoned the great man forthwith to his presence (no small degradation), and, after lecturing him sharply on his unmilitary conduct, ordered him to parade his recruits for the purpose of their being drafted into the flank company; "and as they are such fine fellows," he added, "I suspect you will have few left." . . . His *gentlemen* followers in six months cared no more for their *chief* than for any other officer in the regiment. It was found that more than two-thirds of his men were suited to the flank companies, and were accordingly drafted into them.

Admitting that the clansmen were kittle cattle, one cannot help feeling that a man of Woodford's type was peculiarly unfitted for the difficult task of handling them. A member of an old family connected with Northamptonshire and Leicestershire, he was quite a typical Englishman of the governing caste. Crosthwaite, the eulogist of his son John, describes him as a "man of great ability and force of character, a soldier, a scholar, and a patriot of no common order." Pryse Gordon admits that he was "an active clever officer," but adds that he was a "strict disciplinarian." He had learned his soldiering in the Grenadier Guards—just think of a smart English Guardsman being put in charge of six hundred raw Highland lads—and he had fought under Wolfe at Quebec, finding it, probably, inconceivable that any man could hesitate over such points as Cameron raised, when the flag was in danger. His stern sense of duty and his equal lack of tact had been illustrated in 1780 by his being the first officer to order on his own responsibility the soldiers to fire on the followers of his wife's favourite brother, Lord George Gordon—an indiscretion which sent him into hiding for a time. I fancy that the Duke of Gordon, a man of strong "horse-sense," was not long in regretting his nepotism in selecting Woodford, for he tried to get a billet for him before he had long begun his command, writing to Pitt, on October 14, 1793 (P.R.O.: *Chatham Papers*, 139) :—

Dear Pitt,—I have just seen by the Papers that Captain Hill, who had the Fort Major's place at the Tower, is dead. I wish much to get something for my friend Colonel Woodford ; and, if you are not already under any promise for that place, I shall be very much obliged to you to bestow it on him.

Woodford found himself in much greater difficulties when he had to communicate the orders that the regiment was to march into England. To the average Scot the road to the South is the traditional road to Fortune. But to the Highlanders of this period the South had most unpleasant prospects, thanks largely to the dishonesty of the War Office, which had drafted Fencibles, totally in defiance to the terms of their enlistment, into regiments of the line and regiments of the line into transports, bound for the hungry maws of the Indies, East and West. Unluckily for the War Office, the Celt has a highly retentive memory, and the tragedy of the Black Watch in 1743, followed by similar refusals to go abroad on the part of the Seaforth Highlanders in 1778, detachments of the 42nd and 71st in 1779, and the Atholl Highlanders in 1783, had left a deep impression.

When the word came in 1794 for the Scots Fencibles to embark, the Southern Fencibles, commanded by Lord Hopetoun at Ayr, mutinied and declined. Pryse Gordon tells us that their decision communicated itself to the other regiments " like an electric shock." He goes on to say (*Personal Memoirs*, i., 150-1) :—

Ours [the Northern Fencibles], being locked up in the Castle [of Edinburgh], had less communication with the malecontents [sic], and was the last to exhibit discontent ; but at length the soldiers were seen in knots talking Gaelic with an air of mystery. The Lieutenant-Colonel [Woodford] fancied himself actually a Highlander, and, piquing himself on his popularity, he imagined that his eloquence would bring the men to reason. He marched them by detachments into the garrison chapel, and, mounting the pulpit, lectured away with great vehemence for a couple of hours, but, as might have been expected, without effect ; and it was evident to every one but himself that he was throwing away his time.

Pryse Gordon, who clearly did not like Woodford, advised him to summon the Duke as "the only chance of checking a mutiny that was ready to break out every moment, but he continued lecturing for three days, when he found that his eloquence had no good effect, and at length he despatched an express to Gordon Castle, where his Grace was, and in eight and forty hours, he arrived." His Grace on his way south supped (March 16, 1794), with Captain Finlason, " leaving [Aberdeen] in a very fine night and in perfect health." Finlason, in recording this, adds :—

I hope the Duke will lead the way to England and show an example worthy to be imitated in times of partial disaffection and undue influence, and to poison the minds of ignorant men. I hope it may not be necessary for his Grace to embark in person. I think it [he?] is by far too great value on sea.

On reaching Edinburgh, the Duke had the regiment paraded. Pryse Gordon tells us that :—

He explained in a few words the nature of the service they were called for, "the defence of their country"; and he trusted that any soldier who was such a disloyal dastard as to refuse such service he would step out of the ranks, and he should have his discharge, for, though they were raised for the defence of Scotland, England was now in danger, and none but cowards would refuse the call. He could assure them that, wherever they went, they would find him at their head ; and, if they preferred marching to England by land, rather than being transported by sea, that they had their choice. This short harangue was received with the greatest applause, and every bonnet was elevated, and every voice cheered, that they were ready "to follow his Grace to the world's end."

Thus terminated the dreaded mutiny [Stewart makes no reference to it]; and, though this gratified our little Colonel [Woodford], it was evident by his sour looks that he was somewhat mortified to find that a few words had produced effects which his eloquence had been unable to accomplish in three days.

By a strange irony, England, so far from being a promised land for Woodford, proved his undoing, for when he reached his native shore he got into a divorce scrape.

The Duke writes to Menzies, April 3, from Edinburgh that he is on the point of marching the regiment off to Leith where they were to embark. Lord Adam Gordon advised him to precede the men by land, so that they could get good quarters. The men embarked for Portsmouth in five transports, "with the utmost good will and cheerfulness and not one man of the whole in liquor." They had, however, a bad start, for owing to bad weather they were kept rocking about in the transports for two days before they actually sailed.

The journey to England was worth taking, for it proved the occasion of a unique honour. When stationed in Kent, the regiment was ordered to London, which had seen no Highland regiment since the tragic visit of the Black Watch in 1743 (Stewart's *Highlanders*, 2nd ed. ii., 324). The King himself had never seen a Highland regiment, so he reviewed the Fencibles with interest. The Duchess of Gordon and her daughters were present among the Royal spectators, wearing Highland bonnets and Gordon tartan plaids. The Royal party paid particular attention, on the initiation of the Duchess, to the sergeant-major, Dugald Campbell, who is described as "a most superb specimen of the human race." Pryse Gordon (*Memoirs*, ii., 287) assures us that his fine martial figure was "much admired by the Royal party, and by thousands of females who were present on the occasion." In 1793 Campbell at the age of 18 deserted his father's forge to wield the claymore. "I happened to be at Gordon Castle when the young hero descended from the mountains to enroll his name under the banners of his Grace," from whom his father, a pistol and dirk maker, at Fort-William, rented a farm. In 1797 the Marquis of Huntly presented him with a commission in the Gordon Highlanders, with whom he served in all its hard campaigns in the Peninsula and elsewhere. His noble patron got him permission to retire on his full pay shortly after the battle of Waterloo, where Campbell had been severely wounded.

The review was a source of immense pride to Woodford, for he referred to it four years later in addressing the regiment on June 4, 1798 :—

The favourable reports made of this regiment excited in His Majesty a wish to see one so highly talked of. He reviewed us, on our march in Hyde Park, but to mark his Royal favour, he met you, who had come so far to serve, at the Horse Guards, and himself led at your head to the ground of the review, an honour most distinguished and never to be forgotten. You were the first Highland regiment, too, the King ever saw; he admired your dress; he praised our steady adherence to the garb of old Gaul, and was gratified in every point of our appearance and discipline that day.

Sir Alexander Woodford, the colonel's son, has left a charming little reminiscence of the regiment (J. Fisher Crosthwaite's *Brief Memoir of Sir J. G. Woodford*, 1881 ; p. i.) At Christmas, 1794, he joined his father, who was stationed at Shoreham, with the Fencibles. They stayed at Portslade House. In 1795 he and his mother went to Sittingbourne, and the regiment was turned out to receive her, then formed into eights, and afterwards danced reels. The colonel's little boys, who were just 13 and 10 years old respectively, walked down the ranks and shook hands with every man.

This pretty domestic picture makes it difficult to understand why Woodford, so severe a disciplinarian with others, should have been so lax himself as to have run off the rails with the wife of his paymaster, Captain Charles Gordon, laird of Wardhouse. She was Katherine, daughter of Major James Mercer of Auchnacant (who had been in the previous regiment of Northern Fencibles), and had married Wardhouse, as his second wife, at St. Paul's Church, Aberdeen, in 1781. Woodford and she were accused of having carried on during the whole time the regiment was in England—at Hythe between June and November, 1794; at Shoreham and Southwick Barracks, November, 1794-May, 1795, during part of which time her husband commanded a detachment of the regiment at Seaford; at Hastings, May-October, 1795; and at Blatchington Barracks, October, 1795—January, 1796. Mrs. Gordon finally had a natural daughter, Sophia, born in Edinburgh in August, 1796. Gordon got a divorce in the Edinburgh Commissary Court, January 5-6, 1797 (*Edinburgh Consistorial Decreets*, vol. 23: printed verbatim in the *Huntly Express*, March 31, 1911).

When the regiment returned to Scotland—it got orders to march north on April 9, 1796, five companies from Blatchington and five from Eastbourne (*W.O.* 5: 70)—and got into encampment at Ayr, the injured laird of Wardhouse, not content with his divorce, took the law into his own hands and assaulted Woodford in the streets of Ayr, though Pryse Gordon makes no reference to the scandal, being much too taken up with "my friend Lord Montgomery." Gordon was court-martialled at Ayr on July 5 ("and following days"), 1797, Colonel the

THE NORTHERN FENCIBLES, 1793-99.

Earl of Darlington (who was raised to the Dukedom of Cleveland in 1833) acting as President. The case was so important that *The Times*, at that time very sparing in provincial news, dealt with it (August 19, 1797, p. 3, col. 4) to the extent of half a column. Gordon was charged under three different counts :—

(1) With violently assaulting and striking Colonel Woodford, his commanding officer on the street of Ayr upon the fifteenth day of June last, in breach of the 5th Article of the second section of the Articles of War.

(2) For ungentlemanlike behaviour in running behind and violently striking and wounding his said commanding officer with a stick in the nature of a bludgeon, when he was in no state of self-defence, in breach of the 22nd Article of the 16th section of the Articles of War.

(3) For disobedience of orders and breach of arrest in refusing to return with the adjutant to Head-quarters, and going to Edinburgh in breach of the 21st Article of the 16th section of the Articles of War.

It was an unhappy affair, for Woodford's superior officer, the Duke of Gordon, must have sided not only with his sister (Lady Susan Woodford) but with his injured clansman, the laird of Wardhouse. Moreover, the Duke's uncle, Lord Adam Gordon, was Commander-in-Chief of the Forces in Scotland. In the circumstances it is not surprising that the sentence of the Court, promulgated at Edinburgh from the Adjutant-General's Office, August 17, 1797, was of the nature of a hush-up, as follows :—

The Court, upon full consideration of the evidence and the whole matters before them, were of opinion that the Prisoner is guilty upon each of the charges exhibited against him in breach of the Articles of War, on which the said charges are laid, and that he is liable to punishment accordingly ; on which account they adjudged him to be cashiered. But, in consideration of the aggravated circumstances attendant upon the case from an unfortunate family difference [the divorce case] the Court humbly requested General Lord Adam Gordon to recommend to his Majesty that the punishment may be so far mitigated that the prisoner Captain Gordon shall only be obliged to give in his resignation to Lt. Col. Woodford for him to forward to his Colonel, the Duke of Gordon.

The whole of the proceedings of the aforesaid General Court Martial having been laid before the King, His Majesty has been pleased to signify to General Lord A[dam] Gordon that from the peculiar circumstances of the case—in which His Majesty sees much to lament and

much to blame—he has not thought fit to rectify the sentence of Court
Martial in its extent with reference to each of the Articles of the charge;
but, considering it to be inconsistent with the harmony of the Corps, and
in point of example with the necessary support of discipline that Captain
Gordon should retain his commission in the Regiment of North Fencible
Highlanders, His Majesty is pleased to direct that it be signified to him
that His Majesty has no farther occasion for his services as Captain in
the said Regiment.

It is General Lord Adam Gordon's order that the foregoing charges
and sentence, with His Majesty's pleasure signified thereupon, be circulated to the Regular and Fencible Forces in North Britain, and entered
in the Order Books of the respective corps. By General Lord Adam
Gordon's command.

The hush-up took the form of Gordon's being appointed paymaster
to the 2nd battalion of the 1st Foot (Royal Scots) a few months later
(March 15, 1798).

The whole episode was, of course, fatal to the maintenance of
discipline, especially after Woodford's rigidity at the beginning of his
career; so it is not astonishing that the recalcitrant Cameron, who had
given trouble in Edinburgh in 1794, should have taken advantage of the
Colonel's downfall, not, of course, out of any love for the Gordons,
but simply on his own behalf. Pryse Gordon gives a vivid picture of
Cameron (*Memoirs* i., 145):—

He had been bred, if not born, in France, owing to the misfortunes
of his family, who had been obliged to emigrate, and did not see his
mountains until he was an adult. His father had been very popular,
and the return of his representative was hailed with joy. Many of the
old Jacobites were still living, and they puffed up the stripling with
ideas of chieftainship and power which no longer existed. His father
had been so much loved by his tenants that after his estates were
forfeited, they raised annually a handsome sum which was remitted to
France to support him, and he died before the estates were restored.

Unfortunately, the young chief had imbibed false notions of his own
consequence and of the altered state of the Highlands, and his education
had been neglected; he took but little pains to make himself acquainted
with the statistics of his own country; he had quite the air and manners
of the Frenchman, though he had been some years in an academy in
England. Nothing could be more unlike a Highland chief; in his
exterior he would better have graced a levee at Holyrood than the head
of a regiment in the field: he was tall and elegantly formed, and
extremely graceful—more of Adonis than Mars, and quite unlike a

native of Lochaber. Such was the hero who called out his clan on the commencement of the French Revolution to join the standard of the Cock of the North.

Young Cameron may have been all this, but he clearly had the support of his more sober headman. A striking proof of this is afforded by an angry letter which Donald Cameron of Lochiel wrote from Glasgow, March 6, 1798, to the Duke of Gordon relative to Dundas's scheme for a proposed force called the "Grampian Brigade," to be described later on :—

[I] am clearly of opinion that every exertion in the present time must be used by those who have power and interest in the Highlands : and as far as relates to myself, I am ready to come forward, not only on account of the situation of my country, but the great satisfaction I shall feel at leaving your Grace's regiment [the Northern Fencibles], which I am perfectly dissatisfied [with], and am not the only one : I am convinced if all the circumstances were known to you, you would not be surprised.

In reply to your Grace's question whether the men would go to Ireland, I don't know what they would do. They have already been asked by Lieut.-Col. Woodford and refused him. Nothing, my Lord Duke, would have induced me to be in this corps but the idea of affording my neighbour, the Duke of Gordon, every assistance in my power, which, I hope, will always be the case. Therefore should it so happen that I am called on by your Grace to come forward according to the Plan proposed, I shall expect that same friendly assistance from you by which each of us ought at all times to be governed.

The trouble came clearly out a few days later when Captain John Cameron was court-martialled in Edinburgh, March 12-26, 1798, on various charges of insubordination :—

For throwing a disgraceful aspersion on the character and conduct of the officers commanding companies, in publicly declaring to his commanding officer in the presence of many officers that he would prove that there were but three officers paying companies who were not in-debted to their men, and some of them to the amount of £50 and upwards.

The Court held the charge "frivolous. Such an aspersion appears not only unwarrantable, from the books, and the certificate rolls of the companies, but was hurtful to His Majesty's service in affecting and lessening, if not actually destroying, the confidence soldiers ought to repose in the honour and integrity of their officers, was at the same time subversive of subordination and obedience."

Y

For threatening to bring this accusation forward only in case the officers persisted to demand full subsistence of their companies, and for not giving the information at a proper time, or in a proper manner, to his commanding officer.

The Court held his conduct " censurable."

For exciting and promoting in the barracks at Glasgow in March, 1797, a combination against the lieutenant-colonel [Woodford], his commanding officer, and for making an unjustifiable, unauthorised, and improper use of his Colonel's, the Duke of Gordon's, name to aid and sanction his purpose on that occasion.

For disrespectful, improper, and slighting behaviour to his commanding officer in the line of his duty.

The Court held that the fact of promoting a combination among the officers had been proved by the prisoner's own admission: " yet in respect of the peculiar circumstances of this case the formal reconciliation which had taken place between the parties and the time that had elapsed between the alledged offence and the bringing forward the present charges, they are of opinion that no immorality attaches to Captain Cameron on these accounts."

Of the latter part of the charge, the alledged improper use made by him of the Duke of Gordon's name the Court entirely acquit Captain Cameron of the same.

On the entire number of charges Cameron was " reprimanded," but the King was pleased to remark on the " great inconvenience resulting to the Service from bringing before General Courts Martial, charges which after a long and solemn investigation turn out to be light and frivolous ": and it is General Lord Adam Gordon's order that the foregoing articles of charge, opinions and sentence, be circulated and read to all the regular Fencible and militia forces in Great Britain.

The plain fact is that the Camerons were jealous of the Duke. Lochiel had seen a regiment of the line, the 79th or Cameron Highlanders, raised in 1793 by Allan Cameron of Errach, who added 780 men to it in Inverness-shire in 1798. So he decided to have a Fencible regiment of his own. On June 8, 1798, he asked the Duke to let him have thirty of his men from the Northern Fencibles. The Duke replied on June 11 (*Scottish Review*, xvii., 132 ; original in Gordon Castle) :—

Dear Lochiel,—I recd. your letter of the 8th, along with one of the same date from the Lord Advocate, acquainting me of his having received the Duke of York's approbation of your offer to raise a corps of Fencibles, and wishing to allow you some assistance from my Regt. I have every inclination to do what is agreeble to you and the Lord Advocate. But I really can't think of parting with so many men as you propose. The situation and circumstances are very different now from what they were in 1795, when I gave some aid to Coll. Baillie [in raising the Inverness Fencibles] at the particular request of Mr. Dundas, and he paid me five guineas for each man given over to him. The strength of my regiment at that time was much superior then to what it is now, and the men were much easier replaced. At present I do not consider myself at liberty to comply with your request to such an extent, as it would in great measure anihilate the regiment. I would not undertake to get others in their place at present, when almost all the young men are engaged in the Militia and Volunteer Companies, and I think it of great consequence to have my regiment as complete as any other Fencible Company in Scotland: I shall, however, make you welcome, to thirty of the men you brought to the Regiment, including such as may be non-commissioned officers, which number, you must be sensible, is more than I can well spare, and I hope will be sufficient to furnish you with drills. However, I must beg leave to stipulate no men to be taken from either the flank companies without the approbation of the Lt. Col.

Lochiel made the same request on July 24, 1798, and on September 8, the Duke again refused, although " it really gives me pain to be a third time under the necessity of refusing your requests." But in the end, Lochiel gratified his ambition by raising in 1799, a regiment called the Lochaber Fencible Highlanders, which is described by Stewart (*Highlanders*, 2nd ed. ii., 353-367). It did not, however, last long, being reduced after a sojourn in Ireland, in July, 1802.

The Camerons were not the only officers whom Woodford failed to manage, for he got into trouble with the surgeon, Ralston Caldwell, who proceeded to flout him. The case was investigated at a General Court of Inquiry, and on April 8, 1798, Lieutenant-General Sir Robert Abercromby (Lochiel's father-in-law) gave it as his opinion that Caldwell had not established his first three charges and that the fourth was frivolous. He expresses his " disapprobation of the rash and unbecoming attack made by Surgeon Caldwell on the conduct of his commanding officer, and he strongly recommends him to confine himself in future to the performance of the duties of his station."

At this time four companies of the Northern Fencibles were at Kirkcaldy, three at Dunfermline, two at St. Andrews and one at Falkirk. The return on July 31, 1798, was 31 sergeants, 22 drummers and 493 rank and file.

The Northern Fencibles officially closed their career on April 2, 1799, at Ayr, though the last muster is for the period, March 25-April 15, 1799 (*W.O.* 13 : 3,901). The officers then were as follows, rank and file then stood at 495, of whom 443 were privates :—

Commandant.	Lieutenant.	Ensign.	Privates.
{ Col. the Duke of Gordon { Adj. James Brown { Surg. James Bennet	James McKilligan Donald Macpherson Duncan Macpherson Alexander Robertson	Alexander Taylor	46
Lieut.-Col. Woodford	Robert Gordon	Alexander Stuart	44
Major Donald Cameron	John Gordon	James Bisset	44
Captain Daniel Gordon	William Mitchell	George Cumine	43
„ George Gordon	William Scott (Paymaster)	Humphrey Grant	47
„ Pryse L. Gordon	William Marshall	Alexander Macdonald	42
„ William Abercrombie } Gordon (Quarter-Master)	Alexander Gordon	Thomas Bennet (Assist. Surgeon)	43
„ Alexander Macdonald (Only Coy. with Pipers)	Ronald Macdonald	John Macpherson	47
„ Alexander Robertson	George Anderson		44
„ Robert Smith	Alexander Todd	Robert Gordon	43

The payment of the officers for the last 22 days amounted to £837 7s. 6d., and that of the men to £611 17s. 10d., the total expense including extras being £2,273 13s. 4d. (*W.O.* 13 : 3,901).

The Duke still had Woodford on his back, for he tried once more to get a billet for him from Pitt, to whom he wrote from Gordon Castle, September 22, 1799 (*Chatham Papers*, 139) :—

Dear Pitt,—I see by the Papers that Mr. Orde, Receiver General at Martinique, is dead. I beg to put you in mind of Col. Woodford ; and, if you have not already fixed upon a successor, I should be very much obliged to you to appoint him to it.

Poor Woodford did not, however, trouble his Grace long, for he died at Edinburgh on Sunday, April 17, 1800, being buried in Holyrood Abbey within a few feet of his wife's kinswoman, Lady Jean Gordon, the long suffering wife of Bothwell.

An index to all the documents dealing with the internal economy of the Northern Fencibles is preserved at the Record Office (*W.O.* 2 : 36 : p. 123).

STRATHSPEY REGIMENT OF FENCIBLE HIGHLANDERS.

1793: RAISED BY SIR JAMES GRANT OF GRANT: DISBANDED 1799.

One of the Fencible organisations of 1793 brought a new factor into the field in the shape of the Grants, who, as near neighbours of the Duke of Gordon, made the recruiting efforts of his Grace increasingly difficult.

Sir James Grant was in quite a different position from the Duke, whose senior he was by five years. The Grants had sided with the Government in the Jacobite struggle, and Sir James's father, Ludovick, had joined Cumberland at Cullen, though he was not at Culloden. So much did they aid the Government that, when Sir James succeeded in 1773, he found the estates so embarrassed that he had to sell some of them, and the Exchequer admitted that he had a claim for £12,540 expended on the public service. It was probably for this reason that he did not raise a regiment in 1778 like the Duke, but as M.P. for Banffshire (1790-95), and Lord-Lieutenant of Inverness-shire (1794-1809), he found himself closely in touch with the actualities of politics and county affairs, which launched him into the recruiting business. Sir James by all accounts fully merited the epithet "The Good" attaching to his name; and yet it cannot be said that his own particular regiments, the Strathspey Fencibles, 1793-99, and the Strathspey Regiment, 1794-95, were very successful, for the first was disfigured by two abortive mutinies, and the second soon dissolved into other regiments. The reason probably was that Sir James was not closely enough associated with either regiment, as the Duke of Gordon was with all his levies. Sir James had far too much to do with his Parliamentary and county duties; and when he left Parliament it was to take up the post of General Cashier of the Excise in Scotland (1795-1811).

He started off gaily enough under a Letter of Service, March 1, 1793, for a regiment of Fencibles, consisting of eight companies. By April 9, he had got 24 sergeants, 24 corporals, 10 drummers, two pipers, 480 privates, and as many as 150 supernumeraries (*W.O.* 1 : 1,059).

Stewart tells us (*Highlanders*, ii., 312) that 41 of the men were from the Lowlands of Scotland, three from England, and two from Ireland, and that 70 supernumeraries were discharged in May, 1793.

Sir James was delighted with the result, and wrote, April 9, from headquarters at Forres, to the Commander-in-Chief (*W.O.* 1 : 1,059):—

As yet, neither the drums, arms, or cloathing are come down, which is of the less consequence as I am convinced His Majesty would think it improper to withdraw many of the men who are engaged from the necessary labours of the spring, to whom we gave such assurance. The seed time has been very backward this season, and makes it indispensably necessary to give all possible indulgence to the Farmers. By the period allowed us, however, in our Letter of Service, I trust all inconveniences of this nature will be remembered. In the meantime, as many of my friends to whom I could not give commissions have exerted themselves to assist me and promote His Majesty's service, allow me humbly and earnestly to request that His Majesty will honour me with two additional companies, which I have the greatest reason to believe may also be completed within the limited time. . . . The spirit is now high.

On April 11, he wrote that the recruiting had gone on with such uncommon alacrity "that he wanted to raise a second battalion."

The first expenses of the regiment for the period June 5-December 24, 1793, were as follows (*W.O.* 24 : 578, p. 39):—

Pay	. .	.	.	.	.	.	.	£5,515 18 1½
Clothing	.	.	.	.	.	.	.	1,062 9 5½
Agency	.	.	.	.	.	.	.	101 2 11½
Allowances	.	.	.	.	.	.	.	354 8 8¾
Accoutrements	.	.	.	.	.	.	.	643 15 4

Total £7,677 14 7¼

The full pay bill for the year 1794 is set forth in *W.O.* 24 : 593 : p. 49:—

Colonel and Captain	.	.	.	.	.	£502 10 0
Lieutenant-Colonel and Captain	.	.	.	.	291 6 0½
Major and Captain .	.	.	.	.	.	257 0 7½
Seven Captains more	.	.	.	.	.	1,199 9 7
Captain-Lieutenant	.	.	.	.	.	79 19 4
Eleven Lieutenants	.	.	.	.	.	879 12 8

£3,209 18 3

								£3,209	18	3
Eight Ensigns	.	.	.	.	.	.	.	502	12	10
Chaplain	.	.	.	.	.	.	.	114	4	8¾
Adjutant	.	.	.	.	.	.	.	68	10	10
Quartermasters	.	.	.	.	.	.	.	79	19	4
Surgeon	.	.	.	.	.	.	.	68	10	10
Mate	.	.	.	.	.	.	.	59	19	5¾
Sergeants (32)	.	.	.	.	.	.	.	584	0	0
Corporals (30)	.	.	.	.	.	.	.	365	0	0
Drummers (20)	.	.	.	.	.	.	.	243	6	8
Fifers (2)	.	.	.	.	.	.	.	24	6	8
Privates (570)	.	.	.	.	.	.	.	5,201	5	0

Total £10,521 14 7½

The subsequent cost of the regiment was as follows (the odd figures are not given):—

	Pay.	Clothing.	Agency.	Total.
1795-6	£9,635	£1,781	£259	£16,311
1796-7	11,970	1,459	242	13,671
1797-8	15,303	1,715	192	17,260
1798-9				17,667

The regiment, which bore the number One in point of precedency, as arranged at Edinburgh, June 9, assembled at Forres in the end of April, but it was not until June 5 that it was finally inspected and embodied by Lieutenant-General Leslie. The first muster roll at the Public Record Office (*W.O.* 13 : 3,944) is for the period June 5-June 20, 1793, and shows a muster of 600 privates, of whom 60 were Grants, 10 were Gordons, and exactly 200 bore surnames beginning with " Mac." The officers, whose commissions were dated March 1, 1793, to synchronise with the Letter of Service, were as follows (*W.O.* 25 : 156, pp. 187-9: and also *W.O.* 25 : 160 : 226 : 242):—

COLONEL.

Sir James Grant of Grant, March 1, 1793.

LIEUTENANT-COLONEL.

Alexander Penrose Cumming, March 1, 1793. Laird of Altyre: afterwards took the additional name of Gordon. He had been in the Northern Fencibles of 1778, but having married Sir James Grant's sister, Helen (1754-1832), he took post with the Grants in 1793, instead of with the Gordons.

MAJOR.

John Grant, March 1, 1793.

CAPTAINS.

Robert Cumming, March 1, 1793.

Simon Fraser, March 1, 1793.

John Grant, March 1, 1793; Major, February 17, 1794.

Alexander Macdonell, March 1, 1793; resigned, May 9, 1794.

John Rose, March 1, 1793.

CAPTAIN-LIEUTENANT.

John Grant, March 1, 1793. He wrote from Tammore, March 10, 1794 (*W.O.* 1 : 1,072):—"I am a very old officer, having entered the army at the age of 16 in 1760 as ensign by purchase: went out in the 4th Division of Independent Companies to Senegal, where on 11 Nov., 1761, I was appointed Lieutenant. In 1763, was reduced and remained on half pay till 1775, when I was appointed as one of the additional Lieutenants of the 42nd, but owing to bad health had to retire. I served five years during the last war in the Duke of Gordon's Regiment of Fencibles and commanded a company. At present tho' the oldest Captain in Sir James Grant's Fencibles, I am only Captain-Lieutenant." He became Captain, May 9, 1794, *vice* Alexander Macdonell.

LIEUTENANTS.

R. Grant Clarkson, May 23, 1794; resigned by June 3, 1795.

Alexander Grant, gent., June 3, 1795, *vice* Mackay.

Allan Grant, March 1, 1793; Captain-Lieutenant, May 9, 1794.

Francis William Grant, March 1, 1793, fourth son of Sir James; succeeded to the Earldom of Seafield, 1840, on the death of his brother Lewis (1767-1840), who was the first Earl of the Grant line. On February 14, 1794, he was appointed Captain in the 97th, or Strathspey Regiment; on November 29, 1794, Major of the Fraser Fencibles; and on January 23, 1799, Lieutenant-Colonel of the 3rd Ayrshire Fencibles.

James Grant, March 1, 1793; Captain, June 20, 1794, *vice* John Grant, who resigned.

John Grant, sen., March 1, 1793.

John Grant, jun., March 1, 1793; left by January 20, 1794.

John Grant, June 3, 1795, *vice* Hugh Macdonald.

William Grant, March 1, 1793.

Hugh Macdonald, ———, promoted by June 3, 1795

James Macdonell, March 1, 1793.

Ronald Macdonell, March 1, 1793.

Thomas Macdonell (from Ensign, late North Carolina Volunteers), June 20, 1794, *vice* John Grant, jun.

James Mackay (from Lieutenant, late King's American Rangers), June 20, 1794, *vice* James Grant; resigned by June 3, 1795.

Theodore Morison, June 3, 1795, *vice* Clarkson.

John Urquhart, March 1, 1793.

ENSIGNS

Harry Cumming, March 1, 1793

Simon Fraser, December 6, 1798

Alexander Grant, March 7, 1794, joined Howe's Regiment by August 5, 1795

Duncan Grant, March 1, 1793, Lieutenant, March 7, 1794, *vice* F W Grant

Duncan Grant, jun, March 1, 1793

James Grant, March 1, 1793, Ensign 85th, May 28, 1794

James Grant, August 28, 1794, *vice* John Grant

James Grant, August 5, 1795, *vice* Alexander Grant

John Grant, March 1, 1793, resigned by June 20, 1794

Robert Grant

William Grant, May 11, 1797 (*W O* 25 47, p 44), Lieutenant, December 6, 1798, *vice* Reynolds

William Ogilvie.

John Rose

Thomas Steel, June 3, 1795, *vice* John Grant

Thomas Stephen, June 20, 1794, *vice* John Grant, jun

Maxwell Stewart

CHAPLAIN

James Grant, March 1, 1793

ADJUTANT

James Watson, March 1, 1793

QUARTERMASTER

Angus Sutherland, March 1, 1793, succeeded by James Carmichael, who on April 12, 1804 became Quartermaster of the Inverness, Banff, Elgin and Nairn Militia (*H O* 50 59) —

SURGEON

Peter Grant, March 1, 1793, succeeded by William Ogilvie

The regiment spent all its time—indeed, insisted on doing so—in Scotland, its service being confined to towns in the south It first marched, *via* Aberdeen, to Glasgow, and was stationed in turn at Paisley, Linlithgow, Dumfries, Musselburgh (1795), Dundee, Ayr, Edinburgh, Irvine (1798), and then back to Edinburgh where it was disbanded

The real command of the regiment was in the hands of Sir James's brother-in-law, Alexander Penrose Cumming of Altyre, who did not prove a much greater success than Woodford did with the Northern

z

Fencibles. If it had been easy to raise, it was difficult to regulate, as Sir James soon learned to his sorrow. The first trouble arose out of the question of the out-pensioners of Chelsea who had joined the regiment and whose pensions had been withheld. Sir James Grant wrote to Sir George Yonge, April 19, 1794, that the withholding had "occasioned extreme dissatisfaction, that, if not granted to them by Government for the past so as to put them on a footing with the other [Fencible] regiments, the effect may be extremely disagreeable " (W.O. 1 : 1,072). He enclosed a more minute letter which he had sent to the agents of the regiment, Ainslie and Fraser, Cleveland Row:—

The pensioners in the Hopeton, Argyle, and, I believe, the Gordon Fencible Regiments, having received their pensions, those in my regiment are in extreme dissatisfaction that it is refused to them ; and, as in all the confusion that has happened in the Regiment about going south, these men (the pensioners) have behaved uncommonly well, I must entreat that Sir George Yonge and Sir George Howard may take their case into consideration. As those in the other regiments have got it, there can be no good reason for withholding it from them [the Strathspey Fencibles], and, if it is owing to inaccuracy in sending up the lists, that inaccuracy should not militate against those who were accurate. . . .

The men are so enraged, and with some reason, at the exception with regard to them that I expect, if Government does not allow it, I must pay it out of my own pocket—which, I assure you, has already been drained sufficiently. . . . They attack me upon it, and say it is a shame, I should not allow those of my regiment to be deprived of what is given to others.

But discontent spread to a much larger section of the corps, arising out of a proposal to extend their service out-with Scotland, as set forth in a letter to Sir James from Dundas, dated the Horse Guards, September 27, 1794 (Fraser's *Chiefs of Grant*, ii., 561):—

Sir,—In the present state of the military services of this country, it is very essential, as speedily as possible to collect every species of force that can be appropriated to general service. This object would be materially promoted if a number of Fencible corps could be formed under an engagement to serve not only in Great Britain, but, if necessary, in Ireland. The effect of such a levy would be to enable His Majesty to withdraw from Ireland and appropriate for general service the regular regiments which, without such a substitute, it will be necessary to leave in Ireland for the defence of that kingdom.

I have taken the liberty of making this communication to you, because, perhaps, you may be able to suggest some officer of your corps, willing with your approbation to undertake the raising of a new corps of the nature I have described; and, if any of the privates of the corps of fencibles commanded by you should be willing to enlist as volunteers in such a corps, not only will no objection be made to their doing so, but a bounty of five guineas, in addition to what they have formerly received, will be allowed as an acknowledgement for their zeal in turning out as volunteers. They will likewise be assured of being brought back to Scotland at the conclusion of the war and disbanded in their own country.

If, in consequence of this measure, your corps should be deprived of any part of its present strength, His Majesty will be advised to allow you a bounty of ten guineas per man to replace those who may offer as volunteers for the newly proposed corps.

It has occurred to me that perhaps it may prove an additional encouragement to the raising these corps, if each person undertaking to raise a corps should have it in his power by means of it to aid either his own or the promotion of a friend in the army; and, with that view, His Majesty will be advised to give one step of promotion of permanent rank, either to the person himself who raises the corps, or to any one other officer now in the Army, recommended by him for one of the commissions in the corps, provided the person to receive such step is not at present of a higher rank than that of Major in His Majesty's service.

I am aware that one material obstacle to the proposition I now make is the difficulty of finding officers to undertake the service; but I flatter myself the zeal which has so conspicuously manifested itself throughout the kingdom in various other modes of service, will not be wanting for the very essential service I now propose. But, if there should be any deficiency of officers for the purpose of carrying on the service, the deficit may be supplied by appropriating to it the service of officers who, having raised independent companies, are at present unemployed in any other service.

Sir James was quite keen on the idea, for he wrote to Dundas from Castle Grant, October 11, 1794 (*W.O.* 1 : 1,096):—

My being at Inverness at a county meeting prevented my answering the letter you did me the honour to write relative to the new Fencible Corps to serve in Great Britain and Ireland. I shall be exceedingly happy that my son, Captain Francis William Grant, engage to raise one of these Corps as Lieutenant Colonel Commandant, having permanent rank of a Major on the Establishment of the Army— provided the Bounty he gets will at all enable him to raise the men, as I find from what I have experienced that men are with great difficulty, without extraordinary Bounty, to be got in Scotland; and, tho' I would accept of any individual Fencible man willing to accompany him, and expect full liberty in regard to these as you mention, yet I would be very much afraid of making such a general proposition, especially in the quarters they are now in. Therefore his engagement should be perfectly independent of any aid he may afterwards get from volunteers from the Fencible Corps under my command. You will please let me know the plan and number of men, and the highest Bounty, and on what footing the officers in general are to be as to rank and half pay. You will likewise be pleased to direct one letter to Castle Grant and another to Edinburgh under Mr. McKenzie of Exchequer's cover in case, as is possible, I may be obliged to go to Edinburgh.

Dundas apparently advised the Duke of Gordon that he might expect to have the Northern Fencibles raided for this purpose, but, though the Duke was his personal friend, he got a prompt refusal in the following strong letter written from Gordon Castle on October 16, 1794 (*W.O.* 1 : 1,096) :—

Your letter of September 25, having been sent to the camp at Hythe, did not reach me till the end of last week. It has since occupied much of my attention, and I confess I am still very much at a loss how to answer it.

After the repeated exertions I have made to meet His Majesty's views, I hope I shall not be suspected of want of zeal in the recruiting service if I withhold my consent to the measure proposed of allowing men to be enlisted from my Regiment to make up a new Fencible Corps to serve in Ireland.

My motives for undertaking to raise the Fencible Regiment are, I daresay, fresh in your recollection. I came under that engagement, because I considered it my duty to step forward in support of the King and Constitution. A considerable part of the Regiment was enlisted from my own estate, and composed in a great measure of officers and men who followed me from attachment to my family and in the fullest confidence that they would never be required to serve but under my command, or go out of Scotland except in case of an invasion. When the King called upon them to go to England, I was at some pains to persuade them to comply with His Majesty's wishes, and it was very flattering to me that my personal influence among them was not on that interesting occasion exerted in vain.

In this situation, I hope I shall be excused from the disagreeable task of being employed to urge them to go still further ; and, indeed, I am very doubtful how far it would be prudent to propose it ; nor can I take it upon me to be responsible for the consequence of attempting it ; for I look upon myself as pledged, not only to the men themselves, but to many of their connections and friends in this country, who would certainly consider it as a breach of faith in me; and in my opinion it must ultimately injure His Majesty's service.

However, if Government, notwithstanding of this, shall think it expedient to allow gentlemen [Sir James Grant, his son, and Lieutenant-Colonel Simon Fraser] who undertake to raise this new corps the liberty to enlist men from my Regiment, I must submit to it; but I fairly acknowledge that I shall regret the loss of every man who may be induced to leave it, because I well know that it will not be in my power to get men to supply the deficiency thereby occasioned, for the £10 10s. of Bounty proposed; nor scarcely upon any terms.

My estate was so much drained of men to make up my own Regiment [the Northern Fencibles of 1778], Lord Huntly's Independent Company [for the Black Watch, 1790], and his regiment afterwards [the Gordon Highlanders, 1794], that I have not been able to complete my own Loyal Companies—far less can I now come under fresh engagements, when the demand for men is increasing every hour, and, more especially as the difficulty of finding Fencibles is become much greater in consequence of those originally enlisted for that purpose having been taken out of the Kingdom, which, of course, must lessen their confidence in any promises of a similar nature made to them in future.

I understand Major Gordon of my Regiment has already applied to you, and that Major Baillie, my oldest Major, has gone to London to give in his proposals for a corps [the Inverness Fencibles]. It is but justice to me to declare that they are both good officers, and very deserving of His Majesty's attention, and I have no doubt they will make every exertion in their power to promote the service. But I cannot take it upon me, consistent with what I have already said, to suggest any officer to undertake to raise a Fencible Corps agreeable to the plan proposed for recruiting men from my Regiment.

Sir James, however, had reckoned without his own rank and file, for this must be the cause of the trouble which Stewart says broke out at Linlithgow in 1794, though the regiment seems to have been at Dumfries in that year and at Linlithgow in the previous one. The men were sounded as to whether they would serve out of Scotland. Stewart, always on the defensive, treats their attitude gingerly (*Highlanders*, ii., 312):—

Measures were accordingly taken, but unfortunately not with that care, precaution, and ample explanation, so necessary when men's feelings and prejudices are to be consulted, and any previous agreement or understanding to be altered or renewed on another and different basis. In this case, when the commanding officer issued the orders on the subject, some officers thought it unnecessary to offer any explanation to their men ; others entirely mistook the meaning and import of the proposals. The consequence was a degree of jealousy and distrust ; and, as busy and meddling advisers are not wanting on such occasions, the soldiers became alarmed ; they knew not what to believe, or what was intended ; and even the explanations of those officers who understood the nature of the proposed measure lost much of their effect.

The result of the whole was a division and difference of opinion among the men ; some were for volunteering, others opposed it ; the proposal was therefore abandoned and no volunteering took place. But it was not the mere volunteering and the consequent loss of more general and extended duty that was so much to be regretted, as the want of confidence which this misunderstanding caused, and the effect it had on the conduct of the men for a considerable time afterwards. However this unpleasing and unexpected circumstance passed away ; and by the presence of Sir James Grant, who hurried up to join his regiment when he heard of the affair, it was in some measure forgotten and confidence re-established.

An unfortunate episode occurred to men of the regiment when stationed at Dumfries, "the only warlike affray that occurred in Scotland during the whole volunteer and fencible era," as Kay tells us (*Edinburgh Portraits*, i., 278, where a "contemporary chronicle" is quoted), forgetful of the episode of the Ross and Cromarty Rangers at Aberdeen on the King's Birthday in 1802.

On the evening of the 9th June (1795), the civil magistrates of Dumfries applied to the commanding officer of the 1st Fencibles for a party to aid in apprehending some Irish tinkers, who were in a house about a mile and a half from the town. On the party's approaching the house and requiring admittance, the tinkers fired on them and wounded Sergeant Beaton very severely in the head and groin ; John Grant, a Grenadier, in both legs, and one Fraser, of the Light Company, in the arm ; the two last were very much hurt, the tinkers' arms being loaded with rugged slugs and small bullets. The party pushed in to the house, and, though they had suffered so severely, abstained from bayonetting the tinkers, when they called for mercy. One man and two women in men's clothes were brought in prisoners. Two men in the dark of the night made their escape ; but one of them was apprehended and brought in next morning, and a party went out upon information to apprehend the others. Fraser's arm received the whole charge, which it is believed saved his heart. One of the soldiers died of his wounds.

The leader of the tinkers named John O'Neill was brought to Edinburgh for trial. He was a Roman Catholic, and at this time a number of genteel Catholic families being resident in Dumfries, they resolved to be at the expense of defending O'Neill on the ground that he was justified in resisting any attempt to enter his own house. With this view they prevailed on the late Mrs. Riddell of Woodley Park to go to Edinburgh and procure counsel. Mrs. Riddell was a great beauty, and a poetess of no inconsiderable note. She wrote a critique on the poems of Burns, and materially assisted Dr. Currie in writing the life of the poet. She found no difficulty in obtaining the services of Henry Erskine, without fee or reward ; but, notwithstanding, O'Neill was found guilty, and condemned to be hanged. The good offices of Mrs. Riddell, however, did not terminate here. She applied to Charles Fox ; and, through him, obtained a commutation of his sentence.

Soon after the affair with the tinkers, " an unhappy state of insubordination " broke out among the Strathspey Fencibles at Dumfries (Fraser's *Chiefs of Grant*, i., 456). Stewart is at a loss to account for it. He wonders whether it was the severe code of punishment, which he strongly deprecated for Highlanders, or whether the men believed that they had been " teased with long drills and fatiguing discipline, not required for soldiers who were never to meet an enemy, or perhaps not very necessary for any service, whether the individuals themselves were of a character different from, and inferior to," cases he had mentioned, " or whether, as is most probable, some unpleasant recollections of the affair at Linlithgow still existed." In any case, there occurred at Dumfries a circumstance, " very trifling in itself, originating in a remark by a soldier in the ranks, which might pass for a joke, or a piece of wit, according as the thing was taken." Some of the men were immediately put under arrest and threatened with flogging. While Stewart considered the lash necessary to restrain " the unprincipled and shamelessly depraved who sometimes stand in the ranks of the British army," he also held that it " struck a Highland soldier of the old school with a horror that would have rendered him despicable in his own eyes and a disgrace to his family and name." So a party of the Strathspeys defied their officers and released the prisoners. As in the previous year, Sir James was summoned, but he arrived too late, and the breach of discipline could not be overlooked ; and the regiment was marched to Musselburgh, where Corporal James Macdonald with Privates Alexander Fraser, Charles Mackintosh, Duncan Macdougall and A. Mackintosh were tried and found guilty of mutinous conduct. The corporal was sentenced to be flogged—though he was subsequently pardoned—and the four privates to be shot. The execution was carried out on Gullane Links on July 16, 1795, in presence of the Scotch Brigade (afterwards the 94th Regiment), the Sutherland, Breadalbane and Strathspey Fencibles. When the prisoners arrived on the ground, they were told that only two were to suffer and that two were to draw lots. Fraser was not allowed to draw, as he had been the most violent. The fatal chance fell on Charles Mackintosh, who was shot with Fraser. The other two men were drafted into regiments abroad. Stewart was so shocked by the treatment of the men that he tells the story twice in his *Sketches* (ii., 315, 416), adding that it afforded

another striking instance of the necessity of paying a due regard to the feeling of soldiers, and of treating them as men of good principles, whose culpability may proceed more from mistaken notions than from depravity. It also affords a striking instance of the paramount call, on those under whose direction they are placed in their native country, that their treatment be not such as to loosen and destroy those finer feelings and render the people desperate, regardless of their own character, disaffected to the Government, and transplant a spirit of hatred and revenge, in place of the fidelity, confidence and attachment of other times.

Despite these very sensible remarks, it is clear that the laird of Altyre was very proud of his share in the business, for it is repeated in Burke's Peerage year after year that he received the thanks of the Commander-in-Chief "for suppressing a mutiny at Dumfries, 1794."

The regiment was disbanded at Edinburgh in April, 1799, at which time the officers were as follows (*W.O.* 13 : 3,394):—

Commandant.	Lieutenant.	Ensign.
Col. Sir James Grant.	James Grant (Capt.-Lieut.).	Simon Fraser.
Lieut.-Col. A. P. Cumming.	James Watson (Adj.).	Alexander Grant.
Major John Grant.	John Grant (Surgeon).	Robert Macdonald.
Captain Robert Cumming {	Alexander Grant. John Grant.	
„ Allen Grant.	William Grant.	John Grant.
„ John Grant (sen.).	Charles Grant.	Patrick Lee.
„ John Grant (jun.).	Thomas Stephen (Assistant Surgeon).	John Grant.
„ William Grant.	Robert Urquhart.	John McInnes.
„ None. (Light Company.)	{ Thomas Macdonald. { William Manford.	
„ John Rose.	James Carmichael (Q.M.).	John McGregor.

There is a picture of the Strathspey Fencibles in Kay's *Portraits* (i., 277). An index to official correspondence about the regiment appears in *W.O.* 2 : 1.

THE 97TH: OR INVERNESS-SHIRE REGIMENT OF FOOT.

1794: RAISED BY SIR JAMES GRANT OF GRANT: DRAFTED 1795.

Whether on his own initiative, or under pressure from the War Office, Sir James Grant raised a regiment of the line, the 97th, or Strathspey Regiment, within a year of raising his Fencibles, and it was inspected and embodied at Elgin by Major-General Sir Hector Munro. Stewart calls it the "Strathspey Regiment," but the War Office calls it the "Inverness-shire Regiment of Foot." It seems to have been contemplated to call it the "Inverness-shire Volunteers," for, at a meeting of the County of Inverness, July 15, 1794, with Sir James in the chair, it was resolved to support Lieutenant-Colonel Simon Fraser, late of the 71st, in raising a regiment of 600 foot and that "the corps be called the Inverness Volunteers to distinguish them from Sir James Grant's, which is denominated the Inverness-shire Volunteers" (*W.O.* 1 : 1,098)—unless indeed the latter be a third regiment raised by Sir James.

The 97th was really a failure from the very first, being in no sense a local regiment. It was, in fact, typical of all the worst abuses of regiment-raising of the period, righteously denounced by Mr. Fortescue (*History of the Army*, vol. iv., part i., pp. 212-3), when battalions were raised like gourds, and "were no sooner formed than they were disbanded and drafted into other corps," while a "scandalous traffic" was carried on in the matter of the officers' commissions. Even the faithful Stewart (*Highlanders*, ii., 216), with all his immense admiration for Sir James— "honourable, humane and hospitable in his private character, as well as a kind and generous landlord to a numerous and grateful tenantry"— admits the failure of the 97th :—

Though the corps was numerically completed to 1,000 men within the stipulated time, all of them were not of that class which formed the Fencible corps. The Lieutenant-Colonel, Major, and others of the officers were not natives of the north, and without local knowledge or influence; their commissions depending on their success in recruiting, their principal object was to procure a sufficient number capable of passing muster, and, as money in manufacturing towns effected what influence did in the north, many men were recruited whose character and constitution could bear no comparison with men of regular and hardy habits raised in the agricultural districts. However, there were among them a number of very good men ; the flank companies were excellent.

It may be doubted whether the corps ever contained 1,000 men. The first muster roll at the Record Office (*W.O.* 12 : 9,655), covering the period February 8, the date of the Beating Order, to June 10 " being the day preceding that of the inspection and establishment of the Regiment," showed the following results :—

Present - - - - -	182
Absent - - - - -	427
" Non-effective since " - - -	106
Total - -	715

Of this number, 12 were Grants, 15 were Frasers, and 138 bore surnames beginning with " Mac."

Commissions were given to several men bearing the name of Grant ; but north countrymen were not a *sine qua non*: think of a Major with the name of Scroggs commanding the gallant Grants! The officers from first to last were as follows (*W.O.* 12 : 9,655 ; *W.O.* 25 : 157 : 158 : 160 : 161 : 214 : 215) :—

COLONEL.

Sir James Grant, February 8, 1794, without purchase, permanent rank, or half pay.

LIEUTENANT-COLONEL.

Denzil Onslow, May 29, 1794. He had been promoted from the 1st Foot Guards to be Major by purchase in the 19th, or North Riding Regiment of Foot, May 28, 1794, and became Lieutenant-Colonel of the 97th next day ; but he left by November 15, 1794.

MAJORS.

William Bain (from Major of the 67th), August 12, 1794, *vice* Houghton ; Lieutenant-Colonel, November 15, 1794 ; he retired by December 21, 1795.

Henry Harcourt (from Captain, R.H.G.), Major by purchase, *vice* Grant, December 23, 1795.

Daniel Houghton, February 8, 1794 ; he had got a Captaincy in the 82nd from half pay to the 101st, September 29, 1793 ; and joined the 67th by August 12, 1794.

—— Scroggs (from Captain, 39th), December 16, 1795.

CAPTAINS.

William Alcock (from Captain, Independent Company), *vice* Baillie, May 13, 1795.

Hugh Baillie (from Lieutenant, 93rd), February 13, 1794; joined the 86th by May 13, 1795.

James Colquhoun (from Lieutenant, 66th), February 12, 1794.

Francis William Grant (from Independent Company), February 14, 1794; left by April 1, 1795, to join the Fraser Fencibles. Son of Sir James Grant, and afterwards Earl of Seafield.

James Grant (from Lieutenant, Independent Company), February 8, 1794; retired by September 19, 1794.

John Grant (from Lieutenant, Independent Company), February 10, 1794; Major, November 15, 1794; retired by December 23, 1795.

John Josiah Hall (from Lieutenant, 36th), September 30, 1795, *vice* Price.

John Lamont (from Lieutenant, Independent Company), February 11, 1794.

Holt Mackenzie (from Lieutenant, 26th), September 19, 1794, *vice* James Grant.

Barrington Price (from Captain, half pay, 93rd), July 15, 1795, *vice* Forbes; left by September 30, 1795.

Edward Charles H. Sheppard (from Lieutenant, 1st Life Guards), by purchase, December 23, 1795, *vice* Grant.

Patrick Stewart (from Lieutenant, 80th), February 9, 1794; Major, November 15, 1794, *vice* Bain; Lieutenant-Colonel, December 16, 1795, *vice* Bain.

CAPTAIN-LIEUTENANT.

Alexander Forbes (from Lieutenant, 98th), October 9, 1794; Captain, April 1, 1795, *vice* F. W. Grant; exchanged by July 15, 1794.

Alexander Rose (from Lieutenant, 98th), October 9, 1794.

LIEUTENANTS.

Edward Carroll (from Ensign, 107th), April 22, 1795; retired by October 21, 1795.

Henry Cumming (from Scotch Brigade), February 9, 1794.

George de Passou (from Ensign, 60th), by purchase, December 9, 1795, *vice* Wilton; he joined the 6th Dragoon Guards by December 23, 1795.

James Grant (from Lieutenant, 21st), February 8, 1794; Captain-Lieutenant, April 1, 1795.

James Grant (from Ensign, 41st), February 11, 1794; joined Keppel's by July 15, 1795.

John Grant (from Ensign, 85th), February 12, 1794.

John Grant (from Ensign, 95th), February 14, 1794; Captain, November 15, 1794, *vice* John Grant, promoted Major.

Lewis Grant (from Ensign, 95th), February 15, 1794; joined Myers' Regiment before July 15, 1795.

Peter Grant (from Ensign, Independent Company), September 3, 1794; exchanged by April 22, 1795.

John Hay (from Ensign, Independent Company), February 16, 1794; Lieutenant, Royal Glasgow Regiment, August 15, 1795.

Fleming Kearney (from Ensign, 124th), April 7, 1795; rejoined the 124th by May 6, 1795.

Alexander Macpherson (from Ensign, 100th), September 29, 1795; joined the 40th, January 9, 1796.

Hugh Macpherson (from Ensign, Independent Company), April 22, 1795, *vice* P. Grant; joined the 78th by July 29, 1795.

Oliver Moore (from Lieutenant, 6th Dragoon Guards), December 23, 1795, *vice* de Passou.

Alexander Rose (from Ensign, Independent Company), February 10, 1794.

John Rose (from Ensign, Independent Company), February 13, 1794.

William Rose (from Ensign, Independent Company), September 3, 1794; Captain, November 15, 1794, *vice* Patrick Stewart.

John Wilton (from Lieutenant, 83rd), July 1, 1795; he "refuses," and was replaced by de Passou, December 9, 1795.

ENSIGNS.

Robert Croke (from half pay, 94th), September 15, 1794, *vice* Charles Grant; joined the 106th before January 21, 1795.

Thomas Fraser, February 12, 1794; Lieutenant, July 15, 1795, *vice* John Grant.

James Geddes, April 1, 1795; Lieutenant, August 15, 1795, *vice* Hay. Joined the 40th, January 10, 1796.

Alexander Grant (from Volunteer), November 18, 1795, *vice* Macpherson; Lieutenant, 86th, August 12, 1796.

Charles Grant, February 13, 1794; exchanged by September 15, 1794.

Francis Grant, December 17, 1794, *vice* William Grant.

James Grant (from Sergeant, 53rd), September 25, 1794; Lieutenant, July 15, 1795, *vice* James Grant; joined the 40th, January 6, 1796.

John Grant (from Ensign, Strathspey Fencibles), February 8, 1794; Lieutenant, April 1, 1795.

Peter Grant, February 14, 1794; Lieutenant, December 23, 1795; joined the 40th, January 12, 1796.

Peter Grant (from Volunteer), July 15, 1795.

Robert Grant (from Volunteer), August 15, 1795; Lieutenant, December 23, 1795, *vice* Macgregor; Lieutenant, 111th Foot, January 20, 1796.

William Grant, February 15, 1794, *vice Stewart*; joined the 109th by December 17, 1794.

Duncan Macdonell, September 26, 1794; Lieutenant, July 15, 1795, *vice* Lewis Grant; joined the 40th, January 7, 1796.

Charles George Macgregor (from Sergeant), July 15, 1795.

James Grant Macgregor (from Lieutenant, Northampton Militia), February 9, 1794; Lieutenant, May 6, 1795, *vice* Kearney; joined the 88th by December 23, 1795.

Lachlan Macpherson, May 6, 1795.

—— Macpherson (from Volunteer), July 29, 1795; one of these Macphersons died by November 18, 1795.

William Robertson, July 15, 1795; Lieutenant, October 21, 1795, *vice* Carroll; joined the 40th, October 24, 1795.

William Stuart, February 11, 1794; joined the 106th by February 15, 1794.

Alexander Ward (from Volunteer, 126th), June 16, 1795, *vice* Grant (who joined the 133rd).

CHAPLAIN.

John Grant, February 8, 1791.

SURGEON.

Alexander D. Campbell, February 8, 1794.

ADJUTANT.

Hugh Roy, February 8, 1794; Ensign, January 21, 1795, *vice* Croke; Lieutenant, July 29, 1795, *vice* Macpherson.

QUARTERMASTER.

Angus Sutherland, February 8, 1794; apparently the same man as was Quartermaster of the Strathspey Fencibles. He resigned and was succeeded by Sergeant Matthew Grant (from the Strathspey Fencibles), June 3, 1795.

Sir James Grant seems to have worked his two regiments together for he wrote to Dundas from 2 Fludyer Street, December 10, 1794, as follows (*W.O.* 1 : 1,096):—

The letter received this day from the War Office makes it of still more consequence that the augmentation of my Fencible officers should be held and approved by His Majesty, the same as those of the Northern Fencibles.

I must likewise request that I may be allowed to take any man

I may have to discharge in consequence of the limitation of my Fencible Regiment to the 97th, or allow them to go with my son to a Fencible regiment optional to them, as I have in view of his engaging for a majority with permanent rank for a sum of money with a deduction for any men he may bring.

Stewart says that the 97th was ordered to the South of England in 1794 and served a few months as marines on board Lord Howe's fleet in the Channel. The last muster roll is for the period June-December, 1795, when the regiment was at Chatham, the figures being

Present	-	-	-	-	0
Absent	-	-	-	-	140
"Non-effective since" -		-		-	381
	Total		-	-	521

The Marines got 95 men on November 13, 1794, and 69 men on November 23. The rest were drafted into other regiments, notably the 21st, 74th and 42nd, the last of which, according to Stewart, got the two flank companies when embarking for the West Indies. Many men were discharged altogether. Seven Lieutenants transferred to the 40th Foot (*W.O.* 25: 161 p. 409).

The same mismanagement which had marked the life of the 97th, dogged it on its deathbed, as the following puzzled epistle which Major John Grant, then in command, wrote from Hilsea on December 2, 1795, to the Secretary for War, serves to show:—

In obedience to your letter of 23rd Novr., 113 men of the 97th Regiment have been drafted into the 42nd Regiment and several have volunteered entering the Marine Corps. I observe by your letter that the utmost care must be taken that all the just claims of the men be settled in a satisfactory manner before they are drafted. I therefore beg leave to state to you the impracticability of settling thoroughly with at least one half of our men owing to five of the officers who pay Companies being at sea, viz., two in the Mediterranean, one in the West Indies, and two at Quiberon Bay, and not a vestige of the books of their companies left behind; and many of the men belonging to those companies are here, and have not made any clearance whatever, further than money on account since the Regiment embarked as Marines in April last. It was with the utmost difficulty that I prevailed on some of those men to join the 42nd Regiment or Marines until they were finally settled and cleared with. The same difficulty will occur when those at

Quiberon Bay, etc., arrive, as they are mixed detachments of the whole Regiment.

In this situation, I beg leave to submit to you how I am to act, as the Regiment by your letter is to be discontinued after the 24th inst. ; and in the present situation it is obvious that no clearance can be made when pay officers are not on the spot.

THE NINETY-SECOND: OR GORDON HIGHLANDERS.

1794: RAISED BY THE 4TH DUKE OF GORDON: STILL FLOURISHING.

The Gordon Highlanders form the fourth and last regiment re-cruited by the 4th Duke of Gordon; they are, with the exception of their 3rd battalion, the sole remnants of the great recruiting efforts in the north-east of Scotland in the period under review; and they have had by far the most distinguished career of any of those efforts.

The Duke, who was sixty-one when he undertook this final effort, had become quite an expert recruiter, but even he found increased difficulty in raising the regiment. It was probably a perception of this difficulty that had stayed his hand from tackling a regiment of the line four years before, when, with an eye to providing a post for his son-in-law, Colonel Charles Lennox (1764-1819), afterwards Duke of Richmond, who had married Lady Charlotte Gordon, his Grace's eldest daughter, in 1789, he had suggested a similar scheme to Pitt. Writing from Gordon Castle on May 3, 1790, he said (*Chatham Papers*, bundle 139):—

Dear Pitt,—I wrote to Dundas about a fortnight ago, in which I begged of him to let me know if he had heard that any new levies were likely to be raised; but as yet I have not received his answer. By a letter I had last post from Colonel McLeod a regiment of 2000 men has been accepted of, and he expects to be called upon to fulfill his engagement in case a war shall take place.

As I wish upon all occasions to show my attachment to His Majesty, I beg you will mention my desire of raising a regiment of Highlanders to consist of a thousand men to be commanded by my friend Lennox, with the rank of colonel and the nomination of the officers. Should this proposal meet with His Majesty's approbation, I beg you will let me know as soon as possible. I am with the greatest esteem and regard, dear Pitt, your very faithful and obedient servant.

Nothing came of this proposal, perhaps because Pitt remembered that his father, Lord Chatham, had been bitterly attacked by Lennox's uncle, the 3rd Duke of Richmond, who denounced him in 1766 as "an insolent Minister." Perhaps it was because Lennox was still in disfavour for his

An Officer of the Gordon Highlanders
Drawn in the dress by T. Mansion and R. Eschauzier

duel on May 26, 1789, with the Duke of York, which had resulted in his having to transfer from the Coldstream Guards to the 35th Foot, the regiment in which his Grace of Gordon's two sons began their military career.

The Duke, as we have seen, modified his 1790 proposal by raising an Independent Company for his elder son, the Marquis of Huntly, who took it to the Black Watch. In that regiment, and subsequently in the Scots Guards, Huntly got an insight into soldiering. He saw active service in Flanders, though his father was " a little vexed about his going to Holland," and John Stuart, of Pittyoulish, writing in March, 1793, shared the same feeling—" not that I wou'd be affraid of his lordship if 20,000 well disciplined Highlanders was about him." Short of being a King and a Crœsus, it was not possible for the Duke to raise anything approaching 20,000 men, but he did the next best thing: he raised a regiment of regulars for his boy. It would, indeed, have been difficult for the Duke to find a better asset for any recruiting effort, because the Marquis had many attributes of a popular leader; he was young (only four and twenty), handsome, good-natured and soldierly.

The official proposal for the Duke to raise a regiment was written in a letter by Lord Amherst, who had been fighting hard in America when the Duke was raising the 89th in 1759, and who had become Commander-in-Chief in 1788. Dating from St. James's Square, January 24, 1794, Amherst wrote to the Duke :—

My Lord,—The King, having been pleased to approve of the raising of some regiments in N. Britain agreeably to the plan of Lord Seaforth's in the last war, I beg the favour to know if it will be agreeable to Your Grace to raise a regiment of 1000 men, the regiment having a Lieut.-Colonel Commandant and two Majors, the two Majors appointed by the King, and leaving to Your Grace the recommendation of the other officers. The plan of the particulars shall be transmitted immediately to Your Grace if it meets with your accepting the offer.

The Duke's acceptance was sent from Gordon Castle on February 2, 1794, an auspicious occasion, for it was the birthday of the Marquis, and indicates that his Grace—who had the true Gordon eye for good stage management—intended the regiment as a birthday gift to his heir. He wrote Amherst thus (*Gordon Castle Papers*):—

My Lord,—I had not the honour to receive Your Lordship's letter of the 24th of last month till yesterday owing to the great fall of snow

B2

which retarded the course of the post for several days. Upon every former occasion it made me very happy to prove my zealous attachment to the King by promoting his wishes as far as lay in my power, and I think it my duty, more particularly on the present emergency, to comply with His Majesty's pleasure by accepting of the offer he has made me, and I shall do my utmost endeavours to assist Lord Huntly in raising the regiment, to whom I wish the command to be given. He will set out for London as soon as the roads are passable for a carriage, in order to settle the terms with Your Lordship, of which I am ignorant, but I trust they will be such as not to put me to great expense on account of my circumstances, which really will not admit of it.

The Letter of Service for the raising of the regiment was sent from the War Office, February 10, 1794, by Sir George Yonge, Secretary for War, the same day on which the mandate for the Argyll and Sutherland Highlanders was issued (*Ibid.*):—

My Lord,—I am commanded to acquaint you that His Majesty approves of your Grace's offer of raising a Regiment of Foot to be completed within three months upon the following conditions:—

The Corps to consist of one company of Grenadiers, one of Light Infantry, and eight Battalion Companies.

The Grenadier Company is to consist of one captain, three lieutenants, four sergeants, five corporals, two drummers, two fifers, and 95 privates.

The Light Infantry of one captain, three lieutenants, four sergeants, two drummers, and 95 privates.

And each Battalion Company of one captain, two lieutenants, one ensign, four sergeants, five corporals, two drummers, and 95 privates;

Together with the usual staff officers, and with a serjeant major, and quartermaster serjeant, exclusive of the serjeants above specified. The captain lieutenant is (as usual) included in the number of lieutenants above mentioned.

The corps is to have three field officers, each with a company; their respective ranks to be determined by the rank of the officer whom your Grace shall recommend for the command thereof. If the person so recommended for the command is not at present in the army, he will be allowed temporary rank during the continuance of the regiment on the establishment but will not be entitled to half pay on its reduction.

His Majesty leaves to your Grace the nomination of all the officers, being such as are well affected to his Majesty, and most likely by their interest and connections to assist in raising the corps without delay; who, if they meet with his Royal approbation, may be assured they shall have commissions as soon as the regiment is completed.

The officers, if taken from the half pay, are to serve in their present ranks; if full pay, with one step of promotion. The gentlemen named for ensigncies are not to be under sixteen years of age. The quartermaster is not to be proposed for any other commission.

In case the corps shall be reduced after it has been established, the officers will be entitled to half pay.

The pay of the officers is to commence from the dates of their commissions: and that of the non-commissioned officers and private men from the dates of their attestations.

Levy money will be allowed to Your Grace in aid of this levy at the rate of five guineas per man for 1064 men.

The recruits are to be engaged without limitation as to the period or place of their service.

None are to be enlisted under five feet four inches, nor under 18 years or above 35. Growing lads from 16 to 18, at five feet three inches will not be rejected.

The non-commissioned officers and privates are to be inspected by a general officer, who will reject all such as are unfit for service, or not enlisted in conformity with the terms of this Letter.

His Majesty consents that on a reduction the Regiment shall, if it be desired, be disbanded in that part of the country where it was raised.

In the execution of this service, I take leave to assure Your Grace of every assistance which my office can afford.

The first important duty was to allot commissions, and the difficulty was not to get officers but to winnow them, for the applications were far in excess of the vacancies. Indeed, in November, 1793, that is to say, three months before the raising of the regiment was officially authorised, thirty applications for commissions were sent in. The following is a list of all the disappointed applicants for the first allotted commissions :—

MAJORS.

Captain Baillie, brother-in-law of Cosmo Gordon of Cluny. Captain Fraser of Fraserfield. Captain John Gordon-Cuming of Pitlurg, then serving in the Northern Fencibles. Major Urquhart, late of the 14th Regiment, brother of the laird of Craigston.

CAPTAINS.

Lieutenant Forsyth, 72nd Regiment. Lieutenant Horn and Lieutenant Houston, both of the 37th. Lieutenant Macdonald of Keppoch, suggested by Todd, one of the Duke's factors. Lieutenant Lewis Macdonald, brother of Glengarry. Alexander Mackay, of the Reay family. Lieutenant Ewan Macpherson of Coullachie. Lieutenant Hugh Macpherson of Inverhall, who was in the Northern Fencibles.

Lieutenant John Mercer, 63rd Regiment. Lieutenant Stuart of Urard, from Atholl. Mr. Seton, Rumgay, Fife.

CAPTAIN-LIEUTENANT.

Lieutenant John Gordon. Captain J. Grant, Rippachy.

LIEUTENANTS.

William Gordon, in Minmore. Mr. Macdonald, yr. of Achbriachlan. Ensign Alexander Stewart, of the 79th Regiment.

ENSIGNS.

Sergeant Innes, Glenlivet, of the Northern Fencibles. Mr. Ray, at Sherifftown.

SURGEONS.

Patrick Mushet. Alexander Reid.

CHAPLAINS.

Rev. James Gordon, Bellie, for his son. Rev. George Gordon, Aberdeen. Mr. Grant, Kirkmichael. Mr. Grant, Laggan. Rev. Thomas Ross, Kilmonivaig.

Some of the applications make curious reading. For instance, Duncan Stewart wrote from Belfast, on February 8, to the Duke of Gordon (*Gordon Castle Papers*):—

My Lord,—Coming to this place with two of my sons in the 79th Regiment, the Quarter-master department being in their charge, they were both young and unacquainted, [and] I had to attend them to see the regiment clothed and accoutred: and seeing here in the public papers that Your Grace was to raise a regiment, I have presumed to address and solicit your Grace for a lieutenancy for one of them in your regiment, which I hope is to be commanded by Lord Huntly. I will engage to make men for the step. It's most likely your Grace may not recollect me, tho' I am one of your Lochaber tenants and a feuar of Gordonsburgh. Mr. Tod, the factor, I have wrote to him on this business. He will inform your Grace respecting me.

On February 10, 1794, an application was made by the Rev. George Gordon, Aberdeen, for the Chaplaincy (*Ibid.*):—

Perhaps I am wrong, but it strikes me that my having been the Marquis's first preceptor, if it does not give me some sort of natural claim for the Chaplaincy, at least furnishes an excuse for my thinking of it.

Gordon had to wait nine years for a post, being appointed chaplain to Fort George, December 7, 1803. Three of his sons became surgeons in the H.E.I.C., and a fourth was in the Artillery.

On March 4, the Rev. William Gordon, Urquhart, applied for the Chaplaincy (which he got):—" I can assure you that independent of the emoluments it would much gratify my pride to be my young Chief's chaplain." He came of military stock,.for his uncle James was a Lieu-tenant-Colonel in the Bengal army, and was killed at Bijaigarh in 1800; his twin brother, Captain John Gordon in Laggan, had been in the Northern Fencibles; his son, William, who died in 1881, was an army surgeon; two of his grandsons were in the army; and a great-grandson is now in the Indian army.

Still another Gordon was most pertinacious. This was John Gordon, Coynachie, who had entered the Northern Fencibles in 1778. Coynachie gave two sons (including General John Gordon, Culdrain) and four grandsons (including General Cosmo Gordon, Culdrain) to the services. On February 16, he wrote to the Duke (*Ibid.*):—

My Lord Duke,—When I had the honour of seeing your Grace at Gordon Castle the other week, I mentioned that I had made proposals to Lord Huntly for raising what number of men might be required for the Captain-Lieutenancy of his regiment, and, altho' his Lordship did not positively say that that was to be the appointment, yet he was pleased to say that I should be in his regiment in some line or other. As the raising of the regiment must be an expensive undertaking, if your Grace and Lord Huntly would trust me with the paymastership I would cheerfully do the business for one half of the emoluments that might arise from the office. I cannot pretend to be a good accountant, but shall be answerable for the accounts of the regiment being kept exact, and I am certain that I would have his lordship's interest in view as [well as] any other that can be appointed.

Next day, on February 17, he wrote from Tullich, where he had been " holding forth in strong terms for recruiting " (*Ibid.*):—

I find there will be many applications for commissions, but his Grace would need to be careful in not appointing too many in one neighbourhood, because if they engaged for me they will go to logger-heads and spoil the recruiting.

It would be highly necessary that I knew if I was to be appointed: I cannot recruit with success or courage if not principally concerned, and being so much cut up at the last business makes my influence with the young lads of less consequence. If my finances would answer, I would not be the least affraid to raise my proportion for a company, independ-ent of subaltern, if the rank was allowed from half pay.

On March 14 he wrote to Menzies, the Duke's factotum, more freely:—

If there is nothing more for me but a lieutenancy, it will he a damn'd poor appointment. However, I'm content: if I persist in going I will get much better terms from other colonels. I have enlisted about 16 men, but I'm in an awkward situation with some of them. I subsist them, but has [sic] given very little of their bounty untill the Marquis approves or not. I have none half so bad as I see with other parties. If I don't go into the regiment, I will not insist on my own friends going, and has not attested them untill I'm certain, as I know they would not go with any other person whatever.

He was given the Captain-Lieutenancy. "I therefore am certain," writes Huntly, on March 23, "he will do what he can." On June 24, Captain Finlason writes to Menzies (*Ibid.*):—

Our friend Coinachy was put in orders as paymaster. I certainly did say everything in his favours possible. I think well of him, and I was the more inclined to do him good offices that you joined and wished it. I shall be happy to give him all the instructions in my power. I went and ordered the proper books for him.

One of the successful applicants was Lieutenant Simon Macdonald of Morar from the half pay of the 76th Regiment. James Fraser of Gortuleg writes, February 15, to Charles Gordon of Braid soliciting a commission for Macdonald (*Ibid.*):—

[He] is in point of ffriends and connections extremely well calculated to raise a company: and it would be particularly agreeable to him to be promoted in any corps to be raised by the Marquis of Huntly, as his brother is a captain in the first Royals, and owes much to Lord Adam Gordon, both from his original introduction and promotion in that regiment. Independent of his own tribe, which are numerous, and his remaining property [being] by no means inconsiderable, he is by inter-marriage particularly connected with the Glengarry branches.

When it came to the rank and file, Huntly was confronted by precisely the same difficulties as his father had had to face in recruiting for the Northern Fencibles in 1778 and 1793—especially in the matter of a rival regiment and of bounties. In addition, the young Marquis was unable to be present in person at the early stages of the recruiting, for he had injured his leg at Gordon Castle, and was laid up at Edinburgh in Walker's Hotel, having apparently gone south for medical advice. His friends became so agitated that he sought to allay their fears by advertising in the *Aberdeen Journal*, March 23:—

Lord Huntly presents his respectful compliments to the gentlemen who have obligingly interested themselves in his regiment. He sincerely thanks them for their exertions, and flatters himself that he will soon be permitted by his physicians to go to the north, and to have the honour to co-operate with them in person. In the meantime he requests that the recruits already enlisted may be sent to the headquarters at Aberdeen, where Major Erskine is appointed to receive them.

Despite Huntly's placid attitude, Captain John Gordon, writing from Huntly, March 27, declared that it would "retard the recruiting amazingly." Captain Finlason, who had to face the difficulty in Aberdeen itself, where a rival regiment was being formed, felt the Marquis's non-appearance very keenly. In March he wrote to Menzies, "I should not be surprised if the Prince of W., etc., etc., have him by the arm yet." As late as May 17, Finlason writes again to Menzies (*Gordon Castle Papers*):—

Good God, why will he not come and be the Lion in his own cause? I wish to God I was stopped and officers appeared. It does not answer for me (not an officer in the regiment) to carry on such an oppositional business. Unsupported, too, is dreadful. I have not even a serjeant to keep my irregulars in order.

These letters prove that the presence of a personality was still of value, despite the fact that the spirit of clanship had largely died out.

Even more serious than the Marquis's prolonged absence was the raising of another regiment in Aberdeenshire, namely, the 109th, for which Letters of Service were granted to Alexander Leith-Hay, of Rannes, on April 4, 1794, within a few weeks of the mandate to the Duke. The keenness of the rivalry was strikingly shown by Hay's adopting the name "The Aberdeenshire Regiment," which Finlason had suggested to the Duke (March 1) as the name which should be used by his Grace's corps. On March 11, Finlason reports that Hay "is to assume the name of the Aberdeen Regiment. I once hinted that to your graceful Marquis." Next day he writes to Menzies:—"The Aberdeen Regiment will be upon us, and we should get strong before they start." So keenly did the Duke's supporters feel on the point that Finlason sent Professor Patrick Copland of Marischal College to remonstrate with the Lord Provost on the preference shown by the Town Council to Hay's corps. Copland reported (*Ibid.*):—

I told him that whatever name might be given to Colonel Hay's regiment, the Marquis was surely the one with which the Town of Aberdeen would be most connected. I at length learned the truth of the matter: which is, that Hay's friends have strongly urged some of their connexions in the Council to accept of a sum of money privately to be given in their name as a bounty. I took the liberty of saying that if this was the case, I was certain the Magistrates would never be guilty of such meanness as thus to impose on the public. He agreed that they ought not, and promised that if it was again brought forward (which he believed it would) he should certainly oppose it and he hoped successfully. . . . The Provost told me besides that he and the Magistrates had been strongly urged by the Colonel's friends to sign a letter they had drawn out, recommending him in the warmest terms to Mr. Allardyce as under the patronage of the town, and approving of his regiment being named as you mention. This has been refused, has been altered and again presented I think twice; and to avoid being teazed longer, they have this afternoon [March 15] given him what one of the baillies called to me a "milk and water" letter, merely mentioning that from their regard to His Majestie's service, it would be agreeable to the magistrates if Mr. Allardyce would give Coll. Hay any assistance which might have been in his power while in London. I hope, however, the Duchess will have secured Allardyce before the Colonel's arrival, which in the present case will not, I believe, be difficult because his friends and the colonel's in general are not on the same side of the question.

In all likelihood the Duke's corps would have been known as the Aberdeenshire Regiment but for Hay's intervention. The first time I have noted the name "The Gordon Highlanders," is in an account of June 17. The regiment, it may be remembered, was numbered the 100th till October, 1798, when it became the 92nd.

The great crux of the situation, however, was the question of finance. The point is particularly interesting in the case of the Gordon Highlanders on account of the famous, and possibly immortal, story that the Duchess got recruits by giving them a kiss and a guinea. The first appearance of the kiss story which I have been able to find occurs in 1858 in the Rev. Archibald Clerk's *Memorial of Colonel John Cameron of Fassifern*, where it is stated that the kiss was conferred in "*rare* cases" (p. 23).

It is said that the celebrated Duchess herself was more active and more successful than any of her vassals or friends: that, equipped in semi-military costume, she rode from farm to farm, from hamlet to hamlet of her extensive estates, by an eloquent tongue rousing the martial ardour of her tenantry : and in *rare* cases where this failed offering the bribe of a kiss from her own lips.   Such a bribe always proved irresistible.

On the other hand it is not mentioned by Stewart in his *Sketches of the Highlanders*, 1822, though he says the Duke, the Duchess, and the Marquis recruited " in their own persons "; nor by Browne, *History of the Highlands*, 1838 ; nor by Cannon in his official history of the regiment, 1851.   The first circumstantial version of the story appears in William Grant Stewart's *Lectures on the Mountain*, 1860 (Ser. i., p. 62).

In a crowded market at Tomintoul, dressed in Highland bonnets and feathers, tartan scarfs, short tartan petticoats and pantaloons, in a circle formed by their attendants, appeared some of those young, gay and lovely ladies [the Duchess's daughters], afterwards the consorts of ducal coronets ; and danced with any young man willing to wear a cockade, to the music of the bagpipes ; and at the end of each reel handed to each of their partners a guinea and a cockade, in the name of King George and Huntly.   Candidates for the honour of a dance crowded around emulous for the next vacancy, and in spite of the remonstrances and lamentations of female friends, they bounded in rapid succession into the enchanting circle, going in as civilians and coming out as soldiers.   At the end of the day the noble marquis and his fair assistants had reason to be satisfied with the day's sport—scores of young men, the finest of the Fair, having become stricken, proud, no doubt, come what might, they had been partners for once with " Nighean Duchd Gordon " (the Duke of Gordon's daughter).

A circumstantial-looking testimony to the kiss-story is given by a correspondent, " G. T.," who, writing in the late Mrs. Simpson's interesting *Souvenir of Sympathy*, 1900, says :—

My grandmother, aged 97 years, told me, with her own mouth, that she stood one day beside the plainstones in the Old Square at Elgin and saw the Duchess ride up in search of men for her regiment, and seeing a fine young fellow standing in front of the old jail—which occupied the place which the water fountain now holds—she waved her hand for him to approach her, which he did, and after a little talk with him, she dismounted and approached him with a sovereign held between her teeth.   The gallant lad wiped his mouth, and the next moment the coin was transferred and held between his teeth, she remarking—" You will get maha to-mo'o " (you will get mare [more] to-morrow, or mae to-mo'o).   She could not pronounce the letter " r."

Lieutenant-Colonel Greenhill Gardyne is inclined to stand by the tradition, which he summarizes thus (*Life of a Regiment*, i, 14):—

C2

She rode to the country fairs in Highland bonnet [now in possession of the 2nd Gordons] and regimental jacket (it was not unusual in those days of military enthusiasm for ladies to wear the uniform of their husbands' or brothers' regiments). It is told how she gave a kiss to the men she enlisted—a fee more valued than the coin by which it was accompanied, as in the case of a smart young farmer at Huntly market, who took the shilling and the kiss, and then paid "smart" [that is £1 which a recruit forfeited if he repented his bargain before being sworn in], saying, "A kiss from your Grace is well worth a pound note." Sometimes she is said to have placed a guinea between her lips. There was in a Highland village a young blacksmith remarkable for his strength and good looks. Recruiters for the Guards and Line had in vain tried to enlist him, but he could not resist her Grace! He took the kiss and the guinea; but to show it was not the gold that tempted him, he tossed the guinea among the crowd. [Colonel Greenhill Gardyne goes on to note that when a Gordon Highlander was wounded in battle a Highland comrade would say, "Och cha n'eil ach pog eile o'n Bhan Diuc," or, as an Aberdonian would facetiously put it— "Mind, lad, ye got a kiss o' the Duchess o' Gordon for that."]

In a letter to the present writer, dated December 2, 1908, he adds :—

It is quite true that there is no actual legal evidence that the Duchess kissed the recruits; nor is it, I fancy, supposed by anyone that she kissed all of them, which would have been rather much of a good thing even for a woman of her temperament. But I do think it quite probable that she did kiss some individuals. One old Peninsular soldier, a particularly respectable old man, said he had himself heard it referred to by a soldier to a wounded comrade, I think, more than once; and so many old people believe it that I thought there must be a foundation for it. But I never thought of suggesting that the kiss or the guinea was the only bounty received by the men.

The Duchess may or may not have kissed the men—she certainly had just that touch of Bohemianism to do so; but we have proof positive that her eldest daughter, Lady Madelina Sinclair, not only did not do so, but was angry at the suggestion that she did, for her husband, Sir Robert Sinclair, writing from Fort George on June 22 about his recruiting experiences in Caithness, says (*Gordon Castle Papers*):—

I met with great opposition from the [Caithness] Fencibles. . . . At last they were reduced to the necessity of saying something false, which was truly ridiculous—that Lady Madelina marched thro' Thurso in the filibeg and hose and enlisted men with a kiss and a guinea in her mouth; which she very properly, at Lord Caithness's table, etc., made a very laughable joke of.

The interesting point about this denial is this, that, while the story is told of the Duchess—even on the picture-cover of the latest official recruiting pamphlet—by way of distinction, it was said of her daughter by way of disparagement; and not a single document at Gordon Castle refers to her Grace's feat.

On the other hand, there seems to be little doubt that the Duchess took a keen personal interest in the recruiting arrangements. The second battalion of the Gordons still possess the diced cap which she wore, not unlike the feather bonnet in shape, and the Duke of Richmond and Gordon treasures at Gordon Castle the yellow silk recruiting flag (used by her in recruiting for a second battalion in 1803), which he has illustrated (both sides) in collotype in the inventory of his war trophies, 1907, and describes as follows (p. 41):—

On one side the achievement of the United Kingdom of Great Britain and Ireland as displayed by George III. (the quarterings being, 1 and 4 England, 2 Scotland, 3 Ireland en surtout Hanover surmounted with the Electoral Bonnet). Beneath is a military trophy which includes three medallions, showing respectively St. Andrew, the Cross and Rays, and the Thistle. From each side of the trophy springs a Union Wreath of Roses, Thistles and Shamrocks encircling the Royal Arms. Above all, the motto in an escroll, " Pro Patria."

The other side displays in the centre a shield, with the British lion roused, whose body supports an oval shield with the words " To Arms." Underneath the shield is a military trophy including the distinctive details of two broadswords in saltire, hilts downwards, surmounted by a representation of the feather bonnet of the 92nd showing a fess chequey of red, white, and green resting on a plaid of Gordon tartan, from each side of which springs a Union Wreath of Roses, Thistles, and Shamrocks. On the plaid is the motto, " For Our King and Country." Above the shield is a stag's head and neck affronteé proper, attired or, issuing out of a Marquis's Coronet (Marquis of Huntly's), and surmounted by a similar coronet with the motto in an escroll, " Animo non Astutia." Size, 6 ft. 3 in. by 5 ft. 10 in. [The feather bonnet shown is the earliest authentic representation of the headgear of the 92nd.]

Of one thing we may be sure—the Duchess was temperamentally incapable of adopting some of the recruiting practices of the day. A writer in *Public Characters* for 1800 (p. 503), in a very free and easy sketch of her Grace (in which no mention is made of the kiss) tells us:—

She heard of practices that were carried on in a certain part of Scotland very inconsistent with the rights of British subjects—for instance, confining poor men in cellars to compel them to inlist as soldiers, although there was no Act in force at that period of the war that permitted involuntary levies.

When she came to London some time after, she mentioned that mode of recruiting. One day, she happened to be at a rout where Mr. Fox was present, when she related to the company an anecdote she had heard. It seems in the regiment, of which part had been levied in the manner we have above mentioned, there was a good deal of contumacy in learning the discipline. It happened drilling that a sergeant was very severely beating a poor fellow near a town, through which her Grace had to pass on her way to the south. On inquiry what crime had drawn upon the sufferer such severity—" No crime at all, please your Ladyship," replied the sergeant, " this is the way in our corps of making folunteers " [sic]. Her Grace, in reciting this story, expressed such sentiments as humanity would dictate on such a subject, and added some observations concerning the cellars.

Mr. Fox, hearing this short narrative with the accompanying remarks, immediately declared that the conduct of the principal in this species of recruiting demanded a serious inquiry, which he would set about instituting. Her Grace intreated him not to proceed on her information and before he had time or opportunity to investigate the truth through other channels, other public business interfered and prevented the reconsideration of the cellar adventures.

It is certain that Her Grace could not have got a drummer, much less a full blown private, for a guinea, even if she had kissed him. Indeed, the experience of the Marquis in getting men was far more severe than anything his father had encountered. The latter had gone the length of three guineas for the Northern Fencibles in the previous year, but that was no good whatever in the case of the Gordons, for the simple reason that, while soldiering in the Fencibles was a mere interlude in a man's career, it became his life-work in a regular regiment like the Gordons. The Government itself offered five guineas, but even that was not enough, and it had to be supplemented by the Marquis from the price of commissions. Cox and Greenwood, the army agents of Craig's Court, London, wrote about the point on February 11, 1794 (*Gordon Castle Papers*):—

The terms of the Letter of Service are such as, with the produce of the appointment and the Bounty, admit of £20 per man, and that at a very moderate calculation; but we think that no more than £15 ought to be allowed to the recruiting officer, and we should hope that the colonels raising the several corps will agree to this, as there must be service expences and contingencies which cannot otherwise be provided for

On March 1, they condescended to figures, calculating, on the basis of other new regiments, that £22,850 could be raised from commissions, and £5,586 was due from Government, thus making a bounty of £26 14s for each man The figures ran thus —

1st Majority	£2,000
2nd ,,	2,000
7 Companies at £1,500 each	10,500
1 Captain-Lieutenancy .	800
2 eldest Lieutenancies at £300 each	600
17 next in rank at £250 each .	4,250
2 youngest Lieutenancies at £200 each	400
2 eldest Ensigncies at £350 each	700
2 next in rank at £300 each	600
4 youngest Ensigncies at £250 each	1,000
	£22,850
Levy money allowed by Government for 1,064 men at £5 5s each .	5,586
	£28,436

which being divided by 1,064, the number of men to be raised, produces a fund of £26 14s per man

On March 8, Cox and Greenwood wrote more minutely about the allocation of the money (*Gordon Castle Papers*) —

We think it necessary to mention to you that, excepting about one half of the levy money which will be issued from the War Office, there will be no other fund to ensure the various demands for the recruiting, but such as may arise from the deposits to be made by the several officers who are to obtain commissions in the corps, and that it will therefore be requisite as these gentlemen may be approved of by your Grace or by Lord Huntly that their respective proportions of the purchase money should be immediately lodged

The colonels of the other regiments proceed precisely upon this plan, being aware of the inconvenience which must otherwise be experienced in completing their respective corps.

On March 14, 1794, J M[enzies?] pointed out to Cox and Greenwood that Lord Amherst had stated that levy money would be issued "at the rate of £5 for each man and the pay of the regiment from the date of the beating order to be allowed in aid of the recruiting" (*Ibid.*):—

From this I should humbly conceive that his Grace and Lord Huntly were entitled to touch immediately the whole levy money at the above mentioned rate and three months' subsistence of the regiment. Otherwise where is the allowance held forth in aid of the recruiting?

Cox and Greenwood replied to this particular query on March 26 (*Ibid.*):—

About one half of the sum for levy money will be issued immediately . . . and this, together with the amount of the actual subsistence of the men will be all the Fund that can be ·obtained from Government towards the recruiting till the Regiment may have got half of the men, when all the remainder of the levy money will probably be issued.

The increment on the Government allowance varied with different regiments according to the state of the labour and the bounty market. Unfortunately for the Marquis, the increment was run up sometimes to four times the Government bounty by the acute recruiting rivalry of the 109th Regiment, which had captured the patronage of the Town Council of Aberdeen. The worst of the opposition fell upon Captain Finlason, who was conducting not only the financial affairs of the Northern Fencibles in Aberdeen, but the recruiting for the Gordons. As early as February 22, that is to say, within a month of the issue of the War Office mandate, Finlason wrote as follows (*Ibid.*):—

I struggle hard to make a good bargain, but I may as well attempt to change the system of the whole army as to ask recruiting officers here to alter their terms; but I flatter myself no other party has done the same execution here in the same time, and I give you my word there have not been ten minutes passed this day without my knocker going to all fellows, drunk and sober.

On March 30 he made another plaint—Finlason was always complaining about something (*Ibid.*):—

If friends to one Corps [Hay's] advertise gratuitys, the other, [the Marquis's], will find some to do so too. It becomes necessary in such a case and there is no help. It is inflaming the reckoning on both sides: but the Marquis will chuse to keep his ground I daresay.

The rivalry was felt in the country districts, for Gordon in Coynachie wrote on March 14 (*Ibid.*):—

If Colonel Hay's beating orders come to this country before the Marquis makes his appearance, it will knock our recruiting on the head. Every man that has any inclinations expects such high bounty money from him.

A similar difficulty faced the Duke's son-in-law, Sir Robert Sinclair, who enlisted ten drummers at Fort George. Writing to Menzies on March 19, he said (*Ibid.*):—

Do let me know if the Marquis raises his bounty when he comes, as very fine lads laugh at 12 guineas. There is this day a beating order come to Campbelltown to inlist for Colonel Graham's corps at 18 guineas, and very fine lads [do] not stick at that. It has alarmed me much, being near me. The drummers get no bounty, but I give them cloaths, almost to the amount of the King's [bounty].

Coynachie Gordon, in writing from Huntly, March 27, says (*Ibid.*):—

You may as well suppose that we could remove Gordon Castle on our shoulders as get men without paying them their bounty down. They are so knowing with that line now.

It was essentially true of recruiting in those days that every man had his price, though we now have no data to decide why it differed. It was certainly not a mere matter of a change in the buyers (that is to say, different recruiting officers), for the same officer is found paying a varying scale. Here are some of the figures selected as showing that the demand for bounties was widespread, and not conditioned by geography. For example, one would have thought that the Badenoch men, as fine specimens of Highlanders, would have been easy to recruit. The list of bounties paid there, however, dispels that idea. The following were some of the bounties paid to Badenoch recruits (*Ibid.*):—

Clark, Alexander	£21	0
M'Pherson, John	"	"
Cattanach, Alexander	£18	18
M'Intyre, Alexander	"	"
M'Pherson, Peter	£17	2
Cattanach, Malcolm	£17	1
Davidson, Malcolm	£16	0
M'Pherson, Ewan	£15	0
M'Nair, John	£13	6
Ross, Andrew	£13	2
Davidson, Paul	£12	18
Gordon, Donald	"	"
Macdonell, John	"	"

M'Intosh, John	£12 18
M'Intosh, Lachlan	,, ,,
M'Intyre, James	,, ,,
M'Pherson, Donald	,, ,,
M'Pherson, Donald	,, ,,
Robertson, Donald	,, ,,
Ross, David	,, ,,
Cameron, John	£12 12
Fraser, Angus	,, ,,
M'Gillivray, Benjamin	,, ,,
M'Pherson, Alexander	,, ,,
M'Pherson, Alexander	,, ,,
Reid, Alexander	,, ,,
M'Pherson, Duncan	£10 16
M'Intosh, Duncan	,, ,,
M'Pherson, Andrew	£10 10
M'Pherson, Ewen	£6 6
M'Intosh, Lachlan	£5 5

The bounties paid at Peterhead were just on the same scale (*Ibid.*):—

Greig, Francis	£24 3
Brook, Robert	£16 16
M'Donald, Alexander	,, ,,
Shewan, John	,, ,,
M'Veagh, John	£14 14
M'Pherson, John	,, ,,
Matheson, Alexander	,, ,,
Sangster, James	,, ,,
M'Veagh, John	£12 12
Young, James	£11 0
Foreman, Andrew	£8 8
Milne, James	,, ,,
Renton, John	£5 5

The price of recruits tended to go up as the days slipped by (*Ibid.*):—

March 20.—James Taylor	£10 10
,, 28.—Alexander Dibby	£12 12
April 10.—Thomas Thomas	,, ,,
,, 29.—Alexander Gordon, Rothes . . .	£14 14
May 15.—William Lorimer	,, ,,
,, 19.—James Baxter	£17 17
,, 24.—John Reynolds	£21 0
,, 27.—Donald Urquhart	£19 19
June 14.—Edward Douarty: " Brought Mr. Alex. Garden from Banff in his place "	£21 0

June 14.—James Simpson, Fochabers £17 17
 „ 15.—Charles Cameron, "cousin to Glenco" . . £15 15

This last figure, £15 15s., was ultimately fixed by the War Office, in a letter of February 21, 1795, as the limit for recruits enlisted for general service, "the high bounties offered to the new levies being judged extremely prejudicial to the recruiting for the Navy"; but it may be doubted whether this by-law was strictly observed.

The total paid out for bounties in 1794 from the exchequer at Gordon Castle was £2,478 12s. 5d., including

Badenoch bounties £442 17 6
Lochaber bounties 96 12 0
Contingent expenses in Badenoch and Lochaber . . 185 13 7
Fochabers bounties 115 7 6
Peterhead bounties 164 6 0
Mr. Tod's "Highland expenses" 500 0 0

These figures, of course, do not include the men raised by other captains of companies, dealing only with those for whom the Marquis of Huntly was directly responsible. One wonders what has become of the balance-sheets of the other companies. It is probable, however, that they all would tell the same tale.

Besides these sums, a further amount of £560 12s. 2d. was paid out in bounties and expenses in 1797. We have no details of any precise addition to the regiment, although Lieutenant-Colonel Gardyne mentions a draft of recruits arriving at Gibraltar in April of that year. They were probably raised in response to the big territorial scheme which Dundas proposed (February 22, 1797). A second battalion was raised for the Gordons in 1803 in response to the Army Reserve Act, by which 50,000 additional men were to be added to the army, by conscription, Scotland contributing 6,000. This second battalion totalled 1,113, but the only note of expense we have is the sum of £958 15s. 10d., paid between May 1 and November 2 to the Forsyths of Huntly for clothing. A letter from the Forsyths, dated January 9, 1804, shews that the men "paid full value for their kilts."

In addition to bounties, the Marquis had sometimes to acquiesce in a *quid pro quo*, such as the following, which was propounded by James Gordon, who wrote from Croughly to Menzies on June 14 (1794) (*Ibid.*):—

D2

I find Peter Gordon cannot prevaill on either of his younger broyrs. to go with the Marquis. In my presence he used all his endeavours to perswade his younger broyr. to goe, but to no purpose; and as that is the case, to please the Marquis, he will goe himself. He wishes to get possession of Ffourdmouth, as he has nothing to support his wife and two orphants, except the possession and small cover there, one which is reather greatly under burden, so that his wife, etc., cannot be supported without the possession in his absence: and in the event of his going he wishes if his friends can find anoyr. passable man to goe in his place some time hereafter to gett his discharge.

On June 15 the Marquis gave a bounty of £2 2s. to Gordon and £18 18s. to his wife. In some cases the recruit's relatives had to be pacified. In this way the father of Neil M'Millan got £12 12s., while Neil himself got £8 8s., bringing up his price to £21.

Sometimes the *quid pro quo* was put forward on behalf of a community. Thus George Bell, writing from Coclarachie, March 26, 1794, speaks about the clothing of the regiment:—"I think the profits of a Huntly regiment should be given to Huntly folks, and I hope you [John Menzies] are of the same opinion, and will on proper occasions say so" (*Ibid.*). Huntly himself clearly recognised this method of bargaining, for he wrote from Edinburgh, March 23, that "Forsyth should exert himself, as he is to have the shirts to make."

A frank admission of the difficulty of getting recruits was forthcoming from Lieutenant M'Killigin, who wrote from Banff to Menzies, April 3, about a man John Joass (*Ibid.*):—

I consider [him] a very excellent recruit. He was put into prison here suspected of things not of an agreeable nature, but, as times go, soldiers must be admitted whose character will not bear particular inquiry. Mr. Forbes, the sheriff's substitute, has given me a preference, and in other respects been most ready and obliging as the getting the man liberated was attended with some difficulty. I have given him an order on you [Menzies] for his bounty of five guineas, and have also paid expenses on his imprisonment amounting to £3 7s. Add to this half a guinea I was obliged to promise one of the town's officers to endeavour to bring him to agree to enlist.

The Marquis in pursuit of men came into sharp collision with employers and their apprentices. A typical case is stated by Miss G. Gordon, who, writing to Menzies, March 2, says that a nineteen-year-old apprentice of Provost Robinson, Banff, had enlisted with the Sea-forths, but on his indenture being produced he was given up (*Ibid.*) : —

But as Mr. Robinson has had great trouble and been put to expense with this man, they have no objections to let him go to Lord Huntly for ten guineas, provided they can get eight guineas of the bounty in order to make up their loss. . . . [Men] do not like going to be killed, they say. I offered a fine handsome and stout young man twelve guineas, but no money would make him go.

Sometimes the masters were not averse from being paid off, for Alexander Black, blacksmith at Buckie, got £4 4s. for delivering up the indenture papers of James Wilson, who himself cost £10 10s.

Examples of other incidental expenses constantly occur, as, for example (*Ibid.*) :—

June 17.—To William Christie, wright, for his trouble and expenses in keeping a boy who came to enlist but was found to be diseased . . .	£1 1 0
May 27.—To George Urquhart, for bringing his brother Donald, whose bounty was £19 19s. . .	£1 1 0

Even when he had captured his men, the Marquis had to humour them. In certain cases he even increased the bounty, as shown in the entry under date July 3—" To Donald Macpherson, enlisted on March 12, ordered by your lordship over and above £8 8s. formerly paid by Menzies, and £7 7s. at Aberdeen," the further sum of £5 5s., bringing up the price of Macpherson to £21. Everything seems to have been done to make the recruits as happy as possible, as these payments prove (*Ibid.*) :—

June 4.—To A. Bayne, for playing the fiddle to the recruits at Gordon Castle	£0 17 6
June 15.—To William Gordon, of the New Inn, Aberdeen, for four hogsheads of porter for the recruits	£16 10 0
July 1.—To A. Bayne and Robert Bremner, for playing the fiddle on February 7, May 24, June 20 .	£1 10 0
July 15.—To Peter Weir, in Bogs, price of bull, baited and roasted and given to the recruits . .	£3 15 0

Some of the recruits had little perquisites, as, for example, John Baxter, who got five shillings for "drummbeting" at two markets at Keith, two at Elgin, and one at Botriphnie. Drum beatings, however, were cheap, for only two shillings were paid for "diffrant" beatings at Fochabers from January 1 to April 29.

Examining the recruiting progress in the different centres, we find that Captain Finlason, stationed at Aberdeen, had probably the hardest task of anybody. On February 25 he told Menzies he was willing to do everything in his power in the "two fold business, but they are clashing circumstances and will operate against each other." In the first place, he was face to face with the fiercest element of the competition with the 109th, and in the midst of a people who were biassed in favour of his rival. Then he had to carry on his work without the personal help of the man chiefly involved, the Marquis of Huntly. One sees him hard at work in his office, which was apparently in his house, dashing off letters at night after his day's work to Menzies—now hopeful, now in the depths of despair. A clear idea of his moods will be got by a chronological arrangement of his varying sentiments (*Ibid.*):—

February 22.—I have been in the lower storey of my own house from morning to night [but he found some compensation in having got five men]. The gentlemen have been striped [sic] to the buff—and critically inspected as men never were.

March 1.—I have had nibblers from morning to night of this day, and I think three have taken the bait. Monday is the first attesting day, so we do not count our chickens.

March 2.—I had a full parade in my court this morning, before they set off with pipe and drum for the display of a Friday.

March 3.—I am really much concerned that the Marquis does not come north instantly, as I cannot see how the material business of raising the regiment can be set going and put fairly on leg, but in this country under the Duke's influence, after his Grace has received all the necessary previous information to be collected by the Marquis on the spot and in the agents' power to communicate. It is obvious that Sir J[ames?] G[rant?], or any undertaker who has been at the fountain head and a disciple under agents so long and versant in the publick market and traffick of the day, must start with every advantage. To such a one, I am sure the undertaking a regiment is a profitable thing, independent of patronage.

March 11.—This day I engaged George Gordon from the Cabrach, late a tenant of the Duke. He was dislodged by Coinachie or Mr. Bell, and says he has £48 due him on bills from good men for the stocking of his farm sold. He is a tight Light Infantry man, 26 [years of] age. But I had him to engage thro' many windings—(1) a recommendation to the Marquis to sollicit the Duke for his former task to him on or after his discharge from the army: (2) an application to you or Mr. Bell for some tenement or bigging for his wife till his return: (3) promotion if he deserves it: besides (4) ten guineas bounty and three guineas to his pilot, Sergeant Reid. This hero of the Cabrach says he is highly related here [Aberdeen], viz., to the Rev. Mr. Sheriffs and his brother, the advocate. To-morrow he goes in high dress with his sword by his side to announce his new profession.

March 24.—I got on very slowly in numbers here. Had it not been for the enterprises of a new corps, I had been about 40 strong, instead of 32 as I stand. Had the Marquis come among us long ago, it would have been above 100 men in his way taking the country all over.   .   .   . Every gauger in Scotland is employed for [Graham of Balgowan]. So between that and the Hay Corps we are sadly off: and no Marquis to support.

March 30.—A damned cheat (I believe he is), W. Stewart, an old deer stalker of the Duke's, made me believe he could get men in the Cabrach, etc. I ventured 20s. with him, and he is returned a clean ship: wants more money, but he shall rather get a rope. Do you know this fellow or his character?

April 1.—[Colonel Hay beat up for the first time]. The town is in a roar. We shall catch nothing till it settles. Nothing less than 30 guineas is spoken of; so we must have patience.   .   .   .   A bounty from the County will soon be noticed for the Aberdeenshire Regiment. Lord Huntly's friends must equal it and not be outdone. For one emissary we have on foot, they have a hundred. The whole town is for them. We have no one to assist us.   .   .   .   For God's sake, lay every oar in the water. Secure all the Strathbogie men. The Aberdeenshire Regiment will be about your ears, if every friend of the Marquis does not act with heart and hand and stop at no bounty.

April 6.—All people here are acting for [Hay], and the connection made with [Francis Garden of] Delgaty by his brother [Peter Garden] being second Major is powerful in Aberdeenshire.   .   .   .   I hear Pitfour and Allardyce assisted [Colonel Hay] strongly. He found great difficulty after he went to London.

April 14.—The whole town high and low are at work for the Aberdeen Regiment. To-morrow Hay gives a great dinner.

May 2.—The Gordon recruits in Aberdeen were being drilled by a sergeant major of the Northern Fencibles.

June 24.—The Marquis gave a dinner on Sunday to Sir Hector Munro, Lord Kintore, Lord Inverury, [the] Provost of Aberdeen *for his great services*, Colonel Hay, Colonel Morison, etc., etc., etc. The most of the company drank enough.   .   .   .   Eighty seven men were secured here, whose attestations I have, besides a world of trouble I had in and about them. My house [was] never empty for five weeks from nine in the morning to ten at night. It was like an alehouse or gin shop.

July 1.—I went to town the day before the last division of Lord

Huntly's regiment marched, to settle my recruiting account, which was accurately done by Captain Gordon, paymaster. . . . I delivered 86 attestations, besides 2 pipers instructed. Major Erskine was present and was pleased to think my men cheap, tho' at 16 guineas each, all expenses included. They would have been much lower had it not been for a certain interference: but you will consider what opponents I had, and how the market was raised all at once, and many of the bringers would accept nothing less than three guineas per man. . . . The Marquis, after paying for my men, is £726 in pocket.

As in the case of the Northern Fencibles in the previous year, some of the tenants on the ducal estates took concerted action. The *Aberdeen Journal* of April 28 announced:—

At a meeting of some of the Duke of Gordon's tenants in the Parish of Kirkmichael and Strathdown, it was resolved, in testimony of their gratitude and attachment to the noble family under which they and their predecessors had lived for generations, to exert themselves to assist in enlisting volunteers for the Marquis of Huntly's regiment, and for that purpose they resolved to give three guineas of additional bounty over and above every other bounty, to any good recruit from their own country, who shall voluntarily enlist with the Marquis of Huntly, or with Captain John Gordon of Coynachie, or with any of the subscribers to the present bounty for his lordship's behoof ; and they also resolved to give the same additional bounty to every good recruit from any other country who shall voluntarily enlist with James Gordon in Craughly [Croughly], Robert Macgregor in Delavorar, or William Stuart in Bellantruan, for the Marquis of Huntly's Regiment.

The hand of the Gordons must have been considerably strengthened by the Duke's appointment as Lord-Lieutenant (1794-1808). Dundas wrote to him from Whitehall, May 14, 1794 (*Gordon Castle Papers*):—

His Majesty, having been pleased to appoint Lord Lieutenants and High Sheriffs for the different counties in Scotland, and having fixed upon your Grace for the execution of those offices in the county of Aberdeen, I think it proper to explain to you the object of these appointments. When I first advised his Majesty to adopt this measure, I had in contemplation the double object of defence against a foreign enemy and the preservation of internal tranquillity against any who, either in conjunction with foreign enemies or actuated by their own evil dispositions, might be inclined to disturb it.

The first of those objects is, I trust, already sufficiently provided for by the various levies of Fencible Corps, both horse and foot, which have been already raised or are now raising in consequence of the zeal and loyalty which has so conspicuously manifested itself in the different parts of Scotland, and, if any circumstance should occur to render any more general array of the County necessary, the powers vested in you by your Commission as His Majesty's Lieutenant will enable your Grace to regulate that array so as to give an effectual aid to the regular Force which might be employed in such an emergence. . . .

You will perceive that it has been likewise in contemplation to attend to the wishes of any towns upon the coast which may be desirous to arm for their local defence; and if any considerable towns, other than those upon the coast, should be desirous of forming from their respectable and loyal inhabitants Volunteer corps, it is His Majesty's pleasure that you should receive such propositions and transmit them to his Majesty's consideration.

This appointment probably quickened the instinct of the family to fend for itself, for Sir Robert Sinclair of Stevenston, who had married the Marquis's sister, Lady Madelina Gordon, in 1789, joined the recruit hunt at this time. Sir Robert, who was Governor of Fort George, was in close touch with the whole military situation. He began his recruiting work at Huntly, as we learn from a letter, written on May 25, by John Gordon, Coynachie, to Menzies (*Ibid.*):—

The number of men certain enlisted at Huntly during the time Sir Robert and the Marquis was there altogether does not exceed ten, including the time Sir Robert went to Aberdeen. There [sic] names is [sic] as follows:—

M'Killican Mackie	}Enlisted by Sir Robert Sinclair.
Reynolds, John Hay, William	}Enlisted by Lord Huntly.
Fife Fordyce	}Enlisted by Mr. Davidson.
Shand	Miss Bisset's man. Lady Madelina has his attestation.
Brown, James	Enlisted by Knockespock.
Wanes, W. Milne, Peter	}Enlisted by Gordon, Coynachie.

Then Sir Robert turned to his native heath, where he had to face the formidable opposition to the Caithness Fencibles, just as Captain Finlason had had to struggle against the Aberdeenshire Regiment. Sir Robert was greatly aided in his work by his charming wife (who outlived him by 54 years). He wrote some excellent letters on the progress of his work; the following are the most telling points (*Ibid.*):—

Murkle, June 1. (To Menzies):—I begin my operations to-morrow. I understand my farmers have agreed to give me a man each, six in number. To-morrow, my estate of Murkle is to come in here, and I mean to try them, tho' the country I find much drained by the Fencibles. Tuesday, I go to another propperty at Brabster, where I am in hopes of success. Wednesday, the King's birthday, I give a hogshead of porter in the town of Thurso: may have an effect as I have published at the church doors this day. Thursday, I shall be active as possible about the parish of Ray, where I have propperty. Friday, I dine with the Caithness Fencibles. I think I have brought things more to a bearing between them and me than I could have expected and I make no doubt, if any man preferred high bounties they would assist me. Lord Caithness asked Lady M. and I to dine at the mess, Friday the market day, and Lady Caithness and some other ladies meet Lady M. On Friday last, I gave a glass of whisky to the Fencibles in the afternoon and all the officers attended my party in beating up. I got a most excellent recruit on the street, 5 ft. 6 inches, to begin with. Saturday next, I mean to dine with Mr. Sinclair of Holbournhead, and then to go to Mr. Innes of Sandside, near my propperty in the parish of Ray, where by being in the neighbourhood I may get a man to come in. I then go to Lord Caithness's and some other gentlemen.

Murkle, June 5. (To the Marquis of Huntly):—Bounties are high here and the devil to pay with the Fencibles. I can hardly find a man to attest, let alone justice from the Justices of the Peace in the country. However, I have determined to yield to none of them. . . . My propperty has dissatisfied me very much by all the young men keeping back, but I would feign hope they will still come forward, as I have thro' some of tacksmen let them know my mind. But at the Thurso market and the King's birthday Lady M[adeline] and I have done a little. . . . I gave a hogshead of porter yesterday, and the Fencibles seem to be astonished we are doing so well.

June 19, 1794. (To Menzies):—Tell Huntly my estate, like all others here, is much drained. I tryed to turn them out, but the young men ran to the hills. This happen'd to Lord Caithness and Sir John [Sinclair] likewise here: so it is pretty well what we have done. I regret much not having been sooner in the county.

Fort George, June 22, 1794. (To Menzies):—It gives Lady Madelina and I great pleasure to think the Marquis has been so successful. We arrived here at 12 o'clock at night the night before last, having made the most wonderful good passage from Caithness in a fishing boat ever known. We catched a good wind, and were in Caithness at Mr.

Sinclair's at half past three in the afternoon and here at 12 at night, which saved us four cursed tedious days' journeys. My success in Caithness was not quite up to my expectations as my farms did not turn out men: but I have excellent recruits. There is here 11 capitals [men] —one adjudged to me which I have advertised as a deserter in Caithness, having absconded: and one given against me by two justices, which, I am certain by the steps I have taken, is mine. . . . I had a dreadful hard drinking campaign, but am in perfect health notwithstanding. Tho' I have few men, I have the satisfaction to think *my friend*, Sir John Sinclair, did not get a man to the Fencibles from the day I entered the county till I left it. It is quite drained. If I had gone in two months ago, I was credably assured Sir John would have been puzled to get one man. The Fencibles were offering money to their officers to get off to go with Lady Madelina.

Sir Robert died at Fort George on August 4, 1795, and on August 16 Major Baillie wrote to Menzies (*Ibid.*):—

I have to request that you may be so good as to acquaint the Duchess of Gordon, with my most respectful compliments, that I have done the utmost in my power to arrange for Sir Robert's recruiting business with the Caithness legion to the best advantage. All those that could be proved are to be transferred to the Marquis's regiment (5 in number).

The regiment was at last completed, and the recruits began to march on Aberdeen, which has been selected as the rendezvous, and still remains the depot of the regiment. A curious glimpse of the clannishness of some of the sections is borne out by the fact that when the Lochaber men started out for Gordon Castle on or about June 9, 1794, Baillie Cameron, of Gordonsburgh, accompanied them part of the way. He wrote on June 9 (*Ibid.*):—

They have to a man petitioned not to be sent with Captain Cochrane's countrymen, and indeed refused to go with them, as they are afraid they would get them a bad character by the road, and I have agreed to their request, in hopes that Lord Huntly will have no quarrell with them on that account. I had a compleat whisky meeting at Highbridge on Saturday with Mr. Ross and all his neighbours. I am sorry to say that I got no attestations filled up there, but returned loaded with promises to be implemented at the market. What it may produce I know not.

Sergeant David Nicol, who enlisted at Edinburgh, March 12, 1794, and who left a very interesting (manuscript) diary of his experiences,

E2

tells us that every man on joining at Aberdeen passed General Munro separately, running 50 paces. The recruits found lodgings at from two shillings to half a crown a week. Oatmeal was tenpence a peck, and beef twopence a pound. Butter could be had at fourpence to fivepence a pound (of 28 ozs.), and the best Hollands gin cost twopence a gill.

In the end all difficulties were overcome, and the Marquis, or, rather, his helpers and servers, who lacked his easy-going philosophy, had the satisfaction of seeing the rival 109th obliterated within two years, by being drafted into other regiments. The Gordons were embodied, 750 strong, at Aberdeen on June 24, 1794, a red letter day in the military history of the north, for it was the date chosen for laying the foundation stone of the barracks on the Castle Hill, which remains to this day the depot of the regiment and still shelters the precious Description Register giving full particulars of the first men to enter the Gordons. The Marquis, attended by the Brethren of seven Lodges of Freemasons, the Magistrates, and everybody who was anybody, marched to the spot from Lodge Walk by Marischal Street, the Quay, and " up the hill by the new road," returning to the New Inn by North Street, Queen Street and Broad Street. The *Aberdeen Journal* of the day tells us that :—

On this occasion there was the greatest concourse of people that has ever been known in this city. Wherever the procession passed all the windows, balconies, and streets were crowded ; but, notwithstanding the vast multitude, and the hazardous situation of the Castlehill and the tops of the adjoining houses to which many were led by their curiosity, the whole concluded without the smallest accident happening to any person.

The regiment was reviewed next day by General Sir Hector Munro, who had been an officer in the Duke's first regiment thirty-five years previously, and set out at once for Fort George, where on July 8 and 9, Nicol tells us that on the march to the Fort the regiment halted at Old Meldrum, when Lord Kintore gave the men cold punch and bread and cheese. Turriff was passed on March 23, Banff on March 25, Cullen on March 26, and Elgin on March 27. At Fochabers the Duke entertained the men at the principal inn, and the officers at the Castle. At Nairn they were met by the Governor of Fort George, Sir Robert Sinclair, who had helped to raise them, "Lord Huntly and his sister " [mother ?] were present, she being dressed in a regimental jacket and bonnet. On July

10, the regiment embarked with the second battalion of the 78th Regiment and the Inverness-shire Highlanders for Southampton, which was reached on August 16. The *Journal* of the period, in recording the embarkation, tells this delicious story :—

The men went on board in the highest spirits. The Marquis of Huntly, who may boast of one of the finest bodies of men in the service, embarked with them. He showed an alacrity of service by jumping into the first boat, and so great was the eagerness of his men to follow their noble commander, that the boat had nearly been overset ; and the air resounded with cheers from those left on the beach until his lordship was on board the transport. Every man appeared to be perfectly sober, an Irish gentleman excepted [there were 51 Irishmen in the regiment], who swore by J—— that though he was half-seas over already, he would not quit the land without a quid of tobacco ! [Nicol says twelve Irishmen were absent at the embarkation, but "mostly joined after."]

The transports set sail on July 18, and passed Aberdeen, which must have been on the outlook for them, on the evening of July 21. Nicol says the men were very angry on seeing windmills on the Norfolk coast working on Sunday! The regiment was not to set foot again in Scotland for eight years.

It seems (from the Order Book of 1794) that when stationed at Hilsea Barracks the regiment was alarmed by a " misunderstanding," and twenty guineas were offered for the discovery of the person who had created it. Sergeant Nicol states that the story was that Lord Huntly had sold the regiment to the East India Company, and the men, who believed the gossip, proposed among themselves to march back to Scotland.

As a matter of fact it was on European service that the regiment began its career, sailing from Southampton on September 5 for Gibraltar, which was reached on September 26. We get a glimpse of the life on the Rock from a letter written from Gibraltar on November 21, 1794, by Gordon in Coynachie, who was not an easy man to please (*Gordon Castle Papers*) :—

There cannot be a worse place for a paymaster. He cannot get a farthing but the greatest risk of loosing by the meanness the troops are kept and the damn'd coin, that is perhaps not two days of the same value. Everything is dear but wine, which the 100th Regiment takes a good spell of sometimes.

From Gibraltar the regiment went to Corsica, June 11, 1795. The Marquis sailed for England on December 20, 1795, but when three days out his ship was captured by a French privateer, and he did not reach England till September, 1796. This was the month in which the regiment left Corsica, and by a remarkable coincidence one of the four transports, the " Granby," in which it sailed to Gibraltar was captured by a Spanish vessel, with two staff officers, three sergeants and 48 rank and file. This affair, however, was counterbalanced a little later by an adventure recorded in a memorial which Alexander Phimister sent to the Marquis of Huntly on October 17, 1797 (*Ibid.*):—

In the year 1794 your petitioner inlisted in your lordship's regiment. Upon June 21, 1796, your petitioner had the misfortune to lose his eyesight, and on September 1, 1796, he was ordered for Giberalter [from Corsica], where I was ordered for England. And on the passage coming to England wee fell in with a Spanish brig, and captured her by Captain Puget; and when we come to England she was estimate at £15,000 stg. All our names was inserted in the prize list, which my name was along with the others aboard. But I have gott none of the money as yeat. May it therefore please your lordship to take the above premesses into your consideration, and see if you'l be pleased to do for your petitioner so as he may have his proportionable part of the prize money.

During its sojourn in Gibraltar, the regiment got alarmed at the prospect of being "drafted"—that is to say, distributed among other corps; and only the influence of the Marquis averted that catastrophe. Henry Dundas wrote on the point to Lord Huntly from Wimbledon, December 3, 1796 (*Scottish Review*, xvii., 130):—

Dear Huntly,—I should have wrote to you sooner on the subject of this letter, but different interruptions have prevented me. You know that your regiment is considerably beyond the line of those which are kept up on the limited establishment. The latest number not drafted is the 90th, and the only exemptions is your regiment and one at the Cape, which we could not spare from that quarter at present. Your Regiment will still be continued undrafted, and at Gibraltar till the Peace; but you will recollect that the only ostensible ground of doing so is that it is a Regiment raised by your family, which would therefore be hard to draft, as the same exertions which raised it were able to keep it at its full compliment [sic]. In consequence of a conversation I had with the Duke of York, I think it right to mention these particulars to you with a view that you will omit no exertions on your own bottom to keep your Regiment complete to its full establishment. I need not tell you that in a Regiment circumstanced as yours is, it is impossible to give to it any of the men levied under the Act of Parliament. It being, however, a material part of the garrison of Gibraltar, it is very essential that you should exert yourself both for your credit and to prevent your Regiment from being drafted, and, allow me to add, to prevent any reflections being cast on those who, it may be said, ought to have drafted yours at the same time they did the others below the number 90.

The Marquis followed this advice, for the next document bearing on this subject is an "advertisement" by order of the Marquis of Huntly, which, according to a certificate appended to it, was read at the kirk doors of Kingussie and Advie on Sunday, January 22, 1797. It ran (*Scottish Review*, xvii., 130-1):—

His Lordship, being anxious to have a few young handsome fellows to complete his Regiment, entreats and expects the assistance of his friends in Badenoch. He can assure such young men as are willing to go along with him that the Regiment is *not* to be drafted during the war, and that they may depend on every attention from him while they continue in service; and that on their return to the country they and their relations will have preference upon equal terms, from the Duke of Gordon for such farms on his estate as they are inclined to settle upon. His Lord-ship will be found at Aviemore during the whole of the day on Monday.

How his friends supported Huntly on this occasion, and what were the inducements offered to recruits is set forth in a letter which Cluny Macpherson wrote to Todd from Cluny on February 22, 1797 (*Scottish Review*, xvii., 131):—

My namesake, Thomas Macpherson, the refractory fellow in Ballgown, has at last come to his senses, and brought his son Malcolm here this morning, a volunteer for the Marquis's Regiment. His terms are as moderate as could be expected (and I have promised him they should be granted), as he only asks what Lord Huntly offers to every other person, vizt., a half aughteen part of land (free of services) where he at present resides, or in the place of Gorstial, with as much land contiguous to it as will make up an half aughteen part; the latter of the two he much prefers, and I think by far the most eligible situation for him, as our friend Mr. Grant has already two pensioners saddled upon him, and in my opinion it would be a hardship to burden him with any more. I shall accommodate his eldest son with an half aughteen part at Gaskinloan, near the farm which his father wishes to get. I need not mention that the place of Gorstial and Bloragiebeg is part of the farm of Delchullie, at present occupied by subtenants, of which Mr. Mitchell is Manager, as factor for Parson Robert's son; and I make no doubt

that he will readily provide for Thomas Macpherson on your applying
to him, for he is a very good tenant, although he happened to forget
himself on the present occasion.

With respect to bounty money, the father leaves that matter totally
to his Lordship. I mentioned to Lord Huntly at Gordonhall that, as
the boy was young and weak, I wished his Lordship to take him into
his own service ; but, as he had no way for him at the time, he promised
to write to your son to employ him or to get one of his brother officers
to take him as a servant. I must therefore, my good Sir, beg your
attention to this matter, and procure a proper letter for the boy. His
father requested of me to say that he hoped you would have the goodness
to antedate his attestation, and as the boy attends school, he hopes Lord
Huntly will indulge him with remaining in the country as long as any
of his other recruits.

If the Marquis is at the Castle, pray make my best respects to him,
and tell him that I have not forgot my toast when we were all so tipsy
at Pitmain, and can with truth assure you that few of his Lordship's
friends has a higher esteem for Gillidow Glenamore than your humble
servant.

The rumour that the regiment was to be drafted was, of course,
fatal to recruiting ; and Todd had to contradict it in emphatic terms.
Writing to Baillie Cameron from Fochabers, February 11, 1797, he
said (*Scottish Review*, xvii., 130-1) :—

The story of Lord Huntly's regiment being drafted into [the] 42nd,
is an infamous falsehood, and you'll see it contradicted in all the papers
by authority. Some of his Lordship's rivals in the recruiting line have
thought such a tale might be of service to them, but I can assure you that
Lord Huntly has the most positive assurance from the highest authority
that his regiment shall not be drafted during the war.

The regiment arrived in England again on May 15, 1798, and was
at once sent to Dublin. During its stay in Ireland it became immensely
popular, not only with the people but with other troops. In January,
1800, a memorial was presented to the Marquis Cornwallis, Lord-Lieutenant of Ireland, from the Protestant non-commissioned officers and
men of the Glengarry Regiment to the number of 300, offering to serve
the King as "a distinct battalion or as a battalion with any other
regiment in any way that may be conducive to the service in any part of
the British Dominions (East and West Indies excepted), and the only
reward we ask for so doing is that we will be commanded by our late
Lieutenant-Colonel, Charles Maclean, etc." M'Lean and the officers,

writing from Nenagh, January 15, 1800, expressed to the Marquis of
Huntly the wish to be attached to his regiment in the event of the
Government accepting their new services, and asking him to apply to the
Duke of York and to Cornwallis for permission   Huntly replied on
January 29 from Gordon Castle accepting the offer gladly so far as he
was concerned   The Glengarry Fencibles were reduced in 1802

On April 2, 1800, four privates of the North Lowland Fencibles
—William Anderson, John Thomson, Malcolm M'Lean and James
Angus; all belonging to Huntly—wrote from Downpatrick to the Marquis
that they wished to join the line —

> We have volunteered our services the second time in order to be
> under your lordship's command, but we have been taken no notice of
> We therefore hope your lordship will be so good as to do all in your
> power for us, as we have been so bold as to write to H R H the Duke
> of York concerning your lordship's regiment   My lord, we think it very
> hard to see our native country in such danger from foreign arms, and
> so many young lads only waiting the favourable opportunity to serve
> His Majesty when the greatest danger appears, only with the choice of
> your regiment   We have had the offer of a volunteer bounty for 12 or
> 14 guineas to be taken as Riflemen agreeable to the Duke of York's
> orders   in consequence of which, there is about 120 turned out, and if
> there was any encouragement given by our officers, the strength and pick
> of our regiment would follow the example of their comrades   As we are
> all Scotchmen, we would wish to be distinguished as such

One can thoroughly understand the point of the petition, for the
Marquis was personally very popular   Grant Stewart tells a story in
illustration of this.—

> Among the candidates who pleaded for a commission [in 1794] was
> a young man, who, as far as his face was concerned, was not recom-
> mended by their Graces, being dark and swarthy, and much disfigured
> by the smallpox   The Marquis being particular as to the personal
> appearance of his officers, the candidate was humourously told of his
> disqualifications , but, nothing daunted by the rebuff, he was determined
> to accompany the Gordon Highlanders as a volunteer   One day as the
> Marquis was making an inspection of the regiment in line, his sharp eye
> rested on a figure dressed in the Highland garb, smart bonnet, and staff
> in hand, who took his place at the end of the line   The inspection being
> over, his lordship sent for the volunteer, and a conversation to the
> following effect, as we are told on good authority, took place between
> his lordship and his follower   "Well, Grant, pray what have you come

here for?"　"Just to be a soldier, my lord," answered the volunteer. "Oh, don't you know that you are too ugly for a soldier?" said his lordship. "Maybe I am, my lord, but perhaps I may be of use in frightening the French" "Well, well, poor fellow," said the Marquis, "as you are determined to smell gunpowder, you must be humoured in your wish." The ready mother wit displayed by the volunteer in his interview with the Marquis so pleased his lordship, that he soon became a commissioned officer and favourite of his lordship, who found much amusement in his strong good sense and caustic vein of humour.

The Marquis seems also to have looked after promising privates, for there is a receipt at Gordon Castle, dated September 7, 1798, for the school fees (seven shillings) which he paid to Mr. Lorimer for Duncan Macdonald, a private of the regiment. An illustration of the popularity of the Gordon family appears in an (undated) memorial which was sent by George Catto, "now under sentence of seven years' transportation on board the 'Prudentia,' hulk, at Woolwich," to the Duke of Gordon, as follows (*Gordon Castle Papers*):—

Your Grace's unfortunate petitioner is a native of Rhynie. When young in life, he took a shop in the town of Huntly, where he continued a leather merchant until the beginning of the French war. Having drawn large sums at the office of Mr. George Davidson on a tanner in Dundee, he became bankrupt, and the drafts in course came back on him. The drawer made him fail in business and come into this nation. He lived one year with a Scotch drover at Woodford in Essex, after which he engaged himself into His Majesty's Royal Laboratory, Woolwich, where he continued until the day he came by the misfortune he is here for, which was for driving away three Scotch heifers off Epping Forest. He was tried at Chelmsford gaol the 17th day of July, 1795, and cast for death before Alexander M'Donald, Lord Chief Baron: but by the letters from His Majesty's foreman at the works at Woolwich, I was respited for seven years' transportation. He had a letter dated 3rd of May from your Grace's factor at Cocklarachy, assuring him that he had wrote to London to her Grace to endeavour to get him a conditional pardon to serve his Majesty in Army or Navy, which letter he sent accompanied by a petition to her Grace the 21st day of May. Your Grace's petitioner most humbly intreats of you to take this unhappy situation under your eye, so that by your great interest he may be once more released from the chains of bondage and slavery and be enabled to regain the character he has lost, by standing in defence of his most Gracious Sovereign and Country; and then shall have reason to bless you till the last moment of his breath.

The regiment received its baptism of fire in Holland, losing heavily between Bergen and Egmont-op-Zee on October 2, 1799 Colonel Greenhill Gardyne has gone elaborately into this episode in the Walcheren expedition, which the Duchess with a sound historic sense afterwards described as " that fatal crusade " (*Add MSS* 37282, f 123) The figures in the return as preserved at Gordon Castle differ, however, from those in *The Life of the Regiment* (1, 72-75) —

Company	Killed	Wounded	Missing
Colonel's .	2	5	
Lieutenant-Colonel's .	8	8	10
Major's .	7	21	
Captain Cameron's	8	18	
Captain Ramsay's	15	20	12
Captain Paton's	7	16	
Captain Gordon's .	10	20	7
Captain M'Lean's	10	20	1
Captain M'Donald's .	5	16	3
Captain Grant's .	4	13	
	76	157	33

Gordon M'Hardy, an Ensign who was killed, was the son of the late John M'Hardy and his wife Mary M'Donell, residing at Kingussie. She had been left with no money and six children, and the Marquis of Huntly had taken her eldest boy as a cadet In December, 1799, she sent a petition to the Marquis asking for help Huntly himself was rather severely wounded, and the bullet was not extracted till seven years afterwards. The *Aberdeen Journal* of April 16, 1806, records the circumstances —

On Tuesday, the 8th inst , the Marquis of Huntly had a considerable attack of fever, accompanied with severe pain, in that part of his back, · where suspicion lay, that an extraneous body was lodged. This hourly increased, and a considerable fluctuating tumour made its appearance On pressure, a hard substance was felt, which pointed out the necessity of its removal Accordingly, in the forenoon of Friday, the 10th, a simple incision was made into the tumour, and along with fully three ounces of purulent matter, a broken piece of leaden bullet was discharged, ragged in its surface, and pointed at one end, about the size of a small raisin flattened His Lordship bore the operation with his well known fortitude ; and it must be very pleasing to all ranks of people to know that this noble gallant officer, who has so long suffered violent attacks of pain from having bled in his country's cause, has now every prospect of a complete recovery; but with a heart still ardent to expose himself again to danger when his services are required. Let Britain have confidence when she has such sons.

By April 23, Huntly had so far recovered as to be able to "take an airing in his carriage."

The regiment was not long idle, for it sailed for the East on August 30, 1800, touching at Malta (December 1—January 2 or 3) on the way. While here, Coynachie Gordon sent a letter to the Marquis on December 18 (*Gordon Castle Papers*):—

I wrote your lordship from Tetuan Bay, respecting an exchange on half pay 'twixt Major Honyman and me. He was very anxious to know if it could be accomplished. It is by no means of being tired of the army, affraid of service or climate that I would wish it, but merely from the situation of my family. However, if your lordship could procure an exchange with any person that would pay the difference, but without making any stipulations, I authorise your lordship to make any agreement you think eligible. I would give a 100 guineas that Honyman could be brought in for it. There can be no reason for refusing him, but being older in the army than Napier. I confess he is young, but Colonell Erskine puts it on the footing that he had pledged himself to the captains that he would never allow it: which you must see is a very lame excuse, as it does not interfere with their promotion in any degree, and I'm certain it is not for the regard for myself or service that he did not part with me. It is impossible to sell out on account of Captain Cameron, and I have refused to do it for various reasons. The utmost request I have to ask your lordship in case of accidents is to get the pension and allowance from Government settled on my wife and family. . . . [Malta] would be as safe [as] to be taking a wee drapy of Miss Mellis's bottle at Strabogy.

Almost the only other document of interest at Gordon Castle after this date is another letter written to Menzies by Coynachie, now a Major, from Colchester, August 3, 1804:—

We expect the French over every day. I don't know if you have any fears or dread of them in Scotland. I wish to God we had peace on some terms, or other. I am perfectly tired of the service, and what makes it so disgusting to one who has served so long as I have done and purchased everything is, altho' Col. Robertson is to be placed on half pay, I find that I will not succeed to the promotion. I sent a memorial to the Duke of York to that effect but received an answer from his R.H. secretary, saying that Col. Robertson would be replaced by one from the half pay. I wish the Marquis would stir them up about it. I would take your advice and sell out altogether, but it is an improper time to ask it just now when the enemy is expected, and were you in my situation you would think it extremely hard to sell for the regulation, and that I would not get at present. I do not believe I could sell the company. The 2nd battalion is so much against the sale of commissions. If I could obtain leave to sell and name a successor, I could get just 4,000 guineas for the majority. Do you think if this campaign was over, would the Duke give his interest along with the Marquis of Huntly to get me leave to sell without restriction? If I do not quit the service, I must unavoidably give up farming. Its a perfect drudgery on Mrs. Gordon and the same time a loosing bargain.

The career of the regiment in war belongs to the history of the Nation (and is dealt with in a bibliography set forth at the end of the present volume) rather than of the Family. The career of the first two Battalions may be summarised in the following list of the principal campaigns and battles in which they have been engaged, the " honours " on the colours being marked with an asterisk, while the figures show the Battalion concerned. This list (from John S. Farmer's *Regimental Records*, p. 197) may be supplemented easily by the student from Captain C. B. Norman's *Battle Honours of the British Army* (1911):—

1761 - -	Belle Isle		1813 - -	Maya
1762 - -	Portugal		*1813 - -	Pyrenees (2)
1778-83 -	America		*1813 - -	Nive (2)
*1791-1806	India (1)		1814 - -	Gâve
1792 - -	Seringapatam		*1814 - -	Orthes (2)
1795-97 -	Malabar and Goa		1815 - -	Quatre Bras
*1799 - -	Mysore (1)		*1815 - -	Waterloo (2)
1799 - -	Sedaseer		1815 - -	Netherlands
*1799 - -	Seringapatam (1)		*1835 - -	South Africa (1)
1799 - -	Helder		1857-58 -	Indian Mutiny
1799 - -	Crabbendam		*1857 - -	Delhi (1)
1799 - -	Bergen		1857 - -	Bulundshuhur
*1799 - -	Egmont-op-Zee (2)		1857 - -	Agra
1799 - -	Quiberon		1857 - -	Cawnpore
1800 - -	Ferrol		*1858 - -	Lucknow (1)
*1801 - -	Mandora (2)		*1878-80 -	Afghanistan (2)
*1801 - -	Egypt (2)		*1879 - -	Charasiah (2)
1801 - -	Alexandria		*1879 - -	Kabool (2)
1803 - -	Gujerat		*1880 - -	Kandahar (2)
1804 - -	Malwa		1881 - -	Transvaal
1805 - -	Bhurtpore		*1882-84 -	Egypt (1)
1807 - -	Copenhagen		*1882 - -	Tel-el-Kebir (1)
1808-14 -	Peninsula (2)		*1884-85 -	Nile (1)
*1809 - -	Corunna (2)		1884 - -	El Teb
1809 - -	Flushing		1884 - -	Tamai
*1811 - -	Fuentes d'Onor (2)		*1895 - -	Chitral
1811 - -	Arroyo dos Molinos		*1897-98 -	Tirah
*1812 - -	Almaraz (2)		1899-1902	South Africa
*1813 - -	Vittoria (2)		1914 - -	" The Great War "

It must not be forgotten that the Gordon Highlanders still bear the crest of the house which raised them—a striking, if rare, reminder of feudal times, when all our army was equipped by the great landlords, as a sort of rent for the broad acres which the King entrusted to their keeping.

THE MUSTER ROLL.

The Gordon Highlanders are peculiarly fortunate in possessing as they do at Castlehill Barracks an elaborate register (" Description Book ") of all the first recruits to the regiment in 1794. Indeed, the preservation of this invaluable document is little short of a miracle. An absurd custom for long committed to regiments the keeping of their records— the absurdity resulting from the fundamental fact that the soldier's business is destruction and not preservation; that his life is essentially nomadic. Yet regiments were not wholly to blame, for the War Office itself has been a great sinner. Thus in 1825 an Order was issued that certain documents were to be destroyed. What these documents were I cannot discover. The Horse Guards in 1824 looked with grave displeasure on any destruction of records by officers of regiments, but it is clear that such destruction took place. The attitude of official indifference was not attained till a much later date. However that may be, the sad fact remains that Colonel John MacDonald, who commanded the regiment 1828-46 (his grand-uncle commanded it at Waterloo, and an uncle was killed in the Pyrenees), states in a memorandum (*Life of a Regiment*, ii., 1) that the original books " had been considered as waste paper "— probably under this War Office Order of 1825—but he " afterwards saved such as remained." They lay for years at his house, Dunalastair, in Rannoch, until his son, General Alastair McIan MacDonald, sold that fine estate, and the books were then taken to his London house in Park Lane. He lent them to Lieutenant-Colonel Gardyne for the purpose of writing *The Life of a Regiment*. When he was taken ill, his sisters, at the suggestion of Lieutenant-Colonel Gardyne, allowed them to go back to the regiment, and they are now in admirable condition, together with other records (detailed in the bibliography at the end of the present work). It is, therefore, to Lieutenant-Colonel Gardyne that we are indebted for the preservation of the Description Book of 1794. Those for the years 1795-1817 have vanished, but the series at the Public Record Office begins at 1818 (*W.O.* 25 ; 529).

The transcript printed here was made in October, 1907, by Mr. John Milne, LL.D., to whom a debt of gratitude is due by military students for his laborious work.   It was intended to be presented as a supplement to "Gordons under Arms," issued by the New Spalding Club.   That book, however, proved too large for the inclusion of the register.

The Description Book is a large folio, in an excellent state of preservation at Castlehill Barracks, and is lettered "Description Book 92nd Reg., No. 1."   It contains the roll as dated June 25, 1794, and gives (1) the recruit's name; (2) the date of his attestation; (3) his age; (4) his height; (5) the colour of his eyes and complexion; (6) his birthplace; (7) his trade; (8) his fate.   The register is arranged alphabetically, as conditioned by the date of attestation.   Thus in the "A's," James Allardice comes first because he enlisted on March 5; while James Allan comes last because he enlisted in June.   For the sake of easy reference I have rearranged this (omitting the colour of the eyes entry) on strict alphabetical lines.   The register contains several entries relating to enlistments in 1795 and subsequent years.   One finds that 879 men 'listed in 1794, the rate of progress being:—

Feb.	March.	April.	May.	June.	July and Dec.
33	204	249	269	87	37 men

Unfortunately, details of the non-commissioned officers are not given, but many of the men may be recognised in the roll of privates.

The first fact of interest is the average height of the men in the 1794 Description Book.   For the following calculations I am indebted to Mr. Duff MacWilliam, the painstaking historian of the Black Watch. Of the 940 names of privates on the roll, the heights of 914 are stated and work out at an average of 5 ft. 5.51088 ins., approximately 5 ft. 5½ ins.   In 1911, the average height of recruits in the British Army was 5 ft. 6.2 ins., and that of the period 1901-1910 was 5 ft. 6.1 ins.   Only six men in 1794 were six feet or over, whereas in January, 1890, eight men of a total of 622 in the second battalion were 6 ft. and over (*Life of a Regiment*, ii., 379), and nine of the 841 men of the first battalion were six feet and upwards (*Ibid.*, ii., 321).   The six men of 1794 who were six feet and upwards were:—

William Black, Kintore	-	-	Sawyer	-	6 ft.
Robert Ferguson, Cumbernauld	-		Weaver	-	6 ft.
Alexander M'Gregor, Laggan	-		Soldier	-	6 ft.
George Shanks, Glasgow	-	-	Shoemaker	-	6 ft.

George Smith, Kilmarnock   -   Weaver   -   6 ft. 2 in.
David Wood, Dyke (Moray)   -   Labourer   -   6 ft. 4 in.

Several little boys joined the Regiment, chiefly as drummers :—

		Age.
4 ft.	—Duncan M'Millan	11
4 ft. 1 in.	—Robert Watt, Banff - - -	9
4 ft. 7 in.	—William Allardice, Aberdeen - -	13
4 ft. 7½ in.	—Gordon M'Intyre, Edinburgh - -	13
4 ft. 8 in.	—Duncan M'Donald, Aberdeen - -	12
4 ft. 9 in.	—William Dowlin, Falmouth - - -	12
4 ft. 9 in.	—Allan M'Pherson, Argyll - - -	12
4 ft. 10 in.	—David Ross, Inverness - - -	12
4 ft. 10 in.	—Angus Sutherland, Sutherland - -	13
4 ft. 10 in.	—Thomas Wilson, Stirling - - -	12
4 ft. 10 in.	—Peter Wright, Glasgow - - -	14
4 ft. 10½ in.	—John M'Kenzie, Cromarty - - -	13
4 ft. 11 in.	—Angus Henderson, Kilmally - -	15
4 ft. 11 in.	—Colin M'Donald, Petty - - -	12
4 ft. 11 in.	—John M'Kay, Reay - - -	12

Some of the individual averages are interesting, as follows :—

442 Labourers - - - - - -	5 ft. 5·23 in.
243 " Macs " - - - - -	5 ft. 5·1 in.
35 Macphersons - - - -	5 ft. 5·714 in.
34 Camerons - - - - - -	5 ft. 4·68 in.

The men (the origins of 894 are stated) hailed from every county in Scotland except three, Inverness contributing the greatest number, namely 240, and Aberdeen coming next with 124. For the purposes of calculation, Cairnie, Gartly, Glass and the Cabrach are assigned to Aberdeenshire, and Bellie and Boharm to Banffshire ; Kirkmichael is treated as Banffshire, Cromdale as Elginshire, and Abernethy as Inverness-shire. The average height worked out in counties is not of great interest because we have not the same number of men in each county to deal with, but it may be given :—

County, etc.	No. of Men.	Average Height. Ft.	In.	County, etc.	No. of Men.	Average Height. Ft.	In.
Aberdeen - -	124	5	5·0827	Kinross - -	1	5	8·5000
Argyle - - -	31	5	6·0645	Lanark - - -	62	5	5·8105
Ayr - - -	17	5	6·7206	Linlithgow - -	7	5	6·4286
Banff - -	82	5	5·8598	Nairn - -	6	5	2·5417
Bute - -	1	5	8	Orkney - -	1	5	7·5000
Caithness -	25	5	4·8800	Peebles - -	3	5	7·3333
Clackmannan -	15	5	5·9166	Perth - -	22	5	6·1250
Dumbarton -	5	5	8·8500	Renfrew - -	25	5	6·4400
Dumfries -	3	5	8·2500	Ross and Cromarty	23	5	3·9130
Edinburgh -	33	5	4·7803	Stirling - -	38	5	5·5724
Elgin - -	29	5	5·5862	Sutherland -	13	5	4·0961
Fife - -	9	5	6·9167	Wigtown - -	2	5	6·2500
Forfar - -	5	5	5·2000	England - -	9	5	5·7222
Haddington -	6	5	6·6666	Ireland - -	51	5	6·1324
Inverness -	240	5	5·2031	Wales - -	2	5	7·2500
Kincardine -	4	5	7·5000	Germany -	1		?

There are 361 different surnames in the Roll, 61 of which are prefixed by "Mac-." The more important are as follows :—

39 Macdonald	13 Macmillan	8 Campbell
4 Macdonell	13 Robertson	8 Ferguson
35 Macpherson	12 Mackenzie	8 Grant
34 Cameron	12 Maclean	8 Mackinnon
18 Stuart	12 Ross	7 Anderson
16 Gordon	12 Smith	7 Forbes
15 Fraser	12 Thomson	7 Macgregor
15 Mackay	11 Mackintosh	7 Maclellan

The trades of 913 are given, showing that 442, almost one-half of the men, were unskilled artisans, being vaguely described as "Labourers." There was a great dearth of trades in the Highlands, most of the artisans belonging to the southern part of the country. The specified avocations (186 men were weavers) may be roughly classified thus :—

Agriculture -	13	Dress -	93	Slates -	6
Books -	4	Food -	15	Stones -	11
Building -	29	Leather -	32	Textile	215
Coals -	10	Metals -	33	Tobacco	1
Combs -	4	Pottery -	3	Wood	27

The individual occupations were as follows :—

Apothecary -	1	Fisher -	1	Printer -	1
Armourer -	1	Flaxdresser -	1	Rope spinners -	2
Bakers -	3	Founder -	1	Saddler -	1
Barbers -	6	Gamekeeper -	1	Sailor -	1
Blacksmiths -	17	Gardeners -	8	Sawyers -	5
Bleacher -	1	Glass-blower -	1	Servants -	7
Bonnetmaker -	1	Goldsmith -	1	Sheriff officer -	1
Bookbinder -	1	Hat makers -	2	Shoemakers -	31
Braziers -	2	Hatters -	2	Skinner -	1
Butchers -	5	Hosiers -	2	Slaters -	6
Cabinetmaker -	1	Labourers -	442	Soldier -	1
Carpenters -	5	Maltster -	1	Spinner -	1
Carter -	1	Masons -	11	Spoonmakers -	2
Cattle dealer -	1	Merchants -	2	Staymaker -	1
Chaise driver -	1	Millers -	2	Stockingmakers -	6
Chapman -	1	Millwright -	1	Tailors -	42
China mender -	1	"Miln driver" -	1	Thread manufacturer	1
Clerk -	1	"Minder" -	1	Thread twiners -	3
Coal miners -	8	Musicians -	2	Tobaccospinner -	1
Combmakers -	2	Nailers -	5	Turner -	1
Confectioners -	2	Nailsmiths -	3	"Twist-miller" -	1
Coppersmith -	1	"Padler" -	1	Waiter [tide?] -	1
Coppersmith printer	1	Paper maker -	1	Weaver ("Inkle") -	1
Cork cutter -	1	Pensioner -	1	Weavers -	185
Cotton spinners -	4	Pipe maker -	1	Wheelwright -	1
Cutler -	1	Piper -	1	Wine cooper -	1
Excise-officer -	1	Plasterer -	1	Wool combers -	20
Farmers -	4	Potters -	2	Wrights -	13

The average age of the 1794 recruits was 23, the youngest being a boy of nine (Robert Watt, Banff), and the oldest, Robert Clauron, a Haddington man, 47, serving till he was 52.

Curiously enough a complete list of all the first officers, with the dates of their commissions, has never been printed. The following list of officers is made up from a Succession Book at Castlehill Barracks and two Public Record documents (*W.O.* 25; 158, pp. 31-2; *W.O.* 25; 214). The first official announcement of the first officers is dated from the War Office, July 19, 1794, the commissions themselves being antedated:—

COMMANDING OFFICER.

George (Gordon), Marquis of Huntly (from Lieutenant-Colonel, 3rd Foot Guards), Lieutenant-Colonel Commanding, February 10, 1794; Colonel Commanding, May 3, 1796. Son of the 4th Duke of Gordon, born February 2, 1770; died s.p. May 28, 1836, when the Dukedom became extinct.

MAJORS.

Charles Erskine (from Captain, 41st Foot), February 10, 1794; Lieutenant-Colonel, May 1, 1795; died of wounds at Alexandria, March 13, 1801. Son of James Erskine of Cardross by Lady Christian Bruce, daughter of William, 8th Earl of Kincardine; had served in the 25th, 16th and 77th.

Donald Macdonald (from Captain, 18th), August 20, 1794; retired March 11, 1796. Laird of Boisdale.

CAPTAINS.

John Cameron (from Lieutenant, 93rd), February 13, 1794; Major, April 5, 1801; Lieutenant-Colonel, June 23, 1808. Son of Sir Ewen Cameron; born 1771; of Fassifern; killed at Quatre Bras, June 16, 1815 (Clerk's *Memorial*, 1858; Alexander Mackenzie's *History of the Camerons*, 284-368).

Alexander Gordon (from Lieutenant, 90th), May 29, 1794; Major, July 9, 1803, 14th Battalion of Reserve. Son of Alexander (Gordon), Lord Rockville; grandson of the 2nd Earl of Aberdeen; and nephew of Hon. William Gordon, who raised the 81st Regiment; killed at Talavera, July 28, 1809 (*Gordons under Arms*, No. 184).

Simon Macdonald (from Lieutenant, 81st), February 12, 1794; Major, May 1, 1796, retired January 16, 1799. Laird of Morar. He had served in the American War with Macdonald's Highlanders.

William Mackintosh (from Lieutenant, 88th), May 22, 1794; killed in Holland 1799. Of Aberarder. He had been in the Northern Fencibles for a time.

Alexander Napier (from Lieutenant, 7th Fusiliers), February 12,

1794, Major, March 12, 1796, *vice* Macdonald, Lieutenant-Colonel, April 5, 1801; killed at Corunna, January 16, 1809 Of Blackstone

Andrew Paton (from Lieutenant, 10th), February 15, 1794, joined 45th Regiment, September 1, 1804

Hon John Ramsay (from Lieutenant, 57th), February 14, 1794, wounded in Holland, 1799, and Egypt, 1801; went on half pay, 1804 Son of George, 8th Earl of Dalhousie, born 1775, died 1842; had six sons in the Services, including the 12th Earl of Dalhousie

CAPTAIN-LIEUTENANT

John Gordon, February 12, 1794 (from Lieutenant, 81st), Captain, June 20, 1797, Major, January 17, 1799, retired January 1, 1805, as Brevet Lieutenant-Colonel Son of John Gordon, in Auchmair, born 1751, farmed Coynachie, died 1827 (*Gordons under Arms*, No 909)

LIEUTENANTS

Thomas Forbes (from Ensign, 80th), August 6, 1794, killed at Toulouse as Lieutenant-Colonel of the 45th, April 10, 1814 Son of Rev George Forbes, minister of Leochel, afterwards of Strathdon, brother of Sir Charles Forbes, 1st Bart of Newe

George Hamilton Gordon (from Cornet, 6th Dragoons), Captain of Foot, January 27, 1795, died 1841, origin unknown (*Gordons under Arms*, No 574) Succeeded by William Gordon, July 1, 1795 (from Ensign, 133rd)

Peter Gordon (from Ensign, Independent Company), May 29, 1794, Captain, April 5, 1801 He belonged to Binhall, Huntly, and died at Colchester Barracks, April 22, 1806 He is entered in *Gordons under Arms* as "Patrick" (No 1,140)

Patrick Grant (from 2nd Lieutenant, 23rd), February 10, 1794, Major, June 23, 1808; retired November 25, 1812, died at Keith, 1817

Archibald Macdonell (from Ensign, 79th), February 11, 1794, became Lieutenant-Colonel of Veterans, died in Lochaber, 1813

John Maclean (from Ensign, 2nd battalion Royals, where he was only one day), May 1, 1794, fought in Egypt, Lieutenant-Colonel, 27th, 1808 Son of John Maclean, who belonged to the Achat, or Urquhart, group of the family His eldest brother was James, minister of Urquhart, and his sister Elizabeth married Rev John Gordon, minister of Speymouth, two of whose sons entered the Army (*Gordons under Arms* Nos 453-4, and 1,464) Maclean was made K C B, April 15, 1815, and died January 31, 1848 (Seneachie's *Account of the Clan MacLean*, 1838, pp 255, 256-8)

James Macleod (from Ensign, 2nd Royals), May 1, 1794

Evan Macpherson (from Ensign, 78th), September 12, 1794 He came from Ovie, Badenoch, and died in 1823 as Governor of Sheerness.

William Maxwell (from Ensign, Independent Company), August 20, 1794; joined the 23rd Dragoons by June 16, 1795.

Patrick Ross (from Ensign, Independent Company), May 13, 1794; joined 101st. Succeeded January 28, 1795, by William Erskine (from Lieutenant, 92nd).

Alexander Stewart (from Ensign, 79th), February 11, 1794; joined the 67th. Succeeded January 12, 1796, by Stephen Webb (from Lieutenant, 67th), who was succeeded, February 27, 1796, by Thomas Christopher Gardiner (from Ensign, 9th). Laird of Auchnacone; died in Appin, 1854.

ENSIGNS.

George Davidson, February 11, 1794; Lieutenant, June 16, 1795, *vice* Maxwell; rose to be Captain. He became Captain of the Huntly Volunteers, from half pay, February 18, 1804, and Major of the Strathbogie, Huntly and Drumblade Volunteers, May 26, 1804; joined the 42nd, July 28, 1807; killed at Quatre Bras, 1815.

Charles Dowle (from Northern Fencibles), February 10, 1794; killed in Egypt, 1801.

Alexander Fraser, February 13, 1794; killed in Holland 1799.

Edward Fullarton, February 17, 1794; Lieutenant, 101st, March 10, 1795, being succeeded by Alexander Macpherson; who was succeeded August 5, 1795, by John Macpherson.

Archibald Macdonell, February 12, 1794. He came from Garvabeg, Badenoch, and died in Canada.

James Mitchell, February 15, 1794, suggested by Todd; Major, March 30, 1809; Lieutenant-Colonel, June 13, 1815; retired September 1, 1819. He came from Auchindaul, Lochaber, and died in Lochaber 1847.

Maxwell Stuart, February 16, 1794; joined the 109th by March 10, 1795; succeeded March 10, 1795, by John Evatt, who joined the 81st, and was succeeded April 29, 1795, by James Forbes Macdonell.

William Todd, February 14, 1794. Son of Todd, the factor at Fochabers.

CHAPLAIN.

Rev. William Gordon, February 10, 1794; retired December 1796. Son of James Gordon in Laggan; minister of Urquhart, 1769-1810; died July 18, 1810 (*Gordons under Arms*, No. 1,415).

SURGEON.

William Findlay, from Hospital Mate, August 13, 1794; Apothecary to the Forces, April 4, 1800; died in Egypt, 1801.

ADJUTANT.

James Henderson (from Independent Company), February 10, 1794; Lieutenant, October 1, 1794. Nicol says he was "a very stern man."

QUARTERMASTER.

Peter Wilkie, February 10, 1794; died 1806. Lieutenant-Colonel Greenhill Gardyne says he died 1806, but there was a Peter Wilkie promoted Major, November 4, 1819, retiring September 24, 1823.

SERGEANTS.

(From Muster Roll, June 25-December 24, 1794, Castlehill Barracks.)

Alexander Cameron.
Dougald Cameron.
John Davie.
Alexander Dobbie.
Peter Ferguson.
George Gordon.
William Hay.
John Kennedy.
Angus McBain.
Alexander McGrigor.
Angus McIntosh.
John McIntosh.
Lachlan McIntosh.
Alexander McIntyre.
Duncan McKinlay.
James Macpherson.
James Martin.
John Mitchell.
John Reynolds.
James Ross.
William Sinclair.
Alexander Smith.
Alexander Stewart.
Donald Stewart.
George Still.
James Wilson.

Q.M.S. L. McPherson.

CORPORALS.

(From Muster Roll, June 25-December 24, 1794, Castlehill Barracks.)

James Allardice.
Alexander Anderson.
William Beedie.
Alexander Cameron.
John Cameron.
Andrew Campbell.
Duncan Dewar.
William Gordon, sen.
William Gordon, jun.
John Hendry.
John Lamond.
Donald McBarnet.
John McDonald.
Colin McInnes.
Lachlan McIntosh.
Kenneth McKenzie.
Hugh MacPherson.
Charles McVie.
John Miller.
Daniel Park.
John Robertson.
William Robertson.
John Sime.
John Sinclair.
Andrew Symmers.
John Taylor.
James Wood.
William Younger.

DRUMMERS.

(From Muster Roll, June 25-December 24, 1794, Castlehill Barracks.)

William Allardyce.
Alexander Bremner.
William Dove.
William Dowlin.
Alexander Forbes.
Thomas Fraser.
James Hadden.
Angus Henderson.
Duncan McDonald.
Gordon McIntyre.

John McKenzie.
John McKilligan.
Allan McPherson.
John Martin.
Ebenezer Monteith.
William Monteith.
David Ross.
Hugh Ross.
Thomas Wilson.
James Wright. Peter Wright.

PRIVATES.

Name.	Age.	Height.	Birthplace.	Trade.	Career.	Attest.
Abraham, William	28	5 ft. 7¾ in.	Annan	Labourer		May 22
Adam, David ..	35	5 ft. 8 in.	Stirling	Stocking maker	Dis. 24 Feb., 1799	April 1
Adam, James ..	30	5 ft. 7 in.	Paisley	Weaver	Dis. 20 May, 1800	April 18
Adams, George ..	33	5 ft. 9½ in.	Kirkliston	Labourer		May 6
Aitchison, Robert	37	5 ft. 7 in.	Use [Ewes], Dumfries	Sadler	Trans. 61st Reg., 28 Oct., 1794	March 27
Aitken, John ..	27	5 ft. 5½ in.	Kilbarchan	Weaver		May 21
Aitken, Robert ..	21	5 ft. 8¼ in.	Paisley	Weaver		April 3
Allan, James ..	18	5 ft. 4½ in.	....		Trans. 2nd Batt. 25 Nov.,1803	?
Allen, James ..	33	5 ft. 5 in.	Dunshachlan, Meath	Merchant	Dis. 27 May, 1802	June 10
Allen, Jonathan ..	18	5 ft. 2 in.	Huntly	Weaver	Enlisted by Lieut. Davidson	April 27
Allen, William ..	19	5 ft. 8 in.	Falkirk	Carter	Dis. 24 Feb., 1799	June 8
Allerdice, James ..	22	5 ft. 9¾ in.	Gamrie	Labourer	Enlisted by Lord Huntly; dis. 24 Feb., 1799	March 5
Allerdice, John ..	28	5 ft. 5 in.	Gartly	Weaver	Enlisted by Lord Huntly; trans. 2nd Batt. 25 Nov., 1803	March 29
Allerdice, William	13	4 ft. 7 in.	Aberdeen	Weaver	Enlisted by Lord Huntly; trans. 2nd Batt. 25 Nov., 1803	March 31
Allison, James ..	34	5 ft. 3¾ in.	Glasgow	Labourer	Dis. 4 May, 1802	March 20
Anderson, Alex. ..	29	5 ft. 4 in.	Aboyne	Wright	Dis. 4 May, 1802	March 7
Anderson, George ..	34	5 ft. 8 in.	Turriff	Weaver		March 12
Anderson, James ..	18	5 ft. 4 in.	Paisley	Weaver	Dis. 27 May, 1802	May 2
Anderson, James ..	19	5 ft. 3½ in.	Colston, Cromar	Weaver	Dead 4 Jan., 1799	May 7
Anderson, John ..	32	5 ft. 10¾ in.	Aghadowey, Londonderry	Cotton spinner	Dis. 8 June, 1796	May 27
Anderson, Wm. ..	18	5 ft. 7 in.	Larbert	Mason		April 1
Anderson, Wm. ..	19	5 ft. 11 in.			Trans. 2nd Batt. 25 Nov., 1803	?
Angus, James ..	19	5 ft. 8 in.	Mortly [Mortlach]	Labourer	Dead 27 Dec., 1799	May 20
Annand, William ..	15	5 ft. 3 in.	Bechelvail [Belhelvie]	Weaver	Dis. 24 Feb., 1799	April 4
Ardbuckle, John ..	34	5 ft. 11 in.	Cambuslang	Sawer	Dis. 10 June, 1795	April 1
Atinborough, Wm.	18	5 ft. 6½ in.	Dunbanon	Nailer		Nov. 1795
Baillie, Francis ..	34	5 ft. 4 in.	Doress, Inverness	Weaver	Dis. 9 June, 1797	May 10
Bain, Alexander ..	18	5 ft. 5 in.	Wick	Spoon-maker		April 12
Bain, William ..	35	5 ft. 4½ in.	Kippen, Stirling	Weaver		May 21
Balfour, James ..	25	5 ft. 9½ in.	Calduff, Donegal	Butcher	Trans. 61st Regt. 28 Oct., 1794	May 25
Banks, George ..	35	5 ft. 5 in.	Glasgow	Shoemaker	Enlisted by Lord Huntly; dis. 30 June, 1798	April 16
Banks, John ..	18	5 ft. 3 in.	Edinburgh	Shoemaker	Deserted 16 June, 1799	Feb. 25
Barclay, Alex. ..	24	5 ft. 8½ in.	Leith	Labourer	Enlisted by Ensign Fraser; dead 3 Feb., 1809	April 5
Baxter, James ..	20	5 ft. 7½ in.	Bellie	Weaver	Dead 18 Feb., 1795	April 14

Name.	*Age.*	*Height.*	*Birthplace.*	*Trade.*	*Career.*	*Attest.*
Baxter, John ..	17	5 ft. 3 in.	Bellie	Labourer	Discharged	March 12
Baxter, William ..	29	5 ft. 5 in.	Duffus	Blacksmith	Trans. 2nd Batt. 25 Nov., 1803	March 20
Baxter, William ..	17	5 ft. 6¾ in.	Bellie	....	Enlisted by Lord Huntly	Feb. 14 1798
Beaton, Daniel ..	16	5 ft. 3½ in.	Portree	Weaver	Dead 12 April, 1799	May 3
Beaton, Murdoch ..	35	5 ft. 5 in.	Portree	Weaver	Dis. 20 May, 1800	Sept. 15
Beattie, Alexander	16	5 ft. 3 in.	Aberdeen	Servant		March 9
Beattie, John ..	16	5 ft. 4 in.	Disercreal, Tyrone	Weaver		May 3
Beatton, Murdoch	35	5 ft. 4 in.	Connan	Labourer	Enlisted by Lieut. E. M'Pherson; dead 6 Nov., 1794	May 9
Beidie, William ..	29	5 ft. 6½ in.	Benholm	Weaver	Sergeant, 1813	Feb. 28
Berry, Joseph ..	34	5 ft. 7¼ in.	Christchurch, Hants	Woolcomber	Dis. 30 June, 1798	April 11
Bethune, John ..	28	5 ft. 8 in.	Kilmonivaig	Labourer		Feb. 22
Biggam, James ..	18	5 ft. 5½ in.	Cambleton, Argyll	Taylor	Died 25 Feb., 1809	May 16
Birnie, William ..	19	5 ft. 11½ in.	Old Deer	Blacksmith		April 21
Bisset, Robert ..	16	5 ft. 1 in.	Alloa	Weaver		May 29
Black, Alexander ..	26	5 ft. 5 in.	Falkirk	Weaver		May 16
Black, William ..	23	6 ft. 0 in.	Kintore	Sawer	Dead 31 May, 1796	Feb. 21
Black, William ..	35	5 ft. 6½ in.	Kilmallievick, Argyll	Labourer	Late 74th Regt., 2 months' service	May 10
Blaikie, John ..	40	5 ft. 8½ in.	Kirnton, Midlothian	Taylor	61st Regt., 11 years 2 months	Oct. 26
Blair, Thomas ..	16	5 ft. 7 in.	Gifford, Haddington	Baker	Enlisted by Ensign Fraser; dead 5 Oct., 1799	April 3
Booth, William ..	17	5 ft. 3 in.	Dundonald	Labourer		May 6
Boyd, Adam ..	22	5 ft. 5½ in.	Kilmarnock	Bonnet-maker		April 12
Boyd, Hugh ..	26	5 ft. 5 in.	Kilmally	Labourer	Dead 18 Sept., 1795	May 6
Boyd, James ..	16	5 ft. 2 in.	Falkirk	Weaver		April 18
Boyle, Hugh ..	23	5 ft. 4½ in.	Broad Island, Antrim	Labourer	Dis. 4 May, 1802	May 9
Bowie, John ..	29	5 ft. 9 in.	Ratha, W. Lothian	Servant	Dead 25 March, 1828	March 25
Bremner, Alex. ..	14	5 ft. 4 in.	Stirling	Nailsmith	Enlisted by Lord Huntly	April 25
Bremner, George ..	15	5 ft. 0 in.	Bellie	Labourer	Dis. 5 Aug., 1798	March 4 1795
Bremner, John ..	23	5 ft. 7¾ in.	Rothes	Labourer	Died 7 Oct., 1799	June 14
Brimner, Andrew ..	16	5 ft. 2 in.	Speymouth	Labourer	Enlisted by Lord Huntly	March 28 1798
Brodie, William ..	16	5 ft. 3½ in.	Banff	Labourer	Enlisted by Lord Huntly	April 17 1798
Brook, John ..	16	5 ft. 3 in.	Old Deer	Cutler		June 29
Brook, Richard ..	16	5 ft. 3½ in.	Paisley	Weaver	Dis. 20 May, 1800	April 14
Brook, Robert ..	21	5 ft. 6½ in.	Peterhead	Labourer	Trans. 46th Regt. 2 Nov., 1794	April 28
Brown, Æneas ..	17	5 ft. 4 in.	Depadlin, Londonderry	Labourer	Deserted 14 Dec., 1797	April 29
Brown, Andrew ..	..	....	....	....	Enlisted by Major M'Donald; dis. 3 Nov., 1794	April 14
Brown, Dugald ..	19	5 ft. 8½ in.	Whiteburn, Linlithgow	Gardener	Dis. 10 June, 1795	April 21
Brown, James ..	16	5 ft. 2 in.	Cairney	Labourer		May 14
Brown, James ..	26	5 ft. 6 in.	Deskford	Labourer		July 7
Brown, John ..	30	5 ft. 7 in.	Paisley	Weaver	Dead in Harwich of his wounds	April 4
Brown, Malcolm ..	25	5 ft. 8½ in.	Comrie	Taylor	Died 15 Feb., 1798	June 16
Brown, William ..	25	5 ft. 8 in.	Inveraven	Shoemaker	Dis. 24 Aug., 1799	March 2
Brown, William ..	18	5 ft. 3 in.	Cairney	Labourer	Late West Fencibles; 5½ months' service; dis. 9 June, 1797	May 10
Bruce, James ..	32	5 ft. 6 in.	Dundee	Labourer	Dead 27 Aug., 1799	March 19
Brukmire, John ..	18	5 ft. 4 in.	Temple Patrick, Antrim	Weaver	Dis. 1 Feb., 1808	May 1
Bryce, Robert ..	21	5 ft. 8½ in.	Kinross	Weaver	Trans. 2nd Batt. 25 Nov., 1803	April 17
Buchan, John ..	17	5 ft. 2½ in.	Dyce	Weaver	Dis. 24 May, 1807	April 17
Buchan, John ..	28	5 ft. 7 in.	Glasgow	Labourer		April 25
Buchannan, Norman	22	5 ft. 10½ in.	Skye	Labourer	Died of his wounds, 3 Feb., 1800	May 15
Buchannan, Thos.	15	5 ft. 2½ in.	Alloa	Weaver		April 28
Cairns, James ..	18	5 ft. 6 in.	Paisley	Shoemaker	Prize list, 1813	May 11
Calder, Andrew ..	38	5 ft. 10 in.	Foveran	Labourer	Enlisted by Capt. A. Gordon; dis. 23 June, 1800	April 30
Calder, Marquis ..	16	5 ft. 6 in.	Watton, Caithness	Weaver		May 31
Calder, William ..	21	5 ft. 4½ in.	Dunnet, Caithness	Labourer	Dead 18 Sept., 1795	June 4

Name.	Age.	Height.	Birthplace.	Trade.	Career.	Attest.
Cameron, Alex	.. 18	5 ft. 4 in.	Kilmally	Labourer	Enlisted by Captain J. Cameron	April 8
Cameron, Alex.	.. 19	5 ft. 5 in.	Kilmally	Labourer	Dis. 27 May, 1802	April 10
Cameron, Alex.	.. 18	5 ft. 4 in.	Kilmally	Labourer	Trans. 2nd Batt. 25 March, 1803	April 11
Cameron, Alex.	.. 24	5 ft. 6 in.	Ardnamurchan, Argyll	Labourer	Enlisted by Captain J. Cameron	April 27
Cameron, Alex.	.. 19	5 ft. 8½ in.	Kilmally	Labourer	Dead 28 Aug., 1795	May 6
Cameron, Alex.	.. 18	5 ft. 3 in.	Kilmanivaig	Labourer		May 20
Cameron, Allen	.. 24	5 ft. 8 in.	Kilmally	Labourer	Dead 11 Oct., 1799	Sept. 14
Cameron, Angus	.. 21	5 ft. 4½ in.	Mushirlock, Inverness	Servant	Enlisted by Lord Huntly; dis. 24 Feb., 1806	April 9
Cameron, Charles	.. 16	5 ft. 4 in.	Kilmally	Labourer		May 6
Cameron, Charles	.. 16	5 ft. 4 in.	Kilmally	Labourer	Ensign 18 Feb., 1799. " A most distinguished officer. 3rd Reg., J. M'Donald." Dis. 6 March, 1799	June 9
Cameron, Charles	.. 16	5 ft. 4½ in.	Kilmally	Labourer	Dis. 30 June, 1798	June 10
Cameron, Daniel	.. 34	5 ft. 3½ in.	Morvain, Argyll	Labourer	Dis. 10 June, 1795	June 8
Cameron, Donald	.. 22	5 ft. 5 in.	Kilmally	Labourer	Enlisted by Captain J. Cameron; deserted 16 June, 1799	April 9
Cameron, Donald	.. 17	5 ft. 2 in.	Kilmanivaig	Labourer	Enlisted by Lord Huntly; trans. 9th R.V. Batt. 15 Oct., 1806	April 22
Cameron, Dougald	22	5 ft. 7 in.	Kilmally	Farmer	Enlisted by Captain J. Cameron	April 27
Cameron, Duncan	.. 19	5 ft. 4 in.	Kilmally	Labourer	Dead 2 Oct., 1799	May 2
Cameron, Duncan	.. 18	5 ft. 5 in.	Kilmally	Labourer	Dead 20 Nov., 1796	May 13
Cameron, Duncan	.. 16	5 ft. 3 in.	Kilmanivaig	Labourer		May 27
Cameron, Evan	.. 17	5 ft. 4 in.	Kilmally	Labourer	Enlisted by Captain J. Cameron; dead 23 Dec., 1800	April 8
Cameron, Evan	.. 20	5 ft. 5 in.	Kilmally	Labourer	Enlisted by Captain J. Cameron	April 12
Cameron, Evan	.. 28	5 ft. 5 in.	Kilmally	Taylor	Dis. 31 Oct., 1800	May 1
Cameron, Evan	.. 22	5 ft. 5½ in.	Kilmally	Labourer		May 10
Cameron, Evan	.. 18	5 ft. 6 in.	Kilmally	Taylor	Dead 2 Nov., 1799	May 24
Cameron, Hugh	.. 16	5 ft. 3½ in.	Fortingall	Labourer		May 7
Cameron, John	.. 16	5 ft. 2½ in.	Alloa	Weaver	Dead 20 Sept., 1809	Jan. 22 1795
Cameron, John	.. 25	5 ft. 4 in.	Kilmally	Labourer	Dead 22 Oct., 1794	March 5
Cameron, John	.. 14	5 ft. 2 in.	Kiltarlity	Labourer		March 8
Cameron, John	.. 19	5 ft. 3 in.	St. Cuthbert's Edinburgh	Bookbinder		March 14
Cameron, John	.. 19	5 ft. 5 in.	Kilmally	Labourer		April 9
Cameron, John	.. 21	5 ft. 5 in.	Kilmally	Taylor		May 1
Cameron, John	.. 20	5 ft. 10 in.	Kincardine, Inverness	Taylor		May 20
Cameron, John	.. 18	5 ft. 5 in.	Kilmally	Labourer		June 2
Cameron, Robert	.. 21	5 ft. 4 in.	Falkirk	Blacksmith	Enlisted by Lord Huntly	May 21
Cameron, William	.. 32	5 ft. 4½ in.	Abernethy	Labourer	Dis. 30 June, 1798	June 13
Campbell, Andrew	24	5 ft. 9 in.	Muthel, Perthshire	Labourer	Deserted 6 April, 1799	March 12
Campbell, Charles	19	5 ft. 4 in.	Reay	Labourer		April 1
Campbell, Donald	.. 34	5 ft. 2½ in.	Redcastle, Ross	Twist miller	Dis. 27 May, 1802	March 25
Campbell, Donald	.. 18	5 ft. 7 in.	Barra, Inverness	Labourer	Enlisted by Captain J. Cameron	April 26
Campbell, Donald	.. 20	5 ft. 6½ in.	Halkirk	Labourer	2nd Battalion	June 6
Campbell, Wm.	.. 16	5 ft. 6½ in.	Farr	Weaver		March 31
Campbell, Wm.	.. 21	5 ft. 6½ in.	Dowrass, Sutherland	Labourer		April 1
Campbell, Wm.	.. 19	5 ft. 5 in.	Reay	Labourer	Trans. Reay Fencibles, 24 April, 1799	June 14
Card, Francis	.. 35	5 ft. 7½ in.	Flamborough, York	Labourer	Dead 10 Sept., 1797	Aug. 1
Catherwood, Don.	.. 15	5 ft. 3 in.	Lisson, Tyrone	Taylor	Dead 2 Oct., 1799	June 7
Cattanach, Alex	.. 23	5 ft. 9 in.	Kingussie	Labourer		May 22
Cattanach, Donald	16	5 ft. 3 in.	Kingussie	Labourer	Dead 4 Oct., 1799	March 11
Cattanach, John	.. 16	5 ft. 4 in.	Kingussie	Labourer	Enlisted by Lieut. M'Lean	April 15
Cattanach, Malcolm	22	5 ft. 6 in.	Kingussie	Labourer	Dis. 27 May, 1802	May 3
Chalmers, Alex.	.. 15	5 ft. 1½ in.	Glasgow	Weaver	Trans. 2nd Batt.	May 5
Chapman, James	.. 30	5 ft. 11 in.	Kilbarchan, Renfrew	Weaver		April 14
Cherry, James	.. 22	5 ft. 6½ in.	Glasgow	Hosier	Dead 25 Jan., 1799	May 6
Chisholm, Roderick	25	5 ft. 3½ in.	Kilmorach, Inverness	Carpenter	Enlisted by Lord Huntly; dead 2 Oct., 1799	April 14
Christie, John	.. 16	5 ft. 4 in.	Strichen	Woolcomber		March 5
Clark, Alexander	.. 18	5 ft. 8 in.	Kingussie	Taylor	Ensign 19 Feb., 1799; dis. 6 March, 1799	May 22

Name.	*Age.*	*Height.*	*Birthplace.*	*Trade.*	*Career.*	*Attest.*
Clark, James ..	15	5 ft. 1½ in.	Cross, Inverness	Labourer	Enlisted by Lord Huntly; trans. 2nd Batt. 25 Nov., 1803	April 14
Clark, William ..	18	5 ft. 7½ in.	Lochwinnoch, Ren.	Weaver		May 26
Clarkson, William	35	5 ft. 7 in.	Ecclesmachan, Linlithgow	Turner	Enlisted by Ensign Fraser; dis. 1 April, 1804	April 8
Clauron, Robert ..	47	5 ft. 4½ in.	Haddington	Labourer	Dis. 24 Feb., 1799	May 1
Cochran, Walter ..	23	5 ft. 9 in.	Aberdeen	Flesher	Dis. 4 May, 1802	March 25
Cock, James ..	16	5 ft. 3 in.	Alloa	Slater		May 5
Cock, Richard ..	15	5 ft. 3½ in.	Edinburgh	Hairdresser		March 31
Conely, Patrick ..	20	5 ft. 4 in.	Castle Blen, Monaghan	Labourer		May 24
Couper, John ..	20	5 ft. 7 in.	Tarland	Gardener	Dis. 27 May, 1809	July 16 1795
Couts, John ..	17	5 ft. 3 in.	Aberdeen	Taylor		March 31
Couvile, John ..	22	5 ft. 7 in.	Lisson, Tyrone	Weaver	Deserted 16 June, 1799	June 6
Craig, John ..	15	5 ft. 3½ in.	Glasgow	Labourer	Dis. 30 June, 1799	April 13
Craigan, John ..	18	5 ft. 4 in.	Rhynie	Labourer	Enlisted by Captain J. Gordon; dead 19 Jan., 1799	March 25
Craigan, William ..	15	5 ft. 8 in.	Cairny	Labourer		April 3
Crawford, Hugh ..	16	5 ft. 3½ in.	Stewarton, Ayr	Weaver		April 14
Cross, Alexander ..	16	5 ft. 4 in.	Eastwood, Lanark	Weaver		April 12
Cruickshank, John	23	5 ft. 4 in.	Dunbenan	Mason	Dead 30 Sept., 1809	March 21
Cruickshank, John	27	5 ft. 3 in.	Glass	Labourer		April 29
Cruickshank, Wm.	18	5 ft. 6½ in.	Glass	Taylor	Trans. 66th Regt. 13 March, 1798	April 5
Cummin, George ..	30	5 ft. 10 in.	Kirkmichael	Labourer	Dis. 1 Feb., 1799, to be Ensign in Northern Fencibles	Dec. 2
Cummin, James ..	33	5 ft. 11½ in.	Elgin	Wright	Dis. 27 May, 1802	April 7
Cumming, James ..	34	5 ft. 6½ in.	Clackmannan	Weaver	Dis. 27 May, 1802	March 28
Cunningham, Alex.	26	5 ft. 7½ in.	Alisonford E. Lothian	Servant	Dis. 7 June, 1802	March 25
Cunningham, John	25	5 ft. 9 in.	Ardhallan, Argyll	Wright		May 26
Cunningham, Wm.	23	5 ft. 9½ in.	St. Cuthbert's Edinburgh	Blacksmith		March 26
Curray, Donald ..	20	5 ft. 6 in.	North Uist	Labourer		May 17
Dallas, William ..	29	5 ft. 5 in.	Golspie	Gardener		March 24
Darlin, David ..	17	5 ft. 5 in.	Edinburgh	Slater	Dis. 25 Nov., 1804	March 12
David, John ..	24	5 ft. 9½ in.	"Terynissel," Aberdeen	Labourer		April 21
Davidson, John ..	15	5 ft. 2 in.	Kinel, Angus	Labourer		April 12
Davidson, Paul ..	35	5 ft. 8 in.	Kingussie	Labourer	Dead 15 Feb., 1795	May 22
Davidson, Robert	23	5 ft. 6¾ in.	Stabletown, Cumberland	Labourer	Dis. 20 May, 1800	July 11
Davidson, William	35	5 ft. 5 in.	Kingussie	Labourer	Dis. 10 June, 1795	April 15
Dawson, Thomas ..	20	5 ft. 6¼ in.	Inverness	Taylor		March 25
Deans, Robert ..	34	5 ft. 7 in.	Knockando	Weaver	Dead 4 Nov., 1794	May 10
Derrach, John ..	20	5 ft. 10 in.	Lech, Tyrone	Labourer	Dead 27 Aug., 1799	May 5
Deutalsop, William	35	5 ft. 6½ in.	Londonderry	Weaver	Dis. 9 June, 1797	May 7
Dewar, Andrew ..	21	5 ft. 3¾ in.	Dunfermline	Weaver	Dead 6 Feb., 1802	July 1
Dewar, Duncan ..	35	5 ft. 7¾ in.	Dall, Perth	Gardener	Trans. 37th Regt. 16 March, 1798	May 2
Dey, Alexander ..	16	5 ft. 8¼ in.	Forgie	Labourer	Dead 24 Jan., 1809	May 3
Dickie, William ..	35	5 ft. 9 in.	East Calder	Labourer	Dis. 30 June, 1798	April 22 1796
Dignan, John ..	..	....	....	....	Dis. 6 Oct., 1800	May 25
Dobbie, Alexander	22	5 ft. 9½ in.	Bellie	Labourer	Enlisted by Lord Huntly; dead 2 Oct., 1799	March 2
Docharty, Simon ..	26	5 ft. 7 in.	Coumber, Londonderry	Weaver	.	March 2
Donald, James ..	16	5 ft. 0 in.	Old Deer	Weaver	Dead 2 Oct., 1799	May 14
Donaldson, Robert	30	5 ft. 8½ in.	Eastwood, Renfrew	Weaver	Dis. 20 May, 1800	May 24
Douglas, John ..	20	5 ft. 10¾ in.	Kilpatrick	Taylor	Dis. 24 Feb., 1799	May 15
Dow, James ..	24	5 ft. 5 in.	Alloa	Labourer		March 20
Dowarty, Simon ..	24	5 ft. 9 in.	St. Ninian's, Stirling	Merchant		June 14
Dowie, James ..	15	5 ft. 1 in.	Linlithgow	Labourer	Dead 10 Sept., 1809	May 28
Dowlin, William ..	12	4 ft. 9 in.	Falmouth, Essex [sic]	Labourer	Dis. 4 May, 1802	April 24
Downie, James ..	35	5 ft. 7½ in.	Glasgow	Blacksmith	Dis. 30 June, 1798	April 16
Downs, John ..	22	5 ft. 5 in.	Antrim	Labourer		May 13
Duffes, John ..	..	....	....	....	Enlisted by Lord Huntly	May 12 1798
Dunbar, Alex. ..	16	5 ft. 3 in.	Duffus	Labourer		March 28
Duncan, Edward ..	28	5 ft. 8¼ in.	Saline, Clack.	Weaver	Dis. 27 May, 1802	May 10

Name.	Age.	Height.	Birthplace.	Trade.	Career.	Attest.
Duncan, George	..	....	....	....	Enlisted by Lord Huntly	..
Duncan, James	22	5 ft. 10½ in.	Salino	Weaver		May 10
Duncan, James	24	5 ft. 6 in.	Montrose	Chaise-driver	Dis. 27 May, 1802	May 16
Duncan, John	15	5 ft. 2½ in.	Kincardine O'Neil	Padler		May 18
Duncan, John	15	5 ft. 4 in.	Dollar	Weaver	Dead 2 Oct., 1799	May 28
Dunlop, William	35	5 ft. 9 in.	North Quarter, Lanark	Weaver	Dis. 10 June, 1795	May 11
Durward, John	34	5 ft. 6¾ in.	Garvock	Blacksmith	Dis. 30 June. 1798	Feb. 26
Edmond, Thomas	29	5 ft. 3¾ in.	Balfron, Stirling	Smith	Dead 16 Oct., 1799	June 11
Eisdale, Thomas	27	5 ft. 10½ in.	Stevenston, Ayr	Miner	Dis. 27 May, 1802	April 5
Ellis, Alexander	33	5 ft. 4¾ in.	Fordyce	Plasterer	Dis. 27 May, 1802	April 26
Ellis, Alexander	28	5 ft. 2 in.	Gartly	Mason	Dead 14 Oct., 1794	June 29
Ellis, John	17	5 ft. 10 in.	Cairney	Weaver	Dis. 27 May, 1802; rejoined at Malta 12 Dec., 1800; after being left at home to be dis. and was since discharged	March 11
Evans, Richard	23	5 ft. 7 in.	Northkep, Flint	Butcher	Trans. 10 Aug., 1810	April 18
Ewing, John	18	5 ft. 7 in.	Glasgow	Weaver		April 20
Ewing, Peter	17	5 ft. 4 in.	Clunie, Aberdeen	Labourer		Aug. 28 1796
Farlow, Walter	35	5 ft. 6 in.	Donegal	Weaver	Dis. 20 May, 1800	March 3
Fee, Henry	..	..	....	....	10 months' former service, 128th Reg.; dead 13 March, 1801	June 10 1795
Fergus, James	35	5 ft. 4 in.	Glasgow	Weaver	Dis. 30 June. 1798	June 7
Ferguson, James	20	5 ft. 10½ in.	Ardersier	Weaver		April 14 1795
Ferguson, James	..	..	....	....	10 months' former service, 128th Reg.; deserted 23 March, 1799	June 10 1795
Ferguson, John	35	5 ft. 5 in.	Kilmarnock	Weaver	Dis. 10 June, 1795	May 2
Ferguson, John	27	5 ft. 5 in.	Alva, Stirling	Labourer	Dis. 9 June, 1797	May 27
Ferguson, Malcolm	26	5 ft. 5½ in.	North Uist	....	Killed in Holland, 10 Sept., 1799	..
Ferguson, Patrick	30	5 ft. 5 in.	Armagh	Sawer		May 10
Ferguson, Peter	21	5 ft. 9 in.	Kilmally	Labourer		April 27
Ferguson, Robert	18	6 ft. 0 in.	Cumbernauld, Dumbarton	Weaver	Dis. 23 June, 1800	May 8
Fimister, Alex.	25	5 ft. 3½ in.	Alves	Labourer	Dis. 9 June, 1797	May 25
Findlay, Alex.	..	....	....	....	Dead	..
Findlater, Wm.	20	5 ft. 7½ in.	Fyvie	Taylor	Dis. 27 May, 1802	April 6
Flamingham, Nicolas	25	5 ft. 5 in.	Stewarton, Tyrone	Labourer		June 4
Fleming, James	17	5 ft. 5½ in.	Dunipace	Labourer		April 14
Fleming, John	20	5 ft. 7 in.	Dunipace	Wright	Trans. 24 March, 1804	April 7
Forbes, Alexander	33	5 ft. 6½ in.	Chapel of Garioch	Taylor		March 9
Forbes, Alexander	25	5 ft. 4 in.	Daviot, Inverness	Labourer	Dead 28 Aug., 1826	April 25
Forbes, Andrew	12	5 ft. 0 in.	Newmachar	Labourer	Trans. 3rd Argyll L. Militia, 31 Dec., 1809	April 16
Forbes, Hary	20	5 ft. 3 in.	Strathdon	Labourer	Dead 22 Dec., 1795	July 19
Forbes, James	18	5 ft. 8 in.	Inveravon	Labourer		April 9
Forbes, John	22	5 ft. 4 in.	Strathdon	Labourer		Sept. 16
Forbes, William	17	5 ft. 4 in.	Kilmorack, Inverness	Hatter	Dead 23 Aug., 1795	March 20
Fordice, Alexander	16	5 ft. 3 in.	Drumblade	Labourer	Dead 15 Oct., 1795	May 15
Foreman, Andrew	17	5 ft. 3½ in.	Crimond	Labourer	Dis. 10 June, 1795	March 22
Fraser, Angus	20	5 ft. 3 in.	Inverness	Labourer		Feb. 28
Fraser, Charles	16	5 ft. 3 in.	Ardersier	Servant		June 7
Fraser, Donald	23	5 ft. 9½ in.	Calder	Labourer	Enlisted by Lord Huntly; dead 2 Oct., 1799	March 12
Fraser, James	34	5 ft. 5 in.	Fordyce	Woolcomber	Dis. 27 May, 1802	Feb. 21
Fraser, John	16	5 ft. 2 in.	Ardersier	Labourer	Dead 2 Oct., 1799	March 29
Fraser, John	32	5 ft. 3 in.	Kiltality	Labourer	Dead 19 Oct., 1794	April 16
Fraser, John	28	5 ft. 6 in.	Dunfermline	Excise officer	Dis. 30 June. 1798	May 6
Fraser, John	16	5 ft. 3 in.	Beaulie	Spinner		May 20
Fraser, Peter	26	5 ft. 7 in.	Huntly	Labourer	Dis. 20 May, 1800	March 6
Fraser, Thomas	34	5 ft. 6½ in.	Kirkhill, Inverness	Weaver	Dead 11 Feb., 1799	Feb. 28
Fraser, Thomas	15	5 ft. 3 in.	Inverness	Labourer		April 16
Fraser, Thomas	15	5 ft. 2½ in.	Portsmouth	Weaver		May 1
Fraser, William	17	5 ft. 5½ in.	Croy	Labourer		April 14
Fraser, William	16	5 ft. 4½ in.	Daviot, Inverness	Labourer		May 7
Fraser, William	26	5 ft. 4¾ in.	Kirkhill, Inverness	....	Enlisted by Lord Huntly	Aug. 21

Name.	Age.	Height.	Birthplace.	Trade.	Career.	Attest.
French, John ..	28	5 ft. 6 in.	Crawford Jones, Lanark	Wright		May 24
Fyfe, William ..	18	5 ft. 5½ in.	Huntly	Labourer		May 8
Galloway, Alex. ..	36	5 ft. 9 in.	Stirling	Weaver	Dead 2 Oct., 1799	April 18
Gardner, James ..	14	5 ft. 2½ in.	Denny	Labourer		May 10
Gardner, William	21	5 ft. 7¾ in.	Glasgow	Weaver		April 18
Geddes, James ..	19	5 ft. 6¾ in.	Rathven	Labourer	Dis. 31 Oct., 1800	April 19
Geddes, John ..	22	5 ft. 11¼ in.	Raffin, Banff	Glassblower	Trans. 10 Aug., 1810	April 7
Gemble, John ..	24	5 ft. 5¾ in.	Kilmarnock	Shoemaker		April 4
George, Robert ..	16	5 ft. 3 in.	Marnoch	Labourer		July 16
George, William ..	25	5 ft. 2 in.	Tunay,? Banff	Labourer		June 24
Gibb, Joseph ..	16	5 ft. 3 in.	Huntly	Weaver	Trans. 2nd Batt. 25 Nov., 1803	March 18
Gibson, William ..	25	5 ft. 5 in.	Stewarton, Tyrone	Carpenter		June 5
Gilchrist, John ..	26	5 ft. 6¾ in.	Paisley	Shoemaker	Dis. 3 Nov., 1795	June 12
Gilles, Alexander	23	5 ft. 8 in.	Rothes	Taylor	Trans. 10 Aug., 1810	May 14
Gilles, Donald ..	20	5 ft. 5 in.	Durinish, Inverness	Weaver	Dead 2 Oct., 1799	May 30
Gilles, Douglas ..	35	5 ft. 5 in.	Ardnamurchan, Argyll	Labourer	Discharged	Aug. 26
Gilles, Duncan ..	32	5 ft. 4 in.	Ardnamurchan	Chapman	Dis. 8 June, 1796	June 22
Gilles, Duncan ..	20	5 ft. 4 in.	Glenelg, Inverness	Labourer		July 3
Gilles, Evan ..	20	5 ft. 7 in.	Glenelg	Labourer		July 3
Gilles, Hugh ..	18	5 ft. 5½ in.	Barra, Inverness	Labourer		April 26
Gilles, John	17	5 ft. 4 in.	Erles, Inverness	Weaver	Trans. 24 June, 1805	March 31
Gillespie, John ..	25	5 ft. 3 in.	Aberdeen	Woolcomber		April 23
Gillespie, William	25	5 ft. 3 in.	Stranraer	Wright	Dis. 8 June, 1796	April 23
Gordon, Alexander	17	5 ft. 6 in.	Cairney	Labourer	Dead 4 Nov., 1799	Feb. 17
Gordon, Alexander	21	5 ft. 8 in.	Inveravon	Labourer	Trans. 2nd Batt. 25 Nov., 1803	March 16
Gordon, Alexander	17	5 ft. 5 in.	Mortlach	Labourer		April 19
Gordon, Alexander	30	5 ft. 6 in.	Inveravon	Labourer	Dead 19 Dec., 1795	June 18
Gordon, Charles ..	20	5 ft. 5 in.	Glass	Labourer	Dis. 26 Feb., 1800, he having found a man in his place	Feb. 17
Gordon, Donald ..	21	5 ft. 5 in.	Inch, Inverness	Labourer	Dis. 27 May, 1802	May 21
Gordon, George ..	26	5 ft. 4 in.	Cabrach	Labourer	Dis. (date not known)	March 12
Gordon, John ..	18	5 ft. 6 in.	Glenbucket	Weaver	Trans. 2nd Batt. 25 Nov., 1803	March 2
Gordon, John ..	16	5 ft. 4 in.	Inveravon	Taylor		April 6
Gordon, John ..	34	5 ft. 4½ in.	Cabrach	Shoemaker	Dis. 10 June, 1795	April 18
Gordon, John ..	17	5 ft. 3 in.	Rayne	Bookbinder	Dis. 27 May, 1802	June 24
Gordon, Peter ..	21	5 ft. 7 in.	Inveravon	Blacksmith	Dis. 1 Aug., 1803	June 2
Gordon, Peter ..	26	5 ft. 7 in.	Kirkmichael	Labourer		June 14
Gordon, William ..	20	5 ft. 5 in.	Urquhart, Ross	Taylor	Dead 2 Oct., 1799	March 20
Gordon, William ..	22	5 ft. 6 in.	Inveravon	Labourer	Trans. 25 Nov., 1803	March 28
Gordon, William ..	19	5 ft. 8 in.	Inverury	Labourer	Trans. 2nd Batt. 25 Nov., 1803	April 16
Goudie, John ..	34	5 ft. 6 in.	Paisley	Weaver	Enlisted by Ensign Fraser; dis. 27 May, 1802	April 7
Gow, Alexander ..	18	5 ft. 4½ in.	Gamrie	Labourer	Dead 2 Oct., 1799	April 17
Graham, James ..	16	5 ft. 3¼ in.	Glasgow	Weaver		March 7
Grahame, Murdoch	19	5 ft. 4 in.	Snisort, Inverness	Labourer		July 12
Grant, David ..	24	5 ft. 4 in.	Tarbet, Ross	Labourer	Dis. 10 June, 1795	July 5
Grant, James ..	35	5 ft. 3½ in.	Mortlach	Woolcomber	Dis. 10 June, 1795	March 15
Grant, James ..	15	5 ft. 3 in.	Glenduff, co. Down	Labourer		May 24
Grant, John ..	20	5 ft. 3 in.	Kirkmichael	Weaver	Dead 2 Oct., 1799	March 19
Grant, John ..	19	5 ft. 6½ in.	Ruthven	Labourer	Dis. 26 May, 1800	May 29
Grant, John ..	..	....	....	....	From S. Fencibles, 5 years' service; 61st Reg., 11 years' service; dead 2 Oct., 1799	Oct. 29
Grant, John ..	20	5 ft. 7 in.	Inveravon	Labourer	Dead 2 Oct., 1799	Sept. 4 1797
Grant, William ..	23	5 ft. 4 in.	Inveravon	Labourer		June 10
Gray, James ..	31	5 ft. 6 in.	Kilmodack, Perth	Weaver		March 24
Greach, David ..	16	5 ft. 4 in.	Auchendore	Weaver	Dis. 23 June, 1800	April 18
Greenhorn, John ..	28	5 ft. 8 in.	Polmont, Stirling	Collier	Deserted 9 July, 1794	May 26
Grieg, Andrew ..	17	5 ft. 4½ in.	Bachern, Banff	Labourer		March 18
Grieg, Francis ..	23	5 ft. 7¾ in.	Peterhead	Woolcomber	Trans. 24 June, 1805	April 22
Grieg, James ..	16	5 ft. 3 in.	Dundurcas	Labourer		March 20
Grieg, Thomas ..	14	5 ft. 2 in.	Laswade	Papermaker		April 24
Gunn, Adam ..	34	5 ft. 4 in.	Kildonan	Woolcomber		May 10
Gunn, Alexander ..	24	5 ft. 2½ in.	Halkirk	Weaver	Dis. 24 May, 1800	May 10
Gun, George ..	..	....	....	....	From N. Fencibles, 5 years' service; 61st Regt., 11 yrs.' service; dis. 27 May, 1802	Oct. 29

Name.	*Age.*	*Height.*	*Birthplace.*	*Trade.*	*Career.*	*Attest.*
Gunn, John	32	5 ft. 5 in.	Kildonan	Labourer	Dis. 10 Jan., 1795	May 26
Gunn, Peter	19	5 ft. 11½ in.	Huntly	Weaver		March 21
Hadgin, Thomas	34	5 ft. 5 in.	Lisburn, Antrim	Weaver	Dis. 27 Nov., 1795	April 23
Halbert, Robert	29	5 ft. 11½ in.	Irvine	Weaver	Dis. 27 May, 1807	April 9
Hall, William	16	5 ft. 3½ in.	Rhynie	Coalier		May 30
Hamilton, John	16	5 ft. 8 in.	Linlithgow	Shoemaker	Dead 6 March, 1799	May 24
Hart, Edward	18	5 ft. 7 in.	Cumber, Derry	Carpenter		May 27
Hay, George	24	5 ft. 8 in.	Inverpeiling, Banff	Labourer	Deserted 9 June, 1794	April 18
Hay, James	17	5 ft. 3 in.	Glenbucket	Weaver	Trans. 2nd Batt. 25 Nov., 1803	April 16
Hay, James	35	5 ft. 6½ in.	Calder, Lanark	Weaver		May 6
Hay, William	28	5 ft. 10½ in.	Rhynie	Labourer	Enlisted by Lord Huntly; dead 10 Feb., 1799	May 15
Hemdry, John	19	5 ft. 10 in.	Alloa	Weaver	Dead 2 Oct., 1799	April 9
Henderson, Angus	15	4 ft. 11 in.	Kilmally	Labourer		April 30
Henderson, Robt.	16	5 ft. 2 in.	Huntly	Labourer		March 1
Henderson, Robt.	19	5 ft. 8 in.	Dumblane	Weaver	Dis. 8 June, 1796	May 10
Henderson, Thos.	35	5 ft. 6 in.	Perth	Weaver	Enlisted by Ensign Fraser; dis. 30 June, 1798	March 25
Henderson, Thos.	35	5 ft. 5 in.	Halkirk	Taylor	Trans. 2nd Batt. 25 Nov., 1804	March 29
Henderson, Wm.	17	5 ft. 5 in.	Stirling	Weaver		April 25
Henderson, Wm.	20	5 ft. 7 in.	Thurso	Labourer	Dis. August, 1805	May 11
Herkless, David	32	5 ft. 2 in.	Musselburgh	Shoemaker	Enlisted by Major M'Donald	April 17
Hodgert, Alex	16	5 ft. 4½ in.	Cambleton, Argyll	Weaver		March 29
Hogg, George	28	5 ft. 9 in.	Clackmannan	Carpenter		March 24
Hollingsworth, And.	39	....	St. Paul's, Dublin	Musician	Previous service: 46th Regt., 26 years; dead 8 Jan., 1796	Nov. 3
Horn, James	20	5 ft. 7 in.	Gartly	Labourer		April 3
Hunter, John	21	5 ft. 9½ in.	Stow, Edinburgh	Labourer		April 2
Hutchison, John	28	5 ft. 11½ in.	Baneff, Dunfermline (?)	Weaver	Dis. 30 June, 1798	April 13
Hutchison, Thos.	17	5 ft. 3¾ in.	Edinburgh	Sailor		May 6
Innes, Alexander	18	5 ft. 7½ in.	Inveravon	Labourer		June 10
Innes, John	20	5 ft. 9 in.	Inveravon	Labourer		March 11
Innes, John	21	5 ft. 4½ in.	Wick	Confectioner		March 18
Innes, Robert	34	5 ft. 6 in.	Kirkmichael	Labourer	Dis. 20 May, 1800	May 27
Irvine, James	30	5 ft. 5 in.	Armagh	Weaver	Dis. 27 Aug., 1802	March 17
Irvine, Matthew	21	5 ft. 0 in.	Ulco, Antrim	Labourer		May 9
Jack, Coats	16	5 ft. 3 in.	Glasgow	Weaver		May 15
Jack, James	26	5 ft. 10 in.	Glasgow	Weaver	Enlisted by Ensign Fraser; deserted 9 July, 1794	April 4
Jamieson, George	..	....	....	....	Enlisted by Major M'Donald; dead 6 Dec., 1796	April 12
Jamieson, James	19	5 ft. 9 in.	Feteresso	Labourer	Dead 2 Oct., 1799	April 30
Jamieson, James	34	5 ft. 4 in.	Greenock	Sheriff Officer	Dis. 30 June, 1798	June 15
Jardine, Samuel	19	5 ft. 8½ in.	Answorth, Stafford	Coppersmith	Deserted 26 July, 1796	May 17
Joss, John	28	5 ft. 6 in.	King-Edward	Farmer		April 3
Kelly, Walter	35	5 ft. 6 in.	Almadock, Perth	Slater	Dead 24 Dec., 1795	April 1
Kennedy, Alex	17	5 ft. 5½ in.	Kilmallie	Labourer	Trans. 21 Oct., 1809	April 10
Kennedy, Alex.	19	5 ft. 3 in.	Kilmanivaig	Labourer	Trans. to 95th Regt. 25 Dec., 1803	April 18
Kennedy, Angus	35	5 ft. 5½ in.	Maybeg, Inverness	Miln Driver	Dis. 24 Feb., 1799	April 19
Kennedy, Evan	18	5 ft. 5 in.	Kilmallie	Labourer	Dis. 1 Feb., 1808	April 5
Kennedy, Evan	16	5 ft. 4 in.	Kilmallie	Taylor		May 6
Kennedy, John	21	5 ft. 10½ in.	Boleskine	Labourer	Enlisted by Lieutenant E. M'Pherson	Feb. 22
Kennedy, John	35	5 ft. 5 in.	Kingussie	Labourer	Dis. 10 June, 1795	April 13
Kennedy, Neil	20	5 ft. 7½ in.	Kilmanivaig	Labourer		April 22
Kerr, James	15	5 ft. 1¾ in.	Daviot, Inverness	Labourer	Dead 17 Feb., 1799	Feb. 18
King, Richard	24	5 ft. 5½ in.	Prestonpans	Mason		April 22
Kinmouth, John	22	5 ft. 5½ in.	Dunning	Weaver	Dead 23 Sept., 1795	March 25
Kinnaird, Wm.	..	....	....	....	Taken prisoner in Holland; struck off 31 May, 1800	..
Knox, John	26	5 ft. 8½ in.	Renfrew	Weaver	Trans. 2nd Batt. 2 Nov., 1803	May 15
Laing, Alexander	26	5 ft. 5¾ in.	Aberdeen	Hairdresser	Dis. 24 May, 1800	Feb. 22
Lamont, John	21	5 ft. 3¾ in.	Knapdale, Argyll	Weaver	Dis. 4 May, 1802	May 2
Lapsley, William	18	5 ft. 4 in.	Midlothian	Weaver	Dis. 12 Dec., 1803	Feb. 25
Lattimore, John	29	5 ft. 5 in.	Antrim	Weaver	Dis. 4 May, 1802	March 27
Ledingham, Geo.	19	5 ft. 5 in.	Insch	Labourer	Dead 24 Aug., 1795	April 29
Legg, James	17	5 ft. 6 in.	Fordyce	Labourer	Deserted 4 Sept., 1794	April 28
Leitch, Alexander	16	5 ft. 4½ in.	Nairn	Labourer		April 21
Leith, Andrew	19	5 ft. 5¾ in.	Grange, Antrim	Weaver		March 17

Name.	*Age.*	*Height.*	*Birthplace.*	*Trade.*	*Career.*	*Attest.*
Leslie, George ..	16	5 ft. 8 in.	Rothes	Labourer	Dead 1 Jan., 1796	April 3
Leslie, Robert ..	20	5 ft. 6½ in.	Ellistown, Ross	Weaver	Deserted 9 July, 1794	May 6
Leslie, William ..	16	5 ft. 10½ in.	Mortlach	Miller	Dead 8 Oct., 1809	..
Liddle, John ..	34	5 ft. 4 in.	Lanark	Labourer	Dis. 27 May, 1802	April 5
Loan, William ..	28	5 ft. 5½ in.	Drummore, co. Down	Blacksmith	Enlisted by Lieut. Stewart	May 16
Lourimore, Hugh ..	23	5 ft. 9 in.	Stanyfair, Antrim	Weaver	Deserted 9 July, 1794	May 27
Lourimor, Wm. ..	36	5 ft. 6 in.	Banff	Labourer	Dis. 30 June, 1798	May 15
Lourimore, Wm. ..	16	5 ft. 3½ in.	Forgie	Stocking-maker		June 21
Lumsdale, John ..	28	5 ft. 7¾ in.	Baillie, Banff	Labourer		..
Lyon, James ..	16	5 ft. 5 in.	Dundureas	Labourer		May 14
Lyon, Robert ..	21	5 ft. 7 in.	Kilbride, Lanark	Baker	Dis. 20 May, 1800	April 10
M'Allister, Alex. ..	34	5 ft. 6 in.	Johnston, Renfrew	Weaver	Dis. 1 April, 1805	March 9
M'Arthur, Peter ..	27	5 ft. 10½ in.	Calder	Labourer	Dead 16 April, 1796	March 27
M'Arty, William ..	18	5 ft. 6 in.	Brigh, co. Down	Labourer	Dis. 10 July, 1797	May 16
M'Bain, Alexander	16	5 ft. 4 in.	May, Inverness	Labourer		March 18
M'Bain, Angus ..	40	5 ft. 7¾ in.	Moy	Labourer	Dead 14 Feb., 1806	May 9
M'Beath, George ..	35	5 ft. 6½ in.	Lathron	Labourer		March 1
M'Callum, James ..	29	5 ft. 6½ in.	Alloa, Clackmannan	Skinner	Dead Aug., 1802	April 8
M'Carmet, Donald	18	5 ft. 6 in.	Kilmanivaig	Labourer		May 26
M'Cormick, Gilbert	22	5 ft. 8 in.	Killihoman, Argyll	Slater	Deserted	March 27
M'Cormick, Neil ..	28	5 ft. 5 in.	South Uist	Labourer		May 8
M'Dermid, John ..	15	5 ft. 2½ in.	Islay, Argyll	Labourer		May 10
M'Donald, Alex. ..	17	5 ft. 10 in.	Dores, Inverness	Labourer	Trans. 2nd Batt. 25 Nov., 1803	March 15
M'Donald, Alex. ..	22	5 ft. 6 in.	Alvie	Shoemaker	Dead 22 Feb., 1809	March 18
M'Donald, Alex. ..	19	5 ft. 1½ in.	Rothiemurchus	Labourer	Dis. 30 June, 1799	April 21
M'Donald, Alex. ..	21	5 ft. 7 in.	Ardnamurchan, Argyll	Cotton spinner		April 30
M'Donald, Alex. ..	38	5 ft. 6 in.	Inverness	Labourer	Dis. 24 Jan., 1803	May 1
M'Donald, Alex. ..	20	5 ft. 7 in.	North Uist	Labourer	Dis. 27 May, 1802	May 10
M'Donald, Allen ..	35	5 ft. 7 in.	Tyrie, Argyll	Labourer	Dis. 20 May, 1800	March 10
M'Donald, And. ..	35	5 ft. 6 in.	Larbert	Shoemaker	Deserted 9 July, 1794	May 14
M'Donald, Angus ..	18	5 ft. 4 in.	Bolleskine	Labourer	Dead 2 Oct., 1799	May 29
M'Donald, Angus ..	25	5 ft. 7 in.	Glenelg, Inverness	Labourer	Dead 5 March 1799	July 13
M'Donald, Angus ..	16	5 ft. 0 in.	Ardnamurchan, Inverness	Taylor	Dis. 27 June, 1802	Aug. 25
M'Donald, Colin ..	12	4 ft. 11 in.	Petty, Nairn	Taylor	Dead 19 Oct., 1794	March 4
M'Donald, Donald	35	5 ft. 8½ in.	Ardnamurchan, Inverness	Labourer	Dis. 27 May, 1802	Aug. 25
M'Donald, Donald	16	5 ft. 2 in.	Ardnamurchan, Inverness	Labourer	Dead 20 Aug., 1797	Oct. 18
M'Donald, Donald	34	5 ft. 6 in.	Small Isles, Inverness	Labourer	Dis. 24 May, 1800	Dec. 18
M'Donald, Donald	15	5 ft. 0 in.	Ardnamurchan, Inverness	Labourer	Dead 15 May, 1796	Feb. 24 1795
M'Donald, Dougald	19	5 ft. 10 in.	Ardnamurchan, Argyle	Cotton spinner	Dis. 20 May, 1800	April 30
M'Donald, Duncan	12	4 ft. 8 in.	Aberdeen	Labourer	Trans. 2nd Batt. 25 Nov., 1803	March 16
M'Donald, Duncan	16	5 ft. 2½ in.	Croy	Labourer		April 23
M'Donald, Evan ..	19	5 ft. 0 in.	Ardnamurchan, Inverness	Carpenter		June 22
M'Donald, Hugh ..	22	5 ft. 3 in.	Canongate, Midlothian	Hatmaker		March 15
M'Donald, Hugh ..	16	5 ft. 3½ in.	Inverness	Labourer		April 21
M'Donald, James ..	16	5 ft. 4½ in.	Nairn	Labourer	Trans. 2nd Batt. 25 Nov., 1803	May 8
M'Donald, John ..	30	5 ft. 5½ in.	Lairg	Woolcomber	Dead 12 June, 1796	March 15
M'Donald, John ..	19	5 ft. 7 in.	Laggan, Inverness	Labourer	Dead 23 Sept., 1809	March 28
M'Donald, John ..	16	5 ft. 3½ in.	Kilfinan, Argyll	Shoemaker		April 18
M'Donald, John ..	16	5 ft. 4 in.	Forres	Thread manufacturer		May 30
M'Donald, John ..	21	5 ft. 9 in.	Strathdon	Wright	Deserted 19 July, 1799	Sept. 22
M'Donald, John ..	20	5 ft. 6½ in.	Ardnamurchan, Inverness	Weaver		Oct. 18
M'Donald, John ..	18	5 ft. 1 in.	Ardnamurchan, Inverness	Labourer		Nov. 19
M'Donald, Neil ..	19	5 ft. 4 in.	Barra, Inverness	Labourer	Trans. 10 Aug., 1810	March 12
M'Donald, Neil ..	22	5 ft. 8 in.	Culloden	Labourer	Dis. 20 May, 1800	March 28
M'Donald, Robert	19	5 ft. 7 in.	Laggan	Labourer		March 16
M'Donald, Ronald	28	5 ft. 6 in.	South Uist	Labourer	Promoted to Ensign	May 5
M'Donald, Ronald	20	5 ft. 4 in.	Bracadel, Inverness	Labourer	Dis. 1805	Aug. 2
M'Donald, Ronald	17	5 ft. 5 in.	Ardnamurchan, Inverness	Labourer	Dead 2 Oct., 1799	Dec. 29
M'Donell, Donell ..	18	5 ft. 4 in.	Abertarfe, Inverness	Labourer	Enlisted by Lieutenant E. M'Pherson	Feb. 21

Name.	*Age.*	*Height.*	*Birthplace.*	*Trade.*	*Career.*	*Attest.*
M'Donell, Evan ..	23	5 ft. 6 in.	Kilmanivaig	Labourer	Dead 2 Oct., 1799	March 12
M'Donell, John ..	17	5 ft. 4 in.	Kilmanivaig	Labourer		March 9
M'Donell, John ..	16	5 ft. 3¼ in.	Kilmanivaig	Labourer		June 2
M'Dougald, Dougald ..		....	....	....	Enlisted by Major M'Donald; dis. 10 June, 1795	April 26
M'Eachin, Angus ..	32	5 ft. 2 in.	Strath, Inverness	Labourer	Dis. (date not known)	July 14
M'Eachin, John ..	18	5 ft. 0 in.	Ardnamurchan, Inverness	Labourer	Dead 10 Nov., 1799	June 21
M'Ewan, James ..	17	5 ft. 5½ in.	Losse, Perth	Wright		May 19
M'Farlane, And. ..	19	5 ft. 8¾ in.	Gorbals	Coalhewer	Dead 2 Oct., 1799	May 30
M'Farlane, John ..	16	5 ft. 4 in.	Glasgow	Labourer	Dis. 24 Jan., 1796	April 8
M'Findlay, Wm. ..	34	5 ft. 9½ in.	Kilpatrick, Dunbarton	Nailer	Deserted 9 July, 1794	May 10
M'Garvie, Mundy ..	35	5 ft. 6 in.	Argyll, Tyrone	Labourer	Dead 7 Oct., 1794	May 3
M'Ghee, James ..	34	5 ft. 5 in.	Baillieston, Antrim	Weaver		May 7
M'Gie, James ..	16	5 ft. 4½ in.	Glasgow	Labourer	Trans. 2nd Batt. 25 Nov., 1803	June 10 1795
M'Gie, William ..	17	5 ft. 3 in.	Insch, Abd.	Labourer	Trans. 2nd Batt. 25 Nov., 1803	Aug. 26
M'Gilvray, Ben. ..	16	5 ft. 0 in.	Bolleskine	Taylor		March 11
M'Gilvray, Evan ..	36	5 ft. 7 in.	Ardnamurchan, Inverness	Labourer	Dis. 8 June, 1796	July 7
M'Gilvray, John ..	18	5 ft. 10½ in.	Ardnamurchan, Inverness	Labourer	Dis. 20 May, 1800	Dec. 10
M'Glashan, Arch. ..	33	5 ft. 8 in.	Ardnamurchan	Labourer	Dead 1 Nov., 1796	March 16
M'Gowan, Alex. ..	17	5 ft. 6 in.	Bocharn, Banff	Taylor		May 5
M'Grath, Henry ..	25	5 ft. 7 in.	Achim, co. Down	Labourer	Dis. 10 June, 1795	May 20[30?]
M'Gregor, Alex. ..	30	6 ft. 0 in.	Laggan, Inverness	Soldier	Dis. 24 Jan., 1803	March 2
M'Gregor, Alex. ..	16	5 ft. 3 in.	Cromdale	Labourer		March 19
M'Gregor, Alex. ..	16	5 ft. 4 in.	Nairn	Labourer		May 23
M'Gregor, Alex. ..	26	5 ft. 8 in.	Laggan	Labourer	Dis. 24 May, 1800	May 31
M'Gregor, Charles	20	5 ft. 7 in.	Inveravon	Labourer		April 2
M'Gregor, John ..	29	5 ft. 6 in.	Paisley	Weaver	Enlisted by Capt. Napier; dis. 31 Oct., 1800	May 7
M'Gregor, Wm. ..	35	5 ft. 4 in.	Cabrach	Taylor	Dead 30 Aug., 1796	March 10
M'Grewar, John ..	17	5 ft. 4 in.	Bolleskine	Labourer	Dead 30 Oct., 1795	June 14
M'Hardy, Charles ..	17	5 ft. 2 in.	Strathdon	Weaver		Aug. 31
M'Innes, Andrew ..	16	5 ft. 3 in.	Ardnamurchan, Inverness	Labourer	Deserted 26 Feb., 1799	July 14
M'Innes, Donald ..	15	5 ft. 2 in.	South Uist	Labourer	Dis. 10 July, 1797	Sept. 28
M'Innes, Ewan ..	35	5 ft. 6 in.	Kilmallie	Labourer	Dis. 30 June, 1798	March 12
M'Innes, John ..	35	5 ft. 4½ in.	Ardnamurchan, Inverness	Labourer		June 5
M'Intosh, Andrew	16	5 ft. 3 in.	Ardersier	Labourer		March 18
M'Intosh, Angus ..	30	5 ft. 10¾ in.	Petty	Labourer		May 17
M'Intosh, David ..	15	5 ft. 0 in.	Pitsligo	Labourer		March 7
M'Intosh, Gardner	25	5 ft. 9 in.	Newbattle, Edinburgh	Minder		March 29
M'Intosh, James ..	16	5 ft. 5 in.	Midmar	Labourer	Trans. 46th Regt., 2 Nov., 1794	April 1
M'Intosh, John ..	20	5 ft. 6 in.	Abertarfe, Inverness	Shoemaker		March 4
M'Intosh, John ..	16	5 ft. 2 in.	Canongate, Edinburgh	Labourer	Dis. 4 May, 1802	April 24
M'Intosh, John ..	19	5 ft. 0 in.	Kingussie	Labourer	Dis. 30 June, 1798	May 22
M'Intosh, Kenneth	26	....	Durness, Caithness	Weaver	9 years' previous service; with 46th Regt.; dead 2 Oct., 1799	Nov. 3
M'Intosh, Lachlan	22	5 ft. 7 in.	Laggan	Labourer	Dead 22 Nov., 1795	May 30
M'Intosh, Lachlan	22	5 ft. 7 in.	Kingussie	Labourer		June 2
M'Intyre, Alex. ..	37	5 ft. 5 in.	Ardekalen, Argyle	Labourer		March 21
M'Intyre, Alex. ..	18	5 ft. 8 in.	Kingussie	Weaver	Trans. 9th R. V. Batt. 29 Nov., 1805	May 23
M'Intyre, Donald ..	23	5 ft. 3 in.	South Uist	Labourer	Dead 18 Oct., 1799	April 17
M'Intyre, Evan ..	28	5 ft. 6 in.	South Uist	Labourer	Dis. 8 June, 1796	May 21
M'Intyre, Gordon ..	13	4 ft. 7½ in.	Edinburgh	Goldsmith	Trans. 66th Regt. 10 June, 1795	March 6
M'Intyre, James ..	35	5 ft. 7 in.	Kingussie	Labourer		May 22
M'Intyre, William	15	5 ft. 2 in.	Nairn	Labourer		March 11
M'Invine, Duncan	34	5 ft. 6 in.	Kilcalminel, Argyll	Labourer		May 5
M'Kay, Archibald	18	5 ft. 7½ in.	Hughall, Antrim	Inkle weaver		May 15
M'Kay, Donald ..	18	5 ft. 6½ in.	Bellie	Labourer	Dead 29 Oct., 1794	March 16
M'Kay, Donald ..	19	5 ft. 7 in.	St. Nicolas, Aberdeen	Shoemaker		March 25
M'Kay, Donald ..	21	5 ft. 3 in.	Cromarty	Stocking-maker	Dead 10 June, 1799	May 8
M'Kay, Findlay ..	21	5 ft. 4½ in.	Fullerman, Ross	Weaver	Dead 19 Jan., 1799	May 15

Name.	Age.	Height.	Birthplace.	Trade.	Career.	Attest.
M'Kay, Hugh	18	5 ft. 4½ in.	Thurso	Weaver	Dis. 27 Aug., 1802	March 28
M'Kay, John	16	5 ft. 5 in.	Thurso	Staymaker	Dis. 29 Aug., 1796	March 12
M'Kay, John	15	5 ft. 2 in.	Derness, Ross	Weaver	Dead 3 Dec., 1799	April 25
M'Kay, John	15	5 ft. 2½ in.	Kilcarnan, Ross	Labourer	Dead 2 Oct., 1799	May 28
M'Kay, John	12	4 ft. 11 in.	Reay	Labourer	Trans. to Reay Fensibles for another man, 24 April, 1799	June 10 1795
M'Kay, Robert	17	5 ft. 4½ in.	Kintall, Sutherland	Weaver	Dis. 24 May, 1807	March 27
M'Kay, Robert	23	5 ft. 6 in.	Inveravon	Labourer		June 4
M'Kay, Stephen	19	5 ft. 4 in.	Edinburgh	Founder	Dead 22 Dec., 1795	March 1
M'Kay, Thomas	..	....	....	....	Enlisted by Major M'Donald; dis. 30 June, 1798	March 12
M'Kay, William	15	5 ft. 2 in.	Sutherland	Weaver	Dead 4 March, 1799	April 2
M'Keachin, Dun.	17	5 ft. 4 in.	Kilmallie	Labourer		March 11
M'Keachin, Hugh	18	5 ft. 4 in.	Ardnamurchan	Labourer	Dis. 24 Feb., 1799	April 21
M'Keachnie, Alex.	16	5 ft. 4 in.	Glasgow	Weaver		May 12
M'Kenzie, Alex.	19	5 ft. 4 in.	Ferintosh, Ross	Labourer		May 5
M'Kenzie, Alex.	18	5 ft. 3½ in.	Birnie	Labourer		May 9
M'Kenzie, Donald	14	5 ft. 2 in.	Rosskeen	Labourer	Dis. 30 July, 1803	May 23
M'Kenzie, Duncan	27	5 ft. 9 in.	Kilmallie	Labourer		March 19
M'Kenzie, John	18	4 ft. 10½ in.	Cromarty	Labourer	Trans. 2nd Batt. 5 Nov., 1803	Feb. 18
M'Kinzie, John	19	5 ft. 6 in.	Bolleskine, Inverness	Armourer		March 18
M'Kenzie, John	34	5 ft. 4 in.	Mortlach	Gardener	Dis. 24 Feb., 1799	March 28
M'Kenzie, John	22	5 ft. 6 in.	Liberton, Edinburgh	Labourer	Trans. 10 Aug., 1810	May 6
M'Kenzie, John	18	5 ft. 6 in.	Inverness	Labourer		May 23
M'Kenzie, Keneth	17	5 ft. 7½ in.	Duthil	Weaver		May 3
M'Kenzie, Murdoch	19	5 ft. 7½ in.	Lochcarron, Ross	Piper		Aug. 12
M'Kenzie, Wm.	16	5 ft. 3½ in.	Annis, Ross	Labourer	Dis. 24 May, 1807	March 12
M'Kerin, Archibald	28	5 ft. 6 in.	Knapdale, Argyll	Weaver		March 10
Mackie, William	16	5 ft. 2 in.	Marnoch	Weaver	Died in Ireland	May 15
M'Killican, Ben.	20	5 ft. 6 in.	Pettie	Weaver	Dead 25 Sept., 1795	May 8
M'Killican, John	15	5 ft. 1 in.	Croy, Nairn	Labourer	Discharged	April 8
M'Killop, Hugh	35	5 ft. 5 in.	Kilmoor, Argyll	Weaver	Dis. 9 June. 1797	May 17
M'Killop, John	16	5 ft. 3 in.	Bolleskine, Inverness	Labourer	Dis. 3 Nov., 1795	March 22
M'Killop, John	16	5 ft. 4 in.	Lorn, Argyll	....	Dis. 27 May, 1802	May 4
M'Kinlay, Duncan	28	5 ft. 9 in.	Lochgoie, Argyll	Labourer	Enlisted by Ensign Fraser	March 20
M'Kinnon, Alex.	24	5 ft. 7 in.	Glenelg	Labourer	Dis. 27 May, 1802	Dec. 18
M'Kinnon, Donald	17	5 ft. 5 in.	Kilmallie	Labourer	Dis. 31 Oct., 1800	March 11
M'Kinnon, Donald	19	5 ft. 5 in.	Barra, Inverness	Taylor	Trans. 10 Aug., 1810	March 12
M'Kinnon, Donald	18	5 ft. 6 in.	Kilfinchan, Argyll	Labourer	Dead 27 Aug., 1799	April 20
M'Kinnon, Donald	30	5 ft. 5 in.	Muck, Argyll	Labourer	Dis. 27 May, 1802	June 23
M'Kinnon, Donald	28	5 ft. 8 in.	Fleat, Skye	Labourer		Aug. 12
M'Kinnon, John	22	5 ft. 3½ in.	Mull	Labourer	Dead 2 Oct., 1799	May 2
M'Kinnon, John	19	5 ft. 2 in.	Ardnamurchan, Inverness	Labourer	Dis. 24 May, 1800	Aug. 20
M'Kormick, Pat.	22	5 ft. 5 in.	Glenevy, Antrim	Labourer	Dis. 30 June, 1798	May 18
M'Lachlan, Wm.	28	5 ft. 8 in.	Kilpatrick, Dumbarton	Weaver	Dis. 31 Oct., 1800	April 8
M'Lamont, James	28	5 ft. 4 in.	Colmonel, Ayr	Weaver	Dis. 4 May, 1802	April 5
M'Lean, Alexander	17	5 ft. 8½ in.	Barra, Inverness	Fisher	Enlisted by Captain J. Cameron; dead 6 Oct., 1796	March 12
M'Lean, Alexander	19	5 ft. 8 in.	Inverness	Labourer		May 15
M'Lean, Alexander	35	5 ft. 6½ in.	Islay	Labourer		May 16
M'Lean, Allen	37	5 ft. 9½ in.	Mervin, Argyll	Labourer	Dead 6 Feb., 1797	June 18
M'Lean, Donald	16	5 ft. 0½ in.	North Uist	Labourer	Dis. 27 May, 1802	May 18
M'Lean, Donald	35	5 ft. 9 in.	Ardnamurchan, Inverness	Taylor		June 5
M'Lean, Duncan	25	5 ft. 9 in.	Kilmuir Easter, Inverness	Labourer	Dis. 27 May, 1802	April 4
M'Lean, Findlay	24	5 ft. 6½ in.	Laggan, Inverness	Labourer		March 14
M'Lean, John	34	5 ft. 4 in.	Alvie	Labourer		Feb. 18
M'Lean, John	18	5 ft. 5 in.	Inveravon	Labourer	Dis. 1 Feb., 1808.	Feb. 18
M'Lean, John	20	5 ft. 8 in.	Barra, Inverness	Labourer	Dead 3 Feb., 1799	March 12
M'Lean, John	15	5 ft. 4 in.	Ardnamurchan, Inverness	Labourer	Dis. 27 May, 1802	June 6
M'Learon, Alex.	18	5 ft. 5½ in.	Inverary	Mason		March 12
M'Learon, Arch.	19	5 ft. 4 in.	Edinburgh	Wright		March 28
M'Learon, John	16	5 ft. 1½ in.	Kincardine, Perth	Shoemaker		May 31
M'Lealion, Arch.	23	5 ft. 7 in.	Inverness	Labourer		May 15
M'Lellan, Donald	30	5 ft. 4 in.	South Uist	Labourer	Dis. 8 June, 1796	June 20
M'Lealon, Donald	34	5 ft. 0 in.	Glenelg	Labourer	Dead 7 Jan., 1799	Aug. 26
M'Lellan, Hugh	22	5 ft. 7½ in.	Terfergus, Argyll	Weaver	Dead 29 Sept., 1795	April 5
M'Lellan, John	33	5 ft. 6 in.	South Uist	Labourer		May 6
M'Lellan, John	15	5 ft. 2 in.	Coutin, Ross	Labourer		May 29
M'Lellan, Patrick	22	5 ft. 7 in.	Glasgow	Shoemaker		June 17

Name.	*Age.*	*Height.*	*Birthplace.*	*Trade.*	*Career.*	*Attest.*
M'Clay, Charles ..	16	5 ft. 4 in.	Girvan	Weaver	Enlisted by Ensign Fraser; dead 2 Oct., 1799	March 14
M'Leod, Alexander	18	5 ft. 4 in.	Troternish, Inverness	Labourer	Dead 27 Aug., 1799	March 12
M'Leod, Alexander	26	5 ft. 6½ in.	South Uist	Labourer	Dead 14 Jan., 1799	May 20
M'Leod, Hugh ..	22	5 ft. 6 in.	Durness	Taylor	Exchanged to Reay Fencibles for another man, 24 April, 1799	..
M'Leod, John ..	18	5 ft. 6 in.	Kilmuir, Inverness	Labourer	Dis. 20 May, 1800	June 3
M'Leod, John ..	30	5 ft. 7 in.	Portree	Labourer	Dis. 27 May, 1802	July 21
M'Leod, Neil ..	28	5 ft. 5 in.	Durinish, Inverness	Labourer	Dead 27 Aug., 1799	May 19
M'Liesh, Donell ..	25	5 ft. 4½ in.	Antrim	Labourer	Dis. 30 June, 1798	May 25
M'Luskie, William	25	5 ft. 4 in.	Errageturan, Tyrone	Labourer		May 9
M'Master, Allen ..	17	5 ft. 4½ in.	Kilmallie	Labourer	Trans. 2nd Batt. 25 Nov., 1803	April 30
M'Master, Arch. ..	20	5 ft. 3½ in.	Ardnamurchan, Inverness	Labourer	Dead 2 Oct., 1799	Nov. 22
M'Millan, Alex. ..	17	5 ft. 4 in.	Kilmallie	Labourer		March 10
M'Millan, Dougald	16	5 ft. 3½ in.	Kilmally	Labourer	Dis. 31 Oct., 1800	June 7
M'Millan, Duncan ..	20	5 ft. 6 in.	Kilmally	Weaver		April 3
M'Millan, Duncan ..	11	4 ft. 0 in.	....	Labourer		July 26
M'Millan, Evan ..	22	5 ft. 9 in.	Kilmally	Labourer		March 10
M'Millan, Evan ..	30	5 ft. 10 in.	Kilmallie	Labourer		April 5
M'Millan, Evan ..	20	5 ft. 4 in.	Kilmallie	Labourer		May 8
M'Millan, John ..	21	5 ft. 9½ in.	Kilmallie	Weaver	Dis. 1 Feb., 1808	March 9
M'Millan, John ..	20	5 ft. 6½ in.	Barra, Inverness	Labourer		March 12
M'Millan, John ..	21	5 ft. 7 in.	Kilmallie	Labourer	Enlisted by Captain J. Cameron	April 21
M'Millan, John ..	21	5 ft. 6 in.	Down, co. Down	Tobacco spinner	Lost left arm; dis. 29 Jan., 1800	April 22
M'Millan, Lachlan	23	5 ft. 5 in.	South Uist	Labourer	Dis. 6 Sept., 1802	June 9
M'Millan, Neil ..	22	5 ft. 8½ in.	Kilmally	Labourer	Dis. 24 Jan., 1803	June 8
M'Nab, James ..	32	5 ft. 6 in.	Aberdour, Fife	Weaver	Dis. 20 May, 1800	April 5
M'Nair, John ..	18	5 ft. 4½ in.	Kilmanivaig	Labourer	Dis. 8 April, 1804	June 2
M'Neal, John ..	17	5 ft. 6½ in.	Barra, Inverness	Labourer	Dead 2 Oct., 1799	April 26
M'Neil, John ..	17	5 ft. 6½ in.	Greenock	Shoemaker	Trans. 9th R. V. Batt. 15 Oct., 1806	May 15
M'Neil, Rodrick ..	19	5 ft. 4½ in.	Barra, Inverness	Taylor	Dead 2 Oct., 1799	March 12
M'Nichol, Donald	36	5 ft. 8 in.	Port Mentieth, Perth	Blacksmith	Dis. 27 May, 1802	April 22
M'Nichol, John ..	..	....	....	....	Enlisted by Major M'Donald; dis. 30 June, 1798	March 11
M'Phee, Alexander	22	5 ft. 6 in.	Kilmallie	Labourer	Dead 2 Oct., 1799	April 26
M'Phee, Angus ..	23	5 ft. 5 in.	Kilmally	Labourer	Dead 2 Oct., 1799	March 12
M'Phee, Duncan ..	35	5 ft. 5 in.	Kilmallie	Labourer	Dead 18 Nov., 1794	May 6
M'Phee, John ..	22	5 ft. 7 in.	Kilmallie	Labourer		May 13
M'Pherson, Alex. ..	35	5 ft. 8 in.	Ardnamachan	Labourer	Enlisted by Lieutenant E. M'Pherson	Feb. 24
M'Pherson, Alex. ..	34	5 ft. 7½ in.	Ardnamurchan	Labourer	Deserted 24 Feb., 1799	May 12
M'Pherson, Alex ..	26	5 ft. 4 in.	Laggan	Taylor	Dis. 24 May, 1800	May 23
M'Pherson, Allen ..	12	4 ft. 9 in.	Ardnamurchan	Labourer		May 13
M'Pherson, Alex. ..	17	5 ft. 6 in.	Kingussie	Labourer	Dead 24 May, 1801	May 30
M'Pherson, Andrew	19	5 ft. 4½ in.	Laggan	Labourer	Trans. 2nd Batt. 25 Nov., 1803	May 31
M'Pherson, Angus	28	5 ft. 5 in.	Laggan, Inverness	Labourer		March 5
M'Pherson, Donald	17	5 ft. 4 in.	Kingussie	Labourer		March 5
M'Pherson, Donald	17	5 ft. 4 in.	Kingussie	Labourer	Dis. 31 Dec., 1795; dead 11 Oct., 1799	March 15
M'Pherson, Donald	20	5 ft. 10 in.	Laggan	Labourer		May 21
M'Pherson, Donald	27	5 ft. 8½ in.	Kingussie	Labourer	Dead 8 Jan., 1799	May 22
M'Pherson, Donald	25	5 ft. 9¾ in.	Laggan	Labourer	Dis. 14 Oct., 1798	June 3
M'Pherson, Duncan	20	5 ft. 6 in.	Laggan, Inverness	Barber	Dis. 12 Aug., 1797	March 11
M'Pherson, Duncan	30	5 ft. 8 in.	Laggan	Labourer	Dead 17 Nov., 1794	May 23
M'Pherson, Duncan	16	5 ft. 3 in.	Laggan	Labourer		May 30
M'Pherson, Evan ..	30	5 ft. 4½ in.	Laggan, Inverness	Labourer	Dis. 27 May, 1802	March 14
M'Pherson, Evan ..	14	5 ft. 0 in.	Laggan	Labourer		June 10
M'Pherson, Hugh ..	24	5 ft. 6 in.	Laggan, Inverness	Clerk		March 3
M'Pherson, James	17	5 ft. 4 in.	Laggan, Inverness	Labourer		March 24
M'Pherson, James	21	5 ft. 11 in.	Laggan, Inverness	Labourer	Dead 20 Jan., 1796	May 20
M'Pherson, John ..	30	5 ft. 6 in.	Kingussie	Labourer	Trans. 10 Aug., 1810	March 16
M'Pherson, John ..	19	5 ft. 10½ in.	Laggan	Labourer	Ensign 20 Feb., 1799; dis. 6 March, 1799	May 22
M'Pherson, John ..	20	5 ft. 4 in.	Durinish, Inverness	Labourer	Dead 24 Oct., 1799	May 30
M'Pherson, John ..	26	5 ft. 4½ in.	Laggan	Labourer	Dis. 24 Feb., 1799	Aug. 15
M'Pherson, Lach. ..	23	5 ft. 8 in.	Laggan, Inverness	Labourer	Dis. 14 Oct., 1798	March 2

Name.	Age.	Height.	Birthplace.	Trade.	Career.	Attest.
M'Pherson, Lach. ..	35	5 ft. 5 in.	Croy	Butcher	Dis. 30 Jan., 1798	April 6 1795
M'Pherson, Lach. ..	20	5 ft. 7 in.	Laggan, Inverness	Labourer	Dead 4 Sept., 1809	May 16
M'Pherson, Mal. ..	22	5 ft. 5 in.	Kingussie	Labourer	Dead 4 Jan., 1796	March 16
M'Pherson, Mal. ..	29	5 ft. 11 in.	South Uist	Labourer		June 2
M'Pherson, Peter ..	22	5 ft. 5 in.	Laggan	Labourer		May 23
M'Pherson, Robert	16	5 ft. 4 in.	Laggan, Inverness	Labourer	Dis. 24 Feb., 1799	March 14
M'Pherson, Thos. ..	28	5 ft. 7½ in.	Inch, Inverness	Labourer		March 14
M'Pherson, Thos. ..	19	5 ft. 6 in.	Inveravon	Labourer	Trans. 2nd Batt. 25 Nov.,1803	May 30
M'Pherson, Thos. ..	18	5 ft. 3 in.	Laggan	Labourer		June 14
M'Pherson, Wm. ..	16	5 ft. 3 in.	Kingussie	Labourer		Feb. 22
M'Queen, James ..	16	5 ft. 4 in.	St. Nicholas, Aberdeen	Labourer	Dis. 30 June. 1798	Nov. 12
M'Queen, Malcolm	16	5 ft. 3 in.	Kilmuir, Inverness	Labourer		July 4
M'Robbie, James ..	17	5 ft. 4 in.	Aberlour	Labourer	Dead 24 Oct., 1797	March 16
M'Sween, Sween ..	23	5 ft. 6½ in.	Snizort	Labourer	Dis. 20 May, 1800	May 30
M'Tavish, Angus ..	25	5 ft. 5 in.	Bolleskine, Inverness	Labourer		March 12
M'Vey, John ..	19	5 ft. 7½ in.	Ramshorn, Lanark	Weaver	Dis. 27 May, 1802	May 12
Mair, Alexander ..	35	5 ft. 6½ in.	New Milns, Ayr	Blacksmith	Dis. 10 June, 1795	May 3
Malloch, George ..	15	5 ft. 3 in.	Negurting, Perth	Dieper bleacher	Dead 23 Dec., 1795	May 15
Malven, Charles ..	27	5 ft. 9½ in.	Diple	Mason	Dead 7 March. 1809	April 17
Manson, Andrew ..	32	5 ft. 9 in.	Thurso	Labourer	Dis. 27 May, 1802	June 9
Manson, Donald ..	16	5 ft. 3½ in.	Obreck, Caithness	Labourer	Dead 26 Oct.. 1794	March 16
Manson, Donald ..	16	5 ft. 4 in.	Olrig, Caithness	Labourer		June 4
Marriner, James ..	19	5 ft. 4 in.	Kilmore, co. Down	Labourer		April 23
Marron, John ..	17	5 ft. 3½ in.	Antrim	Labourer		April 1
Marshall, William	35	5 ft. 3½ in.	Mortlach	Woolcomber	Dis. 30 June, 1798	April 18
Martin, James ..	34	5 ft. 7 in.	Kinethmont	Woolcomber	Dis. 30 June. 1798	Feb. 24
Martin, James ..	14	5 ft. 0 in.	Huntly	Ropemaker		March 16
Martin, John ..	16	5 ft. 3 in.	Inerat, Inverness	Labourer	Dead 6 Oct.. 1799	June 29
Martin, Murdoch ..	20	5 ft. 8½ in.	Tromper, Inverness	Labourer	Dis. 20 May, 1800	July 28
Martin, William ..	34	5 ft. 10½ in.	Glasgow	Weaver	9 years' 9 months' service in 26th Regt.; dis. 24 Feb., 1799	March 29
Mason, John ..	34	5 ft. 8 in.	Federessie, Kincardine	Woolcomber	Dead 15 May, 1796	Dec. 29
Mathison, Alex. ..	29	5 ft. 4½ in.	Clyne	Labourer	Dead 30 April, 1796	May 12
Mathison, Donald ..	22	5 ft. 5½ in.	Snizort, Inverness	Labourer	Dis. 31 Oct., 1802	July 13
Mathieson, John ..	21	5 ft. 3 in.	Inverness	Weaver	Dead 2 Oct., 1799	March 8
Middleton, Alex ..	17	5 ft. 4 in.	St. Nicholas. Aberdeen	Baker		April 16
Miller, John ..	35	5 ft. 10 in.	Glasgow	Weaver		April 4
Miller, John ..	16	5 ft. 9 in.	Munkland, Lanark	Weaver	Dead 1 April, 1790	April 28
Miller, William ..	17	5 ft. 4½ in.	Dunnet, Caithness	Taylor	Dead 2 Oct., 1799	April 15
Milne, James ..	17	5 ft. 6 in.	Edinburgh	Slater		April 16
Milne, James ..	17	5 ft. 2 in.	New Machar	Combmaker		April 21
Milne, Laughlan ..	22	5 ft. 7 in.	Banff	Gardener		May 16
Milns, Patrick ..	32	5 ft. 7 in.	Rhynie	Labourer		May 15
Mirrlees, George ..	33	5 ft. 3½ in.	Westkirk. Edinburgh	Wright	Dis. 24 Feb., 1799	March 29
Mitchell, Alex. ..	15	5 ft. 2½ in.	Glasgow	Hairdresser		May 12
Mitchell, James ..	35	5 ft. 5 in.	Kennethmont	Shoemaker	Dis. 30 June, 1798	April 12
Mitchell, John ..	24	5 ft. 7 in.	Borowness, Linlithgow	Weaver	Dead 10 Nov., 1809	March 29
Mitchell, William	30	5 ft. 3½ in.	Glasgow	Weaver	Dis. 30 June, 1798	March 23
Mitchell, William	17	5 ft. 2 in.	St. Nicholas. Aberdeen	Weaver	Dis. 12 Oct., 1805	April 10
Mochrie, John ..	26	5 ft. 4½ in.	Forfar, Banff [sic]	Weaver	Dis. 23 July, 1794	April 12
Moir, James ..	22	5 ft. 7 in.	Rhynie	Labourer	Trans. 2nd Batt. 25 Nov.,1803	May 22
Monk, Archibald ..	24	5 ft. 7 in.	South Uist	Labourer		May 10
Monro, Hector ..	16	5 ft. 2½ in.	Alness	Labourer	Dis. 3 Nov., 1800	May 15
Monro, Hugh ..	28	5 ft. 4½ in.	Kennethmont	Woolcomber	Dis. 4 May, 1802	April 3
Monro, Lewis ..	19	5 ft. 6 in.	Inveravon	Weaver	Dis. 10 June, 1795	March 12
Monro, William ..	..	....	....		Enlisted by Major M'Donald ; dis. 27 May, 1802	April 13
Monro, William ..	16	5 ft. 3 in.	Clatt	Labourer		April 24
Montague, Thomas	16	5 ft. 4 in.	Arrigel, co Tyrone	Weaver	Dead 31 Oct.. 1795	April 26
Montague, Peter ..	19	5 ft. 10½ in.	Bavaigh, Derry	Labourer		May 1
Montague, Thomas	30	5 ft. 5 in.	Argyle, co. Tyrone	Weaver	Dis. 9 June. 1797	May 16
Montgomery, Ed. ..	19	5 ft. 8 in.	Shankle, Armagh	Sawer		April 14
Montgomery,Murdoch	25	5 ft. 6 in.	Portree	Labourer		July 12
Montieth, Ebenezer	12	5 ft. 2 in.	Stirling	Labourer	Dead 2 Oct., 1799	April 25

Name.	*Age.*	*Height.*	*Birthplace.*	*Trade.*	*Career.*	*Attest.*
Montieth, William	16	5 ft. 3 in.	Stirling	Gardener	Dis. 25 June, 1809	April 25
Moody, William ..	35	5 ft. 8 in.	Kilwinning, Ayr	Weaver		May 24
More, David ..	19	5 ft. 9½ in.	Leith	Labourer		April 17
Morgan, James ..	33	5 ft. 6¾ in.	Dumfermline	Taylor	Dis. 30 June. 1798	May 5
Morgan, James ..	25	5 ft. 8½ in.	Lissen, Tyrone	Weaver	Dead 23 Jan.. 1810	June 6
Morrice, Robert ..	29	5 ft. 8 in.	Rothsay	Labourer	Dis. 27 May, 1802	May 1
Morrison, Alex. ..	24	5 ft. 3 in.	Barra, Inverness	Labourer	Dis. 8 June. 1796	April 26
Morrison, Andrew	17	5 ft. 3½ in.	Comrie	Labourer	Dead 2 Oct.. 1799	May 6
Morrison, George ..	28	5 ft. 7 in.	Turriff	Thread-twiner		Feb. 28
Morrison, George ..	16	5 ft. 4 in.	Eddirachilles, Sutherland	Labourer	Dis. 24 April, 1799; exchanged for another man to the Reay Fencibles	Sept. 16
Morrison, John ..	22	5 ft. 10¾ in.	Turriff	Thread-twiner		April 1
Morrison, Rodrick	17	5 ft. 2¼ in.	Harris	Weaver	Dead 22 Feb., 1809	May 24
Mortimore, Wm. ..	27	5 ft. 10¾ in.	Belly, Banff	Cabinet-maker		March 1
Morton, John ..	20	5 ft. 7¾ in.	Tormenny, Derry	Labourer	Dis. 28 Aug.. 1795	May 10
Mour, John ..	30	5 ft. 5 in.	Campsie	Gardener	Trans. 61st Reg., 28 Oct., 1797	May 27
Munro, Donald ..	..	....	....	....	Dis. 24 Feb., 1799	Feb. 28
Murchie, James ..	30	5 ft. 8½ in.	Bochern, Banff	Labourer	Trans. 5th R. V. Batt., 24 May, 1807	April 5
Murdoch, Alex. ..	23	5 ft. 7¼ in.	Down, Perth	Weaver		April 9
Murdoch, James ..	25	5 ft. 8 in.	Ruthven	Labourer		April 1
Murdoch, Malcolm	38	5 ft. 4 in.	Kilmadock, Perth	Weaver	Dis. 30 June. 1798	June 8
Murray, John ..	33	5 ft. 3 in.	Cairney	Weaver		March 5
Murray, John ..	28	5 ft. 5½ in.	Strechen, Aberdeen	Weaver	Dis. 27 May, 1802	April 22
Murray, John ..	16	5 ft. 4½ in.	Glasgow	Potter		June 8
Murray, William ..	20	5 ft. 3 in.	Fordyce	Weaver		March 2
Ness, Robert ..	21	5 ft. 8 in.	Auchtermuchty	Weaver	Enlisted by Lord Huntly; dead 22 July, 1795	April 14
Newlands, James	25	5 ft. 8 in.	Aberlour	Labourer	Dead 27 Aug., 1795	April 12
Nichol, Daniel ..	30	5 ft. 7½ in.	Lesmaingo, Lanark	Weaver	Enlisted by Major M'Donald	April 11
Nichol, William ..	24	5 ft. 4 in.	Mortlach	Weaver		May 1
Nicol, John	16	5 ft. 2 in.	Banff	Stocking-weaver		June 30
Nicols, Robert ..	29	....	Gibralter	....	Previous service in 32nd Reg., 18 years 1 month; in 61st Regt., 1 yr., 10 mths.	June 10 1795
Nicolson, John ..	34	5 ft. 4 in.	Snisort	Labourer	Dis. 30 June. 1798	July 16
Nicolson, John ..	34	5 ft. 6 in.	Portree	Farmer	Dis. 30 June. 1798	Aug. 6
Norrice, Robert ..	15	5 ft. 8½ in.	Glasgow	Potter	Dis. 24 May, 1807	June 8
Park, Daniel ..	26	5 ft. 7 in.	Calder	Slater		April 1
Park, John	34	5 ft. 4½ in.	Glasgow	Nailer		May 23
Parker, William	23	5 ft. 8 in.	Kilbarchan, Renfrew	Shoemaker	Trans. to 9th R. V. Batt., 24 Feb., 1806	May 28
Paterson, Andrew	17	5 ft. 2½ in.	Redcastle	Spoon-maker	Dead 28 Feb., 1799	April 18
Patterson, Alex. ..	18	5 ft. 8½ in.	Stirling	Nailmaker		May 23
Patterson, George	25	5 ft. 10 in.	Stirling	Nailer	Dead 24 Dec., 1795	May 27
Patterson, William	21	5 ft. 11 in.	Stirling	Blacksmith	Dis. 20 May, 1800	May 23
Paul, Robert ..	34	5 ft. 4½ in.	Glasgow	Rope-spinner	Dis. 30 June. 1798	May 1
Petrie, James ..	35	5 ft. 9½ in.	Biggar	Nailer	Dis. 30 June. 1798	March 18
Petrie, John ..	32	5 ft. 7 in.	Manmuir, Forfar	Taylor	Enlisted by Ensign Fraser	May 5
Pettigrew, John ..	17	5 ft. 4 in.	Airdrie	Weaver		March 2
Philp, Charles ..	16	5 ft. 5 in.	Kennethmont	Taylor	Dead 9 July, 1794	May 29
Pirrie, William ..	35	5 ft. 5 in.	Ruthven	Labourer	Dis. 24 Feb.. 1799	May 17
Porter, Hugh ..	26	5 ft. 7 in.	Bellivoi, Ireland	Weaver	Dead 2 Oct., 1799	May 9
Powrie, Robert ..	16	5 ft. 2 in.	Blyth, Perth	Shoemaker		April 15
Rhaeburn, Thomas	34	5 ft. 7 in.	Boyndie	Cattle-dealer	Dis. 10 June, 1795	April 19
Rainey, John ..	29	5 ft. 4 in.	Old Deer	Woolcomber	Dis. 10 July, 1797	March 1
Ralph, James ..	16	5 ft. 2½ in.	Alves	Labourer	Deserted 28 Aug., 1797	April 25
Ralph, William ..	34	5 ft. 4 in.	Alves	Weaver	Dead 6 Aug., 1794	May 8
Ramsay, Samuel ..	17	5 ft. 3½ in.	Spynie	Labourer	Dead 23 Feb., 1807	June 20
Rankine, Donald ..	21	5 ft. 4 in.	Kilmally	Weaver	Enlisted by Captain J. Cameron; dis. 24 May, 1807	April 10
Rankine, James ..	18	5 ft. 4 in.	Airdrie	Weaver	Enlisted by Ensign Fraser; dead 5 Oct., 1799	March 28
Rankine, James ..	25	5 ft. 5 in.	Glasgow	Stocking-weaver	Trans. 10 Aug., 1818	April 28
Reid, Alexander ..	20	5 ft. 6 in.	Thurso	Labourer	Dis. 30 June. 1798	Feb. 28
Reid, Lawrence ..	32	5 ft. 3½ in.	Pennycook	Weaver		March 24

Name.	Age.	Height.	Birthplace.	Trade.	Career.	Attest.
Reid, William ..	31	5 ft. 6 in.	Larbert	Coalier	Dis. 27 May, 1802	May 27
Relie, Edward ..	34	5 ft. 8 in.	Ralduff, Cavan	Labourer		May 29
Rennie, David ..	16	5 ft. 4½ in.	Newcastle	Labourer		April 6
Rennie, John ..	17	5 ft. 3½ in.	Fintry, Stirling	Shoemaker		July 1
Rennie, Theodor ..	10	5 ft. 7½ in.	Dumbennan	Farmer		June 11
Rettie, Alexander ..	26	5 ft. 0 in.	New Deer	Butcher	Dis. 30 June, 1798	March 8
Reynolds, John ..	26	5 ft. 9 in.	Cabrach	Labourer		May 15
Riach, John ..	10	5 ft. 4½ in.	Aberlour	Labourer		March 11
Riach, John ..	24	5 ft. 6½ in.	Strathdon	Labourer	Dis. 4 May, 1802	June 13
Riach, William ..	17	5 ft. 4 in.	Kirkmichael	Labourer	Dead 14 Oct., 1795	June 6
Ritchie, Robert ..	18	5 ft. 7½ in.	Duffus	Labourer	Dis. 8 June, 1796	March 18
Robb, Colin ..	35	5 ft. 6 in.	Loggie, Stirling	Labourer	Dis. 27 May, 1802	May 19
Robertson, Arch. ..	19	5 ft. 5 in.	Edinburgh	Copperplate printer		March 4
Robertson, Donald	28	5 ft. 5 in.	Inch, Inverness	Labourer	Dis. 1 Feb., 1808	June 2
Robertson, Finlay	29	5 ft. 6 in.	Tain	Labourer	Trans. 24 Jan., 1808	April 17
Robertson, James	35	5 ft. 6 in.	Nielston, Renfrew	Labourer	Dead 13 June, 1797	May 20
Robertson, George	10	5 ft. 7 in.	Kairn, Aberdeen	Labourer	Trans. for service abroad, 19 May, 1810	March 29
Robertson, James	16	5 ft. 2½ in.	Stirling	Weaver	Dead 1 Nov., 1799	April 3
Robertson, John ..	18	5 ft. 7½ in.	Newhills	Labourer	Dead 29 Sept., 1795	March 5
Robertson, John ..	36	5 ft. 5 in.	....	Weaver	Left in England	March 19
Robertson, Patrick	30	5 ft. 4½ in.	Hadington	Wright	Dis. 30 June, 1798	March 28
Robertson, Robert	33	5 ft. 7 in.	Paisley	Weaver		April 4
Robertson, Wm. ..	33	5 ft. 6½ in.	Old Machar	Woolcomber	Dis. 27 May, 1802	Feb. 24
Robertson, Wm. ..		....	Aberdeen	Mason	Dead 18 Nov., 1796	May 12
Robertson, Wm. ..	35	5 ft. 9½ in.	Rutherglen	Weaver	Dead 27 Nov., 1795	June 29
Robson, William ..	35	5 ft. 6 in.	Skene	Woolcomber		March 8
Rogers, John ..	28	5 ft. 3½ in.	South Leith	Cork cutter	Enlisted by Major M'Donald; dis. 9 June, 1810	April 16
Ronalds, Alex. ..	22	5 ft. 5½ in.	Falkirk	Taylor	Enlisted by Ensign Fraser; dead 9 Oct., 1799	March 29
Ronalds, Thomas ..	24	5 ft. 4½ in.	Rhynie	Shoemaker	Dead 1 March, 1800	April 19
Roney, Donald ..	22	5 ft. 6½ in.	Killan, co. Down	Labourer	Enlisted by Lieut. Stewart	May 24
Roseside, John ..	22	5 ft. 9½ in.	Campbleton	Weaver	Dis. 24 May, 1800	April 9
Ross, Alexander ..	18	5 ft. 5½ in.	Forres	Labourer		May 12
Ross, Andrew ..	17	5 ft. 4 in.	Laggan	Labourer	Dis. 27 May, 1802	May 22
Ross, David ..	12	4 ft. 10 in.	Inverness	Labourer		Feb. 19
Ross, David ..	25	5 ft. 3½ in.	Inverness	Weaver	Dead 10 Aug., 1810	April 12
Ross, David ..	19	5 ft. 2 in.	Dornoch	Weaver	Dead 30 June, 1798	May 12
Ross, David ..	20	5 ft. 3½ in.	Laggan	Labourer		June 2
Ross, Hugh ..	12	5 ft. 0 in.	Reay	Labourer		March 26
Ross, James ..	20	5 ft. 8½ in.	Rosemeveu, Ross	Blacksmith	Trans. 61st Regt., 28 Oct., 1794	April 8
Ross, John ..	16	5 ft. 2 in.	Old Machar	Weaver	Dead 31 Oct., 1795	April 16
Ross, John ..	22	5 ft. 3 in.	Daviot, Inverness	Weaver	Trans. 10 Aug., 1810	June 7
Ross, John ..	19	5 ft. 8 in.	Olrig, Caithness	Labourer		June 5
Ross, William ..	18	5 ft. 2½ in.	Croy	Labourer	Dis. 4 May, 1802	April 4
Roxburgh, John ..	35	5 ft. 0½ in.	Newton Stewart	Shoemaker	Dead 20 Oct., 1799	May 28
Russell, John ..	23	5 ft. 8 in.	Monkland, Lanark	Weaver		April 8
Sangster, James ..	24	5 ft. 11 in.	Peterhead	Labourer		April 28
Scott, George ..	24	5 ft. 6½ in.	Gartly	Labourer	Trans. 2nd Batt., 25 Nov., 1803	Feb. 17
Scott, Robert ..	39	5 ft. 7 in.	Derry	Miller	Dis. 30 June, 1798	March 19
Seebright, George		....	....	....	Dis. 10 June, 1795	Oct. 27
Shand, Alexander	20	5 ft. 10½ in.	Speymouth	Labourer		April 12
Shand, John ..	30	5 ft. 5 in.	Turriff	Shoemaker		April 5
Shand, Robert ..	28	5 ft. 9 in.	Rhynie	Labourer		May 12
Shanks, George ..	29	6 ft. 0 in.	Glasgow	Shoemaker	Trans. 61st Regt., 28 Oct., 1794	April 25
Shanks, Hugh ..	21	5 ft. 6 in.	Kilbrachan	Weaver	Dis. 30 June, 1798	May 14
Sharp, James ..	21	5 ft. 5 in.	Invertown, Banff	Labourer		July 5
Sharp, John ..	25	5 ft. 5 in.	Drumelzier, Peebles	Printer	Dis. 27 May, 1802	March 20
Shaw, Alexander	21	5 ft. 8 in.	Kilmorich, Argyle	Labourer	Dead 3 Jan., 1799	March 11
Shaw, Peter ..	21	5 ft. 4 in.	Incrat, Inverness	Labourer		June 25
Sheddan, James ..	16	5 ft. 2 in.	St. Cuthberts, Edinburgh	Labourer	Trans. to 2nd Batt. 25 Nov., 1803; dead 22 Sept., 1809	April 8
Short, Alexander	35	5 ft. 4½ in.	Glasgow	Shoemaker	Dis. 10 June, 1795	May 17
Shuan, John ..	18	5 ft. 4½ in.	Lonmay	Labourer	Trans. 10 Aug., 1810	April 22
Sibbald, Thomas ..	28	5 ft. 11 in.	Brughton, Tweeddale	Shoemaker		April 22
Sime, Daniel ..	30	5 ft. 8 in.	Maybole	Labourer		May 21
Sime, David ..	18	5 ft. 5 in.	Dundee	Labourer		June 6
Sime, John ..	27	5 ft. 6 in.	Elgin	Labourer	Dead 26 Sept., 1795	May 10
Simpson, James ..	17	5 ft. 8 in.	Bellie	Labourer		May 18
Simpson, Peter ..	19	5 ft. 7 in.	Old Machar	Combmaker	Dead 2 Oct., 1799	April 3
Simpson, Thomas ..	17	5 ft. 3 in.	Edinburgh	Hairdresser	Dead 24 Aug., 1798	May 2
Sinclair, David ..	20	5 ft. 7½ in.	Stronsay	Wheelwright		May 9

Name.	*Age.*	*Height.*	*Birthplace.*	*Trade.*	*Career.*	*Attest.*
Sinclair, George	20	5 ft. 9½ in.	Bower, Caithness	Weaver		June 12
Sinclair, John	20	5 ft. 8½ in.	Blackford, Perth	Mason	Trans. R. Wy(?) A. 24 March, 1804	March 24
Sinclair, Peter	16	5 ft. 5 in.	Reay	Labourer	[Dis.?] 27 May, 1802	March 9
Sinclair, William	37	5 ft. 8 in.	Reay	Wine cooper	Dead 27 Aug., 1799	April 12
Skeen, Joseph	29	5 ft. 4½ in.	Tarland	Woolcomber		March 15
Skeen, William	32	5 ft. 5 in.	Inverkeithnie	Hairdresser		May 10
Slimman, Andrew	20	5 ft. 11 in.	Falkirk	Miner	Trans. 10 Aug., 1810	May 15
Smellie, John	34	5 ft. 11½ in.	Dalserf, Lanark	Weaver	Dis. 30 June, 1798	May 3
Smith, Alexander	21	5 ft. 7 in.	Turriff	Weaver	[Dis.?] 30 June, 1798	March 7
Smith, Alexander	21	5 ft. 7 in.	Dunlichity, Inverness	Labourer	Dead 25 Nov., 1795	March 18
Smith, Alexander	..	....	....	....	Enlisted by Major M'Donald; dead (date not known)	May 1
Smith, Andrew	..	....	....	....	Enlisted by Major M'Donald; dis. 8 June, 1796	April 19
Smith, Findlay	20	5 ft. 4½ in.	Daviot, Inverness	Taylor		April 25
Smith, George	35	5 ft. 6½ in.	Coldstone, Aberdeen	Woolcomber	Dis. 30 June, 1798	March 2
Smith, George	27	6 ft. 2 in.	Kilmarnock	Weaver	Dis. 24 May, 1800	April 4
Smith, John	32	5 ft. 4½ in.	Strachan, Aberdeen	Taylor	Dis. 10 June, 1795	March 28
Smith, John	37	5 ft. 9 in.	St. Philip's, Gloucester	Labourer	Enlisted by Ensign Fraser; dis. 3 Nov., 1795	March 31
Smith, John	19	5 ft. 3 in.	Mary Culter	Smith		April 19
Smith, Robert	34	5 ft. 8 in.	Newmilns, co. Tyrone	Weaver	Dis. 24 Feb., 1799	March 19
Smith, William	20	5 ft. 2 in.	St. Ninian, Stirling	Nailsmith	Dead 31 May, 1799	April 14
Smout, George	21	5 ft. 8½ in.	Ellon,	Labourer		May 2
Snaddon, John	32	5 ft. 6 in.	Shaws, Fife	Weaver	Enlisted by Lieut. M'Lean; dis. 10 June, 1795	May 12
Sochling, C. Augustus	27	....	Hess Castle, Reutlin, Germany	Musician	Dis. 16 May, 1798	Nov. 3
Stewart, Alex.	24	5 ft. 11½ in.	Kilmanivaig	Labourer		Feb. 25
Stewart, Alex.	23	5 ft. 8½ in.	Mortlach	Labourer	Dis. 1 April, 1805	May 3
Stewart, Alex.	34	5 ft. 5 in.	Portree	Labourer		June 11
Stewart, Archibald	34	5 ft. 3 in.	North Uist	Woolcomber	Dis. 8 June, 1796	April 15
Stewart, Daniel	23	5 ft. 8 in.	Blair Athol	Waiter		March 20
Stewart, Donald	21	5 ft. 8 in.	Kirkmichael	Labourer	Dead 17 Sept., 1809	April 3
Stewart, James	19	5 ft. 8 in.	Greenock	Labourer	Trans. 9th R.V. Batt. 27 May, 1807	March 11
Stewart, James	19	5 ft. 6 in.	Mortlach	Labourer	Dead 2 Oct., 1799	July 8
Stewart, James	23	5 ft. 6 in.	Slate, Inverness	Taylor	Dead 2 Oct., 1799	Sept. 27
Stewart, John	33	5 ft. 6 in.	Kirkmichael	Labourer		June 4
Stewart, John	24	5 ft. 10 in.	Inveraven	Labourer		June 6
Stewart, John	33	5 ft. 4 in.	Kilmore, Inverness	Labourer	Dis. 30 June, 1798	Aug. 26
Stewart, Lewis	35	5 ft. 6 in.	Inveraven	Labourer	Dis. 10 June, 1795	June 5
Stewart, Norman	17	5 ft. 3 in.	Inverness	Labourer		July 10
Stewart, Robert	16	5 ft. 4 in.	Cairney	Labourer		March 4
Stewart, Robert	16	5 ft. 2 in.	Kirkmichael	Labourer	Deserted 27 June, 1794	March 2
Stewart, William	36	5 ft. 7 in.	Fortingall	Labourer		Feb 25
Stewart, William	20	5 ft. 10 in.	Glenavy, Antrim	Apothecary	Dis. 10 June, 1795	April 26
Still, George	27	5 ft. 5½ in.	Aberdeen	Woolcomber	Dead 21 Jan., 1796	April 17
Stronach, Thomas	20	5 ft. 4 in.	Cairney	Labourer		Feb. 27
Sutherland, Angus	13	4 ft. 10 in.	Saggie, Sutherland	Labourer	Dead 3 Oct., 1799	Nov. 1
Sutherland, James	17	5 ft. 5 in.	Thurso	Weaver	Dead 2 Oct., 1799	May 10
Sutherland, Wm.	..	....	Ardersier, Inverness	Labourer	Dis. 30 Jan., 1798	Oct. 22
Symers, Andrew	23	5 ft. 7 in.	Keig	Weaver		Feb. 24
Symons, Alexander	16	5 ft. 7 in.	Cairney	Labourer		May 31
Symons, James	18	5 ft. 5½ in.	Keith	Shoemaker	Discharged	April 18
Swan, William	34	5 ft. 8 in.	Liberton, Edinburgh	Sawer		April 2
Swanson, David	16	5 ft. 3¾ in.	Elach, Caithness	Labourer	Trans. 9th R.V. Batt. 15 Oct., 1806	June 14
Tait, Andrew	35	5 ft. 5 in.	Hilsborrow, co. Down	Weaver	Dis. 24 Feb., 1799	May 3
Taylor, James	17	5 ft. 7¾ in.	Bellie	Labourer	Dis. 10 June, 1799	March 20
Taylor, John	19	5 ft. 5 in.	Forres	Hosier	Dead 2 Oct., 1799	May 3
Teisdale, John	16	5 ft. 4 in.	Dalserf, Lanark	Weaver	Dead 28 Aug., 1795	April 8
Thoburn, George	22	5 ft. 6 in.	Traquire, Tweed-dale	Weaver		April 16
Thomas, Thomas	35	5 ft. 7½ in.	Lanbaden, Cardigan	Pensioner	Dead 29 May, 1795	April 10
Thomson, Alex.	21	5 ft. 5 in.	Oldmacher	Weaver	Dead 10 Jan., 1796	April 5
Thomson, Alex.	34	5 ft. 5½ in.	Kintyre, Argyle	Shoemaker	Dead 8 Jan., 1796	April 5
Thomson, Alex.	18	5 ft. 4 in.	Glasgow	Weaver		May 15
Thomson, David	..	....	....	....	Enlisted by Major M'Donald; dead 2 Oct., 1799	April 23
Thomson, David	23	5 ft. 8 in.	Falkirk	Labourer	Dead 22 May, 1795	May 6
Thomson, George	33	5 ft. 4 in.	Forgue	Taylor	Dis. 30 Jan., 1798	Feb. 24

Name.	*Age.*	*Height.*	*Birthplace.*	*Trade.*	*Career.*	*Attest.*
Thomson, James ..	16	5 ft. 4 in.	West Quarter, Lanark	Weaver	Enlisted by Ensign Fraser	April 8
Thomson, James ..	35	5 ft. 7¾ in.	Dalserf, Lanark	Cotton-spinner	Enlisted by Capt. Fraser; dis. 20 May, 1800	April 9
Thomson, James ..	34	5 ft. 3¼ in.	Elgin	Taylor	Dis. 10 June, 1795	May 12
Thomson, Peter ..	37	5 ft. 5 in.	Falkirk	Labourer	Dis. 27 May, 1802	May 5
Thomson, Thomas	26	5 ft. 6¾ in.	Humbie, Edinburgh	Labourer	Dis. 20 May, 1800	April 24
Thomson, Thomas	31	5 ft. 10¾ in.	Annan	Labourer	Enlisted by Marquis of Huntly; former service: 5 yrs. 5 mths., 81st Regt.; 11 yrs. 5 mths, 61st Regt.; dis. 9 Nov., 1796	Nov. 3
Tod, Andrew ..	25	5 ft. 9 in.	Leslie, Fife	Confectioner	Dis. 16 March, 1798	Oct. 21
Tod, James ..	26	5 ft. 9 in.	Ellon	Labourer		March 28
Tugh, Matthew ..	21	5 ft. 4½ in.	Aberdeen	Servant		March 15
Turnbull, George	47	5 ft. 11 in.	Dunbar	Labourer	Dead 21 Feb., 1795	April 22
Turner, Alexander	18	5 ft. 6 in.	Glasgow	Blacksmith		May 21
Turner, Archibald	15	5 ft. 2 in.	Glasgow	Nailsmith	Deserted 16 Dec., 1798	May 23
Turner, James ..	35	5 ft. 6½ in.	Greenock	Blacksmith	Dead 28 July, 1795	May 18
Urquhart, Alex. ..	19	5 ft. 3¼ in.	Cromarty	Taylor	Dead 18 June, 1796	May 21 1795
Urquhart, Donald	20	5 ft. 6½ in.	Cromarty	Labourer		May 13
Urquhart, George ..	18	5 ft. 4 in.	Cromarty	Labourer	Dead 15 Sept., 1809	April 15
Urquhart, John ..	38	5 ft. 5 in.	Invery, Inverness	Stocking-maker	Dis. 10 June, 1795	May 24
Vickerman, Fred ..	25	5 ft. 5½ in.	Edinburgh	Labourer	Trans. 10 Aug., 1810	April 3
Walker, James ..	15	5 ft. 2½ in.	Gartly	Weaver		April 25
Wallace, George ..	19	5 ft. 4 in.	Edinburgh	Woolcomber		March 2
Wallace, John ..	16	5 ft. 4 in.	Gorbals	Weaver		March 6
Wands, William ..	17	5 ft. 6 in.	Botrifney, Banff	Labourer		May 15
Watson, Adam ..	22	5 ft. 5½ in.	Duffus	Servant		April 23
Watson, John ..	23	5 ft. 5 in.	Cromarty	Taylor	Dead 2 Oct., 1799	March 8
Watson, Thomas	19	5 ft. 8 in.	Gorbals	Weaver	Trans. 46th Regt. 2 Nov., 1794	March 20
Watson, Walter ..	14	5 ft. 1 in.	Glasgow	Weaver		April 11
Watson, William ..	30	5 ft. 8½ in.	Clackmannan	Labourer	Dis. 31 Dec., 1799	March 12
Watson, William ..	18	5 ft. 8 in.	Slamaunan, Stirling	Labourer	Dead 22 Dec., 1795	May 23
Watt, Alexander ..	27	5 ft. 8 in.	Crief	Mason	Dead 4 Feb., 1799	March 29
Watt, Alexander ..	28	5 ft. 8¼ in.	Keith	Hatmaker	Trans. 9th R.V. Batt. 29 March, 1805	April 27
Watt, James ..	16	5 ft. 4 in.	Stirling	Labourer		April 10
Watt, John	22	5 ft. 7½ in.	Gartly	Millwright	Dead 13 Nov., 1795	March 17
Watt, John	20	5 ft. 8 in.	Crief	Mason	Dead 17 Nov., 1794	March 20
Watt, John	17	5 ft. 6 in.	Deskford	Labourer	Dead 23 Dec., 1795	July 8
Watt, Nathaniel ..	24	5 ft. 7 in.	Rothes	Mason	Dis. 1 June, 1803	March 1
Watt, Robert ..	9	4 ft. 1 in.	Banff	Labourer		May 24
Webster, Cusine ..	19	5 ft. 5½ in.	Dunfermline	Weaver	Dis. 27 March, 1802	May 19
Weir, James ..	16	5 ft. 4 in.	Kirkintilloch	Weaver	Dis. 21 May, 1800	May 14
White, William ..	16	5 ft. 3¼ in.	Glasgow	Weaver	Dead 18 Jan., 1796	Jan. 9 1795
Whiteford, David	17	5 ft. 5 in.	Beith, Ayr	Weaver		May 19
Whiteford, John ..	16	5 ft. 4 in.	Beith, Ayr	Labourer		May 14
Whyte, James ..	30	5 ft. 4 in.	Glasgow	Weaver	Dead 18 Nov., 1797	April 3
Whyte, James ..	18	5 ft. 4½ in.	Falkirk	Coalhewer		May 18
Whyte, William ..	20	5 ft. 5 in.	Falkirk	Labourer	Dis. 20 May, 1800	May 12
Williamson, Mal.	35	5 ft. 4 in.	Glasgow	Weaver	Dis. 10 June, 1795	April 29
Willie, Wilson ..	22	5 ft. 10½ in.	Govan	Weaver		April 22
Wilson, Evan ..	25	5 ft. 6 in.	South Uist	Labourer		May 8
Wilson, Hugh ..	28	5 ft. 5 in.	Paisley	Weaver	Dis. 1 April, 1803	May 20
Wilson, James ..	32	5 ft. 8 in.	Glass	Flaxdresser	Dead 24 Feb., 1799	March 5
Wilson, James ..	23	5 ft. 3 in.	Bellie	Blacksmith	Dead 2 April, 1798	May 18
Wilson, John ..	19	5 ft. 8½ in.	Gravesend, Kent	Labourer	Deserted 24 Sept., 1794	March 6
Wilson, Montgomery	16	5 ft. 3¼ in.	Liberton	Labourer		April 25
Wilson, Robert ..	18	5 ft. 3 in.	Fyvie	Weaver	Dead 6 Sept., 1798	March 12
Wilson, Thomas ..	12	4 ft. 10 in.	Stirling	Labourer	Dis. 24 June, 1797	April 25
Wilson, William ..	30	5 ft. 11 in.	Keith	Gamekeeper	Dis. (date not known)	March 30
Wilson, William ..	34	5 ft. 5½ in.	Glasgow	Maltster	Dis. 9 July, 1802	May 8
Wood, Alexander	28	5 ft. 6½ in.	Aberdeen	Wright	Dead 2 Oct., 1799	April 11
Wood, David ..	28	6 ft. 4 in.	Dyke, Moray	Labourer	Dead 20 March, 1795	April 9
Wood, James ..	35	5 ft. 7 in.	Glasgow	Shoemaker	Enlisted by Ensign Fraser; dead 3 Oct., 1799	April 20
Wright, Archibald	21	5 ft. 6 in.	Drumgull, co. Down	Weaver	Dead 19 Jan., 1809	May 11
Wright, James ..	15	5 ft. 3¼ in.	Clackmannan	Weaver	Trans. 6th R.V. Batt. 24 June, 1805	March 17
Wright, Peter ..	14	4 ft. 10 in.	Glasgow	Pipemaker	Dis. 24 June, 1797	April 20

Name.	Age.	Height.	Birthplace.	Trade.	Career.	Attest.
Young, James	20	5 ft. 8½ in.	Ordiquhill	Brazier	Trans. 6th R.V. Batt. 24 May, 1807	March 1
Young, James	30	5 ft. 4 in.	Slains	China mender		Aug. 28
Young, John	25	5 ft. 0 in.	Ordiquhill	Brazier		March 1
Young, John	20	5 ft. 0 in.	Gorbals	Slater		March 28
Young, John	34	5 ft. 7½ in.	Irvine	Hatter	Dis. 20 May, 1800	April 26
Young, William	30	5 ft. 8¼ in.	Fenwick, Ayr	Weaver		April 3
Young, William	14	5 ft. 2½ in.	Paisley	Shoemaker		June 24
Younger, William	20	5 ft. 8 in.	Clackmannan	Wright		Feb. 20

THE 109TH: OR ABERDEENSHIRE REGIMENT OF FOOT.

1794: RAISED BY ALEXANDER LEITH-HAY: DRAFTED 1795.

The 109th Regiment, of small north-country importance in itself, as it very soon vanished from the Army List, is interesting for three specific reasons. In the first place, it affords one the opportunity of noting how the family of Leith, which raised it, came to power, especially in the annals of soldiering. In the second, it illustrates the strong family rivalry which was at the back of so much of the regiment-raising in the second half of the eighteenth century. Last of all, it shows up the hugger-mugger methods of the military authorities, who, having put an officer to the trouble and expense of raising a corps, soon found they had so little use for it that they drafted it into other corps, greatly to its creator's chagrin, to the discouragement of similar enthusiasts, and to the discontent of the folk of the countryside which had supplied the men.

The raising of the 109th, excellent as it was in view of the urgent need of troops for national defence, was carried out with a sense of rivalry against the Duke of Gordon that bore the suspicion of strong animus. What the cause of this may have been it is difficult to decide. The Leiths had been settled in Aberdeenshire probably as long as the Gordons, who had gone north in the beginning of the fourteenth century from Berwickshire—the Leiths had come from Midlothian—on the forfeiture of David de Strabolgi, Earl of Atholl. A picturesque echo of the latter's fate and of the Leith rivalry with the Gordons has come down to our time in the claim of Lieutenant-Colonel A. H. Leith of Glenkindie for the barony of Strabolgi. But the Gordons had taken to the Services long before the Leiths. The first of the Leiths to enter the Army seems to have been Alexander of the Bucharne family, who fell as an Artillery officer at the siege of Havannah in 1762. It is probable that the activities of a soldier's life had been introduced into the family by this officer's grandfather, Major Walter Ogilvy, son of Sir

Patrick Ogilvy, Lord Boyne. However that may be, the Leiths suddenly rose from the duties of local lairds to the distinction of arms, as the accompanying table shows.

Having put in a brief apprenticeship to soldiering, the Leiths decided to combine it with territorial influence. The first to do so was Lawrence Leith of the Bucharne family, who got a commission in the Duke of Gordon's Regiment, the 89th, in 1759; but when the Duke was countered in 1778 by his kinsman, Colonel William Gordon, with the 81st, Alexander Leith (afterwards Leith-Hay), of the Leith-hall family, and his more famous brother, James, took post in it, and conducted recruiting in the ducal domain itself, greatly to the Duke's anger.

The dislike of the Gordons may have been inherited with the appearance of a Strachan bride among the Leith-hall Leiths, for the family of Glenkindie, as staunch Covenanters, had suffered severely at the hands of the Gordons, and even at the end of the 17th century the old feud was carried on by the lawless conduct of the laird of Glenbucket against his neighbour at Glenkindie. Another form of the vendetta occurred in 1738-40, when John Leith of Leith-hall (the father of Alexander Leith-Hay) and his uncle, Patrick Leith, brought a lawsuit over money alleged to have been lent to the impecunious Arthur Gordon of Law, who was said to have borrowed largely from John Leith, IV. of Leith-hall. Leith's widow had taken James Gordon, the laird of Clashtirum, for a second husband, and she and her brother-in-law, Gordon of Drumwhindle, father of Colonel Charles Gordon of the Atholl Highlanders, supported Gordon of Law, the defender in the action.

Between 1778, when the 81st was raised, and 1794, Alexander Leith had become quite a county personage, for he not only held Leith-hall, but he had succeeded to Rannes in 1789 (taking the additional name of Hay in consequence), and had been served heir in other properties to different relatives. He was thus in a position to have a regiment of his very own, instead of helping to officer a Gordon's. Not only so, he decided to be equal to the double effort of the Duke, for, while he raised the 109th as the Leith answer to the 92nd (or 100th as it then was), his brother James raised (in 1795) the Aberdeenshire Fencibles to match the Northern Fencibles raised by the Duke in 1793.

The year 1794 found Leith-Hay not only a laird on a big scale

but an officer with Army rank, for he had been appointed a Lieutenant in the 7th Dragoons on his birth, and a Captain at the age of ten.

On March 8, 1794, he wrote from Leith-hall to Sir George Yonge, at the War Office (*W.O.* 1 : 1,072):—"In the beginning of the war I offered to raise a regiment of Highlanders and will still undertake to raise one on the same establishment and terms with those now going on in Scotland." His offer was on this occasion accepted, and he got his Letter of Service on April 2, 1794. Having kissed the King's hand, he immediately left London for Aberdeen to recruit. As we shall see, his ambition, starting gaily off, was soon curbed, for his regiment lived only eighteen months, being drafted in September, 1795, into the 53rd.

At the beginning, he got much support from a certain section of the county gentry and from the town of Aberdeen. Finlason, recruiting for the Gordons, became panic-stricken. He had suggested the name "Aberdeenshire Regiment" for the Gordons, and was alarmed when he heard on March 11 that Hay was to adopt that designation. As a matter of fact, Hay won the day, and his successes became a perfect nightmare to Finlason, whose letters to Gordon Castle are one long wail as to his encroachments. On March 12, Finlason wrote—"The Aberdeenshire Regiment will be upon us," the smallness of the Gordon bounty troubling him especially (*Gordon Castle Papers*):—

If friends to one Corps (Hay's) advertise gratuitys, the other, the Marquis's, will find some to do so too. It becomes necessary in such a case, and there is no help. It is inflaming the reckoning on both sides, but the Marquis will chuse to keep his ground, I daresay.

The situation was, however, approached with a sense of humour by George Bell, Coclarachie, who wrote on March 28 as follows (*Ibid.*):—

> On Thursday,
> We'll convene the farmers round
> Our hills and preach up Bon-Accord ;
> Say, what we mean is for their good
> And serving of their Lord.

And if we be in luck, we may hear the remainder of this elegant ditty from our friend Captain Leith, who, I think and hope, is hearty in the cause, notwithstanding of his intimacy and friendship with Colonel Hay. Although, as you say, our appearance will convince the publick of our attachment, yet I'm afraid the money of others will be an argument with the young fellows of a nature as convincing as our perswasions.

Captain Forsyth raises a company either for the Marquis or Colonel

Hay—for the latter, I suppose, as he made the first offer; but nothing need be feared from him, as his brothers in London raise the men, and he does not propose braving odium here and only to pick up straggling doggs, and even this only privately, for, if he be in opposition to the Marquis, his father will not admit of a publick appearance.

The lairds took sides at once. To begin with, a meeting held at Aberdeen under the chairmanship of Leith of Freefield voted Hay its cordial support. On April 17, another meeting of freeholders, Commissioners of Supply and others, appointed a working committee to support Hay, and offered a substantial bounty—which Hay, however, declined on the ground that the Government grant was sufficient. General Sir A. J. F. Reid, who made a special study of the 109th, notes (*Aberdeen Journal*, December 11, 1907) that

The Colonel [Hay] was so popular that one market day as many as eighteen men joined him. Mr. Skene of Skene brought a large contingent drawn from his own estates and obtained at Rood Fair, Montrose, where he had liberally regaled all and sundry at the Market Cross. The Earl of Aberdeen was at Tarland to help on the work [May 21, 1794], and, punch being distributed in great abundance in the street, a number of "very fine young men" were enlisted [*Aberdeen Journal*, May 26, 1794]. The regiment was complete by the beginning of September.

The officers of the 109th from first to last were as follows (*W.O.* 25; 156, 157, 158, 159, 160, 161, 162, 214, 215, 224, 226, 766):—

COLONEL.

Alexander Leith-Hay (from half pay 104th), Lieutenant-Colonel Commanding, April 2, 1794; Colonel Commanding, October 1, 1794. Son of John Leith of Leith-hall; succeeded to that estate and also to Rannes; married, 1784, Mary, eldest daughter and co-heiress of Charles Forbes of Ballogie, and had General Sir Andrew Leith-Hay (1785-1862) and Rear-Admiral John James Leith (1788-1854); died May 16, 1838.

MAJORS.

Erskine Fraser (from Major, 34th), April 2, 1794; Lieutenant-Colonel, October 1, 1794, *vice* Hay; retired by September 19, 1795. Laird of Woodhill; married Elizabeth Forbes (1766-1813), and had an only son, Colonel William Fraser, 43rd Regiment (1796-1872). Erskine Fraser died January 21, 1804, aged 37 (Munro's *Old Aberdeen* ii., 223).

Peter Garden (from Captain, 57th), April 3, 1794; Lieutenant-Colonel, September 19, 1795, *vice* Fraser. Younger son of Peter Garden of Delgaty and Troup, who, marrying a Glenlyon Campbell, assumed the additional name of Campbell   His grand-aunt, Jean, married Alexander Leith of Freefield, and was the mother of Garden Leith

CAPTAINS

Thomas Philip Ainslie (from Lieutenant, 31st), April 4, 1794, Major, September 19, 1795

Alexander Irvine (from Lieutenant, 84th), August 21, 1794.

Alexander Leith (from Lieutenant, Independent Company), November 27, 1794

James Mackenzie (from Lieutenant, 93rd), April 6, 1794

Charles Stewart (from Lieutenant, 71st), April 3, 1794, joined 109th, September 2, 1795

William Stopford (from Lieutenant, 54th), September 19, 1795

George Sutherland (from Captain, Independent Company), April 2, 1794

William Whalley (from Lieutenant, Independent Company), April 5, 1794, Major, 106th, November 5, 1794.

CAPTAIN-LIEUTENANT

James Morrison (from Lieutenant, Independent Company), November 27, 1794, Captain, November 29, 1794, *vice* Whalley

LIEUTENANTS

John Fraser (from Ensign, 84th), April 9, 1794, joined 53rd, September 7, 1795.

Francis Grant (from Ensign, 97th), April 28, 1795, *vice* William Grant, joined 53rd, September 14, 1795

Johnston Grant (from Ensign, 106th), November 30, 1794. Captain, by purchase, December 16, 1794, in 107th

William Grant (from Ensign, 97th), November 28, 1794, joined 53rd, September 8, 1795

John Leith (from Ensign, 106th), August 24, 1795, *vice* George Leith declines

Thomas Leslie (from Lieutenant, 78th), December 12, 1794, *vice* Mackintosh

Arthur Lloyd (from Lieutenant, 110th), April 27, 1795 ; joined 53rd, September 15, 1795

Phineas Mackintosh (from Ensign 78th, which he joined, aged 17, February 11, 1794); November 27, 1794, Lieutenant, December 12, 1794, 78th.

William Ponsonby, joined 53rd, September 10, 1795.

Maxwell Stuart (from Ensign, 100th), April 2, 1794, dead by April 1, 1795

Francis Wemyss (from Ensign, 84th), June 21, 1794, died before February 9, 1795

Thomas Williamson (from Ensign, Independent Company), April 2, 1794; Captain-Lieutenant, November 29, 1794; Captain, September 29, 1794.

John Wynne (from 110th), May 27, 1795, joined 53rd, September 16, 1795.

ENSIGNS.

Francis Philip Bedingfield (from Volunteer), February 25, 1795, *vice* Nicoll; joined 106th by April 22, 1795.

William Brocky, April 1, 1795, *vice* George Leslie; Lieutenant, same day; he was Surgeon's Mate; joined 53rd, September 8, 1795.

William Byres, April 4, 1794; Lieutenant, February 19, 1795, *vice* Wemyss.

Hugh Douglas (from Sergeant-Major), August 24, 1795.

John Grant, April 1, 1795, *vice* Lushington; joined 53rd, September 7, 1795.

Andrew Leith-Hay, April 2, 1794; Lieutenant, November 29, 1794, *vice* Williamson; joined 53rd, September 9, 1795; served in the Peninsular War as A.D.C. to his uncle, Sir James Leith, and wrote a *Narrative* of that war. Elder son of Colonel Alexander Leith-Hay (*supra*), born 1785; Governor of Bermuda, 1838-41; knighted 1834; wrote the *Castellated Architecture of Aberdeenshire*; died October 13, 1862 (*D.N.B.*).

Alexander Leith, April 1, 1795, *vice* Thomas Leslie; joined 53rd, September 6, 1795.

William G. Leith, April 6, 1794; joined 53rd, September 3, 1795.

George Leslie, April 5, 1794; Lieutenant, April 1, 1795, *vice* Stewart; joined 53rd, September 13, 1795.

Thomas Leslie, April 3, 1794; joined 78th (apparently rejoined 109th as Lieutenant, December 12, 1794); joined 53rd, September 11, 1795.

Charles Lushington, November 27, 1794; joined 101st by April 1, 1795.

Phillip Nicolli, October 15, 1794; joined 106th by February 25, 1795.

John Smith (from Volunteer), February 25, 1795, *vice* Hay; joined 53rd, September 5, 1795.

Ludovick Stewart, April 22, 1795, *vice* Bedingfield.

John Vispre, January 14, 1795; Lieutenant, August 24, 1795; joined 53rd, September 17, 1795.

CHAPLAIN.

Robert Shepherd, April 2, 1794.

SURGEON.

James Bannerman, April 2, 1794.

ADJUTANT.

William Deans, April 2, 1794; Ensign, February 19, 1795.

QUARTERMASTER.

William Skene, April 2, 1794.

The first pay roll of the regiment (there are only two at the Record Office) covers the period, April 2-September 4, 1794, and designates the corps "H.M. 109th (or Aberdeenshire) Regiment." The state of the muster was a follows (*W.O.* 12: 10,003):—

	Sergeants.	Corporals.	Drummers.	Privates.
Present - - -	17	12	15	230
Absent - - -	6	3	2	152
Non-effective since -	9	15	5	228
Totals -	32	30	22	610

There were only three privates named Hay, and 33 Macs. Curiously enough there were 11 Gordons:—

Sergeant John Gordon	-	-	-	Attested June 1, 1794.
Corporal James Gordon	-	-	-	„ April 2, 1794 (dead).
„ John Gordon -	-	-	-	„ April 14, 1794.
Private George Gordon	-	-	-	„ May 21, 1794.
„ Hugh Gordon -	-	-	-	„ April 21, 1794.
„ James Gordon -	-	-	-	„ June 13, 1794.
„ James Gordon -	-	-	-	„ June 24, 1794.
„ John Gordon -	-	-	-	„ May 6, 1794.
„ John Gordon -	-	-	-	„ July 21, 1794.
„ Maxwell Gordon	-	-	-	„ May 20, 1794.
„ William Gordon	-	-	-	„ July 13, 1794.

The regiment was inspected and passed at Aberdeen, September 5, 1794, by General Sir Hector Munro, when colours were presented to it from the county. It marched south by divisions, and by the end of September was concentrated in Dundee, embarking at Burntisland for Southampton, which was reached, October 26. It went to Jersey in April, 1795 (*W.O.* 5: 71: p. 68), returning to England in July, 1795, to join a force, fixed at twenty regiments, assembling at Nursling Common, Southampton, under General Sir Ralph Abercromby, for a descent on the West Indies.

Some trouble with officers occurred at this time, though all I know about it is from the Commander-in-Chief's letter, dated August 18, 1795 (*W.O.* 3: 14: p. 145):—

My Dear General [Gordon],—I laid before His Royal Highness and have the pleasure to acquaint you that he approved entirely of your conduct relative to Captain Leith and Lieutenant Leslie of the 109th

Regiment, and of the lenity you had thought proper for the reasons assigned in your letter to show them.

While the regiment was at Nursling Common an order came that it was to be drafted into the 53rd, now the 1st battalion of the Shropshire Light Infantry. The Colonel protested, but all in vain, for he had not the influence of a man like the Duke of Gordon. On August 20, 1795, he wrote from London " To the County of Aberdeen " as follows (*Morning Chronicle*, September 1):—

My Lords and Gentlemen,—It is impossible for me to express to you my feelings at this moment, when I find myself called upon to address you on a subject most painful and unexpected.

When I had the honour, by your zeal for the King's service, and your kindness towards me, of becoming Colonel of the County Regiment, I considered my situation of a nature to require my best endeavours to render the Corps worthy of that protection which you so liberally evinced towards it; and I can venture to assure you, that (notwithstanding various unfortunate circumstances), by the activity of my Officers, it had arrived at a state of discipline which permitted me to flatter myself the time was at hand when they should, in the field, testify their love of their country. At the instant we expected to be sent on actual service, figure my astonishment at being informed that Government had resolved to draft the Aberdeenshire Regiment, in violation of the faith pledged to me in my Letter of Service, and by me held out as an inducement to our countrymen to enlist into the regiment, *viz.*, that when the regiment should be disbanded, it should take place in the county where it was raised.

I lost no time in coming to town, and now have the honour to state to you the measures I have taken, and the grief I have in finding them ineffectual. I represented to his Royal Highness the Duke of York, and to Mr. Dundas, his Majesty's Minister for the War Department, that if the King had no further use for the service of the 109th Regiment, as a Corps, they would be pleased to solicit, in consequence of the particular situation in which we were raised, that the men might be permitted to turn out Volunteers, and choose the regiments into which they might enlist, and such as did not wish to serve in any other regiment, might be sent home—or that the regiment might be disbanded entirely ; and, last of all, I stated that I should be exceedingly sorry, if it could be supposed I had any idea in this application, except that the faith which was pledged to the men, should be preserved; assuring them, that I was perfectly ready and willing to go with the Corps to any part of the world, without receiving pay for myself as Colonel of the Aberdeenshire Regiment.

Permit me now to request you will do me the justice to believe I have been entirely actuated by the most ardent wish to preserve faith with the County and my Regiment, not an individual of whom but was ready to serve in any part of the world.

I trust that such steps may still be taken as the wisdom of the County may think right, to restore those men, if it is their wish, to the County, instead of being incorporated with any other regiment whatever.

I must in justice to Mr. Ferguson, mention to you, that every exertion hath been used by him, with administration, on this occasion, although unsuccessfully.

The *Morning Chronicle*, then edited by the famous Aberdeen journalist, James Perry (1756-1821), strongly supported Hay in an editorial note introducing his letter (September 1):—

However necessary for the public service it may be to draft the men from new Regiments into old, it is much to be lamented that measures were not taken to obviate the discontents which it was easy to see it must occasion among the men who understood the terms of their enlisting to be that they should not be drafted. Nothing can be more dangerous than for the Government of a country to be suspected of breaking faith with those who are to fight in its defence. The late Mutiny of the Manchester and Birmingham Regiments in Dublin is imputable to this cause alone; and although the mutiny has been quelled, every military man knows that many of the men will carry their discontents to the regiments into which they may be drafted, and, instead of proving good soldiers themselves, corrupt others who but for such communication would have become good soldiers.

All protests, however, were in vain, and the 109th ceased to exist officially on September 24, 1795. The question afterwards came up in Parliament. On November 20, 1795, General Fitzpatrick moved " That there be laid before the House a copy of the Letter of Service for raising the 109th, or Aberdeenshire Regiment, commanded by Colonel Hay," and this was ordered to be done (*Morning Chronicle*, November 21). On November 26, he expressed his belief that the disbandment was contrary to the spirit of the Letter of Service, and moved for copies of the correspondence between Hay and the Secretary at War or any other of the Ministry to be laid on the table (*Ibid.*, November 27). General Macleod seconded this motion because he understood that the conditions upon which the regiment was raised were that the men when they were disbanded should be disbanded into their own country, or near their own homes, whereas they were drafted and dispersed to other regiments, which made it impossible for all to be disbanded in their own country, or near their own homes, and consequently there appeared to be a breach of faith upon the part of the Government. On the other hand, Alexander Allardyce (1743-1801), of Dunnottar, M.P. (from 1792 to 1801) for the Aberdeen District of Burghs, told the House that no complaints had been made from Aberdeen : which called up General Macleod to explain (*Ibid.*, November 27).

An index of various documents dealing with the internal economy of the regiment appears in the War Office documents at the Public Record Office (*W.O.* 2 : 36 : p. 162).

The number 109th had been used for a regiment (1761-63) raised by a Perthshire man, Major John Nairne (died 1782), who but for the attainder of his Jacobite father would have been 4th Lord Nairne : it was raised, however, chiefly in Herts and Middlesex. Major Nairne gave its colours to his cousin, the Duke of Atholl, and they are still at Blair Castle (*Military History of Perthshire*, i., 67). As if to celebrate the centenary of this corps, the number was revived in 1861, when the 3rd (Bombay) Regiment, raised in 1854, was so numbered. It is now the second battalion of the Leinster Regiment, the first battalion of which was the 100th—originally the number of the Gordon Highlanders.

ABERDEENSHIRE FENCIBLES: OR PRINCESS OF WALES'S.

1794: RAISED BY JAMES LEITH: DISBANDED 1803.

So pressing was the nation's need for additional troops in the last decade of the eighteenth century that while Leith-Hay was raising his line regiment, the 109th, his younger brother, Major James Leith, set about raising a Fencible regiment in Aberdeenshire.

The appearance of Leith on the scene marked a new condition of affairs in the troubled world of recruiting. The big territorial landlords had said their say as it were, and the Government were now utilising military officers with a territorial background. Leith himself had no land, but he was connected with the landed gentry. His real qualification was his soldiership, which proved to be of a very high order. The younger son of John Leith of Leith-hall, and the brother of Alexander Leith-Hay of Leith-hall and Rannes, he was born in 1763, and entered the 21st Foot as 2nd Lieutenant in 1780. He then got a company in 1782 in the 81st, commanded by the Hon. William Gordon, and thus understood the spirit of rivalry to the Duke of Gordon early in his career. He transferred to the 50th in 1784, and was promoted to be Captain of an Independent Company of Foot on March 19, 1794 (*W.O.* 25: 157: p. 124).

On October 25, 1794, he got a Letter of Service authorising him to raise a regiment of Fencibles of ten companies—one Grenadier, one Light Infantry, and eight Battalion Companies. His was only one of six new regiments authorised within one week, for similar commissions were granted on October 20, to James Durham and Archibald Douglas; on October 25, to Major H. M. Clavering, and Lieutenant-Colonel M. H. Baillie; and on October 30 to Major William Robertson of the 4th Fencibles, the Letters of Service being identical in each case (*W.O.* 4: 155: pp. 42, 45). Although the beating orders were for Great Britain, "yet it is to be understood that the recruiting shall be confined to Scotland." The men were to serve in any part of Great Britain and

Ireland, and a bounty of £10 10s. was to be paid for each approved recruit, and the regiment was to be completed in three months. The Government made four separate recruiting grants in 1794 and 1795 aggregating £10,500 (*W.O.* 2 : 1 : p. 186). The War Office took up a strong attitude as to the scale of bounties, and in a Circular Letter denounced the high bounties offered to the new levies as being "extremely prejudicial" to the Services. Any officer convicted of exceeding the official bounty, £15 15s. for the Line and £10 10s. for Fencibles was to forfeit his commission. Leith was only too ready to accept the conditions, for he wrote to the War Office, January 28, 1795 (*W.O.* 1 : 1,087) :—

I have the honor to acknowledge the receipt of your letter on the subject of the terms held out to the Fencible Corps now raising. I beg leave to assure you that I have ever paid since I have been a soldier the strictest attention to act in conformity to my instructions. Although I was very particular in mentioning the danger of inlisting men on such terms as the advertisements alluded to held out, I have sent a circular letter to the officers of the Aberdeenshire Fencible Regiment again to put them on their guard. I am sorry to observe that advertisements have [been] appearing in this country. They have been published by agents recruiting for some corps in this country. I considered it my duty, even before your letter, to remonstrate in the strongest terms against a step which might lay the foundation for a mutiny ; but I have only to regret that there is not some method of punishing those people who presume on the thought of their being civilians to treat with impertinence a remonstrance which I conceive myself so well authorised to make.

I have found no data about the progress of the recruiting, but Leith must have met with competition, for the Loyal Inverness Fencible Regiment of Infantry, raised by John Baillie of Dunain, late of the Northern Fencibles, under Letter of Service, November 21, 1794, was partly recruited in Aberdeenshire by its Lieutenant-Colonel, John Gordon-Cuming of Pitlurg, who had also been in the Northern Fencibles. Pitlurg arrived in Aberdeen on March 5, 1795, in connection with recruiting (*Aberdeen Journal*) ; and "got a great number of his townsmen," although the nomenclature of the recruits shows that they were largely Highland. Thus out of 545 privates there were 151 Mac.s, 17 Campbells, 8 Camerons, 6 Chisholms, with 6 Grants and 5 Gordons (*W.O.* 13 : 3,859). The officers included George Gordon, John Gordon (son of Robert

Gordon, in Auchmair), and Charles Irvine (1756-1819), second son of Alexander Irvine, XVII of Drum. Leith's corps, on the other hand, had only 31 Mac.s among its 417 privates, and not a single man of the name of Leith (*W.O.* 13: 3,792).

The regiment was put on the establishment on July 23, 1795—on the previous day its band was present at the presentation of colours to the Aberdeen Volunteers on the Links—as H.M. Aberdeen Fencible Regiment of Foot; but later in the year the title was changed to the Princess of Wales's, or Aberdeen Highland Fencible Infantry. It was sent to Ireland at once, and on September 24, 1795—the very day when Leith's brother's regiment, the 109th, came officially to an end—it was transferred to the Irish Establishment (*W.O.* 4: 164: p. 82), so that it lost its local bearings. In view of this fact, I give only the officers who were first appointed, for the others have no northern interest. The following list of officers is made up from various sources, notably *W.O.* 25: 225: pp. 353-5; 25: 160, p. 239; *London Gazette*, August 8, 1795:—

COLONEL.

James Leith (from Independent Company), October 25, 1794; commanded the regiment throughout its whole career.

LIEUTENANT-COLONEL.

Archibald McNeil, October 25, 1794; became Colonel of "a" Fencible Regiment, January 23, 1799.

MAJOR.

William Cunningham (from 4th Fencibles), October 25, 1794.

CAPTAINS.

Abraham Bunbury, October 25, 1794.

Thomas Burns, October 25, 1794; served during the whole career of the corps.

William Dawson, October 25, 1794; joined 2nd battalion Argyll Fencibles by April 12, 1800; succeeded by Captain-Lieutenant Francis Lamont.

Alexander Farquharson, October 25, 1794; died February 10, 1800, when he was succeeded by Alexander Boyd from the Essex Fencibles.

Hon. William Hay-Carr, October 25, 1794. Born 1772; took the additional name of Carr in terms of the will of his maternal grandfather, Sir William Carr, of Etal; succeeded his brother, 1798, as 17th Earl of Erroll; Lieutenant-Colonel, Aberdeenshire Militia, October 21, 1802; died 1819.

Lawrence Leith, October 25, 1794. Son of Leith of Bucharne; formerly in the 89th, raised by Colonel the Hon. William Gordon; died at Bucharne, December 17, 1795.

James Morrison, October 25, 1794; resigned by January 12, 1796.

CAPTAIN-LIEUTENANT.

Thomas Stewart, October 25, 1794; resigned by January 12, 1796.

LIEUTENANTS.

Alexander Boyd, October 25, 1794.

Matthew Alexander Bunbury, October 24, 1794. Apparently a member of the well-known Irish family.

Andrew Clerk, October 24, 1794; resigned by June 8, 1799, when he was succeeded by Hugh Maclean (from Ensign, 1st battalion Breadalbane Fencibles), who subsequently got his company and remained to the end of the corps.

John Cunningham, October 25, 1794.

Adam Darling, October 25, 1794.

John Donald, October 25, 1794; resigned by February 23, 1799; succeeded by Ensign Ferguson.

William Douglas, October 25, 1794; Surgeon's Mate; Surgeon, September 28, 1779, *vice* Kerr.

Robert Duncan, October 25, 1794.

William Gilbert, October 25, 1794; superseded by March 14, 1799.

William Marcus Henderson, October 25, 1794; Captain of a Fencible Regiment, January 25, 1799.

George Kerr, October 25, 1794; dismissed the service by General Court Martial by October 23, 1800, when he was succeeded by Ensign Andrew Gallagher.

Francis Lamont, October 25, 1794; became Captain-Lieutenant, September 21, 1795 (succeeded by Ensign George Duguid); and on March 12, 1800, Captain, *vice* Dawson. He was subsequently Lieutenant in the 21st Foot, and in 1804 became Adjutant of the Aberdeen Volunteers (*H.O.* 50; 93).

Francis Leith, October 25, 1794.

Ernest Leslie, October 25, 1794; subsequently became Captain.

James Mackinnon, October 25, 1794.

Robert Moir, October 25, 1794.

Thomas Mitchell, October 25, 1794.

Hugh Rose, October 25, 1794; subsequently became Captain; and was succeeded as such, September 21, 1799, by Lieutenant Hector Maclean, who remained to the end of the corps.

John Skene, October 25, 1794; joined H.E.I.C. by July 1, 1801, when he was succeeded by Henry D'Anvers, who became an Ensign, April 11, 1800.

Thomas William Thurstans, October 25, 1794.

John Wilson, October 25, 1794; became Captain, and remained to the end of the corps.

ENSIGNS.

John Brown, October 25, 1794; resigned by August 17, 1795.

James Craigie, October 25, 1794; Captain-Lieutenant in the last muster, 1863.

Charles Crow, October 25, 1794.

William Dyce, October 25, 1794.

James Ferguson, October 25, 1794; Lieutenant, February 23, 1799, *vice* Donald; succeeded as Ensign by Francis Montgomery, March 12, 1799.

Alexander Gordon, October 25, 1794; afterwards in the Caithness Legion (*Gordons under Arms*, No. 186).

James Reynolds, October 25, 1794.

Jacob Wagner, October 25, 1794.

CHAPLAIN.

Walter Chalmers, October 25, 1794.

SURGEON.

George Kerr, October 25, 1794.

SURGEON'S MATES.

John Donald, October 25, 1794.

William Douglas, October 25, 1794.

ADJUTANT.

Francis Lamont, October 25, 1794.

QUARTERMASTER.

Thomas Stewart, October 25, 1794.

The first muster roll, for the period July 23, 1795—July 11, 1796, shows the following figures (besides 30 desertions) :—

	Sergeants.	Corporals.	Drummers.	Privates.
Present	28	41	19	266
Absent	14	9	3	151
	42	50	22	417

After this period the number of privates dwindled as follows (*W.O.* 13 : 3,792):—

January 12—March 31, 1796	374
April 1—September 30, 1796	368
October 1, 1796—March 31, 1797	377
April 1—September 30, 1797	362
October 1—March 31, 1798	365

The last muster of all, however, shows a rise, the figures reaching 431.

The whole career of the regiment was spent in Ireland. Leith's nephew, Andrew Leith-Hay, tells us (*Memoirs of the late Lieutenant-General Sir James Leith*, p. 14):—

During the Rebellion [in Ireland] he was conspicuous for his activity and firmness of mind, and those qualities that found full scope for development in the mercy and forgiveness extended to many of the unfortunate objects of mistaken feeling, whom circumstances placed in his power; and it is no slight eulogium that, during scenes where so much bloodshed was inevitable, Colonel Leith's leniency never became in the slightest degree questioned. His regiment was in the highest state of discipline, and its appearance upon every occasion evinced the professional knowledge of its commanding officer.

Perhaps it was Leith's instinct for discipline that led to the court-martialling and dismissal of at least three officers—George Kerr, Surgeon; Richard Kennon, who became Ensign, January 3, 1799; and Captain-Lieutenant Quin (*W.O. Letter Book* 21, p. 356).

The regiment was disbanded at Naas, April 8 and 11, 1803, the officers then being:—

Company.	Lieutenant.	Ensign.	Men.
Col. James Leith			43
Lieut.-Col. Thomas Purefoy			41
Major Thomas Burns	William Douglas	Thomas Miller	47
Captain Oct. 25, 1794.	Lieutenant Oct. 25, 1794.	Ensign June, 1801.	
Capt. Adam Donaldson	William Ratcliffe		43
	Lieutenant Feb. 23, 1799.		
	John Gallagher		
	Ensign June 30, 1801.		
Capt. Ernest Leslie	Allan Maclean		42
Lieutenant Oct. 25, 1794.	Ensign Mar. 14, 1799.		
Capt. Hector Maclean	John Middleton		44
Captain Sept. 21, 1799.	Ensign Mar. 12, 1799.		
Capt. Hugh Maclean	Andrew Gallagher		43
Lieutenant June 8, 1799.	Lieut. Oct. 23, 1800.		
Capt. George Maxwell	John Minty	L. Grant Coghlan	44
	Ensign Mar. 12, 1799.	Ensign July 1, 1801.	
Capt. John Usher	Francis Montgomery		41
Capt.-Lieut. May 1, 1800.	Ensign Mar. 12, 1799.		
Capt. John Wilson	Humble Lawson		46
	Lieutenant Feb. 23, 1799.		

The pay rolls will be found in *W.O.* 13: 3,792, 3,793, and 3,794. Documents relating to the Corps are indexed in *W.O.* 2: 1: p. 186.

Leith had a very brilliant career during the last thirteen years of his life, especially in the Peninsula, being knighted in 1813 for his "distinguished conduct in the action fought near Corunna, and in the battle of Busaco for his noble daring at the assault and capture of

Badajos by storm ; and for his heroic conduct in the ever memorable action fought on the plains of Salamanca, where in personally leading the fifth division to a most gallant and successful charge upon a part of the enemy's line, which it completely overthrew at the point of the bayonet, he and the whole of his personal staff [including his nephew and A.D.C., Andrew Leith-Hay] were severely wounded."   He was again wounded at the siege of San Sebastian.   He was appointed Commander of the Forces in the West Indies and Governor of the Leeward Islands in 1814, and died of fever at Barbados, October 16, 1816.   The story of his life is told in two books by his nephew, Sir Andrew Leith-Hay :—

Memoirs of the late Lieutenant-General Sir James Leith, G.C.B., with a Precis of some of the most remarkable events of the Peninsular War.   By a British Officer : Barbados ; printed for the author by W. Walker, 1817 : 8vo., pp. 24.

A Narrative of the Peninsular War.   By Major [Andrew] Leith-Hay, F.R.S.E., in two volumes ; illustrated ; Edinburgh, Daniel Lizars, 1831.   Small 8vo. ; Vol. I. pp. xvi., 317 ; Vol. II. pp. viii., 301.

BANFFSHIRE (DUKE OF YORK'S OWN) FENCIBLES.

1798: RAISED BY ANDREW HAY OF MONTBLAIRY: REDUCED 1802.

The Banffshire Fencibles, raised under Letter of Service, July 26, 1798, are remarkable for the fact that they were the only Fencible regiment of the north-east of Scotland to serve on the Continent of Europe. They were raised by Andrew Hay of Montblairy, in the parish of Alvah, son of George Hay of Montblairy, a cadet of the Hay of Rannes family, and under conditions very similar to those of the Aberdeen Fencibles, commanded by Major James Leith, who also traced to the Hays of Rannes.

Born 1762, Hay had put in nearly twenty years in the army before he raised the regiment, which was altogether a much more professional force than the earlier corps of Fencibles. He had begun in the 1st Foot in 1779, and had subsequently served in the 88th, the 1st (a second time), and the 72nd. He had married (at Montcoffer, April 2, 1784) Elizabeth Robinson, daughter of William Robinson, the manufacturer of Banff, who had been murdered by some soldiers of the guard there April 10, 1771 (Cramond's *Annals of Banff* i, 221, 237). Raeburn immortalised the lady in a classic portrait (now owned by the American connoisseur, Mr. E. T. Stotesbury), which fetched 21,200 guineas at Christie's in 1912. The Robinsons who figure among Hay's Fencible officers were probably relatives of his wife. In 1794, Hay's own sister, Dorothea, married the famous "Tiger" Duff (1742-1803), so that he was intimately connected with Banffshire. He went on half pay of the 93rd in 1794, and was appointed from that to raise his regiment of Fencibles.

The regiment consisted of ten companies—one Grenadier, one Light Infantry, and eight Battalion companies. By the Letter of Service (given in full in *W.O.* 4: 172, pp. 195-9) the regiment was to serve "in any part of Europe, but not beyond it." There was a further provision:—

The men are not to be draughted [sic], and in the event of their being ordered out of Great Britain, His Majesty consents that they shall not be reduced abroad, but be brought back in a corps and disbanded in the county where they were principally raised, or as near thereto as possible.

We have no data as to the progress of recruiting, but the first muster roll, dated July 27, 1798—March 28, 1799 (*W.O.* 13 : 3,806), gives the names of 742 privates, who were inspected at Barnstaple on March 29, 1799, by Major-General Whitelocke; but the muster roll of March—April shows that many of these had been drafted or discharged, for the figures there stand at 442 men. This roll also shows that the regiment was largely recruited out of Scotland :—

51 Men were enlisted in Scotland.	18 Men were drafted to the 16th Foot.
78 „ „ „ England.	5 „ „ „ 22nd Foot.
30 „ „ „ Ireland.	1 „ „ „ 40th Foot.
	5 „ „ „ Navy.

The cost of the regiment between July 28, 1798, and March, 1799, was :—

$£5,554$ 15 11¾ in Pay.
$£5,772$ 2   0   in Levy Money.

The total cost between March and December, 1799, was £15,350 18s. 3d. (*W.O.* 24 : 604):—

Pay	.								.	£12,632 16 8
Clothing	.	.	.	.	.	.	.	.	.	1,461 3 2
Agency	.	.	.	.	.	.	.	.	.	152 18 1
Allowances	.	.	.	.	.	.	.	.	.	440 16 9
Accoutrements	.	.	.	.	.	.	.	.	.	663 3 7

Hay's officers, who are not easy to identify, have one remarkable feature. Unlike the officers of many Fencible regiments, who seem to have used the Fencibles as a back door to the regular army, they stuck to the regiment from its start to its finish, very few changes having taken place in its three years of life. They were as follows (*W.O.* 25 : 70, 168 and 224):—

COLONEL.

Andrew Hay, December 29, 1798; commanded the regiment throughout its whole career.

LIEUTENANT-COLONELS.

Francis John Wilder (from Major, 9th Foot), December 29, 1798, with permanent rank in the army. Joining the 35th Foot, he was succeeded, April 30, 1801, by

Brevet Colonel Ronald Craufurd Ferguson (from 31st Foot), the laird of Raith (1773-1841), who became General in 1830, and married (1798) Jean, the natural daughter of Sir Hector Munro. He was the grandfather of Sir Ronald Craufurd Munro-Ferguson of Novar. Ferguson was succeeded July 25, 1801, by

Nicholas Nepean (from half pay of the late 93rd). Born 1755; died 1823; became a Lieutenant-General and Governor of Cape Breton; brother of Sir Evan Nepean (1750-1822), Lord of the Admiralty, who was created a baronet in 1802.

MAJOR.

John George Ogilvie (from Captain, Loyal Essex Fencibles), December 29, 1798. He was superseded and succeeded, June 9, 1801, by Henry Zouch (from Lieutenant-Colonel, half pay 121st).

CAPTAINS.

Stewart Black (from Lieutenant, Angus Fencibles), January 2, 1799. Became Captain in the Forfar Volunteers, 1803 (*H.O.* 50: 93).

John Bourke, January 3, 1799; remained to the end.

Colin Campbell, December 31, 1798; resigned and was succeeded, May 9, 1800, by Captain Alexander Riddell.

Thomas Glisson, January 1, 1799; resigned and was succeeded, May 16, 1800, by Captain-Lieutenant James Grant, late of the Strathspey Fencibles.

James Scott Hay, December 28, 1798; resigned and was succeeded, July 3, 1801, by Charles Staples (from Captain, of late 3rd Staffordshire Militia), who remained to the end.

William Ramsay (from Major, half pay of the Marines), August 5, 1799.

George Taylor (from Lieutenant, Rothesay and Caithness Fencibles), December 30, 1798.

CAPTAIN-LIEUTENANT.

Joseph Barningham (from Lieutenant, half pay, 40th), January 4, 1799. He was Adjutant, and resigned by January 21, 1801, when he was succeeded as such by Ensign Moyle.

LIEUTENANTS.

James Barwick, January 1, 1799; became Captain, and remained to the end.

Andrew Christie (from Surgeon, 6th Dragoons), December 31, 1798; Surgeon of the Regiment, December 29, 1798.

Edward Clark, January 4, 1799; remained to the end.

Jacob Cooper (from Ensign, half pay, 5th Regiment, Irish Brigade), January 6, 1799; Quartermaster, December 29, 1798; resigned and was succeeded, April 23, 1800, by Ensign Hunter.

James Darcus, (from Captain, half pay, 7th West Indian Regiment), December 30, 1798; resigned and was succeeded, January 9, 1800, by Ensign Archibald Fletcher.

Thomas Lauder, January 5, 1799; resigned and was succeeded, March 14, 1800, by Ensign Hewerdine.

James McKilligin (was also Paymaster). Son of George McKilligin (1728-98), who settled in Banff from Alness; entered the army in 1785 and went to India. He was afterwards Major in the Banffshire Local Militia, and Provost of Banff, 1831-3. He married Jane Pelham, had three sons and two daughters, and died, on the same day as his wife, January, 1837, both being buried in Banff churchyard (Cramond's *Annals of Banff*, ii., 338).

James Mackintosh (from Captain, half pay, late Sheffield Regiment), December 29, 1798.

Henry Maxwell, January 7, 1799; remained to the end.

John Mill, January 8, 1799; remained to the end.

James Robinson, January 3, 1799.

Alexander Stevens, January 2, 1799.

ENSIGNS.

James Brown, January 1, 1799; resigned and was succeeded, November 21, 1799, by Volunteer William Smith, who joined the 63rd Foot, and was succeeded, February 3, 1801, by H. Harrington.

Edward Dester, January 4, 1799. There was also a private of the same name in Captain Stewart Black's company.

Archibald Fletcher, December 29, 1798; Lieutenant, January 9, 1800, *vice* Darcus; succeeded as Ensign by Alexander Reid; succeeded as Lieutenant, April 18, 1800, by James Harris (from Captain, Birmingham Light Infantry), who was superseded by April 16, 1801, for being absent without leave.

James Hewerdine, December 30, 1798; Lieutenant, March 14, 1800, *vice* Lauder; Quartermaster, July 23, 1800, *vice* John Williamson, who had been appointed from the late Roxburgh Fencible Cavalry.

John Hunter, December 31, 1798; Lieutenant, April 23, 1800, *vice* Cooper.

Thomas Moyle, January 3, 1799; Lieutenant, April 16, 1801, *vice* Harris; succeeded as Ensign, by Volunteer John Barningham.

George Robinson, January 2, 1799; acted as Assistant Surgeon.

Thomas Russel, January 5, 1799; perhaps of the Rathen family.

The regiment, for some reason not explained, got the sub-title of "Duke of York's Own," which is surprising in view of the fact that the Loyal Inverness Fencibles, commanded by Colonel John Gordon-Cuming of Pitlurg, had already received the sub-title, the "Duke of York's Royal," as a mark of the King's approbation for its offer to join Sir Ralph Abercromby in Egypt or to serve in any part of the Empire.

The regiment was inspected at Barnstaple by Major-General Whitelocke, March 29, 1799, and went on to Jersey, returning to England, December 9, 1799, when it was stationed at Portsmouth. On May 1, 1800, it embarked for Gibraltar, where it spent the rest of its career, being discharged at Gosport in May, 1802. The officers then were (W.O. 13 : 3,808):—

Company.	Lieutenant.	Ensign.	Men.
Col. Hay		John Barningham	33
Lieut. Col. Nepean July 25, 1801.	James Hewerdine	John Hay	37
Major Henry Zouch June 9, 1801.	Edward Clark	Thomas Russel	42
Capt. James Barwick	George Robinson	John Potton Sept. 5, 1801.	39
Capt. Stewart Black	James McKilligin	Edward Dester	34
Capt. John Bourke	{ John Mills { John Hunter		35
Capt. James Grant May 16, 1800.	Andrew Christie	Samuel Kennedy Feb. 10, 1801.	40
Capt. Alexander Riddell May 9, 1800.	{ Alexander Stevens { Henry Maxwell		41
Capt. Charles Staples July 3, 1801.	Thomas Moyle	Alexander Reid Jan. 9, 1800.	35
John Williamson Capt.-Lieutenant Oct. 6, 1801.	James Robinson		36

After the reduction of his Fencible regiment, Hay was appointed Lieutenant-Colonel of the 16th battalion of the army of reserve, afterwards of the second battalion of the 72nd, and in 1807 of his old corps, the 1st Royals, whom he commanded at Corunna; his despatches from Spain in 1808 are preserved at the Record Office (W.O. 1 : 229). He commanded a brigade in the stupid Walcheren expedition, and returned in 1810 to the Peninsula, where he did yeoman service during the next four years. His son, George, was killed at Vittoria, June 21, 1813; his A.D.C., Captain James Stewart, son of Andrew Stewart of Auchlunkart, died (September 2, 1813) of the wounds he received at San Sebastian while reconnoitring with Hay; and Hay himself fell in the sortie from Bayonne, April 14, 1814. He is commemorated in the Cimetière des

Anglais at Bayonne by a flat stone (originally in St. Etienne Church, and illustrated photographically in the *Graphic*, April 17, 1914) bearing this inscription :—

This tomb is placed by the officers of the 3rd Battalion, 1st or Royal Scots, as a testimony of respect to the memory of the late Major-General A. Hay, commanding the 1st Brigade, 5th Division, British Army, who gallantly fell in defence of the ground in which his body was deposited on the night of the 14th April, 1814, aged 52 years.

Another inscription on the monument at Bayonne reads :—

Sacred to the memory of Major-General Andrew Hay, of Mount-blairy, in Scotland, who fell at Bayonne on the night of the 14th of April, 1814, while repelling gallantly a sortie of the enemy.

The lineal descendant of an ancient Scottish family, he was in private life respected and beloved. But the respect and love of friends, the enjoyments and the honours of private life and every ordinary object of ambition disappeared before his passion for military fame. Fitted for camps, as well by temper as by spirit, cheerful, ardent, vigilant and brave, he distinguished the whole of his military career by an elevated sense of the duties of a soldier, signal intrepidity, promptitude and zeal.

He lived to see his country triumphant ; but, being himself amongst the latest victims of war, he has left a memory dear to his associates-in-arms ; while as a companion of Wellington and a partner in his victories, he has bequeathed his renown among the heroes of his time as a grateful solace to his friends and a sacred inheritance to his children.

This stone also records the premature fate and early fame of Major George Hay, who fell in the decisive battle of Vittoria, in the heroic discharge of his duty as Aide-de-Camp to his father. It is erected by Mrs. Elizabeth Hay as the only memorial which the affectionate distress of a wife and a mother can consecrate to the valour of a husband and a son.

There is also a monument to Hay in St. Paul's Cathedral, executed by Humphrey Hopper, which has been much criticised, bearing the inscription :—

Erected at the public expense to the memory of Major-General Andrew Hay. He was born in the county of Banff, in Scotland, and fell on the 14th of April, 1814, before the Fortress of Bayonne in France in the 52nd year of his age and the 34th of his service, closing a military career marked by zeal, prompt decision, and signal intrepidity.

ABERDEENSHIRE MILITIA: NOW 3RD BATTALION GORDON HIGHLANDERS.

1798: RAISED UNDER THE SCOTS MILITIA ACT OF 1797.

The Aberdeenshire Militia, raised under the Act of 1797—the first measure in Scotland creating a Territorial force nearest to the type we now have—is peculiarly interesting as being the only corps (with the sole exception of the Gordon Highlanders, to which regiment it is attached) now existing of the many which were raised in the restless recruiting panics of 1759-1814. Its history, partly interrupted by periods of neglect, falls into five main periods:—

1798-1802—Raised under the Act 37 Geo. III. cap. 103: eight companies, including Banff; numbered the 6th North British Militia.

1803-1816—Reconstituted as the 55th North British Militia, and increased to 10 companies under 42 Geo. III. cap. 91, Banff being assigned to Inverness, Elgin and Nairn; continuously embodied, 1803-14, and quartered in many parts of the country.

1817-1855—Period of neglect, represented by only four bundles of pay rolls at the Record Office (*W.O.* 13: 17-20) as against 16 for the period 1798-1814 (*W.O.* 13: 1-16).

1855-1882—Became 89th Regiment of Militia.

1882 to the present time—3rd Battalion Gordon Highlanders.

The Militia Act of 1797 provided for 6,000 Militia to be raised in Scotland, but this number was whittled down owing to the unpopularity of the measure. August 1, 1797, was the date for initiating the Act, but it had to be postponed to March 1, 1798. The number to be raised was reduced to 5,468, and ultimately it was resolved to call out only half that number, 2,734 (*H.O.* 50: 29), the proportions from the northern counties being as follows:—

Aberdeen	-	-	-	244	Nairn	-	-	-	12
Banff	-	-	-	65	Inverness	-	-	-	95
Elgin	-	-	-	47	Kincardine		-	-	52

Unfortunately, we know nothing about the recruiting, for there are no letters at the Record Office bearing on the subject as there are (*H.O.* 50: 29) from the southern counties of Scotland. Colonel Innes in his sketch of the regiment (1884) does not even hint that the Militia was anywhere unpopular. Yet the disinclination to serve personally was so strong that as early as June, 1798, substitutes were advertised for in the *Journal*, a " handsome " bounty being offered.

The regiment was embodied on July 5 and mustered 280 men, which was less than the King demanded (324). The latter number, according to a return of 1797, was to have been made up thus (*H.O.* 50: 29):—

	Men.	Captains.	Lieuts.	Ensigns.
Aberdeen - - -	254	4	6	4
Banff - - -	70	1	3	—

So far as the officers went, the Gordons had the " guidin' o't," inasmuch as George (Gordon), 5th Earl of Aboyne, representing the leading junior line—he was yet to succeed to the Marquisate of Huntly—was appointed Colonel and held the command for 36 long years. At this time the Marquis of Huntly was commanding the Gordon Highlanders, and his father, the 4th Duke of Gordon, commanded the Northern Fencibles. This Gordon beginning—particularly emphasised in 1804, when no fewer than nine of the 39 officers bore the surname Gordon—is very interesting in view of the fact that the regiment has ultimately become associated with the Gordon Highlanders. The officers were as follows (*W.O.* 13: 1; and *Militia List* for 1801):—

COLONEL.

George (Gordon), 5th Earl of Aboyne, April 23, 1798. Born in 1761, he entered the 1st Foot Guards in September 2, 1777, as an Ensign, and became Captain in the 81st Regiment, raised by the Hon. William Gordon, on December 26, 1777. He was subsequently in the 2nd and 35th Foot and Coldstream Guards (*Gordons under Arms*, No. 518). He was created Baron Meldrum of Morven in the peerage of the United Kingdom in 1815, and succeeded to the Marquisate of Huntly on the death of the 5th Duke of Gordon in 1836. He died in 1853.

LIEUTENANT-COLONEL.

David MacDowall Grant, May 23, 1798. Laird of Arndilly.

MAJORS.

Francis Garden of Troup, April 23, 1798 (*London Gazette*). He seems, however, to have resigned soon. His elder brother, Peter, was Major in the 109th.

William Rattray, July 23, 1798.

CAPTAIN-LIEUTENANT.

Charles Adamson, May 16, 1798; Captain, May 1, 1799. He gave evidence in favour of the prosecution in the trial of the Ross and Cromarty Rangers, January 6, 1803, at which time he was living at Kirkhill, Nigg. Died February 25, 1841; buried in Old Machar Churchyard, the stone recording several of his family (Munro's *Old Aberdeen*, ii., 242).

CAPTAINS.

Robert Bartlett, May 24, 1798. Son of James Bartlett of Afforsk; married Janet Grant of the Elchies family (*Aberdeen Journal* N. and Q., ii., 60).

Adam Gordon, May 23, 1798; resigned August 19, 1799.

Peter Gordon, May 21, 1798.

George Leith, May 24, 1798; acted also as Paymaster.

Keith Turner, May 25, 1798. Son of John Turner, of Turnerhall and Tipperty, whom he succeeded in 1802. He married, 1804, Anna Margaret, only child of George Riddoch, H.E.I.C. Civil Service, and died in 1808 (Temple's *Fermartyn*, 554). His grandson, Colonel John Turner, commanded the regiment in 1883.

LIEUTENANTS.

John Annand, May 26, 1798.

William Deas, May 24, 1798.

William Donald, May 23, 1798.

H. George Forsyth, May 28, 1798.

George Gordon (formerly of H.E.I.C.) May 22, 1798; Captain, May 1, 1799.

Charles Grant, May 21, 1798.

John Grant, May 25, 1798; Ensign, 85th, October 25, 1798, *vice* C. Whyte (*W.O.* 25 : 226, p. 785).

Robert Moir, May 29, 1798.

William Skene, October 25, 1798.

Alexander Young, May 27, 1798.

ENSIGNS.

Robert Anderson, May 25, 1798.

John Emslie, May 23, 1798; Lieutenant, July 5, 1799. Lieutenant, Inverness, Banff, Elgin and Nairn Militia, December 24, 1802.

William Lindsay, May 26, 1798; Lieutenant, July 6, 1799.

George Sangster, October 26, 1798.

Benjamin Vaughton, May 22, 1798; Lieutenant, May 1, 1799.

ADJUTANT.

Benjamin Vaughton, May 22, 1798.

QUARTERMASTER.

William Skene, May 21, 1798. He gave evidence for the prosecution in the Ross and Cromarty Rangers trial, January 6, 1803.

PAYMASTER.

George Leith, July 5, 1798. A note in the index to Militia documents (*W.O.* 2: 79, p. 113) gives a reference to the Militia Account Book, No. 5, p. 7, which does not now exist—" Captain Leith and his sureties to continue responsible till the appointment of another Paymaster," Captain Adamson (*Ibid.* No. 5, p. 67).

SURGEON.

William Robertson, May 21, 1798; succeeded December 1, 1798, by John Ritchie.

The eight companies as contained in the first muster roll were commanded as follows (*W.O.* 13: 1):—

Company.	Lieutenant.	Ensign.	Men.
Col. Lord Aboyne			35
Lt.-Col. D. MacDowall Grant	John Grant	William Lindsay	36
Major William Rattray	H. G. Forsyth	William Skene	36
Captain Robert Bartlett	William Donald	Robert Anderson	35
Captain Adam Gordon	Charles Grant	Alexander Maclean	35
Captain Peter Gordon	{ William Deas { Alexander Young		34
Captain George Leith	George Gordon	Robert Moir	35
Captain Keith Turner	John Annand	John Emslie	34

The regiment was called The Aberdeenshire, or 6th North British Militia, and was inspected by Major-General Hay on October 8, and then marched to Montrose. It moved in the spring of 1799 to Dundee, and received its colours on July 1, 1800. The following figures as to the cost of its maintenance are interesting (*W.O.*, 24: 603, 604, 605):—

						Pay.	Clothing.
May—Dec., 1798	-	-	-	-		£6,830	£1,012
Jan.—Dec., 1799	-	-	-	-		16,179	1,683
Jan.—Dec., 1800	-	-	-	-		16,281	1,683

It may be noted that the non-commissioned officers and men wore " long gaiters," for which Lord Aboyne got a special allowance (*W.O.* 2: 2, p. 355, and *W.O.* 2: 79: p. 113).

A detailed balance sheet for the year 1799 shows how the entire cost of the regiment, £18,635, was apportioned (*W.O.* 14, 604):—

	Per Day.	Per Year.
Colonel - - - - -	£1 6 6	£483 12 6
Lieut.-Col. and Captain - -	0 15 11	290 9 7
Major and Captain - - -	0 14 11	257 0 5
Captains (3) - - - -	2 7 1	859 5 5
Captain-Lieutenant - - -	0 4 8	85 3 4
Lieutenants (9) - - - -	2 2 0	766 10 0
Ensigns (6) - - - -	1 2 0	401 10 0
Adjutant - - - - -	0 4 0	73 0 0
Quartermaster - - - -	0 4 8	35 3 4
Surgeon - - - - -	0 4 0	73 0 0
Sergeant-Major - - -	0 2 0¾	37 12 9¾
Quartermaster-Sergeant - -	0 2 0¾	37 12 9¾
Sergeants (24) - - - -	1 17 6	684 7 6
Corporals (24) - - - -	1 8 6	520 2 6
Drummers (18) - - -	1 0 7½	376 8 1½
Privates (563) - - - -	28 3 0	10,274 15 0
Various allowances - - - - -	- - -	874 0 0

On October 1, 1801, the Peace of Amiens was concluded, being subscribed on March 2, 1802, and on April 30, the regiment was disembodied at Aberdeen. But the difficulties facing the country did not disappear, and on June 26, 1802, a new Act (42 Geo. III. cap. 91) was passed raising the Scots Militia from 5,768 to 7,950 men. The county of Aberdeen was separated from Banffshire, which allied itself with Inverness, Elgin and Nairn, and had to maintain a battalion of 640 ballotted, subject to a supplementary levy of 960, that is to say one-half the original number. The latter were known as the Old Militia, and the augmentation was the Supplementary Militia. The title of the regiment was also changed to " The Aberdeenshire, or 55th Regiment of Militia," and it was so called until 1855.

As there had been difficulty in getting men under the Act of 1797, so difficulty was encountered in getting officers under the Act of 1802. This difficulty is the subject of a letter, which the Duke of Gordon, as Lord-Lieutenant of Aberdeenshire, wrote to the Home Secretary, January 13, 1803 (*H.O.* 50: 57):—

Your lordship [Hobart] will hardly give me the credit when I inform you that I have not had a single application for a company from any gentleman in the county, qualified for that appointment. Finding that to be the case, I wrote to many gentlemen to solicit their acceptance of companies and received refusals from every one except Sir John Gordon [of Park, who by the way had no right to the baronetcy].

This inadequate supply of officers is vividly brought out by the state of the first muster roll, March-April, 1803 :—

Company.		Lieutenant.			Ensign.
Col. Earl of Aboyne -	-	Alexander Young	-	-	Ben. Vaughton.
None	-	William Lindsay	-	-	Alexander Gordon.
None	-	John Duguid -	-	-	Andrew Affleck.
None	-	Alexander Robertson		-	Alexander Anderson.
None	-	Robert Christie	-	-	Robt. Chas. Grant.
None	-	Charles Grant	-	-	John Law.
None	-	John Marshall	-	-	John Cruickshank.
None	-	Robert Moir -	-	-	James Gordon.
None	-	Thomas Sangster -		-	None.
Captain Wm. Gordon	-	Francis Thompson		-	None.

Gradually, however, the ranks filled. It would be interesting to know how the captaincies were supplied in view of the lack of "gentlemen." The first officers were (*H.O.* 50, 57 ; *London Gazette*, 1803 ; *Militia List*, 1803, 1804) :—

COLONEL.

George (Gordon), Earl of Aboyne, October 28, 1802.

LIEUTENANT-COLONEL.

William (Hay), 17th Earl of Erroll, October 28, 1802. He had previously been in the Aberdeenshire Fencibles. A second Lieutenant-Colonel, John Baird, late Lieutenant-Colonel, 53rd, was added, October 21, 1803.

MAJORS.

Harry Gordon, November 1, 1802. Laird of Knockespock ; born in Philadelphia, 1761 ; served in the H.E.I.C. army, 1777-1788 ; died 1836 (*Gordons under Arms*, No. 628 ; his Militia appointment is not noticed there, however). He was succeeded by

George Gordon, June 27, 1803 ; resigned May 6, 1807. Laird of Hallhead.

Keith Turner, June 8, 1803. Formerly Captain, late Aberdeenshire Militia.

CAPTAINS.

David Campbell, July 28, 1803 ; Captain, late Caithness Legion (*H.O.* 50 : 57).

Robert Corbet, June 1, 1803 ; Major *vice* George Gordon, May 6,

1807. He had been 14 years in the 5th Dragoon Guards, three of them as Captain. He died 1804.

Daniel Gordon, May 2, 1803; Captain-Lieutenant, May 1, 1799, Aberdeen Militia; Captain, October 18, 1798, Northern Fencibles (*q.v.*). He resigned on being appointed an Adjutant to the Recruiting Staff of Great Britain, and was succeeded, April 2, 1808, by Lieutenant Lindsay.

"Sir" John Gordon, November 1, 1802. Son of "Sir" Ernest Gordon, "bart.," of Park; died unmarried at Rothbury, Northumberland, June 10, 1804 (*Gordons under Arms*, No. 951). He was succeeded by Captain James Boyd (from the Guards), July 23, 1804.

William Gordon, May 2, 1803 (qualifying "in terms of the Militia Act"). Lieutenant, July 4, 1795, Gordon Highlanders (*q.v.*).

William Alexander Gordon (from half pay, 2nd battalion, 85th), May 2, 1803. Captain, December, 1797, Northern Fencibles (*q.v.*).

George Primrose, June 27, 1803.

William Todd (from Captain, half pay, 40th), May 2, 1803; resigned and succeeded April 2, 1804, by Robert Moir.

LIEUTENANTS.

Alexander Anderson (from half pay, 42nd), May 2, 1803.

John Brown, October 2, 1802.

Robert Christie, December 25, 1802; resigned and succeeded, December 1, 1804, by Ensign Alexander Gordon.

John Duguid, November 1, 1802.

Charles Grant, January 8, 1803.

William Lindsay, July 30, 1802; Captain, April 2, 1804, *vice* Daniel Gordon.

John Marshall, January 18, 1803. His father was worth £1,000 (*H.O.* 50: 57).

Robert Moir, November 1, 1802; Captain, April 2, 1804, *vice* Todd. His father was worth £1,000.

Alexander Robertson, November 1, 1802.

Peter Simpson, November 1, 1802; appointed to the Army of Reserve, and succeeded by Ensign Charles Middleton, January 21, 1804.

Francis Thompson, January 8, 1803. He had £300 a year (*H.O.* 50: 57).

Alexander Young, November 1, 1802; Captain, April 2, 1804. His father was worth £1,000.

ENSIGNS.

Charles Adamson, May 25, 1803; became Paymaster; Lieutenant, July 18, 1803.

Andrew Affleck, March 12, 1803.

James Anderson, March 6, 1803.

Alexander Cameron, June 1, 1803 ; Lieutenant, July 18, 1803.

William Chalmers, June 1, 1803 ; Lieutenant, July 18, 1803.

John Cruickshank, October 2, 1802 ; Lieutenant, May 7, 1803 ; resigned and succeeded June 27, 1803, by Donald Fraser, Ensign late Inverness Fencibles. Father worth £500.

Alexander Gordon, November 1, 1802 ; Lieutenant, December 1, 1804, *vice* Christie. His father was worth £500.

James Gordon, January 8, 1803.

Robert Charles Grant, November 1, 1802.

John Law, October 6, 1802 ; Lieutenant, June 1, 1803. His father was worth £500.

ADJUTANT.

Benjamin Vaughton, November 1, 1802 ; removed to an Invalid Corps ; succeeded by William Rattray (from Major, late Aberdeenshire Militia), May 7, 1803, with rank of Captain.

QUARTERMASTER.

Alexander Cameron, March 6, 1803.

SURGEON.

Neil Sutherland, November 1, 1802, March 6, 1803.

PAYMASTER.

· Charles Adamson.

The difficulty of getting officers had its counterpart in the strong dislike of personal service among ballotted men, so that the Duke of Gordon had to inform the Secretary for State, July 22, 1803, that " a very great proportion of the persons drawing paid penalties " according to the Act (*H.O.* 50: 57). The number of men in the muster of April 21, 1803, was 408 effectives and 232 wanting.

The regiment mustered at Aberdeen on April 21, 1803, with 415 men (who increased to 592 by September), and on June 12, marched for Fort George, which was reached on July 2. On July 6, two officers were detached to take charge of the Supplementary levy at Aberdeen. This is almost the only fact we know about the Aberdeen Supplementary Militia, though there is one bundle of odds and ends about it at the Record Office (*W.O.* 13: 2,471). Mr. Fortescue states that in Scotland, as in London, this force was a " farce."

It was several months before the list of officers was filled up, for even in the September-October, 1803 list, a Captain is missing. I have added the commissions in this roll to show how slowly they dropped in (*W.O.* 13 : 6):—

Company.	Lieutenants.	Ensigns.
Col. Earl of Aboyne	Alexander Young Capt. April 2, 1804 Charles Grant Robert Gordon July 18, 1803	
Capt. David Campbell	John Duguid Charles Adamson	Charles Middleton July 28, 1803
Capt. Robert Corbet	Donald Fraser June 27, 1803 George Marshall July 18, 1803	Philip Gordon August 24, 1803
Capt. William Dawson	Charles Gordon July 18, 1803 Alexander Anderson July 18, 1803	John Grant En. July 28, 1803 Lieut. April 2, 1804
Capt. Daniel Gordon	John Marshall Alexander Cameron July 18, 1803	Robert Winchester En. August 9, 1803 Lieut. April 2, 1804
Capt. W. A. Gordon	Alexander Skene July 18, 1803 George Sangster July 28, 1803	Donald Macpherson August 24, 1803
Capt. George Primrose	Robert Christie William Chalmers July 18, 1803	John Clark En. August 24, 1803 Lieut. June 25, 1804
Capt. Patrick Stewart	Peter Simpson James Gordon July 18, 1803	William Gordon August 24, 1803
Capt. William Todd	John Law Alexander Gordon	John Clyne Lieut. April 2, 1804
	Robert Moir Capt. April 2, 1804 William Lindsay Capt. April 2, 1804 Archibald Hyndman July 18, 1803	

The cost of the regiment in 1804 (when there were 960 privates) was as follows (*W.O.* 24 : 609):—

Pay	-	-	-	-	-	-	-	£26,996 13	10½
Agency	-	-	-	-	-	-	-	141 9	4½
Captains' allowances	-	-	-	-	-	565 0	0
Clothing	-	-	-	-	-	-	2,796 3	7
		Total	-	-	-	-	£30,499	6 10

The first ten years of the regiment were spent in quarters all over the country as follows:—

1803, July—1803, November - - -	Fort George.
1803, July—1806, May - - -	Edinburgh.
1806, May—1807, May - - -	Haddington.
1807, May—1809, May - - -	Musselburgh.
1809, May—1810, May - - -	Edinburgh.
1810, May—1811, November - - -	Berwick.
1811, November—1812, December - -	Dalkeith.
1812, December—1813, February - -	Glasgow.
1813, February—1813, March - - -	Carlisle.
1813, March—1813, June - - -	Liverpool.
1813, June—1814, January - - -	Norman's Cross, Dover.
1814, January—1814, August - - -	Tower of London.

It marched out of the Tower on August 23, 1814, and arrived on September 17 at Aberdeen, where it was disembodied on September 23. It assembled again at Aberdeen on July 25, 1815, and continued embodied till February 24, 1816, but it had dwindled. Thus while the muster, beginning in 1803, had been 455, and had risen in 1809 to 814, and in 1811 to 1,003, it fell in 1815 to 217 men. The rise in 1809 had been effected under the Act of 1807 (47 Geo. III. cap. 71) for replenishing the Militia by raising a number equal to three-fourths of the quota under the Act of 1802. Aberdeenshire answered to the call thus by March, 1808 (*H.O.* 50: 181):—

District.	Apportionment.	Number levied.
Aberdeen - - - - - -	113	102
Alford - - - - -	46	46
Braemar - - - - -	37	37
Deer - - - - - -	80	80
Deeside - - - - -	35	35
Ellon - - - - - -	28	28
Garioch - - - - -	41	41
Huntly - - - - -	48	46
New Machar - - - - -	10	10
Turriff - - - - -	40	40

From 1816 to 1855 the regiment was quite neglected. The Crimean crisis reanimated it, however. From 1855 to 1882 it was known as the Royal Aberdeenshire Highlanders, or 89th Regiment of Militia. It signalised this change by adopting Gordon tartan (while stationed in Dublin) in 1858. Gordon tartan was selected in compliment to Lord Aberdeen, Lord-Lieutenant of Aberdeenshire at the time, through whose application the title "Highlanders" was conferred. Thus while the regiment was raised under the Lord-Lieutenancy of the Duke of Gordon, and first commanded by George (Gordon), Earl of Aboyne, it got its tartan in honour of the third ennobled Gordon of the north, George, Earl of Aberdeen. It was not till 1874, however, that the kilt was adopted.

This foreshadowed the attachment as third battalion to the Gordon Highlanders in 1882. The association of the Militia with the Gordons had been practically marked by the fact that in 1807 the 92nd was one of four regiments (the others were the 29th, 71st and 72nd) to which the Militia could volunteer, up to the number of 251. But there had been a connection before that, for at a meeting of the Lieutenancy on February 10, 1804, it was stated (*H.O.* 50: 93) that "the whole men hitherto raised for this country are now serving in the 92nd Regiment, and the Lieutenancy have the satisfaction to know that no claim has been, or can justly be, made by any of them for any part of their Bounties."

Besides Colonel Innes's printed sketch, there is an index to correspondence about the regiment at the Record Office (beginning *W.O.* 2: 79; and a series of pay rolls, *W.O.* 13: 1-25; *W.O.* 13: 2,471).

BANFFSHIRE MILITIA FORCE.

Banffshire has never been a Militia unit. From 1798 to 1802 it was attached to the county of Aberdeen, and from that date onwards to the counties of Inverness, Elgin and Nairn, the quota of the component parts being, in June 1803, as follows (*H.O.* 50: 59):—

	Original Number.	Supplementary.	Total.
Banff - - - -	179	89	268
Inverness - - - -	384	192	576
Elgin - - -	138	69	207
Nairn - - - -	43	21	64
	744	371	1,115

It is beyond my purpose to go minutely into the history of the regiment as attached to Inverness, but one may note that officers were as difficult to get as in Aberdeenshire. Thus Lord Fife wrote to Lord Hobart from Fife House, April 4, 1803 (*H.O.* 50: 59):—

I could only get one Captain [for the Militia] with property required for qualification by the Act that would accept of a Commission. I, therefore, appointed Captain John Watt to a Company. He was first a Lieutenant in the [Newmill] Volunteers, both active and attentive; he afterwards raised an Independent Company and always had his men and arms perfectly regular and in good order. He has a very valuable farm, and I am perfectly certain, taking all those together, few men of property are better qualified.

The officers are given with a full description of their previous service in a letter to the Secretary of State by Sir James Grant, dated April 9, 1803 (*H.O.* 50: 59). The following list is made up from this source and also from the (printed) *List of the Officers of the Militia of the United Kingdom*, for 1804:—

COLONEL.

Sir James Grant, November 1, 1802. Raised the Strathspey Fencibles and 97th Regiment (*q.v.*). Succeeded by his son, Francis William Grant, January 21, 1803.

LIEUTENANT-COLONEL.

Alexander Duff, December 24, 1804. Natural son of Alexander Duff of Hatton; born about 1744; began his career as Lieutenant in 89th Regiment (*q.v.*); Lieutenant, March 21, 1765, 58th; Captain, 1772; Major, 1783; retired on half pay, 1786. Lieutenant-Colonel, Banffshire Volunteers, June 20, 1795; "is still [1803] on the half pay of the late 99th." Laird of Mayen; died 1816 (Taylers' *Book of the Duffs*, 273-77).

MAJOR.

Hugh Rose, December 24, 1802; Lieutenant-Colonel, November 15, 1803. Captain, April 19, 1797, Nairnshire Volunteers; Major-Com., March 29, 1799. A second Major, James Dunbar, was added on December 31, 1803.

CAPTAINS.

William Cumming, December 24, 1802; not previously in the Army.

Garden Duff, December 24, 1802; Major, July 18, 1803; not previously in the Army. Son of John Duff of Hatton; born 1779; died 1858; father of Garden William Duff of Hatton (Taylers' *Book of the Duffs*, 249-51).

Hon. Archibald Campbell Fraser, December 24, 1802; "held a company in the Volunteer Militia set on foot in 1782, called the Caledonian Band." Fraser (1736-1815) was the youngest son of the notorious Lord Lovat, but for whose attainder he would have succeeded to the peerage. His elder brother, Simon (1726-82), raised the 78th Highlanders in 1757, and the 71st in 1775. Archibald supported Fraser of Belladrum in raising the Fraser Fencibles in 1794. He commanded the 1st Local Inverness-shire Militia in 1808, and as such asked Lord Liverpool in 1809 to let the men wear the kilt (*H.O.* 50-59):—" Your memorialist begs pardon and blushes at being called to mention aught as to what may seem to point to himself, because it is well known that in conjunction with Lord Graham in the House of Commons, the grace and favour of His Majesty and Parliament was solicited and procured for the restoration of their garb to Highland men as the reward of their loyalty. The Caledonian Band, immediately filled, were the first Volunteers in the Empire, and gave rise to many other corps." The famous tablet, which he erected in his own memory in the church of Kirkhill, makes the same claims. He outlived all his five sons, and entailed his property on his distant kinsman, Thomas Alexander Fraser of Strichen (1802-75), who was restored to the title and created Baron Lovat in 1837.

John Fraser, December 24, 1802. Captain, December 12, 1770, of the late 48th; Captain, April 18, 1797, Nairnshire Volunteers.

Robert Fraser, June 23, 1803.

Alpin Grant, December 24, 1802. First Lieutenant, Marines, 1760.

George Grant, December 24, 1802. Captain, June 15, 1797, Forres Volunteers.

John McAlister, jun., January 24, 1803; not previously in the Army.

Masterton Robertson, jun., December 24, 1802. Captain, June 15, 1797, Inches Volunteers; Captain, August 30, 1800, late 1st N.B. Militia.

John Watt, December 24, 1802. Captain, 1798, late Balvenie Volunteers.

William Wilson, December 24, 1802; Adjutant.

LIEUTENANTS.

John Chisholm, December 24, 1802. Lieutenant, 1798, Banffshire Volunteers.

James Duff, December 24, 1802; never in Army.

James Elder, December 24, 1802. Lieutenant, June 15, 1797, Elgin Volunteers; Captain, May 21, 1801.

John Emslie, December 24, 1802. Lieutenant, July 5, 1797, Aberdeenshire Militia.

Charles Farquharson, April 30, 1803 (*Militia List*, 1804).

James Grant, December 24, 1802. Entered Army as Lieutenant of the line in 1760; Captain, February 1794, 97th (*q.v.*). Captain, July 24, 1798, Inverallon Strathspey Volunteers.

Robert Lawson, December 24, 1802. Captain, July 24, 1798, Eastern Abernethy Volunteers.

Andrew Macdonald (or McDonell), December 24, 1802. Ensign, May 22, 1797, Glengarry Fencibles; Lieutenant, November 1800.

Archibald Macdonald, December 24, 1802. Lieutenant, May 19, 1798, late 1st N.B. Militia.

Charles Macgregor, December 24, 1802. Ensign, May 19, 1798, 1st N.B. Militia; Lieutenant, October 25, 1798.

ENSIGNS.

Dugald Cameron, December 24, 1802; Lieutenant, June 18, 1803. Ensign, January 13, 1799, late Lochaber Fencibles; Lieutenant, November 1800.

John Gatherer, December 24, 1802. Second Lieutenant, June 15, 1797, late Elgin Volunteers.

Robert Gordon, December 24, 1802. Ensign, May 1796, Northern Fencibles; Lieutenant, October 10, 1798.

Alexander Grant, December 24, 1802. Lieutenant, June 20, 1798, 1st Company, Urquhart Volunteers.

Donald Macdonald, December 24, 1802.

Hugh Macgregor, December 24, 1802. Lieutenant, March 1, 1799, Clan Alpine Fencibles.

Ronald Macgregor, December 24, 1802; also Paymaster and Quartermaster, November 27, 1799, late Strathspey Volunteers; Lieutenant, February 1801.

John Munro, December 24, 1802; Lieutenant, November 9, 1803. First Lieutenant, November 22, 1st South Uist Volunteers; Ensign, June 24, 1800, 1st N.B. Militia.

George Sangster, December 24, 1802. Ensign, 1799, Aberdeen-shire Militia.

Robert Steuart, December 24, 1802. Second Lieutenant, May 11, 1797, Grantown Volunteers; 1st Lieutenant, June 1801.

ADJUTANT.

William Wilson, September 7, 1802. Ensign, December 25, 1762, 72nd; Ensign, September 23, 1763, 56th; Lieutenant, April 18, 1766, 56th; Captain-Lieutenant, July 16, 1778, 39th; Captain, December 26, 1778, 39th, serving 14 years and going on half pay, September 25, 1792; two years in the Volunteers; Major, April 23, 1798, 2nd N.B. Militia.

SURGEON.

Robert Grant, December 24, 1802.

QUARTERMASTER.

James Carmichael, April 12, 1803, with rank of Lieutenant. Quartermaster, 1776, 40th; Ensign, 40th, 1778; Quartermaster and Lieutenant, 1794, Strathspey Fencibles; 2nd Lieutenant, 1802, Inverness-shire Volunteers.

On January 10, 1803, Sir James Grant petitioned that the corps should be called " H.M. Royal Inverness-shire, Banffshire, Elginshire, and Nairnshire Regiment of Militia," and "in consequence be permitted to have blue facings" (H.O. 50; 59).

The administration of the regiment between the four counties was complicated, as appears from a plan forwarded in June, 1803, by Sir James Grant for the appointment of the Supplementary officers (H.O. 50: 94):—

The present establishment of the Regiment is 10 Captains, 10 Lieutenants, 10 Ensigns; but, of course, there remains to be added in consequence of the Supplementary quota, 2 Captains, 14 Lieutenants, 2 Ensigns.

The next consideration is—by whom these additional officers are to be appointed. It is conceived that the fairest way will be that each Lord Lieutenant appoint a certain number of them, in as near a proportion to the number of privates furnished by the respective counties as possible. It is, therefore, proposed that His Majesty's Lieutenants should appoint the additional officers as follows:—

				Captains.	Lieutenants.	Ensigns.
Inverness	-	-	-	I	7	I
Banff	-	-	-	I	3	O
Elgin	-	-	-	O	3	O
Nairn	-	-	-	O	I	I
				2	14	2

The cost of the regiment in 1804 was £35,406 18s. 4d. (*W.O.* 24 : 609).

An index to correspondence dealing with the regiment is preserved at the Record Office (*W.O.* 2 : 80) and the muster rolls 1803-76, are contained in *W.O.* 13 : 1,039-1,054.

VOLUNTEERS IN ABERDEEN, TOWN AND COUNTY,
1794-1802 AND 1803-1808.

The first epoch of Volunteering in this country divides itself into two distinct periods, 1794-1802; 1803-1808. In 1794-1802, the town of Aberdeen had four different groups of Volunteers (aggregating 19 companies); while nine different places in the county contributed 14 more companies. In 1803-8, the town again gave four separate organisations (aggregating 25 companies), while 32 places in the county contributed 28 more. Kintore, Inverurie, Monymusk, Kemnay and Logie-Durno had officers appointed, but companies were never embodied.

Place.	1794-1802.	No. of Companies.
Aberdeen—		
Battery Vols. (1794-1802)		1
Royal Vols. (1794-1802)		5
Light Inf. Vols. (1799-1802)		11
Old Aberdeen (1798-1802)		2
Fraserburgh (1797-1802)		1
Garioch (1798-1802)		1
Gartly (1798-1802)		1
Huntly (1798-1802)		2
Leslie (1798-1802 ?)		1
Oldmeldrum (1799-1802)		2
Peterhead (1795-1802)		4
Rosehearty (1799-1802)		1
Strathdon (1798-1802)		1
		33

Place—	1803-1808.	No. of Companies.
Aberdeen—		
Loyal (Finlason's) (1803-8)		10
Royal (Leys') (1803-7)		8
Gilcomston Pikemen (1803-8)		2
Aberdeen Pikemen (1804-8)		5
Aberdeenshire Battalion (1804-8)		7
(Companies, 7, included below).		
Aberdour (1803-8)		1
Belhelvie (1803-8)		1
Crimond and Lonmay (1803-8)		1
Cruden (1803-8)		1
Drumblade (1803-8)		1
Dyce, Newmachar, Fintray (1803-8)		1
Ellon (1803-8)		1
Foveran (1803-8)		1
Fraserburgh (1803-8)		2
Huntly (1803-8)		2
Kintore, Inverurie (1803) (Officers only)		0
Logie Buchan, Slains (1803-8)		1
Logie Durno (1803) (Officers only)		0
Methlick (1803-8)		1
Monquhitter (1803-8)		1
Monymusk, Kemnay (1803) (Officers only)		0
Oldmeldrum (1803-8)		3
Peterhead (1803-8)		4
Rathen (1803-8)		1
Rosehearty (1803-8)		1
St. Fergus, Longside (1803-8)		1
Tarves (1803-8)		1
Tyrie, Strichen (1803-8)		1
Udny (1803-8)		1
		53

This aspect of Territorial soldiering has already been elaborately dealt with by Mr. Donald Sinclair in his *History of the Aberdeen Volunteers*, published in 1907, where a good deal of space (pp. 30-142) is devoted to the Volunteers and Local Militia of 1794-1814. I do not essay to supersede his matter; for a complete survey of the facts his book must be studied in conjunction with what is set forth here, which supplements his facts chiefly by giving the names of officers from the various Notification Books at the Public Record Office, where Christian names are usually stated in full, and where the commissions almost invariably have a slightly earlier date than in the *London Gazette*, which Mr. Sinclair followed. Secondly, I have gone over all the pay rolls at the Record Office, which had never been examined by the public until I tackled them in April and May, 1914, the bundles having had to be stamped for the first time to enable me to do so. No rolls have been preserved before those for 1797.

I deal first with the 1794-1802 group—Aberdeen stepping out first in the field with two corps in 1794, and Peterhead coming second in 1795—and follow on with an account of the 1803-8 group.

ABERDEEN BATTERY OF VOLUNTEERS (1794-1802).—The first Volunteers in Aberdeen were the Company of Artillery offered by the county and accepted by the King, August 1794 (Sinclair's *Aberdeen Volunteers*, 40). No pay rolls are preserved at the Record Office, but the *London Gazette* of October 7, 1794, contains the names of the officers gazetted.

CAPTAIN.

George Taylor; he retired.

LIEUTENANT.

Arthur Gibbon, succeeded Taylor as Captain, November 17, 1796 (*W.O.* 25: 168: p. 102), and died in 1798.

ENSIGN.

William Gibbon, succeeded Arthur Gibbon as Lieutenant and ultimately became Captain, remaining so to the end. He was succeeded as Ensign in turn by Kenneth Mackenzie, November 17, 1796, and then by Hugh Cochrane, the latter of whom remained to the end.

Mr. Sinclair says that the Company was "afterwards" attached to the Royal Aberdeen Volunteers, but it also had a separate existence as the "Aberdeen Battery of Volunteers," and is inventoried as such in the Public Record Office, where the first pay roll is for the period December 1797—December 1798, and the list for December 1801—April 1802 (*W.O.* 13 : 4,163). The corps was popular, and grew in numbers.

December, 1797—December, 1798	29
July-August, 1798	32
April-May, 1799	38
May-June, 1799	45
June-July, 1799	51
July-August, 1799	58
August-September, 1799	60
December, 1800—February, 1801	60

Adjutant John Emslie left March 30, 1800, and was replaced by Hector Maclean, June 18, 1800.

ROYAL ABERDEEN VOLUNTEERS (1794-1802).—This corps, which is fully described by Mr. Sinclair (*Aberdeen Volunteers*, 42-73), was the only one in Aberdeen which asked for no pay, being composed of the better to do classes and officered by professional men. Consequently, there are no lists of the rank and file at the Record Office, the sergeants, corporals and drummers alone being paid.

The corps arose out of a meeting convened by the Lord Provost, as Deputy Lieutenant. The first we hear of it is on November 4, 1794. Recruits were advertised for, November 25, by the "Aberdeen Volunteer Association," and in December 15, it was announced that the King had accepted five companies. The officers came dribbling in, beginning with two Captains and six Lieutenants, gazetted January 9, 1795 (*W.O.* 25: 159: p. 118). I give these officers all in a group, with the dates of their commissions.

MAJOR-COMMANDANT.

Alexander Moir, Major-Commandant, April 29, 1795 (*W.O.* 25: 159: p. 381), resigned April 1796 on becoming Sheriff-Substitute of Aberdeen. He was laird of Scotstown, was born 1764, married Margaret, daughter of James Gordon of Leicheston, and died 1824 (Mitchell Gill's *Houses of Moir and Byres*, p. 76).

CAPTAINS.

Thomas Bannerman, May 2, 1795; Major, *vice* Moir, April 5; Lieutenant-Colonel, May 11, 1797. Brother of the 6th baronet of Elsick, he was born in 1743, and died 1820. He was a wine merchant in Aberdeen. His son, Sir Alexander Bannerman, M.P. (1788-1864), married Margaret Gordon (1799-1878), famous as "Carlyle's first love" (R. C. Archibald's *Carlyle's First Love*).

William Henderson, Captain, January 9, 1795 (*W.O.* 25: 159: p. 118); retired by April 9, 1796. Apparently the "late Captain of the 4th Regiment of Foot," who died at Aberdeen, November 4, 1809.

George Symmers, Captain, from late 25th Foot, January 9, 1795; died February 14, 1796.

LIEUTENANTS.

Charles Bannerman, January 9, 1795; Captain of the second company, *vice* Symmers, April 9, 1795. Brother of Thomas Bannerman; advocate in Aberdeen; died 1813. His son, Alexander, a school-fellow of Byron in Aberdeen, entered the H.E.I.C.S.

William Black, May 11, 1797.

Alexander Brebner, January 9, 1795; Captain, May 11, 1797. Laird of Learney; he was the partner and the brother-in-law of Thomas Leys. He died in 1823. The late Colonel Thomas Innes was his grandson.

Alexander Dauncy, January 9, 1765; Captain of the 3rd company, *vice* Henderson, retired, April 5, 1796. He became Lieutenant-Colonel of the Aberdeen Light Infantry Volunteers, March 29, 1799. Born 1749; advocate in Aberdeen, died s.p. 1833.

John Dingwall, *vice* Milne, April 5, 1795. Son of Baillie John Dingwall; he was a stocking manufacturer, Provost of Aberdeen (1799-1800), and laird of Ardo and Rannieston. He died s.p., 1836.

John Ewen, *vice* Charles Bannerman, April 5, 1795; Captain, March 29, 1799, *vice* Dauney. He became Captain in the Royal Aberdeen Volunteers in 1803. Ewen, who was a jeweller (1741-1821), is the reputed author of the "Boatie Rows" (*Bards of Bon-Accord*, 329).

Charles Farquharson, May 11, 1797.

Peter Farquharson, May 11, 1797; he was Adjutant. Born in Dundee, he became an advocate in Aberdeen, and died there, 1855, aged 89. His son, Andrew succeeded to Whitehouse, and his daughter, Margaret, married Lieutenant-Colonel John Farquharson of Corrachree.

Charles Gordon, January 9, 1795; Captain, May 1, 1797. Apparently the advocate in Aberdeen, who was born at Peterculter in 1755, and died at Culter House in 1835; and whose brother, Alexander, wrote the classic treatise on puerperal fever.

James Hadden, Lieutenant of the 3rd company, *vice* Dauney, April 5, 1795; he joined the Aberdeen Light Infantry Volunteers in 1799, and was succeeded by William Gibbon. He joined the Royal Aberdeen Volunteers in 1803 as Lieutenant-Colonel. Hadden (1758-1845) was in company with Thomas Leys, and was several times Lord Provost of Aberdeen (Munro's *Lord Provosts of Aberdeen*).

Thomas Leys, January 9, 1795; Captain, May 11, 1797; Colonel of the Royal Aberdeen Volunteers, 1803-7. Leys (1764-1809) was a member of the spinning firm at Gordon's Mills (now Grandholm) in partnership with his brother-in-law, Alexander Brebner of Learney, and James Hadden, and he was laird of Glascoforest (Munro's *Lord Provosts of Aberdeen*, 257, 262; Morgan's *Annals of Woodside*, 60-73).

Alexander Milne, January 9, 1795; Captain, *vice* Charles Bannerman, April 5, 1796; Major, *vice* Thomas Bannerman, May 11, 1797. Died May 19, 1806.

Alexander Moir, May 11, 1797.

ADJUTANT.

David Keith, from Sergeant in the Coldstream Guards, *vice* Farquharson, July 19, 1797 (*W.O.* 25: 164: p. 327).

The battalion was never a big one, and when Major-General Hay inspected it on July 22, 1799, its rank and file stood at 300.

ABERDEEN LIGHT INFANTRY VOLUNTEERS (1799-1802).—This was a working men's corps, in contradistinction to the Royal Aberdeenshire Volunteers, who were recruited from the better-to-do classes, and who received no pay. The corps, which is fully described by Mr. Sinclair (*Aberdeen Volunteers*, 74-81), started with seven companies, under the command as Lieutenant-Colonel of Alexander Dauney, with James Hadden as Major—both of them from the Royal Aberdeen Volunteers. The original seven companies (420 men) as set forth in the first muster is for the period January 25—February 24, 1799 (*W.O.* 13: 4,160).

Company (Captains).	Lieutenants.	Ensigns.	Men.
Alexander Barron	John Johnston (From Feb. 9)	————	60
John Blaikie	{ Arthur Farquhar { George Craig	————	60
James Chalmers	{ Alexander Brown { Thomas Duncan	————	60
James Ferguson	Alexander Duncan	Robert Spring	60
John Johnston	{ Alexander Duthie { Charles Baird { (Captain, Feb. 16)	Alexander Leith	60
James Middleton	William Michie (Resigned, Feb. 6)	James Dick	60

Three new companies were added on February 16, 1799:—

Company.	Lieutenants.	Ensigns.	Men.
Charles Baird	Charles Fyfe	John Allan	58
William Dauney	Thomas Duncan	George Smith	55
Alexander Shirrefs	Alexander Smith	Charles Panton	62

Many changes occurred in the personnel of the officers during the first year as the January-December, 1799, pay roll shows, the rank and file rising from 420 to 1,011 (*W.O.* 13, 4,160):—

Company (Commandants).	Lieutenants.	Ensigns.	Men.
Artillery Company	Francis Dodd James Harvey	————	92
Capt. Charles Baird	Charles Fyfe (Transferred) John Allan (En. till August 16)	George Alexander	86
Capt. Alexander Barron	John Johnston (Promoted Captain) Robert Spring (En. till March 29. Transferred)	George Smith	101
Capt. John Blaikie	Arthur Farquhar (Promoted Captain) Robert Spring George Craig (Resigned)	David Reid	92
Capt. Alexander Brown William Dauney (Promoted Major)	Thomas Duncan George Smith (En. till August 16)	George Barclay	78
Capt. James Chalmers	Alexander Brown (Promoted Captain) James Dick Thomas Duncan (En. till March 29 Transferred)	Robert Smith	102
Capt. James Ferguson Capt. Alexander Duncan	Alexander Duncan (Promoted Captain) John Imrie (1st Lieut. August 16) Robert Spring (En. till March 29)	Robert Caie	103
Capt. John Johnston	Alexander Duthie Charles Baird (En. till March 29)	Alexander Leith	82
Capt. James Littlejohn	Alexander Hall Charles Panton (Transferred) John Imrie (En. till August 16)	Alexander Cooper	92
Capt. James Middleton	William Michie (Resigned) James Dick (Transferred) Charles Fyfe James Dick (En. till March 29)	————	96
Capt. Alexander Shirrefs (Resigned) Capt. Arthur Farquhar	Alexander Smith (Resigned) Charles Panton (En. till August 11)	John Mathieson	87

The pay rolls show that the following sums were disbursed :—

January—December 24, 1799	-	-	-	-	-	-	£2,364
December, 1799—December, 1800	-	-	-	-	-		2,563
December, 1800—December, 1801	-	-	-	-	-		3,624

The last pay roll, for the period March—April, 1802, shows the disbursements as £416 and the number of men as 597, as follows :—

Company.	Lieutenants.	Men.
Artillery	Francis Dodd James Harvey	32
Charles Baird	John Allan Alexander Low	52
Alexander Barron	George Smith William Troup	55
John Blaikie	Robert Spring David Reid	59
Alexander Brown	Thomas Duncan George Barclay	55
James Chalmers	Robert Caie David Chalmers	61
Alexander Duncan	John Imrie Andrew Affleck	58
Arthur Farquhar	Charles Panton John Gordon	57
Alexander Hall	Charles Fyfe James Matthews	60
John Johnston	Alexander Duthie John Law	56
James Littlejohn	Robert Smith Alexander Cooper	52

OLD ABERDEEN (1798-1802).—Old Aberdeen formed a Volunteer Association on May 7, 1798, and on May 22, the officers were appointed :—

CAPTAIN.

Alexander Matheson. Mr. Sinclair (*Aberdeen Volunteers*) says he was a magistrate, and that the corps was really commanded by Gilbert Gerard. Matheson is probably the "Lieutenant" Alexander Matheson who was made honorary burgess, September 29, 1787. He died, February 28, 1800 (*W.O.* 13 : 4,163).

LIEUTENANT.

Rev. Gilbert Gerard, became Major-Commandant of the corps, and remained to the end in 1802. He was the son of Professor Alexander Gerard (d. 1795), Professor of Divinity, and he himself was Professor of Greek at King's College ; he died September 28, 1815. A brother, two sons, a nephew and a grandnephew, Sir Montagu Gilbert Gerard (1842-1905), were all in the Army, the last having a very distinguished career, notably in negotiating the Pamirs boundary dispute, 1895.   Sir Montagu's sisters, Jane Emily and Dorothea, the well-known novelists, both married officers in the Austrian Army (*Scottish Notes and Queries*, 1st ser. x., 8, 61 : xii., 61, 175).

ENSIGN.

Rev. William Jack, M.D. ; Captain, *vice* Matheson, March 28, 1800. He became Provost of Old Aberdeen and Principal of King's College, and died, February 9, 1854, aged 85, having held College office for 60 years (Munro's *Old Aberdeen*, ii., 228).

The first pay roll, March 13—March 24, 1799, shows 77 men.   The number gradually rose as follows : —

	Men.			Men.
March—April, 1799 - -	80		June—July, 1799 - -	119
April—May, 1799 - -	87		July—August, 1799 - -	119
May—June, 1799 - -	111		August—September, 1799 -	120

In the beginning of 1800 the corps was divided into two companies of 60 men each : —

Major—Gilbert Gerard	Captain—Alexander Matheson
1st Lieutenant—William Jack	1st Lieutenant—Robert Eden Scott
2nd Lieutenant—James Gordon	2nd Lieutenant—John Irvine
(Promoted 1st, March 28, 1800)	

These officers remained to the end, except that Matheson's death involved a change, shown in the last pay roll, March—April 1802, when the two companies had 60 men each.

Major—Gilbert Gerard	Captain—William Jack
1st Lieutenant—Robert Eden Scott	1st Lieutenant—James Gordon
2nd Lieutenant—John Irvine	2nd Lieutenant—Robert Low
	(Promoted 1st, March 28, 1800)

The Old Aberdeen Volunteers, described in Mr. Sinclair's *Aberdeen Volunteers* (82-7), were disembodied May 3, 1802, and did not reappear in the 1803 reconstruction.

FRASERBURGH (1797-1802).—The officers were all gazetted, February 16, 1797 (*W.O.* 25 : 168 : p. 34).

CAPTAIN.

William Troup, formerly in the H.E.I.C.   He died, August 23, 1800, and was succeeded in the command in October 2, 1800 by William Fraser, of Memsie (1739-1813).

1ST LIEUTENANT.
Alexander Paton.

2ND LIEUTENANTS.
George Gordon and William Kelman, who remained to the end.

The first pay roll, July 25—August 26, 1798, and the last, December 25, 1801—April 24, 1802, contain 60 men each (*W.O.* 13: 4,164). Paton dropped out before the end, and William Cooper became Ensign.

GARIOCH (1798-1802).—The first pay roll is for the period, October 25—November 26, 1798, with 60 men; and the last, March, 1802—April, 1802, with 60 men (*W.O.* 13: 4,164). The officers were all gazetted on October 25, 1798 (*W.O.* 25: 167: p. 14), and remained to the end.

CAPTAIN.
Alexander Stewart, from Lieutenant, half pay, of the late 89th.

1ST LIEUTENANT.
Peter Beattie.

2ND LIEUTENANT.
Thomas Dawson.

The Garioch was not represented in the 1803 reconstruction.

GARTLY (1798-1802).—This company was embodied, November 1, 1798, with the following officers, gazetted October 25, 1798 (*W.O.* 25: 167: p. 15):—

CAPTAIN.
William Allan.

LIEUTENANT.
Dr. James Christie.

ENSIGN.
George Davidson, jun.

The first pay roll, November 1, 1798—December 24, 1798, shows 60 men. In August or September, 1801, the company was linked with the two Huntly ones under the command of Major James Brodie. The last pay roll, March—April, 1802, shows 57 men. The history of the company has been minutely described, with the full list of names of all its members, by Mr. William Will in the *Huntly Express* (May 1, 1914).

HUNTLY (1798-1802).—It is said that " 800 of the Duke of Gordon's tenants and inhabitants of the town" of Huntly enrolled to serve as Volunteers. The number is probably exaggerated, but one can understand that the cradle of the Gordons in the north was enthusiastic for the movement. As a matter of fact, Huntly raised two separate companies, one in July, and the other in October, 1798.

First Company (82 men) embodied July 27, 1798 :—

CAPTAIN.

James Gordon; resigned, May 26, 1804. Factor for the Duke of Gordon, and tenant of Coclarachy. He had four sons officers in the Navy, and two in the H.E.I.C.S. (*Gordons under Arms*, Nos. 107, 529, 784, 791, 1,155, and 1,236: but his own soldiering is omitted there). He became laird of Littlefolla, and died March 11, 1828. He is fully described in the *Huntly Express*, August 31, September 7, 1906.

LIEUTENANT.

John Innes.

ENSIGN.

Alexander Thomson.

Second Company (64 men), embodied, October 1, 1798; officers gazetted on September 28, 1798 (*W.O.* 25 : 166: p. 43) :—

CAPTAIN.

William Forsyth.

LIEUTENANT.

Alexander Forsyth.

ENSIGN.

William Paterson.

In August, 1801, the two companies and that of Gartly (*q.v.*) were brigaded together under the command of Major Brodie, who had entered the 2nd Queen's in 1792, and had served in the 91st, 106th, 56th, 93rd, 39th, the Perthshire Fencible Cavalry and the 4th, selling out in 1800. The last musters of both companies are for the period March—April, 1802 (*W.O.* 13 : 4,165).

LESLIE (1798-1802?).—This company (not mentioned by Mr. Sinclair and unrepresented by any pay rolls at the Record Office) had the following officers gazetted, December 17, 1798 (*W.O.* 25: 226: p. 825):—

CAPTAIN.
George Willis.

LIEUTENANT.
—— Jamieson.

ENSIGN.
Alexander Orrock.

This company may never have been actually embodied.

OLD MELDRUM (1799-1802).—Although "upwards of 230 inhabitants of Old Meldrum, and the parish of Old Meldrum," enrolled themselves as Volunteers in November, 1797 (Sinclair's *Aberdeen Volunteers*, 119), their services were apparently not utilised till April and May, 1799. The officers were:—

MAJOR-COMMANDANT.
James Urquhart, July 22, 1799. He remained to the end in 1808. He was laird of Meldrum, an advocate in Edinburgh, and died s.p., June 17, 1835, aged 77, being succeeded by his cousin, Beauchamp Colclough Urquhart (d. 1861).

1st Company—

CAPTAIN.
James Garioch (from Lieutenant, half pay, 87th), June 10, 1799; continued till 1808. He was laird of Gariochsfield, practised medicine at Old Meldrum for upwards of 40 years, and died at Milton of Durno, August 25, 1818, aged 78.

LIEUTENANT.
John Manson, June 10, 1799.

ENSIGN.
James Duncan, June 10, 1799. A John Duncan became Ensign, July 10, 1800, and remained to the end.

2nd Company—

CAPTAIN.
John Gordon, July 22, 1799, served without pay; replaced, October 30, 1799, by Lieutenant Simpson.

1ST LIEUTENANT.
Thomas Simpson, July 22, 1799; remained to the end (as Captain).

2ND LIEUTENANT.

James Forbes, July 22, 1799; became Lieutenant. James Duncan was appointed July 10, 1800 (*W.O.* 25 : 169: p. 215).

The first pay list of the 1st Company, April 13—26, 1799, shows 57 men, and in the last, March—April, 1800, gives 60.

The first pay list of the 2nd Company, May 20—December 24, 1799, shows 66 men, who rose in 1800 to 78, and fell in the last, March 25—April 24, 1802, to 60. The companies were disembodied, May 8, 1802.

PETERHEAD (1795-1802).—As a vulnerable seaport town, Peterhead rose to arms in March, 1795, when it was decided to raise one Artillery and three Infantry Companies, the officers being gazetted, April 8, 1795, but there are no pay rolls till the period July 25—August 24, 1798. A fresh start was made in 1797 when the three infantry companies were brigaded under one Commandant, Major John Ramsay. The companies were officered thus :—

Artillery Company: 1st pay roll, July—August, 1798 (80 men); last, December, 1801 (80 men). Pay, December, 1800—December, 1801—£476. The (ten) Bombardiers served without pay.

CAPTAIN.

William Ferguson, April 8, 1795. Son of Robert Ferguson; born 1722; naval officer; afterwards shipmaster, Peterhead; married Isabella Arbuthnot (1725-1812); died March 1, 1806 (*Records of the Clan Ferguson*, 288-9; Henderson's *Epitaphs*, i., 371-2).

LIEUTENANTS.

James Hutchison, April 8, 1795. Son of Robert Hutchison, whalefisher; married Jane, daughter of Captain William Ferguson; died June 4, 1822 (Henderson's *Epitaphs*, i., 372).

James Arbuthnot, April 8, 1795. Apparently son of Thomas Arbuthnot (1727-73), and historian of Peterhead, who died February 9, 1829, aged 62 (Henderson's *Epitaphs*, i., 370).

The first pay roll of the three Infantry Companies is for the period July 25—August 24, 1798 (with 50 men each), and the last for March—April, 1802 (with 50, 48 and 50 men respectively). At first, Major Ramsay had a company of his own; but in 1798 he assigned it to a

separate officer, and concerned himself with the general command.   The
three companies cost in pay from first to last £4,767 :—

December, 1797—July, 1798	-	-	-	-	-	-	-	£693
July, 1798—December, 1798	-	-	-	-	-	-	-	574
December, 1798—December, 1799	-	-	-	-	-	-	-	1,494
December, 1799—December, 1800	-	-	-	-	-	-	-	1,496
December, 1801—April, 1802	-	-	-	-	-	-	-	510

1st Infantry Company—(50 men in 1798 : 89 in 1801)—

MAJOR.

John Ramsay.   He gave up his company in 1798 to command the
three companies generally, and did not join the 1803 movement.

CAPTAIN-LIEUTENANT.

Donald Mackintosh (from half pay of the 4th, or King's American
Foot), April 8, 1795; appointed to command the company as Captain,
September 27, 1798 (*W.O.* 25 : 226 : p. 289), in place of Ramsay, who
assumed general command.   He was succeeded by Alexander Robertson,
who had formerly been a Sergeant.

LIEUTENANT.

William Forbes, May 3, 1797.

2nd Infantry Company—(50 men in 1798 : 85 in 1803)—

CAPTAIN.

John Hutchison, April 8, 1795.

LIEUTENANT.

Gilbert Alexander, December 21, 1796.   Apparently tanner at
Peterhead ; originally Quartermaster, as which he was succeeded by
James Forbes.

James Forbes, originally Adjutant ; Lieutenant, December 21, 1796.

3rd Infantry Company—(50 men in 1798 : 81 in 1803)—

CAPTAIN.

Alexander Elles (Lieutenant, April 8, 1795), December 21, 1796
(*W.O.* 25 : 168 : p. 179).

LIEUTENANT.

Thomas Arbuthnot, December 21, 1796, *vice* Elles.   He was ap-
parently the merchant who died April 8, 1820, aged 76, and whose sister,
Margaret of Rora, married her cousin, Thomas Arbuthnot, a Jacobite
(Henderson's *Epitaphs*, i., 369, 370).

Thomas Robertson, died May 29, 1804.

ROSEHEARTY (1799-1802).—This company, according to the statement (October 1, 1799) of its Captain, was raised by Thomas Russel of Rathen in February, 1799. The first pay roll, May 3—May 26, 1799, shows 57 men, and the following officers who remained to the end:—

CAPTAIN.

Thomas Russel, laird of Rathen; formerly in the Northern Fencibles, and then in the Banff Volunteer Artillery. He wrote, October 1, 1799, asking for pay as an officer.

LIEUTENANT.

William Milne.

ENSIGN.

John Cowie.

The last pay roll, March-April 1802, contains 57 men (*W.O.* 13 : 4,167).

STRATHDON (1798-1802).—The officers of this company (which is not given by Mr. Sinclair) were gazetted December 12, 1798 (*W.O.* 25 : 226 : p. 84):—

CAPTAIN.

Alexander Forbes (from Lieutenant, late 93rd); remained till 1802.

1ST LIEUTENANT.

George Forbes.

2ND LIEUTENANT.

John Forbes; he replaced George Forbes by March, 1799, and was replaced by Robert Gordon by June, 1800, the latter remaining to the end. Alexander Anderson was appointed 2nd Lieutenant by March, 1799, and remained to the end.

The first pay roll, December 25, 1798—January 24, 1799, shows 67 men, and the last, April—December, 1802, gives 62. The pay for December, 1799—December, 1800, was £400 (*W.O.* 13 : 4,167).

THE VOLUNTEER RECONSTRUCTION OF 1803-8.

The reconstruction of the Volunteer force in 1803 found Aberdeen, town and county, putting 53 instead of 33 companies into the field.

On November 5, 1803, the Duke of Gordon, as Lord Lieutenant, sent the Secretary of State a very interesting return of the Volunteer force in Aberdeenshire (*H.O.* 50 : 57). It shows:—

Infantry Companies	= 42	:	Establishment - - - -			2,928
Artillery ,,	= 2	:	,, - - - -			120
	Field Officers - -	5	Sergeants -	-	- 140	
	Captains - - -	41	Corporals -	-	- 120	
	Subalterns - -	99	Drummers	-	- 58	
	Staff Officers - -	3	Rank and File	-	- 3,042	

Corps.	Commandant.	Raised.		Privates.
Aberdeen Vol. Infantry	Lieut.-Col. Finlason	21st May, 1803		800
Aberdour	Capt. William Leslie	15th October, 1803		60
Belhelvie	,, John Scott	,,	,,	80
Crimond and Lonmay	,, Thomas Laing	,,	,,	60
Cruden	,, George Gordon	,,	,,	60
Drumblade	,, Andrew Paterson	,,	,,	60
Dyce, Newmachar, Fintray	,, John Paul	,,	,,	80
Ellon	,, John Leith Ross	,,	,,	80
Foveran	,, George Thomson	,,	,,	60
Fraserburgh Artillery	,, William Kelman	,,	,,	60
Fraserburgh Infantry	,, William Fraser	21st May, 1803		82
Gilcomston Pikemen	Lieut. James Chalmers	15th October, 1803		120
Huntly	Capt. George Reynolds	,,	,,	60
Kintore and Inverurie	,, Benjamin Lumsden	,,	,,	80
Logie Buchan and Slains	,, James Watson	,,	,,	80
Logie Durno	,, Robert Harvey	,,	,,	60
Meldrum	Major James Urquhart	,,	,,	180
Methlick	Capt. Ludovick Grant	,,	,,	60
Monquhitter	,, Archibald Cumine	,,	,,	60
Monymusk and Kemnay	,, David Robertson	,,	,,	80
Peterhead (Indep.) Infantry	,, William Scott	,,	,,	60
,, Infantry	Major John Hutchison	20th June, 1803		240
,, Artillery	Capt. James Hutchison	15th October, 1803		60
Rathen	,, Alexander Henderson	,,	,,	60
Rosehearty	,, William Milne	,,	,,	60
St. Fergus and Longside	,, Thomas Kilgour	,,	,,	60
Strathbogy Infantry	,, James Gordon	,,	,,	60
Tarves	Lieut. James Hay	,,	,,	60
Tyrie and Strichen	Capt. Andrew Anderson	,,	,,	60
Udny	,, John Marr	,,	,,	60

An even more interesting return was made on October 1, 1803, showing the position of the Militia and Volunteer quotas of the shire side by side. In forwarding it, Thomas Burnett, clerk to the Lieutenancy, wrote to the Secretary of State (*H O.* 50: 57) —

I have to acknowledge the honour of a Circular Letter from Mr Carew of the 16th ulto, reminding me that no Abstract of the Subdivision Rolls for the County of Aberdeen has hitherto been transmitted, as required by the Statute 43rd Geo III, Cap 96

I took the earliest opportunity of communicating the Circular to the Lieutenancy of this County, and should not have omitted to pay the strictest attention to that Section of the Act appointing a Return to be made of the Subdivision Rolls, had the Lieutenancy considered it expedient to carry its other compulsory provisions into execution

On receipt of the Circular from the Right Hon Lord Hobart, dated the 3rd and 18th August last, not a moment was lost in forwarding by every exertion the Voluntary Enrollments thereby recommended   In consequence of the measures adopted for this purpose, I have the satisfaction to acquaint you that the inhabitants of the different Districts in this county came forward with the utmost alacrity and unanimity, and enrolled themselves to the extent specified in the Return which I have the honor to inclose

The arrangement of these Voluntary Offers has been completed by his Grace, the Lord Lieutenant, in terms of Lord Hobart's Circular above alluded to, namely to the extent of six times the Quota of Militia raised in the County, exclusive of the Supplementary number, and the different Volunteer Corps accepted of by His Majesty

Under the circumstances and while numerous other public measures respecting the Militia and Army of Reserve were in agitation, the Lieutenancy were induced to suspend the execution of the foresaid Statute from a perfect conviction that it would tend to perplex the different individuals concerned and might in the same measure check the public spirit and alacrity so conspicuously manifested in the numerous Voluntary Enrollments throughout the County

I am desired, however, to assure you that all these circumstances will not prevent the Lieutenancy from carrying the Act into immediate execution, should you consider such a measure necessary, after the steps which have already been taken and approven of by His Majesty

This return—"Volunteer enrolments, and apportionment of Volunteers in the County of Aberdeen, agreeable to Lord Hobart's Circular of August, 1803 "—shows that the quota of Volunteers allotted to the county was 3,840, of whom 1,120 were already embodied

District and Parish. I		Quota of Militia in each Parish	Full quota of Vols in each Parish	Total in each District	No. of Vol offers in each Parish	Total Vols in each District
Crathie and Braemar	-	9	54	—	324	—
Glenmuick, Tullich, etc		8	48	—	290	—
Aboyne, Glentanner	-	4	24	—	145	—
Birse - - -	-	7	42	—	97	—
Logie Coldstone	-	4	24	—	153	—
Tarland and Migvie	-	5	30	—	57	—
Coull - - -	-	3	18	—	49	—
				240		1,115
II						
Kincardine o' Neil -	-	8	48	—	142	—
Lumphanan - -	-	4	24	—	68	—
Midmar - -	-	6	36	—	96	—
Cluny - - -	-	3	18	—	44	—
Skene - - -	-	6	36	—	187	—
Drumoak - -	-	2	12	—	82	—
Peterculter - -	-	3	18	—	103	—
Newhills - -	-	7	42	—	107	—
				270		918
III						
St Nicholas or Aberdeen		80	480	—	1,008	—
Oldmachar - -	-	37	222	—	910	—
				1,212		3,951
IV						
Strathdon - -	-	4	24	—	303	—
Cabrach - -	-	3	18	—	52	—
Glenbucket - -	-	2	12	—	30	—
Towie - -	-	3	18	—	75	—
Cushnie - -	-	2	12	—	24	—
Leochell - -	-	2	12	—	39	—
Kinnethmont - -	-	3	18	—	103	—
Auchindoir - -	-	2	12	—	65	—
Rhynie - -	-	2	12	—	50	—
Kildrummy - -	-	2	12	—	54	—
Kearn - -	-	1	6	—	16	—
Clatt - -	-	3	18	—	17	—
Tough - -	-	2	12	—	56	—
Keig - -	-	2	12	—	18	—
Alford - -	-	4	24	—	55	—
Tullynessle - -	-	2	12	—	32	—
Forbes - -	-	1	6	—	13	—
				240		1,002

District and Parish. V.	Quota of Militia in each Parish.	Full quota of Vols. in each Parish.	Total in each District.	No. of Vol. offers in each Parish.	Total Vols. in each District.
Leslie	3	18	—	42	—
Insch	8	48	—	60	—
Culsalmond	6	36	—	60	—
Glass	6	36	—	98	—
Gartly	7	42	—	60	—
Drumblade	6	36	—	60	—
Forgue	11	66	—	80	—
Cairney	9	54	—	160	—
Huntly	18	108	—	240	—
			444		860
VI.					
Fyvie	15	90	—	145	—
King Edward	9	54	—	76	—
Monquhitter	9	54	—	106	—
Auchterless	9	54	—	31	—
Turriff	13	78	—	142	—
			330		500
VII.					
Logie Durno	8	48	—	100	—
Daviot	5	30	—	85	—
Inverury	5	30	—	145	—
Keith-hall and Kinkell	6	36	—	42	—
Kemnay	3	18	—	69	—
Kinnellar	2	12	—	62	—
Kintore	5	30	—	122	—
Meldrum	9	54	—	174	—
Monymusk	7	42	—	170	—
Oyne	4	24	—	84	—
Premnay	3	18	—	59	—
Rayne	8	48	—	100	—
			390		1,112
VIII.					
Udny	10	60	—	117	—
Tarves	12	72 }	—	633	—
Methlick	7	42 }			
Foveran	9	54	—	170	—
Ellon	13	78	—	284	—
Logie Buchan	5	30	—	84	—
Cruden	8	48 }	—	252	—
Slains	6	36 }			
			420		1,540

District and Parish. IX.				Quota of Militia in each Parish.	Full quota of Vols. in each Parish.	Total in each District.	No. of Vol. offers in each Parish.	Total Vols. in each District.
Longside	-	-	-	9	54	—	49	—
Peterhead	-	-	-	20	120	—	90	—
St. Fergus	-	-	-	9	54	—	130	—
Crimond	-	-	-	3	18	—	62	—
Loanmay	-	-	-	6	36	—	67	—
Raethen	-	-	-	7	42	—	103	—
Fraserburgh	-	-	-	10	60	—	164	—
Pitsligo	-	-	-	4	24	—	80	—
Aberdour	-	-	-	5	30	—	88	—
Tyrie	-	-	-	4	24	—	101	—
Strichen	-	-	-	6	36	—	143	—
New Deer	-	-	-	15	90	—	16	—
Old Deer	-	-	-	18	108	—	133	—
						696		1,226
X.								
Belhelvie	-	-	-	6	36	—	129	—
Dyce	-	-	-	2	12	—	22	—
Fintray	-	-	-	3	18	—	36	—
Newmachar	-	-	-	4	24	—	83	—
Bourty	-	-	-	3	18	—	53	—
						108		323
						3,840		10,514

The above numbers are exclusive of Guides, Pioneers, and Persons who have agreed to furnish horses, carts, etc., amounting to 783, making total of voluntary offers for the County of Aberdeen   -   -   11,297

The note of the 1803 reconstruction was the unifying of the patriotism of the parishes into five groups:—

Aberdeenshire Battalion—Cruden, Ellon, Foveran, Logie-Buchan and Slains, Methlick, Tarves and Udny.

Crimond grouped with Lonmay, Rathen, St. Fergus and Longside.

Fraserburgh (2 companies) grouped with Aberdour, Rosehearty, Tyrie and Strichen.

Meldrum—Three companies.

Strathbogie—Huntly (2 companies) and Drumblade

The Volunteer force of Aberdeen, town and county, transferred itself in 1808 into the Local Militia (five battalions).

LOYAL ABERDEEN VOLUNTEERS, or Finlason's Fencibles (1803-8), described by Mr. Sinclair in his *Aberdeen Volunteers* (98-103), were raised by the veteran soldier, William Finlason, who had begun his soldiering in the Duke of Gordon's first regiment, the 89th, in 1759, and who had spent much of his time in recruiting for the last regiment raised by his Grace. Finlason made his offer in the spring of 1803, and by June 1, "above 300" privates enrolled. The first parade was upon the Links on July 29 (*H.O.* 50: 57), when Finlason offered to lead the corps to "any part of Great Britain in case of Invasion." The officers, commissioned on May 21, 1803, are notable for the number of old Army men who were appointed (*W.O.* 25: 170: p. 52). Some supplementary particulars on this list are given in a letter by the Duke of Gordon to the Secretary of State, July 17, 1803 (*H.O.* 50: 57), and some additional officers are supplied by a return of the Duke.

LIEUTENANT-COLONEL.

William Finlason, from Captain, half pay late 89th (which he had joined in 1759). He had spent all his life in the Service (for a time in Dominica). He was the son of John Finlason (born at Dysart, 1708, died at Aberdeen, 1774), Collector of Excise at Aberdeen, by his wife, Anne (1710-73), only daughter of Alexander Gordon of Aberdour. He married Elizabeth Aird, and died in 1817.

MAJORS.

Edmund Filmer, from Captain, half pay 84th; replaced September 27, 1803, by William Black, who remained to the end. Born in 1765, Filmer was the fourth son of the Rev. Sir Edmund Filmer, 6th bart. of East Sutton, Kent. He married, 1794, Emelia (died 1854), daughter of Professor George Skene of Marischal College, and died in 1810, his only son, Edmund (1809-57), becoming 8th bart.

Hay Livingston, from Captain, half pay 13th, with six years' actual service; became Lieutenant-Colonel, November 22, 1803 (*W.O.* 25: 206: p. 61). He replaced Filmer in command of a company, and remained to the end. He had a son, Alexander, M.A. of Marischal College in 1818.

CAPTAINS.

James Bannerman, from half pay, 109th, six years' actual service; he had also been Lieutenant, East and West Lothian Fencible Cavalry; left before the end.

Thomas Burnett; remained to the end.

Alexander Fraser, from half pay, 109th, with eight years' service in the Line and Militia; remained to the end.

William Gilbert, from Captain, 52nd, 10 years' service; transferred to the Stirlingshire Militia July, 1806, and was succeeded as Captain by Henry Lumsden (*H.O.* 50 : 150).

James Moir, from Lieutenant, late Southern Fencibles; remained to the end.

James Roy, from Ensign, half pay 94th, eight years' actual service; remained to the end.

Charles Skene, from Lieutenant, half pay 35th; remained to the end.

LIEUTENANTS.

David Chalmers, became Captain, *vice* Filmer, September 27, 1803 (*W.O.* 25 : 204 : p. 257), and remained to the end.

George Cheyne, *vice* Maclachlan, resigned September 27, 1803.

Alexander Duthie, *vice* Chalmers, September 27, 1803.

John Emslie; formerly Lieutenant, Aberdeen Militia.

Robert Charles Grant, September 27, 1803; remained to the end.

John Imrie, September 27, 1803; resigned by April 1804.

Henry Lumsden; became Captain, 1806, and remained to the end. He acted as Paymaster. He was succeeded as Lieutenant by Ensign James Blackhall, who was succeeded as Ensign by John Morrison.

George Mackenzie; became Captain, and remained to the end.

Peter Maclachan (one list calls him " Robert," and another William); resigned.

Thomas Sangster; remained to the end.

William Skene (*W.O.* 13 : 4,162).

ENSIGNS.

Alexander Abercrombie, December 3, 1803; remained to the end.

Charles Baird, December 3, 1803; remained to the end.

Andrew Bonniman, December 3, 1803; remained to the end.

Alexander Booth; became Lieutenant.

John Brown; remained to the end.

John Duguid, December 3, 1803.

James Dyce; became Lieutenant and remained to the end.

Hugh Fullerton; remained to the end. Apparently the Aberdeen advocate who died in 1846, aged 66.

Robert Gibb; remained to the end.

Alexander Grant, September 27, 1803; Lieutenant, *vice* Imrie; resigned April 3, 1804 (*W.O.* 25 : 206 : p. 61). He was succeeded as Ensign by George Gordon.

Charles Grant, from Ensign, half pay 94th; remained to the end.

George Logan, September 27, 1803.

John Middleton; remained to the end.

James Morrison.

William Ogilvie, September 27, 1803; resigned and succeeded by John Gordon, April 3, 1804.

James Sherriffs appears in the first pay roll (*W.O.* 13 : 4,162), but gives way in the next one, September—December, 1803, to James Turriff.

George Shinnie, April 3, 1804.

James Simpson.

Alexander Smith; remained to the end.

James Spalding, September 27, 1803; remained to the end.

William Stewart.

James Turriff; remained to the end.

QUARTERMASTER.

William Skene, from Ensign, half pay 109th.

ADJUTANT.

Andrew Affleck; remained to the end. He had been seven years in the Southern Fencibles (*H.O.* 50 : 205), and in 1799 was made Adjutant of the Royal Aberdeen Volunteers.

CHAPLAIN.

Rev. George Gordon, D.D., December 24, 1803. He was minister of the second charge, Aberdeen, and died 1811, aged 59. He had three sons in the Indian Army (*Gordons under Arms*, Nos. 202, 540, 969). The Maxwell Gordon who was in Finlason's corps in 1808 was probably his son, who became minister of Foveran, and who died in 1840 aged 46. The Gordon McRobie (died 1818), who was also in the corps, was son-in-law of the Rev. George Gordon.

SURGEON.

Dr. William Livingstone, M.D., December 24, 1803. He died in 1822.

ASSISTANT SURGEON.

Dr. Ligertwood and Dr. William Donaldson appear in the 1808 list.

On September 14, 1803, Finlason, whose tetchiness about his rights resulted in his writing scores of letters to the authorities from time to time, wrote on behalf of the Captains (*H.O.* 50 : 57):—

We are field officers with companies in the Aberdeen Volunteers, from half pay and with very old rank in the Army. When we made an offer of our services in that corps we certainly did conceive from the proposed conditions of service from Lord Hobart of March 31 last that, being from half pay, though field officers at the same time Captains of companies, we should be entitled to constant pay not higher than that of Captain.

R2

The first pay roll, June 11—26, 1803 (£209), shows that there were 764 men in the ten companies. These numbers had risen to 886 in the next roll, June 25—September 24, 1803, when they were commanded as follows (*W.O.* 13: 4,162):—

Company.	Lieutenants.	Ensigns.	Men.
Lieut.-Col. Finlason	{ Alexander Booth { William Stewart	James Spalding	83
Major Edmund Filmer	{ James Morrison { Hugh Fullerton	————	96
Capt. James Bannerman	{ James Simpson { John Emslie	George Cheyne	89
„ Thomas Burnett	{ Charles Grant { Alexander Duthie	Robert Charles Grant	88
„ Alexander Fraser	William Skene	————	85
„ William Gilbert	{ Thomas Sangster { Charles Baird	————	84
„ Hay Livingston	{ Alexander Smith { James Dyce	————	85
„ James Moir	{ John Brown { John Middleton	William Ogilvie	86
„ James Roy	David Chalmers	James Sherriffs	90
„ Charles Skene (Grenadier Coy.)	{ Henry Lumsden { George Mackenzie { Robert Gibb	————	87

The last pay roll is for December 25, 1807—September 24, 1808, when the companies were officered thus, the rank and file standing at 1,081, as against 764 in 1803:—

Company.	Lieutenants.	Men.
Colonel William Finlason	{ John Whyte { Maxwell Gordon	104
Capt. Thomas Burnett	{ Charles Grant { Robert Charles Grant	110
„ David Chalmers	{ John Brown { James Dyce	113
„ Alexander Fraser	{ William Skene { Alexander Smith	112
Lieut.-Col. Hay Livingston	{ James Morrison { Hugh Fullerton	113
Capt. Henry Lumsden	{ Thomas Sangster { Charles Baird	100
„ George Mackenzie	{ James Spalding { James Blackhall	103
„ James Moir	{ John Middleton { Gordon McRobie	110
„ James Roy	{ Alexander Abercrombie { George Davidson	109
„ Charles Skene	{ Robert Gibb { James Grant	107

ROYAL ABERDEEN VOLUNTEERS (1803-6).—The reconstruction of the Volunteers, which had found the working men corps in the Loyal Aberdeen Volunteers as enthusiastic as ever, was received by the unpaid battalion, the Royal Aberdeen Volunteers, in anything but a gallant mood. Mr. Sinclair, who describes the corps (*Aberdeen Volunteers*, 104-110), finds the circumstances rather obscure; and there is one link in the story which has escaped his notice, namely the intervention of Dr. Dauney, the Colonel of the Royals.

On July 27, 1803, a letter was addressed by "Civis" (John Ewen?) "To the gentlemen who composed the late Battalion of Royal Aberdeen Volunteers." On August 10, Dauney wrote the following letter to the Duke of Gordon, as Lord Lieutenant of the county (*H.O.* 50: 57):—

I had the honour of transmitting to your Grace as far back as the 7th April last an offer from 25 officers of the late Royal Aberdeen Light Infantry (which consisted of 600 rank and file) to re-embody the Corps to the extent of 400; which offer your Grace was pleased to forward to Lord Hobart, Secretary of State. On the 26th of the same month the persons concerned in the above offer met and came to the resolution of withdrawing it. . . . The chief reason was that at the above period there was every appearance of an accommodation taking place with the French Government. Now, however, that war seems inevitable and that the enemy will in all probability attempt an invasion, it becomes the duty of all ranks to stand forth in defence of their country. I am, therefore, authorised to renew the offer of the 7th April made by the officers above mentioned to re-embody the Corps to the number of 400 rank and file on the same terms as to extent of service, pay and allowance as the 2nd Regiment of the Royal Edinburgh Volunteers, but subject to the ballots for the Militia and Army of Reserve.

Your Grace will be fully sensible of what consequence it may be to have as many bodies of regular Volunteers on the coast as possible; and that their services may be reasonably expected to be more efficient on that footing than under the late Act for the Levy *en masse* [43 Geo. III. cap. 96, July 27, 1803]. If in these views your Grace shall be disposed so far to approve of the tender here made as to forward it for his Majesty's gracious consideration, the men, in the event of being accepted of, will be got together immediately, and every effort made to prepare them for repelling the Enemys of their country.

As they will consist of tradesmen and others resident in Aberdeen, who entirely depend on the wages of their industry for their subsistence, it would be impossible for them to dedicate sufficient time for learning the military dutys without receiving the same indemnifications as the

Edinburgh Regiment. Their offer of service was made at as early a period as possible, and they hope the present renewal of it will be considered the same as the original tender.

Dauney's demand for the Militia Ballot and for pay proved fatal to his proposal. On August 18, the members of the corps were called together in the Town House to serve without pay; and the following resolution was adopted and forwarded by the Duke of Gordon to the Secretary of State on August 25 (*H.O.* 50 : 57) :—

We, the Persons subscribing, inhabitants of the City of Aberdeen and its neighbourhood, feeling it to be the bounden duty of every British subject at this momentous crisis when the country is threatened with a foreign invasion to press forward in its Defence ;

Do hereby make a tender to His Majesty of our Military Services and agree to enroll ourselves as a Volunteer Corps, to serve without pay and to furnish our own Clothing, to be trained in the use of Arms and to march to any part of Great Britain for the defence thereof, in case of actual invasion on the appearance of an enemy in force upon the coast, and for the suppression of any rebellion or insurrection within the same, arising or existing at the time of any such invasion ;

It being understood that Government shall furnish arms and accoutrements, and pay one Adjutant and the necessary number of Sergeants and Drummers with reasonable allowance for contingencies.

Subsequent meetings were held on September 21, October 19, and November 3 and 9, and the " Corps of Gentlemen Volunteers serving without pay," were asked on November 23 to assemble in Gordon's Hospital. As a matter of fact, the " Gentlemen Volunteers " did not serve without pay, the officers only giving their services gratis, the men receiving the following amounts (*W.O.* 13 : 4) :—

October-December, 1803	-	-	-	-	-	£133
December, 1803—December, 1804	-	-	-	-	770
December, 1805—December, 1806	-	-	-	-	443

The command of the regiment was given to Thomas Leys; but Dauney was not daunted, for he wrote to the Duke of Gordon, July 23, 1804, about a meeting held that day by persons desirous of embodying a corps of " Riflemen or Sharpshooters," to the extent of 300 or 400 men (*H.O.* 50 : 93). This proposal was never adopted, so that Dauney really disappears from the scene in April 1803.

The first officers were gazetted October 5, 1803, though the majority of the commissions at this period were dated October 15.   They were as follows (*W.O.* 25 : 205 : pp. 370-1) :—

LIEUTENANT-COLONEL COMMANDING.

Thomas Leys, from the old Royals.

LIEUTENANT-COLONEL.

James Hadden, from the old Royals.

MAJOR.

John Dingwall, from the old Royals.

CAPTAINS.

Alexander Crombie.
Alexander Brebner, from the old Royals.
John Ewen, from the old Royals.
Charles Farquharson.
Charles Gordon, from the old Royals.
Gavin Hadden, brother of Lieutenant-Colonel James Hadden ; born 1778 ; Provost of Aberdeen (for the first time) 1820-1 ; died 1857, in his 88th year.
Alexander More ; probably a relative of George More of Raeden.
Alexander Pirie.

LIEUTENANTS.

Duncan Davidson ; apparently laird of Inchmarlo, who died 1849.
William Gibbon.
Francis Gordon ; probably laird of Kincardine O'Neil and Craig, who was an advocate in Aberdeen, and had begun his career in 1784 as an Ensign in the 68th Foot at the age of 12, dying at Aberdeen in 1857, aged 85.
George Hogarth ; apparently the laird of Woodhill, who died 1848, aged 73.
John Low ; advocate in Aberdeen ; died unmarried 1817, aged 49.
Robert Tower.
James Young, jun.
John Young.

ENSIGNS.

Robert Abercrombie.
William Carnegie ; born 1772 ; Town Clerk of Aberdeen 1806 ; died unmarried 1840.
David Dingwall ; apparently son of Baillie John Dingwall.
James Hardie ; advocate and City Chamberlain of Aberdeen ; died unmarried 1840, aged 67.
James Littlejohn.
Alexander Low.
Robert Morice ; advocate in Aberdeen, where he died 1834, aged 59.
James Young.

CHAPLAIN.

Rev. James Shirrefs, D.D. He was minister of the West Church, Aberdeen.

SURGEON.

Hugh Macpherson, M.D.

QUARTERMASTER.

James Hardie.

ADJUTANT.

Francis Lamont, March 14, 1804 (*W.O.* 25: 206: p. 210). He had been Lieutenant and Captain in the Aberdeen Fencibles, 1795-1800, and Lieutenant in the 21st Foot, and on its half pay till it was reduced in 1802 (*H.O.* 50: 593).

The first pay roll (439 men) is for the period " to December 24, 1803," and shows how the companies were officered (*W.O.* 13: 4,162):—

Company.	Lieutenants.	Ensigns.	Men.
Capt. Alexander Brebner (Grenadier Coy.)	John Low	Alexander Low	59
„ Alexander Crombie (2nd Coy.)	John Young	William Carnegie	56
„ John Ewen (6th Coy.)	Francis Gordon	Robert Abercrombie	60
„ Charles Farquharson (Light Infantry Coy.)	George Hogarth	Robert Morice	45
„ Charles Gordon (5th Coy.)	James Young, jun.	James Hardie	55
„ Gavin Hadden (1st Coy.)	Robert Tower	David Dingwall	49
„ Alexander More (3rd Coy.)	William Gibbon	James Littlejohn	57
„ Alexander Pirie (4th Coy.)	Duncan Davidson	James Young	58

The career of the regiment was not much more enthusiastic than its beginnings, for it did not like some of Windham's regulations, and ceased to exist, as far as drills were concerned, in December, 1806, though the staff carried on until June, 1807 (at an expense of £46). The last pay roll is for December, 1805—December, 1806, from which it will be seen that all but one of the original Captains remained, and that there were 354 men:—

Company.	Lieutenants.	Ensigns.	Men.
Capt. Alexander Crombie	John Young	William Carnegie	50
„ John Ewen	Francis Gordon	Robert Abercrombie	46
„ Charles Farquharson	George Hogarth	James Hardie	54
„ Charles Gordon	James Young	Thomas Black	54
„ Gavin Hadden	Robert Tarras	James Forbes	50
„ John Low	Alexander Low	David Dingwall	43
„ Alexander More	William Gibbon	Joseph Hogarth	49
„ Alexander Pirie	Duncan Davidson	James Young	48

On June 1, 1807, Colonel Leys wrote to the Duke of Gordon announcing the end of the corps (*H.O.* 50: 160):—

It is with much concern that I am under the necessity of stating to your Grace on the part of myself, the Officers, and Corps of the City of Aberdeen Volunteers that, after repeated attempts since the Regulation [of] 12th July, 1806 [apparently as to allowances], we find it out of our power to maintain the Corps in that state of efficiency which can alone render it useful to the country. We, therefore, beg leave to tender our resignations to his Majesty and humbly to request his gracious acceptance.

We at the same time beg leave to assure your Grace that nothing would have induced us to make the present request but a conviction that the Corps can no longer answer the purpose of its institution.

We also beg leave humbly to express in the strongest manner our attachment to his Majesty and our readiness to contribute our services in every way they can be useful to His Person and Government.

GILCOMSTON PIKEMEN (1803-8).—This corps, fully described in Mr. Sinclair's *Aberdeen Volunteers* (111-113), was raised at a public meeting August 19, 1803, and formed into two companies, the first pay roll being for December, 1803. The officers were all gazetted October 15, 1803 (*W.O.* 25: 205: p. 370):—

CAPTAIN-COMMANDANT.

James Chalmers; son of the founder of the *Aberdeen Journal*; born 1741; died 1810.

Left Company (60 men)—CAPTAIN.

James Chalmers (the Commandant); remained to the end.

LIEUTENANT.

John Rae; replaced by John Cadenhead, who remained to the end.

ENSIGN.

John Cowie; replaced by James Reid, who remained to the end.

Right Company (60 men)—CAPTAIN.

William Paterson; remained to the end.

LIEUTENANT.

John Cadenhead jun.; was transferred to the Left Company, and replaced by Thomas Gordon, who remained to the end.

ENSIGN.

Andrew Milne; does not seem to have taken up his commission for he is not in the pay rolls, where we find in his place Alexander Cromar, who remained to the end. Another subaltern, Andrew Hogg, though figuring in the return of November 19, 1803, appears in none of the pay rolls.

CHAPLAIN.

Rev. Dr. James Kidd, December 3, 1803 (*W.O.* 25 : 205 : p. 430).

The corps abandoned the pike (on the recommendation of the Duke of Gordon, October 10, 1807) and became Light Infantry Volunteers (*H.O.* 50 : 160). The last pay roll, December 25, 1807—September 26, 1808, shows the strength of the companies at 62 and 63 respectively (*W.O.* 13 : 4,165).

ABERDEEN PIKEMEN (1804-8).—This corps, which consisted mostly of ship-carpenters and workmen in the Footdee district (*H.O.* 50 : 93), and is described by Mr. Sinclair (*Aberdeen Volunteers*, 113-115), was started in April, 1804. The first officers were gazetted April 18, 1804 (*W.O.* 25 : 206 : p. 281) :—

LIEUTENANT-COLONEL.

Alexander Tower (1753-1813). Born 1753; son of a cooper; owner of Ferryhill; M.P. for Berwick on Tweed, 1806; Colonel, 5th Local Militia; died 1813.

MAJOR.

George Storey.

CAPTAINS.

James Buchan; Alexander Gibbon; Arthur Gibbon; John Gill; Alexander Hall.

1ST LIEUTENANT.

Alexander Fiddes, September 7, 1804.

2ND LIEUTENANTS.

Alexander Innes; James Midcalf; William Stephen; John A. Younghusband. All gazetted September 7, 1804.

ADJUTANT.

Alexander Cooper, September 1804. He had first served in the Angus Fencibles, then in the Angus Militia in 1798, and subsequently as a Sergeant in the 1st Royals (*H.O.* 50 : 93).

Mr. Sinclair says that the corps numbered throughout "about 400" (the number was only 300); and that it attached itself to Finlason's corps. The first pay roll is for April 18—December 24, 1804, but shows only one company, the others appearing in the rolls for December, 1803—December, 1804 (*W.O.* 13 : 4,163) :—

Company.	Lieutenants.	Ensigns.	Men.
Capt. James Buchan	William Stephen	——	60
„ Alexander Gibbon	Alexander Fiddes	——	59
„ Arthur Gibbon	John A. Younghusband	——	60
„ John Gill	Alexander Innes	——	54
„ Alexander Hall	James Midcalf	——	60

In October, 1807, the corps became the Aberdeen Light Infantry Volunteers (*H.O.* 50 : 160). During the course of its career it took to itself Ensigns, but did not materially increase its numbers, the last pay roll, December 1807-September 1808, showing :—

Company.	Lieutenants.	Ensigns.	Men.
Capt. James Buchan	William Stephen	Alexander Walker	60
„ Alexander Gibbon	Alexander Fiddes	John Byres	60
„ Arthur Gibbon	James Ross	Adam Esson	60
„ John Gill	Charles Fyfe	Leslie Cruickshank	60
„ Alexander Hall	John A. Younghusband	——	60

ABERDEENSHIRE BATTALION OF VOLUNTEERS (1804-8).—This battalion was composed of seven companies, the nucleus of it being the (three) companies of Udny, Tarves and Methlick, commanded by Major Sir William Seton, 6th bart. of Pitmedden (died 1818). He was appointed Lieutenant-Colonel, January 11, 1804, and was succeeded, September 26, 1804, by Major John Leith-Ross of Arnage, previously in command of the Ellon Company. On July 27, 1807, the Earl of Aberdeen became Lieutenant-Colonel. The companies, which became linked in a battalion in June, 1804, and will be described alphabetically later, were as follows (*W.O.* 13 : 4,163) :—

Parish.	Men in 1804.	Men in 1808.
Cruden	62	59
Ellon	68	82
Foveran	40	43
Logie Buchan and Slains	63	58
Methlick	60	58
Tarves	79	67
Udny	50	58
	422	425

S2

The Chaplain of the battalion, Rev. Thomas Tait, was gazetted January 17, 1804, and the Adjutant, William Duff, March 7, 1804 (*W.O.* 25 : 206 : p. 210). The latter had been twenty-four years in the 42nd, and had joined the Clan Alpine Fencibles in 1799 (*H.O.* 50 : 93).

On April 19, 1804, the Secretary of State sanctioned, on the Duke of Gordon's recommendation, the increase of the battalion from 460 to 500 men so as to entitle it to a Sergeant-Major (*H.O.* 50 : 93).

ABERDOUR (1803-8).—This company started as an independent unit. The officers were appointed in 1803 :—

CAPTAIN.

William Leslie, August 22, 1803, from Lieutenant, half pay, of the late 115th Foot (*W.O.* 25 : 166 : p. 304); remained to the end. Perhaps William Leslie of Coburty, who died 1814, aged 69, or his son William, who died 1819, aged 37 (Jervise's *Epitaphs*, i., 55).

1ST LIEUTENANT.

Patrick Gordon, August 22, 1803 ; left before the end.

ENSIGN.

Andrew Youngson, December 3, 1803 (*W.O.* 25 : 205 : p. 569); resigned ; replaced, May 24, 1804, by James Bisset, who remained to the end. Rev. Andrew Youngson (1726-1809) was minister of Aberdour.

The offers of some of the old Volunteer companies were at first declined, the Government confining the number to 1,000. Curiously enough this refusal referred to some of the coast parishes. In the summer of 1803 the commanding officers of Fraserburgh, Peterhead (two companies) Aberdour, Strichen, Rosehearty, Crimond, Longside, and Rathen offered their services—" judging it to be a period in which every loyal subject ought to stand forth to oppose the attacks of that implacable enemy which had for years been a scourge to all Europe." They renewed their offer in August in the terms of Lord Hobart's circular of August 3, and obtained the enrolment of their respective companies, and then " were surprised that there were neither pay nor contingent allowances whatever " to corps accepted under that regulation. On March 21, 1804, they forwarded, through the Duke of Gordon (who thought their " situation rather unpleasant "), a memorial which said :—

When the Memorialists look around and see other Volunteer Corps and Companies, some of them in the same Town, which are doing no more duty than the Corps under the Memorialists' command, and receive 84 days' pay in the year, officers and men, and £40 for each 80 men of contingent allowances, they cannot help thinking their situation exceeding hard and different.

On the most economical plan, no officer could furnish himself with a uniform under ten guineas; a commanding officer still more, no contingent expense being allowed him in teaching drummers, procuring arms, postage, and other items. Thus, the nine Memorialists resolved (*H.O.* 50: 93):—

That while their Hearts glow with every sentiment of Loyalty and attachment to the Sovereign under whom they enjoy the Blessings of Liberty and Wholesome Laws; and that, however much it must press upon their feelings, they must, unless their situations are taken into consideration and some remedy provided, have recourse to that most disagreeable necessity resigning their situation, and come forward in defence of their Country in a way that will not injure in so material a degree the interests of themselves and their families.

The Duke of Gordon recommended (*H.O.* 50: 93), January 7, 1804, that the company (60 strong), with those of Rosehearty, Tyrie and Strichen, should be linked to that of Fraserburgh (*q.v.*). The last pay roll, December, 1807—September, 1808, shows 67 men. Benjamin Williamson was then the Ensign (*W.O.* 13: 4,164).

BELHELVIE (1803-8).—This company, consisting nominally of 80 men, began and ended with 76. It was commanded by the following officers, all gazetted October 15, 1803 (*W.O.* 25: 205: p. 369):—

CAPTAIN.

John Scott. Mr. Sinclair calls him "of Drumside," and says that he was specially asked by the Deputy Lieutenants to accept.

LIEUTENANT.

John Lumsden. Farmer of Eggie; died 1833, aged 52 (Henderson's *Aberdeenshire Epitaphs*, i., 150).

William Stephen, jun. (at Milden), was gazetted Ensign, but appears in none of the pay lists, which are very poorly kept, the first being simply headed "pay list for ten days' exercise in 1804." The corps was drilled along with the Dyce, Newmachar and Fintray Company.

CRIMOND AND LONMAY (1803-8).—The officers of this company were all commissioned, October 15, 1803 (*W.O.* 25 : 205 : p. 370):—

CAPTAIN.

Thomas Laing; remained to the end.

LIEUTENANT.

James Scott.

ENSIGN.

John Geddes; replaced by 1804 by John Hay, when James Godsman was the Quartermaster.

The first muster pay roll, November 14—December 24, 1803, shows 60 men, and the last, December, 1807—September, 1808, shows the same. But only the Captain remained among the officers, the other two places being blank (*W.O.* 13 : 4,164).

In December, 1803, the Crimond and Lonmay Company was battalioned (as right company) with those of Rathen and of St. Fergus and Longside, under the command of Major Alexander Harvey, who ultimately became Lieutenant-Colonel of the 2nd Regiment of Local Militia.

CRUDEN (1803-8).—The officers were gazetted October 15, 1803 (*W.O.* 25 : 205 : 307):—

CAPTAIN.

George Gordon. Laird of Hallhead?

LIEUTENANT.

Peter Murray.

ENSIGN.

Robert Johnston. Probably related to the farming family in Sand End of Cruden (Jervise's *Epitaphs*, i., 317).

The first pay roll, November 22—December 24, 1803, shows 57 men. In June, 1804, it formed the second company of the Aberdeenshire Battalion, with 62 men. The last pay roll, December, 1807—September, 1808, shows 59 men, Gordon being still in command (*W.O.* 13 : 4,163).

DRUMBLADE (1803-8).—This company was brigaded with the Huntly group of Volunteers (*q.v.*). The officers were gazetted October 15, 1803 :—

CAPTAIN.

Andrew Paterson; he succeeded George Davidson in command of the three companies.

LIEUTENANT

Alexander Patillo.

ENSIGN

William Macdonald

The first pay roll is dated June 29, 1804—46 men (*W O* 13 . 4,165)

DYCE, NEWMACHAR, AND FINTRAY (1803-8)—Dyce and New-machar interested themselves in the Volunteer movement of 1797, for the farmers in these places held a meeting at Aberdeen on February 24, 1797, with the farmers of eight other parishes and made an offer of their carts and horses for transport. But a Volunteer Company was not formed until the 1803 movement   The first pay list " 1802—December, 1803," shows 80 men   The number fell to 72 in 1803-4, and stood at 74 in December, 1807—September, 1808   The (nine) pay lists (*W O* 13 4,164) are poorly kept, the first giving officers being dated August 18, 1804   The officers were gazetted October 15, 1803, and remained to the end :—

CAPTAIN

John Paul   Mr Sinclair says he was at Overtacktown of Dyce.

LIEUTENANT

John Melvin   " In Lochills of Newmachar" (Sinclair's *Volunteers*, 132)

ENSIGN

John Skene.   " Son to Peter Skene in Wester Fintray " (*Ibid*, 132).
The corps was drilled with the Belhelvie Company.   On September 26, 1808, 62 of the men agreed to transfer to the Local Militia, although the quota was only 54—24 from Newmachar, 18 from Fintray, and 12 from Dyce (*H O* 50 181)

ELLON (1803-8)—The officers were gazetted October 15, 1803 (*W O* 25 205 . p 367) —

CAPTAIN

John Leith-Ross, Lieutenant-Colonel of the Aberdeenshire Battalion, *vice* Seton, September 26, 1804   Laird of Arnage ; died May 15, 1839 (Temple's *Fermartyn*, 496-7)

LIEUTENANT

James Mair ; succeeded Leith, October 15, 1803 , Captain, *vice* Leith-Ross, March 14, 1804 (*W O* 25 206 p 210)

ENSIGN.

Francis Murray; remained to the end; succeeded Mair as Lieutenant, and was succeeded as Ensign, March 14, 1804, by Thomas Mair.

The first pay list, November 14—December 24, 1803, shows 72 men. In January 1804, the Ellon corps formed the 4th Company of the Aberdeenshire Battalion. The last pay list, December, 1807—September, 1808, gives 82 men (*W.O.* 13 : 4,163).

FOVERAN (1803-8).—The first officers were gazetted October 15, 1803 (*W.O.* 25 : 205 : p. 367):—

CAPTAIN.

George Thompson; in a general return of November 19, 1803 (*H.O.* 50 : 57), William Milne is given as the Captain.

LIEUTENANT.

Alexander Thomson.

ENSIGN.

Alexander Harvey.

There are no pay rolls until it joined the Aberdeenshire Battalion as the 6th Company, June 1804, by which time all the officers had changed:—

CAPTAIN.

Alexander Forsyth.

LIEUTENANT.

George Stodart.

ENSIGN.

John Mearns.

The first pay roll, June—July, 1801, shows 40 men. The last pay roll, December, 1807—December, 1808, shows 43, but Forsyth had dropped out (*W.O.* 13 : 4,163).

FRASERBURGH (1803-8).—As a seaport town, Fraserburgh met the 1803 movement enthusiastically, increasing its one company to two (one of them Artillery). The Infantry Company officers were gazetted May 21, 1803 (*W.O.* 25 : 204 : p. 138):—

CAPTAIN.

William Fraser of Memsie; remained to the end.

1ST LIEUTENANT.

George Gordon.

2ND LIEUTENANT.

William Cooper; resigned and replaced November 24, 1803, by George Milne (*W.O.* 25 : 205 : p. 367).

ENSIGN.

John Gordon; not gazetted till December 3, 1803.

The first pay roll, June 25—September 24, shows 87 men. The last, December, 1807—September, 1808, giving Milne and Gordon as Lieutenants and Lewis Chalmers as Ensign, shows 96 (*W.O.* 13 : 4,164).

The company was linked—on the recommendation of the Duke of Gordon, forwarded to the Secretary of State on January 7, 1804 (*H.O.* 50 : 93)—with those of Aberdour, Rosehearty, Tyrie and Strichen, Captain Fraser being appointed Major-Commandant, January 13; and it absorbed the Artillery Company in December, 1806 (*H.O.* 50 : 160), the whole battalion numbering in January, 1807, 355 men.

The Artillery Company officers were gazetted October 15, 1803 (*W.O.* 25 : 205 : p. 370):—

CAPTAIN.

William Kelman.

1ST LIEUTENANT.

William Jamieson; replaced by William Mackay, December 24, 1803.

2ND LIEUTENANT.

John Alexander; resigned; replaced by James Cooper, March 7, 1804, and then by Charles Simpson.

The first pay roll in 1803 shows 60 privates. On December 9, 1803, Kelman asked for an augmentation of twenty as pikemen (*H.O.* 50 : 57). In 1804 there were 77 men, and in the last pay roll, December 25, 1807—September, 1808, there are 80 men. In 1808 the equipment consisted of two brass fieldpieces, ammunition, a waggon and 40 stand of small arms (*H.O.* 50 : 181).

HUNTLY (1803-8).—In the reconstruction of 1803, the Huntly Volunteers were grouped with those of Drumblade; and the two were associated under one general command with the Strathbogie Company. The first pay roll, December 25, 1804—December 24, 1805, shows 52 men (*W.O.* 13 : 4,165). The officers were :—

CAPTAIN.

George Davidson (from Lieutenant, Gordon Highlanders, in which he had served from 1794 to 1804), February 17, 1804; Major-Commandant of the Strathbogie, Huntly and Drumblade Volunteers, May 26, 1804; resigned, July 28, 1807, on joining the 42nd. He was killed at Quatre Bras, June 16, 1815.

LIEUTENANT.

George Reynolds, October 15, 1803 (formerly in the Northern Fencibles); succeeded Davidson in the command of the company.

ENSIGN.

William Allan, October 15, 1803.

The Strathbogie Company was officered thus, the commissions being dated October 15, 1803 :—

CAPTAIN.

James Gordon, formerly in command of the 1st Huntly Company of 1798-1802. He resigned in 1804, and was succeeded by John Innes (from half pay of the 73rd), who remained to the end.

LIEUTENANT.

William Paterson, formerly Ensign in the 2nd Huntly Company of 1798-1802; he remained to the end.

ENSIGN.

Alexander Will; remained to the end.

The first pay roll is dated June 29, 1804—49 men (W.O. 13: 4,165). The Huntly Companies of 1798—1800 have been minutely described by Mr. William Will in the *Huntly Express*, April 10-May 8, 1914.

KINTORE AND INVERURIE (1803).—The officers of this company (80 men), which was attached to that of Logie Durno, were gazetted October 15, 1803 (W.O. 25 : 205 : p. 369):—

CAPTAIN.

Benjamin Lumsden. Apparently the laird of Kingsford who died in 1856, aged 83.

LIEUTENANT.

William Mollison.

ENSIGN.

George Mackie (or Mackay).

There are no pay rolls at the Record Office, the company like that of Monymusk (*q.v.*) never having been embodied.

LOGIE BUCHAN AND SLAINS (1803-8).—The first officers were gazetted October 15, 1803 (*H.O.* 50: 57):—

CAPTAIN.

James Watson.

LIEUTENANT.

George Gray.

ENSIGN.

George Muir.

There are no pay rolls till it joined, in June 1804, the Aberdeenshire Battalion as 7th Company, by which time all the officers had changed:—

CAPTAIN.

David Brown.

LIEUTENANT.

William Midler.

The first muster pay roll, June—July, 1804, shows 63 men; the last, December 1807—December 1808, shows 58 (*W.O.* 13: 4,163).

LOGIE DURNO (1803).—The officers of this company (60 men) which was attached to the Kintore and Inverurie Company, were gazetted October 15, 1803 (*W.O.* 25: 205: p. 369):—

CAPTAIN.

Robert Harvey.

LIEUTENANT.

James Brown.

ENSIGN.

Alexander Bisset.

There are no pay rolls at the Record Office, the company like that of Monymusk (*q.v.*) never having been embodied.

MELDRUM (1803-8).—In the reconstruction, Old Meldrum raised three instead of two companies, which were accepted October 15, 1803, Urquhart still remaining in command. All the officers were gazetted October 15, 1803 (*W.O.* 25: 205: p. 368):—

1st Company (57 men)—CAPTAIN.

James Garioch, continued from the Old Meldrum Company, 1802. *W.O.* 25: 205: p. 368, calls him " Sir," instead of Dr.

1ST LIEUTENANT.

John Duncan, continued from 1802; ultimately replaced by John Ingram, who remained to the end.

2ND LIEUTENANT.

George Shepherd, gazetted October 15, 1803, does not seem to have taken up his commission, for his name appears in no pay roll, his place being occupied first by William (not George as gazetted) Williamson, and ultimately by George Robertson, who remained to the end.

2nd Company (57 men)—CAPTAIN.

John Manson, formerly Lieutenant under Dr. Garioch; remained to the end.

LIEUTENANT.

Alexander Manson; remained to the end.

ENSIGN.

John Ingram; replaced by John Hunter, who remained to the end.

3rd Company (60 men)—CAPTAIN.

James Duncan.

1ST LIEUTENANT.

Alexander Barnett.

2ND LIEUTENANT.

William Connon; all these three officers remained to the end.

The first pay roll is for the period prior to December 24, 1803. The last is for December 25, 1807—September 24, 1808, and shows the strength of the three companies as 57, 57 and 58. James Porterfield, Sergeant-Major of the corps, was for many years in the Black Watch.

METHLICK (1803-8).—The officers were gazetted October 15, 1803 (*W.O.* 25: 205: p. 367):—

CAPTAIN.

Ludovick Grant.

LIEUTENANT.

Robert Moir.

ENSIGN.

James Pirie; resigned; succeeded by William Duguid, December 15, 1803.

At first the company formed a unit with those of Udny and Tarves. By June, 1804, it formed the 5th Company of the Aberdeenshire Battalion with 60 men, by which time Robert Moir was Captain, and Duguid, Lieutenant. The last pay roll, December, 1807—September, 1808, showing Moir still in command, has 58 men (*W.O.* 13: 4,163).

MONQUHITTER (1803-8).—This company was founded August 19, 1803, when the heritors and crofters met, and " 108 stout young men enrolled themselves as Volunteers " (Sinclair's *Aberdeen Volunteers*, 129). But according to a return of December 1, 1803 (*H.O.* 50: 57), only 67 men enrolled themselves on this date. The first muster roll, certified by Captain Cumine at Millfield, August 24, shows 60 privates. The officers were gazetted October 15, 1803 (*W.O.* 25 : 205 : p. 364):—

CAPTAIN.

Archibald Cumine, from half pay 34th Foot; remained to the end. Apparently laird of Auchry, who died at Edinburgh, January 24, 1834, in his 81st year.

LIEUTENANT.

Joseph Johnstone; replaced in 1805 by Ensign Mitchell, who remained to the end.

ENSIGN.

William Mitchell; replaced in 1805 by Alexander Cruickshank, who remained to the end.

The last pay roll, June 27—July 20, 1808, gives 60 privates.

MONYMUSK AND KEMNAY (1803).—This company arose out of a memorial signed by 200 effective men at Monymusk, July 28, 1803, and forwarded by Sir Archibald Grant, 4th bart. of Monymusk, to the Lord Lieutenant (*H.O.* 50 : 57):—

We, the undersubscribing tenants, sub-tenants and other residenters in the estate of Monymusk, sensible of the very great service it may be of [sic] to our country to give every assistance in our power to forward the passage of troops, their baggage, artillery and ammunition from one part of the country to another, in case of any invasion by an enemy,

Do therefore voluntarily make offer of our carts [to the number of 120] and horses to assist in transporting any of his Majesty's troops that it may be found necessary to march through this part of the country in order to repel any enemy that may be landed on our coasts. And we do hereby empower Sir Archibald Grant, our landlord, to call together our horses and carts upon the above event taking place, by such signals as shall hereafter be agreed upon.

And, whereas, in the event of an invasion, we consider it the duty of every Briton to stand forth in defence of his King and country, we who are above the age of sixteen and under that of sixty years, voluntarily offer to march under the command of Sir Archibald Grant, our heritor, one of the Deputy Lieutenants of this district, to whatever place or landing on the coasts of this country within the northern military district shall be made or attempted by an enemy, and give any assistance in our power to repel said invasion as becomes loyal subjects. And in order that this our voluntary offer may be the more effectual, we all agree, as soon as the said Sir Archibald Grant can procure arms for us from Government, immediately to meet within our own parish for four hours every week to be trained in the use of arms.

The officers were duly gazetted October 15, 1803 (*W.O.* 25 : 205 : p. 364) :—

CAPTAIN.

David Robertson.

LIEUTENANT.

Cumming Laing.

ENSIGN.

George Shewan.

The company, so rhetorically heralded, never existed so far as rank and file were concerned. The reason is stated by the Lord Lieutenant in a letter of April 3, 1805 (*H.O.* 50 : 125) :—

Although the officers of Monymusk, Kemnay, Logie Durno, Kintore and Inverurie were gazetted in consequence of my recommendation, founded upon that of my Deputy Lieutenants, yet the Volunteers were not embodied on account of the resignation of most of the officers soon after the names appeared in the *Gazette.* To obviate the inconvenience which might have from thence arisen to the Volunteer system of this country, I considered it my duty to recommend the establishment of a Volunteer corps in a part of the country more exposed than the district in which the Volunteers of Monymusk, etc., were to be embodied ; by which means the Volunteer quota of Aberdeenshire has been kept up.

PETERHEAD (1803-8).—In the reconstruction of 1803, Peterhead increased its companies from four to five—one Artillery, three Infantry, brigaded together, and an independent company—and the number of men rose from 230 to 446.

Artillery Company (" Peterhead Battery Volunteers "), 60 men ; 1st pay roll, December 25, 1803—December 1804 (60 men) ; last pay roll, December, 1807—December, 1808 (57 men) : —

CAPTAIN-COMMANDANT.

James Hutchison, October 15, 1803 ; previously Lieutenant in the 1798—1802 Company ; remained to the end.

1ST LIEUTENANT
James Arbuthnot, October 15, 1803, previously Lieutenant in the 1798—1802 company, remained to the end.

2ND LIEUTENANT
James Robertson, October 15, 1803, replaced before the end by James Henderson

The three Infantry Companies of 1798-1802 remained as a unit ("Peterhead Infantry Volunteers") under a new commandant, and with several changes in the officering of the companies   The first officers were all gazetted June 25, 1803 (*W O.* 25 205 p 79; although the *London Gazette* fixes the date as August 23, 1803)

MAJOR-COMMANDANT
John Hutchison (previously in command of the 2nd Company), remained to the end

1st Infantry Company. 1st pay roll, July 2—December 24, 1803 (82 men), last muster, December 1807—September 1808 (86 men).—

CAPTAIN
Alexander Elles, formerly of the 3rd Company; remained to the end

1ST LIEUTENANT
Gilbert Alexander; formerly of the 2nd Company, remained to the end

2ND LIEUTENANT
George Arbuthnot, remained to the end

ENSIGN
Robert Hutchison, gazetted December 3, 1803; remained to the end

2nd Infantry Company. pay rolls of same date, began with 88, and ended with 85, men ·—

CAPTAIN
Hector Maclean (from Lieutenant, half pay of the 103rd Foot), became associated with the Aberdeen Light Infantry August 23, 1808

1ST LIEUTENANT
Thomas Robertson, died March 29, 1804

2ND LIEUTENANT
James Elles; remained to the end, becoming 1st Lieutenant, while William Arbuthnot was appointed 2nd Lieutenant

ENSIGN.

James Marshall, gazetted December 3, 1803; replaced by Robert Mackie.

3rd Infantry Company: pay rolls of same date; began with 80, and ended with 89, men.

CAPTAIN.

Donald Mackintosh, formerly of the 1st Company; remained to the end.

LIEUTENANTS.

Alexander Robertson and Robert Cordiner; both remained to the end.

ENSIGN.

Alexander Gordon, gazetted December 3, 1803; replaced by John Henderson.

QUARTERMASTER.

William Arbuthnot.

SURGEON.

Robert Jamieson.

In addition to these three companies, there was a fourth one of Infantry quite independent, the "Company of Peterhead Volunteers." It contained 60 men. Its first pay roll is from October 18—December, 1803; and its last, December, 1807—December, 1808. Its first officers were all gazetted October 15, 1803 (*W.O.* 25 : 205 : p. 369) :—

CAPTAIN.

William Scott, jun.; remained to the end.

LIEUTENANT.

James Brown (from Ensign, Northern Fencibles).

ENSIGN.

James Gordon; resigned and replaced by Adam Arbuthnot (*W.O.* 25 : 200 : p. 241), who was ultimately replaced by John Gilchrist.

RATHEN (1803-8).—The officers in this company were gazetted October 15, 1803, as follows :—

CAPTAIN.

Alexander Henderson; died by October 6, 1808, and was replaced by Lieutenant William Mackay, who was replaced as Lieutenant by William Lawrence (*H.O.* 50 : 181).

LIEUTENANT.
Robert Smith
ENSIGN
William Mackay

The first pay roll, November 14—December 24, 1803, and the last, December, 1807—September, 1808, show 60 men each (*W O* 13 4,164). In December, 1803, the company was linked (as left company) with those of Crimond and Lonmay, and of St Fergus and Longside into one battalion under Major Alexander Harvey

ROSEHEARTY (1803-8)—This company started as an independent unit   The first officers were gazetted October 15, 1803 (*W O* 25 205 p 367), and remained to the end —'

CAPTAIN
William Milne, from Lieutenant in the 1798-1802 company
LIEUTENANT
John Cowie, from Ensign in the 1798-1802 company
ENSIGN
James Milne

The company became attached in 1804 to the Fraserburgh Battalion (*q v*) with 60 men, and ended its career, September, 1808, with 65   Very few of the pay rolls have been preserved (*W.O* 13 · 4,164)

ST FERGUS AND LONGSIDE (1803-8)—The officers of this company were gazetted October 15, 1803 (*W O* 25 · 205 · p 368) —

CAPTAIN
Thomas Kilgour, who remained to the end
LIEUTENANT
Thomas Logan, acted as Paymaster
ENSIGN
James Fraser

The first pay roll, November 14-December 24, 1803, and the last, December 1807-September 1808, show 60 men each (*W O* 13 . 4,164)   But in the last roll there is neither Lieutenant nor Ensign   In December 1803, the company was linked (as centre company) with those of Crimond and Lonmay, and of Rathen, under the command of Major Alexander Harvey.

TARVES (1803-8).—The officers were gazetted October 15, 1803 (*W.O.* 25: 205: p. 367):—

LIEUTENANT.

James Hay; made Captain before the end of the year.

ENSIGN.

John Hay; made Lieutenant before the end of the year; succeeded as Ensign by Alexander Knox.

At first it formed a unit with the companies of Udny and Methlick. The first pay roll, November 16-December 24, 1803, shows 66 men. By June, 1804, it formed the third company of the Aberdeenshire Battalion with 79 men, and it ended, December, 1807—December, 1808 list, with 67, the two Hays still holding their positions (*W.O.* 13: 4,163).

TYRIE AND STRICHEN (1803-8).—This company started as an independent unit. The first officers were appointed October 15, 1803 (*W.O.* 25: 205: p. 369):—

CAPTAIN.

Andrew Anderson; remained to the end.

LIEUTENANT.

John Duguid.

ENSIGN.

Alexander Gavin; resigned; replaced, May 12, 1804, by John Woodman; who replaced Duguid, who in turn was succeeded by James Shearer. Gavin was probably Dr. Alexander Gavin (1776-1841), who had been a surgeon in the Navy, fighting at Copenhagen (Jervise's *Epitaphs*, ii., 140).

There are only two pay rolls for the Company in 1803 and 1804. In 1804 it became attached to the Fraserburgh Battalion (*q.v.*) with 60 men, and ended, December, 1807—September, 1808, with 70 (*W.O.* 13: 4,164).

UDNY (1803-8).—The officers were gazetted October 15, 1803 (*W.O.* 25: 205: p. 367); all of them remaining to the end.

CAPTAIN.

John Marr.

LIEUTENANT.

Robert Temple.

ENSIGN.

Thomas Davidson.

At first it formed a unit with the companies of Methlick and Tarves. The first pay roll, November 23—December 26, 1803, shows 58 men. By June 1804 it formed the first company of the Aberdeenshire Battalion with 50 men. The last pay roll, December, 1807—September, 1808, has 41 men (*W.O.* 13 : 4,163).

VOLUNTEERS IN BANFF, TOWN AND COUNTY, 1794-1808.

Banffshire, as Mr. Fortescue says, has "never lacked military enter-prise." Closely in touch with the ducal family of Gordon, it had seen a great deal of soldiering, and standing as it does on the coast, it had the problem of defence brought prominently in front of it. Consequently it took up the Volunteering movement with vigour; and yet with a certain drawback in the matter of its Lord Lieutenant, Lord Fife. His family were still in the process of emergence from small beginnings, and his sway, as we shall see, was disputed, with bad effects on the movement. Besides the jealousy of Lord Fife shown by some of the lairds (and his jealousy of the Duke of Gordon), there was jealousy between the towns of Banff and Macduff. In 1794, when the magistrates of Banff, knowing that Macduff had no battery and would be more likely to become the objective of an enemy than Banff itself, wanted to draft 40 men of the Breadalbane Fencibles from Banff to Macduff—a sub-sidiary reason being that the poor people of the former town were over-burdened with billetting—Macduff would not have it; and on November 17, 1794, the two baillies, John Sangster and George Hunter, sent the following "cavalier letter" to the officer commanding the Fencibles (*Banff Town Council Papers*):—

The inhabitants of Macduff are determined not to accept of the Breadalbane Fencible Regiment to lie here until such time as there is a route from the Commander in Chief for Scotland [Lord Adam Gordon]. When that comes, we can assure you that the troops that may be sent here will get every accommodation that the inhabitants of Macduff can afford. When they are order'd here, we expect that proper officers will come along with them to keep peace and good orders.

The Banff magistrates therefore (December 8, 1794) petitioned the Commander-in-Chief to treat the two towns as a unit for military purposes.

The Volunteer movement was taken up by the county in the two periods in the following way (the town of Banff alone contributing to the movement of the initial year 1794):—

1794-1802.	1803-8.
Banff (Town) 5 Companies	Banff (town) Independent Company
Aberlour and Boharm (Independent)	1st Battalion (Banff town : 6 Coys.)
Alvah	2nd Battalion
Balveny (Independent)	Boyne
Boyne (2nd Batt.)	Cullen
Cullen (1st Batt.)	Grange
Enzie (4 Companies ; 2nd Batt.)	Marnoch
Forglen (2nd Batt.)	Portsoy
Grange (1st Batt.)	Rothiemay
Keith (Independent)	
Macduff (1st Batt.)	
Newmill (Independent)	
Portsoy (1st Batt.)	
Rothiemay	

The 1794-1802 list is probably not complete, for Lord Fife says (*H.O.* 50: 59) that he raised "twenty one companies of Volunteers"; but the places given are all of which we have records.

BANFF (1794-1802).—There had been some sort of fort at Banff from time immemorial. During the War of Independence, Banff Castle gave both Edward and Bruce a great deal of trouble. It seems to have been particularly accessible from the sea, and even when the whole northern district was strongly for Bruce, Banff Castle held out for Edward; one of the reasons being that it was revictualled (1300-9) by the English fleet, which was seldom away from the Scots coasts between 1308 and 1312. It was therefore not till the winter of 1309-10 that Bruce succeeded in capturing the Castle. The first we hear of a properly equipped battery in modern times is on August 17, 1780, when we learn that Captain Fraser, Engineer for Scotland, had given it as his opinion that a battery of six or eight 18-prs. placed upon a battery to be erected at the north end of Seatown lands would effectually protect the harbour and bay as well as the town (Cramond's *Annals of Banff*, i., 329). On March 30, 1781, it was announced that Captain Marr, engineer, had planned a battery of nine embrasures (it was dismantled in 1815) and the work was at once begun (*Ibid.* i., 329-330). The next thing was to man it ; and for this purpose the Town Council wrote to the Convener of the Trades, February 26, 1782 (*Banff Town Council Papers*):—

At it is necessary to get some of our inhabitants trained to manage
the cannon of the Battery for defence of the Town and Harbour, the
Magistrates are of opinion that the younger of our Householders and the
stout apprentices of the Trades will be the people most proper for this
purpose ; and, although no attendance will be necessary after they have
learned how to manage the cannon but in times of necessity, the
Magistrates are of opinion that the Householders and the Masters of
the apprentices who engage for this service should be freed from the
burden of quartering soldiers, and that, upon this account, the soldiers
should be billeted upon the other inhabitants who do not perform this
service ; and, besides, those who behave well should have the freedom
of the Town.   The Magistrates will therefore be glad if you would call
a meeting of the Trades and report to the Council to-morrow such of
them or their apprentices as are willing to engage in this service.

The result of this application seems to be the origin of the estimate
(*Annals of Banff*, i., 330) that 426 were fit to bear arms and that 23
had intimated their willingness to work the battery.

When the regular Volunteer movement began in 1794, Banff was
early in the field.   On August 6, the Town Council resolved (*Banff
Town Council Papers*) : —

That in the present situation of this country, it is the duty of all
loyal subjects to come forward and express their sentiments in the
strongest manner, and, as far as in them lyes, to strengthen the hands of
the Executive Government in order to enable them to presserve the
Constitution of the Kingdom against all enemies whether open or con-
cealed, foreign or domestic.

And that for this purpose, it is proper and expedient that the
Inhabitants of this Burgh (who have been always Loyall) have a posible
opportunity of testifying their loyalty to his Majesty and the Constitution, and of enrolling themselves for the defence of both in the terms
proposed by the Lord Lieutenant.

And therefore appoint a General Meeting of the Inhabitants be
called to assemble in the Court House on Wednesday next at eleven
o'clock forenoon for the purpose above mentioned.

And declare that the proposed inrollment shall be entirely voluntary,
and shall be considered as an honourable mark of distinction, and that
no person shall be admitted to enroll himself until he first take the oaths
to Government and subscribe a declaration expressive of his resolution to
maintain the laws and constitution of the country as present established
or to be enacted in future by authority of Parliament, as well as to
support the Magistrates and other judges of the country in the preserva-

tion of the peace thereof, and suppression of all riots, tumults or seditious meetings or assemblies therein.

Resolved that those who shall enroll themselves as above shall not be obliged on any pretence (unless in case of actual invasion by a foreign enemy) to go without the Liberties of the Burgh, and that they shall only be obliged to attend once a week for harassing the military exercise, unless called out to actual duty. And that in case of actual invasion they shall march under the command of the Lord Lieutenant or the Officers appointed by him to any part of the Country. And that, however soon a competent number shall enroll themselves, the Provost in name of the Council shall apply to the Lord Lieutenant for arms to them, and to name proper officers.

On August 11, 1794, Peter Cameron, writer in Banff, writing to George McKilligin, Deputy Lieutenant, said (*Ibid.*) : —

I have seen the resolutions which I understand you mean to submit to the consideration of the inhabitants of this Burgh on Wednesday next, and I do highly approve of the loyal principles and measures of safety therein mentioned. But, as I am obliged to be out of town on that day, permit me in this manner to request that you will consider me as an enrolled person and willing at all times to promote and inforce by every means in my power the salutary objects contained in those resolutions, according to their true spirit and common meaning.

The next we hear of the Volunteers is on October 8, 1794, when :—

The Magistrates and Town Council of Banff, sensible of the blessings they enjoy under the present Government, beg leave to offer their assurance of loyalty and attachment to his Majesty, his family and the present Constitution of Great Britain, and that they will to the utmost of their power support and assist his Majesty in the prosecution of the just and necessary war in which this country is at present engaged : and would further beg leave to recommend to his Majesty Lieutenant-Colonel James Edward Urquhart (whose attachment to Government and the happy Constitution of this country the Magistrates and Council are perfectly sensible of) as a most fit and proper person for raising a Regiment of Infantry for his Majesty's service. And the Magistrates and Council (in case such permission is granted) do resolve and agree to give every aid and assistance in their power to Lieutenant-Colonel Urquhart in raising and completing his Regiment ; and they do further humbly request the Right Honourable General Lord Amherst, Commander in Chief, to present this present Resolution and recommendation to his Majesty.

In thanking the Town Clerk, who had forwarded this minute, William Urquhart of Craigston, the Lieutenant-Colonel's brother, wrote October

8, 1794 (*Banff Town Council Papers*):—" It is just what I wanted and I imagine will do perfectly for him." But, for some reason or other, this " regiment " was not raised, and Urquhart seems to have had nothing to do with the movement.

On February 28, 1795, the Town Council resolved to raise a company (*Ibid.*) :—

The Magistrates and Council, taking into their consideration the present state of this country, and the probability that his Majesty's regular troops may be encamped or removed to a distance from this place, whereby the same may be left without protection, and considering also that the Incorporated Trades of this Burgh have offered to raise a Company of Infantry from their own numbers for the internal defence of the Town, which offer has been accepted by Government :

Therefore the Magistrates and Council, in order to testify their loyalty to his Majesty and their attachment to our glorious Constitution, resolve and do hereby humbly make offer to his Majesty to raise a Company of men to serve for the internal defence of the place, as well as to man the Battery for the protection of the Harbour. . . . The Council order the Chamberlain to commission for the use of the Town three hundred-weights of gunpowder from Aberdeen if it can be had there.

On March 19, the Provost laid before the Council two letters from Lord Fife to him, accompanying a letter from the Duke of Portland to the Earl notifying his Majesty's acceptance of the Volunteer company. The Council informed Lord Fife that it would be highly gratifying to them that McKilligin and Robertson, clothiers in Banff, should be employed to furnish the clothing to the company, " as they know that these gentlemen have an opportunity of supplying the clothing on equally good, if not better terms than any other." The Council name and appoint the Provost, Baillies, Dean of Guild ; Convener, Mr. Brown ; Assessor, Provost Robinson ; with Captain Russel, Mr. John Smith, Wright, and Mr. Isaac Cooper as a Committee to correspond with Lord Fife and to settle with him everything regarding the two Companies, the procuring arms for them, with proper accoutrements, and also to suggest to his Lordship such uniform as would be agreeable to the corps. On April 4, Fife informed the Council that he had used his interest with the Duke of Portland to obtain pay for the Trades, as well as the Town Council, Company.

The Artillery Company was commanded and drilled by Thomas Russel of Rathen, who had begun his career in the Northern Fencibles. At this time he was a corporal of an Invalid Company of Artillery, and was stationed on recruiting service at Fort George. Considering him a "very discreet, well behaved man," the Town Council asked the Commander-in-Chief for his services, and these were granted by Lord Adam Gordon, April 28, 1795. On the previous day the Council had authorised the Chamberlain to get three carts of gunpowder from Aberdeen.

Unfortunately, there are no muster rolls of these companies at the Record Office, and Dr. Cramond, with the usual indifference of the local historian to this subject, dismisses the movement in a small type note, in which he says "Among the Burgh Records is a bundle of about fifty papers relating to measures for the defence of the country at this critical period." He also gives an illustration of a badge bearing the words "Banff Volunteers; Independent Company" (*Annals of Banff*, ii., 414). I have, however, had the privilege of examining all those papers, which are full of interest although they contain no musters.

The officers appointed in 1795 (with the changes effected in 1797) were as follows:—

COMMANDANT.

Alexander Duff, May 20, 1795, Major-Commandant (*W.O.* 25: 160: p. 24); March 7, 1797, Lieutenant-Colonel Commandant. The natural son of Alexander Duff of Hatton (1718-64), he had begun his career in the Duke of Gordon's first regiment, the 89th, in which he got a Lieutenant's commission, October 12, 1760, and on its disbandment joined the 58th as Lieutenant in 1765. He became Captain in 1772, and Major in 1783, retiring in 1786. Having, in 1785, married his cousin, Jane Abernethy (1751-1805), one of four sisters owning the estate of Mayen, he settled in the north after retiring from the Army, buying up the shares of his sisters-in-law, and becoming laird of Mayen. He died in 1816 (Taylers' *Book of the Duffs*, i., 273-8).

CAPTAINS.

James Reid, March 25, 1795; Adjutant, March 2, 1797. His pay for the latter post was stopped by the War Office in December, 1800, but Reid went on with the duties all the same till he was replaced in 1801 by his son, also James Reid (*W.O.* 13: 4,183).

Thomas Russel, March 24, 1795. Laird of Rathen; he had been formerly in the Northern Fencibles. In May, 1796, he was appointed a

Lieutenant of Invalids at Sheerness "as a remuneration for former services." In February 1799, he raised a company at Rosehearty but rejoined the Banff Company in 1803, retiring 1808. He died in 1827 aged 85.

James Bartlett (from Lieutenant, half pay of Steele's late Independent Company of Pioneers), February 16, 1797 (*W.O.* 25 : 168 : p. 339); Major, March 2, 1797 (*vice* Duff).

Archibald Young, June 6, 1797. Apparently the laird of Kininvie.

1ST LIEUTENANTS.

Isaac Cooper, March 25, 1795. Teacher of music and dancing at Banff from 1783 to about 1811, when he is said to have died suddenly when playing "Robin Adair."

George Forbes, March 25, 1797; Captain, April 8, 1797, *vice* Russel. He was Sheriff-Substitute.

Alexander Stronach, May 20, 1795.

Lewis Cruickshank, February 16, 1797.

Alexander Robinson, June 6, 1797.

Thomas Wilson, April 8, 1797, *vice* Forbes. Made Burgess of Banff, September 26, 1797.

2ND LIEUTENANTS.

John Grant, May 20, 1795; 1st Lieutenant, January 31, 1797, *vice* Stronach, promoted.

John Smith, March 25, 1795.

George Wilson, March 25, 1795; superseded; replaced by Alexander Smith, October 30, 1800 (*W.O.* 25 : 169).

Arthur Scott, January 31, 1797, *vice* Grant.

James Fraser, February 16, 1797.

James Laird, June 6, 1797.

CHAPLAIN.

Rev. Peter Forbes, March 2, 1797.

QUARTERMASTER.

John Fraser, March 2, 1797.

SURGEON.

———— Gould, March 2, 1797.

Although the Artillery Company was raised in 1795, the Battery does not seem to have been equipped till 1797, when stores were despatched north (March 4) by the "Friendship," commanded by William Milne (*Banff Town Council Papers*):—

ABERLOUR AND BOHARM (1798-1802).—There is no pay roll for this company at the Public Record Office, but the following officers were appointed August 22, 1798 (*W.O.* 25: 226: p. 697):—

CAPTAIN.
James Leslie (from Lieutenant, of late 115th).

1ST LIEUTENANT.
Patrick Gordon (laird of Aberlour?).

2ND LIEUTENANT.
James Falconer.

ALVAH, BOYNE, AND FORGLEN (1797-1802).—All these three places supplied a company each under the general command of Andrew Hay, and the first commissions were dated June 20, 1797 (*London Gazette,* 1797):—

MAJOR-COMMANDANT.
Andrew Hay.

CAPTAINS.
Peter Cameron, from Ensign on half pay of the late Scots Brigade, having served five years on full pay; Robert Falder.

1ST LIEUTENANTS.
Thomas Grant; Alexander Milne (who went to the 15th Foot and was succeeded October 31, 1798, by Quartermaster John Innes); Alexander Watson.

2ND LIEUTENANTS.
William McIntosh; John Milne (went to the 15th Foot and was replaced October 31, 1798, by Quartermaster John Fraser); John Wilson (all from the *London Gazette* of 1797); William Watson replaced John Wilson, who retired August 16, 1797 (*W.O.* 25: 164: p. 363).

The first muster roll is for the period August—September, 1798 (*W.O.* 13: 4,187), by which time some changes had taken place:—

Company.	Captains.	Lieutenants.	Ensigns.	Men.
Alvah	Peter Cameron	Thomas Grant	John Milne	58
Boyne	Andrew Hay	Alexander Watson	William Watson	55
Forglen	Robert Falder	Alexander Milne	William McIntosh	54

In October, 1798, Major James Duff got the command of the Alvah Company.

X2

BALVENY (1798-1802).—The first muster is for December, 1798—January, 1799, containing 63 men, and the last for March—April, 1802, containing 57 (*W.O.* 13 : 4,189). The officers were all gazetted August 1, 1798 (*W.O.* 25 : 166 : p. 261).

CAPTAIN.

Alexander Cameron (from half pay of the late Scotch Brigade). In June 1799, he exchanged with Captain Watt, of the Newmill Company.

1ST LIEUTENANT.

John Marshall; remained to the end.

ENSIGN.

William Macgregor; remained to the end.

The company does not seem to have been incorporated with the 1803-1808 force.

CULLEN (1797-1802).—Officers were gazetted May 3, 1797, as follows (*W.O.* 25 : 164 : pp. 113, 264):—

CAPTAIN.

Thomas Rannie.

1ST LIEUTENANT.

James Smith.

2ND LIEUTENANT.

Robert Johnstone; retired and was replaced June 21, 1797, by Alexander Wilson, who was a nephew of John Wilson, Chief Magistrate and land steward to Lord Findlater; and also related to Captain Rannie. Alexander Wilson was ultimately suspended, as he became "remiss in his duty," as Lord Fife states in a curious letter quoted later on.

This company became part of the 1st Battalion in 1798, but was handed over to the 2nd Battalion, March 24, 1800.

ENZIE (1797-1802).—The Enzie supplied four companies to the Volunteer movement of 1797, the first muster roll being for the period December 25, 1797—July 24, 1798 (*W.O.* 13 : 4,187). The first officers are given in the *London Gazette* of 1797:—

CAPTAIN-COMMANDANT.

Sir George Abercromby; resigned and replaced January 10, 1798, by Captain Thomas Booker (*W.O.* 25 : 165 : p. 164). Booker came from the 60th Foot, and was probably the officer who married the Duke of Gordon's youngest sister, Lady Catherine Gordon (1751-97).

CAPTAINS.

George Geddes; John Gordon; resigned and replaced June 20, 1798, by James Macgregor, from half pay, late 75th (*W.O.* 25: 166: p. 160); Alexander Innes, who died September 15, 1799, and was replaced November 13, 1799, by Alexander Robertson, from half pay late 89th.

1ST LIEUTENANTS.

James Bennett; Alexander Coull; George Lyman [Symon?], who retired and was succeeded September 21, 1797, by William Anderson (*W.O.* 25: 164: p. 447).

2ND LIEUTENANTS.

Andrew Brodie; retired and was replaced by John Hay (*W.O.* 25: 164: p. 447); William Clark; James Gordon; William Ogilvie.

The officers in the first muster roll are arranged as follows:—

Company.	Lieutenants.	Ensigns.	Men.
Capt. Thomas Booker	{ William Anderson { John Hay	———	62
„ John Gordon (Cairnfield)	James Wiseman	John Gordon	61
„ Alexander Innes	{ Alexander Coull { William Clark	———	61
„ George Geddes	James Bennett	William Ogilvie	61

These companies became part of the 2nd Battalion.

GRANGE (1797-1802).—This was the fifth company of the 1st Battalion. The following officers were appointed on January 26, 1797 (*W.O.* 25: 168: p. 277), though the *London Gazette* gives the date as January 31:—

CAPTAIN.

Alexander Stronach (from Lieutenant, Rothiemay Company).

1ST LIEUTENANT.

John Watt; transferred to the Newmill Company, and succeeded by Alexander Robertson.

2ND LIEUTENANT.

Alexander Robertson; succeeded by George McHattie.

KEITH (1798-1802).—The *Aberdeen Journal* of the period tells us that " in less than two hours [in 1798] two companies of Volunteers were enrolled in Keith to serve in the counties of Aberdeen, Banff, and Moray. Three hundred horses and 200 carts are also offered by the inhabitants of Keith and its neighbourhood." As a matter of fact we have the actual record of but one company. The first muster roll of this company is for the period October 25—November 24, 1798, containing 86 men, and the last is for March—April, 1802, containing 60 men (*W.O.* 13 : 4,189). The officers were commissioned on August 1, 1798 (*W.O.* 25 : 160 : p. 263), and remained throughout :—

CAPTAIN.

John Forsyth. In 1802 (Sinclair's *Aberdeen Volunteers*, p. 123) the company presented Captain Forsyth with a sword as a token of their esteem.

1ST LIEUTENANT.

James Roy. He was a solicitor, of whom an amusing account is given in Gordon's *Chronicles of Keith* (p. 183).

2ND LIEUTENANT.

John (or George) Morison.

The company was not incorporated in the 1803-1808 force.

MACDUFF (1798-1802).—This company came late in the field, being created apparently when the 1st Battalion was organised to contain Banff town, Cullen and Grange. Its first appearance (62 men) in the pay rolls is for the period December 25, 1798—January 24, 1794, with the following officers :—

CAPTAIN.

James Fyfe.

LIEUTENANTS.

T. A. Jamieson, and James Wilson.

NEWMILL (1798-1802).—This company was raised May 24, 1798. The first muster roll is for the period December 25, 1798—January 24, 1799, containing 67 men, and the last is for March—April, 1802, containing 59 men (*W.O.* 13 : 4,189). The officers were all commissioned on August 1, 1798 (*W.O.* 25 : 160 : p. 263) :—

CAPTAIN.

John Watt (from Lieutenant of the Grange Company). In June 1799, he exchanged with Captain Alexander Cameron of the Balveny Company. In 1803 he joined the Inverness-shire Militia.

1ST LIEUTENANT.

John Simpson; remained to the end.

2ND LIEUTENANT.

William Pirie; remained to the end.

The company was not incorporated in the 1803-1808 force.

PORTSOY (1798-1802).—This company also came late into the field, being created apparently when the 1st Battalion was organised to contain Banff town, Cullen and Grange. Its first appearance (62 men) in the pay rolls is for the period December 25, 1798—January 24, 1799, with the following officers:—

CAPTAIN.

David Greig.

LIEUTENANT.

Robert Knight.

ENSIGN.

John Taylor.

ROTHIEMAY (1797-1802?).—There are no pay rolls for this company, but Alexander Stronach was Lieutenant of it before he was transferred to Grange on January 26, 1797; and John Grant was appointed Lieutenant of the Rothiemay Company in place of Stronach on the same date (*W.O.* 25: 168: p. 277).

THE COMPANIES BATTALIONED (1798-1802).—A further step in organisation was reached under the Act of 1798 when the companies of the county were arranged in two battalions, Portsoy and Macduff appearing, apparently, for the first time; while Aberlour, Balveny, Keith and Newmill remained as independent companies outside those two Battalions. The two Battalions were made up as follows:—

1st BATTALION.	2nd BATTALION.
Banff—	Alvah Company
Trades Company	Boyne ,,
Artillery ,,	Enzie (4 Companies)
3 other Companies	Forglen Company
Cullen Company	
Grange ,,	
Macduff ,,	
Portsoy ,,	

The officers of the 1st Battalion were allotted as follows :—

Commandant.	Lieutenants.	Ensigns.	Men.
Col. the Earl Fife	{ Arthur Scott { John Chisholm	——	62
Lt.-Col. Alexander Duff (4th, or Commandant's Coy.)			
Major and Capt. James Bartlett (6th, or Major's Coy.)	{ Lewis Cruickshank { James Fraser	——	61
Capt. James Reid (1st, or Banff Trades Coy.)	Isaac Cooper	John Smith	62
„ George Forbes (2nd, or Banff Artillery Coy.)	Thomas Wilson	George Wilson	66
„ James Fyfe (3rd, or Macduff Coy.)	} T. A. Jamieson } James Wilson	——	62
„ Alexander Stronach (5th, or Grange Coy.)	} Alexander Robertson } George McHattie	——	62
„ David Greig (7th, or Portsoy Coy.)	Robert Knight	John Taylor	62
„ Thomas Rannie (8th, or Cullen Coy.)	James Smith	Alexander Wilson	63
„ Archibald Young (9th, or Banff Coy.)	Alexander Robinson	John Laird	61

The thoroughly local, not to say civilian, character of the Volunteers at this time is borne out by Lieutenant-Colonel Duff's note in the January—February, 1799, pay roll (*W.O.* 13 : 4,185):—

From the severity of the weather the men have not been regularly exercised, but they have done duty more than equivalent to it by clearing the public roads for upwards of two miles, which were rendered impassable by the heavy fall of snow ; this being requested by the Deputy Lieutenants of the County.

The pay of the 1st Battalion for three successive years amounted to :—

1799	-	-	-	-	-	-£4,395	1801	-	-	-	-	-	-£4,299
1800	-	-	-	-	-	4,402	1801, December—1802, April	-	1,417

The first brigade statement of the 2nd Battalion is for the period December 1798—December 1799, for which the total pay was £3,799 (as against £4,370 for December 1799-December 1800), the Battalion being under the command of Lieutenant-Colonel James Duff.   The companies were commanded thus (*W.O.* 13 : 4,187):—

Commandant.	Lieutenants.	Ensigns.	Men
Andrew Hay (Boyne Coy.)	Alexander Watson	William Watson	58
Capt. Peter Cameron (Alvah Coy.)	Thomas Grant	John Milne	60
„ Robert Falder (Forglen Coy)	John Fraser	William McIntosh	60
„ Thomas Booker (Enzie Coy.)	{ William Anderson { John Hay	——	65
„ George Geddes (Enzie Coy.)	James Bennett	William Ogilvie	67
„ James Macgregor (Enzie Coy.)	James Wiseman	John Gordon	61
„ Alexander Robertson (Enzie Coy.)	{ Alexander Innes { Alexander Coull	William Clark	60

The pay of the 2nd Battalion from December 1800 to December 1801, amounted to £4,465 (*W O* 13 4,188), and the men in the last roll, December 1801—April 1802, numbered 499

THE TWO BATTALIONS (1803-8)

The Volunteer movement found a warm supporter in the Lord Lieutenant of the county, James (Duff) 2nd Earl Fife, although at this time he was 74 years of age   He wrote to the Secretary of State on March 14, 1803 (*H O. 50: 59*) —

During the late war I raised twenty one companies of Volunteers, and it is but doing justice to say that there was not a more regular body of men in His Majesty's army   From long experience and a perfect knowledge of the county I cannot recommend a more perfect measure than the Volunteers raised within six or eight miles of the sea coast, not only as a constitutional defence but also for the suppression of every kind of lurking which exists in the country

But he found some difficulty among the people, for he wrote again to Lord Hobart on April 4, 1803 (*H O 50 59*).—

I have transmitted to the country the conditions for raising Volunteers with every recommendation in my power, but I am much afraid few officers will come forward from the difference of the present conditions to the former.   They are often put to considerable expense, and, besides, many of those formerly in the Volunteer Corps have gone into the Militia [although he had great difficulty in getting Captains for that establishment]

On April 9, 1803, the Deputy Lieutenants meeting at Banff offered to raise two battalions for the county of eight companies each, with headquarters respectively at Banff and Cullen   It was proposed that the Banff Battalion should have 400 men, and the Cullen 480 men   It was stated at the same meeting that there were six "great guns" at Banff, 12- and 18-prs, and two field pieces, so one of the companies of the Banff Battalion was to be Artillery   The offer was accepted on June 20, 1803, the terms of service being the military district where the Battalions were situated, and; in case of invasion, any part of Great Britain   These Battalions were known respectively as the 1st and 2nd Banffshire Volunteer Infantry

Although the first officers' commissions are dated June 20, 1803, they were not issued by the War Office till May 8, 1804 (*W.O. 25. 205* pp 153-5)   On August 1, 1803, Lieutenant-Colonel Bartlett, commanding the 1st Battalion, sent in the names of the field and staff officers and five Captains "whose services were accepted by His Majesty prior to the 25th June." He suggested that it "would be very obliging if they were gazetted without further loss of time and their commissions dated about the time of their acceptance" (*H.O.* 50 : 59). On October 17, Lord Fife forwarded another list containing five Captains, thirteen Lieutenants, and six Ensigns for the 1st Battalion, with six Captains, twelve Lieutenants, and six Ensigns for the 2nd. The officers, all dated June 20, 1803, were as follows :—

1st BATTALION (Banff).
Colonel—Earl Fife
Lieut.-Col.—James Bartlett
Major—Alexander Stronach
Captain—Peter Cameron
   ,,   David Souter
   ,,   Stewart Souter (of Melrose)
              (Major, Nov. 9, 1803: d. 1839)
   ,,   Archibald Young
Lieutenant—William Bruce
   ,,   Lewis Cruickshank
   ,,   John Cowie
   ,,   John Cuming
   ,,   James Fraser
   ,,   Thomas Grant
   ,,   Alexander Robinson
   ,,   Alexander Ross
   ,,   John Ross
   ,,   John Sangster
Ensign—Isaac Cooper
   ,,   Peter Grant
   ,,   Andrew Morison
   ,,   James Simpson
   ,,   George Smith
Chaplain—Rev. Alexander Walker
Adjutant—James Reid
Quartermaster—John Fraser
Surgeon—James Williamson

ARTILLERY COMPANY.
Captain—Thomas Russel
Lieutenant—George Forbes
   ,,   George Wilson
2nd Lieutenant—Thomas Wilson

2nd BATTALION (Cullen).
Colonel—Earl Fife
Lieut.-Col.—George Garden Robinson
Major—[Not nominated]
Captain—James Fyfe
             (Marnoch Coy.)
   ,,   John Harden
             (Rothiemay Coy.)
   ,,   John McBean
             (Portsoy Coy.)
   ,,   James McKilligin
             (Cullen Coy.)
   ,,   Thomas Stewart
             (Boyndie Coy.)
   ,,   John Watt
             (Grange Coy.)
Lieutenant—Richard Bloxham
   ,,   James Donald
   ,,   James Duff
   ,,   John Gatherer
   ,,   James Laird
   ,,   John Longmore
   ,,   William Mackintosh
   ,,   Alexander Robertson
   ,,   Arthur Scott
   ,,   James Smith
   ,,   Alexander Watson
   ,,   William Watson
Ensign—James Bruce
   ,,   John Conn
   ,,   John Fraser
   ,,   John Fyfe
   ,,   George MacHattie
   ,,   Alexander Robertson
Adjutant—Robert Falder
Quartermaster—James Simpson
Surgeon—James Smith

The officers who were subsequently appointed to the two Battalions are enumerated in a return of 1809 with the date of the commission (*H.O.* 50 : 182) :—

CAPTAINS
W D Bruce, July 12, 1808, Alexander F Williamson, July 15, 1808, George Wilson, July 15, 1808

LIEUTENANTS
John Fyfe, July 25, 1805, George Smith, September 1, 1806, James Simpson, September 1, 1806, Andrew Morison, June 24, 1807, George Smith, July 12, 1808, Andrew Longmore, July 12, 1808, William Gordon, August 27, 1808

ENSIGNS
William Cowie, January 21, 1805, Alexander Mackintosh, May 19, 1805, James Grant, July 25, 1805, Alexander Harper, June 24, 1807, William Robertson (no date), John Stronach, July 12, 1808, Alexander Duff, July 12, 1808, George Dawson, July 15, 1808

QUARTERMASTERS
James Grant, March 13, 1805, Thomas Wright, July 18, 1805

SURGEON
James Rainey, March 12, 1808

In addition to these two Battalions, Banff raised an independent and unpaid company

At this period Banffshire felt itself peculiarly unprotected   Thus Lord Fife wrote, July 31, 1803 (*H O* 50 59) —

There is not a military man of any other description [than Volunteers] in this county at present, though we have nearly forty miles of sea coast, very liable to be attacked by the enemy, and on many parts of which in our present situation even a small privateer might do much damage

In March, 1797, the Lord Lieutenancy had proposed to erect alarm stations at six points along the coast, but as a matter of fact only one was ever erected, and that was done by Francis Garden at Trouphead Garden also erected a fort on his property at a place called Fort Fiddes On June 21, 1804, Garden wrote from Troup House to Lord Fife (*H O* 50 94).—

The small fort erected here at my own expense and formerly reported to your Lordship [this report does not seem to have been preserved], having been inspected, highly approved of, and reported to the Earl of Moira by Major General the Marquess of Huntly, and his Excellency having been pleased to order amunition for the same, I beg leave to suggest to your Lordship the propriety of haveing it well man'd, and,

Y2

as I understand the Banff Battery Company are forty men short of the complement allow'd by Government, that it will be in your Lordship's power to permit me to raise that number in this corner as a Detachment from the Banff Battery Company to man the Fort for the protection of this part of the coast. If the above proposal meets with your Lordship's approbation, I shall take the liberty of recommending an officer to command the detachment.

Lord Fife was quite keen on the proposal, for, in forwarding Garden's letter to Lord Hawkesbury two days later, he says that the fort had been erected.

in a situation extremely well calculated to annoy an enemy and commanding a bay in which trading vessels would be apt to run for protection from privateers, should any appear on this coast. I am, therefore, very desirous that the augmentation he suggests should be made to the Battery Company in Banff, in order that I may be enabled to send the detachment he wants with an officer to take charge of the fort in question.

Mr. Garden's exertions for the protection of this part of the coast have been very spirited, and I trust your Lordship will agree with me in the opinion that this measure ought to be adopted. I have, therefore, to request that your Lordship will lay this before the King, and if it meets with His Majesty's approbation, give the necessary directions for carrying it into effect.

To meet the defenceless condition of the coast, Sea Fencibles were proposed. According to Fife's letter of July 31, 1803 (*H.O.* 50: 59), an offer of this kind was made by Banff (the actual offer is not preserved), and "if Government sees it proper to accept of the same, another company will be raised at Macduff." Again on August 31, 1803, Fife wrote to Charles Yorke (*H.O.* 50: 59):—

I beg to enclose an offer for raising a company of Sea Fencibles at Cullen and to the westward of that [the enclosure is not preserved]; and, if the proposal is approved of by you and accepted by his Majesty, I have to recommend the officers therein named to command the same. I am not acquainted with either Captain Hay or Lieutenant Wood, but both are strongly recommended to me as meritorious officers, and I have no doubt but they will do credit to the recommendations they have got.

None of these proposals for Sea Fencibles was accepted, and, as we shall see, Cullen adopted a very lukewarm attitude with regard to Volunteers.

BANFF: LOYAL COMPANY (1803-8):—The Loyal Banff Company of Volunteer Infantry, as it was called, was an independent unit, differing from the two county battalions in that the men took no pay and clothed themselves. It arose out of the following memorial to the Lord Lieutenant, August 8, 1803 (*H.O.* 50: 59):—

We, the subscribers, young men residing in the town and parish of Banff, actuated by a sense of the duty we owe to our sovereign and our country at the present crisis, when an ambitious, despotic, and cruel enemy dares to threaten no less than the annihilation of all these sacred and invaluable privileges which we enjoy as Britons, purchased to us by the blood and established by the wisdom of our brave, victorious and patriotic ancestors, hereby voluntarily and unanimously associate ourselves together into one body for the purpose of being instructed in the military discipline, in as far as may be judged necessary as conforming with the intentions of His Majesty's Government, as expressed in the late Act of Parliament for the General Defence of the Realm [43 Geo. III.], chap. 96, passed 27th July, 1803.

This company, which rose by 1804 to 80, drilled on the bowling green of the Castle, in granting the use of which the minister of Banff, the Rev. Abercromby Gordon, wrote, August 1803 :—

The Banff Volunteers, I trust, may never be called to the field of battle; but, if in the course of Divine Providence their active exertions are required to repel the invasion of an exasperated and rancorous enemy, I am confident they will quit themselves like men and Britons,

To which the Volunteers replied (Cramond's *Annals of Banff*, i, 347):—

We feel much disappointed that the duties of your sacred profession prevent you from joining us as a fellow soldier; but, while we contemplate this circumstance with regret, we cannot help rejoicing to think that, should it please Divine Providence to put our courage to the test, the good wishes and the intercessions of such a man with the Supreme Ruler of events will attend on and be employed to guard us in the hour of danger from the hostile attacks of our implacable enemy.

The officers of this company were gazetted August 22, 1803 (*W.O.* 25: 205: p. 156) :—

CAPTAIN.

Patrick Rose; he was sheriff clerk.

1ST LIEUTENANT.

John Smith.

2ND LIEUTENANT.

George Imlach; remained to the end.

SURGEON.

John Whyte ; remained to the end ; died in 1831, aged 61.

It is apparently this company's uniform which is described by Dr. Cramond (*Annals of Banff*, i., 346):—

The cap made of leather is similar to the Light Infantry cap and is surrounded from ear to ear with a boarskin, having a pure white feather at the left side. The collar or cap of the coat is dark, royal blue, with two pieces of gold lace and buttons. The wings at the shoulders are white cotton fringes. The cuffs and facings are of the same blue with the cap and have a small edging of white. There are 16 buttons on the front of the coat, eight on each side ; two are pretty close and betwixt them and the other two there are about 3½ inches distance and so on. The pantaloons extending nearly to the ankle bone are of white Russia duck and the half gaiters are about three inches above the ankle. The tails of the coat, which of course is scarlet are short and in shape similar to those of established corps ; and the stock about the neck [is] a regimental one.

In spite of this enthusiastic send off, the Loyal Company of Banff Volunteer Infantry dwindled away, till in 1805 it numbered only 30 men. Captain Rose left it and was replaced in command by his 1st Lieutenant, John Smith, the 2nd Lieutenant, George Imlach, moving up a step and being replaced by James Wright. In the summer of 1805 Smith left, and Wright was replaced by James Paterson, leaving Imlach the only original officer. In the same year the company made proposals to be taken over by the 1st Banffshire. Lord Fife seconded the request in a letter to Lord Hawkesbury, May 3, 1805 (*H.O.* 50: 125), and the last list is for the period June 25—September 24, 1805 (*W.O.* 13: 1,488).

It is not clear, however, whether the company actually joined the 1st Battalion, but it was still in some kind of suspended animation in 1808, when it ended its career finally by declining to be transferred to the Local Militia. On September 19, 1808, Lord Fife announced this decision to the Secretary of State, and it was followed up by a letter to himself, written on September 23, and signed by the officers of the company, Captain Imlach and Lieutenants Wright and Paterson. The letter is worth quoting, for it is typical of the kind of rhetoric in theory which (as in the case of the Monymusk Volunteers) tends to collapse in practice. The letter runs (*H.O.* 50: 182):—

My Lord,—We received by Mr Souter, Deputy Lieutenant, a communication of the determination of Government, that, unless the Banff Company of Volunteer Infantry should agree to volunteer their services for the Local Militia of the county, it would be expedient to discontinue them as a separate Corps, owing to their reduced number

We consequently deemed it proper to submit to the consideration of the members of the Company assembled for that purpose whether they would now come forward and commute their service as required We have, therefore, to communicate to your Lordship in name of ourselves and the Company, that our first determination in this case would have been to have solicited your Lordship's recommendation to Government that His Majesty would have been graciously pleased to continue our services as a Volunteer Corps had we any confident hopes of being able to make up our number to nearly the original establishment of the Company, but at present we do not see a prospect of accomplishing that which to us would be a most desirable object

It would have been our evident wish during the continuance of this just and necessary war to have stood together in our military capacity and to the best of our ability [to] have discharged those duties as soldiers, to the performance of which we pledged ourselves when, through your Lordship's recommendation, our Sovereign was graciously pleased to accept our humble, but willing, services   This object, however, we must reluctantly relinquish, as the paucity of young men in this place who would be inclined, or could afford, to furnish the necessary military equipment together with the general preference of the Local Militia service, render its attainment so uncertain that we could not pledge ourselves to your Lordship to effect it

After mature consideration and having taken the sense of the individual members of the Company upon it, we find that we cannot as a body come forward and offer our services to your Lordship for the Local Militia, but have reason to conceive that, in the event of the dissolution of the Corps by Government, all those members of the Company, whose avocations in life would permit their giving the attendance requisite in that service, will as individuals be ready to offer themselves for enrolment to the officers commanding the Banffshire Battalions under your Lordship

The consideration that under the regulations in the Local Militia for the County the members of the Corps might not continue associated together in one Company has doubtless operated towards preventing a majority of them from commuting their service, as well as the more essential cause that their civil employments would prevent their giving that attendance required by the Local Militia Law for a constant period of successive days to military exercise, in place of the accommodation in respect of time afforded in the other service

We beg to claim the permission of assuring your Lordship that it proceeds not from diminution of zeal in our country's cause or backwardness to comply with the wishes of Government in joining our brethren in arms in a new and more efficient service for the country, but from these causes which we cannot obviate; and we humbly beg leave to say that, if ever a foreign enemy should land on British ground, our most ardent desire shall be to follow up our original engagement by soliciting the permission of joining the ranks of the Militia of our County to meet and endeavour to repell him.

THE 1ST BATTALION (1803-8).—The main difference between the Battalions of 1798 and 1803 was that Cullen was transferred from the 1st to the 2nd (in 1800) and that Captain Peter Cameron (in command of the Alvah Company in 1798) was transferred from the 2nd to the 1st. The vacancy in the 2nd Battalion's Majority was ultimately filled up by Captain McKilligin.

Although the commissions are all dated June, 1803, only the Captains appear in the first muster roll (June—September, 1803), the other officers not being given until the September—December, 1803, roll. The officering of the 1st Battalion (which contains 494 men) was as follows:—

Company.	Lieutenants.	Ensigns.	Men.
Lieut.-Col. Bartlett	William Bruce / James Fraser	Isaac Cooper	81
Major Stewart Souter	John Ross / John Sangster	Patrick Grant	81
Capt. Archibald Young	Lewis Cruickshank / Alexander Robinson	George Smith	91
„ Peter Cameron	Thomas Grant / John Cumine	James Simpson	81
„ David Souter	Alexander Ross / John Cowie	Andrew Morison	80
„ Thomas Russel (Artillery Coy.—Gaz. June 20, 1803)	George Forbes / George Wilson	Thomas Wilson	80

Some difficulty arose with its actual commander, Lieutenant-Colonel James Bartlett, who probably would not have been appointed if Alexander Duff of Mayen, Lieutenant-Colonel of the 1798-1802 Volunteers had not joined the Inverness-shire and Banffshire Militia. Hardly had Bartlett been appointed than he sent the following memorial to the Duke of York, as Commander-in-Chief, August 14, 1803 (*H.O.* 50: 59). He does not state his origin, but he may have been one of the Bartletts of Afforsk.

That your Memorialist served as a Volunteer without pay in the 4th, or King's Own Regiment of Foot, during the siege and untill after the surrender of the Island of Martinique in the year 1761; came to Britain and was appointed a Lieutenant of an Independent Company of Foot commanded by the Late Richard Steele, Esquire, which was reduced at the Peace in February, 1763. Since which period, your Memorialist has been, untill within these few years, upon half pay, and resided for many years in the Islands of Grenada, and Carriacou [the largest of the Grenadines], where he purchased a Cotton Plantation, which suffered greatly during the time the French were in possession of those Islands. And soon after their restoration to Great Britain, he disposed of his property and retired in bad health. During his residence in these Islands, your Memorialist was on the Commission of the Peace, and held different public offices, in which he had the honour to obtain the full approbation of General [Robert] Melville, the Earl Macartney, and Lieutenant-General Mathew, during their respective governments. To General Melville, he was for some time, acting Major Brigadier; was Captain in Lord Macartney's Body Guard, at the capture of Grenada, and after its restoration was appointed by Lieutenant-Colonel Mathew, one of his Aides-de-Camp, with the rank of Lieutenant-Colonel.

Your Memorialist has resided at Banff in Scotland since the year 1788; was employed as Resident Commissary to the Camp at Aberdeen* in 1795. In February, 1797, he was appointed a Captain, and in March the same year Major, of the first battalion, Banffshire Volunteers, where he has done constant duty, to the satisfaction of Colonel, the Earl of Fife, and in such manner as to obtain the approbation of the General of the District and all the field officers, occasionally appointed to inspect the Corps; which being now ordered to be disembodied, your Memorialist, after forty years serving His King and Country finds himself and family reduced to a small pittance insufficient for their maintainence; and therefore humbly solicits Your Royal Highness will condescend to recommend him to His Majesty, for the Command of an Invalid Company, or such other appointment as His Majesty shall be pleased to bestow on him.

This memorial is accompanied by testimonials from Lord Fife, Lord Macartney, General Melville, and Lieutenant-General Mathew.

---

*This camp was held at the Canny Sweat Pots on the Aulton Links in the summer and autumn of 1795. It is described in a pamphlet *Hints respecting the state of the Camp at Aberdeen, 1795*, written by Dr. Robert Somerville, surgeon to the Caithness and Rothesay Fencibles, with an introduction by Sir John Sinclair, and printed by T. Egerton, Whitehall, 1795. It was described and illustrated by Dr. F[rank] K[elly] in the *Aberdeen Journal*, July 24, 1908.

On September 3, 1803, Bartlett wrote to Lord Fife as follows (*H.O.* 50 : 59) :—

In consequence of my letter to the Secretary at War of the 14th ultimo, transmitting Copies of my Memorial to His Royal Highness the Commander in Chief with the annexed testimonies of my services, in order to ascertain my claim as being from the half pay to constant daily pay, I have just received a letter from Mr. Bragge in answer, saying that the rules and regulations for the government of Volunteer Corps were framed by His Majesty's confidential servants, and that it is not in his power to deviate from them ; and he further observes that field officers of Volunteer Corps are not allowed to receive pay, either as such or as Captains of companies.

Should this be the case, your Lordship must be sensible that it will be impossible for me to hold the honorable situation to which you have been pleased to appoint me, as I cannot afford to serve without pay ; but I flatter myself by your Lordship's recommendation to Mr. Yorke, His Majesty's Secretary of State, to take my letter to the Secretary at War with the accompanying Memorial into his consideration (and which I have requested Mr. Bragge to transmit) that he will be induced to comply with my request to be put on daily constant pay of Captain at least, if not higher ; but, should the regulations be such as cannot be departed from, I must beg your Lordship to accept my resignation of the Commission of Lieutenant-Colonel Commandant of the 1st battalion, Banffshire Volunteers, and that you will have the goodness to recommend me to be appointed eldest Captain, and that my Commission may be dated at least some days prior to the other Captains of the Corps.

On September 4, Lord Fife forwarded Bartlett's letter to Charles Yorke, then Secretary for War, expressing the hope that his requests should be granted. He added :—

I cannot omit, upon this occasion, representing to you the bad consequences that must ensue to His Majesty's service if these Regulations [about pay] are persisted in, for I am confident that it will be impossible to find gentlemen properly qualified who will accept of commissions as field officers in the Volunteers, if they are not allowed pay ; and I must beg leave to mention the just sense I entertain of the merits and capacity of Lieutenant-Colonel Bartlett from his services during the last war, as Major of the 1st Battalion, and the hope that I entertain from his talents and exertions in the discipline of the present corps ; nor is there anybody who would more willingly offer his services gratis did his situation admit of it. But I am sorry to say, that is far from being the case, and Lieutenant-Colonel Robinson of the 2nd Battalion, and the Majors to both are in the same situation respecting their pecuniary situations.

THE 2ND BATTALION (1803-8)—The 2nd Battalion had its head-quarters at Cullen, and was made up entirely of country companies, the general command being in the hands of George Garden Robinson (1766-1844), son of Provost George Robinson (1743-1827) It is notice-able that four of the six Captains were ex-officers of the Regular Army. The officering of the companies in the September—December, 1803, pay list was as follows, the privates numbering 477 —

Company	Captains	Lieutenants	Ensigns	Men
Boyndie	Thomas Stewart (Transferred 76th)	Alex Watson William Watson	} James Robinson	78
Cullen	James McKilligin (H p Sheffield Foot)	Richard Bloxham John Gatherer	} John Fyfe	89
Grange	John Watt (H p. 8th Foot)	Alex Robertson James Duff	} James Bruce	78
Marnoch	James Fyfe (89th Foot)	John Longmore William Mackintosh	} George Machattie	78
Portsoy	John McBean	James Laird James Smith	} John Fraser	76
Rothiemay	John Harden (of Ardyne died 1810, aged 61)	James Donald (Late 105th Foot) Arthur Scott	} John Conn	78

On July 8, 1803, Patrick Copland, Portsoy, wrote to Sir George Abercromby of Birkenbog, and Adam Gordon of Cairnfield, as Deputy Lieutenants, offering to raise a company of 80 men to be under his command, with John Taylor as 1st Lieutenant, and Forbes Watson as 2nd (H O 50 59), but it apparently was not accepted

The raising of the two county battalions brought out some of the difficulties attaching to Territorial soldiering, illustrating in this particular case two points—the jealousy of Lord Fife as shown by smaller pro-prietors in his county, and, on the other hand, the jealousy shown by Fife of the Duke of Gordon, Lord Lieutenant of Aberdeenshire, who had been a notability when the Duffs had been nobodies

The first we hear of the matter occurs in a letter which Fife wrote from Mar Lodge, August 24, 1803, to Lord Hobart (H O 50 59) ·—

By a letter I have received from Lieutenant-General Vyse [an officer who had given very important advice to the Government on the organisa-tion of the Volunteers], I am given to understand that a proposal has been transmitted to him by the Duke of Gordon, in the name of some other gentlemen, for raising five Volunteer companies of 80 men each in the County of Banff, and that such proposal the General mentions having transmitted to your Lordship

Z2

I, however, trust your Lordship will not in this instance depart from
the usuall mode adopted on such occasions of referring the said proposal
to the Lord Lieutenant of the County for his opinion and report; when,
I am confident, I shall be able to convince your Lordship that I have
acted in this instance, as on every former occasion, with a due sense of
my own duty as Lord Lieutenant and for the good of His Majesty's
Service.

Hurrying back to Duff House, Lord Fife unbosomed himself at
much greater length in an extremely interesting manifesto, headed
" Memorial from the Earl of Fife, His Majesty's Lieutenant for Banffshire," dated August 31 (*H.O.* 50 : 59):—

The Memorialist has received a letter from Lieutenant-General
Vyse, commanding His Majesty's Forces in Scotland, dated 18th current,
mentioning that the General had by that day's post received a Proposition to raise five companies of Volunteers in the County of Banff. This
Proposition, but for the polite attention of the General, the Memorialist
in all probability would never have heard of; and, having come forward
as it has done in a way so contrary to the known and established official
rules of business in the like cases, it is impossible for the Memorialist
to view it in any other light than as an attempt to convey a reflection
on him as Lieutenant of the County in the execution of his official duty
—an attack equally illiberal and ill founded, and which the Memorialist
should have treated with the silent contempt it deserves, if he did not
conceive that in the present times it behoves every official man, not only
to act with the strictest impartiality, but also, when anything like the
reverse is alledged, to vindicate himself from the charge, where, as he
trusts he will be able to shew in the present instance, it is without the
least foundation. On this ground the Memorialist hopes Lord Hobart
will hold him excused for troubling His Lordship with the present
communication.

Lord Hobart will realise that in the months of April and May last,
the Memorialist offered twenty companies of Volunteers to be raised
in the County of Banff on the terms then proposed by the Government;
and the proposition then made will shew it was his intention to establish
several companies of that number in the District, which, in the letter
addressed to Lieutenant-General Vyse, is said to be left in a defenceless
state. But Government not judging the whole number necessary, Lord
Hobart's letter of the 20th of June directed the Memorialist to restrict
the force to twelve companies; and he accordingly selected those from
the offer first made, having at the same time, a due regard that those
companies should be so stationed and so officered as to afford the best
chance of their being efficient and usefull, in case of emergency. And

the Memorialist will venture to say without fear of contradiction that any impartial person acquainted with the local situation of this County, will readily allow that the force, to the extent allowed, could not have been better arranged consistent with the views and orders of Government

Having thus arranged matters in the manner which the Memorialist conceived most conducive to the good of the service, and acting from that motive, and that motive solely and impartially, he was not a little surprised at the receipt of Lieutenant-General Vyse's letter and the information it contained, by which it would appear certain individualls would endeavour to insinuate that a considerable part of the County is intentionally left unprotected, but the fact is, and on investigation will prove to be, that these individuals have only resorted to this plausible pretence to give vent to private pique and disappointment, because in conforming to the orders of Government it was impossible to comply with their wishes, and to this source principally, if not solely, is to be traced the letter to Lieutenant-General Vyse   That the Memorialist is well warranted in this conclusion, a perusal of the correspondence between him and some of the parties alluded to will fully evince, but, as that would occupy more of Lord Hobart's time than it can be expected at present can be bestowed on any object of so little importance, the Memorialist shall content himself with mentioning a few of the leading particulars .—

The district in this county said to be left in an unprotected state is called the Enzie, and situated between the town of Cullen and the river Spey, a distance of eight or ten miles, in which there is neither town nor village except a few fishing stations, and only two resident gentlemen of landed property—Mr [James] Gordon [1779-1843] of Letterfurrie [who in 1806 assumed the (premier Scots) baronetcy of Gordonstoun, extinct, 1908], and Mr Adam Gordon [1773-1847] of Cairnfield [his son Patrick raised the Ludhiana Sikhs], whose estate is about £300 per annum, and who is supposed to have been the principal promoter of the letter to Lieutenant-General Vyse   Neither of the Messieurs Gordons are any way connected with the Memorialist, but as being the only resident proprietors in that part of the country he appointed them Deputy Lieutenants

During last war, Mr Adam Gordon's father, John Gordon of Cairn-field [died 1804], held the same situation, and was also Captain of a [Enzie] company of Volunteers in the late 2nd Battalion, which he continued to hold until from bad health and mental derrangement his situation became such as to induce the son to procure his resignation, and to assume possession of the estate in the father's lifetime   Upon this event, the Memorialist appointed Mr Adam Gordon a Deputy Lieutenant, and also offered to appoint him Captain of the company which his father had resigned. He, however, declined the last, unless the Memorialist would appoint him Major, a situation which he conceived himself qualified to hold from having held a Company for a few months in the Aberdeenshire Militia; but in this wish the Memorialist felt he could not gratify him at that time without putting him over the heads of officers who, without meaning any disrespect to Mr. Gordon, he judged much better qualified to fill that office; and so matters rested till the conclusion of last war.

When the present war broke out, and His Majesty's Ministers issued orders last spring to the Lieutenants of Counties to inroll Volunteers for the defence of the country, the Memorialist, being then in London, conveyed the same to his Deputies in the County with the necessary directions to receive and transmit to him all such offers as might be made; and when in every other part of the County the inhabitants came forward with the greatest spirit and zeal, he was surprised to find that no offer, or report appeared from either Mr. Gordon in the Enzie district, or the Royal Burgh of Cullen; but, as the Memorialist was perfectly convinced that the inhabitants of these districts were equally well affected as their neighbours, he, as already stated, offered Twenty Companies, having it in contemplation to station at least one, and probably two of them, in the Enzie; and on the 23rd of June wrote to Mr. Gordon, offering to appoint him Major to the second battalion if Government should accept of the number offered. Mr. Gordon's answer of the 24th of that month is not very explicit, but seems to point at a separate command.

On the 25th of June the Memorialist received a letter from Lord Hobart dated the 20th of same month stating that His Majesty had been graciously pleased to accept the services of 960 Volunteers for this County to be formed into twelve companies of 80 men each, thus reducing the number of companies from twenty to twelve. His Lordship at the same time mentions that the King's confidential servants judged it proper not to accept of any more Volunteers for this County on the terms on which the number above mentioned were to serve. Being thus restricted, the Memorialist was, of course, obliged to acquaint many of the officers who had offered to serve that he could not appoint them, but he still resolved and actually recommended Mr. Adam Gordon as Major of the second Battalion, whose head quarters is at Cullen and within a few miles of his residence.

By a letter of the 2nd current, Mr. Gordon declines accepting of the Majority and for the first time offers to raise five companies in the Enzie to be commanded by himself on the terms of the twelve companies which Government had previously accepted. Lord Hobart will at once perceive that, after the orders His Lordship had himself transmitted to the Memorialist on the 20th of June, it was impossible to listen to this proposal   He was, however, willing to do justice to the apparent spirit and zeal of Mr Gordon, and, as the offer made could not be accepted, recommended to him to raise a company of Sea Fencibles, and, which being also declined by him, the Memorialist then wrote to Mr Gordon requesting he would endeavour to enroll his five companies on the terms contained in Lord Hobart's circular letter of the 3rd August, but to this last communication he has as yet received no answer

Having concluded this tedious detail as to Mr Gordon, the Memorialist is sorry to intrude further on Lord Hobart's time, but, as he has also met with a good deal of trouble from certain people in the town of Cullen, with whom Mr Gordon now seems to act, he hopes he will be excused for briefly stating a few circumstances relative thereto

During last war there was a company of Volunteers established in that town under the command of a Captain Thomas Rannie, who is a near connection of Mr John Wilson, the Chief Magistrate of the town and land steward to the Earl of Findlater   Of this company, Alexander Wilson, nephew to Mr John Wilson, was first Lieutenant, who became so remiss in his duty as to call forth from the officer commanding the Battalion several very sharp admonitions, which having failed of the desired effect he was at last superceded, and it was strongly suspected that his Captain (Rannie) had frequently returned him present when absent, and which there was the more reason to believe was true, as Captain Rannie, tho' charged, did not come forward as he ought to have done with a proper vindication

Be that as it may, the Memorialist naturally considered Mr Rannie as a very unfit person to recommend again for a commission, and certainly resolved not to do so if he had offered in time   However he did not make any offer untill the 23rd of June, and long before that period Captain McKliggin [McKilligin], an officer in the Army on Captain's half pay, was on the recommendation of Mr Abercromby of Glassaugh, the only resident gentleman of landed property in that neighbourhood, appointed to the company, and Mr Stables and Mr Smith, both residing in Cullen and having been officers in the former company, I recommended as Lieutenants   Captain McKliggin upon his appointment was ordered by the Memorialist to wait on Mr Wilson, the Chief Magistrate, to intimate the same and require his aid in inrolling the men; but to his surprise found that Mr Wilson not only refused his assistance, but told him that he would give every opposition in his power, because his friend Mr Rannie was disappointed in his expectations of being Captain, and certainly Mr Wilson has been as good as his word, for it can be clearly proved that he availed himself of his situation of land steward to the Earl of Findlater to keep back the men from inrolling, threatening to dispossess such of them as did so with Captain McKliggin, of their houses, and actually made many of them

who had inrolled withdraw their names. [Rannie states in a letter of
June 30, 1803 (*H.O.* 50: 59), that only four men offered themselves as
Volunteers to McKilligin, when he visited Cullen. "The men have since
voluntarily come forward to the number of 100 and upwards to serve
under their former officers."] The same unwarrantable conduct was also
on the same ground extended to the town of Portsoy which is likewise
the property of Lord Findlater. However, Captain McKliggin and
Captain McBane, who is appointed to the Portsoy Company, have both
succeeded in raising two very fine companies in the neighbourhood of
these towns.

From what has been stated it is hoped that Lord Hobart will now
be convinced that the Memorialist is well warranted in saying that not
the defence of the country, but the pique and disappointment of
individuals has given rise to the offer made to Lieutenant-General Vyse,
and the censure thereby evidently meant to be conveyed. But that a
neighbouring Lord Lieutenant should have so far gone out of his way
as to take a lead in it, as he seems to have done, is still to the Memorialist
matter of great surprise. His Grace is well acquainted with the whole
County of Banff. Let him impartially review every part of it with the
provision made for its defence, and then turn his eyes to his own County
and draw a comparison. If [this is] impartially done, the Memorialist is
confident he will not have cause to blush at the result. Let His Grace
[the Duke of Gordon] say, if he can, if in any one appointment made in
the County of Banff, the Memorialist has allowed party or political con-
siderations to interfeere with his duty as Lieutenant. His Grace best
knows how far he has acted from the same motives in his county, and
impartial men will judge.

It is strange, when His Grace is so much alarmed, that he did not
apply to the Earl of Moray, Lieutenant of Morayshire, to re-establish
the company of Volunteers which were in Fochabers last war. This
village is at the door of Gordon Castle, and nearly surrounded by His
Grace's park. If on that side he thinks himself secure, His Grace has
not much to fear from the other, for at Cullen within twelve miles there
is one company and other five in the neighbourhood. Between that
and Gordon Castle a company of 100 men and upwards of Sea Fencibles
will be established if accepted by the Government, and, considering how
narrow the Moray Firth becomes there, it is not likely that any of the
enemie's ships of much force will venture up. His Grace making use of
Lord Findlater is also very extraordinary. That nobleman is at present
abroad, and if he was here, the Memorialist will venture to say he would
be very well satisfied with the arrangements that have been made, and
is confident that his Lordship will not be well pleased at the part his
land steward and other managers have acted on this occasion, and has
the more reason to think so that Lord Findlater by a letter at the end

of last war to the Memorialist approved highly of the dismissal of Lieutenant Wilson and of everything done respecting Cullen

The Memorialist has one of the largest properties in Aberdeenshire, and has some reason to expect that he might, like other proprietors, have been consulted on the arrangements for its defence   He, however, never was; but on that ground makes no complaint, conceiving that the Lord Lieutenant appointed by the King is the best judge, and, being responsible, will do what is proper.   It was on this principle, and from a dislike to interfeere in the province of others that the Memorialist refused to listen to complaints made from the inhabitants of his village of Turnff in Aberdeenshire, who last War offered to raise two companies of Volunteers, and were refused to be recommended on the ground that they were situated too far from the sea, from which the village is distant only eight or ten miles, and nearer to the coast than any other Volunteer station, Aberdeen, Peterhead, Fraserburgh and Rosehearty only excepted, and that, too, at a time when Volunteer Corps were established at the distance of thirty, forty and fifty miles from any part of the Aberdeenshire coast

This Memorial having already swelled beyond the size intended, the Memorialist shall only further detain Lord Hobart untill he mention that the different letters and correspondence establishing the facts contained in it will be sent him if he should think it worth his while to procure them.

The Banffshire Volunteers had something to say about the much discussed and muddled bill which Charles Yorke introduced in the spring of 1804 to consolidate all the existing Acts concerning the Volunteers (44 Geo III, cap 54)   On March 27, 1804, Lieutenant-Colonel Robinson, commanding the 2nd Battalion, wrote to Yorke about it, being, as he said, "very fond of the Service"   He was particularly interested in the disposal of the guinea allowed to the men on permanent duty.   He wrote ($H O$ 50 94) —

Mr Kinnaird observed that in Scotland, which he had just left, when he had been on permanent duty, no such thing as the marching guineas had ever been heard of   I here must beg leave to say that Mr Kinnaird is misinformed as I received them from the Collector of the Cess for the county nearly two months ago, and I am proud to think that I have anticipated your wishes by disposing of the guineas in the following manner, viz

A great coat of stout cloth, including making and materials	£0	17	9
A knapsack properly painted	0	4	0
	£1	1	9

If another guinea were allowed each man, I should lay it out in the following manner, to remain in the store, until we were ordered to take the field, *viz.*

One pair strong shoes	.	.	.	.	.	.	.	.	£0 8 0
One pair strong stockings	.	.	.	.	.	.	.	.	0 3 6
Two flannel waistcoats	.	.	.	.	.	.	.	.	0 8 0
One water canteen	.	.	.	.	.	.	.	.	0 0 10
Turn screws and pickes	.	.	.	.	.	.	.	.	0 0 8

$$£1 \quad 1 \quad 0$$

Mr. Pitt's observations, I make no doubt, are perfectly just in regard to Volunteers in England, who can at any time raise money to purchase great coats, but that is by no means the case in the battalion which I have the honour to command, which (with a very few exceptions) consists of young unmarried men from 18 to 28 years of age, who have no command of money and nothing to trust to but their own daily labour.

The sacrifices made by some of the Banffshire Volunteers is brought out in a letter by Bartlett, who wrote to Lord Fife, October 27, 1804, showing that 31 non-commissioned officers, 12 drummers and 461 privates had attended permanent duty at Banff for fifteen days. But nineteen salmon fishers had not put in an appearance (*H.O.* 50 : 94) :—

The nineteen salmon fishers could not, without ruinous consequences to their employers and themselves, attend constantly, but were drilled two days in the week and being members of the Corps may be considered as entitled to the allowance for necessaries.

The Banffshire Volunteers came to an end in 1808, the last pay sheet of the 1st Battalion representing the period June 27-July 10, 1808, and that of the 2nd Battalion, December, 1807—September, 1808. There was very little change among the officers. Captain McBean, Portsoy Company, was replaced at the very end by his Lieutenant, and several of the subalterns fell out, and the 2nd Battalion had lost several officers altogether by the end. The privates in the 1st Battalion had fallen from 494 to 467 men, and those of the 2nd Battalion from 477 to 468, which shows that Volunteering was popular. The officers in the last pay roll are as follows (*W.O.* 13 : 4,188) :—

1st Battalion—last pay sheet, June 27-July 10, 1808 —

Company	Lieutenants	Ensigns	Men
Lieut.-Col. Bartlett	{ James Fraser { Alexander Robinson	Isaac Cooper	78
Major Peter Cameron	{ Thomas Grant { George Smith	Patrick Grant	80
Capt. David Souter	{ Alexander Ross { John Ross	William Cowie	81
„ Stewart Souter	{ James Simpson { A F Williamson	George Wilson	76
„ Archibald Young	{ Lewis Cruickshank { Andrew Morrison	Alexander Harper	78
„ Thomas Russel	{ George Forbes { George Wilson	Thomas Wilson	74

2nd Battalion—last pay sheet, December, 1807—September, 1808 ---

Company	Lieutenants	Ensigns	Men
Major McKilligin (Cullen Coy)	——	————	78
Capt. James Fyfe (Marnoch Coy)	——	———	—
„ John Harden (Rothiemay Coy)	Arthur Scott	John Conn	78
„ James Smith (Portsoy Coy)	——	———	78
„ Alexander Robertson (Grange Coy)	{ Alexander Robertson { James Duff	William Robertson	78
„ Thomas Stewart (Boyndie Coy)	Alexander Watson	Andrew Longmore	78

A3

LOCAL MILITIA: ABERDEENSHIRE, 1808-1816.

The Scots Volunteers were converted into Local Militia under the Act, 48 Geo. III. cap. 150, passed on June 30, 1808, the formal birth of the force being September 26, 1808. The measure, which has been explained in the introduction, aimed at making the Volunteers approximate the condition of the Militia and Regular soldiers and the response of Aberdeenshire can be described only as fair, for the Volunteer quota of the County, 3,840, was over 700 short. There were some angry refusals to join the new force, at least in one part of the County—the seventh sub-division which included among other places Monymusk, Inverurie, Kintore, Kemnay and Logie Durno. All these places had joined the 1803 Volunteers, so far as the gazetting of officers was concerned, but never had the companies actually embodied. This is all the more ironic as Monymusk had been one of the first places to come forward with a desire to serve couched in high-flown rhetoric. Curiously enough, we hear nothing of this trouble with the Local Militia until June, 1813, when the story is set forth in a statement from Lord Huntly as Lord Lieutenant, to the Secretary of State, in which he says (*H.O.* 50: 292):—

In June, 1809, the proceedings of the Lieutenancy within the seventh sub-division were most illegally obstructed by a numerous body of the lower classes of the people, who, instigated by bad advice, came forward in a most tumultuous manner, and by open violence actually prevented the Deputy Lieutenants from carrying into effect the enrolment of Local Militia. Upon the occasion, the gentlemen who attended as Deputy Lieutenants were put in the most imminent personal danger; nor could they with safety complete the enrolment of a subsequent meeting without military assistance. The most active rioters on the occasion were brought to a criminal trial, and sentence of transportation passed against them.

The men tried at the Circuit Court at Aberdeen, September 22, were Alexander Mitchell, James Skene, Alexander Jessamin and John Burgess, and they were charged with obstructing proceedings of the sub-division meeting of Lieutenancy held at Pitcaple on June 15 (*Aberdeen Journal*, September 27 and October 4, 1809) They were accompanied by a great number of people, many of whom were armed with sticks and bludgeons, and they rushed into the room where the officials were meeting Two of the accused, after using the "most insolent and disrespectful language" to one of the Deputy Lieutenants, (who repeatedly attempted to address and offer explanation to, the rioters), "brandished their sticks or bludgeons and attempted to strike him therewith." It was pleaded that the riot was due to a misunderstanding of one or two clauses of the Act It was also stated that there was no preconcerted plan or combination for any violent purpose, and that, although some of the people were intoxicated and perhaps conducted themselves in a rude or disrespectful manner, they "neither intended nor committed any violent act" A third line of defence was set up, namely that Volunteers were invited to be enrolled, so as not merely to get the benefit of the bounty provided by the Act, but also to avoid the necessity of the ballot, Volunteers, accordingly having tendered their services, went to Pitcaple to be enrolled, so that in the circumstances the ballot appeared inconsistent with the terms of the Act But these defences were not accepted, and the four prisoners were condemned to seven years' transportation

Lord Huntly, continuing his letter, maintained that —

The evidence adduced on the trial established in the most satisfactory manner the correctness and moderation by which the conduct of the Deputy Lieutenants had been actuated, and in justice to them the Lord Lieutenant signified his approbation of their proceedings in a letter published in the newspapers of the County

Although many of the inhabitants of the parish of Monymusk, in which Sir Archibald Grant's property is situated, were particularly active in the disturbances, and although one of his own servants was among those brought to trial, the Lord Lieutenant had occasion to regret that he thought proper to absent himself from the meeting at which the proceedings were obstructed, and this regret could not fail to be increased, when it was understood, that, with the exception of one meeting, Sir Archibald Grant has ever since declined to afford any assistance or to co-operate with the other Deputy Lieutenants of the District in execution of their duty as Magistrates

Whether any other districts acted in a similar way I cannot say. Lord Huntly was chary of mentioning these internal dissensions to the Secretary of State; but, as we shall see, Grant did not end his opposition to the start of the force.

Lord Huntly felt from the start that there would not be much difficulty in getting the men to transfer, so far as the coastwise Volunteers were concerned, but he wrote to the Secretary of State on September 23, 1808 (*H.O.* 50: 181): "In the interior part of Aberdeenshire where there are no towns sufficiently large to accommodate a regiment of 700, I would take the liberty of proposing to reduce the establishment to a number at least not exceeding 500 men. On this footing I would be able to form one Regiment of 800, three of 700, one of 500 and one of 400, making up 3,840," the quota of the county. This expectation at first was not realised, for a return of November 30, 1808, showed the following figures (*H.O.* 50: 208):—

Return of the number of men who offered to transfer their services from the Volunteer Corps and are now enrolled and serving in the Local Militia of that County on November 30, 1808, made up in obedience to the Secretary of State's circular of November 14.

CORPS.	Effective Volunteers who offered to transfer their services into the Local Militia.	Persons enrolled and serving in the Local Militia on Nov. 30, 1808.
Aberdeen Volunteers - - -	800	704
Aberdeen Light Infantry Battalion -	300	340
Gilcomston Battalion - - --	108	125
Peterhead Volunteers - - -	238	238
„ Independent Company -	60	60
Crimond, St. Fergus, etc. - - --	180	202
Monquhitter Company - - -	60	60
Strathbogie Battalion - - -	144	144
Fraserburgh „ - - -	339	336
Meldrum „ - - -	171	171
Belhelvie Company - - -	60	60
Dyce, Newmachar, etc., Company -	62	62
Aberdeenshire Battalion - - --	343	343
Peterhead Artillery - - - --	66	60
	2,931	2,905

The deficiencies and arrangement of the corps are set forth in another return, forwarded on November 24, 1808 (*H.O.* 50: 181):—

ARRANGEMENT OF CORPS   HEADQUARTERS

1st Regiment of Aberdeen Volunteers who have transferred their services into the Local Militia—Lieut.-Col Finlason -		800	City of Aberdeen
Aberdeen Light Infantry Battalion transferred—Lieut.-Col Tower - - -	300		
Gilcomston Company - - - - -	108		
Dyce, etc, ,, - - - -	62		
Belhelvie ,, - - - -	60		City of Aberdeen
	——		
	530		
Wanted to complete by ballot or volunteers - - - -	170		
	——	700	
Aberdeenshire Battalion transferred -	343		Aberdeen or Ellon and neighbourhood
The Earl of Aberdeen - - - -	457	800	
	——		
Fraserburgh Battalion transferred—Lieut.-Col Fraser - - - - -	339		Fraserburgh and neighbourhood
Meldrum Corps - - - - -	171		
Huntly Corps (Strathbogie) - -	144		
Monquhitter Company - - -	60		Turriff and neighbourhood, or Old Meldrum and neighbourhood
	——		
	714		
Wanted to complete - - -	86		
	——	800	
Peterhead Corps—Major Hutchison - -	238		
Crimond, Lonmay, etc - -	180		
Peterhead Independent Company - -	60		
,, Artillery ,, - -	60		Peterhead and neighbourhood
	——		
	538		
Wanted to complete - - -	202		
	——	740	
Total of quota - - -	3,840		

Lord Huntly adds the following note to the return —

For maintaining the above establishment and supplying such deficiencies as may arise, the Lieutenancy have divided the County into ten districts and apportioned the quota in the respective parishes upon the principles fixed by the Local Militia Act The men, when the full numbers have been completed to be placed on the different parishes either by ballot, or by such other mode as may be deemed most fair and equitable

These figures, however, increased so that the number of the five Regiments in the first pay rolls, June—July, 1809, stands as follows —

1st Regiment - - - - - - - - -	800
2nd ,, - - - - - - - -	659
3rd ,, - - - - - - - -	743
4th ,, - - - - - - - -	796
5th ,, - - - - - - - -	612
	——
	3,610

This figure was only 230 men short of the Volunteer quota of the county.

The first corps assenting to transfer were announced in a letter of August 3, 1808 (*H.O.* 50: 181):—1st Aberdeen Volunteers, Aberdeen Light Infantry, Fraserburgh Battalion, Monquhitter, Peterhead Volunteers and the Independent Company, Crimond, St. Fergus, Longside, Rathen. The Fraserburgh men agreed (June 4, 1808) to transfer "on condition that they are commanded by their own officers and that their officers get their present rank." This desire has been echoed in the recruiting efforts of 1914 in the shape of the regiments of "pals."

Each corps was to consist of 10 companies, with the following staff:—1 Lieutenant-Colonel Commandant, 1 Lieutenant-Colonel, 2 Majors, 10 Captains, 22 Lieutenants, 8 Ensigns, 1 Chaplain, 1 Adjutant, 1 Quartermaster, 1 Surgeon, 1 Assistant Surgeon, 1 Sergeant-Major, 40 Sergeants, 10 drummers, and 40 Corporals.

Once started, the Local Militia suffered only one serious inconvenience in the course of its short career; and this came once again from Sir Archibald Grant of Monymusk. In January, 1813, a meeting of Lieutenancy was held within the seventh sub-division for the purpose of ballotting for Local Militiamen under the reduced establishment. At the meeting, where, as Lord Huntly complained to the Secretary of State (*H.O.* 50: 292), "the proceedings were conducted with perfect accuracy and impartiality," the name of Sir Archibald Grant's son was drawn among others ballotted at the time. Upon receiving notice of this circumstance, Sir Archibald, without having attended the meeting or making any inquiry as to its proceedings, not only entered a formal protest with the clerk of General Meetings, but also addressed a letter to the Secretary of State under date February 4:—

A very singular occurrence having lately taken place relative to the Local Militia of this County, I take the liberty of stating to your Lordship the following facts.

In the end of November or beginning of December, 1812, fourteen or fifteen people liable to serve in the present Local Militia went to John Shand, District Clerk to the 7th or Garioch Division of this County, and there entered their names as Volunteers to serve as Local Militiamen for the parish of Monymusk under the new Act. They chose one of the Aberdeen Regiments to serve in, and, when called upon, did on the 22nd of December attend and attest at Aberdeen, being first desired to stand at a side and shew how many men came forward from the parish of Monymusk. On the evening of the said day, David Sherriffs also attested before the Provost of Aberdeen for said parish Thus, as the quota of the parish is only thirteen (the first Local Militia being nineteen and a small fraction), three men volunteered and were attested, more than were required from the parish [Under the Act when men voluntarily enrolled themselves in any parish, the ballot was to be held only for the number deficient of the quota]

Though sole proprietor of the parish and therefore liable to any penalties contained in the Act, I gave myself no trouble respecting the proceedings of the Lieutenancy, knowing that the parish had volunteered more than their quota But I was this morning officially informed by the schoolmaster of the parish that, notwithstanding of what I have already stated, the District had a few days ago ballotted ten men from the parish, among whom is my eldest son, James Grant [afterwards 5th bart, 1791-1859] Twenty six men are therefore taken from this parish instead of thirteen, and the parish is thus punished for volunteering by having a double portion drawn from it, while those parishes who have not volunteered their quota are rewarded by having that quota diminished from them and added to those who had volunteered Such surely was never the intention of the Act

I heard this strange doctrine advocated some time ago, and therefore wrote to the General Clerk, Mr Burnett, stating that it was impossible to ballot upon a parish which had furnished its quota of Volunteers to the New Militia, and received for answer that "the Lieutenancy had not yet determined upon their procedure" From this it would appear that some of the Deputies conceive that they are entitled to manufacture the Act to suit their own purpose

As my son is personally interested, I hope it will plead my excuse for troubling you on this subject I am and always have been a firm friend to the present Ministry, I am known both to Lord Melville and Sir William Grant It will, therefore, be with very great reluctance if I am forced to bring this matter before Parliament, but it is a duty I owe, not only to my son, but to my tenantry to see them get justice, where they are so grievously oppressed Of the statement of the facts I am certain, and the procedure of the Lieutenancy cannot but appear to you a gross violation of the Law Though I am myself one of the number, I have myself for some time declined to act, and I do not chuse that my name should appear in sanctioning measures which seem to me to be so totally contrary to the meaning of the Local Militia Act, as most of those which have been carried into execution respecting it, appear to have been

May I therefore request the honour of your Lordship's opinion respecting the legality of the measure above stated

P.S.—To show your Lordship that I am not fastidious in refusing to act or quirking about trifles, in the parish of Monymusk 40 men are liable; two thirds of nineteen, being thirteen, are the quota. In the adjoining parish of Kemnay, eleven are liable, eight are declared to be the quota and are drawn. The simplest rules of arithmetic must show a gross inaccuracy in the original apportionment.

On February 6, 1813, the baronet wrote again to the Secretary of State (*H.O.* 50: 292):—

Since I had the honor of addressing you I find that in respect to the letter I sent you respecting the Local Militia, I had received complete misinformation from the schoolmaster of the parish who attended the ballot; but so completely had he blundered that the whole men liable for this parish are summoned to a wrong day. I, therefore, hope you will excuse the trouble I put you to.

On February 10 and 17 the Lieutenancy discussed the question at great length and desired Grant to apologise for having ("under the impression that the quota of Local Militia for Monymusk was completed by offer of Voluntary service") declared that the ballot was illegal. But the laird declined. Not only so; he wrote once more to the Secretary of State, June 1, 1813, declaring :—"Of many of the measures of these gentlemen I am profoundly ignorant and, were I better acquainted with others of them, there would be nothing strange if I was to entertain different views of the law from them." On which, the Lord Lieutenant forwarded the whole correspondence to the Secretary of State.

The formal disembodiment of the Local Militia was April 24, 1816, but as a matter of fact there had been no training after June 30-July 13, 1813, and on July 6, 1814, the Thanks of Parliament were voted to the Volunteers and Local Militia who had been formed during the course of the war. There were only five trainings of the Aberdeen Regiments— in 1809, 1810, 1811, 1812 and 1813. All these are dealt with in pay rolls at the Record Office, but unfortunately after the first rolls of 1809, we do not learn how the companies were officered. Pay rolls for the officers and sergeants exist for the years 1814, 1815, 1816. The papers at the Record Office are very nondescript in character and in actual shape.

I now proceed to summarise the personnel of the five different Regiments into which Aberdeenshire was divided.

1ST REGIMENT.—This Regiment, stationed at Aberdeen, was composed of what had been the Loyal Aberdeen Volunteers, commanded by

Finlason, to whom the command was again given The commissions are dated January 21, 1809 (*London Gazette*, March 25, 1809) The chief officers were —

COLONEL

William Finlason, January 21, 1809

LIEUTENANT-COLONEL

Charles Skene, January 21, 1809

MAJORS

Alexander Fraser, January 21, 1809
James Moir (Roll, June 27—July 24, 1809)

ADJUTANT

Andrew Affleck, May 6, 1809

SURGEON

James Selby, May 1, 1809

QUARTERMASTER

James Grant, January 21, 1809

CHAPLAIN

Rev George Gordon (Roll, June 27—July 24, 1809)

The officers were allotted to the companies as follows, according to a return of June 27-July 24, 1809 (*W O* 13 . 3,394) It will be seen that four of the Captains of the Volunteers were transferred, one became Lieutenant-Colonel, and two others became Majors, while five Lieutenants were promoted to command companies —

Company	Lieutenants	Ensigns	Men.
Capt Thomas Burnett	Robert Gibb / James Grant	———	81
„ David Chalmers	George Davidson (He resigned)	John Shepherd	79
„ James Dyce	Gordon McRobie	———	80
„ Hugh Fullerton	John Middleton	Alexander Hay	80
„ Henry Lumsden	Charles Baird	Maxwell Gordon	80
„ George Mackenzie	James Spalding	James Anderson	80
„ James Morison	Robert Charles Grant	Charles Chalmers (Lieut , May 20, 1810)	80
„ Thomas Sangster	John Whyte	———	80
„ William Skene	James Blackhall	James Cruickshank (Lieut , May 23, 1812)	80
„ Alexander Smith	Charles Grant	———	80

B3

The following officers were subsequently appointed as Ensigns :—

George Benzie, January 19, 1813.
David Gill, July, 1810.
Alexander Gordon, June 15, 1813.
William Gordon, May 23, 1812.
William Paton, June 28, 1813.

Finlason states, March 17, 1815 (*H.O.* 50: 312), that the arms of the Regiment were consigned to Bridewell as a place of greater safety than any private store.

2ND REGIMENT.—This Regiment was made up of the companies at Peterhead, Crimond, Lonmay, Rathen, St. Fergus and Longside, and had its headquarters at Peterhead. The commissions were dated January 21, 1809. The field officers were :—

COLONEL.

Alexander Harvey, January 21, 1809; formerly in command as Major-Commandant of the Crimond Volunteer Battalion.

LIEUTENANT-COLONEL.

John Hutchison, January 21, 1809; formerly in command of the three Volunteer Infantry Companies at Peterhead.

MAJOR.

John Gordon, January 21, 1809. Natural son of the 3rd Earl of Aberdeen; born 1787; laird of Cairnbulg; died 1861. Of his six sons two became Generals, one was a Vice-Admiral, and one a Captain in the Gordon Highlanders, while three of his grandsons and one great-grandson are in the Army (*Gordons under Arms*, Nos. 222, 237, 273, 339, 989, 1,007, 1,036, and 1,459).

ADJUTANT.

David Campbell, May 6, 1809; had been connected with the Peter-head Volunteers.

SURGEON.

Robert Jamieson, January 21, 1809.

QUARTERMASTER.

Alexander Ross, January 21, 1809; formerly Sergeant in the Peterhead Volunteers; James Hutchison was appointed Quartermaster, June 7, 1813.

The companies were officered as follows in the pay roll of June 30—
July 27, 1809 (*W.O.* 13 : 3,395):—

Company.	Lieutenants.	Ensigns.	Men.
Capt. Gilbert Alexander (Jan. 21, 1809)	Adam Arbuthnot (Jan. 21, 1809)	James Hutchison, senr.	64
„ George Arbuthnot (Jan. 21, 1809)	⎰Robert Mackie (Jan. 21, 1809) ⎱Alexander Peterkin	——	74
„ William Arbuthnot (July 3, 1809)	Alexander McHardy	James Kilgour	64
„ Robert Cordiner (April 26, 1809)	⎰Robert Hutchison (Jan. 21, 1809) ⎱Robert Arbuthnot (May 26, 1809)	—— —	74
„ James Elles (April 26, 1809)	John Ford Anderson	James Hutchison, junr.	64
„ Thomas Logan (June 20, 1809)	James Godsman	William Pirie	63
„ Donald McIntosh (Jan. 21, 1809)	John Hay	James Skelton (Lieut., Oct. 26, 1812)	65
„ William McKay (Jan. 21, 1809)	William Lawrence	William Scott	64
„ Alexander Robertson (Jan. 21, 1809)	James Fraser	George Skelton (Lieut., Oct. 26, 1812)	64
„ James Scott (May 26, 1809)	John Gilchrist (April 26, 1809)	James Arbuthnot	63

The following Ensigns appear in the return of January 21, 1814:—

Alexander Hutchison, October 26 1813.
James Innes, October 26, 1813.
Alexander Ogston, April 3, 1811.
Hope Peterkin, June 1810.
James Scott, October 26, 1813.
John Skelton, June 1810.

The pay of this Regiment throughout its career was as follows:—

1811	.	.	. £761	1814	.	.	. £600
1812	.	.	. 1,254	1815	.	.	. 545
1813	.	.	. 628	1816	.	.	. 196

3RD REGIMENT.—This Regiment comprised the Aberdeenshire
Battalion representing Cruden, Ellon, Foveran, Logie Buchan and Slains,
Methlick, Tarves and Udny, but the officers were not attached to the
companies assigned to them in that corps. The first commissions were
dated January 21, 1809 :—

COLONEL.

George, 4th Earl of Aberdeen, January 21, 1809; resigned on or before March 16, 1811, when he was succeeded by his kinsman, previously the Lieutenant-Colonel, George Gordon, of Hallhead. Lord Aberdeen (1784-1860) never held any other military post, devoting himself to politics and becoming Prime Minister (*Gordons under Arms*, No. 541).

LIEUTENANT-COLONEL.

George Gordon, January 21, 1809, succeeding to the Colonelcy March 16, 1811. Son of Robert Gordon, of Hallhead, and Lady Henrietta Gordon, he was born in 1761 and died in 1823 (*Gordons under Arms*, No. 542). He was succeeded, May 25, 1811, by Alexander Gordon (born 1781), previously a Captain, who was a son of James, of Rosieburn, and who emigrated to Canada (*Gordons under Arms*, No. 192).

MAJOR.

A[lexander?] Forbes Irvine, 1809. Apparently the 19th Laird of Drum (1777-1861), who was connected with Buchan by succeeding in right of his mother, Jean Forbes, to the estate of Schivas, Methlick, which he sold to Lord Aberdeen (Wimberley's *Family of Irvine of Drum*, 55-56). James Wilson succeeded him as Major, May 29, 1813, being associated with the Hon. Robert Gordon, appointed Major, September 28, 1813. Gordon (1791-1847) was the brother of the 4th Lord Aberdeen, and spent his life in diplomacy. His name does not occur in *Gordons under Arms*.

ADJUTANT.

Robert Moir, May 6, 1809.

SURGEON.

James Perry, 1809; succeeded by Peter Smith, 1809; succeeded by James Perry, June 19, 1813.

CHAPLAIN.

Rev. Thomas Tait, 1809. He was minister of Ellon, and died there September 6, 1810; his wife, Elizabeth Gordon, died January 8, 1804.

QUARTERMASTER.

Thomas Mair, April 13, 1809. He resided at Dudwick.

The companies were officered as follows in the pay roll of July 3-30, 1809 (*W.O.* 13: 3,396), the names of the Volunteer companies to which the officers were originally attached being placed beneath such of them as transferred their services :—

Company	Lieutenants	Ensigns	Men
——	Thomas Davidson	——	75
——	⎧William Duguid ⎨ (Methlick Coy) ⎩Henry Lamond	——	75
——	William Charles Hay	John Montgomery	70
— —	Thomas Mair (Ellon Coy)	George Muir (Foveran Coy)	75
Capt John Duncan	John Mearns (Foveran Coy)	——	75
„ James Hay (Tarves Coy)	Francis Murray (Ellon Coy)	Alexander Garden	75
„ James Mair (Ellon Coy)	John Hay (Tarves Coy)	George Stodart (Foveran Coy)	74
„ Alexander Manson	——	George Brown	74
„ Robert Moir (Methlick Coy)	——	John Garden	75
——	Robert Temple (Udny Coy)	James Wilson	75

The following officers were subsequently added or promoted, and appear in a return of January 21, 1814 ·—

Company	Lieutenants	Ensigns
Capt John Cumming (May 2, 1810)	⎧George Brown ⎨ (May 9, 1813) ⎩George Cuming (No date)	Thomas Fiddes (May 29, 1813)
„ Harry Lamond (May 2, 1810)	William Duguid (Jan 21, 1809)	John Mair (May 29, 1813)
„ George Mudie (July 1, 1810)	John Garden (May 2, 1809)	Charles Ruxton (May 29, 1813)
„ Francis Murray (May 2, 1810)	Thomas Ligertwood (No date)	James Ruxton (May 29, 1813)
„ George Stodart (July 1, 1811)	James Mudie (May 9, 1813)	William Scott (May 29, 1813)
——	George Muir (May 9, 1813)	James Torrie (May 29, 1813)
——	James Wilson (May 9, 1813)	——

4TH REGIMENT—This Regiment was composed of the Strathbogie, Old Meldrum and Fraserburgh Battalions, and comprised Huntly, Drumblade, Old Meldrum, Fraserburgh, Cuminestown, New Pitsligo and Aberdour Most of the officers were commissioned on January 21, 1809 ·—

COMMANDANT.

Lieutenant-Colonel William Fraser, December 1808 (from the Fraserburgh Battalion); laird of Memsie, who died at Fraserburgh, September 10, 1813, in his 74th year He was succeeded in the command, September 28, 1813, by James Urquhart, who had been Lieutenant-Colonel in December, 1808, but was granted a full Colonelcy on becoming Commandant

LIEUTENANT-COLONEL.

James Urquhart (Old Meldrum Battalion), December 1808; promoted to the command as stated, and was succeeded as Lieutenant-Colonel by James Wilson, who had been a Captain since December 1808. He became Colonel, September 28, 1813.

MAJORS.

William Kelman (Fraserburgh), and Archibald Cumine (Monquhitter), both December, 1808. William Milne, June 26, 1811, who was a Captain, January 21, 1809.

ADJUTANT.

James Donald, January 21, 1809. May 6, 1807.

SURGEON.

Charles Leslie, January 21, 1809. Physician in Fraserburgh; married April 21, 1818, Elizabeth, daughter of William Fraser of Memsie.

CHAPLAIN.

Rev. William Fraser, January 21, 1809. Minister of Tyrie; died September 6, 1819, aged 69.

QUARTERMASTER.

John Gordon, January 21, 1809. Brevet-Lieutenant, April 9, 1810.

The companies were officered as follows in the June 25-July 22, 1809, pay roll (*W.O.* 13: 3,397). Beneath some of the names is placed the Volunteer company to which the officer belonged:—

Company.	Lieutenants.	Ensigns.	Men.
Capt. John Cowie (Rosehearty Coy.)	William Connon (Old Meldrum Batt.)	James Cardno	79
„ James Duncan (Old Meldrum Batt.)	Alexander Barnett (Old Meldrum Batt.)	Anthony Donald	81
„ James Garioch (Old Meldrum Batt.)	John Ingram (Old Meldrum Batt.)	George Robertson	80
„ John Innes (Huntly Coy.)	Alexander Patillo (Drumblade Coy.)	George Smith	79
„ William Leslie	James Bisset	Andrew Youngson	80
„ William Mackay (Fraserburgh Batt.)	ʃCharles Simpson	————————	80
	John Murison		
„ John Manson (Old Meldrum Batt.)	John Hunter	George Taylor	79
„ William Milne	James Shearer (Tyrie and Strichen Coy.)	Alexander Milne	80
„ William Milne	James Milne	Lewis Chalmers (Fraserburgh Coy.)	78
„ Andrew Paterson (Drumblade Coy.)	Alexander Cruickshank	Francis Maitland	80

The officers appointed or promoted subsequent to these are given in a return of January 21, 1814:—

Company.	Lieutenants.	Ensigns.
Capt. James Bisset (June 15, 1812)	Anthony Donald (June 15, 1812)	James Barber (July 6, 1810)
„ John Ingram (June 27, 1811)	Francis Maitland (June 27, 1811)	Phineas Donald (June 15, 1812)
„ Alexander Pattillo (June 27, 1811)	George Taylor (June 27, 1811)	George Geddes (June 27, 1811)
	Robert Webster (June 27, 1810)	George Howie (June 27, 1810)
		John Thain (June 27, 1811)
		Alexander Walker (June 26, 1811)

Mackay, the Captain of the Fraserburgh Company, got into trouble, for on January 29, 1810, Huntly wrote to the Secretary of State that most of the charges brought against Mackay for conduct "highly unbecoming an officer and subversion of military discipline," were proved, and he asked for the Captain's dismissal (*H.O.* 50: 235).

5TH REGIMENT.—This Regiment was composed of the Aberdeen Light Infantry (originally Pikemen), the Gilcomston Light Infantry, Belhelvie, Dyce, Newmachar and Fintray, and had its headquarters in Aberdeen. Its first officers were gazetted January 21, 1809:—

COLONEL.

Alexander Tower (of the Aberdeen Light Infantry), January 21, 1809; succeeded, March 20, 1813, by James Stewart of Balmanno.

LIEUTENANT-COLONEL.

Thomas Burnett, April 12, 1813.

MAJOR.

Alexander Gibbon (of the Aberdeen Light Infantry), January 21, 1809; succeeded, June 4, 1813, by William Skene.

ADJUTANT.

Hector Maclean, May 6, 1809.

SURGEON.

William Dyce, January 21, 1809. Died at Aberdeen, March 10, 1835, aged 65.

CHAPLAIN.

Rev. Alexander Thom, January 21, 1809. Minister of Nigg, where he died July 11, 1843, aged 86.

QUARTERMASTER.

George Coutts, January 21, 1809.

The companies are only half officered in the first pay roll, June 27-July 24, 1809 (*W.O.* 13 : 3,398) :—

Company.	Lieutenants.	Ensigns.	Men.
	⌠William Brown	———	67
	⌡Alexander Allan		
	⌠James Reid	—————	69
	⌡John Byres		
	Alexander Walker	—————	70
Capt. Leslie Cruickshank	—————	—————	67
,, Alexander Fiddes	———	—————	63
(Abdn. Light Inf.)			
,, Charles Fyfe	———	John Booth	70
(Abdn. Light Inf.)			
,, William Paterson	Adam Esson	—————	68
(Gilcomston Light Inf.)			
,, John Paul	————	George Moir	69
(Dyce Coy.)			
,, John Scott	James Bartlett	—————	69
(Belhelvie Coy.)			

The officers appointed or promoted subsequent to this are contained in a return of January 21, 1814 :—

Company.	Lieutenants.	Ensigns.
Capt. John Byres (June 16, 1813)	⌠John Booth (May 23, 1812) ⌡George Lumsden (May 23, 1812)	William Rettie (Feb. 2, 1813)
	Patrick Mitchell (June 29, 1813)	James Walker (Feb. 2, 1813)
Capt. James Reid (Nov. 5, 1809)	George Moir (May 23, 1812)	Thomas Wilson (Feb. 2, 1813)
,, John Smith (June 16, 1813)	James Simpson (June 29, 1813)	—————
	George Wilson (June 12, 1813)	—————

The Battalion clerk, according to a letter of July, 1815, was under arrest for some reason not stated.

LOCAL MILITIA: BANFFSHIRE, 1808-1816.

The transformation of the Banffshire Volunteers into Local Militia seems to have been effected without much trouble. Only one body of

Volunteers, the Loyal Banff Company, declined to "commute," but
in any case it was already moribund   The men of the Artillery
Company of the 1st Battalion were displeased because they now got
the same pay as the Infantry, resenting it as an implication that "they
had been guilty of some fault of which they are not conscious" (June 15,
1809, *H O* 50 209)   The rest, however, was plain sailing, for Banffshire had only two battalions to handle   According to a return of
November 1, 1808, the 1st Battalion transferred 519 men, and the 2nd,
495 men (*H O* 50 189)   The officers of the 2nd Battalion agreed to
transfer on August 6, 1800 (*H O* 50 182)

The companies varied in size from 76 to 91 men, the latter being
the size of the Artillery Company   The officers were gazetted January
21, 1809 —

COLONEL

James Bartlett, from the command of the 1st Battalion, resigned
through ill-health, August 2, 1809

LIEUTENANT-COLONEL

George Garden Robinson, from the command of the 2nd Volunteer
Battalion, succeeded Bartlett as Colonel   He was succeeded as Lieutenant-Colonel by Captain Thomas Duff Gordon of Park (1790-1855),
who was Lieutenant-Colonel of the Inverness, Banff, Elgin and
Nairn Militia, 1812-55 (*Gordons under Arms*, No 1,590)

MAJORS

Alexander Stronach, and Stewart Souter, both from the old
Volunteers

ADJUTANTS

James Reid and Robert Falder, May 6, 1809

SURGEONS

James Smith and James Rainey

CHAPLAIN

Rev Abercrombie Gordon (1758-1821), minister of Banff

QUARTERMASTERS

Thomas Wright and James Grant

The thirteen companies were commanded as follows, according to a muster roll of June 25-July 24, 1809 (*W.O.* 13 : 3,471) :—

Company.	Lieutenants.	Ensigns.	Men.
Capt. William D. Bruce	{ Alexander Robertson { James Duff	William Robertson	76
„ Peter Cameron	Thomas Grant	Patrick Grant	82
„ George Forbes (Artillery Coy.) Sheriff-Sub. of Banff	{ George Wilson { Thomas Wilson	[Alexander Wright] (1810)	91
„ James Fyfe	{ John Longmore { William Mackintosh	Alexander Mackintosh	76
„ [George Gerrard] (1810)	{ James Fraser { Alexander Robinson	Isaac Cooper [Writer of " Strathspeys "]	76
„ John Harden	Arthur Scott	John Conn	76
„ James McKilligan (Patrick Ross, 1810)	{ John Gatherer { John Fyfe	Alexander Duff	76
„ John MacBean	James Smith	Alexander Harper	76
„ David Souter	{ Alexander Ross { John Ross	————————	76
„ Thomas Stewart	John Watson	John Stronach	78
„ Alex. F. Williamson [Ex. with P. Cameron, 1810]	{ Andrew Longmore { George Smith	————————	——
„ George Wilson	James Simpson	George Dawson	76
„ Archibald Young	{ Lewis Cruickshank { Andrew Murison	William Gordon	82

A letter of June 9, 1813 (*H.O.* 50 : 292) announced the resignation of Captain Gerrard, who became Ensign of the 12th Foot, and James Gordon, Lieutenants John Fyfe, Andrew Longmore, William Mackintosh and Alexander Robertson, together with Ensign John Conn, Isaac Cooper and John Stronach.

THE TROUBLES OF THE STRATHSPEY FENCIBLES.

A SUPPLEMENTARY NOTE ON THE ATTACK ON AND BY THE GRANTS

Since the chapter (pp 173-184) dealing with the Strathspey Fencibles was printed off, I have received some additional material through the courtesy of Mr G. W Shirley, honorary secretary of the Ewart Public Library, Dumfries, based largely on contemporary reports in the *Dumfries Weekly Journal*

It appears that the attack made on the Fencibles by the tinkers O'Neill, who lived at the Stoup, near Dumfries, was due to the fact that some constables, assisted by a party of the Fencibles, had been sent on Tuesday night, June 9, 1795, to arrest the two sons of John O'Neill, Henry and Arthur, under the Comprehending Act The O'Neills fired seven shots on the Fencibles, wounding a sergeant and two privates, one of whom, John Grant, had to have his leg amputated The crowd then burned and demolished the O'Neill's house, and in the confusion Henry O'Neill escaped He is described in an advertisement as "aged about 22 years of age, 5 feet 9 or 10 inches high, a stout well-made man with dark hair hanging loose, dark complexioned, and a little pitted by the smallpox, had on when he escaped a blue jacket, striped vest and white trowsers, a small round cap and tied shoes He is supposed to have gone the road towards Edinburgh in order to inlist into some corps, or as a sailor" He seems to have got right away, and at the Circuit Court, opened on September 7, he was outlawed His victim, John Grant, meantime had died in the Dumfries and Galloway Infirmary, August 16, and was buried at Dumfries, August 17, the funeral being attended by the Magistrates and a party of the Durham Rangers The two other men who were injured recovered, and Sir James Grant sent a donation of ten guineas to the Infirmary to mark his gratitude "The Gentlemen at their last County meeting" gave these two men fifteen guineas, and a similar sum was subscribed to them by the Magistrates of the town. John O'Neill not only had his death sentence commuted, but he brought an action against the Magistrates at the end of 1800 " on account of a mob having demolished and burned his house." The case was still in dispute in March, 1803.

The emeute which occurred on Thursday evening, June 11, two days after the O'Neill attack, is described at length in the *Dumfries Weekly Journal* of June 16:—

One of the men [of the Strathspey Fencibles] having been confined for impropriety in the field when under arms, several of his comrades resolved to release him ; for which purpose they assembled round and endeavoured to force the guard room ; but they were repelled by the adjutant and officer on guard, who made the ringleader a prisoner.

The Commanding Officer of the regiment immediately ordered a garrison court-martial, consisting of his own corps and the Ulster Light Dragoons. When the prisoners were recommended back from the court to the guard room, their escort was attacked by fifty or sixty of the soldiers with fixed bayonet. The escort, consisting of a corporal and six men, charged them in return, and would not have parted with their prisoners, but at the intercession of the Sergeant Major, who thought resistance against such numbers was in vain. The mutineers then sent up a shout, and a part of them ran away with the prisoners.

The Lieutenant-Colonel [A. P. Cumming] and Major [John Grant], on hearing the noise, ran down to the street ; and the former seeing the way the prisoners had gone, followed and retook them. They submissively agreed to go with him to confinement ; but, when they had reached the middle of the street, he was surrounded by a great number, who charged him with fixed bayonets, in every direction. The Major did his utmost to beat down their bayonets on the left, and Captain John Grant, jun., was near him on the right equally exerting. The mutineers like cowards were encouraging one another to push on, and had enclosed the three officers in a very narrow compass, when one of the most violent, approaching the Lieutenant-Colonel's breast and threatening to be through him, he was under the necessity of pulling out a pistol, and presenting it at his head. The fellow immediately ducked, and the whole fell back, as if they had received the word of command. Many of the officers had by this time joined, and order was soon restored.

They [the mutineers] were paraded at the Dock, the Mutiny Articles read, and a forcible speech made by the Lieut. Collnel [sic]. They were then ordered, as a mark of returning duty and allegiance, to face to the right and march under the colours ; which was immediately complied with. The ranks were then opened, and six of the ringleaders

picked out, sent to the guard under an escort, and the affair reported
to the Commander-in-Chief   The regiment has since received a route
to march to be encamped on the East Coast

It is but justice to add that this (the only unlucky business) excepted, no corps ever quartered in this place behaved themselves with
such propriety of conduct and demeanour, and so entirely conciliated the
good will of the inhabitants, not a single complaint having yet been
made against any individual of the regiment

The same journal announced on June 30 that the mutineers " are
arrived. at Edinburgh under a strong escort and lodged in the Castle."
The court-martial on the five prisoners—given as Charles McIntosh,
Lauchlin (not " A," as given by Stewart) McIntosh, Duncan Macdougal,
James Macdonald and Alexander Fraser—was begun at Musselburgh
Camp, under the presidency of Colonel William Wemyss of the 2nd
Fencibles on July 6, and concluded on July 10, the men being defended
by John Grant, W S   The proceedings, says the *Journal*, were conducted " with much solemnity and precision, and with great humanity
to the unhappy prisoners "   On Sunday, July 12, the sentence of the
court was intimated to them by the Rev Mr McGregor, all being condemned to death except James Macdonald, who was to receive 600
lashes   The execution on July 17, is described in the *Dumfries Weekly
Journal* of July 21, 1795 —

The prisoners were on Friday last conveyed from Musselburgh
jail about six o'clock in the morning in two mourning coaches, accompanied in the first by the Rev Mr McGregor, and in the second by
the Rev Mr [James] Grant, Chaplain to the Strathspey Fencibles,
escorted by a party of the 4th Regiment of Dragoons [now the 4th
Hussars], the Strathspey, the Breadalbane, and a detachment of the
Hopetoun Fencibles, and followed by the Sutherland Fencibles, with
two field pieces and a party of Artillery   The four coffins were conveyed in a cart immediately after the coaches

They arrived on Gullen [sic] Links about twelve o'clock, where they
found three or four troops of Dragoons, and two battalions of the
Scotch Brigade from the camp at Dunbar formed on the ground   After
the troops were drawn up and the detachment from the Grants destined
to put the sentence into execution being placed in their centre, and a
company of the Scotch Brigade in their rear, the prisoners then walked
up to the ground, accompanied by the two clergymen   Upon their
arrival, General Hamilton, the commander of both camps, ordered the
sentence of the court-martial to be read by Captain Taylor, one of his

Aide-du-Camp [sic]; after which, Mr. Grant, Chaplain of the Regiment, sung Psalms and prayed. That being finished, Captain Taylor read the approbation of the Commander-in-Chief of the sentence on Alexander Fraser, and three other prisoners under sentence of death, *viz.*—Lauchlin McIntosh, Duncan Macdougall and Charles McIntosh were to draw lots; the lot fell upon Charles McIntosh.

The sentence was then put in execution. Fraser was a little turbulent and was obliged to be bound hand and foot before the sentence could be executed. McIntosh submitted to his fate with the utmost calmness.

We are happy to observe that everything was conducted with the utmost regularity and order. The crowd of spectators from every quarter was very great.

GORDON HIGHLANDER ROLL OF HONOUR, 1815

THE FATAL CASUALTIES AT QUATRE BRAS AND WATERLOO

As a contribution to the centenary celebration of Waterloo, which sounds again with the noise of guns, I have thought it well to make a little diversion from the main topic of this book by giving the names of those Gordon Highlanders who fell at Quatre Bras (June 16) and Waterloo (June 18, 1815)

It is not easy to be precise on the losses in the two battles, for the authorities differ, and the official Casualty Lists do not give the date when a man who died of wounds was actually wounded According-ing to Captain C B Norman (*Battle Honours of the British Army*, p 195), the Gordon Highlander casualties were —

	Officers killed	Officers wounded	Men killed	Men wounded
Quatre Bras - -	4	20	35	226
Waterloo - - -	—	6	14	96
	4	26	49	322

Lieutenant-Colonel Greenhill Gardyne (*Life of a Regiment*, 1, 458-460), citing the papers in possession of the regiment, gives a total of 82 killed and died of wounds (excluding officers)

The register of casualties as preserved at the Public Record Office (*W O 25 2,119*) gives 78 actually killed or died of wounds (besides two captured), excluding officers, the names appearing in several returns

The official list (*W O 25: 2,119*) contains eight names not in Lieutenant-Colonel Greenhill Gardyne's, but his one contains 12 not in the other I have included these in square brackets

It need scarcely be added that *k* means killed, *d of w*, died of wounds, and *c*, captured The names not in the Gardyne list are marked with an asterisk The first casualty list (June 25—July 24, 1815) is signed by Donald Macdonald, Lieutenant-Colonel, at the camp near Paris —

COMMISSIONED OFFICERS.[1]

Name.	Birthplace.	Trade before Enlistment.	Date of Casualty.	Prize Money.	Next of Kin.
Cameron, John, Lieut.-Col.	...	....	d. of w., June 17	....	......
Grant, W. C., Capt. ..	....	....	d. of w., June 27 (at Brussels)	....	......
Little, William, Capt. ..	...	....	k., June 16	....	......
Chisholm, J. J., Lieut. ..	...	....	k., June 16	...	......
Becher, Abell, Ens. ..	...	....	k., June 16	....	......
Macpherson, J. M. R., Ens.	....	....	k., June 16	....	....

NON-COMMISSIONED OFFICERS.

Name	Birthplace	Trade	Casualty	Prize	Next of Kin
Taylor, David, Sergt.-Maj...	Perth	Shoemaker	k., June 18	Peninsula	married
Dunbar, Alex., Sergt. ..	Elgin	Weaver	k., June 16	,,	m. Mary ——
[Mackenzie, Kenneth, Sergt.	Ross	....	....		
Paterson, John, Sergt. ..	Aberdeen	Sail-maker	k., June 16	Peninsula	stepson of James Greig
Cameron, James, Corp.	Banff	Labourer	k., June 16	,,	aunt, Eliz. Mitchell
[Fraser, Donald, Corp. ..	Inverness	....	....	....	....
Gibb, James, Corp.	Alyth	Mason	d. of w., June 20	....	......
Grubb, James, Corp.	Monymusk	Labourer	k., June 16	Peninsula	m. Anne ——
Ledingham, John, Corp. ..	Banff	,,	k., June 16	....	married
Ross, Donald, Corp.	Ross	,,	k., June 16	Peninsula	father, William
Russell, James, Corp.	Elgin	Tailor	k., June 16	,,	brother, Alexander

PRIVATES.

Name	Birthplace	Trade	Casualty	Prize	Next of Kin
Appleton, William	Stokerley	Labourer	d. of w., June 27	Peninsula	......
Beaton, Peter	Inverness	,,	k., June 18	,,	father, Malcolm
Benson, Thomas	Newcastle	Brushmaker	k., June 16	,,	married
*Black, William	Dunfermline	Labourer	d. of w., Oct. 2 (at Brussels)	,,	......
Breddon, Robert	Monaghan	Weaver	k., June 16	....	......
Bremner, John	Huntly	Labourer	k., June 16	Peninsula	......
Brown, Charles	Forfar	,,	d. of w., July 17	,,	......
Burnet, John..	King-Edward	Tailor	d. of w., Aug. 9 (at Antwerp)	,,	......
Burnet, William	Fyvie [Tyrie ?]	Labourer	k., June 16	....	... ..
[Cameron, Donald	Inveravon	....	....	....	......
Cameron, Donald	Kilmallie	Labourer	d. of w., July 17	Peninsula	brother, John
Campbell, Colin	Reay	,,	k., June 16	,,	......
Carr, John	Kirkintilloch	Weaver	k., June 18	,,	married
Cockburn, George	Edinburgh	Cutler	k., June 18	,,	mother, Mary
Duncan, Lachlan	Westminster	Labourer	d. of w., June 24	....	......
Duncan, Robert	Huntly	,,	k., June 16	Peninsula	......
Dustan, Peter	Buckie	,,	d. of w., Aug. 15 (at Antwerp)	....	......
Elliot, Robert	Castlebar	Weaver	k., June 16	Peninsula	m. Honora ——
Fisher, Donald	Birmingham	Brass-founder	k., June 16	,,	......
Fitzpatrick, John	Cavan	Blacksmith	d. of w., Sept. 13	....	......
Fraser, John	Beauly	Labourer	k., June 16	Peninsula	m. Helen ——
Fraser, William	Logie	,,	k., June 16	,,	......
Glenny, John	Edinburgh	Shoemaker	k., June 16	,,	......
Gow, Donald	Perth	Weaver	k., June 16	....	......
Graham, Davie	Creich	Labourer	k., June 16	....	married
*Graham, William	Glasgow	Weaver	c., June 17	Peninsula	......
Grant, Alexander	Talbert [Tulloch ?]	Carpenter	d. of w., Aug. 4 (at Antwerp)	,,	......
Grant, John	Perth	Stocking-maker	k., June 18	,,	father, John
Grant, Lewis	Kingussie	Labourer	d. of w., July 24	....	......
[Griffin, Timothy	Kilmorack	....	....	....	......]
Gunn, Peter	Huntly	Weaver	c., June 17	Peninsula	......
Higgins, Charles . ..	Belfast	,,	k., June 16	,,	......
Hutton, James	Forfar	,,	d. of w., July 3	,,	......
Kennedy, Alexander ..	Glengarry	Tailor	k., June 16	,,	......
*Kirkwood, Thomas ..	Dunipace	Labourer	d. of w., Aug. 28	....	......

Name	Birthplace	Trade before Enlistment	Date of Casualty	Prize Money	Next of Kin	
Lamont, Archibald	Mull	Labourer	d of w , July 6	Peninsula		
M'Callum, John	Rinton	,,	k , June 16	,,		
[MacCrackin, William	Inch, Galloway	.				]
Macdonald, Donald	Urquhart	Labourer	k , June 16	Peninsula		
Macdonald, James	Glasgow	Ropemaker	k , June 16			
Macdonald, William	Inverness	Tailor	k , June 16 .	Peninsula		
[Macdonald, William	Dunfermline					]
MacGowan, Patrick	Belfast	Labourer	k , June 16	Peninsula		
McGrigor, William	Urquhart	,,	k , June 16	,,	father, William	
M'Intosh, William	Abernethy	,,	k , June 13			
⁹Mackay, Donald	Renfrew	Goldsmith	k , June 16			
Mackay, Roderick	Urquhart	,,	k , June 16	Peninsula		
McKenzie, John	Inverness	,,	d of w , July 16			
*M'Lachlan, Duncan	Argyll	,,	d of w , June 24	Peninsula	son of Dongald	
M'Lean, William	Nairn	,,	k , June 16	,,		
M'Lellan, Angus	Uist	,,	d of w , July 6	,,		
M'Leod, Malcolm	Skye	.,	d of w , July 29 (at Antwerp)	,,		
M'Leod, Roderick	Kilmorie	,,	k , June 16	,,	m Hannah ——	
M'Neil, Thomas	Dumfries	,,	k , June 18	Peninsula	father, Alexander	
M'Swine, John	Kilmuir	,,	d of w , July 2 (at Antwerp)			
Marshall, William	Glasgow	Weaver	k , June 16		sister, Elizabeth	
Masterton, Charles	Forfar	,,	d of w , July 9			
Mathers, John	Forfar	Labourer	d of w , July 17	Peninsula		
Mathieson, Donald	Creich	,,	d of w , June 28 (at Antwerp)	,,		
[Millar, Robert ·	Dunfermline					]
Mollison, James	Aberdeen	Labourer	k , June 16	Peninsula	father, Herod	
*Munro, Andrew	Ross	Shoemaker	k , June 16		father, William	
Munro, John	Aberdeen	Blacksmith	k , June 18	Peninsula	father, Robert	
⁹Munro, Peter	Inverness	Weaver	d of w , July 5			
*Munro, Peter	Inverness	Labourer	d [of w ?], July 5	Peninsula		
Orr, Mathew	Ayr	Clerk	k , June 16			
Pirrie, Robert	Old Machar	Shoemaker	k , June 16	Peninsula	mother, a widow	
Reid, William	Rogart	Labourer	d of w , June 25 (at Brussels)			
[Ross, Donald	Fearn					]
[Ross Donald	Tain					]
Ross, John	Ross	Labourer	k , June 18		cousin, Kenneth Ross	
Simpson, Duncan	Latheron	,,	k , June 16	Peninsula	father, John	
[Skinner, Donald	Edderton					]
Smith, Finlay	Inverness	Labourer	k , June 16	,,	mother, a widow	
Stewart, John	Blantyre	,,	k , June 16	,,	sister, Bessy	
Stewart, William	Lanark	,,	k , June 16		father, Norman	
Sutherland, Alexander	Elgin	Tailor	k , June 16	Peninsula	brother, Peter	
[Thomson, James	Renfrew					]
Whitaker, John	Stratford [Essex]	Labourer	k , June 18	Peninsula	father, John	
[White, Frederick	Glasgow					]
*Wilson, William	Ganveg	Labourer	d of w , June 24			
⁴*Yates, Samuel	Durham	Tailor	k , June 16		.	
⁵Ziegher, Frederick	Germany	Musician	k , June 16			

⁹ Returned afterwards as rejoined regiment, June 23
³ A supplementary list gives his birth as Aberdeen He is marked simply "dead" It should be noted that the birthplaces given by Lieut -Col Greenhill Gardyne often differ from those in the P R O Casualty Register
⁴ Though returned at first as killed, he was later entered as having rejoined his regiment on July 7, 1815
⁵ Spelt " Zugner" in the Index to Casualties (W O 25 2665).

THE HEIGHT OF THE GORDON HIGHLANDERS.

The average height of 914 of the first recruits to the Gordon Highlanders in 1794 was 5 ft. 5½ ins. (see *supra*, p. 229). Dr. J. F. Tocher, to whom I have submitted the lists, sends the following comment on the figures :—

I find the standard deviation from the mean, for the 914 recruits, to be 2.76 inches, which is very similar to the figures I get for Scottish populations of the present day. I find, for instance, that 2.72 is the standard deviation for the entire insane population for all Scotland, and 2.7 to be the standard deviation from the mean for the general normal population for all North-East Scotland. This is what we should expect. There is no reason that I can think of why there should be any change in the distribution of stature in Scotland during the past hundred years.

In 1900 the average height of a large sample of the Aberdeenshire rural population was found to be 5 ft. 5.72 ins. It would be interesting to know what the average stature of recruits from the Aberdeenshire rural population is to-day. Since the standard has been lowered, quite possibly the average stature will not be any greater than the average stature for recruits in 1794. The following table shows the average stature of various classes in Great Britain :—

	Inches.
Cambridge Students	68·86
English Sons	68·86
Roxburgh and Selkirk Volunteers	67·89
English Fathers	67·74
Aberdeenshire Rural	67·72
General Hospital	67·16
Criminals, New South Wales	66·88
Scottish Insane	65·86
English Criminals	65·54
Scottish Criminals	64·84

The calculation of the first recruits' heights was wrongly given (on the authority of an accountant in Banff) in my little book on the Gordon Highlanders issued by the Banffshire Field Club in 1913, as

5 ft. 3⅔ ins, and when the *Daily Chronicle*, reviewing the book (July 9, 1913), printed these figures, a controversy broke out in several newspapers, some of the writers expressing great surprise, and others even greater anger, at the suggestion that the Gordon Highlanders of 1794 were " dwarfs " Although the correct calculation, 5 ft 5½ ins, makes them somewhat taller, it does not bear out the theory of many of the correspondents (and nearly all the artists of old prints) that the Gordons and the Highlanders generally of that day were gigantic men   For instance, Lord George Beauclerk describes the men of Campbell's Highlanders in a report of May 10, 1760, as " in general very low size, but very fit for service excepting a few old men and some boys " (*W O* 1 : 614)   Again, here are some facts about the height of Highlanders in the latter half of the eighteenth century (cited by the present writer in the *Daily Chronicle*, Nov 28, 1913, and worked out in detail as regards the Jacobite prisoners in the *Globe*, Oct 30, 1913) —

						Ft	In
1746	-	-	79 Jacobite prisoners in London		-	5	6 45
1775	-	-	89 Fraser Highlanders -	-	-	5	5 17
1778	-	-	295 Northern (Gordon) Fencibles -	-	-	5	6 02
1793	-	-	216 Northern (Gordon) Fencibles -	-	-	5	6 25
1794	-	-	914 Gordon Highlanders -	-	-	5	5 51
1901-10	-	-	Average of our Army recruits	-	-	5	6 1
1911	-	-	Average of our Army recruits	-	-	5	6 2

Many of the criticisms put forward were really founded on a theory, highly popular some time ago, that we had " degenerated," but the requirements of the Great War have done much to dispel that illusion Thus Colonel F. N Maude has pointed out (*Sunday Times*, Nov 8, 1914), that to obtain anything like 800,000 men in face of the " preposterous " physical conditions demanded—5 ft 6 ins in height, perfect eyesight, and good teeth—is an " exploit of which any nation in the world might be proud " He goes on to say that the 5 ft 6 ins standard is, in fact, the standard of the Russian Grenadier regiments and of the Prussian Guard, while the normal standard for infantrymen in both these countries is as low as 5 ft 1 25 ins, whereas our minimum for thirty years at least before the war was 5 ft 4 ins for infantrymen

It would be unnecessary to refer to the matter at all but for the widespread belief that the big man makes the best soldier— notwithstanding the prowess of Japan—and that the Highlanders have been giants. It is not without its significance that the late Laureate's grandson, Mr. Alfred Tennyson, in his novel, *A Portentous History*, 1911, makes a doctor in the Highlands responsible for this statement (p. 283) :—

The world likes those huge, fair men with slow pulses and sleepy movements. They're no good. Their hearts can't keep it up—after forty, anyway. The blood all goes to feeding the remote extremities of the body. It hardly reaches their brains. Give me the swift, mad tumult of the short man's circulation and the big stomach, set well in between the thighs, which shows a good digestion and a capacity for always attaining nourishment. That keeps the nerves sound and the brain clear, gives the Napoleonic brain-in-compartments organisation. Give me the short-legged, short-necked, short-tempered man. He gets on.

THE GORDON HIGHLANDERS, 1794-1914

A BIBLIOGRAPHY OF ALL THE BATTALIONS, AND VOLUNTEERS

Though this book does not profess to be a complete history of northern territorial soldiering down to date, it is possible, and highly desirable, to summarise the developments of the century since 1814 (when the Volunteering movement stopped) in the shape of a bibliographical survey of the widely distributed material bearing on the period The 92nd is the only remnant, besides the old Aberdeenshire Militia, of the regiment-raising prior to 1814, and it has formed the nucleus of the Territorial soldiering in the north-east, round which clusters the Volunteering system, dormant between 1814 and 1859

The " Gordon Highlanders " now consist of the following battalions, the dates of their establishment being given   The list does not include the four reserve battalions for the Territorials, nor the four battalions (8, 9, 10, and 11) raised for " Kitchener's Army "—all to carry on the " Great War " with Germany, 1914—and therefore not permanent

    1st—The old 75th, Stirlingshire   -   -   -   -   -   (1787)
    2nd—The old 92nd, Gordon Highlanders   -   -   -   (1794)
    3rd—The old Aberdeenshire Militia   -   -   -   -   (1798)
    4th—The old 1st V.B G H , Aberdeen City· now T F - (1859-60)
    5th—(Buchan and Formartin) Territorial Force , the old
        2nd and 3rd V B G H   -   -   -   -   -   (1860-72)
    6th—(Banff and Donside) T F ; the old 4th and 6th
        V B G H.   -   -   -   -   -   -   -   (1860-68)
    7th—(Deeside Highland) T F , the old 5th V B G H   - (1860-62)
        The Shetland Companies, T F , the old 7th
        V B G H   -   -   -   -   -   -   -   (1900)
        Allied , the 48th Highlanders, Toronto   -   -   (1891)

The bibliography is arranged, under battalions, chronologically according to the dates of publication and not to that of the events described.

1ST BATTALION, THE OLD 75TH (raised 1787 : linked 1881).

1787-1876—Pay and Muster Rolls (P.R.O.: *W.O.* 12 : 8,130-8,190).

1822—Stewart's *Sketches of the Highlanders* (2nd ed., ii., 171-176).

1838—Browne's *History of the Highlands* (iv., 319-320).

1857—*Indian Mutiny Services* (Records at the War Office).

1862—Murray's *Scottish Regiments* (pp. 199-204).

1862—MacKerlie's *Scottish Regiments* (p. 14).

1875—Scott Keltie's *Scottish Highlands* (i., 616).

1888—Richards' *His Majesty's Army* (i., 240-3).

1890—*1st Battalion Gordon Highlanders Standing Orders* (Colombo: printed at the *Times of Ceylon* Steam Press), 1890: 8vo, pp. 36; appendix xxxii.

The preface is signed by F. H. Neish, then Adjutant (Lieutenant-Colonel, August, 1911). There is a copy in the British Museum.

1891-92—*Sociability*: the Gordons' Chronicle and Monthly Magazine of the Social and Literary Club.

The Club was founded by a few non-commissioned officers and men of the 1st Battalion, and the first issue of the magazine appeared in Colombo, July, 1890, under the editorship of Lance-Corporal A. Dobie, who was succeeded during 1891 by Corporal D. B. Thomson. The magazine, to which the sub-title " The Gordons' Chronicle " was added in January, 1891, was continued till June, 1892, when it was succeeded by *The Tiger and Sphinx*. There is a copy in the British Museum for April—December, 1891, inclusive.

1892-98—*The Tiger and Sphinx*: Gordon Highlanders' Chronicle. 4to.

This magazine was a continuation of *Sociability*, and continued to be edited by Corporal Thomson. It was recognized as the regimental paper, and was taken over in June, 1893, by Lieutenant F. H. Neish. The last number appeared in September, 1898. Nos. 5 and 6 are in the British Museum.

1898—*The Campaign in Tirah, 1897-1898*: an account of the expedition against the Orakzais and Afridis under General Sir William Lockhart, G.C.B., based (by permission) on letters contributed to the *Times* by Colonel H[enry] D[oveton] Hutchinson. (London: Macmillan) 8vo, pp. xv., 250; seven maps and plans, and 21 illustrations.

This is the best book on the campaign, in which the 1st Battalion formed part of the 2nd Division, 3rd Brigade, and in which they distinguished themselves at Dargai, October 20, 1897. The charge filled the newspapers for weeks, and was the direct cause of J M Bulloch's taking up the history of the Regiment (*Illustrated London News,* October 30, 1897) and of James Milne's writing his little monograph Other books were written on the campaign, notably by L J Shadwell, R G. Thomsett and A. C. Yate, - all officers The books on the campaign are given in Francis Edwards' *Naval and Military Catalogue,* 1907-1908 (pp 454-5), a unique bibliography which ought to be consulted by students desirous of following up any particular campaign in which the Gordons have been engaged. Colonel Hutchinson, who was Director of Staff Duties at the War Office, 1904-8, had previously translated into native languages several of the drill manuals of Lieutenant William Gordon (1840-93) of the Scots Guards and afterwards of the Gordon Highlanders

1898—*The Ladder of Life or Gordons to the Front* A Military Domestic Drama in four acts, by Charles Rogers and William Boyne · produced at the Borough Theatre, Stratford, E , May 30, 1898

This play, which never was produced in London, deals with Dargai

1898—*Our British Empire. or the Gordon Highlanders* A Romantic Military Drama in five acts, by C A Aldin produced at the Royal Muncaster Theatre, Bootle, August 1, 1898

This play deals with Dargai, and Piper Findlater figures in it

1899—*A Greeting to the Gordon Highlanders from the Gordons of Haddo House,* September 30-October 2, 1899. (Aberdeen . printed for Walker & Company, by the *Journal*) 4to, pp 38 and a cover

This prettily produced pamphlet was issued (at the expense of Lord Aberdeen) in connection with the 1st Gordons' march through Aberdeenshire on their return to Scotland after a long absence, and to mark their first visit to the Territorial district with which they had become associated in 1881 Two hundred strong, they left Edinburgh under the command of Lieutenant-Colonel Downman (killed at Magersfontein, December 11, 1899), on September 11, 1899, and visited Stonehaven, Banchory, Aboyne, Ballater (where colours were presented by the Prince of Wales, September 18), Tarland, Newe, Kildrummy, Breda, Monymusk, Inverurie, Fyvie, Hatton, Brucklay, Haddo House, Parkhill, Aberdeen (reached October 3), and thence by train back to Edinburgh It opens with a welcome by Lord Aberdeen, contains historical notes by D L Presslie, then editor of the *Journal* , and has charming coloured pictures of the new colours presented, the Queen's and regimental colours of the 2nd Battalion (92nd) now in the Aberdeen Town Hall, and the existing colours of the 92nd (on the cover), together with 22 pictures, mostly from photographs, in black and white. Pictures of the colours and the presentation ceremony appeared in the *Graphic*, September 23, 1899, from photographs by W. J. Johnston, Banchory, and R. Milne, Aboyne. Another picture of the old and the new colours, from a photograph by Maclure, Macdonald & Company of Glasgow, appeared in *Black and White*, October 30, 1899.

1903—Lieutenant-Colonel Charles Greenhill Gardyne's *Life of a Regiment* (ii., 222-288).

Curiously enough, the 75th has had no monograph devoted to it, this being by far the most complete account of the regiment.

1914—*A Captain of the Gordons*: Service experiences, 1900-1909. Edited by his mother, Mrs. Margaret Miller (Garrett Mill), and his sister, Helen Russell Miller. (London: Sampson Low, Marston & Company), 1914: 8vo, pp. 315.

This is an affectionately written life of David Skinner Miller (1874-1909), who joined the 1st Gordons as 2nd Lieutenant, March 24, 1900. Most of it consists of his letters home from South Africa, 1900-1902 (pp. 37-133); from Somaliland (1903-4), where he commanded the Somali Mounted Infantry (pp. 153-215); and from India, where he was with his regiment, 1904-1906 (pp. 233-245). He was ultimately appointed Adjutant to the 4th Battalion Gordon Highlanders. There are 16 illustrations, including a Maull and Fox's photographic portrait of Captain Miller in full uniform, and 13 maps.

2ND BATTALION, THE OLD 92ND (raised 1794: linked 1881).

1794-1876—Pay and Muster Rolls (P.R.O.: *W.O.* 12: 9,320-9,392).

1794—Description Book, No. 1 (Castlehill Barracks, Aberdeen).

1794-1850—Description and Succession of Officers (Castlehill).

1794-1806—Services of (453) discharged men (P.R.O.: *W.O.* 25: 1,130).

1794-1865—Monthly Returns (P.R.O.: *W.O.* 17: 213-784).

1798-1817—Muster Master-General's Roll (P.R.O.: *W.O.* 25: 1,331).

1803-1845—Records of Officers' Services (Castlehill Barracks).

1803-1838—   „   „   „   „

1806—Men liable to be sent abroad (P.R.O.: *W.O.* 25: 1,056, 1,057).

1806-1820—Records of Non-Coms. and Officers (Castlehill Barracks).

1809-1817—Casualties, 1st Battalion (P.R.O.: *W.O.* 25: 2,119).

1809-1814—Casualties, 2nd Battn. (P.R.O.: *W.O.* 25: 2,124).

1809-1817—Casualties, indexes (P.R.O.: *W.O.* 25: 2,665, 2,666, 2,882).

1813—Services at St Sebastian and Vittoria (War Office Records)
1817— Casualties, 1st Battalion (P R O *W O* 25 2,120)
1817-1823— „ 1st Battalion (P R O : *W O* 25 2,121)
1818-1827—Description and Succession Book (P R O *W O* 25 529)
1818-1843— „ „ „ (P R O : *W O* 25.530)
1823-1830—Casualties, 1st Battalion (P R O . *W O* 25 : 2,122)
1825-1828— „ Depot (P R O : *W O* 25· 2,125)
1830— „ 1st Battalion (P R O : *W O* 25 2,123)
1826-1842—Description and Succession Book (P R O . *W O* 25 531)
1827-1832— „ „ „ (P R O *W O* 25 532)
1828-1873—Records of Officers' Services (Castlehill Barracks)
1823-1852— „ „ ' „ „
1829— „ „ „ (P R O *W O* 25 803)
1839-1854— „ „ „ (Castlehill Barracks)
1855-1880— „ „ „ „
1857—Indian Mutiny Services (Records at the War Office)
1870—Records of Officers' Services (P R O . *W O* 25 839)
1872— „ „ „ (P R O *W O* 25 867)

1819—*Letters from Portugal, Spain and France* during the memorable campaigns of 1811, 1812, and 1813 , and from Belgium and France in the year 1815 By A British Officer (London printed and sold by T and G Underwood) 1819 8vo, pp 307

This book is believed to have been written by James Hope (probably the one who became an Ensign in the 92nd in November, 1809), who is identified (erroneously, I am given to understand) by Colonel Greenhill Gardyne (*Life of a Regiment*, 1, 210) as nephew of Sir John Hope The author sailed from Monkstown August 31, 1811, and left Passages, December 11, 1813 The book is for the most part very ' vague, but it contains some interesting personal touches in reference to the men of the regiment at Maya (pp 178-184) and Waterloo (pp 240-279), where the writer was wounded in the groin by a musket ball The *Letters from Portugal* was rewritten in narrative form in the anonymous *Military Memoirs of an Infantry Officer*, 1809-1816, published for the author in 1833 (*q v*) Some of the best stories from the two books were reprinted by J M Bulloch in the *Aberdeen Herald and Weekly Free Press*, April 4, 11, 18, 1914

1822—*Sketches of the Character, Manners, and Present State of the Highlanders of Scotland*, with details of the military service of

E3

the Highland regiments; by Colonel David Stewart. (Edinburgh: Archibald Constable & Company): 8vo, 2 vols.

David Stewart of Garth (1772-1829) gave the earliest history of the 92nd (ii., 218-241). In the appendix there is a return of the killed and wounded of the 92nd from 1794 to 1815 (ii., appendix pp. lxxix.), and a list of officers from 1794 to 1820 (ii., appendix pp. lxxii.-lxxiii.). Stewart does not mention the kiss. He also deals with the 89th (ii., 36-40); the Northern Fencibles of 1778 (ii., 305); the Northern Fencibles of 1793 (ii., 323-4), and the 81st (ii., 138-140). All these references are to the second edition.

1833—*The Military Memoirs of an Infantry Officer, 1809-1816.* (Edinburgh: printed for the author by Anderson and Bryce): 8vo, pp. vi., 472. [By James Hope.]

This book, which is not in the British Museum, is simply *The Letters from Portugal*, 1819 (*q.v.*), rewritten in narrative form, some of the incidents being repeated verbatim. It begins, however, with the Walcheren campaign of 1809 (pp. 1-46), and describes the regiment's sojourn in Ireland (48-65, 379). The Peninsular campaign covers the same ground as in the *Letters from Portugal* (pp. 66-377). The rest of the book is devoted to Quatre Bras, Waterloo, and the review which followed. The preface, dated Perth, March 20, 1833, says "it pretends to no eminence as a literary composition; but the Author trusts that it will not be found wanting in accuracy of detail as to facts falling under his notice."

1835-38—*A History of the Highlands and of the Highland Clans*: by James Browne, advocate (Glasgow: A. Fullarton); 4 vols., 8vo.

The 92nd is described at iv., 354-363. A second edition appeared in 1845, the references being the same. Browne's daughter married James Grant, who in *The Romance of War* made the 92nd famous to novel readers.

1842—*The Journal of Sergeant D. Robertson, late 92d Foot*: comprising the different campaigns, between the years 1797 and 1818, in Egypt, Walcheren, Denmark, Sweden, Portugal, Spain, France and Belgium. (Perth: printed by J. Fisher, and sold by J. Dewar and other booksellers) 1842; 8vo., pp. vii., 184.

Duncan Robertson, a native of Dunkeld, entered a company of Volunteers raised by the Duke of Atholl in 1797; then joined the Caithness Fencibles, and went to Ireland; and in 1800 volunteered into the 92nd. He left the Gordons in 1818, "owing to a disappointment" in his promotion and an increase in his family; he returned to Dunkeld, from which he dated his preface, September, 1842. His reminiscences, containing 52,400 words, were edited by the minister of Dunkeld, who did not quite understand the task, so that there are several mistakes, notably the statement that "the Duke of Wellington" gave the famous Waterloo Ball Certain sections of the book were reprinted (apparently from a copy which has been in the possession of Lieutenant-Colonel Greenhill Gardyne for sixty years), in *With Napoleon at Waterloo*, 1911

1846—*The Romance of War*, or the Highlanders in Spain By James Grant, Esq, late 62nd Regiment (London. Henry Colburn) 1846 8vo, 3 vols

1847—*The Romance of War*, or the Highlanders in France and Belgium By James Grant, Esq, late 62nd Regiment (London Henry Colburn) 1847 8vo, one vol

These complementary novels were the first, and remain the best, treatment of the Gordons in fiction, and have done much to popularise the regiment James Grant (1822-87) was the grandson of James Grant, advocate (1743-1835), the last of the Grants of Corrimony, and the son of John Grant (1790-1861), who joined the Gordons as an Ensign in 1809 James Grant wrote no fewer than 56 novels, of which the *The Romance of War* is the best The story is the biography of Ronald Stuart, who joined the Gordons as an Ensign, and the love interest is brought in in the person of Alice Lisle, daughter of Sir Allan Lisle of Inchavon, whom he marries

The two novels have often been published in one volume, the interesting prefaces being omitted and the second volume beginning at chapter 45 without a break Curiously, however, the title of the first novel alone is given A bibliographical account of the novel was given by J M Bulloch in the *Aberdeen Free Press*, April 10, 1914

1851—*Historical Record of The Ninety-Second Regiment, originally termed "The Gordon Highlanders," and numbered The Hundredth Regiment* containing an account of the regiment in 1794, and of its subsequent services to 1850 Compiled by Richard Cannon, Esq, Adjutant-General's Office, Horse Guards Illustrated with plates. London Parker, Furnivall, and Parker, 30 Charing Cross 1851 8vo, pp xliii, 150

This, the earliest history of the regiment, was issued in accordance with the Horse Guards' Order of January 1, 1836, "with the view of doing the fullest justice to Regiments as well as to Individuals who have distinguished themselves by their Bravery in Action with the Enemy" Between 1836 and 1853, Cannon (1779-1865) dealt with 26 Cavalry and 42 Infantry regiments His annotated set with extra illustrations was sold at Hodgson's, Chancery Lane, London, March 29, 1906, by order of the executor of his daughter, Miss Sophia Cannon. His *Record* of the 92nd, which does not give the kiss story, contains four coloured plates.

1858—*Memorial of Colonel John Cameron, Fassifern, K.T.S.*, Lieutenant-Colonel of the Gordon Highlanders, or 92nd Regiment. By the Rev. Archibald Clerk, minister of Kilmallie. Printed for Sir Duncan Cameron, bart., of Fassifern. (Glasgow: printed by Thomas Murray and Son.)

John Cameron (1771-1815) was killed at Quatre Bras. This book deals with the Gordon Highlanders (pp. 20-92, 107-8, 109-110), and is notable as the first book in which the kiss story appeared. The first edition appeared in January, 1858. A second edition with slight alterations (the only one in the British Museum) was published in August, 1858. It contains a portrait of Cameron and a picture of his tombstone at Kilmallie. Both the first editions were issued privately. A third edition was publicly published in 1859. A fourth was ready for publication, and was the first by which the author was to benefit; but it was destroyed by fire when the premises of Thomas Murray were burned down. (Information from the author's daughter, Miss M. Macleod Clerk, Aros, Row, Dumbartonshire).

1862—*An Account of the Scottish Regiments*: with the statistics of each from 1808 to March, 1861; compiled from the old regimental record books and monthly returns of each regiment, now rendered to the War Department [by P. H. MacKerlie]. (Edinburgh: William P. Nimmo): 8vo (p. 16).

1862—*History of the Scottish Regiments in the British Army.* By Archibald K. Murray. (Glasgow: Thomas Murray and Son): 4to.

The author of this book was a Major in the 97th Lanarkshire Volunteer Guards, and the book was published "by request of his brother officers." The 92nd is dealt with at pp. 394-408.

1875—*A History of the Scottish Highlands, Highland Clans, and Highland Regiments*: with an account of the Gaelic language, literature and music. By the Rev. Thomas Maclauchlan, LL.D.: and an essay on Highland scenery by the late Professor John Wilson: edited by John S[cott] Keltie, F. S. A. Scot. (Edinburgh: A. Fullarton and Co.): 2 vols: 8vo.

The work is illustrated with a series of portraits, views, maps, and clan tartans, and upwards of 200 wood cuts, including armorial bearings The 92nd is dealt with in vol 11, 756-66

1888—*Her Majesty's Army* a descriptive account of the various regiments now composing the Queen's Forces, from their first establishment to the present time by Walter Richards, with coloured illustrations by G D Giles (London J S Virtue) · 4to [1888-91]

This work is in two volumes, while a third is entitled *Her Majesty's Army Indian and Colonial Forces* The 92nd is described in vol 1, 243-248 The story of the kiss is recounted

1891—*The Majuba Disaster* · a story of Highland Heroism, told by the officers of the 92nd Regiment Edited by James Cromb (Dundee John Leng and Co) 1891 · 8vo, pp 44

" The desire that their honour and the honour of their corps should be vindicated induced officers of the 92nd Highlanders who were present [at Majuba Hill] to prepare some time ago [the preface is dated January, 1891] the statements from which the details of this pamphlet are now drawn . The 92nd were more strongly represented than any of the other corps engaged" A " freehand sketch " of Majuba Hill by Captain MacBean, and a sketch of the top of Majuba by Major F Fraser, are reproduced in facsimile The pamphlet is bound in a coloured cover, showing an officer in full dress on the battlefield, surveying the dead (who are also in full dress) A second edition, *The Story of Majuba Hill* (pp 59), of smaller shape, was issued by Bryce of Glasgow in 1899

1894—*The Valour Story of a Century Battle History of the Gordon Highlanders* By James Cromb (Edinburgh and Glasgow John Menzies and Co), 1894 · 8vo, 68 , in paper cover

" This pamphlet does not profess to be a complete history of the Gordon Highlanders It simply aims at bringing into collected form a battle story, which after 1850 is to be found only in many different works " It closes with an account of the Centenary Celebrations The author (1847-1901) wrote *The Highland Brigade, The Highlands and Highlanders of Scotland,* and other popular histories His son, David L Cromb, edited an edition of *The Highland Brigade* in 1902 (for Eneas Mackay, Stirling), dedicating it to Sir Hector Macdonald, whose portrait, after Mortimer Menpes, forms the frontispiece Chapter 27 deals with the Gordons at Majuba , chapter 33, at Dargai , chapter 34, at Elandslaagte , and chapter 36, at Ladysmith

1895—*The Gordon Highlanders* printed for Her Majesty's Stationery Office, by Harrison and Sons , price one penny 8vo, pp 12

This forms the 59th part of *Short Histories of the Territorial Regiments of the British Army*, "including the names of officers and soldiers who have won the Victoria Cross or the Distinguished Service Medal; edited by R[obert] de M[ontjoie] Rudolf, I.S.O., of the War Office." The series was issued "in order to interest the population" in their territorial corps. The collected series (726 pp.) appeared in 1905. The kiss story does not appear in this history.

1895—*One of the Best*: a play in four acts by Seymour Hicks and George Edwardes.

This melodrama, produced at the Adelphi Theatre, London, December 21, 1895, showed Captain Dudley Keppel of the Gordons (Mr. William Terriss) accused and degraded like Dreyfus. It was illustrated in the *Sketch* (xii., 525), and is described in William Archer's *Theatrical World of 1895* (pp. 378-382).

1897—*Forty-One Years in India*: from Subaltern to Commander-in-Chief. By Field-Marshal Lord Roberts of Kandahar. (London: Richard Bentley and Son): 2 vols.: 8vo, pp. 511, 522.

This contains the most authoritative account (pp. 342-370) of the work of the Gordons in the famous march from Kabul to Kandahar, August 9-31, 1880. (For other books on the Afghan War, 1879-1880, see Edwards' Naval and Military Catalogue, pp. 450-2).

1897—*The Gordon Highlanders and their Doughty Deeds.*

An article by J. M. Bulloch in the *Illustrated London News*, October 30, 1897, illustrated by W. B. Wollen, R.I. A list of all the versions of what Colonel Mathias said to the Gordons at Dargai appeared in the same journal, December 15, 1897.

1897—*Scotland for Ever! or the Adventures of Alexander McDonnell* by Lieutenant-Colonel Percy Groves, Royal Guernsey Artillery (late 27th Inniskillings); with six illustrations by Harry Payne. (London: George Routledge and Sons.)

This novel, afterwards re-issued under the title *The Gallant Gordons: or "Scotland for Ever"* (8vo, pp. 373), is the autobiography of Alexander Fraser McDonnell, born February 13, 1780, son of Captain Malcolm McDonnell, late of the Black Watch, and his wife, a daughter of Major Alexander Fraser, who had also been in the Black Watch. He got a commission in the Gordon Highlanders, joining the regiment at Blessington, near Dublin, August 12, 1798. His experiences with the Gordons, which included Waterloo, are described in detail (pp. 297-372) and a little history of the regiment is given (pp. 302-305), the kiss story being set forth   McDonnell retired in 1816, and his eldest son joined the regiment before 1821   Payne's illustrations include one of the Gordons at the battle of Alexandria, 1801, and the charge of the Gordons and Greys at Waterloo, which forms the frontispiece

1898—*The Gordon Highlanders   Being the Story of these Bonnie Fighters* told by James Milne   (London · John Macqueen, 1898) 8vo, pp 110

This book was issued in connection with the Gordons' fight at Dargai, and contains eighteen illustrations   Five thousand copies were printed, but it is now rare   The author, a native of Strathdon, is literary editor of the *Daily Chronicle*   He founded the *Book Monthly* in 1903, and still edits it

1898—"*The Gallant Gordons*" · by W B Robertson

An account of the Dargai episode in *Perils and Patriotism* (pp 44-56), published by Cassell in 1898

1898—*A Runaway Girl* · a musical play in two acts, by Seymour Hicks and Harry Nicholls · music by Ivan Caryll and Lionel Monckton lyrics by Aubrey Hopwood and Harry Greenbank

This musical play was produced at the Gaiety, May 21, 1898   Miss Margaret Fraser appeared in it as a Gordon Highlander officer, and reproductions of photographs of her in the uniform were published in the *Sketch* (xxvi, 70, 71)

1898—*Stories of the Gordon Highlanders*   By Charles Lowe

This article, which was suggested by the Dargai affair, appeared in *McClure's Magazine*, New York, April, 1898 (vol x, pp 485-97)   It contains nine illustrations   The author, a Forfarshire man and a graduate of Edinburgh, was for several years *Times* correspondent at Berlin

1900—*General Hector A[rchibald] Macdonald*, C B, D S O, A D C to the Queen, LL D (Glasgow), a biographical sketch by David Campbell [teacher] (London Hood, Douglas, and Howard) 8vo, pp 144. Contains three portraits, including one of Macdonald as an Inverness draper's assistant, and one as Lieutenant in the Gordons in full uniform

1900—*Hector Macdonald*, or the Private who became a General a Highland Laddie's Life and Laurels By Thomas F G Coates (London S W Partridge and Co) 8vo, pp 160 With a portrait

1900—*Hector Macdonald* the story of his life By David L Cromb (Stirling Eneas Mackay) 8vo, pp 158 Contains nine illustrations, including Macdonald's birthplace, and one of him as a Lieutenant in full Gordon uniform. An appendix (pp. 121-158) reprints a number of tributes and poems.

Hector Macdonald was born in 1853, 'listed in the 92nd, August 1870, and became 2nd Lieutenant in the regiment, January 7, 1880; he died by his own hand in Paris, March 24, 1903. The event was the subject of an enormous amount of newspaper comment. Besides the monographs, there is a biography of him by Colonel H. M. Vibart in the Dictionary of National Biography, 2nd supplement; a sketch by Mark Lovell in the Soldiers of the Queen Library, 1900 (pp. 16); and a four page sketch (copy in British Museum) by Wallace Thom (1903).

1900—*Sir George [Stewart] White, V.C.*, the hero of Ladysmith. By Thomas F. G. Coates. (Grant Richards): 8vo, pp. xiv., 290.

Sir George (1835-1912) began his career in the 27th, joined the Gordons August 4, 1863, and was put on half pay, February, 1885, becoming their Colonel, June 28, 1897. His career in the regiment is dealt with by Mr. Coates, pp. 44-109, and his share in the Tirah campaign, pp. 186-204. There are seven pictures, including one of his only son (in full regimentals), James Robert White, D.S.O., who joined the regiment, January 25, 1899, and resigned his commission, 1909.

1900—*Famous British Regiments.* By Major Arthur Griffiths. (London: T. Fisher Unwin): 1900: 8vo.

The 92nd is treated briefly at pp. 118-126. The author (1838-1908), who was an inspector of prisons, was a voluminous author of detective stories (*D.N.B.*, 2nd suppl.).

1900—*A Souvenir of Sympathy*: compiled by H[elen] S[impson], Banff. (Aberdeen: printed at the *Aberdeen Journal* office): 8vo, pp. 199.

This volume, edited by Mrs. Helen Coutts Simpson (1857-1910), St. Helen's, Banff, and issued in connection with the South African War, is an olla-podrida containing several items of interest in connection with the Gordons—a sketch of General Sir Hector Macdonald (pp. 15-27); a gossip about Jane Maxwell, Duchess of Gordon, by J. M. Bulloch (pp. 56-64), reprinted from the *English Illustrated Magazine* of June 1897; and an account of her recruiting in the Old Square at Elgin (p. 168); "The Gordon Plaid," by Charles Murray, reprinted from *Hamewith*; the music of the "Cock of the North"; and "Gordons to the Front," verses by Robert Reid (pp. 70-71). There are 37 illustrations.

1900—*How We Escaped from Pretoria* By Captain [James] Aylmer [Lowthrop] Haldane, D S O Edinburgh William Blackwood and Son) 8vo, pp 126

Captain Haldane, who is the first cousin of Lord Haldane, the creator of the Territorial Force, joined the Gordons on September 9, 1882, becoming Major in 1902, and Major-General, 1914 This volume, which is a reprint from *Blackwood's Magazine*, contains three illustrations, one showing Captain Haldane in Gordon uniform

1901—*The Regimental Records of the British Army* By John S Farmer (London Grant Richards) 1901

A useful and succinct account of the Gordons, both 1st and 2nd Battalions, appears on pp 196-197

1901-1903—*The Life of a Regiment the History of the Gordon Highlanders* By Lieutenant-Colonel C[harles] Greenhill Gardyne (Edinburgh David Douglas) 8vo

This is the completest book about the regiment The first volume, issued in 1901 (pp xxi, 525), deals with the regiment from its formation in 1794 to 1816 It contains 29 illustrations (6 in colour) and 11 maps The second volume (pp xxvii, 415) treats the period 1816-1898, and includes an account of the 75th Regiment from 1787 to 1881, when it became the 1st Battalion of the Gordons It contains 33 illustrations (2 in colour) and 9 maps The author (born 1831) is the son of David Greenhill, H E I C.S, who assumed the additional name of Gardyne in 1864, and he is laird of Finavon, Forfarshire, and Glenforsa, Isle of Mull He joined the Gordons in January, 1851, and transferred to the Coldstream Guards in July, 1855. His son and heir, Alan David, joined the Gordons in 1888 A third volume is in contemplation

1902—*The Highland Brigade* its Battles and its Heroes By James Cromb edited and brought down to the Boer War by David L Cromb (Stirling Eneas Mackay) 1902 8vo, pp 413

This volume, dedicated to Sir Hector Macdonald, devotes the following chapters to the Gordons—27 (Majuba), 33 (Dargai), 34 (Elandslaagte), and 36 (Ladysmith) A complete list of Gordons mentioned in the despatches is given in the appendix

1902—*The Gordons as Campaigners in Africa*

This forms a part (pp 75-84) of *The Gordon Book*, edited by J M Bulloch for the Fochabers Reading Room Bazaar It deals not only with the regiment in South Africa, but with every officer of the name

F3

of Gordon who fought there, this part forming the genesis of the idea
of *Gordons under Arms*, issued by the New Spalding Club, 1912. A
table by J. M. Bulloch, " How the Gordons have suffered," showing every
officer wounded or killed in the South African War, appeared in the
Sphere, August 18, 1900.

1902—"*The Gay Gordons*": *Exploits in Warfare*: Indian and
South African Campaigns.   By Charles Gordon.

This is the title of a series of articles which appeared in the Aberdeen edition of the *People's Journal* from May 3 to September 16, 1902.
The original manuscript, of which copies exist, was much more complete,
being curtailed in the *Journal* because the war had lost immediate
interest.   The author was born in Aberdeen in 1872, though his
father was a Buchan man.   After doing farm work in Buchan, he enlisted
in the 2nd Gordons in 1890.   On leaving the Army he entered the
Edinburgh Post Office.   He settled in Rhodesia in 1903, and now resides
there at Philiphaugh, Makwiro.

1903—*The Gordon Highlanders.*   (No imprint).   N.D: 4¾ in. by
3¾ in.: pp. 12.

This was an official recruiting pamphlet issued in March, 1903.   Part
one tells, in 260 words, the history of the 1st and 2nd Battalions, repeating the kiss story.   The second part gives the conditions of service.
A process block of a private appears on the (green) cover.   A second
edition, 6½ in. by 4¼ in., was issued October, 1913, still repeating the
kiss story, and noting Lieutenant-Colonel Greenhill Gardyne's history
of the regiment.   The cover contains a small reproduction of Skeoch
Cumming's picture of the Duchess of Gordon on horseback recruiting
the men.   It was printed by Gale and Polden, Aldershot, who largely
owe their early success in business to William Gordon (1840-93),
Quartermaster of the Gordons, who compiled a large number of drill
manuals for the firm.

1903-1910—*Materials from Divers Sources for a History of the
Gordon Highlanders of All Battalions*: collected by John Malcolm
Bulloch, and presented by him to the University of Aberdeen.   London,
1903-1910: 4 vols.

This collection (9½ in. by 7½ in.), begun in 1897 with the Dargai
episode, is a series of four scrapbooks with a type title page to each
(printed by Eyre and Spottiswoode).   It contains a mass of newspaper
cuttings and illustrations from many sources bearing on every aspect
of the Gordons, pasted in just as they appeared.   It is not indexed.

1905—*The Gay Gordons* The story of the 2nd Battalion, Gordon Highlanders By Wolmer Whyte (London. John Dicks) N D 8½ in by 4¾ in : pp 46 Price 1d

This was the first and last of a series of popular histories of "Famous Regiments", the author wrote under a pseudonym It repeats the kiss story It has a (yellow) pictorial cover

1907—*The Gay Gordons* a play with music Book by Seymour Hicks, lyrics by Arthur Wimperis, C H Bovill, P G Wodehouse, and Henry Hamilton, music by Guy Jones, A Sablon, Frank E Tours, and Walter Davidson

This two act musical comedy was "presented" at the Aldwych Theatre, Aldwych, London, on September 11, 1907, being "produced" by Mr Seymour Hicks (whose father had been an officer in the Black Watch) Mr Hicks played the part of Private Angus Graeme of the Gordons, who turns out to be an earl, and marries an American millionaire's daughter (Miss Ellaline Terriss), who is masquerading in a Punch and Judy troupe Curiously enough, two ladies in the cast subsequently married into the peerage, notably Miss Sylvia Storey, now Countess Poulett, and Miss Zena Dare, who married the Hon Maurice Brett, of the 6th Battalion Black Watch Mr Cecil Kinnaird, who was also in the cast, was formerly an officer in the 3rd Gordons, and then the 6th Dragoon Guards The music was published by Ascherberg, Hopwood and Crew, and the play was illustrated in *The Play Pictorial*, Vol 10, No 63, pp 137-164 It ran 229 times at the Aldwych, until April 11, 1908, and was played extensively on tour

1907—*Muster Roll of the Gordon Highlanders* transcript of the muster roll "for 183 days, from June 25, 1794, to December 24, 1794," as preserved at the Public Record Office, and copied by Mrs C O Skelton, co-author of *Gordons under Arms*, appeared in *Bon-Accord*, December 19, 1907 The muster rolls at the P R O (beginning *W O* 12 9,320) are missing for the years 1796 and 1797

1908—*The Gay Gordons* some strange adventures of a famous Scots family By John Malcolm Bulloch (London Chapman and Hall) 8vo, pp xi, 295

This was the first book to doubt the "story of a kiss" by the Duchess, which forms the fifteenth chapter (pp 196-206) Another chapter, "The last of his line" (pp 253-267), deals with the first Colonel of the regiment, George, 5th Duke of Gordon

1908—*The Fighting Chance*: four act melodrama. By Edward Ferris and B. P. Matthews.

The play, which deals with the Gordons in the Shundar Pass, and which included Mr. Cecil Kinnaird, a former officer of the 3rd Gordons, as Captain Fraser, was produced at the Lyceum, March 5, 1910, and ran till April 27, totalling 62 performances. It had previously been produced at Wolverhampton, September 21, 1908, as *The Cheat*, but was largely rewritten. It was elaborately illustrated in the *Sketch*, 1910. Mr. Ferris, who was an actor, has since died.

1909—*Gordon Highlanders Old Comrades (London) Association.*

A photographic view (5¼ in. by 10 in.) of this organisation's first dinner held at Masons' Hall Tavern, October 20, 1909, appeared in the *Daily Graphic*, October 22.

1910—*Scotland's Life and Work.*

The section devoted to " Scottish Regiments in the British Army " devotes pp. 615-618 (vol. ii.) to both battalions of the Gordons.

1911—*With Napoleon at Waterloo*: and other unpublished documents of the Waterloo and Peninsular campaigns; also papers on Waterloo by the late Edward Bruce Low, M.A. Edited by MacKenzie MacBride. (London: Francis Griffiths): 1911: 8vo, pp. xi., 249.

This poorly edited compilation contains (1) " With Abercrombie and Moore in Egypt " (pp. 9-68), from the unpublished diary of Sergeant Daniel Nicol, a native of Crossford, Lanark, who 'listed in the Gordons, March 12, 1794 (at Edinburgh, joining at Aberdeen), and was in the employ of Robert Cadell, Scott's publisher from 1819 to 1849, when he died : (2) " The retreat to Corunna " (pp. 71-85), from *The Journal of Sergeant D. Robertson*, 1842 (*q.v. supra*), namely pp. 50-69, with certain omissions : (3) " The Gordon Highlanders in Spain," notably the passage of the Douro and Talavera, from the diary of Nicol (pp. 86-119); (4) " How the British stormed Aray [sic] del Molinos " (pp. 115-119), being pp. 73-80 of Robertson's *Journal*: (5) " What the Gordons did at Waterloo " (pp. 151-166) being pp. 140-162 of Robertson's *Journal* with a few paragraphs omitted: (6) " A British Prisoner in France " (pp. 205-244) from the diary of Nicol, who was captured at Talavera, July, 1809, and not released till May, 1814. There are six articles on Waterloo, several of them by E. Bruce Low, and 32 illustrations, including a black and white reproduction of Andrew Robertson's well known portrait of the 5th Duke of Gordon in the uniform of the Black Watch.

1913—*The Gordon Family and the Regiments Raised by Them.* By J. M. Bulloch : 8vo, pp. 692.

This is an octavo volume of all the articles written by J M Bulloch on this subject It is indexed, was bound in 1913, and is in the author's possession Much of it, contributed to many newspapers, will probably never be reprinted

1913—*The Gordon Highlanders The Story of their Origin* together with a transcript of the first official muster By John Malcolm Bulloch (Banff. Banffshire Field Club) 1913 4to, pp viii, 67

This book (which was bound in Gordon tartan paper boards) forms the basis of the section of the present volume dealing with the Gordon Highlanders It contains a reproduction of M Georges Scott's coloured picture of a Gordon Highlander, and a chronological bibliography of articles on north country soldiering written for various periodicals by J M Bulloch The statistics at pp 36-39 have been corrected in the present volume (pp 229-231) Five hundred copies were issued at half-a-crown, of which 241 were bought by the 2nd Battalion of the Gordons, then stationed in Egypt The statement as to their average height (5 ft 5½ in), incorrectly calculated in the book as 5 ft 3⅔ in, led to a newspaper correspondence in the *People* by Mr Charles Lowe, July 12 and December 7; *Oban Times*, August 21 and 30 (by Mr D Murray Rose), *Scotsman*, by Lieutenant-Colonel John MacGregor, September 20, *Globe*, October 30, and *Daily Chronicle*, where the mistake was corrected by J M Bulloch, November 28, 1913

1914—*British Regiments at the Front* the story of their Battle Honours By Reginald Hodder (London Hodder and Stoughton) 8vo, pp 189

The Gordon Highlanders are one of the seventeen regiments dealt with in this " topically " produced book (pp 118-138), getting more than twice as much space as any of the others The chapter deals chiefly with their work at Waterloo and Dargai The kiss story is repeated—it is a " legend greatly treasured among Highlanders "—with the statement (p 138) that the Duchess said—" Now, lads, whose [sic] for a soldier's life—and a kiss o' the Duchess Jean? "

1914—*How Armies Fight* By " Ubique " (London. Thomas Nelson and Sons) 8vo, pp viii, 490

This remarkable book, which is written by Major Frederick Gordon Guggisberg, C.M G, of the Royal Engineers, now Surveyor-General of Southern Nigeria, was issued originally in 1903, under the title *Modern Warfare* By a prophetic touch, it describes a war between Britain and Germany, declared June 15, 1905, fought out in Belgium under the British leadership of Sir John French, and ending victoriously for Britain,

July 21. The Gordon Highlanders, who are made to play a conspicuous part in the campaign—just as they did in the real war of 1914, when they lost in the opening battle at Mons two officers killed, one wounded and 18 missing, besides 624 men missing—are specially described in the chapter on infantry (pp. 430-1), where the kiss story is repeated—and the exploit with the Greys at Waterloo is enthusiastically told. There are 53 illustrations and 16 maps in three and four colours.

1914—*Britain in Arms*: all about the Military Forces of the British Empire. By F. A. M. Webster, formerly of the 2nd (Herts) V.B. Bedfordshire Regiment and late Royal Field Artillery (T.). (London: Sidgwick and Jackson): 8vo: pp. xvi., 304.

This is a handy guide to the history and uniform of all the forces of the Crown. The Gordons are described (pp. 159-161), with the remark, " The record of the Gordons is so extensive and so brilliant that the space of this book would hardly suffice to deal with it adequately." The kiss story is not retold. The names of the (thirteen) holders of the Victoria Cross are given.

1914—*The British Army Book*. By Paul Danby and Lieutenant-Colonel and Brevet-Colonel Cyril Field, R.M.L.I. (London: Blackie and son): 8vo.: pp. 284.

This excellent book, which contains two coloured and 32 mono-chrome illustrations, contains a chapter (pp. 83-95) on " The Lads in the Kilt," which tells several good and new stories about the Gordon Highlanders.

3RD BATTALION, THE OLD ABERDEENSHIRE MILITIA, raised 1798.

1798-1876: Pay Rolls (P.R.O.: *W.O.* 13: 1-25).

1884—*The Aberdeenshire Militia and the Royal Aberdeenshire Highlanders, now the Third Battalion, the Gordon Highlanders, 1798 to 1882.* By Colonel Thomas Innes. (Aberdeen: printed at the *Aberdeen Journal* Office): 4to, pp. 38.

Colonel Innes (1814-1912) of Learney, served in the regiment, 1855-1882, and wrote this brief account of it, reprinted from the columns of the *Aberdeen Journal*, in connection with the presentation of new colours by the Prince of Wales in 1884. Colonel Innes seems to have seen no Record Office material. A list of officers with dates from 1854-1882 is given (pp. 35-38).

1884—*The Gordons' Gathering*: written for the occasion of the presentation of new colours to the 3rd Battalion, 92nd Gordon Highlanders, by H R H the Princess of Wales, on Aberdeen Links, August 28, 1884

An anonymous broadsheet (no imprint) of twelve verses (four lines each) in broad Scots, probably written by John McIntosh of 13 Union Buildings, air, "Whar the Gaudie Rins"

1884—*Song of the Royal Visit of the Prince and Princess of Wales to Aberdeen.*

A broadside of doggerel, badly printed (without an imprint) on pink paper, containing six eight-line verses and an eight-line chorus It was hawked in the streets on the drenching day of the visit, and is rare

4TH BATTALION (formerly 1st V B G H, raised 1859-60) For other aspects of Volunteering see *infra* (pp. 419-421)

1861—*Ye Nobell Cheese-Monger* an ancient ballad by Geoffrey Chaw ·Sir, jun illustrated by Hans Whole Being, ye Younger (*i e* Sir George Reid, P R S A), MDCCCLXI. second edition 4to, pp 12

This extremely rare booklet bears on the history of the City of Aberdeen Merchants Rifle Volunteers, raised as the result of a meeting of merchants, November 5, 1859 William Stevenson (died May 1, 1877) of Viewfield, a wholesale grocer, who was Captain, became rather remiss in his duties, and something like an emeute occurred among the members of the company To pacify them, Stevenson tried conciliatory measures, including a brass band James Cooper, a clerk with Thomas Baird and colour-sergeant of the company, wrote this skit of 34 four-line stanzas, and Sir George Reid, then a private in the company, illustrated it with eight illustrations The original is in the possession of J M Bulloch Sir George afterwards increased the illustrations to eleven, adding a title page, which showed the citizens pulling down the Duke of Gordon in the Castlegate and putting up "Shochlin' Will, ye Cheese-Monger," in his stead Six of these were facsimiled at Keith and Gibb's, lithographers, where Reid was then employed, and one of the copies came into the possession of John Bulloch (1837-1913), who was a member of the company, and whose copy was coloured and contained two extra drawings by Reid, never reproduced It is now in the possession of J M Bulloch One of these extra sketches shows the difficulty of fitting men with uniforms The other, entitled "Victory," shows Stevenson standing on the carcases of two dead pigs Andrew Gibb, Reid's employer, also had one of the six copies, which was bought at his sale by Lady Reid, the wife of the artist. Mr Skene of Avondow had two

copies, one of which he gave to Mr. Donald Sinclair, the historian of
the Aberdeen Volunteers. The skit is remarkable as the only published
comic-sketches by Sir George Reid. It serves to show the enormous
difference between the National Defence points of view of 1861 and
1914.

1887—*Volunteer Bazaar*, under the patronage of Her Majesty the
Queen in aid of the funds of the 1st Aberdeenshire Artillery Volunteers,
1st Aberdeen Engineer Volunteers, and the 1st Volunteer Battalion
Gordon Highlanders, in the Music Hall, Aberdeen, 21st, 22nd, 23rd, and
24th December, 1887 (no imprint): 4to.

This book contains 72 editorial pages, 20 of pictures (all lithographed), and 37 of elaborately-set advertisement. The literary matter
includes short histories of all the corps concerned (pp. 6-19), programme
of the bazaar (21-51), an account of the Caledonian Asylum, London
(53-7), and a few poems. There are 82 lithographed portraits, including
those of seven patronesses, and the rest officers. The book was produced
by John Avery.

1898—*The Wearin' o' the Green*: dedicated to Alexander Skene,
Esq., of Avondow, Captain of No. 2 Company, 1st A.R.V.; thereafter
B Company, 1st V.B.G.H.: folio: N.D.

This parody on the well known Irish song, signed "Deux," was
written by Dr. Thomas White Ogilvie, Aberdeen (1861-1908), at the
request of Mr. Donald Sinclair, the historian of the Volunteers, and was
sung at the reunion of the No. 2 Company, 1st A.R.V., afterwards B
Company, 1st V.B.G.H., December 2, 1898. It consists of eight verses
of eight lines each, and is printed in *Poems by Thomas White Ogilvie*.
(Aberdeen: William Smith and Sons): 1911.

1900—*Out on the Veldt*: the Muster Roll of the North. (*Evening
Gazette*, Aberdeen, March 21, 23, 26, 27, 28, 29, 31; April 3, 12, 16, 18;
June 18, 19, 20, 21; August 9, 10.)

These valuable lists, compiled by Henry Alexander, jun., contained
the names of 1,201 men sent out to South Africa by the northern counties
from Laurencekirk to Wick. They give some biographical details about
every man. The Aberdeenshire lists contain 526 men. Four Volunteer
service companies were sent to the war between May, 1900, and March,
1902. Their record is set forth in Donald Sinclair's *Aberdeen
Volunteers* (pp. 233-266).

1900—*Roll of Honour*. (*Evening Gazette*, Aberdeen, June 7.)

This is a list (229 names) of the 1st Service Company of the
Gordons in South Africa, which was composed of men from the 1st,

2nd and 4th V.B G H. It was afterwards printed separately on cardboard (28 inches long) The names had previously appeared in "Out on the Veldt" (*supra*)

1901—*A Record of Northern Valour.* How the Volunteers in the counties of Aberdeen, Banff and Kincardine, and the London Scottish Regiment rose in a national crisis (Aberdeen printed and published at the office of the *Aberdeen Journal*) oblong, 7⅛ in by 9⅝ in

This book, published May 14, 1901, and written by William Will, a native of Huntly (now manager of the *Graphic*), is remarkable as containing 399 portraits of the Volunteers who went to the South African War Eight groups show the 1st, 2nd, 4th, 5th and 6th V B G H, the London Scottish, the 1st A R E, and account for 275 of the portraits

.1907—Sinclair's *Aberdeen Volunteers* (pp 150-266 351-354)

1909—Grierson's *Scottish Volunteer Force* (pp 286-291)

1910—Walter Richards' *Territorial Army* (1, 28-32)

5TH BATTALION, BUCHAN AND FORMARTIN (formerly 2nd and 3rd V B G H, raised, 1860-72)

1907—2nd V B G H—Sinclair's *Aberdeen Volunteers* (pp 238, 239, 240, 243, 246-254, 262) This deals only with its services in the South African War

1909—2nd V B G H—Grierson's *Scottish Volunteer Force* (pp 291-3)

This Battalion was built up round the Tarves Company, the first to be formed, February 15, 1860, in the county out of Aberdeen It was first battalioned, 1861, to contain the companies of Ellon, New Deer and Tarves, and was consolidated, 1880, into seven companies—Methlick, Ellon, Newburgh, Turriff, Fyvie, Old Meldrum and Tarves

1894—3rd V B G H—*Records of the 3rd (The Buchan) Volunteer Battalion, Gordon Highlanders·* compiled by Captain and Hon Major James Ferguson. (Peterhead printed by David Scott) 1894 8vo, pp viii, 63, xix

The nucleus of this battalion was the New Deer Company, formed April 12, 1860·. It was first battalioned in 1862, to contain New Deer, Old Deer, Peterhead and Longside, and was consolidated, 1880, into nine companies—New Deer, Peterhead, St Fergus, Old Deer, Strichen, Longside, Fraserburgh, New Pitsligo and Cruden

G3

This volume contains brief accounts of the Peterhead and Fraserburgh Volunteer companies of 1797 (pp. 4-5); the 1859 movement, with various companies up to date (5-63). An appendix gives a full succession of officers, compiled by Captain Patrick L. Davidson, 5th V.B.G.H. The preface is dated Kinmundy, May, 1894. The writer joined the Old Deer Company as Lieutenant, August 19, 1874, became Captain, October 9, 1880, and hon. Major, September, 1889.

1907—3rd V.B.G.H.—Sinclair's *Aberdeen Volunteers* (pp. 240, 242, 355-357). This deals with the South African War and the men who attended the Edinburgh Review of 1905.

1909—3rd V.B.G.H.—Grierson's *Scottish Volunteer Force* (pp. 294-297).

1910—Walter Richards' *Territorial Army* (i., 17-19).

6TH BATTALION, BANFF AND DONSIDE (formerly 4th and 6th V.B.G.H.); raised, 1860-8.

1904—4th V.B.G.H.—"*The Lads of Don*": *Donside Gordon Highlanders, D Company*; 24th August, 1904. (Aberdeen: printed at the *Aberdeen Journal* Office): 8vo, pp. 1-75: adv. pp. 76-93.

The nucleus of the 4th V.B.G.H. was the Huntly Company, formed March 6, 1860. It was first battalioned, 1860, to contain Huntly, Alford, Cluny, Echt, Inverurie, Kildrummy, and was consolidated, 1880, into seven companies—Huntly, Kildrummy, Insch, Alford, Inverurie, Kemnay, Auchmull.

This book, edited by the Rev. Peter Adam, B.D., Acting Chaplain, was got up to defray the expense of clothing the Donside Volunteers "in the true garb of the Gordons." It contains lists of the officers, a roll of the men, and an itinerary of the 1st Service Company in South Africa, with extracts from the diaries kept by two officers. There are 16 illustrations, consisting of local residences and portraits of officers.

1907—4th V.B.G.H.—Sinclair's *Aberdeen Volunteers* (pp. 238, 240, 241, 243-4, 246-251, 254, 256-260; 262; 358-361). This deals with the South African War and the men who attended the Edinburgh Review of 1905.

1909—4th V.B.G.H.—Grierson's *Scottish Volunteer Force* (pp. 297-301).

1907—6th V.B.G.H.—Sinclair's *Aberdeen Volunteers* (pp. 238, 241, 244-6, 251-4, 255, 262, 265, 364-366). This deals with the South African War and the Edinburgh Review of 1905.

The nucleus of the 6th V B.G H was the Banff Company, raised April 18, 1860 A Banffshire Battalion was formed on August 12, 1861, and included Banff, Aberlour, Keith, Buckie, Minmore and Dufftown This battalion was consolidated, 1880, to contain Banff, Aberlour, Keith, Buckie, Glenlivet and Dufftown In 1884 it became the 6th V B G H In 1899 an Aberchirder Company was added In 1891 the battalion adopted Gordon tartan

1909—6th V B G H—Grierson's *Scottish Volunteer Force* (pp 305-307)

7TH BATTALION, DEESIDE HIGHLAND (formerly 5th V.B G H , raised, 1860-62)

1892—5th V B G H.—*Grand Volunteer Bazaar*, under the patronage of Her Majesty the Queen . in aid of the funds of the 5th (Deeside Highland) Volunteer Battalion Gordon Highlanders, in the Music Hall, Aberdeen, on the 8th, 9th and 10th December, 1892 (No imprint) 4to.

This battalion had its nucleus in the Fetteresso Company, raised January 10, 1860 (disbanded 1870) It was battalioned, 1861, with Banchory, Laurencekirk, Fettercairn, Auchinblae, Netherley and Durris , and consolidated, 1880, into ten companies, Banchory, Laurencekirk, Portlethen, Durris, Maryculter, Echt, Tarland, Aboyne, Ballater and Torphins In 1883 Torphins amalgamated with Banchory, and a new company was formed at Stonehaven In 1885 Tarland joined Aboyne

The above volume contains 19 editorial and 13 advertisement pages There are brief accounts of the battalion ; 32 portraits of officers, and ten other illustrations of local buildings—all lithographed

1892—*Statistics of the 5th (Deeside Highland) Volunteer Battalion, Gordon Highlanders*, compiled by Captain Patrick L[eslie] Davidson, 1892 (No imprint) 4to, 20 pp. in a cover Issued as an appendix to the bazaar book.

1898—*Records of the 5th (Deeside Highland) Volunteer Battalion, Gordon Highlanders*. compiled by Major Patrick Leslie Davidson . 1898 · second edition Printed by Cornwall, Aberdeen · 8vo, pp 74.

The writer of this book, who is a younger son of Patrick Davidson of Inchmarlo (1809-81), joined the Banchory Company, October 9, 1886 Tabular lists of the succession of officers are given with second edition, pp 42-73.

1907—Sinclair's *Aberdeen Volunteers* (pp 238, 240, 241, 244-6, 251-

4, 255, 256-260, 262, 264, 361-4). This deals with the South African War and the Edinburgh review of 1905.

1909—Grierson's *Scottish Volunteer Force* (pp. 301-304).

THE SHETLAND COMPANIES (formerly 7th V.B.G.H.; raised, 1900).

1907—Sinclair's *Aberdeen Volunteers* (p. 367). This deals only with the Edinburgh review of 1905.

1909—Grierson's *Scottish Volunteer Force* (pp. 307-8). These companies were raised December 19, 1900.

ABERDEENSHIRE VOLUNTEERS, 1794-1808. (Pay rolls at the Public Record Office, London. "*W.O.*" stands for War Office papers.)

1797-1802 - -	Royal Aberdeen - -	*W.O.*, 13 : 4160
1800-1802 - -	,, ,, - -	,, 4161
1803-1808 - -	1st Aberdeen - - -	,, 4162
1803-1807 - -	Aberdeen City - - -	,, 4162
1799-1802 - -	Old Aberdeen - - -	,, 4163
1803-1807 - -	Aberdeen Battalion - -	,, 4163
1798-1802 - -	Aberdeen Battery - -	,, 4163
1804-1808 - -	Aberdeen Pikemen - -	,, 4163
1803-1808 - -	Gilcomston Pikemen -	,, 4165
1804-1808 - -	Belhelvie - - - -	,, 4164
1803-1808 - -	Crimond and Lonmay -	,, 4164
1803-1808 - -	Dyce - - - - -	,, 4164
1803-1806 - -	Fraserburgh Artillery -	,, 4164
1798-1802 - -	Fraserburgh Battalion -	,, 4164
1798-1802 - -	Garioch - - - -	,, 4164
1798-1802 - -	Gartly - - - -	,, 4165
1798-1802 - -	Huntly - - - -	,, 4165
1803-1808 - -	Monquhitter - - -	,, 4165
1798-1808 - -	Oldmeldrum - - -	,, 4165
1798-1808 - -	Peterhead Artillery - - .	,, 4166
1798-1804 - -	Peterhead Infantry - -	,, 4166
1805-1808 - -	,, ,, - -	,, 4167
1799-1802 - -	Rosehearty - - -	,, 4167
1798-1808 - -	Strathbogie - - -	,, 4167
1798-1802 - -	Strathdon - - - -	,, 4167

The Aberdeen Volunteers are dealt with in the Internal Defence series of Home Office papers at the Public Record Office thus:—

Year.	Year.
1803—*H.O.* 50 : 57	1806—*H.O.* 50 : 150
1804—*H.O.* 50 : 93	1807—*H.O.* 50 : 160
1805—*H.O.* 50 : 125	1808—*H.O.* 50 : 181

The Volunteers of 1794-1808 are dealt with in Mr. Donald Sinclair's *Aberdeen Volunteers* (pp. 30-135).

The names of officers and men in the following pay rolls at the Public Record Office have been printed   Only the first roll of each series has been used   J M Bulloch has also made transcripts (so far unpublished) of all the 1797-1808 Volunteers in the town of Aberdeen —

Corps		Transcriber	Where Published	Date
Aberdeen Battery	- 1798	J M Bulloch	*Aberdeen Weekly Journal*	June 19, 1914
Aberdeen—Gilcomston	1803	„	„ „	April 17, 1914
Old Aberdeen	- - 1798	„	„ „	Nov. 6, 1914
Aberdour -	- 1803	„	*Fraserburgh Herald*	Aug 11, 1914
Belhelvie -	- - 1804	„	*Aberdeen Weekly Journal*	July 17, 1914
Crimond and Lonmay	1803	„	*Fraserburgh Herald*	Sept. 1, 1914
Drumblade	- - 1804	William Will	*Huntly Express*	May 8, 1914
Dyce, Newmachar, and Fintray	- - 1803	J. M. Bulloch	*Aberdeen Weekly Journal*	Aug 21, 1914
Fraserburgh	- 1798, 1803	„	*Fraserburgh Herald*	July 21, 1914
Garioch -	- -	„	*Aberdeen Weekly Journal*	Sept 11, 1914
Gartly	- 1798	William Will	*Huntly Express*	May 1, 1914
Huntly (Gordon's Coy)	1798	„	„ „	April 10, 1914
Huntly (Forsyth's Coy)	1798	„	„ „	April 24, 1914
Huntly (Davidson's Coy)	1804	„	„ „	May 8, 1914
Meldrum (1st Coy) -	1803	J M Bulloch	*Buchan Observer*	Oct. 27, 1914
Meldrum (2nd Coy) -	1803	„	„ „	Nov 3, 1914
Meldrum (3rd Coy) -	1803	„	„ „	Nov 10, 1914
Monquhitter	- 1803	„	*Aberdeen Weekly Journal*	Oct 9, 1914
Old Aberdeen	- - 1798	„	„ „	Nov 6, 1914
Oldmeldrum	- - 1799	„	„ „	Oct 2, 1914
Peterhead Artillery 1798, 1803		„	*Buchan Observer*	July 14, 1914
Peterhead Infantry (1st Coy) - 1798, 1803		„	„ „	July 21, 1914
Peterhead Infantry (2nd Coy) - 1798, 1803		„	„ „	July 28, 1914
Peterhead Infantry (3rd Coy) - 1798, 1803		„	„ „	Aug 4, 1914
Peterhead Independent Coy - - -		„	„ „	Aug 25, 1914
Rathen -	- - 1803	„	*Fraserburgh Herald*	Sept 1, 1914
Rosehearty-	- - 1799	„	*Buchan Observer*	June 2, 1914
Rosehearty-	- - 1804	„	*Fraserburgh Herald*	Aug 11, 1914
St Fergus and Longside -	- - 1803	„	„ „	Sept 1, 1914
Strathbogie	- 1804	William Will	*Huntly Express*	May 8, 1914
Strathdon -	- -	J M Bulloch	*Aberdeen Weekly Journal*	Sept 18, 1914
Tyrie and Strichen	- 1803	„	*Fraserburgh Herald*	Aug. 11, 1914

BANFFSHIRE VOLUNTEERS, 1798-1808. (Pay rolls at the Public Record Office)

1799-1801	-	-	1st Battalion, Banff	-	-	*WO*, 13	4185
1801-1808	-	-	1st „ „	-	-	„	4186
1798-1800	-	-	2nd „ „	-	-	„	4187
1801-1808	-	-	2nd „ „	-	-	„	4188

1798-1802	-	-	Balveny	- - - -	„	4189
1798-1802	-	-	Keith -	- - - -	„	4189
1798-1802	-	-	Newmill	- - - -	„	4189

The Banffshire Volunteers are dealt with in the Internal Defence series of Home Office papers at the Public Record Office thus:—

Year.	Year.
1803—*H.O.* 50 : 59	1806—*H.O.* 50 : 150
1804—*H.O.* 50 : 94	1807—*H.O.* 50 : 160
1805—*H.O.* 50 : 125	1808—*H.O.* 50 : 182

The following pay rolls from the Record Office have been published. J. M. Bulloch has also made transcripts (so far unpublished) of all the Volunteers in the town of Banff:—

Corps.					Transcriber.	Where Published.	Date.
Alvah -	-	-	-	1798	J. M. Bulloch	*Banffshire Herald*	Oct. 24, 1914
Balveny	-	-	-	1798	„	„ „	May 25, 1914
Banff (Loyal)	-	-	-	1803	„	*Banffshire Journal*	Nov. 3, 1914
Boyndie	-	-	-	1803	„	*Banffshire Reporter*	Nov. 4, 1914
Boyne	-	-	-	1798	„	*Banffshire Herald*	Oct. 10, 1914
Cullen	-	-	-	1800	„	*Banffshire Reporter*	Oct. 14, 1914
Cullen	-	-	-	1803	„	„ „	Oct. 21, 1914
Enzie (4 Coys.)	-			1798	„	*Banffshire Advertiser*	Oct. 29, 1914
Forglen	-	-	-	1798	„	*Banffshire Herald*	Oct. 17, 1914
Grange	-	-	1798,	1803	„	„ „	Oct. 31, 1914
Keith -	-	-	-	1798	„	„ „	May 9, 1914
Macduff	-	-	-	1799	„	*Banffshire Journal*	Oct. 27, 1914
Marnoch	-	-	-	1803	„	*Banffshire Herald*	Nov. 7, 1914
Newmill	-	-	-	1798	„	„ „	May 16, 1914
Portsoy	-	-	-	1798	„	*Banffshire Reporter*	May 20, 1914
Portsoy	-	-	-	1803	„	„ „	Oct. 28, 1914
Rothiemay -	-	-	-	1803	„	*Huntly Express*	Nov. 6, 1914

LOCAL MILITIA, 1808-16. (Pay rolls at the Public Record Office.)

1808-1816	-	-	1st Aberdeenshire	- -	*W.O.*, 13 : 3394
„ „	-	-	2nd „	- -	„ 3395
„ „	-	-	3rd „	- -	„ 3396
„ „	-	-	4th „	- -	„ 3397
„ „	-	-	5th „	- -	„ 3398
„ „	-	-	Banffshire -	- -	„ 3407

The following volumes are devoted to the subject in the Internal Defence series of Home Office papers at the Record Office:—

Year.							
1809	-	-	-	Aberdeen	- - -	*H.O.*, 50 : 208
1809	-	-	-	Banff -	- - -	„ 50 : 209
1810	-	-	-	Aberdeen and Banff	- -	„ 50 : 235
1811	-	-	-	Aberdeen	- - -	„ 50 : 255
1811	-	-	-	Banff -	- - -	„ 50 : 256
1812	-	-	-	Aberdeen and Banff	- -	„ 50 : 277
1813	-	-	-	„ „	- -	„ 50 : 292

ABERDEEN DEPOT RECRUITING PAPERS, 1798-1816 These begin with monthly, and later on give quarterly, "pay lists and muster rolls of the Staff of the Aberdeen District and of the recruiting parties belonging to regiments on foreign service, placed under the superintendence of the Inspector General of the Recruiting Service ".—

June, 1798—1810	-	-	-	-	$W O$, 12	12,055
September, 1811—March, 1812	-	-	-	„	12,056
December, 1812— December, 1814	-	-	-	„	12,057
December, 1814—March, 1816	-	-	-	„	12,058

1907—*The History of the Aberdeen Volunteers*· embracing also some account of the early Volunteers of the Counties of Aberdeen, Banff and Kincardine. By Donald Sinclair, solicitor, Aberdeen (*Aberdeen Daily Journal* Office) 1907 4to, pp xxii, 387 60 illustrations

1908—*A History of the Volunteer Forces*, from the earliest time to the year 1860 being a recital of the citizen duty By Cecil Sebag-Montefiore, Captain and Hon Major, 1st Middlesex Royal Engineers (Volunteers) (London· Archibald Constable and Company) 8vo, pp xvi, 420

This is perhaps the most popularly written account of the Volunteers and the intricate legislation relating to them The first two chapters, "The Royal Prerogative and the Citizen Duty," and "The Genesis of the Volunteers" (pp 1-60) sketch the movement in 1757-94 The third chapter (pp 61-94) deals with the Jacobite Rising of 1745-6 There are eight illustrations.

1909—*The County Lieutenancies and the Army, 1803-1814* By the Hon J W Fortescue (London· Macmillan)· 8vo, pp. xx, 328

This book is quite indispensable to every student of Territorial soldiering An "overflow" from the author's encyclopædic *History of the British Army*, which started publication in 1899 and is still unfinished in the seventh volume, it differs from all other books by dealing with all the forces controlled by the Lords Lieutenant, and contains the first, and indeed the only, summary of the Internal Defence series of papers of the Home Office (P.R O H O 50), which run into 326 bulky volumes and bundles of manuscript correspondence received by the Secretary of State from the Lords Lieutenant Mr Fortescue assures us in his preface that the book was "maddening to write," for he had to expound the subject for the first time, and he informed the present writer five years later—"I am rather astonished to think that I ever had the patience to write it." There is an admirable index

VOLUNTEERS, 1859-1908

1909—*Records of the Scottish Volunteer Force, 1859-1908* By Major-General J M Grierson (Edinburgh. William Blackwood and Sons)· 4to, pp xxvi, 372

This is the best book on the subject The author, James Moncrieff Grierson (born Glasgow, January 27, 1859), entered the Royal Artillery, October 9, 1877 The first part (pp 1-118) contains a general account of the Volunteers from 1859 to 1907, the second (pp 119-345) tells the history of every individual corps, the Aberdeenshire portion (pp 154-8, 170-1, 286-308, 344) with a chronological table (pp 346-7) being unusually full owing to the help of his "valuable friend," Major-General Sir A J F Reid, K C B (1846-1913), who, after a brilliant career in India, was Chairman of the County and City of Aberdeen Territorial Association The appendixes (pp 346-372) contain a mass of tabular material There are 47 plates containing 238 separate figures showing uniforms in colour, drawn by the author, 28 being devoted to the Aberdeenshire, Banffshire and Shetland corps A bibliography (pp xix-xx) and list of subscribers (pp. xxi-xxvi) are given General Grierson died in France with the Expeditionary Force, August, 1914

ABERDEEN AND BANFF ARTILLERY, 1859-1908 —Sinclair's *Aberdeen Volunteers* deals with the Aberdeenshire Artillery, raised 1860 (pp 267-292, 370-374) Grierson's *Scottish Volunteer Force* deals with the Aberdeenshire Corps, pp 154-8, devoting a plate showing six figures, and with the Banffshire Corps (pp 133-135) There is a plate showing three figures, including a kilted piper

ABERDEEN ENGINEERS, 1878-1903 —Sinclair's *Aberdeen Volunteers* deals with the Aberdeenshire Royal Engineers, raised 1878 (pp 293-308) Grierson's *Scottish Volunteer Force* deals with it (pp 170-1), devoting one figure to it

ABERDEENSHIRE AND BANFFSHIRE INFANTRY—See under 4th, 5th, 6th, and 7th Battalions, Gordon Highlanders

ABERDEEN AMBULANCE CORPS, 1888-1908

1891—*The Ambulance Corps Bazaar Book* Edited by John B[aptiste] Recaño (Aberdeen Lewis Smith and Son) 8vo, pp 67 (The Ambulance Corps was formed May 13, 1888)

This book, issued at a bazaar got up for the funds of the corps, contains "the story of the Medical Staff Corps" by the Rev James Smith (pp 3-32), with collotype portraits of Surgeon-Major Peter Shepherd (killed in the Zulu War), Drs Alexander Ogston, MacGregor, Mackenzie Booth, Scott Riddell, De Lessert, Rev James Smith, and a coloured picture of a Volunteer Medical Staff Corps corporal There are verses by J M Bulloch and J H. Barron. The editor a native of Gibraltar, was a medical student He is now in the showman business

1907—Sinclair's *Aberdeen Volunteers* (pp 309-315, 368-369)

1909—Grierson's *Scottish Volunteer Force* (p 344)

TERRITORIAL FORCE (formed on or after April 1, 1908)

1909—*The Territorial Year Book and Directory* (London Hodder and Stoughton) 1909 8vo, pp xiv, 294.

This volume is "a handbook for the Territorial Soldier and the Citizen, explaining the rights, duties and obligations of the members of the Territorial Force, the Organisation and Administration of the Territorial System and giving account of all the units of the Force" It appeared again in 1910, and then ceased publication

1910-1911—*His Majesty's Territorial Army* a descriptive account of the Yeomanry, Artillery, Engineers and Infantry, with the Army Service and Medical Corps, comprising the King's Imperial Army of the Second Line By Walter Richards, with illustrations by R Caton Woodville (London Virtue) [1910-11] 4 vols 4to

The 4th Battalion of the Gordons is dealt with in vol 1, 28-32, and the 5th Battalion in vol 1, 17-19 (with coloured illustrations), the 1st Highland Brigade, R F A, is described 1, 15-17, and the Engineers, 1, 17

1913—*Souvenir of Field-Marshal Earl Roberts' Visit to Aberdeen*, August, 1913 being an account of bestowal of Freedom of the City, civic luncheon and presentation of colours to 4th Battalion Gordon Highlanders (T F) (Aberdeen. *Aberdeen Daily Journal* Office)

This is a neat pamphlet of 70 pages, and 34 illustrations One of these shows Lord Roberts inspecting the guard of honour of Depot Gordon Highlanders · another shows Colonel D B D Stewart of the 4th Gordons, three show the presentation of colours to the 4th Gordons, and there are 22 portraits of veterans who accompanied Lord Roberts to Kandahar

H3

ALLIED REGIMENT, THE 48TH HIGHLANDERS OF TORONTO
(raised 1891)

1900—*The 48th Highlanders of Toronto, Canadian Militia*   The
origin and history of this regiment, and a short account of the Highland
regiments from time to time stationed in Canada   By Alexander Fraser,
M A, Secretary to the Citizens' Committee, which raised the Regiment.
(Toronto. E L. Ruddy)· 4to pp 1-96· advertisements, pp 97-128

This Regiment—allied with the Gordons, June 27, 1904, on the
application of its commanding officer—was formed at a meeting of Scots-
men held at Toronto early in 1891, being gazetted (eight companies)
October 16, 1891   The uniform was modelled on that of the Gordon
Highlanders, and manufactured at Inverness, Davidson tartan being worn
in honour of its first commander, John Irvine Davidson (born at Wartle,
1854, and brother of Professor W L Davidson, Aberdeen University),
who spent two and a half years in the 7th Aberdeenshire Volunteers
As many as 152 men were sworn in, October 22, 1891   From 152 to
350 the men came in gradually until May 27, 1892, when the first strength
of the regiment was returned   The first part of Mr Fraser's book deals
with various Highland regiments stationed in Canada, notably the Fraser
Highlanders, the old 78th (pp. 10-22), with an account of the Highland
companies raised in Canada (pp 22-6)   There is a full list of all the first
privates, with a biographical account of the officers, and 61 illustrations
The regiment visited Aldershot in September 1908, under the command of Lieutenant-Colonel Donald Murdoch Robertson, a native of
Glengarry, Ontario, who was appointed senior Captain at its initiation, and
it was quartered with the 1st Gordons. Groups of the regiment appeared
in the *Navy and Army Illustrated*, June 25, 1898, and August 23, 1902 ,
also in the *Sphere*, September 12 and 19, 1908   The documents dealing
with the alliance with the Gordons were printed in the *Aberdeen Weekly
Journal*, July 10, 1914.   The regiment also sent men to fight in the
" Great War" of 1914, reaching Plymouth in October.

The "'Kilties' Band, Gordon Highlanders of Belleville, Canada,"
is "a permanent touring organisation and has no connection with any
regiment, though practically all its members have served in Canadian
regimental bands"   "As a compliment to Scotland's 92nd Gordon
Highlanders, the uniform worn by the Kilties en-tour are [sic] duplicates
of those worn by that famous regiment"   The Band visited this country
in 1904, distributing a large quantity of pictorial advertising literature,
and it played before the King at Balmoral, October 8   It then contained
40 musicians and 16 vocalists, two pipers and five Highland dancers.
The Drum-Major, Donald MacCormack, was 7 ft high

The Gordon Highlanders, D Company, Buffalo City Guard This organisation was established in 1897, and was founded from the St Andrew's Society of Buffalo by James Braik, son of Adam Braik, Mill of Collithie, Gartly. James Braik started life as a gardener at Cobairdy House, and emigrated to America in 1869 He was appointed assistant superintendent of parks in Buffalo, 1887, was Pipe-Major to the Albany Caledonian Club of Buffalo, and died January 16, 1907 When it was organised, the men wore a white tunic and blue trousers, with a " white stripe Glengarry and feather," but in two years it adopted the Gordon tartan kilt Since then it has adopted the scarlet tunic of the Gordons, " the feeling in the States against our scarlet having passed away" The company, now 60 strong, carries rifles, being " the only private organisation in the country which has the privilege to do so" It inherited this right from the City Guard of Buffalo, under a charter from Albany The Guard resigned, leaving the Scots who had joined it in possession of the charter The Mayor has the right to call out the Gordons for his protection, though he has not had occasion to do so Andrew Gilfillan, counsellor at law, Buffalo, whose mother, born in Scotland, was a Gordon, was appointed Captain, February 23, 1908. The 1st Lieutenant at present is Mr William Donaldson, assistant superintendent of parks It was re-uniformed (in Glasgow) in the winter of 1913 " in everything pertaining to the real Gordons."

The Cape Town Highlanders (The Duke of Connaught and Strathearn's Own), who wear the Gordon tartan kilt, were formed in 1882 largely through the enthusiasm of John Scott, who had served in the Scots Guards and the 90th It began as a company of the Duke of Edinburgh's Own Rifles, but ultimately re-started as a complete regiment by itself, being accepted by the Government, April 24, 1885, uniformed in green doublets, Gordon tartan kilt, and Argyll and Sutherland hose-tops At the conclusion of the South African war it adopted in their entirety the uniform and dress regulations of the 1st Gordons, with the exception of the distinctive regimental badges, buttons, etc, and the black thread in the gold lace The regiment, which has seen a great deal of actual fighting, had Sir James Sivewright as its Colonel in 1892 It was illustrated and described in the *Graphic*, June 4, 1910

ICONOGRAPHIA OF THE GORDON HIGHLANDERS.

The illustration of regimental history has been even more inadequately done than the chronicling of it, and as those pictures which have been produced have usually been bought by non-bookish people, they are so rare that it is difficult to make a complete iconographia. Thus the British Museum has no complete copies of such splendid portfolios as Ackermann's, Spooner's, Heath's, Martens', and Reeves' series of costume plates. The best guide to the subject is the *Catalogue of Military Prints, Drawings and Books*, issued by T. H. Parker, Whitcomb Street, London, 1914, containing 3,422 items, and forming the "largest sale catalogue of military prints ever published in this or any other country." A popular pictorial guide to the subject is Mr. Ralph Nevill's *British Military Prints* (Connoisseur Publishing Company, 1909). It contains 146 reproductions (including 24 in colours) and a short bibliography by W. G. Menzies.

The following iconographia does not confine itself, like the dealers, to "old prints and to colour," for it is not merely for art collectors, but for students of history. The old prints are dear—thus £4 10s. is the current market price for L. Mansion and St. Eschauzier's charming (Spooner) coloured lithograph of an officer in the 92nd; but quite modern pictures are becoming unprocurable, usually in direct proportion to their wide distribution. Thus some of the series of coloured picture-postcards are quite out of print. Where they are taken by direct colour photography, they are much more historically accurate, if less artistic, than the old prints.

With the growth of illustrated journalism and the development of photography, an enormous number of pictures in black and white has appeared during the last twenty years, so that it has not been possible to make anything approaching a complete list, though a rough indication of sources has been given.

The arrangement of the material differs from that in the preceding bibliography, for which manuscripts and books have been marshalled in

order of their production The pictures are grouped according to subjects
—uniforms, colours, battles, under the battalions of the Gordons One
cannot help noticing that pictures of the 1st Battalion are, like books
on the subject, miserably poor In fact, the 75th had hardly any pictorial
history till its charge at Dargai The paucity of material is to be
regretted on other than sentimental grounds, for through it we cannot
tell what tartan was originally worn by the 75th Captain John MacRae
Gilstrap of Ballimore has a portrait of his grandfather, Major Colin
McRae of Conchra, in the uniform of the 75th, but the colour is faded
Lieutenant-Colonel Greenhill Gardyne says the colour "looks like
Gordon, though the stripe may be either white or yellow" It is to be
hoped that this tentative iconographia may result in the Aberdeen Art
Gallery specialising on the subject of at least colour-pictures of northern
military uniforms. The measurement given is the extreme edge of the
illustration, the height being noted first

1ST BATTALION

Uniform—1809-10—Sketch of a subaltern, 1809-10, by R Simkin
(*Life of a Regiment*, ii , 245)

1833—Sketch in colour of an officer, Grenadier Company, 10½ in
by 8¾ in, drawn by L Mansion and St Eschauzier, being plate 17 of
Spooner's "Military and Naval Uniforms Upright Series ". 60 plates,
coloured by C. H Martin and C Bowen, and printed by Lefevre 1833-40
A French reproduction of this plate (5¾ in by 4½ in), lithographed
by Destouches, Paris, was published about 1860

1840—Sketch of three (unnamed) figures by Harry Payne (*Life
of a Regiment*, ii , 279)

1857—Sketch of private, by Harry Payne (*Life of a Regiment*,
ii , 269)

1855—Five figures by R Simkin (*Life of a Regiment*, ii , facing
p 289) Since June 18, 1882, the uniform has been the same as that of
the 92nd. A photographic representation of the famous epitaph on the
change from trews to kilt, as erected in Malta, appeared in the *Aberdeen
Weekly Journal*, February 21, 1913

Colours—Colour lithograph (8½ in by 9 in) of the colours as carried
in India and now preserved in the County Buildings, Stirling (Andrew

Ross's *Old Scottish Colours*, 1885, facing p. 101). For colours retired and presented 1899, see *A Greeting to the Gordon Highlanders from the Haddo House Gordons.*

Battles—

1897—*The Charge of the Gordons at Dargai*: oil painting by R. Caton Woodville.

This picture shows Piper Findlater piping while the Gordons charge. The original is now in the keeping of Graves of Pall Mall for the owner, Mrs. Schlette. An engraving of it, 27½ in. by 18½ in., was published by Manzi, Joyeau and Company of Paris; and was reproduced in the Christmas number of the *Graphic*, coloured by Charles Abbott du Pasquier (13½ in. by 20¼ in.), 1909.

1897—*The Gordons at Dargai*: painted by Stanley Berkeley.

This engraving (16 in. by 24 in.) was published by S. Hildesheimer and Company, Ltd.

1897—*Well Done Gordons*: a symbolic drawing, reproduced in three colour process: by C. M. Sheldon.

This plate, 9 in. by 12 in., appeared as a supplement to *Black and White*, October 30, 1897, apropos of the Dargai charge. A great many illustrations of the fight appeared in the illustrated papers of the period. There is one in the *Life of a Regiment*, ii., 352.

2ND BATTALION.

Raising the 92nd—Cap worn by the Duchess of Gordon in recruiting for the Gordon Highlanders: photographed by Ewing, Aberdeen.

This photograph was reproduced in the *Illustrated London News*, October 30, 1897; the *English Illustrated Magazine*, June 1897; and the *Sphere*, May 8, 1909. The cap is in the possession of the 2nd Battalion. It was apparently used as a model by Mr. Skeoch Cumming in his picture of the Duchess recruiting.

The Duchess of Gordon raising the Gordon Highlanders: painted by W. Skeoch Cumming in 1897.

This picture shows her Grace on a white charger distributing favours to recruits. It belongs to Mr. Frank J. Usher, Edinburgh, and was reproduced in the *Sphere*, May 8, 1909 (11½ in. by 8¾ in.), and also as a cover to the official pamphlet of the Regiment, 1913. Another picture of the Duchess recruiting, drawn by William Smith, jun., appeared as a supplement in the Christmas Number of *Bon-Accord*, December 16, 1897.

Uniforms—Coloured lithograph (6¼ in. by 4¼ in); no artist's name is given, forming the frontispiece of the *Life of a Regiment* (vol 1), shows four figures, including a sergeant

1794—Private, drawn in colour by Georges Scott, Paris

This spirited picture appeared as a three colour plate (13 in by 8¼ in.) in the *Graphic* of July 29, 1911; and was reproduced as a four colour plate (7¼ in by 4⅝ in) in *Gordons under Arms*, 1912, and also in *The Gordon Highlanders* the Story of their Origin, 1913 The sporran and the feather bonnet are not quite correct The artist's grandfather was a Scotsman The original painting is in the possession of J M Bulloch, who also owns the copyright.

1813—"92 Regiment oder Gordon Highlanders" drawn in colours by R Knotel.

This picture (7 in by 3¼ in) forms one of the plates (band vi, No 60) of Knotel's *Uniformenkunde*, published by Max Babenzien in Rathenow It also shows privates of the 6th Foot and the Black Watch, and a sergeant of the 87th Foot

1815—Gordon Highlanders at Brussels coloured plate (4⅛ in by 6¼ in) by R Simkin in the *Life of a Regiment* (facing p 423, vol i), shows an officer and seven men on foot, and an officer mounted, in blue trews.

1815—Grenadiers of the 42nd and 92nd coloured aquatint, published in Charles Hamilton Smith's *Costumes of the British Empire* (Colnaghi), folio

1823-1827—The Gordon Highlanders (coloured process plate 6 3-16 in by 4 in). drawn by Graham Glen: frontispiece to vol ii of the *Life of a Regiment*; shows four figures, including an officer in light blue trousers and another in a kilt, a sergeant in a greatcoat, and a drum-major.

1833—Officer. Drawing by L Mansion and St Eschauzier (10⅞ in by 9 in) lithograph in colours from Spooner's Upright Series, 1833-40 Reproduced in colours (7¾ in. by 6½ in) in Ralph Nevill's *British Military Prints* (1909), facing p xxvi

1835—"An Illustrious Stranger in Sight" drawn by C B Newhouse; engraved by Reeve; oblong folio

This crude piece of work represents the battlement of a castle, with a white trousered figure looking over the ramparts with a telescope.

There is a kilted guard of seven men, a piper, a lance-corporal, and an officer examining a book, with a white trousered figure beside him. One figure on horseback is talking to another, both wearing white trousers. This is one of the six colour plates of "Military Incidents" issued in 1835. It is reproduced in monochrome (4 in. by 6 in.) in Nevill's *British Military Prints*, p. 38.

1840—92nd (Highland) Regiment of Foot: Marching Order, coloured lithograph by Lynch after M. Angelo Hayes, R.H.A.: folio. This is one of the set of 51 plates known as Spooner's Oblong Series.

1846—The Highlanders. A large coloured lithograph (17 in. by 12 ½ in.) showing a centre group of officers of Highland Regiments, with small figures of all ranks, outside. Lithograph by E. Walker after M. Angelo Hayes, R.H.A.

1851—Sentries: coloured print (6 1-16 in. by 4 3-16 in.): lithographed by G. E. Madeley.

This plate, facing p. 126 of Cannon's *Historical Record*, shows a sentry and a corporal, both in full uniform. It bears the sub-title "The Advanced Post at Sunrise—The Sentry sees something suspicious and calls the Corporal." There is no date, but the sporran is of the pattern worn by sergeants from 1830 to 1860.

1851—Coloured print (5 ½ in. by 4¾ in.) by G. E. Madeley.

This plate, facing p. 1 of Cannon's *Historical Record*, shows four figures, all in feather bonnets, including an officer, two bandsmen (in white tunics), and a private. No date is assigned to the plate, but it seems to represent the type of uniform worn in 1830.

1853—Officer and group of Privates: lithograph in colours by H. Martens: engraved by J. Harris.

This print is No. 54 of Ackermann's *Costumes of the British Army* (1849-53), and it was published July 1, 1853. Another coloured lithograph of the same type (7⅜ in. by 4¾ in.), and apparently by Martens, shows four officers in the foreground, and a group of men in review order in the background. It was reproduced in monochrome (3¾ in. by 4¾ in.) from a print in the possession of Charles van Noorden, print dealer, in the *English Illustrated Magazine*, June, 1897, side by side with a group of six types of modern Gordons photographed by Gregory of the Strand.

1853—92nd Highlanders: Review Order (12 in. by 9 in.): coloured aquatint by J. Harris after Henry Martens.

This print shows an officer with his company in the background, and forms No 54 of Ackermann's *Costumes of the British Army* The original drawing was bought in 1913 by Colonel W A Scott, C B, Down Street, London, now commanding 9th Gordons, from Robson, the London print sellers   I have to express my indebtedness for some of my notes to Mr F Bathurst (of this firm), whose son, a private in the London Scottish (attached to the Gordons in South Africa), was wounded in the famous fight at Messines, October 31, 1914

1855—Coloured process plate (6⅛ in by 4 in) drawn by Graham Glen in the *Life of a Regiment* (ii, facing p 68), shows five figures —an officer in tartan trews, another in a kilt, a sergeant, a sentry, and a bugler

1866—Officers and men of the 92nd appear in five costume groups, by J Ferguson, lithographed in colours, with other regiments, as follows :—

92nd, 42nd, 71st, 72nd, 74th (7⅞ in by 9½ in)
92nd, two figures, one in drill order and a field officer, 42nd, 78th, 79th (9½ in by 8 in)
92nd, two figures, one in greatcoat and one in full dress ; 42nd, 78th (8⅛ in by 9¾ in)
92nd, 42nd, 71st, 72nd, 74th (7⅞ in by 9⅝ in)
92nd, 74th (7⅞ in by 9½ in)   These were all given in T H Parker, Brothers' *Catalogue of Military Prints* (45 Whitcomb Street, London, 1914), No 9, p 139   I have seen only the second and third

1892—Poster for recruiting purposes   designed and lithographed by Thomson and Duncan, Union Row, Aberdeen.

This was a two-sheet poster showing (1) a private in full uniform with feather bonnet, (2) a private in white tunic and glengarry, and (3) a private in India, with a Hindu servant handing him his rifle

1896—Sketch drawn in two colours by William Smith (8 in by 5½ in)

This drawing, which appeared in *Bon-Accord*, August 20, 1896, shows a sentry in full dress   It is printed in black and white   The artist is the son of William Smith, printer, Aberdeen

1899—Sketches drawn and reproduced in four colours by J. Hoynck

These clever sketches form part of a two-page supplement, " Sketches of the British Army," which appeared in the *Graphic*, September 9, 1899   They show the Gordons "in action," their water-cart,

13

a piper, and other small subjects   The artist, whose full name is J Hoynck van Papendrecht, is a Dutchman

1900—Sir George Stewart White, V.C, as a Gordon Highlander photographed by Window and Grove, Baker Street, London reproduced in colours (10 1-16 in by 7½ in)

This picture was reproduced (p. 16) in *Celebrities of the Army*, edited by Commander Charles N. Robinson, R N, and published by George Newnes   It shows him seated and in a kilt with full regimentals It must have been coloured by hand after being photographed   A black and white reproduction of it appeared in the *Navy and Army Illustrated*, December 10, 1897

1902—A little boy dressed as a Gordon Highlander (not quite correctly) appeared in an alphabet, *Babes of the Empire*, by Thomas Stevens, illustrated by A. H. Collins   published by William Heinemann The verse runs.—

> S comes from Scotland, the land of the cake,
> He's a braw Highland laddie, a soldier to make;
> And the sound of his bagpipes will draw us all forth
> When he comes marching south to the "Cock o' the North"

1903—Captain Harry Vesey Brooke of Fairley · by Robert Brough, A R S A (1872-1905)

This portrait, a three-quarter length, shows Captain Brooke wearing the feather bonnet and full uniform of the Gordons, and was presented to him, August 20, 1903, in recognition of his work in organising the Gordon Highlanders' Memorial Institute, Belmont Street, Aberdeen

1906—Poster in colours for recruiting purposes · designed and lithographed by Thomson and Duncan, Aberdeen (30¼ in by 21 in)

This poster, issued February, 1906, showed three figures (all portraits) of a private (right) in full dress, and a sergeant (left) in white tunic, with Pipe-Major Dunbar and his pipes standing between them A copy of this poster is preserved in J M Bulloch's Scrapbook, *The Gordon Highlanders of all Battalions* (vol iii), now in King's College Library, Aberdeen

1907—Picture post cards · Reliable Series

This was a series of cards issued in colour photography by William Ritchie and Sons, Edinburgh, in January, and twice reissued   They were taken at Castlehill Barracks, and showed (1) a private in full dress; (2) a drummer, with his tiger-skin, (3) piper, (4) bugler; (5) private as

sentry, (6) sergeant, (7) and (8) squad drilling in kakhi tunics   Some
of them were issued with the tunics made of silk and embossed

1909(?)—Picture post cards, "National" Series   No 1,884

These cards, produced from colour photographs and published by
Millar and Lang, Ltd, art publishers, Darnley Street, Glasgow, show a
sergeant, a piper, and a drummer, all in full uniform and in colours

1910—Picture post cards: painted by Harry Payne

This series was issued in colours by Raphael Tuck and Sons, September 23, 1910, in their "oilette" series   They show (1) Field
Officer in kakhi, and Company Officer in drill order, (2) a piper, (3)
sergeant, bandsman, and drummer in review order (4) Captain and
Subaltern with the King's Colour, (5) "swarming down the hill," in
white tunics, (6) "After the review," in full dress

1910—An officer drawn by Frank Dadd, R I

This appears in a three colour process reproduction (12 in by 20 in)
of all the Scots regiments of the line, and was published as a supplement to the *Graphic*, June 19, 1910

1808-98—Sporrans a group of eight

These sketches appear in Lieutenant-Colonel Greenhill Gardyne's
Life of a Regiment (ii, 375), and illustrate the different patterns that
have been worn by officers and men alike   Photographic pictures of the
sporrans of all the Highland regiments at the present time appeared in
the *Sphere*, September 12, 1908, and the *Graphic*, June 18, 1910
Photographic pictures of privates of the first five battalions of the
Gordons appeared in the *Sphere*, April 10, 1899

Colours—Duchess of Gordon's recruiting flag of yellow silk, 1803

This flag, 5 ft 10 in by 6 ft 3 in, in Gordon Castle, was used by
the Duchess in recruiting for a 2nd battalion, and gives the
earliest authentic drawing of the 92nd feather bonnet   Both sides of it
are reproduced in collotype (4⅞ in by 5⅛ in), and it is fully
described (pp 41-42) in the Duke of Richmond and Gordon's *Catalogue
of Weapons, Battle Trophies and Regimental Colours* in Gordon Castle,
1907 (pp 74 50 copies printed)   It was also reproduced in the *Graphic*,
vol 80 p 174   The King's Colour (4½ ft by 5 ft 8 in), and the
Regimental Colour (4 ft 8 in by 5ft 6 in), the second stand of colours
carried by the Gordons, are also in Gordon Castle and are described in
the *Catalogue* (pp 30-1)   The colours of the Northern Fencibles of
1778 and 1793 are also described, and one is illustrated (facing p 32)

1851—Colour print (5⅛ in by 4⅝ in) drawn by Miss McDonald and lithographed by G E Madeley

This plate, facing p 28 of Cannon's *Historical Record*, 1851, shows two sets of colours One cannot be definite, as they are not completely displayed, but they are probably the colours issued December 13, 1830, and retired April 13, 1864, after being carried in the Crimea and India They were taken to Dùnalastair, the home of Sir John Macdonald, who commanded the regiment, and restored by his son, Major-General Alastair Macdonald, being deposited in St Giles's Cathedral, November 14, 1883 They are beautifully lithographed in colours (9¼ in by 10¾ in) in Andrew Ross's *Old Scottish Regimental Colours* (p 112) A second set of colours, issued April 13, 1864, was deposited in St. Giles's, 1883

1901—Poster in colours issued for recruiting purposes designed and printed by Gale and Polden, Aldershot (18¾ in by 21¾ in)

This striking poster illustrated the colours of the 75th and 92nd, showing the flags crossed at the poles, with all their "honours" clearly set forth on each It also gave the badges of the battalions, a corporal in full dress, and photographic portraits of King Edward and Sir George White, both in Gordon Highlander uniform

Heraldry—A Gordon Highlander was chosen by Lord Roberts for the dexter supporter of his Arms, on account of the regiment's valour in the Kabul-Kandahar march, illustrated (in the action at Baba Wali) in the *Graphic*, vol 22, p 389 Sir John Moore proposed to use " a Highland soldier" for one of his supporters in 1804, and asked Lieutenant-Colonel Napier of the Gordons to have a correct drawing of their uniform It is doubtful, however, if he ever used this supporter (*Scottish Notes and Queries*, October 1903)

Battles—Plan of the action at Arroyo del Molinos, October 28, 1811, illustrated (7½ in by 4¾ in) in 4 colours in Cannon's *Historical Record*, facing p 54

1815—Waterloo coloured aquatint (13⅛ in by 19¾ in): by W Heath and T Sutherland, 1836

This shows the positions of the Gordons and 23 other regiments There are portraits of eighteen officers, including that of the Hon. Sir Alexander Gordon, killed at Waterloo (*Gordons under Arms*, No 196)

1815—Private of the Gordons rescuing the colours from the enemy at Waterloo lithograph (10¾ in by 13¾ in) By Francis and S M Gazeau

1815—The Battle of Waterloo coloured print (10⅛ in by 16½ in)

This print, published May 1, 1816, by Whittle and Laurie, 53 Fleet Street, shows a mass of troops There are nine Highlanders standing on the left and four lying dead on the ground They are badly drawn and inaccurate, for, though they are presumably Gordons, they have the blue facings of the Black Watch, but the white hackle of the Gordons A copy is in the possession of Augustin Rischgitz, Linden Gardens, Bayswater Road, London

1815—French Cuirassiers charged and defeated by the Gordons and the Greys at Waterloo aquatint in colours (7⅞ in by 11½ in) By J A Atkinson and M Dubourg, 1815

1815—" The Greys and 92nd Cheered and Huzza'd ' Scotland for Ever ' " drawn by George Jones (7⅝ in by 4½ in) published November 25, 1816, by J Booth, for a *History of Waterloo* (1, 79)

1815—" Gordons and Greys to the Front ". painted by Stanley Berkeley

This picture illustrates the well-known story of the Gordons holding on to the Greys' stirrups at Waterloo The original painting hangs in the Constitutional Club, Northumberland Avenue, London It was published in an engraving by S Hildesheimer and Company, London, in 1897 , and a process reproduction of it appeared (8⅛ in by 4¾ in) in *McClure's Magazine*, New York (x, 491).

1880—The Final Charge at Kandahar led by the Gordons, and supported by the 5th Gurkhas Painted by Vereker Hamilton

This picture represents the charge at the battle of Mazna, September 1, 1880 The painting was reproduced for the first time (7⅞ in by 4¾ in) in *McClure's Magazine*, New York (x, 495) The artist's father, Christian Monteith Hamilton (d 1885), commanded the regiment, and his brother, Sir Ian Hamilton (b 1853), served in it

Monuments—Monolith in the Duthie Park, Aberdeen, to 1st and 2nd battalions, unveiled 1900 , illustrated in the *Navy and Army Illustrated*, December 22, 1900

Memorial window erected in Holburn Parish Church, Aberdeen, in honour of the Gordon Highlanders, including Volunteers, who perished in the South African War · illustrated in Sinclair's *Aberdeen Volunteers* (facing p 266), which describes all the memorials to the Gordons, especially the Volunteers of the Service Companies (pp 263-6)

Castlehill Barracks, Aberdeen

The foundation stone was laid by the Marquis of Huntly June 24, 1794, and the building was completed in 1796 at a cost of about £16,000 The Hospital on Heading Hill was built in 1799 A crude pen drawing of the barracks from Castlebrae was done by an unknown artist, for William Mitchell, bookseller, Aberdeen (whose Gordon descent is given in the *House of Gordon* 11, 307) It was engraved on a card (3⅜ in by 4½ in), and coloured by hand Mr William Walker, author of the *Bards of Bon-Accord*, who has a copy, is of opinion that it was done for Mitchell's notepaper, but abandoned on account of its crudeness The same drawing was reproduced (6⅝ in by 8⅞ in) in the *Aberdeen Weekly Journal*, March 4, 1908, and reprinted in *Aberdeen in Bygone Days* (1910, p 9), where Mr Robert Anderson suggested that the date was 1850 It was afterwards reproduced (3¼ in by 4 7-16 in) in *Aberdeen Street Names* (1911, p 40) by Mr G M Fraser, who dates it twenty years earlier, 1830 A distant view of the barracks from the south-west appeared in a drawing by I Clark, published by Smith, Elder, in 1825, and reproduced in *Aberdeen in Bygone Days* (p 3) An account of the compensation paid for the removal of the Marischal College Observatory, Castlehill, appeared in the *Aberdeen Weekly Journal*, May 29, 1914.

3RD BATTALION

Sir William Schwenk Gilbert as an officer in the Aberdeenshire Militia reproduction (5½ in by 3⅜ in) of a photograph showing him in full kilted regimentals, with his feather bonnet on a table Edith A Browne's *W S. Gilbert* Stars of the Stage series, published by John Lane, London, 1897 (facing p 14)

Gilbert (1836-1911), the dramatist and librettist, held a commission in the Aberdeen Militia, July 7, 1868-April 26, 1878 It may have been this fact which suggested the Bab Ballad on Helen McJones Aberdeen

Captain Hamilton O'Brien Ussher painted by Herman Herkomer

This picture, which hangs in the Strangers' Coffee Room of the Junior Constitutional Club, Piccadilly, of which Captain Ussher was the first secretary (1887-91), shows this officer in full uniform of the 3rd Gordons

4TH BATTALION

1st Volunteer Battalion, Gordon Highlanders drawn in colour by

Major-General J M. Grierson, and lithographed by McLagan and Cumming, Edinburgh (4 in by 5¾ in)

This forms plate xxxv of Grierson's *Scottish Volunteer Force*, and shows (1) Private, 1st Aberdeen R V, 1860-62, (2) Private, No 11 Company, 1st A R V, 1861-62, (3) Sergeant, 1st A'R V, 1862-79, (4) Colour-Sergeant, 1880, (5) Private, 1895-1907 It was on December 8, 1879, that authority was given to change the uniform to one of scarlet doublets with yellow facings, and Gordon tartan trews On February 1, 1884, the title of 1st Volunteer Battalion, Gordon Highlanders, was conferred, and on October 30, 1895, the full uniform of the Gordon Highlanders (less the feather bonnet, which was replaced by the glengarry) was authorised

5TH BATTALION

2nd Volunteer Battalion, Gordon Highlanders drawn in colour by Major-General J M Grierson and lithographed by McLagan and Cumming, Edinburgh (3¾ in. by 3¼ in)

This forms plate xxxvi of Grierson's *Scottish Volunteer Force*, and shows (1) Lieutenant, 6th Aberdeen R V, 1860-64, (2) Private, 2nd A B Aberdeen R.V, 1864-75, (3) Captain, 1880-1908

3rd (The Buchan) Volunteer Battalion, Gordon Highlanders drawn in colour by Major-General J M Grierson lithographed by McLagan and Cumming, Edinburgh (4¼ in by 6¼ in)

This forms plate xxxvii of Grierson's *Scottish Volunteer Force*, and shows (1) Ensign, 5th Aberdeen R V, 1860, (2) Lieutenant, 9th Aberdeen R V, 1860, (3) Lieutenant, 17th Aberdeen R V, 1860, (4) Captain, 20th Aberdeen R V, 1860, (5) Captain, 2nd A B Aberdeen R V, 1863-1868, (6) Captain, 3rd A B, or 3rd Aberdeen R.V, 1872-83, (7) Corporal, 1903-8

6TH BATTALION

4th (Donside Highland) Volunteer Battalion, Gordon Highlanders drawn in colour by Major-General J M Grierson, and lithographed by McLagan and Cumming, Edinburgh (4 in by 6 in)

This forms plate xxxviii of Grierson's *Scottish Volunteer Force*, and shows (1) Private, 10th Aberdeen R V, 1860, (2) Private, 11th Aberdeen R V, 1860, (3) Corporal, 7th Aberdeen R V, 1860, (4) Private, 1st A B Aberdeen R V, 1864-9, (5) Sergeant, 1869-87, (6) Private, 1887-1903, (7) Sergeant, 1903-8

6th Volunteer Battalion, Gordon Highlanders: drawn in colour by Major-General J. M. Grierson, and lithographed by McLagan and Cumming, Edinburgh (4 in. by 4⅛ in.).

This forms part of plate xxxix. of Grierson's *Scottish Volunteer Force*, and shows (1) Corporal, 1st A.B. Banff R.V., 1861-80; (2) Captain, 1887-91; (3) Sergeant, 1891-1908.

7TH BATTALION.

5th (Deeside Highland) Volunteer Battalion, Gordon Highlanders: drawn in colour by Major-General J. M. Grierson, and lithographed by McLagan and Cumming, Edinburgh (3⅞ in. by 2½ in.).

This forms part of plate xxxvi., of Grierson's *Scottish Volunteer Force*, and shows (1) Private, 1st A.B. Kincardine R.V., 1864-76); (2) Private, 1876-1908.

7th Volunteer Battalion, Gordon Highlanders: drawn in colour by Major-General J. M. Grierson, and lithographed in colour by McLagan and Cumming, Edinburgh (4 in. by 1 in.).

This forms part of plate xxxix. of Grierson's *Scottish Volunteer Force*, and shows a corporal, 1900-8.

Territorial Gordon Highlanders: by R. Caton Woodville: reproduced by four colour process (8⅝ in. by 6 in.).

This spirited drawing shows a Territorial Gordon in a feather bonnet and kilt, with troops in the distance. It appears in *His Majesty's Territorial Army*, by Walter Richards, i., 18.

Military and Volunteer Review at the Aberdeen Wapinschaw, July 8, 1862.

At this review there were present 180 of the Depot Battalion, 718 Militia, and 1,631 town and county Volunteers. It was painted by Henry Pont, scene painter at the theatre in Marischal Street, and is reproduced (6 in. by 8⅞ in.) in Donald Sinclair's *History of the Aberdeen Volunteers*, facing p. 340. The painting is in the possession of Mrs. Robert Goldie, Marischal Street, Aberdeen, widow of the painter's nephew.

SOME ADDITIONS.

Page xlviii, last line Before "great" add "great"

Page 296—The original seven companies of the Aberdeen Light Infantry included one commanded by Captain James Littlejohn It is omitted on page 296, though duly included on page 297 The regiment was called (*WO* 13 4,160) the "Royal Aberdeen Light Infantry Volunteers," but I have omitted the word "Royal" so as not to confuse the corps with the "Royal Aberdeen Volunteers." The latter is called by mistake (p. 296, line 18) the "Royal Aberdeen*shire* Volunteers."

Add page 409· 1901.—*The Gordons' Regimental Gazette* monthly magazine, illustrated, (Aberdeen), started May. Six copies up to October, there is a set in the Aberdeen Public Library

Add page 410. 1902—*The Gordon Country* (Aberdeen) An illustrated souvenir issued in connection with the opening of the Gordon Highlanders Institute in Belmont Street.

Add page 414 1914—"Story of the Great War as seen through Gordons, Seaforths, and Camerons' Eyes"—*Aberdeen Weekly Journal*, No 1, December 4

Add page 417. 1892—*3rd (The Buchan) Volunteer Battalion* rules and standing orders (Peterhead)

Add page 435 1914.—"The Rally of the Empire" ($5\frac{3}{4}$ in × $10\frac{1}{8}$ in), three colour plate, by Lionel Edwards, A R C A.; issued also as part of a 1915 calendar by Abdulla, cigarette makers, London : shows 22 military types, a Gordon Highlander being the only kilted regular (*cf* note *supra*, p. xxxviii).

1914.—"The Highlander's Farewell" ($11\frac{3}{4}$ in × 8 in.), four colour plate, by A S Hartrick, A R W S, shows a Gordon Highlander sergeant with a Huntly (?) background, bidding good-bye to his wife and children Issued as one of the "Great War Series, 1914-1915," by George Pulman & Sons, London, copyright by T C. & E C. Jack, Edinburgh

INDEX LOCORUM.

L3

INDEX NOMINUM.

NOTE —Officers have been indexed with the rank which is theirs in the *first* official list in which their names occur, but identified when possible Their frequent changes of regiment made it impossible to follow the ordinary rule of indexing under the latest title —JEAN E 'KENNEDY

Abercromby (Abercrombie)
—, of Glassaugh, 365
—, of Glassaugh, Gen , 7
Alexander, Ens , 312, 314
or Cameron, Anne, 147
George of Birkenbog (?), Lt , 115, 118
Sir George, of Birkenbog, Capt - Comt , 346, 361
or Morison, or Duff, Jean, 7
Sir Ralph, Gen , 147, 259, 274
Robert, Ens , 317, 318
Sir Robert, Lt -Gen , 171

Aberdeen, Countess of
Anne Gordon, 1
Catherine Hanson, 8
Susan Murray, 1

Aberdeen, Earl of
George Gordon, 1st Earl, 1
George Gordon, 3rd Earl, 8, 256, 373
George Hamilton Gordon, 4th Earl , Col , lviii , 285, 321, 379, 380
John Campbell Gordon, 7th Earl, 399
William Gordon, 2nd Earl, 1, 4, 37, 232

Aberdeen Evening Gazette,
Roll of Honour, 416

Aberdeen Herald, 401

Aberdeen Journal, vii , lviii , 10, 11
note, 20, 21, 29, 30, 114, 122
note, 125, 126, 214, 218, 219,
225, 256, 264, 277, 278, 319,
347, 359, 379, 399, 408, 414,
417

Aberdeen Weekly Free Press, 401

Aberdeen Weekly Journal, lxv note,
8, 116, 421, 426, 429, 438, 441

Abernethy
James, Ens , 51
or Duff, Jane, 343

Aboyne, Earl of
Charles Gordon, 4th Earl, 49
George Gordon, 5th Earl *See* Huntly, Marquis of
John Gordon, 3rd Earl, xxv , 49

Abraham
William, 236

Ackermann
Costumes of the British Army, 432, 433

Adam
David, 236
James, 236
Rev Peter, Chaplain,
Lads of Don, 418

Adams
George, 236

Adamson
Charles, Capt -Lt , 278, 279, 284
Charles, Ens (1782), 116
Charles, Ens. (1803), 282, 283

Affleck
Andrew, Adjt , lx , 313, 377
Andrew, Ens., 281, 282, 298

Dowall (Dowle)
Charles, Ens , 149, 234
Lachlan, 123
Richard, 48
Stephen, 48

Dowarty
Simon, 239

Dowie
James, 239

Dowlin
William, Falmouth, 230, 239
William, drummer, 236

Downie
James, 239
Robert, 121

Downman
Lt -Col , 399

Downs
John, 239

Drummond
——, Agent of 89th Foot, 10
Patrick, Lt , 26

Dubourg
——, 437

Duff
Alexander of Davidston, Capt , 7,
8, 11
Alexander of Hatton, 288, 343.
Alexander II of Hatton, 8
Alexander of Mayen, Lt , 8, 9, 288,
343, 350, 358
Alexander, Ens , 353, 386
Alexander, Lt , 26
Arthur, 94
or Morison, Catherine, 8
Garden, Capt , 288
Garden William, 288
George of Edindiach, 60
James, Land Surveyor of Customs,
59, 60
James, Lt , 289, 352, 361, 369, 386
James, Maj , 345
John of Culbin, 7
John of Drummuir, 7
John of Hatton, 288
Katherine of Drummuir, 7
Magdalen, 7

Duff
Patrick, "Tiger," gentleman vol-
unteer, 10, 270
Robert, 59
Robert of Hillockhead, 60
Robert of Logie, Admiral, 8
William of Muirtown, 7
William, Adjt , 322
William, drummer, 120

Duftus (Duffes)
James, Serg , 119
John, 239

Duguid
George, Lt , 266
John, Ens , 312
John, Lt , 281, 282, 284, 336
William, Ens , 330, 381

Dumbreck
John, 137.

Dumfries Weekly Journal, 387, 388,
383

Dunbar
——, Pipe-Major, 434
——, of Duffus, 12
——, Capt., son of Dunbar of
Duffus, 12
Alexander, 239
Alexander, Ens , 116
Alexander, Serg , 392
Archibald, Capt -Lt , 8
James, Maj , 288
John, 137

Dunbar's
Social Life, 12

Duncan
——, Capt , 55
Alexander, deserter, 30
Alexander, Lt , 296, 297, 298
Edward, 239
George, 240
James, Montrose, 240
James, Rothiemay, 34
James, Saline, 240
James, Ens , 302, 303, 330, 382
John, Dollar, 240
John, Speymouth, 35
John, Kincardine O'Neill, 240
John, Ens , 302, 329, 381
John, Provost of Aberdeen, 5, 25
Lachlan, 392
Peter, drummer, 120
Robert, Huntly, 392
Robert, Rhyme, 121

Gordon
    William Abercrombie, Q M , 151, 172
    William Alexander, Lt , 148, 282, 284

Gordon Castle Archives, passim

Gordon Country, 410

Gordon-Cuming   *See* Cuming

Gordon Country, 410, 441.

Gordon Highlanders, 405, 410

Gordon Highlanders Old Comrades' Association, 412

Gordon Highlanders' Standing Orders, 398

Gordons' Gathering, 414

Gordons' Regimental Gazette, 409, 441

Gorry
    John, Capt., 26

Goudie
    John, 241

Gould
    ——, Surgeon, 344

Gourlay
    John, Stirling, 10

Gow
    Alexander, 241
    Donald, 392
    James, 34

Gower, Earl
    xl

Graham, Marquis of
    xlv , lv , 288

Graham (Grahame)
    ——, of Balgowan, 213
    Alexander, 48
    Colin of Draime, 29
    Davie, 392
    James, 241
    Murdoch, 241
    William, 392 and *note*
    William, Lt , 115, 118

Grand Volunteer Bazaar (1892), 419

Grant
    ——, 221
    ——, Delmore, 122
    ——, Mrs , of Laggan, xxxix
    ——, Lurg, Capt , 124
    ——, Minmore, 120
    ——, Tombreakachy, 121
    ——, Capt , 122
    ——, Capt , 225
    ——, Ens., 32
    ——, Maj , xxv.
    Absalom, 34
    Alexander, Duthell, 34
    Alexander, Marnoch, 121
    Alexander Talbert [? Tulloch], 392
    Alexander, Capt , 129
    Alexander, Ens (1794), 177, 184
    Alexander, Ens (1795), 188
    Alexander, Ens (1802), 289
    Alexander, Ens (1803), 312
    Alexander, Lt (1778), 115, 118
    Alexander, " gent ," Lt (1795), 176, 184
    Allan, Lt , 176, 184
    Alpin, Capt , 289
    Sir Archibald of Monymusk, 4th Bart , 331, 371, 374, 376
    Charles, 154
    Charles in Blairfindy, 156
    Charles, Tombreakachy, 122, 124
    Charles, Ens (1780), 117
    Charles, Ens (1794), 188
    Charles, Ens (1803), 312, 314
    Charles, Lt (1778), 47, 50, 53
    Charles, Lt (1799), 184
    Charles, Lt (1798), 278, 279, 281, 282, 284
    Charles, Lt (1809), 377
    David, 241
    David MacDowall of Arndilly, Lt - Col , 277, 279
    Donald, Ens , 51
    Duncan, 137
    Duncan, Abernethy, 121
    Duncan, Ens , 177
    Duncan, Ens , jun , 177
    Francis, Ens , 188
    Francis, Lt , 257
    Francis, Serg , 119
    Francis William   *See* Seafield, Earl of
    George, Capt , 289
    or Cumming, Helen, 175
    Humphrey, Ens , 172
    Humphrey, Lt , 148
    or McBain, Isobel, 124 *note*
    J , Rippachy, Capt , 135, 196
    James, 154
    James, Abernethy, 154 and *note*
    James, Cromdall, 121

Grant

James, Glenduff, 241.
Sir James of Grant, Col., xxxii.,
    xxxvii., xl., 144, 173, 178, 179,
    182, 184, 185, 186, 187, 189,
    (?)212, 287, 290, 387.
James, Keith, 133, 137.
James, Kirkmichael, 121.
James, Lochaber, 154.
Sir James of Monymusk, 374, 375.
James, Mortlach, 241.
James, Tomintoul, 105.
James, Advocate, 403.
Rev. James, Chaplain, 177, 196,
    389, 390.
James, Capt. (1794), 187.
James, Capt. (1800), 274.
James, Ens. (1778), 117, 118, 119.
James, Ens. (1793), 177.
James, Ens. (1794, Feb.), 177.
James, Ens. (1794, Sept.), 188
James, Ens. (1795), 177.
James, Ens. (1805), 353.
James, Lt. (1760), 26.
James, Lt. (1762), 26.
James, Lt. (1793), 176, 184, 272.
James, Lt. (1794), 187.
James, Lt. (1802), 289.
James, Lt. (1809), 377.
James, Q.M., 353, 377, 385.
James,
    Romance of War, 402, 403.
John, 154, 241, 387.
John, Achnahyle, 121.
John in Achnarrow, 121.
John, Glenlivet, 154.
John, Inveraven, 121, 241.
John, Keith, 135.
John, Kirkmichael, 121, 241.
Rev. John, Kirkmichael, 145.
John, Perth, 392.
John of Rippachie, Lt., 105, 115,
    118, 126.
John, Ruthven, 241.
John, Tammore, Capt.-Lt., 133, 176.
John of Tarmore, 158.
John, Capt., sen., 184.
John, Capt., jun., 184.
John, Capt. (1794), 187, 190.
John, Ens., 184, 188.
John, Ens. (1778), 119.
John, Ens. (1793), 177.
John, Ens. (1795), 258.
John, Ens. (1803), 284.
Rev. John, Chaplain, 189.
John, grenadier, 182.
John, sen., Lt. (1793), 176, 184.
John, jun., Lt. (1793), 176.
John, Lt. (1794) (Ens. 85th), 187,
    278, 279.

Grant

John, Lt. (1794) (Ens. 95th), 188.
John, Lt. (1795), 176.
John, Lt. (1797), 344, 349.
John, Lt. (1799), 184.
John, Maj., 175, 184, 388.
John, Q.M.S., 152
John, Surgeon, 184.
John W. S., 389.
Johnston, Lt., 257.
Lewis. See Seafield, Earl of.
Lewis, 137, 392.
Lewis, Lt., 188.
Ludovick, Capt., 306, 330.
Ludovick of Knockando, Capt., 7,
    8.
Ludovick, of Rothiemurcus family,
    29.
Sir Ludovick, 6.
Sir Ludovick of Grant, 173.
Matthew, Q.M., 189.
Patrick, Inverness, 78.
Patrick, Ens., 358, 369, 386.
Patrick, Lt., 233.
Peter, 154.
Peter, Ens. (1794), 188.
Peter, Ens. (1795), 188.
Peter, Ens. (1803), 352.
Peter, Lt., 188.
Peter, Surgeon, 177.
R., Ruthven, 121.
Robert, Cults, 121.
Robert, Elgin, 121.
Robert, Inveraven, 121.
Robert, Kirkmichael, 121.
Robert, Tomintoul, 145.
Robert, Ens., 177.
Robert, Ens. (1795), 189.
Robert, Surgeon, 290.
Robert, tailor, 47.
Robert Charles, Lt., 281, 283, 312,
    314, 377.
Thomas, Lt., 345, 350, 352, 386.
W., Minmore, 121.
W. C., Capt., 392.
William, Cromdall, Inverness, 121.
William, Cromdall, Murray, 121.
William, Inveraven, 121, 241.
William, Tombrackachy, 123, 154.
William, Corp., 120.
William, Ens., 177, 184, 189.
William, Lt. (1793), 176, 184.
William, Lt. (1794), 257.
Sir William, 375.
Graphic, 275, 400, 427, 430, 431, 433,
    435, 436.

Gray

———, Barrackmaster, 122.
Andrew, 48.

PRINTED AT THE ROSEMOUNT PRESS, ABERDEEN

1914, Feb.   6—MS. (*pp.*   1- 42) of this book (*pp.*   1- 36) sent to Printer.
1914, Feb. 28—MS. (*pp.* 43-193)   ,,   ,, (*pp.* 37-128)   ,,   ,,
1914, Mar. 11—MS. (*pp.* 194-275)   ,,   ,, (*pp.* 129-172)   ,,   ,,
1914, Mar. 24—MS. (*pp.* 276-313)   ,,   ,, (*pp.* 173-184)   ,,   ,,
1914, Mar. 27—MS. (*pp.* 314-432)   ,,   ,, (*pp.* 185-252)   ,,   ,,
1914, Apl. 17—MS. (*pp.* 433-514)   ,,   ,, (*pp.* 253-275)   ,,   ,,
1914, May   11—MS. (*pp.* 515-577)   ,,   ,, (*pp.* 276-298)   ,,   ,,
1914, May   26—MS. (*pp.* 578-688)   ,,   ,, (*pp.* 299-337)   ,,   ,,
1914, May   28—MS. (*pp.* 689-806)   ,,   ,, (*pp.* 338-369)   ,,   ,,
1914, June   3—MS. (*pp.* 807-851)   ,,   ,, (*pp.* 370-386)   ,,   ,,
1914, June   8—MS. (*pp.* 860-1,015) ,,   ,, (*pp.* 397-440)   ,,   ,,
1914. Aug. 26—Preface (*pp.* 124)   ,,   ,, (*pp.* xiii.-lxviii.)   , ,,
1914. Dec.   1—Dedication (*pp.* 2)   ,,   ,, (*pp.* vii.-viii.) ,,   ,,

1914, Mar. 2—First proof of book (*pp.* 1-36) received from Printer.
1914, Oct. 17—Second revise of text finished.
1914, Dec. 20—Last proof sent to Printer.